FIT TO FIGHT

FIT TO FIGHT

THE HISTORY OF THE 4TH INFANTRY DIVISION IN WORLD WAR II

1940 — 1946

ROBERT O. BABCOCK

Deeds not Words!
Bob Babcock

Deeds Publishing | Athens

Copyright © 2024 — Robert O. Babcock

ALL RIGHTS RESERVED — No part of this book may be reproduced in any form or by any electronic or mechanical means, including information storage and retrieval systems, without permission in writing from the authors, except by a reviewer who may quote brief passages in a review.

Published by Deeds Publishing in Athens, GA
www.deedspublishing.com

Printed in The United States of America

Cover and interior design by Deeds Publishing

ISBN 978-1-961505-15-5

Books are available in quantity for promotional or premium use. For information, email info@deedspublishing.com.

First Edition, 2024

10 9 8 7 6 5 4 3 2 1

To all the "Greatest Generation" Americans who answered the call to save the world during World War II, and those who supported them.

Especially to those and their Family members who had the honor of serving with the 4th Infantry Division. Those of us who have served since you will always look with pride at the example you set for us and the price you paid without any hesitation.

Steadfast and Loyal

CONTENTS

A Special Tribute to Philippe Cornil	xi
Thanks to Michael Belis	xiii
List of Books Referenced or Quoted	xv
4ID in World War II	1
Training in England	13
Final Preparations	23
Overview of 4ID's Fight Across Europe	37
June 1944	43
July 1944	99
Last Half of July 1944	131
August 1944	167
25 August 1944	213
September 1944	255
October 1944	307
November 1944	329
December 1944	389
January 1945	455
February 1945	513
March 1945	555
April 1945	591
May 1945	653
4ID's Return to USA	683
About the Author	695
4ID Bibliography	697

ABOUT THE TITLE

Steadfast and Loyal, We're FIT TO FIGHT!
The Nation's Finest Soldiers, Keep Liberty's Light
Our Soldiers ROAR For Freedom
We're Fit For Any Test
The Mighty 4th Division, America's Best!

Adopted as the 4th Infantry Division (4ID) song, the words **Fit to Fight** nets out the history of the 4th Infantry Division from our birth on 10 December 1917, to our successful fighting on the battlefields in World War I, our eleven month fight across Europe in WWII, our stand in Cold War Europe in the 1950s, our four and a half years fighting in Vietnam's jungles, our continuing support of Europe in annual REFORGER exercises in the 1971 to 1995 timeframe, our leading edge role in Force XXI as we tested technology and tactics entering the 21st century, our missions in Iraq and Afghanistan from 2003 to 2019, and today's Fort Carson, CO based 4ID ready to deploy to any hot spot around the world where they are needed. To net it out, the 4ID has been fit to fight throughout the 107 years of our existence (as of this writing).

This book focuses exclusively on our 4ID history during the World War II era. That goes from our reactivation on 1 June 1940 to our temporary deactivation in March 1946. This covers training in the United States and England, fighting in Europe from D-Day to VE Day, and return to the States and temporary deactivation.

ABOUT THE COVER

The cover is the last picture of Brigadier General Teddy Roosevelt, Jr. who died of a heart attack on 12 July 1944 after landing in the first wave on Utah Beach on 6 June 1944. When they landed 2,000 yards away from their expected landing site, he famously said to Colonel James Van Fleet, Commanding Officer of 8th Infantry Regiment, "We'll start the war from here." For his calming leadership on D-Day in Normandy, he earned the Medal of Honor.

The citation states:

"For gallantry and intrepidity at the risk of his life above and beyond the call of duty on 6 June 1944, in France. After two verbal requests to accompany the leading assault elements in the Normandy invasion had been denied, Brig. Gen. Roosevelt's written request for this mission was approved and he landed with the first wave of the forces assaulting the enemy-held beaches. He repeatedly led groups from the beach, over the seawall and established them inland. His valor, courage, and presence in the very front of the attack and his complete unconcern at being under heavy fire inspired the troops to heights of enthusiasm and self-sacrifice. Although the enemy had the beach under constant direct fire, Brig. Gen. Roosevelt moved from one locality to another, rallying men around him, directed and personally led them against the enemy. Under his seasoned, precise, calm, and unfaltering leadership, assault troops reduced beach strong points and rapidly moved inland with minimum casualties. He thus contributed substantially to the successful establishment of the beachhead in France."

A SPECIAL TRIBUTE TO PHILIPPE CORNIL

It was 1999 when I received an email from Philippe Cornil, living in Belgium, expressing his interest in the history of the 4th Infantry Division, (I was president and historian of the 4th Infantry Division Association). After a number of emails back and forth over the ensuing months, he said he wanted to fly to Georgia to meet with me in person. It made sense to me, and we set a date in 2000. When I told my wife, Jan, she looked at me as if I'd lost my mind. "Where is he going to stay?" she asked. Shocked, I said, "Here with us, of course. Why not?" Her reply was, "You are going to bring somebody in from a foreign country that you never met and know nothing about to stay here?"

Philippe came, we dealt with the language problem (I speak only English, and his English took a while for me to understand), our whole family loved him, and it started a friendship that lasted until he died in the summer of 2023. While visiting with us, he made Xerox copies of all the daily 4ID WWII After Action Reports (AAR) and took them back to Belgium with him and got them converted to digital format, in both English and French. That selfless work of his made this book possible. (I would be remiss not to thank the 4ID WWII veteran, Corporal William T. Riiska of 4th Reconnaissance Troop Mechanized, 4ID who copied the AARs from the original in the National Archives).

In early June 2002, Philippe invited us to his bed and breakfast home that he had purchased in Ste. Marie du Mont, just off Utah Beach where the 4th Infantry Division landed at H-Hour on D-Day, June 6, 1944. He was a fabulous tour guide and perfect host for our party of four, Jan's mother, our son, Mark, Jan, and me.

Two years later, in 2004 on the 60th anniversary of D-Day, he set up a week-long tour for 12 4ID WWII veterans and their wives or grown offspring. He and I hosted them as their tour guides. Philippe and I both know the 4ID D-Day and beyond history, but we learned a lot from the stories of these WWII vets returning to Normandy, most for their first time since 1944.

Two more times Philippe hosted me as we expanded our tours of 4ID battlefields. In September 2010, he hosted my IBM mentor, Gary Swanson, and me, and in December 2016, on the 70th anniversary of the Battle of the Bulge, he showed me where the 4ID held the southern shoulder of the Bulge in Luxembourg, plus we visited Bastogne.

Sadly, Philippe died in the summer of 2023. Time and distance kept us apart for the past several years and I miss him terribly…a good friend and fellow 4ID history buff. You are missed, Philippe. You made this book possible. You will always be "Steadfast and Loyal."

Philippe Cornil (right) with Bob Babcock, Normandy, France, 60th anniversary of D-Day

THANKS TO MICHAEL BELIS

Michael Belis, 4ID veteran who served in Vietnam in 1970-1971 with C/1-22 Infantry, is the most knowledgeable 4ID historian alive today. Michael has edited for accuracy this book and the *22nd Infantry Regiment in World War II* book by Chaplain Bill Boice. He has been an invaluable friend and resource to me since we met online in 1998. Michael not only pointed out errors or missing facts, but he always has the detail to backup what he tells me. This is a better and more accurate book thanks to Michael Belis. You can see Michael's work online at **www.1-22infantry.org**.

Steadfast and Loyal—Deeds not Words!

(Michael is the author of *Steadfast and Loyal: Medal of Honor and Distinguished Service Cross Recipients of 4th Division in World War One*. Available from **www.deedspublishing.com** and Amazon).

Robert O. Babcock

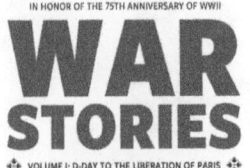

LIST OF BOOKS REFERENCED OR QUOTED

War Stories Volume I: D-Day to the Liberation of Paris by Robert O. Babcock

War Stories Volume II: Paris to V-E Day by Robert O. Babcock

History of the 22nd Infantry Regiment in WWII by Chaplain Bill Boice

Clifford "Swede" Henley's WWII Diary by Swede Henley

History of the Twelfth Infantry Regiment in WWII by Gerden Johnson

World War II WAC by Helen Denton

4th Infantry Division World War II Yearbooks—8th, 12th, 22nd Infantry Regiments, Division Artillery, HQ and Special Troops—published in 1946.

All the above books, except for Swede Henley's diary, are available at **www.deedspublishing.com**, click on Book Store. Most are also available on Amazon.com.

Robert O. Babcock

Utah Beach to Cherbourg, 6 June to 27 June 1944 by US Army Center of Military History. Includes maps, pictures, narrative—Free online—Google: Utah Beach to Cherbourg

4th Infantry Division After Battle Reports—World War II, Copied from National Archives.

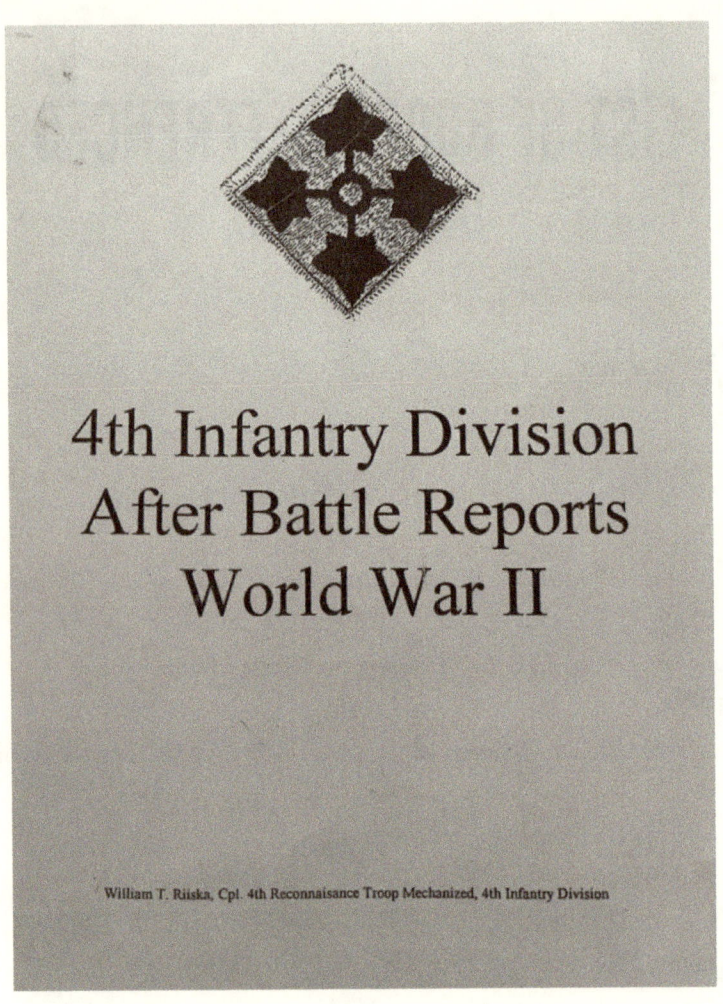

4ID IN WORLD WAR II

1940 TO JANUARY 1944

I have tackled a project to bring the history of the 4th Infantry Division in World War II to all who want to read it. I first created a smaller version of this during the 75th anniversary commemorative year of D-Day to VE Day in 2019-2020, showing it online in monthly and weekly segments. Now, it is in book format, released early in 2024, the **80th anniversary year of D-Day, 6 June 1944**, and to be left as a permanent legacy for anyone at any time who wants to follow the actions of the United States Army's 4th Infantry Division (4ID) in World War II (WWII).

In this first section, I give the story of what our 4ID troops did between June 1940 and January 1944. Then, starting the first week of June (D-Day, 6 June 1944), I switch to detailed after action updates and follow our WWII forefathers in their fight across Europe to victory on 8 May 1945 (VE Day).

I use historic material from the 4ID yearbooks published in 1946, other history books from various authors, stories from memories provided to me in the late 1990's by the 4ID vets who helped win the war in Europe (and published in my *War Stories* book in 2001 and republished as three books in 2014), the official After Action Report of 4ID in WWII, pictures as I can find and use them, and anything else I find that appears to be of interest to those who love the WWII history of the 4ID.

I encourage anyone who reads this book to forward the information to your contacts who have an interest in WWII history, especially the European theater. We don't want to be spam or a nuisance, but I know a lot of people care about WWII history that I am unaware of and do not have contact with.

This book, with an ISBN number for both printed and Kindle e-book formats, will be available worldwide through Amazon and other book outlets. Autographed copies can be purchased through **www.deedspublishing.com** and clicking on Book Store. As long as I am still with us, I'll be happy to autograph these books.

LET'S GET STARTED…

We set the stage with the reactivation of 4ID in June 1940 and follow them through their deployment to England in January 1944. This history comes from the 4ID Yearbooks published in 1946:

Once again war clouds gathered over Europe, and it became necessary to increase the size of the armed forces of the United States.

As part of this expansion, the 4th Division was reactivated on June 1, 1940, at Fort Benning, Georgia, composed initially of the following units: the 8th, 22nd, and 29th Infantry Regiments, 20th, 29th, 42nd, and 44th Field Artillery Battalions, 4th Engineer Battalion, 4th Medical Battalion, 4th Quartermaster Battalion, 4th Signal Company, 4th Reconnaissance Troop, and the 4th Headquarters and Military Police Company. Units of the Division were below strength and training was limited until training areas and aids were pushed to completion.

Then in August 1940, the Division was selected to act as an experimental unit for the development of methods recently demonstrated by the German blitz through Belgium and France, and designated the 4th Division (Motorized), and later re-designated 4th Motorized Division in 1941. Thus began a three-year, wide-open experiment. Initially, equipment was not available although ideas and theories were many and vigorous. The Louisiana Maneuvers of 1941 saw the 4th Motorized Division using trucks, some borrowed, some retrieved from salvage dumps, in lieu of armored half-tracks. Gradually the equipment problem was met, and the now full-strength units were prepared for whatever might be the country's need. Pearl Harbor resolved any doubts; the purpose of the men and the extent of their responsibility was evident.

In the fall of 1941, the 12th Infantry Regiment replaced the 29th Infantry Regiment in the 4th Division. December 1941 saw the Division move to newly-completed Camp Gordon, Georgia. For more than two years, Camp Gordon and Augusta were "home" for the 4th. In July 1942, the Division was withdrawn suddenly from the Carolina Maneuvers, returned to Camp Gordon, and alerted for overseas movement. This was the first in a series of false alarms which, though disturbing, kept personnel aware of the ultimate objective of the continuing intensive training.

Landings were made in North Africa in November 1942, but the 4th continued to assault through Boggy Gut, Georgia. On Christmas Day, the Division again was alerted. Much equipment had been crated, clothing marked, and physical examinations undergone when, at seemingly the last minute, the move was halted. In April 1943, a permanent change of station was ordered. Fort Dix, New Jersey became the next station of the 4th. It was here, on August 4, 1943, that the 4th Motorized Division was reorganized as the 4th Infantry Division, in which form it has remained. (While a motorized division concept made sense, planners overlooked the number of ships it would take to get the men and equipment to the fight. Thus, the 4th Motorized Division missed the North Africa, Sicily, and Italy campaigns due to lack of sea transportation needed).

Early in September 1943, the Division headed south once more, this time to Camp Gordon Johnston, at Carrabelle, Florida, on the shores of the Gulf of Mexico. Here realistic amphibious training was undergone, and familiarity was developed with the variety of assault landing craft and techniques evolved in anticipation of the invasion of *Festung Europa* (Fortress Europe).

Again alerted for overseas movement, the Division shifted to Fort

Jackson, South Carolina in December 1943, where final personnel adjustments were completed.

As the year 1944 opened, the Division moved to Camp Kilmer, New Jersey, a staging area of the New York Port of Embarkation. This last alert "took," and on the morning of January 18, 1944, the 4th Infantry Division put out to sea on troop ships headed to England. On January 29, 1944, their convoy entered the port of Liverpool, England. Within minutes of landing, the mark of the enemy was plain for all to see as troops marched from ships to trains through block after block of bombed homes, warehouses, and docks.

The Division was established in scattered villages in Devonshire with the Division Command Post at Tiverton, near Exeter. Even before unloading had been completed at Liverpool, the Supreme Commander Allied Expeditionary Force, General Dwight D. Eisenhower, and his deputy, Air Marshal Sir Arthur Tedder, visited the 4th. This was but the first in a series of inspections by distinguished British and American higher commanders.

We made welcome additions to the Division family, in the form of the 70th and 746th Tank Battalions, the 65th Armored Field Artillery Battalion, the 1106th Engineer Group, the 377th Anti-Aircraft Artillery (Automatic Weapons) Battalion, the 87th Chemical Battalion Motorized, and the 801st and 899th Tank Destroyer Battalions, which would be with us during the assault and, in some cases, for many months thereafter. For the actual assault, the 1st Engineer Special Brigade would support the Division; therefore, personnel of this Brigade were participants with us in the planning phase and landing exercises.

The following two stories are from War Stories Volume I: D-Day to Liberation of Paris:

Harper Coleman, Tucson, AZ
Camp Gordon Johnston, Florida
Company H, 2nd Battalion, 8th Infantry Regiment

Location: Carabelle, Florida, on the shores of the Gulf of Mexico. Time: October, November, and part of December in 1943. We came by Pullman train from Kentucky to Tallahassee, Florida. From there we were taken by truck to the camp. I was assigned to Company H of the 8th Infantry Regiment, 4th Infantry Division.

The training was all amphibious: we got on and off landing craft out in the Gulf of Mexico, and then back to the beaches of the camp. There was some other training, such as long hikes. One hike was for twenty-five miles in less than seven hours. Quite a few did not make this all the way, but I did. One of the incidents that I remember well happened in the Gulf of Mexico, off Dog Island. We had gone out one night and storms came up. The LCVPs were separated in the storms. The next day the Coast Guard found our craft, along with two others. We were headed toward Mexico, or so they told us. They turned us around and took us back to the right shore on Thanksgiving Day 1943.

After this, sometime in December 1943, we left there and went to Fort Jackson, South Carolina. We were there only a few weeks, mostly to get new equipment and clothing, do some guard duty, and spend a few times in town.

Early in January of 1944, we went to Camp Kilmer, New Jersey. On January 18, we were put out to sea on an English ship. We were about eleven days on the water. The meals were typically English—boiled mutton (sheep) and turnips—none of which was very appetizing. Our lieutenant at the time kept us pretty well supplied with snacks from the officers' exchange, which kept us from getting too hungry. We were offered one meal per day on the ship, and as I recall, we rarely ate it.

When we left New York harbor, everyone was required to stay below deck. Our company, either lucky or unlucky, was part of the guard detail to make sure this was done. I happened to be on deck at the time and saw some of the sights going out of the harbor.

William C. Montgomery, Long Beach, CA
Company A, 4th Medical Battalion
Troopship in January

…From the ferry, we went to a New York pier, a gigantic warehouse-like building, with gangplanks leading up to a ship we couldn't see. Red Cross women gave us coffee and doughnuts while we waited to board. They were angels.

The ship was a large liner called Capetown Castle, formerly on the England-South Africa-India run. It was manned by British merchant seamen, some of whom eked out their wages by selling us baths in the otherwise unused passenger bathrooms. I don't remember any of us took exception to this little racket…

Our quarters had been the Grand Ballroom. Pipe bunks with canvas slings on rope lashings were built up to the ceiling, perhaps six or seven bunks high. We had to fight with our duffel bags and other gear for sleeping room on the narrow canvas.

During the crossing, we were routed out of the bunks each morning for breakfast, given time to go to the commissary when it was open, then mustered out on deck to stand a good part of the day for boat drill. I think the real idea was to get us up and out of the incredible crowding, into the fresh air, and onto the broad decks where discipline was easier to maintain.

Some of our people were so seasick they would not raise their heads and were left in their bunks. The rest of us, when we were in our bunks, played cards or gambled, cleaned weapons, sharpened knives, straightened gear, wrote letters, read, sang, or horsed around.

It was midwinter and the trip was fairly rough. We were on a big ship. I remember looking at the destroyers on the edge of the convoy as they bobbed in and out of sight behind huge seas, wondering how you stayed alive on such a tiny boat. The roughest time was the final night of the eleven-day trip. We anchored in the Irish Sea, probably waiting for port space somewhere. The ship pitched and rolled around violently. I thought it was going to roll completely over several times. Nobody had fallen out of the bunks during the entire crossing, but they did that night.

The next day we finally steamed into what turned out to be Liverpool. I was astonished to see the British dock workers dressed in everyday clothes. In the US, workers doing heavy work like handling ships' lines wore overalls, coveralls, or rough clothing that seemed to be more appropriate.

I remember marching through blacked-out Liverpool that night, so it must have taken some time to unload the ship. We went on a train…

WHO IS THE 4TH INFANTRY DIVISION?

While we 4th Infantry Division (4ID) veterans and Family members are familiar with the accomplishments and some trivia of the 4th Infantry Division, many reading this have no idea who the 4ID is.

The 4ID was formed at Camp Greene, North Carolina on 10 December 1917—two weeks after the 3rd Infantry Division was formed there.

Our 4ID patch is four Ivy Leaves, named after the Roman numeral IV (we old timers know that IV means 4 in Roman numerals, not sure if they teach that any more). In the *History of the 4th Division in the World War* book, there is a statement: "In the language of flowers, ivy means Steadfast and Loyal…" Thus, Major General Cameron gave us the motto—**Steadfast and Loyal**, which remains our true and descriptive motto to this day.

The 4ID deployed to France in May 1918 for entry into World War I. The first casualty of the Division happened in France on May 19, 1918. He was Sergeant Benjamin F. Lair of Company B 12th Machine Gun Battalion, killed in an air raid by German aircraft in the staging camp at Pas-de-Calais. Four days later, we lost more casualties before landing in France when a German U-boat torpedoed one of our troop ships.

The 4ID represented the US on the 4th of July 1918 when selected 4ID units participated in a parade in Paris, down the Champs Elysees. Later in July, we were engaged in our first battle with the Germans. By Armistice Day on 11 November 1918, the 4ID had earned five battle streamers for their actions in World War I.

After a few months of occupation duty in Germany, the division returned to Camp Lewis, Washington in 1919 and was deactivated in 1921.

While on occupation duty, the National 4th Infantry Division Association (4IDA) was formed in Germany in 1919. We celebrated the 100th anniversary of the 4th Infantry Division at Fort Carson, Colorado on 10 December 2017. We celebrated the 100th anniversary of the 4th Infantry Division Association at our 100th reunion in Springfield, Missouri in August 2019.

You read above how we were reactivated in 1940 to fight in World War II. Fast forwarding…our division served Cold War occupation duty in Germany from 1950 to 1956, served as part of STRAC (Strategic Army Command) from Fort Lewis, Washington from 1956 to 1966, served in Vietnam from 1966 to 1970, served at Fort Carson, Colorado from 1970 to 1995 and participated in annual REFORGER (Reinforce Germany) training exercises in Germany, and moved to Fort Hood, Texas from 1995 to 2009. The 4ID served four tours in Iraq between 2003 and 2011, and all brigade combat teams of the 4ID have served tours in Afghanistan and back in Europe as a deterrent against the rising Russian threat.

In August 2019, 4ID Headquarters returned to Fort Carson, Colorado after serving in Afghanistan, their second deployment there. As of the time of this writing in early 2024, the 4ID is still permanently stationed at Fort Carson, Colorado (since July 2009), ready to deploy anyplace in the world where they are needed. 4ID headquarters and the support brigade spent most of 2023 in Poland, leading the NATO contingent during the Russian invasion of Ukraine, and 4ID's 1st Brigade Combat Team was deployed to South Korea. As you read this, they are serving wherever our nation needs them to be. Always Steadfast and Loyal.

SOME INTERESTING TIDBITS ABOUT THE 4ID

Brigadier General Teddy Roosevelt Jr. (pictured on the cover) landed in the first wave of 4ID troops on D-Day, proclaiming, "We will start the war from here" when they landed 2,000 yards off their targeted beach. For his actions that day, he earned the Medal of Honor (there were four other 4ID Soldiers who earned the Medal of Honor in WWII).

Author Ernest Hemmingway attached himself to the 4ID during World War II and is a significant part of our WWII history.

J.D. Salinger, author of *Catcher in the Rye* which many of us read in school, was an interpreter and interrogator with 4ID in WWII.

Dave Thomas, founder of Wendy's Hamburgers, was a cook with 4ID in Cold War Germany in the 1950s.

From 1995 to 2002, the 4ID was, once again, an experimental division in what was called Force XXI, testing equipment, electronics, tactics, etc. that made the 4ID the most lethal division in the world as we entered the 21st century. That is why they were chosen as the assault division to attack into Iraq through Turkey at the start of Operation Iraqi Freedom in March 2003. When Turkey would not allow us to pass through their country, we were delayed and entered Iraq from Kuwait in April 2003. The 4ID was assigned to Saddam Hussein's hometown of Tikrit in 2003-2004 and were the unit, along with special operations forces, who captured Saddam Hussein on 13 December 2003.

Four former 4ID Commanding Generals served as Chief of Staff of the Army: MG John L. Hines (1924-1926), GEN Dennis J. Reimer (1995-1999), GEN Raymond T. Odierno (2011-2015), and as of this writing in 2024, GEN Randy A. George is the current Chief of Staff of the Army (since 2023).

The 15th Sergeant Major of the Army (SMA), SMA Dan Dailey, served three combat tours in Iraq with the 4ID, as Command Sergeant Major (CSM) of 1-8 Infantry, as CSM of 3rd Brigade Combat Team, and as 4th Infantry Division CSM. He served as SMA from January 2015 through August 2019, the second longest serving SMA in history.

YOU ALSO MAY ASK, "WHO IS BOB BABCOCK AND WHAT QUALIFIES HIM TO DO THIS?"

As a young boy growing up in the 1950's, my best friend and I were always playing Army. By my high school days, football and girls replaced playing Army, but my interest in the Army and military history never stopped. My English term paper my junior year in high school was about the D-Day landing in Normandy, France on 6 June 1944. I never dreamed at that time I would one day serve in the 4th Infantry Division.

I served two years with the 4th Infantry Division as a rifle platoon leader and executive officer with Bravo Company, 1st Battalion, 22nd Infantry Regiment during our training at Fort Lewis, Washington (November 1965 to July 1966) and the 4ID's first year of deployment to Vietnam in July 1966 to July 1967. The 4ID is the only active duty division I ever served with. I am a very proud 4ID veteran.

I became an active member of the 4th Infantry Division Association (4IDA) in 1991 and have missed only two reunions since then. In the early days, I sat and listened to the stories of our WWII veterans about their fights in WWII. In 1995, Major General (Ret) John Ruggles, last WWII Regimental commander of the 22nd Infantry Regiment, asked me to take over as leader of their dwindling group of WWII veterans who had formed the "22nd Infantry Regiment Society—World War II" on the troopship returning home from Europe in 1945. He told me to open it up to 22nd Infantry Regiment veterans from all wars. Over the next ten years, I served as president of the 22nd Infantry Regiment Society and listened and collected lots of stories and memories from those WWII vets and others from the Cold War, Vietnam, Iraq, and Afghanistan.

As our WWII vets began to fade away and die, I made it one of my objectives when I became president of the 4IDA in 1998 to preserve their stories. In 2001, I published my first book, *War Stories: Utah Beach to Pleiku,* which has 325 WWII stories, 25 Cold War stories, and 100 Vietnam stories. I also appointed myself as historian of the 4IDA and continue to hold that job 25+ years later. I am tied with our first 4IDA president, from 1919 to 1928, as having served ten years as 4IDA president, between 1998 and 2023.

In 2002, I became a founding official partner of the Veterans History Project, part of the Library of Congress, with my Americans Remembered non-profit organization. We have interviewed hundreds of WWII and other veterans.

During the 60th anniversary of D-Day, I led a group of twelve 4ID WWII veterans and their Family members on a week's tour of Normandy (I learned more from them than they did from me, and I remember what they told me).

In 2009 to 2011, I was hired by the Department of Defense as the 4ID historian, a job that went away with Army downsizing in 2011. Since then, I continue to publish military books and stay in touch with veterans of all wars. I have also served as the liaison between the 4ID Association and the 4ID active duty commanding general and other 4ID leaders from 1998 to 2024 and will continue into the future.

* * * * *

4th Infantry Division Monument at night, Walk of Honor, Fort Moore, GA (formerly Fort Benning)

February, March, April, May 1944
TRAINING IN ENGLAND

TRAINING IN ENGLAND, MARCH 1944

*From the **4ID Yearbook** published in 1946:*

The general operation against Hitler's Atlantic Wall was now crystallized, and the target date determined. For each hour there was a specific job, representing an essential step in preparation for readiness on that target date. Slapton Sands, along the south Devon coast, was cleared of civilians. Water covered an area in the rear of this beach and resembled closely the water obstacle prepared by the Germans, who had flooded the area in the rear of the Normandy beach, which, if all went well, would see us on D-Day. Here landing rehearsals, complete with naval fire support and German air and E-boat opposition, were held many times.

*From Chaplain Bill Boice's **History of the 22nd Infantry Regiment in WWII**:*

England was beautiful, as beautiful, and quaint as old-fashioned and sincere as another century. The 22nd Infantry Regiment, detraining at Devon, was split, and sent to the various camps that could accommodate it. Regimental Headquarters and the 2nd Battalion went to a camp outside the town of Danbury. The 1st Battalion was somewhat inadequately quartered in ancient and forbidding buildings in Newton-Abbott. The 3rd Battalion, plus cannon and anti-tank companies, was stationed some distance away at South Brent in a camp which consisted almost exclusively of Quonset huts. 4th Infantry Division Headquarters was at Tiverton. The nearest English city of any size was Exeter, a favorite shopping place soon to become known to us...

Torquay was the Atlantic city of south England and most of the officers and enlisted men went to Torquay for relaxation, usually to the excellent Red Cross Clubs.

...At a meeting of all the officers of the Division, General Omar Bradley, then commanding the First Army, chosen to storm the beaches, told the officers that originally it had been planned to storm the beach with one United States Infantry Division. This division, picked by the top men of the General Staff, had been the 4th Infantry Division. The officers returned to their Regiments sobered, realizing that theirs was a job from which there was no turning back...

...Training in squad problems, the handling of weapons, camouflage, use of artillery and mortars, assault tactics, pole charges, bee-hives, and the bazooka were given to the men, squad by squad, until they became thoroughly familiar with their particular job. Certain tactics were taught, then company, battalion, regimental, and division problems involving these same tactics were run in order to familiarize the troops with their practical application. Weak spots within the organization were discovered and removed. Officers were shifted in their command. Day by day, the tension increased as it became evident that the long-promised second front would soon be a reality.

Fit to Fight

Following story is from my book **War Stories**
Volume I: D-Day to Liberation of Paris:

Billy Cater, Cambridge, OH
Service Company, 22nd Infantry Regiment
Captain "Big Hawk"

The Regiment was newly-arrived in England and was in the process of drawing all equipment, including vehicles. Captain Hawkins (Big Hawk) was the motor officer and I, as a lieutenant, was his assistant. Our living quarters were in a thin-walled barracks and conversations could be heard through them.

We had a few unassigned jeeps so I could slip out a jeep and several of us could go pub hunting at night. On returning one night, driving blackout, I made a wrong turn, tried to switch back and hit a stone fence head on, but managed to get it back to the motor pool. All I could hear through the wall that night was Captain Hawkins talking about the punishment he would dish out to the guilty party. I made a deal with the medic motor sergeant: he was to really complain but would take the jeep and fix it and I would see that he would be favored forever. Big Hawk and I were good friends, and I could never tell him I was the culprit, even after the war.

(Note: Both Billy Cater and "Big Hawk" are deceased now, but Billy's son and Big Hawk's son are regular readers of this trip down memory lane).

From COL Gerden Johnson's **History of the**
12th Infantry Regiment in WWII:

...The month of March brought new and rigorous training as combat problems got underway amid blinding snowstorms on the freezing windswept wastes of the famous English Moors near Dartmoor. Returning on the 10th of March, there was barely time to pack for another move from the regimental area. On the 13th we temporarily left Exeter, Bye-Pass Camp, Exemouth, and Budleigh-Salterton for two weeks of ship-to-shore training with the U.S. Navy. A rail movement was made to Plymouth where the 12th embarked on three APA's anchored in the harbor... Following extensive practice in organizing boat teams and reaching boat stations in blackout, several days were spent in learning how to debark with full equipment down rope ladders and nets...

...Having completed tactical landings of battalion landing teams, staffs began busily preparing a problem for the entire regimental combat team, while the men got in some well-earned rest as the three APA's began the return to Plymouth. This new problem was called Exercise BEAVER and on March 25th we went over the sides and landed on a strip of beach called Slapton Sands on the southern coast of England. It was our first prelude to invasion. By the next day, all units were back at their stations and normal training was resumed...

ENGLAND, SLAPTON SANDS, APRIL 1944

Training continued in England in April 1944. All the 4ID troops knew that the invasion of France was not if they would do it, but when would they invade. With that understanding, training continued in all aspects of the invasion — naval landing operations, weapons, explosives, medical, communications, support, etc. This would be the largest military operation in history, and the 4ID would be the first division strength seaborne troops to land on French soil.

> *From* **Swede Henley's Diary**, *at the time company commander of Cannon Company, 22nd Infantry Regiment:*

1-30 April 1944

Usual garrison duties except for amphibious operation "Tiger" at Slapton Sands. Another one of those screwed up amphibious operations where the Navy starts, and the Army finishes it up.

Fit to Fight

From COL Gerden Johnson's **History of the 12th Infantry Regiment in WWII:**

It was with great reluctance that Col. Henderson's state of health forced him to relinquish command of the 12th Infantry Regiment. He had contributed much to the regiment...

...the loss of the regimental commander came at a critical time. Into this breach, General Omar N. Bradley stepped in with a request for Col. Russell P. Reeder, Jr..."Red" Reeder, a former football coach at West Point, brought to the 12th Infantry all the punch and drive that had enabled Army to bowl over its opponents on more peaceful fields and drive over the goal line for the prized touchdown. In a remarkably short space of time, Reeder had met and talked with every officer and enlisted man in the regiment. He instilled in them an unshakable faith in themselves and the 12th Infantry and an unsurmountable determination to overcome whatever obstacles might lie ahead...

* * * * *

Meanwhile, in London, a WAC (Women's Army Corps) PFC from South Dakota was busily working in a locked room, typing the orders for a Top Secret operation called Operation Overlord. She was part of a small contingent of WACs who went from the US to England aboard the USS Queen Mary, along with several thousand Army troops, they to prepare for the invasion, the WACs to join General Eisenhower's staff.

In her book, **World War II WAC**, *which I wrote for Helen and published at Deeds Publishing, Helen Kogel Denton describes her job:*

"I was assigned to a small office, with a desk, chair, and a manual Royal typewriter. An armed guard stood outside my office and only admitted officers who could present the proper credentials and identification to him. Officers from the Canadian, British, Australian, and US Armies would come in every morning and give me dictation, with my afternoon being spent transcribing my dictation. Every page I typed had to be stamped TOP SECRET, so I knew I was handling extremely confidential material. The name of the project was OVERLORD. I was making three copies of this material and had to use carbon paper (today's copying machines had not been invented yet). My main concern was not making a mistake since erasing was very difficult. At times, the British officer would take me to the Admiralty, their headquarters, to pick up special material. All of it concerned the movement of troops and supplies which would be involved in the invasion of France.

"At the end of each day, the guard would come into my office, take the ribbon from my typewriter, all the carbon paper I had used that day, and burned it in the fireplace. One of the officers would pick up the pages I had finished, and he was responsible for them after that. I had no idea who handled the pages and never saw them again until I saw them in the binder that was later given to General Eisenhower. My duty was to type it to the best of my ability. I was never asked to retype a page, or make changes, so I assume my work was satisfactory. After the ribbons and carbon paper was burned, and the pages taken away—then I could leave to return to my quarters in the hotel.

"Never did I discuss with my roommate or any of the other girls what I had been working on—nor did they discuss their jobs. It was understood among all of us that we were dealing with highly sensitive and highly classified material. None of us had a "need to know" what the others in our group were doing. We were well indoctrinated with the motto "Loose Lips Sink Ships!" Never would any of us divulge to anyone what our jobs were—and I never talked about it until just before the fiftieth anniversary of the D-Day landing (that was 1994 before she talked about it). All we knew and cared was that we were helping the war effort."

*From the **4ID Yearbook** published in 1946:*

Our first casualties from enemy action were sustained in the course of the final rehearsal when E-boats hit under cover of darkness. So, too, our first

German prisoner was captured during the final preparation—an enemy airman who bailed out of a plane which was shot down over the assembly area.

*Following is a story from **War Stories Volume I: D-Day to Liberation of Paris:***

Thomas A. Welstead, Bal Harbor, FL
HQ, 4th Infantry Division
Tragedy at Sea

Not all of you may know that Slapton Sands was the site of a major tragedy in the preparation for the D-Day invasion. Early on, it was determined by our military leaders that the best way to prepare for an invasion was to find a place that resembled the coast of France and use it for real live combat. The coast at Slapton Sands was almost an exact duplicate of what was to be called Utah Beach. Utah Beach would be assaulted by the 4ID. In order to make the practices realistic, the beach and inland for twenty-five miles had to be evacuated by every living person, including all their possessions. There were some eight small villages in the evacuation area—villages like Torcross, Sherford, and Chillington. Within six weeks, three thousand people had to leave.

Those who lived in this rural farm area traveled very little. Some of the inhabitants had never left their village. When ordered to leave, many of them were lost, since in addition to their unfamiliarity with the area, the government had taken down all road and direction signs. No need to help the enemy if they invaded. These people withstood continuous enemy bombing, incendiary bombs, and bombs with land mines. Now they would have to leave everything—few would return.

The tragedy of Slapton Sands was an operation called "Tiger". The 4th Infantry Division, with its attached units, would assault Slapton Sands as though it was the shore of Normandy, France. Every detail centered on making it as realistic as one could imagine. The invasion would include air bombardment and naval gunfire. "Tiger" was the major pre-invasion exercise and was so realistic that many believed it was the actual invasion itself.

On April 27, 1944, eight LSTs left the Plymouth embarkation area—destination Slapton Sands. Three of these ships would not come back and a fourth struggled to stay afloat. On the morning of April 28, at 0130 hours, all hell broke loose. The convoy was under attack by German E-Boats using torpedoes and surface guns. E-Boats travel at speeds up to 40 knots; LSTs can get up to 8 knots. The confusion aboard those tightly packed ships was enormous. Men were in full battle gear, including gas masks and life preservers, climbing up the ladders and then back down as the captain tried to guess what kind of boats were firing at each other... E-Boats or U-Boats? The panic and helplessness were indescribable.

As dawn broke on the morning of April 28, the sea of bodies floating in the water (many upsides down) was a sight made for no man to endure. Life preservers around the waist instead of under the arms turned many upsides down. The freezing water was no help. Operation Tiger took the lives of 946 servicemen, 749 Army and 197 Navy.

How could such a fiasco happen? Only two vessels were assigned to accompany this convoy: a corvette, the HMS Azalea, and a World War I destroyer, the HMS Scimitar. The Scimitar suffered minor damage in a previous collision and its replacement came to the scene too late. Further, due to a typographical error in the orders, the American LSTs were on a radio frequency different from the corvette and the British naval headquarters ashore. In essence, eight LSTs with highly trained soldiers of the 4ID and its attached units, not to mention the naval personnel, were literally sitting ducks for the German E-Boats. For reasons deemed best by the Allied High Command, the disaster of Operation Tiger would remain a secret.

Largely due to one man who was thirteen years old when Operation TIger took place, the secret was finally broken. Ken Small was born in the little town of Hull—a town that received regular bombing raids of every variety. His beach-combing activities and curiosity led him to conclude that something terrible had happened the night of April 27, and on the morning of April 28. After years of research and investigation, he wrote and published a book called ***The Forgotten Dead***. Thus, the secret was uncovered. On May 31, 1994, Ken Small would participate in the dedication of a bronze relief plaque commemorating those who perished in the sea.

(The majority of those killed were supporting troops, not troops of the 4ID. But any casualty is a major loss).

Operation Tiger was kept secret until long after the war was over. Those 946 casualties were included in the June 1944 casualty reports the Army issued after D-Day. Sadly, that level of security would not survive in this day and age. If you want to read more about the Slapton Sands disaster, you can order Ken Small's book, ***The Forgotten Dead***, on Amazon—available in Kindle and used hard cover and paperback formats.

* * * * *

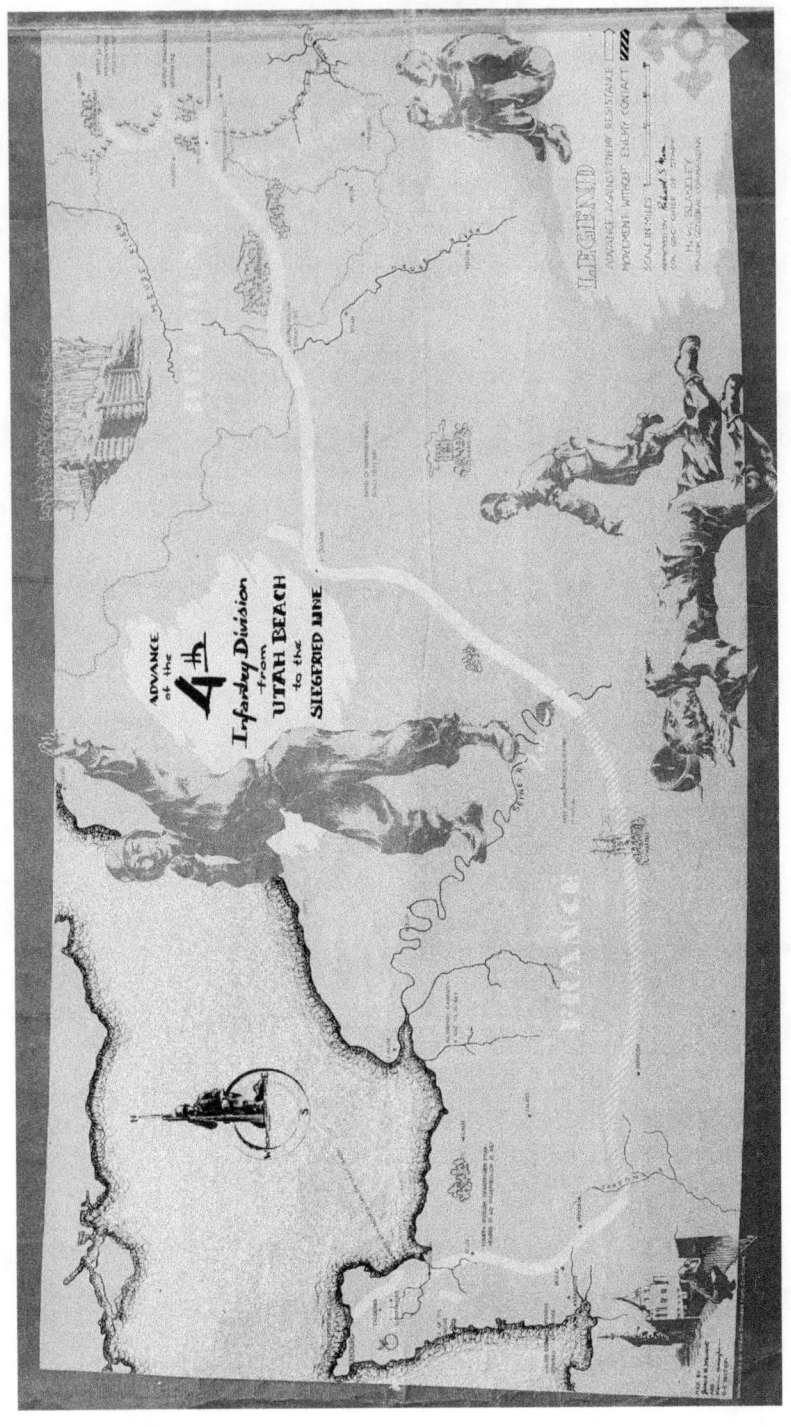

FINAL PREPARATIONS

MAY 1944

*From the **4ID Yearbook** published in 1946:*

Each move to the ports for these rehearsals had been made under complete security restrictions. The final move, during the third week of May, differed in no essential feature from those made previously. Yet it was the insensitive man who did not realize that "this is it."

Arriving in the marshalling areas, units found the areas surrounded by barbed wire and, once inside, none were permitted to exit or contact with any outsider, civilian or military. "Briefing" was begun. United States forces were to attempt landings on two French beaches, one under VII Corps, the other under V Corps. The assault division in the VII Corps plan was the 4th Infantry Division, while the assault element of V Corps, on VII Corps' left, was the 1st Infantry Division, reinforced by one regiment of the 29th Infantry Division. A third area was to be assaulted by British and Canadian forces, to the left of V Corps. By reason of the tide along the Channel coast, the first troops to land would be those assaulting the beach nearest Cherbourg—the 4th Infantry Division.

The mission of the Division was explained; the job for which each man had been prepared was fixed in relation to a given piece of Normandy beach. Models of the assault beach were studied; gas-proof clothing was issued; waterproofing of vehicles and equipment accomplished. During the first few days of June, the troops loaded onto ships for the final pay-off run.

From *Mr. 22nd Infantry (Major Earl "Lum" Edwards)* written by Michael Belis:

As Battalion Commander, Major Earl "Lum" Edwards would hold command over Companies E, F, G, and H of the 22nd Infantry Regiment. In addition to getting 2nd Battalion into a state of readiness for the upcoming assault, Edwards spent a great deal of his time studying a mock-up of the beach on which his Battalion was to land. He was provided with a Nissen hut in which the mock-up was installed, and he was the only one allowed to enter that hut. Daily aerial photos taken of the beach and inland area were brought to him and he studied them all, planning what his moves would be once the invasion got underway in order to achieve his Battalion's objectives. As the 6th of June approached, Major Earl Edwards was as ready as he could be to take 2nd Battalion 22nd Infantry ashore into Festung Europa.

Before he could assault into France, Edwards had another problem he had to deal with. A few days before the actual landing, he suffered from hemorrhoids and was in a great deal of pain from them. He found his ailment gave him considerable trouble in walking. He asked his roommate, Tom Keenan, to report his condition to Colonel Tribolet, the Regimental Commander. He was sure his medical situation would prevent him from making the landings. In his memoirs, Edwards described the resulting events:

"Later in the day an ambulance drove up to our quarters and two medics came in and said that I was to come with them. They helped me to the ambulance where I found Col. Tribolet and the Regimental Surgeon, Dr. Kirtley. We drove away and soon parked in front of a U.S. Field Hospital. Col. Tribolet and Dr. Kirtley went in and soon returned. We then drove a while and parked in front of another hospital.

The same thing happened. So, we drove on to another. This time some medics came out and carried me in and within a short time I was operated on. After an hour or so of recovery, I was carried back to the ambulance which returned me to my quarters, and I was placed again on my bunk. All this time no explanations whatever. I later learned that Col. Tribolet was determined that I would command the 2nd Battalion in the invasion so he and Doc Kirtley decided to take me to a hospital and ask if they would operate on me and immediately release me to their care. If the answer was "no" they simply carried me to another hospital and so on until one agreed.

So, I went into the landings with a large wad of cotton taped to my rear. Fortunately, the salt water and a few artillery rounds cured me. I don't remember ever thinking about it after we landed."

*****

Back in London, WAC PFC Helen Kogel Denton continued to type the D-Day orders, as covered in her book ***World War II WAC:***

We were experiencing some of the worst V-2 bombings that London had endured. If you could hear the noise the bombs made, you knew you were okay. But if the motor shut off, we immediately got under our desk and covered our heads. When the bombs hit, the whole building would shake, and dust flew everywhere. Because the Germans knew where we were working, our compound was hit often. By this time, we were sleeping three stories underground in a bomb shelter in the Square. Every night about dusk (which was around 10:00 PM with wartime double daylight savings time), we would take our blanket and a pillow and head for the shelter. The first floor underground was for people coming in off the street, the second floor was for British people, and the third floor was for the Americans. There was a single cot with a mattress for each of us; we provided the blanket and pillow. Each morning the "all clear" would sound and we would go back to the hotel, dress, and go to work.

Day after day I sat in my tiny office, officers bringing me more material to include in the operations order I was typing—later to be announced to the world as Operation Overlord, the code name of the invasion of

France, or D-Day. Each day the guard came in and repeated the process of taking my ribbon out of my typewriter, collecting all the carbon paper I had used, and burning it in the fireplace. The paper I had typed was taken by an officer and, I assume, locked in a safe. This project kept me busy from late February through April 1944.

When I finished the project I had been working on, I was asked if I would like to take the final work to General Eisenhower. I jumped at the opportunity and was thrilled that I would get to meet him. We often saw the generals, but only to salute and move on — this was quite an honor for me. When he asked if I knew what I had typed, I assured him I did and was honored to have been trusted with such an important job. He told me that one copy of the order would be sent to General MacArthur, to use as a guide in developing a similar plan for the invasion of Japan.

He then asked me if I knew that I had a brother in England. I told him, "Yes, but I have no idea where he is." He responded with, "We know where he is, and we want you to go see him this weekend." He then handed me a pass and permission to take the train to Salisbury, England, where my brother, Jerry, was stationed as part of the 3rd Armored Division. This was quite a thrill as I hadn't seen Jerry since he left home in 1940, four years earlier. We had a wonderful weekend together. Jerry was given a jeep so we could visit some of the countryside. Saturday night we attended a USO dance where I got to meet a lot of his buddies. I stayed overnight with an English family before boarding a train late Sunday afternoon for the trip back to London.

Following is a copy of the order giving Helen time off to visit her brother...

HEADQUARTERS
EUROPEAN THEATER OF OPERATIONS
UNITED STATES ARMY
OFFICE OF THE CHIEF SIGNAL OFFICER, APO 887
RCM DIVISION

6 May 1944

Fit to Fight

SUBJECT: Personnel Off-Duty

To: Commanding Officer, WAC Detachment B

1. Private First Class Helen E. Kogel, A-704xxx, is permitted to have time off this afternoon, 6 May 1944, to check travel status.
2. It would be appreciated if PFC Kogel could be authorized a pass to travel to Salisbury, Wiltshire, tonight and tomorrow, to visit her brother whom she has not seen for 2 1/2 years.
3. Sunday, being her normal day off, will not affect her duty status.

(Signed)
T. J. PALIK
Major, Signal Corps

Back in London, WAC PFC Helen Kogel Denton had some experiences that will be of interest to our readers, as will all her WWII experiences covered in her book, **World War II WAC**, available at **www.deedspublishing.com**. Read on for more of Helen's experiences before D-Day…

With my main project complete and while waiting for the invasion to take place, we took advantage of some time off to see the sights of London, such as Madam Tussauds' wax museum, the Tower of London, Shakespeare's home, the Abbey, and, of course, the USO had canteens and dances at some of the largest gardens (as they were called).

One of my highlights in London was the Saturday I stopped by the USO to see what trips were available. We selected a bus trip to Windsor Castle, the home of King George and his family. When we arrived, the King's flag was flying, indicating he was in residence and that we would only be able to view the outbuildings. We saw the chapel, the carriage house, and one large room that had his paintings in it. As we were walking around the room, the door opened and the King, the Queen, and their two daughters, Elizabeth, and Margaret, walked in. We were astounded when they came up to us and asked who we were and where we were from.

I was the first one in line, and when the King approached me, I didn't know whether to kneel or bow or curtsey, or what the procedure was. So, I just extended my hand in greeting. Then he introduced his daughters, Elizabeth, and Margaret. He asked if I had met Elizabeth since she had just been assigned as a driver for the American Army. Of course, I said, "No, I haven't, but I wish her luck. Maybe I'll see her around."

Never in my wildest dreams did I ever expect to see the King of England and the future Queen of England in my lifetime.

* * * * *

And I will introduce you to another source that I will use throughout this book as I cover the happenings of the 4th Infantry Division's fight across Europe in WWII—the **Diary of Clifford "Swede" Henley** who proudly served with the 22nd Infantry Regiment (we had a brief excerpt from Swede's diary in April). I will introduce it as follows, written by his friend and fellow 22nd Infantry Regiment officer Tommy Harrison who had his secretary type Swede's diary after the war (I thank Swede's two daughters for giving me permission to use this diary):

> *"My name is Cliff Henley. My friends call me Swede, and I was told I am to room with you."*

This was my introduction to Swede. The time was February 1942. The place was Camp Gordon in Augusta, Georgia. His statement, "My friends call me Swede" was ironic because in all the years I have known him, I never knew of anyone who wasn't his friend or didn't like him. The only possible exception to this would have been the Krauts, but they didn't know him personally—at least the way we did. You can bet your bottom dollar though, those Krauts that did get to know him, respected the hell out of him.

I had another roommate, Lt. Dave Henry, who had attended Clemson College at the same time as Swede. Through Dave I learned that Swede had left his mark at Clemson the same way he was to leave his mark with the 22nd Infantry. He was one helluva football player, as well as an excellent boxer. Naturally, he was one of the best-liked men on campus...would you have expected anything less?

In copying Swede's diary, nothing has been changed. If a town or a name is misspelled, it's because it was written that way. The language, at times, was embarrassing to my secretary as she typed the diary; but the language, nonetheless, remains unchanged...

This diary was never intended to be a book. The entries were made by Swede so he could relate these memories to Lila, his wife, and other members of his family back in Sommerville, South Carolina. I can remember the times when I was with Swede, and he would pull out his little book and recall the happenings of the day. This would usually occur late at night or early in the morning after the outposts were set up and all companies had reported they were secure for the night. Between a couple of slugs of cognac, Swede would make his entries.

Now, almost thirty years have passed, but yet in reading his diary, I found myself laughing at Swede's unique way of expressing himself, and once or twice had to wipe away a tear. I am sure you will sense the same emotions as you read the following pages. God—the things you forget...not necessarily wanting to...but time has a way of erasing from your mind, the good as well as the bad, when you don't live them day after day. Somewhere, however, locked in a little corner of your brain, those memories are still there. Swede's diary will trigger those memories.

It is not my intention to write a novel about Swede Henley, although if I were a writer, I would want to do so. I just wanted to print up this diary for him to share it with you. However, I couldn't pass up this opportunity to write something about Swede as a preface to this printing. It is a liberty I couldn't resist to pay homage to a fellow soldier and friend.

Tommy Harrison, New York, New York
January 1973

1-15 MAY 1944: During this period, we were getting all of our equipment, guns, and vehicles ready to go someplace. Destination unknown. Sgt. Horowitz (Supply Sgt.) began receiving equipment to be used only for D-Day operations. Sgt. Haixe (Motor Sgt.) was given orders to waterproof all vehicles. The 105 M3 howitzers were waterproofed. All articles of clothing that were unnecessary were turned in. We knew we were going someplace soon but when and where; God only knows.

15 MAY 1944: We received orders to move to Y-9 sausage in marshaling area and await orders. On the afternoon of the 15th under the command of Captain C. M. Henley, the company left South Brent Post, South Brent, Devon by motor for Y-9 camp. We knew that we were seeing South Brent Post for the last time. All the cooks and unnecessary company headquarters personnel were sent to Denbury Camp, Newton Abbot to join us later. The company command group were — Capt. C. M. Henley Co. Commander, 1st Lt. Frank Eggleston Recon and Executive Officer, 2nd Lt. Edgar Harris Assistant Platoon Ldr. and Recreation Officer, 2nd Lt. John Bullock Supply Officer, 1st Lt. John Ward, Platoon Ldr. 2nd Platoon, 1st Lt. Capelle Platoon Ldr. 3rd Platoon, 2nd Lt. Joseph Kinsinger Platoon Ldr. 1st Platoon, 1st Sgt. Joe Salego — Motor Sgt. Samuel Haire — Supply Sgt. Jacob Horowitz — Communication Sgt. Irwin Lichtman — Platoon Sgt. 1st Plat. Sgt. Evans, Platoon Sgt. 2nd Platoon Sgt. Dufresne, Platoon Sgt. 3rd Platoon Sgt. Froehlich

Section Sgts. Montanaro, Weber, Fatata, Gunst, Skinta, LaBarba. Company strength 7 officers 129 EM.

15 — 31 MAY 1944: Lived in the marshaling area and took life easy and sweating out what was to come, when and where D-Day H-Hour would find us. The Company was briefed on the 22nd but was not allowed to brief the company officers until the 26th and the company the 29th.

Many hours were spent studying the maps of the terrain we were to land on. Plans were made so that everything would work regardless of what happened. Every man knew what he was to do in case the leaders were knocked off. Orders came for the company to load at Dartmouth on Hard "A" on 2nd of June on LCT 2045, an American built LCT with a British crew.

Chaplain Bill Boice in his **"History of the 22nd Infantry Regiment in World War II"** *described the last half of May as follows:*

It was with mingled feelings that the elements of the regimental combat team received orders to move to the marshalling area.

These had been interesting days, charged with tension and anticipation, days when we had come to know and respect the British, and to appreciate this brave island. All equipment was carefully packed and waterproofed. Personal effects, save only that which could be carried, were stored in foot lockers and sent to the Effects Quartermaster in Liverpool for indefinite storage. All documents which might identify the unit were destroyed. No identification other than dog tags or AGO was retained.

On the night of 18 May 1944, the regiment moved by foot under cover of darkness to an assembly area. Then, shivering, and cold, the men were moved by truck to three marshalling areas designated as X, Y and Z, well away from towns and villages on the southern coast of England. Civilians were kept from the area or were required to remain in the area until after the invasion had occurred. The preparation and secrecy surrounding the pre-invasion were of the highest order, and while aware of the impending action, the officers and men of the regiment operated on daily stand-by orders without specific knowledge of invasion plans. An era had passed; preparations were finished. Mail home was curtailed and impounded, heightening the thoughts of loved ones and homes.

Each soldier wondered about his own courage. Yet, there was an eagerness to get into battle, to join the action against the enemy, and there was little expressed fear. It was not even possible to express personal uncertainty in letters; thus, the pressure began inexorably to build. Last-minute equipment was requisitioned and obtained. Quick courses in elementary French, designed to give each man enough knowledge to ask for help in case he was wounded or food if he was hungry, were taught by qualified instructors. There was much joking about the lack of the French phrases most of the men were interested in.

It was while in the marshalling area that the new type of demolition, the Bee-hive, was demonstrated to the assault companies. This new employment of a long-known principle of physics pleased GI's who soon caught on to its use and wanted to demonstrate more times than there were Bee-hives to be used for demonstrative purposes.

Chaplains conducted worship services daily. A regiment that had given little indication of religious interest prior to this time now began to take its religion seriously. Jewish officers remained on duty while Catholic and Protestant men were at divine services. The Jewish Chaplain from Division Headquarters conducted Jewish services for the men of his faith. Attendance increased so sharply as to warn the Chaplains of the magnitude of their spiritual responsibility…

The strength and service of the Chaplains of the Twenty-Second Infantry can never be measured. It is enough to say that during these crucial times officers and men realized as never before the worth of their Chaplains and the seriousness of the task ahead. Spiritual strength counted.

Elements of the Fifth Armored Division ran the marshalling guards and did everything possible to make these last days in Britain as pleasant and comfortable as possible for every member of the Division. By this time, the men knew the impending assault was but a few days away. One soldier remarked that he felt like a turkey prior to Thanksgiving. The remark was greeted with laughter at the time; it ceased to be funny within a matter of days. All mail was impounded, both outgoing and incoming. Sand-tables were constructed to an exact scale of the beach which was to be assaulted. The exact location of the beach, however, was still carefully kept secret, and only the battalion staffs, plus the company commanders involved, knew the place of the assault. Not even they had been told the day or the hour. The sand-tables were placed in tents and carefully guarded as the men were brought into the tents in small groups. They became familiar with the terrain so that they could recognize physical features, either by silhouette or by sight.

The time in the marshalling area seemed incredibly long to soldiers who were keyed to a pitch. At last, orders came to move out and again, under the deep cover of darkness, the companies loaded in trucks and moved slowly over the steep hills of England toward the coast. The trucks halted on back country roads at about 2:00 A. M., and the soldiers, loaded with assault equipment, sat unbelievably cold in the sharp English night. No movement was allowed and there was nothing the weary soldiers could do but miserably await the morning. The night was clear and there was no fog. Lights were prohibited and smoking was allowed only within the covered trucks. A trucking unit provided the soldiers with breakfast put up in paper bags, and hot coffee was supposed to be served. The coffee was cold and bitter. The breakfast consisted of thick, dry slices of English whole wheat bread with cold bologna and a cold hard fried egg. Among other marks of war, surely one part of the English countryside was covered with the brown stains of disdained coffee and the wreckage of the world's worst breakfast.

Prior to dawn, the soldiers dismounted and already weary under their heavy assault loads, they moved up the steep hill and toward the loading harbors. It was with relief, not unmixed with anticipation, that they saw the countless landing craft and assault boats that were to convey them across the channel. It was well past midday when the men got aboard and moved to their cramped quarters below deck. Space was at a premium; officers and men alike crawled into web-laced horizontal bunks barely far enough apart for both the man and his equipment. No men were allowed on deck. Time was spent in final briefing, and impregnating clothing with an evil-smelling preparation to resist gas. Men were warned to expect gas attacks on the beach.

Meals were a problem, and the men became acquainted with the 10-in-1 ration. Better than the K ration, and with a greater variety, the cartons contained canned foods, soluble powdered drink, crackers to take the place of bread, jelly or jam, canned milk, and toilet paper. Of all the ignominy of war, nothing so irritated and amused the men as khaki colored toilet paper. Surely, they felt, this was the last ignominious word in modern camouflage. The ration contained enough food for ten men and thus was called 10-in-1.

From Gerden Johnson's **History of the 12th Infantry Regiment in WWII**:

Early in May test firing of all weapons, trial loadings of vehicles, concentration on new supplies, and waterproofing of vehicles and signal equipment all pointed to the long awaited day. Then one evening General Bradley came to Exeter and addressed all officers of the division. He concluded his remarks with, "I'll see you on the beaches." That sealed it…

In the concise words of the field order and illustrated on large wall maps and aerial photographs, the 12th Infantrymen were told that the 4th Infantry Division with attached troops, supported by air and naval task forces, would assault the Cotentin Peninsula of France on D-Day to capture Cherbourg. Only, the name of Cherbourg was not mentioned at this point for reasons of security…The Naval Task Force would provide lift, protection at sea, gunfire support, and would breach all underwater obstacles. The IX Tactical Air Command would furnish air support.

Commencing at H-hour minus five (hours) on D-Day, the 101st Airborne Division, less certain glider elements, would land by parachute and glider in areas west of Turqueville with the principal mission of assisting the landing of the 4th Infantry Division. At H-hour minus four, the 82nd Airborne Division would land by parachute and glider astride the Merderet River, with one regiment east thereof. It would capture Ste. Marie Eglise and the strongpoint south of Beauzeville Au Plain, making contact with the 101st Airborne Division at that place. It would protect the south and west flanks of VII Corps along the Douve River south and east of Terre De Beauvil.

The regimental order directed that "All units will be alert to recognize and will make every effort to locate, contact, and assist personnel of the 101st and 82nd Airborne Divisions in respective zones of action," and to promptly relieve them…When the doughs had completed their briefing, they were so sure of every detail that enthusiasm reached the highest peak ever seen. They were impatient and eager to get going. The old axiom of instilling supreme confidence by giving the American soldier the whole picture had been proven. The only question left was, "When would D-Day be?"

One final Lum Edwards story for now, from **War Stories Volume I: D-Day to Liberation of Paris:**

General Sir Bernard Montgomery, while inspecting troops of the 22nd Infantry Regiment in England prior to D-Day, asked various officers where they were from in the "Colonies." When Lieutenant Colonel John F. Ruggles was asked, his reply was, "the North East Kingdom, Vermont, Sir!"

Major Earl W. "Lum" Edwards replied by answering, "From the Heart of Dixie, the land of black-eyed peas and grits. Mississippi, Sir!" General Sir Bernard Montgomery was caught off guard, momentarily shocked and stunned by Major Edwards' reply. A brief second was required by the general in order for the bits and pieces to settle. Upon regaining his composure, General Sir Bernard Montgomery replied, "Gad, I thought that was a river!"

* * * * *

This wraps up the training of the 4ID in England prior to D-Day. Hopefully you have felt the work that was being done all over England by the divisions who were destined to fight across Europe to liberate it and the world from the grasp of the Nazi regime of Adolf Hitler.

Next, I will cover the 4ID's fight across Europe that will run from D-Day (6 June 1944) to V-E Day (8 May 1945). I will do my best to help you see the highlights of one division who is representative of all the divisions who liberated Europe and brought an end to the Nazi regime.

I encourage you to share this with anyone you think will enjoy it. One of my favorite quotes of all time is, "If we forget history, we are destined to repeat it." Most of the "Greatest Generation" who made this history are gone now. It is the duty of we who are their offspring to understand and carry on to our Families and friends the history of WWII. If anyone thinks this couldn't happen again, they have their head stuck in the sand (or as we Infantry doughboys would say, up another orifice that I won't spell out.)

Tighten your chin strap and get ready for the historic fight across France, Belgium, Germany, Luxembourg, and deeper into Germany. I'll tell the story to the best of my ability.

Steadfast and Loyal,

— **Bob Babcock,**
Historian and Past President,
National 4th Infantry Division Association

* * * * *

OVERVIEW OF 4ID'S FIGHT ACROSS EUROPE

6 JUNE 1944 TO 8 MAY 1945

Let me give you a feeling for what is ahead of the 4th Infantry Division over the next eleven months. Along with winning the war, our WWII generation paid a high price in casualties.

While the statistics on the casualties we had each month in 1944-1945 will make you cringe, keep in mind, there are people reading this today who can pinpoint the day and month that a loved one…father, uncle, grandfather, husband, friend, classmate was killed or wounded in WWII. I visit the grave of a 1-22 Infantry battalion commander each Memorial Day who was one of the wounded on the day after D-Day; I also located a grave of a Soldier who joined the 4ID on 26 Nov 1944 and was killed on 30 Nov 1944; at least one of our reader's father was killed in June; another reader's uncle was killed in July; an officer who earned the Silver Star and the Distinguished Service Cross in June, was wounded, and came back in September for the penetration of the Siegfried Line, and was killed in the process of earning a second Silver Star; three battalion commanders were hit on 17 Nov 1944 in the Hurtgen Forest, two were wounded and one killed. One of the wounded came back to command the 4ID in Vietnam, and later lost a granddaughter killed in

Afghanistan. Another reader's father was killed in late February 1945, and the list goes on...

These are not statistics, these are American Families, just like yours, who lost loved ones in our nation's wars. As we will cover in more detail at the end of this book, the 4ID had more casualties (killed and wounded) than any other division in the fight across Europe.

Let us never forget, not just on Memorial Day but every day of the year—FREEDOM ISN'T FREE. It is paid for by patriotic Americans who love our country and the American way of life.

These aren't cold statistics; these are life altering experiences for thousands of people. PLEASE take time to reflect on all that have made the ultimate sacrifice for our country, from the early days of the Revolutionary War to those prepared to fight around the world for us today.

* * * * *

Above, I have given us a dose of what our 4ID troops did between January and May 1944. Starting here, we will follow our WWII forefathers in their eleven month fight across Europe to victory on 8 May 1945.

I encourage anyone who reads this book to tell your contacts who have an interest in the 4ID history from WWII about this book. We don't want to be spam or a nuisance, but I know a lot of people care about WWII history that I am unaware of and do not have contact with.

* * * * *

We begin with a summary of what the 4th Infantry Division did between D-Day and V-E Day. My intent is to whet your appetite about what is ahead of us over the next eleven months in 1944 and 1945.

One of my favorite military quotes is: "Any battle is a big one...if you are in it." I can agree with that from my personal experience as an Infantry officer in Vietnam. Whenever someone is shooting at you, it makes a long-lasting impression. I am not negating the personal experiences of any fight, just focusing here on the big picture that made the history books.

Our World War II (WWII) vets had almost daily doses of those big and little battles in their fight from Utah Beach, across France, Belgium, Germany, Luxembourg, and deep into Germany by the end of the war.

The following highlights the big picture fights that history remembers...

D-DAY, 6 JUNE 1944: 4ID, led by the 8th Infantry Regiment, was the first seaborne troops to land on the coast of Normandy, France at H-Hour, 0630 hours.

25 JUNE 1944: 4ID, along with 9ID (9th Infantry Division), liberated the first port in France, Cherbourg.

JUNE AND JULY 1944: Days and days of fighting through the hedgerows and marshland of Normandy took place before and after the liberation of Cherbourg.

25 JULY 1944: 4ID, along with 2nd Armored Division (2AD), were the spearhead divisions in Operation Cobra, the St. Lo breakout where massive air bombardments stunned the Germans as our ground troops broke out of the hedgerows of Normandy and pursued the enemy toward Paris.

25 AUGUST 1944: The 12th Infantry Regiment of 4ID and the French 2nd Armored Division and the rest of the 4ID were the first Allied units to enter Paris. After a day of celebration and clearing out pockets of German resistance, the 4ID continued their pursuit of the retreating Germans. Other units basked in the glory of a liberated Paris; the 4ID had a job to continue.

11 September 1944: A patrol from the 22nd Infantry Regiment became the first Allied unit to breach the daunted Siegfried Line and move across into the German homeland. The next day, other 4ID units, along with

Major General (MG) Raymond O. Barton, our 4ID commanding general, became the first Allied unit on German soil.

NOVEMBER 1944: Starting in early November, the 12th Infantry Regiment of 4ID entered Germany's Hurtgen Forest, to help the 28th Infantry Division. At mid-month, the rest of the 4ID joined the fight which raged non-stop until early December. Virtually every 4ID Soldier I have talked to, when asked what their toughest fight was, quickly said, "The Hurtgen Forest."

16 DECEMBER 1944: While resting and receiving replacements in Luxembourg for losses in the Hurtgen Forest (the average 4ID company had 150% casualties during that fight), the German counterattack that became known as The Battle of the Bulge, hit the weary and battered 4ID troops. Later, General George Patton wrote to MG Barton, 4ID Commanding General, "Your fight in the Hürtgen Forest was an epic of stark infantry combat; but, in my opinion, your most recent fight—from the 16th to the 26th of December—when, with a depleted and tired division, you halted the left shoulder of the German thrust into the American lines and saved the City of Luxembourg and the tremendous supply establishments and road nets in that vicinity, is the most outstanding accomplishment of yourself and your division."

FEBRUARY 1945: Often occupying the same foxholes they dug in September, the 4ID once again penetrated the Siegfried Line and fought through Prum and other German strongholds as the Nazis resorted to defending their homeland against our relentless assault. This pursuit continued through March and April.

8 MAY 1945: After 336 days of combat, punctuated with only short rest periods, the 4ID was deep into Germany when Hitler committed suicide and the Germans surrendered unconditionally.

That is the *Reader's Digest* version of the 4ID's fight across Europe in WWII. Now, stay with me and we'll go blow by blow over what happened in the next eleven months, covering big battles and the little and personal experiences that Soldier's remember.

*****

If you want to read along in some of the books that I will be using as references and take excerpts from for this book, start with these.

War Stories Volume I: D-Day to the Liberation of Paris by Robert O. Babcock

War Stories Volume II: Paris to V-E Day by Robert O. Babcock

History of the Twelfth Infantry Regiment in WWII by Gerden Johnson

World War II WAC by Helen Denton

History of the 22nd Infantry Regiment in WWII by Chaplain Bill Boice

All the above are available at www.deedspublishing.com, click on Book Store.

Utah Beach to Cherbourg, 6 June to 27 June 1944 by US Army Center of Military History

Includes maps, pictures, narrative—*Free online*—*Google:* Utah Beach to Cherbourg

*****

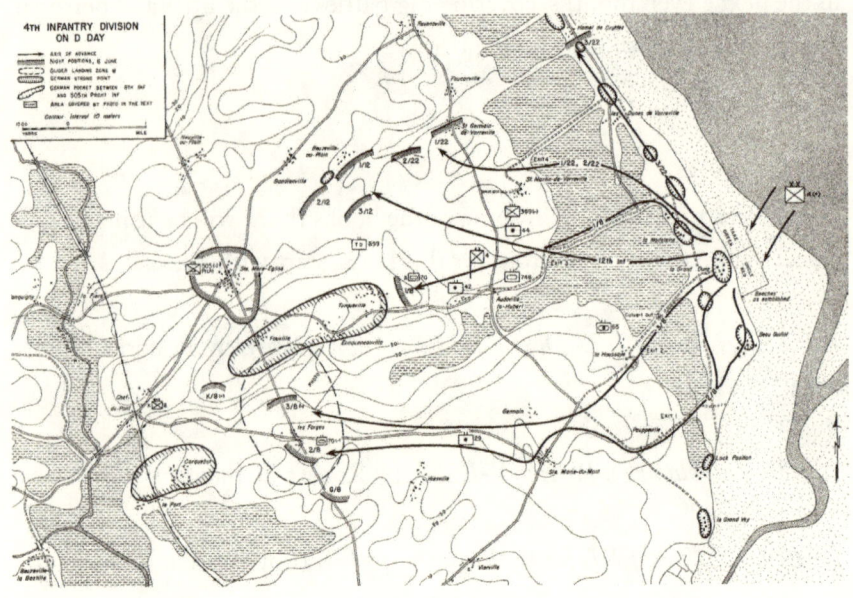

Map — 4th Infantry Division on D Day

BG Teddy Roosevelt Jr. and MG Barton — first 4ID command post on Utah Beach, 6 June 1944

JUNE 1944

D-DAY LANDING ON UTAH BEACH THROUGH THE CAPTURE OF CHERBOURG HARBOR

1-7 JUNE 1944: Since the middle of May 1944, the 4ID, along with the other troops scheduled for the invasion, had been sequestered in marshalling areas in southern England, studying the area they were going to invade, continuing to rehearse, and impatiently waiting for the invasion to come. No one was allowed into or out of the marshalling areas.

D-Day was originally scheduled for 5 June 1944, but bad weather in the English Channel caused the overall Allied Commanding General, GEN Dwight D. "Ike" Eisenhower, to postpone it a day. We'll set the stage for what has been called "The Longest Day" in American history.

From the **4ID Yearbooks issued in 1946:**
JUNE 1 THROUGH JUNE 5, 1944:

The mission of the Division was explained; the job for which each man had been prepared was fixed in relation to a given piece of Normandy beach. Models of the assault beach were studied; gas-proof clothing issued; waterproofing of vehicles and equipment accomplished. During the first few days of June, the troops loaded onto ships for the final pay-off run. From four ports, the flotilla put into the English Channel, formed, and headed toward the coast of France, shepherded by the combined strength of the British and American fleets, and with the air forces fending the enemy from the sky overhead. History assigns few men of any generation a role in so fateful an enterprise. To this already tense scene was added a decision by General Eisenhower and transmitted to the convoy, postponing the assault for 24 hours in the hope that high seas would subside. So, thin fingers of the assault forces turned back in mid-Channel to close into already crowded ports or lay off-shore until, a day later, the movement was resumed. The transports again sailed for the French coast; this time there would be no turning back.

From Chaplain Bill Boice's *"History of the 22nd Infantry Regiment in WWII"*:

During the days of June 4 and 5, the men were given their silk escape map of France and a small compass. Briefing was stepped up, and each man's boat position and duty was carefully reviewed. The assault teams had been broken up into boat teams, since the men would have to transfer from the larger craft to LCI's (Landing Craft Infantry) capable of getting close to the beach. Platoon sergeants were told what to do in the event a part of their team was lost or sunk.

Tension was high. Battle was ahead, but individual reaction was unknown. Most men worried more about their friends than about themselves. Esprit de corps was never better in a fighting unit, and whatever the personal fears the night of 5 June, collectively the men knew they were a great team, and they were confident. The men drifted to fitful slumber, lulled by the steady throbbing of the ship's engines. Their date with destiny would take place on the morrow.

Fit to Fight

*From the **4ID Yearbooks published in 1946**:*

After midnight of June 6, 1944, the transports slowed until they were barely creeping along, following the minesweepers, and at 0200 hours, the ships dropped anchor off the French coast. We were across the Channel. But what of the enemy? Soon—the answer! Heavy flak began to go up and grow in intensity—the German greeting to the airborne landing. The fighting had started. Offshore, with a rough sea running and in darkness, the assault elements climbed down landing nets into the bouncing LCVPs (Landing Craft Vehicle and Personnel). Our planes were pounding the beaches; the orange bursts and crack of the bombs could be seen and heard from the ships. It went on through the dawn. Then the naval barrage thundered down from battleships, cruisers, and destroyers. At the same time, the first assault wave swung into line and headed for shore.

Landing at 0630 hours (H-Hour) on a French beach, named for this operation, Utah Beach (Utah Beach is two miles east of St. Martin-de-Varreville and six miles from Ste. Mere Eglise), the assault units pushed inland as rapidly as possible to reduce the enemy positions behind the beach and to avoid the enemy shells which were beginning to rain down upon the beach. Beach defenses of underwater mines, barbed wire, trenches, machine-guns, 88-mm artillery, automatic tankettes (carrying 300 pounds of TNT and designed to follow runways and crash into our troops), forts with 150-mm and 210-mm guns lay ahead. To increase the hazards of landing, the enemy had flooded the area just behind the beach to a width of 2,000 yards. Only a few roads or causeways ran inland, and it was down these that Americans troops advanced.

It was almost impossible to imagine the fever pitch of excitement that had arisen in the men. Always the drive must be inland—to push the enemy back so as to create a steadily enlarging beachhead. Surprisingly few losses were sustained initially, but they began to mount at an increasing rate as enemy artillery swept the beach. One vital mission of the 4th Infantry Division was to contact the 82nd and 101st Airborne Divisions which had dropped west of the inundated area and around Ste. Mere Eglise. Leading elements of the Division made contact with these paratroopers and reinforced them around Ste. Mere Eglise, as succeeding troops advanced straight in, then flanked to the north on an operation which would eventually cut off the Cotentin Peninsula and roll up the coastal defenses.

JUNE 1944 – D-DAY THROUGH CHERBOURG: The following account of 4ID actions during WWII—from June 6, 1944 through May 8, 1945—comes from official 4ID After Action Reports (AAR) taken from the National Archives—compiled for us by our friend in Normandy, Philippe Cornil. The first AAR report comes from 7 June 1944, guess they were too busy on D-Day to write a report. I will fill in with my own report about D-Day, along with some first-person stories from those who made the landing.

JUNE 6, 1944—D-DAY: Today is one of the biggest days in the proud history of the 4th Infantry Division. It was on June 6, 1944, at 0630 in the morning, that the 4th Infantry Division stormed ashore on Utah Beach on the Normandy coast of France, in the invasion that began the ultimate defeat of Adolf Hitler and the Nazis. It is one of the key days in world history, and our great division was a major player in that event.

Led by the **2nd Battalion, 8th Infantry Regiment**, all three Infantry Regiments of the 4ID (8th, 22nd, 12th) were ashore by early afternoon. Although casualties on Utah Beach were light in comparison to the Airborne forces who had dropped in overnight, and the carnage that the 1st Infantry and 29th Infantry Divisions experienced on Omaha Beach (as depicted in the movie *"Saving Private Ryan"*), the 4ID did have almost 200 killed that day, including 60 men lost when the boat carrying **Battery B, 29th Field Artillery** hit a mine in the water. (Irving Smolens, a longtime friend, now deceased, was in a backup boat with other B/29 Field Artillery Soldiers and helped rebuild the battery after he got to shore).

It was on D-Day that **Brigadier General (BG) Teddy Roosevelt, Jr., assistant division commander of the 4ID**, went ashore with the first wave. When he saw that the landing was 2,000 yards to the left of where they should have landed, he turned to **Colonel (COL) James Van Fleet,**

the 8th Infantry Regimental commander and said, "We'll start the war from here." For his fearless leadership on the beach that day as he encouraged the landing troops, BG Roosevelt earned the Medal of Honor. (Bill Parfitt, now deceased, was Teddy Roosevelt's body guard that day—more about that connection later).

For the next 299 days, the 4ID fought the Germans without relief. No other American division suffered more casualties in the European theater than did the 4ID, and no other division accomplished as much.

Although June 6 was a relatively light casualty day for the 4ID, they suffered over 5,400 casualties during the month of June, far more than any other division, as they battled through the hedgerows and took the port city of Cherbourg.

Unsolicited by me, on June 5, 2003, I received the following note from **Bill Parfitt, BG Roosevelt's body guard,** *describing his memories from D-Day:*

"On this day in 1944 (June 5), I was puking over the side of a landing craft. One just big enough to have a jeep aboard. Getting more scared as I looked about at the tremendous number of boats involved in the landing, which I made about 6:30 the following morning. Can still recall a lot of it, but time takes away some. The damned seasickness was most disruptive to all. I don't remember anyone that didn't get damned sick. We played poker on the hood of the jeep using the invasion money that was given to us...I can remember going over the side of the bigger craft and making it okay. It was so rough that we lost a couple of guys with broken legs trying to transfer.

"I remember the general (BG Teddy Roosevelt, Jr.) and colonels gathering in an area near the Limey soldier driving the landing craft. My memory jumps around as I try to account for the long times spent in line and then approaching the beach. I do remember that the rain had quit when we landed...The jumping off, the cold as hell water, and the rush to the beaches is sorta blurry, but I remember grabbing one of those welded pipe things (obstacles in the water) and reloading my rifle. Don't remember a bit about shooting though. I seem to remember reloading three times this way. The run to the sea wall was quick. Do remember the first meeting of the General with the Colonel behind the sea wall—the one used in the book and movie (*The Longest Day*) for the first meeting. I remember General Teddy without his helmet. Also remember later on when General Hodges chewed his ass for not wearing it. Even then it ended up in the jeep. He detested the steel helmet.

"So, a few memories of the past. Was just thinking, how many of those guys are still alive?—damn few." (Sadly, Bill Parfitt died in November 2005—he is missed. You can see the interview I did with Bill for the Veterans History Project by going to the following web page: **http://lcweb2.loc.gov/cocoon/vhp-stories/loc.natlib.afc2001001.04654/**

If you don't believe in miracles, I think God told Bill to write that note so all our readers could hear the D-Day story from one who made the landing. What better way to feel our great 4ID history—thanks a million, Big Foot! (size 15 shoes)—looking down on us from heaven.

There are lots of key accomplishments and key dates in 4ID history…World War I, World War II, Cold War Germany standing against the Russian threat, Vietnam, more Cold War, four Iraq deployments, including the capture of Saddam Hussein, multiple brigade, and division HQ deployments to Afghanistan, and 4ID elements deployed to Poland, South Korea, and other hot spots around the world. In the fall of 2023, 4ID HQ returned to Fort Carson from a nine-month deployment to Poland. But I doubt that anything will ever happen to take the place of this most memorable day in 4ID history.

From my book, ***War Stories: Volume I—Utah Beach to Liberation of Paris***

I extract these stories. There are 96 pages of first-person accounts of D-Day experiences from 4ID vets in that War Stories book, the largest number of stories from any day in WWII. Space only allows me to use a few of them here.

"We will start the war from here," was the decision made by Brigadier General Teddy Roosevelt, Jr. and Colonel James Van Fleet when they found the lead elements of the 4th Infantry Division had been landed 2,000 yards off their assigned beach. The first Allied seaborne troops to land on D-Day were men of the 4th Infantry Division who landed on Utah Beach at H-Hour (0630 hours) on June 6, 1944. From that "Longest Day," the 4th Infantry Division continued the fight across Europe for the next eleven months until finally achieving total victory over the German war machine.

This section is the longest in our book. The D-Day stories included here are part of a presentation made by our veterans to the National D-Day Museum (now called National World War II Museum) at its Grand Opening in New Orleans, LA, on June 6, 2000. Over one hundred 4th Infantry Division D-Day veterans, organized and led by Bob Babcock, made up the largest organized veterans group at that significant event, paying tribute to all veterans of D-Day. Here are their stories, from my book *War Stories Volume I: D-Day to Liberation of Paris:*

A CHRONOLOGY OF THE 4TH INFANTRY DIVISION, 6 JUNE 1944

Extracted from Chronology 1941-1945, Special Studies, U.S. Army in World War II, by Mary H. Williams, Washington, DC; GPO, 1971. Courtesy of Dr. Robert Sterling Rush, 22nd Regiment Society Historian and former Command Sergeant Major of First U.S. Army and 1st Battalion, 22nd Infantry Regiment.

6 JUNE 1944: Utah Beach—The 4th Div, reinforced by 359th Inf of 90th Div, lands at H Hour, 8th Inf leading and against relatively light opposition secures beachhead; 8th Inf gets some elements to Les Forges crossroads and others to Turqueville area, but enemy retains salient between these and 82nd A/B Div units at St. Mére Eglise. 12th Inf, 4th Div, reaches Beuzeville au Plain area to left of 101st A/B Div and

22nd advances along coast to general line Hamel-deCruttes-St. Germain-de-Varreville.

From War Stories Volume I: Utah Beach to Liberation of Paris.

B.P. "Hank" Henderson, Knoxville, TN
Medic, 22nd Infantry Regiment
Looked Like Coney Island

They had a large tent they called the "Blue Room" where they took us in small groups and briefed us on our mission for D-Day. The 3rd Battalion commander was LTC Arthur S. Teague, one of the finest officers in the army. On June 1, I loaded onto the supply ship for the 3rd Battalion. I was in charge of medical supplies for the assault battalion. My jeep driver, Dago Oliver and I were the only two 22nd Infantry medics on the ship. We spent five days on the English Channel, one of the roughest bodies of water in the world. The last three days I was so sick I hardly knew I was alive.

On the morning of D-Day, June 6, I began to come around at daybreak. We had an English crew manning the ship and one of them came over with some of that British tea in a canteen cup. I drank a little of it. He went back over to one of the other Englishmen and I heard him say, "That big old tall boy is not going to make it." (How wrong he was; I made it through the whole eleven months.)

We had to wait until the first and second waves cleared the beach before we got the signal to bring in the supplies. As we started in and could see the beach, one of the guys from New York said it looked just like Coney Island on a Sunday afternoon. When we got closer, the coastal guns were firing down the beach—that killed the Coney Island ideas real fast.

When the ramp dropped, the lead jeep would not start. It had to come off before the rest of the trucks and jeeps could make it off. I decided I was not staying on that ship loaded with ammunition, so I was the first man off the ship. I went up to the sea wall, which was about three or four feet high, and dug a squatting foxhole where I stayed until all the vehicles were off the ship. I got out of my hole and started up the farm lane that the trucks and jeeps took. About 100 yards up the lane, a buck sergeant was leaning on his antitank gun. I stopped to chat with him. As we were talking, a sniper shot him in the leg.

"Holy mackerel, I got me a million dollar wound!" he said.

I left him a bandage and continued up the farm lane and came to a farmhouse. I had been there less than ten minutes when a woman came out with two young boys, about seven and nine years old. Both of them had real bad forearm burns. I used a whole tube of Unguentine (antiseptic salve) on those two fellows' arms. I put gauze on the arms and then wrapped and taped them really good.

When I finished with the boys, one of our guys came up and said, "Hank, you haven't had anything to eat in a long time."

I said, "This is my fourth day without food."

He had some cheese and crackers left over from a ten-in-one ration. He took my canteen cup around by the barn and got me some cider. My first meal in France was cheese, crackers, and French cider.

Later that evening, I was lying by the side of my foxhole as the glider troops were being towed over. I heard later that most of them were casualties. The Germans had the French people plant big poles in the landing fields and that played hell with the glider troops. The next day, a lone plane strafed our ammunition and blew it all to hell and back. I lay in a foxhole with two men on top of me for 47 minutes — as timed by one of our medical officers.

Harry Bailey (Deceased), Columbia, SC
Company E, 2nd Battalion, 8th Infantry Regiment
Night of June 5-6, 1944

Early morning hours of June 6, 1944 found me on a troop ship with the rest of my company headed for the beaches of Normandy, France. I was a twenty-year old platoon sergeant trying to lead a platoon that had thirty-eight men plus two medics. We had boarded a Coast Guard troop carrier, the APA Barnett somewhere close to Plymouth, England. We set sail with thousands of other ships including big battlewagons, cruisers, and hundreds of destroyers. The night of June 5, we moved all night getting into position at 0200 hours for the invasion. We had a breakfast of beans and bacon and got seasick pills. Then we prepared to go over the side of the ship on rope latticework, which was very hard to do with all the equipment we had to take, plus weapons, ammunition, K rations, and water. Some carried Bangalore torpedoes to blow holes in the barbed wire.

The waves were about ten feet high and the LCVPs were bouncing up and down. Some men got hurt getting into the assault boats. We got loaded and shoved off, joining many assault boats. We circled for about one hour, and then in a line we headed for the beach, which was about twelve miles away. At about 0545 hours we passed the rocket boats that were firing thousands of rockets on the beach that burst like artillery. Just then, the B-26 bombers bombed where we were heading. Our battalion, 2nd Battalion, 8th Infantry Regiment, was the first wave of seaborne troops to land on Utah Beach (the first seaborne troops on any of the five D-Day assault beaches).

Everything happened very fast for this twenty-year-old soldier who felt "like I was in a fog." Then the sailor on the assault boat dropped the ramp and we hit the water, which was about waist deep, and headed for shore. Artillery and small arms fire were all about the beach. My first scout, Douglas Mason, from Michigan, was the first to reach the sand dunes and I ran and dropped down beside him to look to see which way to go. He was immediately killed with a hit to the head by a sniper's bullet. I knew I had to move fast, or I would be next, so I ran forward as fast as I could go. The rest of the platoon followed. The lieutenant, who was platoon leader, when I last saw him, was pointing inland but would not go with us. He left my squad leaders and me to fend for ourselves. Colonel McNeely relieved him and sent him to another company. I was told he was killed on D+2.

We tried to move to where we thought the causeway was but got pinned down by machine gun fire. We finally got moving and had to cross a minefield. I lost two or three men. My medic got his foot blown off. We made it to the causeway at a dead run and started to get fire from a "knee" mortar. A round hit close, and I got shrapnel in my right leg. I didn't know I was hit until a medic saw blood. He gave me a shot and a band-aid.

E Company, 2nd Battalion, 8th Infantry Regiment kept attacking toward St. Marie du Mont. The tanks from the 70th Tank Battalion joined in the fight. One hit a mine and was knocked out. Airborne troopers took twelve prisoners from my company commander. They weren't playing any games. Airborne was called "Big Pockets." The Airborne was in St. Marie du Mont, but we didn't know it. We had the 70th Tank Battalion fire at a belfry, which was visible in the town. We moved into St. Marie du Mont and toward St. Mére Eglise where the Airborne were cut off by enemy forces.

On D+2, we fought our way into St. Mére Eglise under very heavy artillery fire, losing our company commander, Howard Lees, for the rest of the war as well as three or four more men. On the evening of D+2, the 8th Infantry Regiment and the 505th Parachute Regiment caught two battalions of German troops trying to relieve each other and demolished both battalions, killing approximately five hundred men. After the attack, we tried to get some sleep. We had been attacking for almost 72 hours. D+3 found us attacking toward Cherbourg. The count of men at the end of D+3 was fifteen left of our original forty.

When Brigadier General Teddy Roosevelt Jr. died on July 12, 1944, I was picked for his Honor Guard, as well as Captain George Mabry and other men of the 8th Infantry Regiment. In late November 1944, George Mabry earned the Medal of Honor during fighting in the Hürtgen Forest to become one of five men of the 4th Infantry Division to earn the Medal of Honor in World War II: BG Teddy Roosevelt Jr., LTC George Mabry, 1LT Bernard Ray, PFC Marcario Garcia, and PVT Pedro Cano.

Martin King (Deceased), Wills Point, TX
Company H, 2nd Battalion, 22nd Infantry Regiment
Help Us, Lord

On June 3, 1944, at about 1100 hours, Lieutenant Tommy Harrison and I went into a Quonset building with Sergeants Guinn and Pike. What we viewed was an amazing sight for me. There, on a sand display table, was a replica of the French coastline (the landing area) with many, many "to-scale" duplications of every building or bluff. These recognizable coastal features were to be used as landmark references to guide each landing party to their proper section of action.

As Lieutenant Harrison pointed out all the details given to him, I learned that my platoon would be loaded into small landing craft (LCPs) and put ashore at about H-Hour minus 1. Our land reference, an abandoned windmill or silo type structure on the French mainland, would be to our left as we approached the assault area. Our mission was to get ashore, locate two causeways, and, if possible, secure them in order to allow the faster advance of the first and second wave of assault troops to cross over the inundated area. This swamp-like area was about a mile and a half long, up to a mile wide, and five feet deep in places. It was both an excellent antipersonnel and tank barrier. It was subject to being covered with flammable liquid and set afire. It was very important to capture the enemy causeway positions.

At this point, viewing the shoreline replica and reference marks that were to be very important to the whole landing operation, Lieutenant Harrison became very serious in his briefing. He asked for questions and said that this was the time to ask; however, it seemed all we wanted to do was gaze at this table of small scaled-down models and memorize the sight that we would face if the operation was to be a success. "Help us, Lord, help us," Lieutenant Harrison said to us, with an intense stare into my eyes. "Now remember, the landmark structure is to be positioned to your left flank." He repeated this several times. Of course, we would get to review the situation table again the next morning. Thoughts of things past and things yet to come flashed through my mind. Then there were some mini-prayers, I'm sure.

That afternoon, Chaplain Bill Boice arrived in our area and men who wished to do so were gathered for a religious service. We sang hymns while Chaplain Boice played a field organ. I seemed to lead out on the hymns since I had had chaplain's assistant experience stateside. I was loud with it, to say the least. We listened to his message and blessing with an uplifting prayer for God's strength and protection for us in the times ahead. I remember that service to this very day. It is still a memorable experience that I have relived over and over.

By this time, we were equipping ourselves for the events to come. Each man, except the machine gun operators, prepared a backpack with four boxes of .30- caliber ammunition (eighty pounds) to be carried in on the landing. I, too, bore one of these, as did the men, plus all our other equipment.

At dawn on June 6, 1944, H-Hour minus 1 hour or so (about 0530 hours), my platoon and I went over the side and down a rope-net ladder into a smaller landing craft (LCP). The sea was rough, and it took a few attempts for all of us to get aboard. When Sergeant Guinn, the coxswain, and I decided that all were accounted for, we pulled away into a circling rendezvous pattern waiting for the "go ahead" signal. This lasted a few minutes. It was a very impressive sight.

Some rocket launching barges nearby were shooting off their many rockets, sometimes overhead and always toward the shoreline. The coxswain seemed to be very observant and cautious, maybe anxious, but we were all scared and quiet. Suddenly he opened the throttle and sped toward the beach. Gazing ahead, we soon sighted a recognizable feature that resembled our landmark reference. It also appeared to be off to our left flank.

Anxious moments followed. We agreed that this was our action sector, and the coxswain opened the throttle wide open. The windmill silo structure was then very visible to our left. When we were within a hundred yards or so of the beach, he de-throttled, let down the ramp, and shouted, "Get out, get out!" We did. I was first into the water, waist high to me (a six-footer) and the rest of the men followed. It was quite a burden fighting to stand up while wading through rough waves with eighty pounds of ammunition on our backs, but each of us made it. This was about 0550 hours.

Being on land now, we located one causeway but couldn't tell if the other one was to our right or left. A little confusion to say the least, what with some small arms fire directed at us. Alone on a strange beach was never like what we experienced before on our practice runs; however, the firing was going over us and into the water.

We dug in two machine guns and fell in behind a sand dune. If you have ever prayed with your eyes open wide while scanning the horizon, you can imagine what this was like. We waited and waited. The time was getting closer to H-hour, 0630 hours. It seemed like an eternity because no wave of our troops came in behind us.

You know something? I can't remember hearing a single prayer of repentance, just ones of deliverance like, "Lord, please let me get back home." A joking remark that I had heard many times before surfaced in my mind: "Second lieutenants and mop handles are expendable in this man's army." This seemed accurate. Still, there was no wave of friendly troops.

After about an hour and a half, all kinds and sizes of firepower began coming in and going out. We could tell that a real war was happening down the beach to our left. Sergeant Guinn and two men had gone out to scout our position for a causeway to our right. Surprisingly, someone said to look there on the causeway, since coming toward us were six or eight men in uniform, one of them walking with a limp. We thought this to be very strange for the situation we expected at the time. We had been schooled to be very careful of every move, that it might be a trap. Then someone said, "They're paratroopers."

They soon met us and told us that this road was clear for a way inland…only some small arms fire in the distance. These troopers were supposed to have been dropped at St. Mére Eglise but missed their target by seven or eight miles. They had heard the action and came to it thinking it might be some of their outfit. They disappeared down the beach to our right.

We had begun to return fire on two pillboxes as there was more light of day, but all we could do was hold our position and wonder where in the world everybody else was. Near midday, we made contact with men of the 3rd Battalion and learned they had made land to our left, and well out of their proper assault sector.

We would soon find out what a real war was like now that the 3rd Battalion had to clear the beach ahead of them.

The 2nd Battalion Commander, Major Lum Edwards, was to have landed behind us as the second wave following the 3rd Battalion (depending on the amount of success), but they did not come in. The 2nd Battalion, which was my battalion, had landed quite a distance to my left.

Years later, reading Chaplain Boice's book, *History of the 22nd Infantry Regiment in WWII*, the thought came to me that I had taken a fighting unit to war, and no one came. I dislike saying it, but it seems that we learned the meaning of SNAFU (Situation Normal, All F**ked Up), what with bad seas and questionable navigation. Somehow, we got together and soon got into the fight in support of Item and/or King Company.

They hit the first causeway and cleared it. It was a slow go, but we did cross on the causeway and fell in to support the rifle company. Ahead of us, a small tank had hit a mine and was disabled off on the right bank of the road. We looked at them and traveled on into the hedgerows.

Later, in the hedgerow fighting, Martin King was wounded and on June 22, lost his right eye. After recovering in a hospital in England, he led a provisional truck unit and spent until February 1945 convoying supplies to air bases to be flown in support of the fast-moving advance across Europe.

From the 4ID After Action Report from WWII:

(This is a continuation of our daily account of 4ID actions in WWII from the time they landed on Utah Beach on 6 June 1944 until they took the port at Cherbourg on 25 June 1944. There were over 5,400 4ID casualties in that three-week period in 1944).

I will repeat the 7 June 1944—D+1 report since many of us may have overlooked it while reading all the details on D-Day. Keep in mind, D-Day, while among the most famous dates in world history, was the first of an eleven-month string of almost daily battles for the Soldiers of the 4th Infantry Division and all the other Soldiers, Sailors, Airmen fighting across Europe. While D-Day was historically important to the 4ID, the toughest fight for 4ID started on 7 June—D+1...

7 JUNE 1944—D+1: Despite the successful landing, it became quickly obvious that the enemy resistance was increasing; the beachhead was far from secure, and the risk of counterattacks was great, especially from the north and the south. Some positions close to the beach were still in enemy hands and they continued delaying action. D-Day plus 1 was devoted to the destruction of scattered enemy groups and efforts to extend the beachhead.

It would take a week of hard fighting to gain several kilometers and to reach all the initial D-Day objectives.

The attack of the three regiments of the 4th Inf Div began at 0600 AM. The 8th Regiment attacked and reduced the Turqueville salient; severe fights took place for the taking of Ecoquenauville. About mid-afternoon, Sainte Mère Eglise fell completely into the hands of the 8th IR (Infantry Regiment) and the 746th Tank Bn (Battalion) moving to Neuville-au-Plain. The German counterattack toward Sainte Mère Eglise was repulsed by the 82nd Airborne, sustained by some incoming tanks.

The 12th Regiment took Beuzeville-au-Plain and reached the outskirts of Neuville-au-Plain. They were unable to take possession of the town after a sharp engagement.

The 22nd Regiment had the most difficult mission: to reduce the strong points along the beaches and the heavy fortified batteries inland. The strong points consisted of reinforced concrete blockhouses armed with artillery pieces and turreted machine guns, protected by mines, infantry pillboxes, ditches, and wire. Numerous strong points were reduced slowly and at great cost, but not all of them were taken. Fighting in the generally flooded swampland, the regiment fell under the heavy fire coming from the powerful batteries of Azeville (four guns of 105 mm) and Crisbecq (three guns of 210 mm).

The enemy fell back to the general line Taret-de-Ravenoville—Saint-Marcouf—Azeville—Le Bisson. On the beach, the unloading was slow and enemy guns continued to harass the landing operations.

During this second day, 10,735 men (many from the 90th and 9th Infantry Divisions), 1,469 vehicles and 807 tons of supplies were landed, but it was less than the schedule had called for. Ammunition became available in limited quantities.

8 JUNE 1944—D+2: The attack by all three regiments was launched at 0630 against the defenses of the Montebourg area. The 8th and 12th progressed slowly throughout the day. Heavy fires from artillery (88 mm guns), mortar and machine-guns were encountered, and violent fights took place around Neuville-au-Plain, Magneville, and Emondeville.

Faced by stubborn resistance, and after exhaustion of their explosives without destroying the main fortifications and close-in-fighting in the German trenches, the 22nd fell back and, when counterattacked during the afternoon, it was driven back even farther. The only success was the surrender of Taret de Ravenoville. Division Artillery, very active all day long, requested air and naval bombardment to support them. The fires were very effective. At the end of the day, on the beach, all the vehicles were in running condition and sent into the hands of using units.

9 JUNE 1944—D+3: The 8th and 12th Regiments attacked at 0530 toward the high ground east of Montebourg. Progress was continuous but slow at the cost of hard fighting and heavy losses (mainly around Ecausseville for the 8th, and at the Château de Dodainville near Joganville for the 12th). The 22nd launched a new assault on the four powerful forts of Azeville, abandoning the plan to take Crisbecq. Attacked to the rear, the position surrendered after the blowing of the ammunition caused by the flame thrower of Pvt Ralph G. Riley. In mid-afternoon, the 22nd formed with the 70th Tank Bn and 899th TD (Tank Destroyer) Bn, a special task force under command of Brigadier General Henry A. Barber with the mission of attacking in the direction of Château de Fontenay and Ozeville to capture Quinéville. The strong enemy position of Château de Fontenay pinned down the task force.

The weather was bad, and no air support was available. For the first time, the distribution of rations for the infantry was initiated from the beach.

10 JUNE 1944—D+4: Little change in the situation. Strong points along the beaches between Petit Hameau des Dunes and Hameau de Cruttes continued to be in enemy hands. The 8th and 12th Regiments attacked at 0630. Faced throughout the daytime by stiff enemy resistance, they nevertheless reached their objectives (positions around the highways of Montebourg that could not be seized) prior to dark. Attacks (at 0630 and 1745) of the 22nd Regiment in the direction of Ozeville and in the direction of Château de Fontenay fell short and were unsuccessful. (Note: Throughout these After Action Reports, time is expressed in 24 hour military time. Thus, 1745 above is 5:45PM in the time most of our readers are familiar with).

11 JUNE 1944—D+5: Enemy delay and harassing action continued but no counterattacks were experienced. Isolated strong points at Crisbecq and along the beaches were still held by the enemy. The 8th received heavy artillery fire during the day and the night, consolidated and organized positions gained on 10 June. The 12th attacked at 0730 with the objective of taking the high ground to its immediate front. Upon gaining this ground, positions were organized for defense. The 22nd suffered heavy losses in unsuccessful attacks on the Château de Fontenay and Ozeville. The only success was the capture of two more strong points along the beaches. Weather was unfavorable.

12 JUNE 1944—D+6: The enemy resistance decreased and during the afternoon, the strong points at Crisbecq, Ozeville, and Dangueville were vacated. The resistance at Fontenay-sur-Mer remained determined.

The 8th held its positions previously gained. At 2100, an attack to seize and hold Montebourg was partially successful. The 12th organized for defense, launched an attack at 1630 to the northeast. Relieved of its task of containing Fontenay-sur-Mer, the 22nd launched an attack at 1230 on Ozeville behind overwhelming fire power and passed through the village at 1550. The 39th Regiment 9th Infantry Division occupied Crisbecq (at 0820) and Dangueville (mid-afternoon), forcing the enemy to evacuate.

13 JUNE 1944—D+7: Stubborn resistance by small groups of infantrymen continued, fighting from hedgerow to hedgerow. Montebourg was re-occupied by the enemy during the night of 12-13 June and a strong pocket of enemy resistance at Fontenay-sur-Mer was overrun by our forces. Enemy's massed artillery fire was noted for the first time. The 8th held positions. A small task force attempted to reenter Montebourg but after two attempts, it was ordered to only contain the village. The 12th organized defensive positions and launched an attack at 1330 to gain the high ground. The 22nd attacked on Ozeville and advanced to the northeast, to the ridge of the Quinéville-Montebourg highway.

14 JUNE 1944—D+8: After resisting an attack of the 12th Infantry Regiment at about 1600, the enemy launched two counterattacks at 1800 and 2100, both of which were repulsed. The 8th and 12th Regiments held and improved their positions, maintaining constant patrols. The 22nd Infantry Regiment launched a coordinated attack in conjunction with the 3rd Bn of the 39th Infantry (9th Div) to secure Quinéville and the high ground to the northwest. Supported by an aerial bombardment, the attack was successful, the fight ending at 2130. The enemy's main line established on the best natural defenses was broken. The capture of Quinéville and the clearing of the coast also ended the troubles of the unloading on Utah Beach.

Following are more stories from this first full week on French soil from, **War Stories Volume I: Utah Beach to Liberation of Paris.**

Morris Austein, Boca Raton, FL
Company I, 3rd Battalion, 22nd Infantry Regiment
Here They Come!

My most memorable years are of the times I served with I Company, 3rd Battalion, 22nd Infantry. I landed at Normandy at 0630 hours on D-Day. I was in the first wave of the 22nd Infantry on Utah Beach. I was a demolition platoon leader. My first night after moving from the beach was spent behind a waist-high stone wall. We were all nervous and exhausted. We were half asleep around midnight when someone shouted, "Here they come!" We all got excited and started firing in the direction of the noise. We fired until everything got quiet. Checking things out in the morning, we found the place full of dead animals.

The second night I patrolled the hedgerows in the dark. I came face to face with another soldier, not knowing if he was German or American. We turned sideways, and I noticed the cut of his helmet. I raised my rifle the same time he did. We both fired in the excitement. I felt something hit me in the mouth. We missed—it was my rifle butt. Another incident: We were in foxholes in a hedgerow area getting air support in the front lines. One of the planes was dropping a bomb that hung up and didn't drop. As the plane was swinging upward over our lines, the bomb came loose. Fortunately, it didn't explode, but it made a huge crater and the sand rained down for what seemed like an eternity, half burying me.

The final incident crossing my memory is when we were dug in overlooking Cherbourg, and we were getting sniper fire. Young and foolish as we were, I put my helmet on my rifle and raised it. The sniper fired at it. I kept doing it and played with him for a while. Shortly, a group of soldiers came forward to us with a white flag and suitcases. One said, "Me Polish, going to America." I turned the prisoners over to Captain Glenn Walker. I returned to my unit and was talking to my men through a window in the antitank ditch. I was lying flat on my face when a mortar shell landed inches from me, blowing me up and back down into the bottom of the ditch. It was June 27, 1944, and the end of my Army days of combat.

All these incidents made me a fatalist. My number didn't come up, and I still am a fatalist.

Donald Ellis, Richmond, ME
Company G, 2nd Battalion, 8th Infantry Regiment
Lived and Learned

The next day, June 7, 1944 the Company was reassembled, and as we advanced we began to get into the hedgerows. These hedgerows were interwoven and as thick as your wrists. The farmers used these as we would use a fence. The enemy, having been there for some time, had zeroed in their guns and mortars to cover the gate. Some of these areas were fifty to a hundred yards in depth. At times we would fight all day to take one field. After penetrating the area, we would use their foxholes. As we got into the holes, the Germans would drop mortar shells on us because they had zeroed in on those holes, too. We wised up and dug our own holes.

Upon securing our positions, we would establish outposts and then begin our patrols. In the beginning, the patrol would check with the outposts to alert them with a password and counter password to identify us upon return. When we returned, the Germans would attach a couple of their men on the end of our patrol. After catching a couple in the act, we established a procedure of giving the number in our patrol to the outposts. You lived and learned...You've got to realize the Germans had been at war long before we got there. We learned their tricks and counteracted with some of our own.

Montebourg was the first big town we hit. After digging in for the night, Rip Colbath, some others and I, decided we would go into town to scout around. A common practice of the town folk was to hide in cellars of the bombed out houses. When we came in contact with them, they would tell us whether the Germans had left or were hiding out.

In checking out several houses, we entered a partially demolished large apartment building. Entering the cellar, we came upon a large group of French men, women, and children. We spent most of the night there trying to converse with our pidgin French and their poor English. They shared their meager food and wine, and we shared what rations we had with them. Just as it began to get light, we decided to go back to our lines. As we emerged into a large courtyard in a strung out line, a burst of machine gun fire hit and killed one of the two guys ahead of me. My buddy, Rip Colbath, was stitched up. I picked up Rip and took him back to our line. Upon returning to our lines, we were met by a medic and Captain Haley. He radioed HQ that our patrol had discovered the town was very lightly defended. Having learned this information, it precluded a full-scale assault. As a result of this, we earned the Silver Star.

As we captured them, we would immediately separate officers from enlisted men because the privates wouldn't talk with the officers present…

Louis Kaplan, Baltimore, MD
Service Company, 12th Infantry Regiment
Lying In a Ditch

The Personnel Section left Bournemouth, England, for the port of embarkation on or about June 9, D+3. We arrived there the same day, but we ended up doing a lot of waiting. The next night, we boarded an LST and sailed across the English Channel to the Normandy Beach. A strong wind prevented us from landing. During the night, standing on deck, we could see the flashes of fire from our artillery; it was firing from the beach at the enemy.

The next morning, I marveled at the sight. I saw two long breakwaters made up of partially sunken ships. There were many ships with large barrage balloons flying over them, lined up in rows, waiting to land. I watched the tiny minesweepers moving in pairs between the rows of ships to snag mines dropped during the night, or which broke loose from their moorings. The minesweepers rode in pairs because there was a cable extending from one to the other. In the center of the cable was a contraption to snag mines.

After debarking the LST on a quarter-ton truck, my driver drove between white tapes where the area was cleared of mines. On either side were signs in German that read, "Achtung, Minen." We drove past the outskirts of St. Mére Eglise and stopped for the night within earshot of the screaming meemies. I was told that the concussion was so powerful that it broke the blood vessels of anyone near the point of impact and caused internal bleeding. I spent that night lying in a ditch on the side of the road. I was awakened later when a battery of antiaircraft guns sent up a curtain of shells.

Donald Nolan, Lakewood, CA
Company G, 2nd Battalion, 22nd Infantry Regiment
Company Runner

I was on my first day as runner for Company G. Someone, probably the message center officer, pointed in the general direction and said, "Go." There was a sunken road, and on each side were fields with hedgerows. I was about a hundred and fifty yards from the Battalion CP, walking out in the field, when I heard a lot of commotion on the road. I looked through the hedges and was looking into the biggest German tank I ever saw. It was headed toward our CP on the road.

I ducked and headed back to the CP. There was Major Lum Edwards, standing in the hedgerow break, watching our antitank gun and halftrack retreating down the road. What he didn't realize was that the gun was pointing the wrong way and was trying to get turned around. Major Edwards was sort of moaning that his own antitank gun was running away. When the gun finally got turned around, it put at least three .57mm rounds into the tank. I went back to my job and found G Company. That is also the day I met General Roosevelt.

Jim Burnside, Richmond, VA
Company E, 2nd Battalion, 22nd Infantry Regiment
Gallant Paratrooper

I have a vivid memory of an incident that happened in the dim light of dawn on D-Day after our landing on Utah Beach. I had trouble finding some reference points that were given to us. I knew Company E of the 22nd was to advance inland to a macadam road, turn right, and attack toward the fortification of Azeville, but I couldn't find the damn road, only a plowed field. After walking in the field a couple of hundred feet, I suddenly realized what had happened. The Air Corps saturation bombing, intended to blow up underwater obstacles and barbed wire on the beach, had landed too far inland and completely covered the road for several hundred yards. Fortunately, the Navy landed us a mile or so too far to the left, otherwise we would have been under direct fire from the big guns in the Azeville pillbox.

Working cautiously up the road towards Azeville, I became aware of some movement on the road ahead. Holding our fire, we waited to see what was coming. To our astonishment, it was an oxcart with an ox pulling a full load of straw. Astride the ox was a wounded paratrooper who had dropped in the night before D-Day. He had a bandage on one arm and a blood soaked bandage on his forehead. In the cart were five or six of his wounded buddies. As they slowly passed us, looking for an aid station, the paratrooper raised his good arm, holding a Tommy gun. With a big grin he said, "Hi-Ho Silver, fellows." Thus, the gallantry and courage we were to see so often was always served so well by a keen sense of humor.

On a later date (I believe around St. Mére Eglise,) during a lull, Major Lum Edwards, our battalion commander, had cautiously worked his way to a shallow shell hole in the middle of a small field and squatted down to do his morning's duty. A shell landed in the same field. Lum squatted down a little deeper and pulled his helmet down a little further. Wham! Another shell hit a little closer. Lum — never rising up, holding his pants around his ankles in one hand and his helmet on with the other — did the most amazing duck waddle to safety in a nearby hedgerow, accompanied by our hysterical laughter.

'Nuff said. Isn't it amazing how our memories dull the horror of combat that was all around us and keeps the humorous events clear? Good soldiers were a necessity and how fortunate our outfit was to always have some GI in our midst who saw the humor of things and got us laughing—breaking the almost unbearable tension and helping all to keep our sanity. God Bless them.

Carl Morris, Hertford, NC
Company I and HQ, 3rd Battalion, 8th Infantry Regiment
Wine Cellar

This story is just to show you how orders are often carried out to the letter in the field. Company I was prepared to make an attack late one evening but was told not to do so until specific orders were given. In the meantime, they could see the Germans in the distance—in full action. It appeared that they were also preparing to make an attack. Our command post was notified of this situation, but we were still told to hold our fire. When the Germans began to move from their position in the direction of I Company, the CP was notified again. Again, Company I was told to hold their fire. Next, Company I reported that the Germans were walking all over us. The CP responded, "Shoot the bastards." Results…mission accomplished.

At one place, four or five of us got caught under shellfire near a church. For protection, we scrambled to get inside, which was the cellar. When the situation became quiet, we scouted around and came upon a French chateau nearby. Remember, this was grape country. Inside this place was also a cellar that contained racks and racks, fifteen tiers high. It was estimated that there were about sixty thousand bottles of champagne in that cellar. Soon, with a jeep and trailer, we loaded up some hundred and fifty bottles and took them back to our hideout in the church. Knowing that we might be there for several days, we settled down, waiting for ammo and rations. A GI came with supplies. He stayed and had a few drinks that evening. When he left, he was given a couple of bottles of champagne. About noon the next day, he was assumed missing. But later in the evening, he was found lying down on the ground near a small stream of water, passed out like a light. Fortunately, when they sobered him up, he was OK. It so happens that the officers found this out and when it became possible, they sent a large GI truck down there and loaded it up with wine for their big party.

Later, after being hurt scouting with my infantry company, I elected to join the wire section. This job was to help keep communication between the frontline companies and the forward operation post. At one point while checking into the telephone wire for breaks, I spotted a body in a tree about fifty yards ahead. I chanced a shot to see what would happen. Nothing...I was a sharpshooter with a bunch of medals. Did I miss? I don't think so. Anyway, after four or five shots, still nothing happened. To my surprise, that German soldier was tied up in the tree, equipped with a telephone to relay information to his outfit. To my relief, he had been killed a little earlier by our artillery fire.

Louis Kaplan, Baltimore, MD
Service Company, 12th Infantry Regiment
Troop Replacement

I was the Regimental Classification Specialist of the 12th Infantry Regiment. My primary duty was to handle the details of assigning replacement soldiers for those killed, wounded, and or missing in action. Here is a description of the first time in Normandy that I had to go from the rear echelon location of the 12th Infantry personnel section to a combat area to handle the details of replacing soldiers. Captain Arthur A. Edmunds, the Regimental Personnel officer, alerted me to be ready to leave with him. The jeep driver was Glen Steensland, highly trained in night driving.

After leaving the rear echelon, we passed a lightly wooded area from which our artillery was firing at the enemy. We heard many "thunderclaps" but could not see the artillery pieces nor tell from which direction they were firing. Later, after leaving the artillery far behind and as it was getting dark; we came to a crossroad in a desolate area. A military policeman climbed out of his deep foxhole near the crossroad and confirmed the proper road to take.

We arrived at the Regimental CP after dark. There, we were given directions for locating the convoy of replacement soldiers at a designated place on the road. We found the 4th Infantry Division classification specialists with their two-and-a-half-ton-trucks filled with replacement soldiers. They turned over to us the trucks with the soldiers assigned to the 12th Infantry Regiment.

Captain Edmunds guided the trucks to the 12th Infantry Service Company, located near the Regimental CP. Service Company soldiers outfitted the replacement troops with needed equipment and ammo. In the meantime, I was handed the Military Occupation Specialty Forms, one for each replacement. After studying the military skills of the replacements, I used my best judgment in assigning them to the companies that needed them. Quite often, we waited until the next morning before returning to the rear echelon.

James Drennan, Graniteville, SC
HQ, 42nd Field Artillery Battalion
Please Forgive…

Walking into the city of Montebourg on or about June 14, 1944, I felt complete sadness imprinted on my mind.

Dead mothers and fathers holding their dead children was a scene I was not ready to handle. Dead men from D-Day to the Battle of the Bulge have all but faded from my mind, but not the scene in the train or bus station. God, please forgive us.

Franklin Shaw, Santa Fe, NM
Company F, 2nd Battalion, 22nd Infantry Regiment
Date of Rank

I caught up with the company on the morning of D+4, just after the disaster of the Château de Fontenay, to find that Harold Fulton, the company commander and one lieutenant had been killed. Two other lieutenants had been wounded and evacuated, amounting to a total of some ninety men lost. I reported to Jim Beam, whom I knew from the June 1 payroll. He was the XO. He looked at my collar and asked my date of rank. I thought, what kind of chicken outfit is this?

When I told him, he said, "Damn, I rank you by six days. I had hoped you would take over this mess." I became XO and leader of the second platoon. I went up a hedgerow, found fourteen survivors, went back, and secured fifteen replacements. I reorganized the platoon, putting half new, half old veterans in each squad, and moved out within the hour. I lost just one man in a firefight the next day. I myself lasted until I was wounded while on patrol on D+6. Jim Beam, who was wounded and later lost a leg at St. Lô, became my lifelong friend.

My infantry career ended leading a squad. My next command, many years later, was a tank battalion with ninety-one M-48 tanks. It was quite a step up in firepower.

Following is an interview done by David Vindetta of the Morning Call, a newspaper in Bethlehem, PA.

Joe Motil, Bethlehem, PA
Company L, 3rd Battalion, 22nd Infantry Regiment
'The Germans didn't give a damn what they did…'

Six o'clock, we hit the beach. The coxswain on the landing craft said, "I'm taking you right onto dry land," and we went 20 feet right onto the sand. I was out before the ramp was all the way down and ran as fast as I could.

Right away, I saw this little tank coming at me, about four foot high, loaded with explosives. The Germans pushed a button, and it came out of a concrete shell. It was supposed to go out and hit a landing craft, and the explosives would go off, but it malfunctioned and died. I just went around it.

I ran till I got deep into the sand, then I flopped down. The lieutenant came after me and said, "You never ran that fast back in the States."

We weren't under fire at that point. We didn't get hit near as hard as the guys on Omaha Beach.

I upchucked and I threw up blood, too. It was from seasickness. I couldn't even keep water down, couldn't even eat till the third day.

The Germans started firing at us — rifle shots.

We had to go through a section they had flooded with about six feet of water. If I'd gone straight, I would've been up to my neck in water. I went around to the right where I could get a little more protection, where the beach was built up to hold the water. Most all of us were going that way.

We reached a road and saw a German tank coming, but there was a white flag on it. We zeroed in on him, waiting and waiting, and all at once we recognized the guy standing up in the turret was an 82nd Airborne paratrooper. The paratroopers went in the night before, and they had captured the tank somewhere around Sainte-Mere-Eglise.

By late afternoon, we were about two miles inland and started hitting pillboxes. The Germans fired machine guns and mortars from there. I got one pillbox, one of the early ones.

I ran up alone, carrying 10 pounds of TNT and a 3-inch fuse. I ran, dropped, ran, dropped. The Germans were firing, but our men were firing, too. I put my TNT pack against the door, got a match out and lit the fuse. Then I crawled backwards like a crab, as fast as I could go, opened my mouth, and held my ears. I got no more than 10 feet before the explosion blew the door in.

Then the flamethrower came up and shot flame in there. I saw two Germans run out the back, burning and screaming.

That first day we lost one wounded and one killed in my company. The one fella wanted the Luger on a dead German's belt. I yelled at him, "Don't touch it." He reached down to pick it up. He was killed. The Germans booby-trapped their own men.

They didn't give a damn what they did. I saw American paratroopers hanging by wire from trees. The Germans hanged them, then shot them. I dream of that a lot.

There was a sniper in a church steeple shooting at us. I saw him come out, fire, and go back. I zeroed in on that spot with my M-1. I saw his shadow coming and fired. He never fired again.

The second day, we went to a village that was demolished by our bombers. I saw one of our sergeants get hit with a German 88 [an 88 mm shell]. Took his head right off. He was right in front of me.

That night, I saw a paratrooper's chute and thought, oh boy, I'm gonna cover up. I looked at it: C'mon moon, shine a little more. I didn't trust it. I got some string out, tied it on the chute, went back and pulled it. The chute blew up.

Third day, we were pushing through the hedgerows, one after another. The Germans were waiting for us in a village. They ran out from the side of a house with their bayonets fixed on their rifles. We fought hand to hand. I was fortunate enough to know some tricks.

A German officer came at me. I waited for him with my bayonet. When he got close enough, I quick lowered it and pointed it up towards him, and he come toward me to stab me and ran right into my bayonet. I got him in the stomach.

That's something that don't leave you.

Fourth day, we kept going. We were in back of a hedgerow that night, and the Germans were behind a hedgerow in front of us. They fired like heck at us, and we fired back. It quieted down, but I couldn't sleep. After midnight, I told the lieutenant who was with me, "I hear something strange out there." He said, "Whaddaya mean?" I said, "I hear something rattling, like a canteen." There was a little moon out. I looked up and said, "The Germans are crawling in." He said, "OK, let's wait." He gave the order: "Everybody get your grenades."

Finally, we could see them, about 15-20 feet away. "Heave!" Everybody's grenades went over our hedgerow. We threw a lot of them, then got up on the hedgerow and sprayed the whole field with gunfire. The next morning, we jumped off for the next hedgerow. There were a lot of dead Germans in the field.

The fifth day, June 11, we got pinned down. Our radio-man was knocked out. The lieutenant said, "Joe, go back to headquarters and tell them we need artillery fire, and fast." I took off across the field towards a hedgerow. The Germans were firing a machine gun, but they couldn't catch me. Over the hedgerow, a soldier looked up at me and said, "You got 13 lives. Those bullets were behind your heels all the way across."

Running down the road, zing! What the heck, somebody's shooting at me. Bullets whizzing by my ear. A soldier was coming towards me, going to the front with a message. He was just past me when he got hit in the leg. He didn't go down; the sniper's bullet didn't hit the bone. I stopped and came back to him. He said, "I think I know where he's at."

He went into a woods, right under a tree, and shot eight rounds up into it. A body dropped down. I went over to look as he took off the helmet. It was a woman in a German uniform. He said, "That bitch isn't gonna fire no more."

I got back to the colonel and told him what we needed, and I don't think it was 15-20 seconds later, shells were going. He told me to go dig a hole and take a break. That would've been the first night I could get some sleep. I dug the hole and laid back. It's dark, shells are going. Pretty soon I hear, "Incoming!"

One, then the second one. Third one I heard, then I didn't hear it. Get out of this hole! It's gonna hit!

I got up and ran toward the hedgerow, and in back of me, the shell blew. It threw me up against the hedgerow. That's where I laid. I was hit in the right thigh, under the butt, in the back of the knee and the left elbow. There's shrapnel in me yet.

Medics were hollering, "Anybody hurt?" I was yelling for them. I felt my leg was warm; blood was flowing. There was no pain. Somehow I got my belt off, got it under my leg, hooked it and tightened it up as hard as I could.

Medic came and threw a raincoat over me because he had to use a flashlight. He looked and said, "You know you saved your own life."

They put me on an LST [landing ship tank] and took me to England. In a hospital, doctors didn't know what to do. They kept me there for almost a month. My left hand was numb, my right leg was numb, I couldn't walk, I couldn't sleep. Nurses sat with me all night. I was smoking like a fiend.

One day a doctor came in. Nurse told me, "He's the dumbest doctor we ever had." She watched. He got this pocket knife out, opened it up. He wanted to press it on my leg to see if there was life in it. I said, "Doc, if you touch that leg, my left leg is very good, and you're gonna get it right in your face." He went away. The nurse said, "That's the best thing you ever did."

Next morning, I went to a neurosurgeon hospital in England and a doctor examined me and said, "I can save your leg." The operation took six hours. He had to cut from the butt all the way down to the knee to connect the nerves and stitch them together.

He used a local anesthetic, so I was conscious the whole time. Another guy was in the next room. He was watching my operation; I was watching his. He told me, "Joe, they're sewing you up." I said, "They're sewing you up."

They took me back and announced to the fellas in the ward, "Keep quiet, he's gotta sleep." That was the first night I slept since D- Day. I slept for 24 hours. Boy, when I woke up, you should've heard them soldiers yelling, "Thank God, you're here!"

"I try to get most of it out of my mind," Motil said of his combat experience, "but still it never leaves."

Note: Joe Motil was very active in the National 4th Infantry Division Association and in later years would be one of two or three WWII vets in attendance at reunions. He served a term as president of the 4IDA, was an inspiration to all of us veterans from Vietnam and from the Cold War, Iraq, and Afghanistan. Joe died in December 2018, before his 101st birthday. Joe Motil is the person who told me about the "22nd Infantry Regiment Society—World War II" and told me about MG (Ret) John Ruggles. Joe Motil is the person responsible for starting me on this journey of preserving stories of our Greatest Generation...but that is another story for another time.

4ID AFTER ACTION REPORT (AAR)

15-21 JUNE 1944: From the 4ID After Action Reports (AAR) from WWII: **As you read these AARs, you will notice that they are consistent each day.** It starts with a big picture 4ID overview, followed in order by reports from 8th, 12th, and 22nd Infantry Regiments. If you are following a favorite artillery unit, the 29th Field Artillery was in direct support of 8th Infantry Regiment, the 42nd Field Artillery was direct support of 12th Infantry Regiment, and 44th Field Artillery was direct support of 22nd Infantry Regiment. There are lots of other units in the 4ID who worked across the division.

15 JUNE 1944—D+9: Montebourg was reported held by perimeter defense with approximately 100 to 200 men. Hasty positions were being prepared by the enemy along the high ground north and northwest of Montebourg. The three regiments consolidated their positions and patrolled.

Cumulative situation of the build-up on Utah Beach: 99,205 men, 11,131 vehicles, and 30,881 long tons of supplies.

16 JUNE 1944—D+10: The enemy continued to improve defenses southwest of Montebourg. The enemy was greatly disorganized after the capture of Quinéville. The three regiments of the 4th Division improved their defenses and conducted active patrolling to the front and flanks.

17 JUNE 1944—D+11: Little change in the situation. Montebourg was still in enemy hands. The situation of the 8th and 12th Regiments was unchanged. During the night, the 22nd Regiment was relieved by the 24th Cavalry Reconnaissance Squadron and moved to an assembly area in the vicinity of Fontenay-sur-Mer, as Division reserve.

18 JUNE 1944—D+12: The enemy showed only slight activity to the front with the preparation of hasty defenses continuing. Active patrolling was conducted by all the units except for the 22nd Regiment which remained in its assembly area.

19 JUNE 1944—D+13: Enemy defensive positions in depth on the high ground southwest of Valognes consisted of infantry and a few tanks. Montebourg was evacuated. The 8th Infantry launched a coordinated attack in conjunction with 12th Infantry at 0300 and by dark had secured positions (vicinity of La Victoire). Valognes would be bypassed to avoid street fighting. The 22nd Infantry, Division reserve, moved to positions and its 3rd Battalion moved into Montebourg.

20 JUNE 1944—D+14: The enemy was preparing defensive positions in the vicinity of Cherbourg. The 8th Infantry launched a coordinated attack with 12th and 22nd Infantry at 0530 from its positions in the vicinity of Valognes. After that, the 12th reverted to division reserve and followed the advance of the 22nd to an assembly area. The 24th Cavalry Reconnaissance Squadron protected the Division right flank. Very slight resistance was encountered and, in most instances, advancing units were out of contact with the enemy.

21 JUNE 1944—D+15: Concrete and reinforced emplacements were successively occupied by the enemy as its units withdrew to stronger defensive positions around Cherbourg. All strong points along the eastern coast as far north as Quettehou (24th Cavalry Reconnaissance sector) were found free of enemy. The 8th continued the attack from positions in the vicinity of Ruffoses. The 12th attacked and progressed in the vicinity of Gallis until it was stopped by artillery, mortar, and small arms fire. The 22nd attacked at 1600 from its positions in vicinity of Le Theil and captured the high ground. The advance was stopped at 2200 by order.

* * * * *

Following are more first person accounts from 4ID WWII vets of their experiences during this second full week in combat.

From **War Stories Volume I: Utah Beach to Liberation of Paris ...**

Francis W. Glaze Jr., Clearwater, FL
HQ, 8th Infantry Regiment
Military Police Training

As I remember, Bed Check Charlie (BCC) was a twin-engine Henkel airplane, and the engines were purposely out of synchronization. BCC came over at dusk almost every evening for reconnaissance — to draw fire and find gun positions, and to drop antipersonnel bombs on targets of opportunity. That night we were the "opportunity."

These antipersonnel bombs (APBs) were the so-called "cluster bombs." That particular night the cluster was probably a mix of about one hundred small baseball-sized bomblets in a light metal housing. They had three different fuses that were activated on impact when a small central charge exploded, scattering the bomblets over an acre or so. Usually, the fuses were assembled to sense impact, time delay, and motion — the rationale being that the "impact" bomblets would cause the primary casualties, the "time-delay" ones went off as medics and men came to help. The "motion-sensing" bombs were to keep you "loose" in case you thought they were duds and picked them up or kicked them to a side — "Boom!"

That particular night we had forty to fifty German prisoners in a barn near the Regimental CP. I never liked to keep prisoners overnight, so I radioed 4th Infantry Division MPs to come and pick them up by truck. The MPs pulled into the area just as BCC was looking for action. We did not fire to give our position away, but someone on our flank did and alerted BCC to drop a cluster. Then, all hell broke loose.

The lead vehicle was a half-ton with four MPs in it. One of the impact bomblets hit the driver on the head. The two MPs sitting behind were mortally wounded. The driver was decapitated and the MP beside the driver was uninjured but scared "sh-tless." The lone survivor took off running and, to my knowledge, hasn't stopped running since.

To make matters worse, one of the bomblets ignited the hay in the barn, and the barn burned for hours—it seemed like days. BCC circled for a while and then finally went away. I radioed Division MP headquarters and asked for more MPs. Reluctantly, they arrived.

Our Company had five casualties. None were killed, but one was Warrant Officer Joe Powell, one of our old regulars. When he came back to us several weeks later, I never let him forget. He had more garrison time than I did, but I had more combat time than he did. At the time, I was twenty-one, going on one hundred, and he was a regular of twenty years. He realized that combat time was all that counted by our standards.

The next morning, I was "cruising" the area, and one of the "quiet ones," Hugh Jetton, asked me to come and look at his foxhole. I had been haranguing for covers for foxholes but met with typical GI resistance for weeks. Jetton showed me his cover—some boards with six inches of dirt on top. In the middle, on the top, was the neatest little "bomb" crater you ever saw. That was the first time he'd ever covered his foxhole, but now he was a believer. He converted the rest of the Company. They too, wanted to protect the "family jewels."

The Division MPs were very nervous after that. They preferred that we bring the prisoners back. Of course, as you could predict, there was, "No way, Jose…come and get a little combat experience."

Mark Channing, Orlando, FL
Company G, 2nd Battalion, 22nd Infantry Regiment
French Demoiselle

After fifty plus years, events once in sharp focus become blurred or forgotten. But you are pushing for a story, so here goes. By way of background, Lum Edwards pulled me out of Company G into the 2nd Battalion, 22nd Infantry Regiment Headquarters when he found out that I spoke fluent German and very good French. We were not doing any real interrogating, just quickies for possible tactical value before sending prisoners back to the rear.

Here's the first story. I was still with Company G. It took place around D+9 and is a fine example of the concept that opportunities should not be wasted. We had just retaken Montebourg, for the fourth time I think, after a hell of a firefight lasting most of the day. It was late afternoon, and our platoon leader was missing. I was with the search party, and we found him rather quickly. He had a French demoiselle, with skirts hoisted, backed into a doorway, and they were having a good time. Being of the courteous generation, we naturally looked the other way and quickly left. The lieutenant's name will forever remain a secret with me—if I could remember it—which of course, I can't.

My second story isn't even a story. It is just an event that happened, at a guess, sometime around D+15... General Barton produced the event and in the process, made one hell of an impression on a not quite nineteen-year-old kid—me. What he did was simply to have all of us (certainly the battalion and maybe even the entire 22nd Infantry Regiment), gather in an open field to give us a twenty-minute pep talk. He had P47s flying cover, or so he claimed. I thought then, "Boy, that is one crazy SOB." I haven't changed my mind in all these years. Maybe some of the guys can shed more light on this event, including the whys and wherefores.

George Knapp, Westchester, IL
Chaplain, HQ, 12th Infantry Regiment
A Chaplain's View of War

After a few months in England, the 4th Infantry Division made the amphibious landing as invading assault troops on Utah Beach on D-Day, June 6, 1944. Because of severe weather, the invasion had been postponed a day, so we bounced around in the English Channel on that day of waiting. Many soldiers were seasick. I was a bit sick but never missed a meal of those delicious C-rations on the ship. On the morning of June 6, we went down the side of the ship on the rope ladders to the landing craft bouncing wildly on the rough sea. Virginia wonders how I made it down with my Field Altar Communion set in one hand and a personal effects bag in the other. Anyhow, I made it, and the landing craft luckily made it to the beach, and the ramp went down on that sandy beach.

Some assault waves had preceded us, so we witnessed burning vehicles, bomb craters, wounded, dead, and dying soldiers, and other devastations of war. Our goal was to keep moving. It was a numbing shock for me to see the destruction of material and the dead and dying. As a pastor, I had officiated at a number of funerals. All my life, I had seen the deceased all dressed up, with nice caskets, flowers etc. This was different.

In my memory, I can see the paratroopers hanging in the trees of the wooded areas just in from the beach. They had dropped sometime after midnight, and in the darkness their parachutes had become entangled in the tall trees. They had been shot and killed by the enemy as they hung there. I also saw gliders that had landed among the trees, resulting in death or injury to the occupants. One glider was carrying four soldiers with a jeep behind them. When it crashed into a large tree not far above the ground, the jeep broke loose from its moorings, crashing into and killing the men. We had to keep moving, and there was nothing we could do for the men, except breathe a prayer, so we kept on moving. The dead men, by the way, looked as if they had just fallen asleep and were sitting there.

Speaking of trees, two medics and I used a tree trunk that first night to sit around and catch a bit of rest. I was still carrying my field altar and "ditty-bag." My jeep and trailer, with my chaplain's assistant, had landed via a different craft. For days, I had no opportunity to use my jeep trailer as it was commandeered in carrying the wounded.

At first, the three chaplains of the 12th Infantry Regiment stayed with our individual battalions. I was the 3rd Battalion chaplain. After a week or so, orders came from the Division Chaplain that the Commanding General wanted his chaplains to serve at the Regimental Aid Station, but not right at the front lines amidst the fighting. The General said, "I only have fifteen chaplains and if you are killed or wounded, there is no one to replace you." Some served a bit behind the front lines.

The 12th Infantry Regiment did lose one chaplain, killed instantly by enemy shrapnel while he was in the Regimental Command tent. Other chaplains were replaced due to injury, illness, etc.

I received a minor enemy shrapnel injury and was awarded the Purple Heart. I guess my fellow soldiers thought I did a good job, as I was also awarded the Bronze Star. It was not easy, even though I had volunteered for the chaplaincy. After about a week in combat, it almost got the best of me. After hearing a young company commander talk of getting orders to move out again and how exhausted his men were, it hit me emotionally. I just walked across to the other side of the field, lay down and had a good cry. I then said to myself, "Enough is enough. I volunteered for this job, so let's get going."

As history recorded, the 4th Infantry Division had the highest rate of casualties of any outfit that fought in Europe. We had two hundred casualties a day. Some died before they could be evacuated. Besides our prayers and words of comfort and encouragement, we helped the wounded by giving a drink of water, etc. If their hands were wounded, we helped them enjoy a few drags on a cigarette.

Clyde R. Stodghill, Cuyahoga Falls, OH
Company G, 2nd Battalion, 12th Infantry Regiment
Loneliness on a Battlefield

On the days when I carried the radio, it was hard to keep in touch with our latest company commander, although I was always supposed to stay nearby. He frequently told me to wait in a certain place and then would wander off somewhere.

For all practical purposes, that meant the radio was useless. I attributed his determination to keep me at a distance to two things: First, he did not want anyone keeping tabs on his actions when the company was in the attack because he tended to linger behind. Second, he believed the stories about the radio drawing artillery and mortar fire and the antennae pinpointing the location of the key men.

He told me to wait beside a hedgerow one dark and cloudy evening when most of Company G was engaged in a firefight up ahead. The two forward platoons had advanced the length of a field and then turned right, apparently led that way by the Germans. The captain should have been with them. Instead, we were following along with the reserve platoon in the first field, staying close to the hedgerow on the right when he told me to wait there.

I kneeled and watched as the others reached the end of the field fifty yards away, then made the turn at a break in the hedgerow and were gone. An hour of daylight remained, but dark clouds that seemed low enough to reach out and touch had chased away all color so that only blacks and grays remained.

Twilight—the loneliest hour of the day for those away from home, the time when a light glowing in a window should mean friendly faces awaiting, a home-cooked supper, and later, a warm and comfortable bed.

Such thoughts were fleeting, impossible dreams that were best pushed aside. Now a glow in a window meant a building was afire. Supper, if it came at all, would be from a box of cold K-rations. The damp hard ground would provide the only bed—an empty world where comfort was a memory and killing was the norm. That is all that was left.

No feeling of loneliness can equal that of being alone on a battlefield. Soon the firing ceased ahead, and a silence more menacing than any gunfire added to the isolation. No bird chirped in the foliage overhead, no little animal rustled about in the undergrowth. They had sought shelter, leaving me as the lone living creature, in the open.

As the minutes ticked away, I grew apprehensive. Were infiltrators with knives and guns on the prowl? Among the hedgerows, enemy raiding parties and patrols were constantly searching for victims. What could I do if half a dozen Germans suddenly appeared?

Should I wait there, following the orders of an incompetent commander, or should I go ahead and hope to find the company where men with guns were concealed, knowing that to men wary of any movement, I was at risk of being shot by either friend or foe?

The decision was made for me when a man appeared at the far end of the field and beckoned me forward. Elated over not having been forgotten, I ran toward the place where the soldier, who now had vanished again, had stood motioning for me.

I made the turn without slowing down and found myself in a long farm track no more than ten yards wide with hedgerows on each side. Forty yards ahead, a man was waving me on. The same man, I assumed, and I ran on. I had covered half the distance between us when he raised his rifle, grinning as he did so, and only then did I see he was wearing a German helmet. In the gathering darkness, his uniform looked no different from my own.

He had me dead to rights. There was nothing I could do but make a futile dive toward the ground. When a man has his weapon aimed at you and yours is not pointed at him, it's all over but the squeezing of the trigger.

But rather than coming from his rifle, the shot was fired from off to my left. A stunned look came over the German's face as he turned halfway around, the muzzle of his rifle turning with him and drooping toward the ground. He stood that way for several seconds, then slumped to his knees for a moment before slowly falling forward as if he had suddenly grown weary and needed to rest.

As I rose up on my knees, then to my feet, a Company G man came over to me. He guided me to a field on the left where the company was deployed. I asked who had fired the shot, and he told me it was Nick Scala. It seemed he had been watching the German all along, wondering what he was up to until I had come charging around the corner.

I don't know how Nick Scala, who later received a battlefield commission (but at that time was the machine gun section sergeant), scored on the rifle range. There is a vast difference, however, between hitting a paper target and hitting a man when there will be no opportunity for a second shot. At the latter, Nick had few, if any, peers. I was glad that he was such a deadly shot when it counted, but I wished he hadn't waited quite so long to fire. That was Nick's way, though.

Our less-than-competent captain had to have been responsible for the way in which the company was deployed along both sides of the same hedgerow. It made no sense whatsoever. Men were digging in on the opposite side, but on mine, we had taken over slit trenches abandoned by the Germans. That meant we lacked the protection of a hedgerow if Germans returned from the direction in which they had departed. They often did so.

My hole had belonged to an officer. He had left his "dress" cap behind; the kind that had a leather bill and rose to a high peak in front. Below the peak was the SS Death's head insignia. It would have made a fine souvenir, one that in coming years would have been worth a lot of money. I had no way of taking it with me, of course. An infantryman in combat has enough of a load to carry without gathering keepsakes.

A helmet also lay beside the hole. Unless he had fought bareheaded, the officer had been wounded or killed and then carried away by his men. Had he still been on his feet, it was highly unlikely that he would have left his cap behind.

In my exuberance over being back with other men rather than off by myself, and at having watched as Scala killed the German, I did a stupid thing. Acting the fool, I put the German helmet on my head and stood up so that everyone could appreciate my display of ignorance. That came to an abrupt ending when a shot was fired from the other side of the hedgerow. The bullet passed close enough to my head to crack like a pair of boards being slapped together. I turned and peered over the hedgerow and there was Nick Scala. His expression told me what he had thought of my performance. After staring at me for a moment he said, "Don't fool around." I never did again.

AAR – 22-30 JUNE 1944

22 JUNE 1944—D+16: The enemy now defended Fortress Cherbourg. Resistance was stubborn, with the enemy slowly withdrawing from one prepared position to others closer to Cherbourg. Some fire from heavy and medium artillery was received indicating that some guns were moved from the sea coast. A considerable number of prisoners were captured from among enemy troops trying to infiltrate from east to west, attempting to get back within their lines. The 8th (at 0430), the 12th (at 1400) and the 22nd (at 1400) launched attacks and made progress.

23 JUNE 1944—D+17: The defense of Cherbourg continued from the prepared strong points organized in depth. The 8th launched an attack at 0750 and by 2100 had secured its positions, preparing for the next day's attack toward La Glacerie. The 12th attacked at 0830 and took the defended position near the bridge on the Saire river. The 22nd attacked at 0700 and succeeded in capturing all enemy strong points on the high ground in the vicinity of Gonneville. The 24th Cavalry Reconnaissance Squadron contained enemy strong points in the vicinity of the airfield (Maupertus) and in conjunction with artillery, made a feint attack against its western perimeter.

24 JUNE 1944—D+18: The defense of Cherbourg continued, every available man being used in the defense. The 8th attacked at 0900 from the northwest of Ruffoses with heavy artillery fire and considerable opposition. The 12th attacked at 0840, seized numerous strong points and completely disorganized the enemy to their front. This regiment captured upwards of 700 prisoners. The 22nd consolidated the positions and protected the right flank of the Division.

25 JUNE 1944—D+19: Defense was from well-organized artillery and anti-aircraft positions which were well dug in. The enemy surrendered when our artillery fire and automatic fire was brought on him or when his ammunition was depleted. The enemy front no longer existed as a line. The 8th consolidated its positions and patrolled to the east and north plus to the west to establish contact with the 79th Division. The 12th attacked at 0745, drove to the coast and occupied Tourlaville. It seized numerous fortified localities and captured approximately 800 prisoners. The 22nd consolidated its positions, patrolled northward toward the coast during the night of 24-25 June and held it. It also mopped up pockets of resistance and three strong points.

26 JUNE 1944—D+20: Cherbourg was entered by our forces. The enemy fought from prepared emplacements at street corners and corners of buildings. Strong defensive action also continued in the vicinity of the airport at Maupertus. The 8th consolidated the positions, patrolled, and mopped up enemy resistance. The 12th did the same in its own zone of action. The 22nd attacked at 1100 from positions astride the Tourlaville-St-Pierre Eglise road and seized numerous strong points in the vicinity of the airfield.

27 JUNE 1944—D+21: The 8th remained in position in the vicinity of La Glacerie. The 12th effected relief of the 79th Division between 0500 and 1100 in Cherbourg. The 22nd continued the attack against fortifications south and north of the airfield, seized and mopped up strong points toward Cap Lévy.

28 JUNE 1944—D+22: Except for isolated groups and forces in the forts on the harbor, our forces occupied the area along the coast from the center of Cherbourg to the area in the vicinity of Pointe de Barfleur. 1,101 prisoners were taken, bringing the total to 9,705 since D-Day. The 4th took over at 0600 military protection of the city of Cherbourg. One concentration of mass fire Division Artillery fired at Fort Central at 1500.

29 JUNE 1944—D+23: Fort de l'Ouest, Fort Central, and Fort de l'Est surrendered. Over 1,000 more prisoners were taken during the cleanup operation. The 8th and 12th Infantry patrolled and maintained order in Cherbourg as the Division Artillery fired concentrations on Fort Central.

30 JUNE 1944—D+24: The 4th Infantry Division, relieved by elements of the 101st Airborne, moved to an assembly area for reorganization, maintenance, and rest, in the vicinity of Gourbesville. (Editor's Note: They were still in contact with the Germans and maintained security patrols).

CASUALTIES FOR JUNE 1944

Killed or died of injuries: 91 Officers, 1,035 Enlisted Men, Total of 1,126

Missing: 5 Officers, 321 Enlisted Men, Total of 326

Seriously wounded or injured: 202 Officers, 3,058 Enlisted Men, Total of 3,260

Slightly wounded or injured: 47 Officers, 655 Enlisted Men, Total of 702

Total casualties: 5,414.

Prisoners captured: 10,318.

Cumulative situation of the build-up on Utah Beach: 166,839 men, 22,884 vehicles and 108,136 long tons of supplies. (Many new divisions moved across Utah Beach after 4ID assaulted it).

Editor's Note: *Although 4ID did not suffer the magnitude of casualties that were suffered on D-Day (June 6, 1944) by other assault divisions, the 4ID suffered more casualties in the month of June than any other unit, and they accomplished all missions given to them. To put it into perspective, approximately one third of the total strength of the 4ID were killed or wounded in the first 24 days of fighting in the hedgerows of Normandy. And the 4ID would continue the constant fight for another 175 days without relief. By war's end, in eleven months of fighting, they suffered over 30,000 total casualties—about 200% of the division's strength—yet they accomplished every mission given them. Truly a history that we can all be very proud of, just as our current 4ID Soldiers are writing another proud chapter in our 4ID's history.*

Robert O. Babcock

From ***War Stories Volume I: D-Day to the Liberation of Paris*** *...*

Al Miljevic, Havre de Grace, MD
Company F, 2nd Battalion, 22nd Infantry Regiment
Five Days of Captivity

My platoon was several kilometers from St. Mére Eglise, a member of Company F, 22nd Infantry. On or about June 22, 1944, Sergeant Pollock summoned me to the front of the platoon. He and the platoon leader ordered me to proceed as "point man" (we called them "first scout" in WWII) to be on advance patrol. I asked how far was I to go, and the platoon leader's reply was, "Until you meet someone," meaning the Germans.

I then proceeded to advance on the road with a second point man fifteen yards behind me. The main body of our platoon was approximately thirty to forty yards behind us. Along the roadsides were tall hedgerows. I was more concerned about what would be behind the hedgerows than what was on the road in front of me. I noticed a French woman trying to contact me. It appeared she was trying to warn me of something. I halted the column and told the platoon leader about the French woman. He ordered me to continue with the patrol.

The road had a sharp left 70-degree turn. The point man on the right side of the road and behind me could see further up the road ahead then I could. All at once he shouted, "Hit the dirt!" As I looked in front of me, there appeared approximately five German soldiers with machine pistols firing at me. The bullets were hitting the road, and sparks were flying all around my feet. God was with me that day because not one bullet hit me. The other point man and I hit the dirt in a ditch on the left-hand side of the road. As I looked up, I could see the German soldiers on the right side of the road on a high knoll; they had us pinned down.

The point man behind me asked if I could fire at them and he would cross the road and try to divert some of them away from me. As he crossed the road, they fired upon him and hit him in the arm. I heard his rifle hit the macadam. He then ran through the farm house yard. I, too, ran across the road and into the same farm house. In the back yard, there was a small storage shed filled with straw on the floor. I went into the shed with the idea of staying inside until dark and then sneak back to my line. As I looked around the shed, which was dug inside the high knoll, I noticed about half of the roof was missing.

Everything became quiet for about fifteen minutes. Then, through the hole of the roof, a German Infantryman pointed a machine pistol at me at which time I surrendered. For five days, we were strafed by the British spitfires and shelled by the Americans. During the last two days of my captivity, I was semi-conscious. The Germans never left this battlefield. The Allies had the Cherbourg Peninsula cut off, I guess, and there was no escape route for them.

On the morning of June 27, I heard someone say, "Here's one of those sons of bitches." Then I heard them say, "Damn, he's one of ours." If I remember correctly, they were from the 4th Recon platoon. I sure was glad to see them. They then captured the Germans when I pointed out the machine gun position. The captured Germans carried me on a stretcher and mounted me on a jeep. I was headed back to a Battalion Aid Station. I hadn't had anything to eat for five days, and the doctor gave me some water, chewing gum, and a shot of morphine. I was then transported to an evacuation hospital on Utah Beach. From there, I went on an LST to Bournmouth, England and spent several months in the hospital recovering from a collapsed lung.

Bob, I hope if you print this that the soldier who was the second point man, if he is still alive, will contact me. I want to thank him for saving my life. If he did not take them off my back, I would not have made it back home. I can't remember his name after all these years.

Arthur Bart, Boynton Beach, FL
Company E, 2nd Battalion, 8th Infantry Regiment
Caught in a Trap

Joining the 4th Infantry Division as a replacement was the most frightening experience of my life, especially if you're only eighteen years old. Luckily, the GIs in my squad were very comforting and taught me quickly. Constant patrols and slow advances toward Cherbourg provided many hairy moments, but none scarier than the one that happened on June 25, the day that I was wounded.

Our company was the lead on the outskirts of Cherbourg when we found ourselves outflanked by a German unit and caught in a trap inside a hedgerow, which is not a very good place to be caught. The Germans tossed mortars systematically and slowly; the company was being wiped out. One mortar landed so close to me that my watch blew off my hand and five fillings came out of my teeth. My sergeant crawled over to me and told me to try to reach the rear echelon and secure much needed help. I took off my pack, and, with but a rifle in my hand, I dashed across the hedgerow towards the opening. I didn't make it. I ran at least twenty-five yards when a bullet tore through my arm and threw me to the ground.

Knowing that I could bleed to death, I applied a makeshift tourniquet to my arm that temporarily stopped the bleeding. While I lay there sobbing, two GIs scuttled by and asked if I was able to move. I said, "I think so." Together we crawled to the opening, dashed across, and darted into a gully where we searched for an Aid station.

As we proceeded back to where we thought our rear echelon would be, we heard a tank coming down the road. Not knowing if it was German or American, we stayed hidden until we saw the White Star. I rose up, threw a rock with my good arm to get the driver's attention, and asked him for directions to the Aid Station. At the same time, I told him that my company was pinned down and needed help, desperately. Ultimately, the unit was relieved but suffered severely.

We finally found the aid station about a mile down the road. As a result of that action, I spent fifteen months in various hospitals until I was discharged. For this, I received the Purple Heart, the Bronze Star, and memories that I will never forget.

John H. Crowe, Covina, CA
20th Field Artillery Battalion
Accidental Fire

On June 24, 1944, the 12th Infantry Regiment was fighting its way toward the port city of Cherbourg and was getting pretty close. I was a First Lieutenant with the 20th Field Artillery Battalion, a battalion of 155mm howitzers, available for assignment to any of the three regiments of the 4th Infantry Division as needed. On this day, I reported to Lieutenant Colonel John Merrill, the commanding officer of the 1st Battalion, 12th Infantry. They had just seized a second objective at 1540 hours and were consolidating their position, awaiting further orders.

I reported to the colonel in an apple orchard, and he motioned me to join him in a search of the area. My memory of events is hazy here, but I do recall following the colonel, who was behind a bodyguard leading the way. We proceeded in a single file near the wall of a building. As we approached a corner of that building, the colonel motioned the point man to proceed around it. When the bodyguard did this, he drew machine gun fire from another building and one bullet struck him in the abdomen and passed through his body. Colonel Merrill helped the man back out of the line of fire and told me to take care of him.

I did the best I could with the first aid kits we had, tiding him over until the medics arrived. I remember telling him that he appeared to have a clean wound since the bullet had passed completely through him without doing a tremendous amount of damage. If he was lucky, he had a million-dollar wound to save his life. It would take him out of the war.

At some point after this, as best I can recall, I discovered that my radio was inoperable. When I went forward to an infantry unit as a forward observer, I generally traveled in a jeep and was accompanied by the regular driver of that jeep, and a corporal or sergeant who served primarily as a radio operator. On this occasion, the radio operator was Corporal Wier. I sent the driver back to pick up a radio and Corporal Wier stayed with me to await his return. The 1st Battalion's new orders were to jump off at 2000 hours for a third objective.

I don't remember much about my activities prior to the jump off time. I do recall meeting Lieutenant Manuel Herzog, an artillery liaison officer from the 12th Infantry's Cannon Company, during that period. At 2010 hours, the battalion CP group moved out, marching along a road to be used by the battalion's support tanks. I was asked to join this group and would have been there except that I still had to wait for my jeep to arrive with the new radio.

A few minutes later I was standing by the side of the road with Corporal Wier when one of the tanks passed with its top open and the officer in charge riding in it. When he spotted me he said, "If you want to see some good gunnery, come on along." I explained that I had to wait there for my radio and the tank passed out of sight. I later heard that at 2020 hours, just a few minutes after I had spoken to the tanker, the Command Group had somehow come under the direct fire of his tank, accidentally. In this group were Lieutenant Colonel Merrill, Lieutenant Manuel Herzog, Lieutenant James E. Means, the Battalion S-4, two bodyguards, and five scouts. All but three of the party were killed.

When my jeep arrived with the new radio, we proceeded along the road where this accident had occurred and passed the place of the accidental massacre with all the bodies of those killed still there.

For the only time in my war experience, I did not look at these casualties because my imagination was sufficiently active to visualize myself among them. Corporal Wier said as we passed the carnage, "There's that colonel with the mustache." Colonel Merrill had a mustache.

This experience illustrates how pure chance can govern the fate of each of us, especially under circumstances of high risk.

Fit to Fight

Iz Goldstein, Monroe Township, NJ
HQ, 22nd Infantry Regiment
I Remember Ernie Pyle

Iz "Goldie" Goldstein was the first editor of Double Deucer, newsletter of the 22nd Infantry Regiment and an Ivy Leaves (4ID newspaper) editor. This story was published in several magazines.

Dateline: France. D-Day Plus-One. (Just about twenty-four hours after the Utah Beach landing). In an area that was still inhabited by enemy tree snipers who were manufacturing Purple Heart candidates, and featuring lush hedgerows that looked like they just took a mega dose of Miracle Gro, I met Ernie Pyle.

As a GI reporter for the 22nd Infantry Regiment, 4th Infantry Division, I was summoned to escort Mr. Pyle on a battlefield visit.

We had just come off the Utah Beach area, which came at you like an assailant or a vendor of dubious war wares. It even offered an inundated area featuring skeleton headed signs reading, "Achtung Minen!"

Ernie Pyle took the same route that every foot soldier took. The Mr. Pyle that I knew was a frail, humble, quiet man. A class act. Not talkative, a real Gary Cooper type—a gentleman. He injected relaxation to everyone he met. He carried a cheap spiral notebook, the same type that kids had in grammar school, to record his battlefield notes. The stories he filed were unvarnished accounts of dirt, death, and determination from the battlefield. The GIs in my outfit loved him.

During a quiet moment during our foxhole circuit, he questioned me about my family at home. He showed deep concern. He spoke about his wife, Jerry, and how worried he was about her. He was a hell of a reporter, with an ear for the laconic remark that explained everything. He had a way of just listening and putting himself in the other fellow's shoes.

His two prized possessions were an old wool cap that he wore on a head that did not have an abundance of hair. He even wore it when he slept. The other was a small Coleman stove. Everywhere that Ernie went, the stove was sure to go. His reporting was vivid—he was a journalist's journalist.

Goldie added: "The staff of the Double Deucer *had John Cheever, future Pulitzer Prize winner; Linn Streeter, creator of* Archie *cartoon; Joe O'Keefe of* The Washington Post, *and Bill Haggerty of* The Baltimore Sun." —*Bob Babcock*

Robert Williamson, Lakeland, FL
Company F, 2nd Battalion, 12th Infantry Regiment
Taking the Hedgerows

The next morning after D-Day it had stopped raining. We were moved into new foxholes. Across the road, we had no more than gotten there when the Germans started sending in artillery shells, mortars, and screaming meemies again. A lot of the replacements were killed, because by that time, they had the place zeroed in. They really did a lot of damage.

We then stayed at this spot for a few days until we were in better condition to fight the Germans. In a few days we took off across the countryside after "field-fighting" Germans. We took hedgerow after hedgerow and our men were being picked off one after another. They were dying. Some of our men were taken to a hospital but would come back to fight again. Some were sent home, no longer able to fight.

In June we started for Cherbourg, and on June 25, 1944, my division, the 4th Infantry Division, took Cherbourg. After Cherbourg fell, the division prepared for a rest. We were then forced back into the battle when the Germans struck near Carentan, where the 4th Infantry Division relieved the 83rd Infantry Division. The 4th Infantry Division took an awful beating there. The Germans were dug in; they had foxholes in the ground that were at least six feet deep, and their tanks were also dug in.

As we crossed a road, we ran into a hedgerow. One of the fellows looked over the hedgerow too many times in one place. The Germans were watching that place, sighted on it, and the second time he went up to look…bang; a German shot him right between the eyes. I lost a good buddy. We sure hated to lose him. He never did anything out of the way. It sure was a sight a fellow will never forget as long as he lives.

We got over one hedgerow and into the fields, but our problem was to take the next hedgerow. We hit the ground after we got over the first hedgerow from the road and started firing at the next one. We got to our feet, one by one, firing as we went. We ran a little ways and hit the ground again. That is, those of us who were still able to fight.

My BAR man and I got up and a machine gun spit bullets all around us. I got out without getting hurt. My BAR man got it right through his helmet. The bullet just made a mark through his hair. He and I couldn't do it all by ourselves, so we turned around and went up a different hedgerow. I was right behind my squad sarge, and a German stepped out and got my sarge and me. The German got my sarge around the neck and got me in the upper arm before I could get out of the path of the lead sailing through the air. I went to the hospital in England. When I got back to my company, there were a lot of new men there.

John Abraham, St. Ann, MO
Company M, 3rd Battalion, 8th Infantry Regiment
"Combat" Shower

On D-Day, I was a First Lieutenant who led my .30-caliber, water-cooled, machine gun platoon ashore in the first wave at 0630 hours, in support of the rifle companies.

Twenty-one days later, we had fought our way through the hedgerows to Cherbourg. Several days later, when everything was secure, I received word that I could take my men back down the peninsula for showers and clean clothing. We loaded on trucks and drove down to the Merderet River where the quartermaster had set up a large tent with showers inside, pumping water from the river. Needless to say, the men looked forward to enjoying a shower after three weeks of living in the same uniforms and no baths.

The following procedure was followed: The tent containing the showers was enclosed and on each side were flaps. Before entering, the men stacked their rifles, boots, helmets, and gun belts. As they entered, they disrobed, placing their dirty uniforms in piles. So, there were about fifty naked GIs standing in line waiting their turn.

All of a sudden, flying just above the trees, came an ME 109K. In pursuit was a "Spitfire," firing at the German aircraft and bullets were flying all around. The fifty or more GIs in their birthday suits were diving for any cover available. It was all over in seconds. There were no injuries and immediately everyone was laughing and scrambling back in line. All enjoyed their showers and after receiving those welcome clean underwear, socks, and fatigues, they retrieved their equipment, thankful that it all turned out all right.

I am sure there are many stories that veterans try to forget. This is one that we enjoy telling. Any happening that provides a little fun is worth remembering.

From Bill Boice's **History of the 22nd Infantry Regiment in World War II**:

After the fall of Quineville Ridge and Montebourg, the Twenty-Second moved steadily toward the northwest corner of the Contentin peninsula. Casualties were much less, and resistance was crumbling.

Captain Howard Blazzard was having a great time firing German 88's back at the enemy. The Germans often removed the firing pin from an 88, taking it with them. In the event they could recover the position they lost, the pin could be replaced quickly, and the gun used again.

Captain Blazzard found a firing pin intact, and carried it with him, much to the amusement of some of the other officers. But approaching the airport near St Pierre Eglise, he found excellent opportunity to use it. Popping the pin in place in a particularly well-placed gun, he had a wonderful time using German ammunition and a German gun to shoot Germans!

Casualties were heavy approaching the airport as a result of ack-ack fired at short range. Cherbourg was the objective of the Fourth Infantry

Division, but the Twenty-Second Regiment moved to the right of the Twelfth Regiment, securing the eastern section of the peninsula.

Cherbourg fell on 25 June; the harbor was in poor shape and must surely have been a sharp disappointment to the Allied Command since it was to be useless for shipping for many weeks. The Twenty-Second continued to fight for two additional days toward St. Pierre Eglise. As a result of first rate intelligence work and coordinated inter-unit information, the rest of the enemy resistance on the peninsula crumbled, resulting in the surrender of more than 900 German officers and men. The conquest of the Cotentin Peninsula was complete just twenty-one days after D-Day.

The fighting had been bitter and costly. Three hundred and seventy-three enlisted men had been killed and fifteen hundred and sixty wounded. Twenty-three officers had been killed and one hundred and four wounded, for a total of two thousand and sixty casualties in less than one month of fighting, in a regiment whose normal strength was about three thousand two hundred men.

* * * * *

This brings us to the end of the costliest month of World War II for the 4ID. July would be another costly month, as would others, but June ranked at the top. Thus, don't think we had it easy, even though our 6 June 1944 D-Day casualties were relatively light. The fight from D+1 to D+24 was brutal and costly. No other division had the number of casualties that 4ID suffered in June 1944, including D-Day.

German Tank

Last picture of General Teddy

JULY 1944

4ID IN NORMANDY, FRANCE, HEDGEROWS AND ST. LO BREAKOUT

Vicinity of Gourbesville: reorganization and training that covered lessons learned and deficiencies noted.

1 TO 3 JULY 1944—D+25-27: From a retired Lieutenant General whose father served in 4ID in WWII: "Ref 4th ID- June '44. By 1 July my dad had been wounded twice; evacuated to England where he spent 10 days in the hospital; and returned to duty in France. A month later at St Lo as Co Cdr of G/22d he was wounded quite seriously (armor piercing round in the leg—taken out of his stomach) and evacuated again to England where he remained until Feb of 45. He had to fight the bureaucracy and Docs to rejoin his beloved 22d after he had healed. What sacrifices 22d and 4ID Soldiers have made for our Nation through the years! I know my dad's watching down with great pride at 1-22's and 2-22's performance in Iraq. (written during Operation Iraqi Freedom I)."

4 JULY 1944—D+28: Gradual movement of the Division to the south so that an attack could be launched through the lines of the 83rd Infantry Division. The 12th Regiment moved at 1100 by foot and motor to an assembly area in the vicinity of the 90th Infantry Division (Appeville), closing into the area at 2015 hours. Moving of various companies or battalions of other units plus the command post of the Division.

5 JULY 1944—D+29: The 8th Infantry moved from La Lande to another assembly area in the vicinity of Appeville (closed at 2220). The 12th Infantry moved from its assembly area to another in the vicinity of Auvers (closed at 2215). The 22nd Infantry did not move.

6 JULY 1944—D+30: The enemy defended organized log and sand bag emplacements with rifle and automatic weapons, utilizing good fields of fire and covering the narrow corridor through which the leading elements had to pass. The 8th Infantry moved from its assembly area and made preparation for a night attack. The 12th Infantry launched an attack at 0930, seized and secured positions. The 22nd Infantry moved by motor and remained in an assembly area as division reserve.

7 JULY 1944—D+31: The enemy continued to defend from well-organized positions utilizing a maximum of automatic weapons. The 8th Infantry attacked at 0300. The 1st Battalion failed to cross the inundated area due to heavy automatic small arms fire. The 2nd Bn crossed but being in an untenable position at daylight, it was ordered to withdraw to the line of departure. The 12th Infantry attacked at 0630 and advanced slowly against heavy opposition. It prepared to renew the attack at 1400 and after an air bombardment and artillery preparation, it moved forward. The 22nd Infantry remained in division reserve.

*From **War Stories Volume I: D-Day to the Liberation of Paris:***

2 JULY: US First Army commits VII Corps, with 4th, 9th, and 83d Divs under its command, between VIII and XIX Corps.

6 JULY: VII Corps commits 4th Div to W of 83d as attack toward Périers continues against unabated opposition.

Joseph Kraynak, Lansdale, PA
HQ Battery, 29th Field Artillery Battalion
Keeping "The Pipers" Flying

Our next immediate objective after D-Day was to take the port of Cherbourg. This was scheduled to be accomplished in about a week. The fighting got rough, and it took about three weeks until we took the port. During these few weeks, I was exposed to what is referred to as "combat," which was nothing like my idea of what combat would be. From the time of the invasion, it was one long day. I remember thinking how great it would be to fast forward my life about five years and get this one out of the way. It was only then that I really understood why one minute seemed like an hour.

One of the aspects of combat is that there is no end of the day when you bathe, relax, or go to bed. There is no waking up to a new great day and no meals to look forward to. There is neither social life, nor any weekends to recharge your life for the week ahead. There are no plans for your own personal future. There is no medical help for the many minor sicknesses, no family, no toilet...nothing.

The cold winters add much more hardship, which one can feel only by having actually lived it back then. In addition to these miseries, you have the depressing thought that at any time it could be your last day on earth, or you could be wounded. One only had to pass by dead human beings to bring those thoughts to mind and realize how true they were. The thought of a million-dollar wound entered my mind as it did the minds of many other soldiers. That was the kind of wound that was not very serious but could get you out of the mess. I did witness this on a few occasions.

The next seven weeks or so, until we reached Paris, were days of constantly pressing forward. Our "Grasshopper Squadron" was constantly on the lookout for a field large enough for our Piper Cubs to land on and take off. It was always in range of the enemy artillery, and sometimes small arms fire. These fields dictated where we would bed down—either in foxholes or in any available shelter.

After D-Day, the paratroopers who landed in and around St. Mére

Eglise left many dead and wounded from their drop on enemy territory in the dark of the night. I never experienced what this group went through, but there were parachutes just about everywhere you went. The chutes made excellent tents for us with some battlefield alterations. After those six weeks in combat, we felt very much like seasoned troops in comparison with our replacements. Most of our time was spent trying to keep the "Pipers" (Piper Cub airplanes) flying. This kept our artillery fire very effective.

Seeing wounded and dead was constantly a firm reminder of what could happen. After seeing a dead German soldier, I went through his equipment, which at the time, seemed like a very normal thing to do. I found, among other personal things, a letter and a photo of a young woman and a child. It was at that moment I stopped hating German soldiers and I realized his plight and call were no different from mine…

While on the move, the Air Observation, which is what our small unit was called, was in constant search of fields from which we could fly the Pipers. The two-man planes were on call constantly from battalion headquarters to get into the air and direct the artillery on target. It was a very dangerous assignment. I remember several pilots and observers being shot down and killed by small arms fire from the enemy. The flight usually lasted about one hour if our position was close enough to observe the enemy and low enough not to be shot down by enemy fighter planes.

Directing fire presented the problem of being hit by our own artillery, since we were in a direct line between the Artillery and the enemy front lines. We later learned that the Germans, at the first sight of these toy planes, thought it was a joke. It was not long until they realized a strange coincidence: Whenever these "toys" were in the air, our guns were effective and accurate, so immediately they doubled their effort to knock us out of the air.

As pilots were killed or injured, the need for more pilots was crucial. I learned to fly off the record during our training, so once the Battalion Command knew this, they assigned me to fly the mail and communicate between units at the front. This was frightening to me, since I was not trained in navigation, and it was easy to get lost. One wrong turn and you wound up in the German foothills.

Orval H. Mullen, Bradenton, FL
HQ Company, 1st Battalion, 8th Infantry Regiment
"Commo" Man

We fought all the way to Cherbourg, which was not easy by any means. My job was to keep communications by laying wire to the outpost and the front-line company. With all the traffic, the lines would get broken, or the Germans would get in and cut them at night and wait for someone to come in and repair them.

On July 7, before St. Lô, I was wounded in one of the worst shellings that I had ever seen. I was taken back to the beach hospital and the following day flew back to England where I spent the next several months. I was then sent back to HQ Company on December 21, just in time for the Battle of the Bulge, where I was wounded again. This time not badly. I just pulled the shrapnel out, put on a bandage, and went on.

The end came on May 8, 1945. We went on to Bamberg and Le Havre. After that, we were on to the Hermitage and back to the good old USA.

It would be good that no human would ever have to go through what the American troops went through in WWII and all wars. Let's hope that the "higher ups" in these countries around the world will think before starting something like that again.

Jack Fox, Jacksonville, FL
Medic, 1st Battalion, 8th Infantry Regiment
Ernie Pyle Praises the Medics

Jack Fox was with the 1st Battalion, 8th Infantry when Ernie Pyle wrote this article in July 1944

"Forgotten Medics" Ernie Pyle

Praise for the medics has been unanimous ever since this war started. And, just as proof of what they go through, take this one detachment of battalion medics that I was with. There were thirty-one men and two officers (Captain Strawn and Captain Accardo). And in one seven-week period of combat in Normandy this summer lost nine men killed and ten wounded. A total of nineteen out of thirty-three men—a casualty ratio of nearly sixty percent in seven weeks. As one aid man said, 'probably they have been excluded from the Combat Infantryman's Badge (CIB) because they are technically noncombatants and don't carry arms.' But he suggested that if this was true, they could still be given a badge with some distinctive medical marking on it to set them off from medical aid men who don't work right in the lines.

"So, I would propose to Congress or the War Department, or whoever handles such things, that the ruling be altered to include medical aid men in battalion detachments and on forward. They are the ones who work under fire. Medics attached to regiments and to hospitals farther back do wonderful work, too, of course, and are sometimes under shellfire. But they are seldom right out on the battlefield. So, I think it would be fair to include only the medics who work from battalion on forward. I have an idea the original ruling on CIBs was made merely through a misunderstanding, and that there would be no objection to correcting it."

Editor's Note: *The War Department did authorize the Combat Medic's Badge (CMB) which is still awarded today. We Infantrymen who have earned the Combat Infantryman's Badge (CIB) consider the CMB to be equally as important and prestigious an award as is our CIB.*

From Colonel Gerden Johnson's **History of the Twelfth Infantry Regiment in World War II**:

While the 4th Division had been slugging its way northward up the Cotenin Peninsula to wrest the French port of Cherbourg from the Germans, other American units to the south, at the base of the peninsula, had been valiantly preventing the enemy from hurling reinforcements at our rear and had even succeeded in pushing him further south. But the enemy, anticipating our next move, had cunningly flooded vast areas southwest of Carentan and had been busily preparing to make a stand on the high ridges south of St. Lo and Periers, with his outer defense line north of Periers.

In choosing their positions, the Germans had wisely taken advantage of an area soon to become famous as the hedgerow country. The hedgerows of Normandy, according to local legend, were planted by the Romans to protect their small fields from half-civilized local tribes. Hedgerows are mounds of earth with stone and twisted roots imbedded in them, packed tight by the centuries into tough, steep-sided walls. They surround small, irregular fields called "bocages" by the Norman peasants, the earth and stone ramparts themselves being from three to seven feet high, often in double rows with a ditch between them. On top grow the trees and hawthorn thickets, natural fences in peace time, tank traps and natural camouflage in time of war.

The hedgerows made excellent fortifications. A handful of Germans with a few machine-guns hiding behind the hedges could hold off a regiment of infantry. The summer foliage concealed them from the air. A few tanks, strategically placed in the corners of fields under overhanging branches, gave terrific firepower to the enemy infantry. It was suicide country for our tanks. They were channelized in the narrow sunken roads. German anti-tank guns concealed in the hedgerows had merely to wait for the tanks to come into view. And then there was no escape.

Twenty-six hours after the fall of Fort Central, the last remaining bastion in Cherbourg Harbor, the 12th Infantry loaded into quartermaster trucks and wheeled south to join the line which was pushing the Germans all along the southern bulge of the beachhead…

We celebrated the Fourth of July by making a road march south to a forward assembly area in the vicinity of Appeville. 155mm howitzers and 4.2 chemical mortars immediately to our rear crashed all night and brought back sharply the sounds of battle reminiscent of the Cherbourg campaign…

The mission given to the regiment on July 6 was to capture the high ground north of the Taute River. We were in the attack once more, aimed at strengthening the line between the 83rd Division on the left (east) and the VIII Corps on the right (west). On this morning, the enemy was defending with rifles and automatic weapons from organized log and sandbagged emplacements. He was capable of strongly defending his positions by utilizing good fields of fire to cover the narrow corridor through which we had to pass. The 83rd Infantry Division reported that it was in contact with the German 6th Parachute Regiment to the south.

The campaign in the south was to prove an almost new type of combat for us. In the push to Cherbourg, we had the enemy continuously on the run and never gave him a chance to settle down. in addition, we were out front all the way, with plenty of ground on which to maneuver and to exploit our gains. But below Carentan, the enemy had almost a month to prepare his defenses, utilizing to the utmost the inundated area that narrowed the corridor through which we were forced to attack. Into this corridor, he concentrated all the firepower he had accumulated during the past month…

Extremely heavy losses were suffered by the 2nd Battalion of the 329th Infantry Regiment of the 83rd Infantry Division. It was through this sector that Major Richard J. O'Malley led the 2nd Battalion of the 12th Infantry at 0930 hours on July 6. From the time the 2nd Battalion fought its way 1,000 yards into enemy held territory where it was pinned down by heavy well aimed small arms and mortar fire from the front and the right flank, until the regiment was again relieved ten days later, at least one battalion was constantly engaged in bitter combat…

8 JULY 1944—D+32: Fighting a stubborn rear guard action, the enemy withdrew, using scattered interdiction and harassing fires. Preceded by a dive bombing and fifteen minute's artillery preparation, a coordinated attack was made by the 8th Infantry with parts of the 70th Tank Bn, 801st Tank Destroyer Bn, 87th Chemical Bn, and 377th AA Artillery plus Company D of the 22nd Infantry. The 12th Infantry passed to division reserve and remained in its positions, maintaining active patrols to the front and flanks.

9 JULY 1944—D+33: The enemy continued to fight a stubborn delaying action in conjunction with local counterattacks. It withdrew from one prepared defensive position to another and continued to interdict important crossroads and road junctions. A coordinated attack was launched at 0830 and progressed during the day against hedgerow opposition. The 12th Infantry remained in division reserve, except the 1st Bn that was committed to fill the gap between the 8th and the 22nd Infantry Regiments. The first issue of "B" rations was fed; with this issue, all troops not actually in the line were fed hot meals. (This is a month and three days after D-Day when the division was first fed hot meals across the unit).

10 JULY 1944—D+34: Continuing its stubborn resistance, the enemy slowly fell back. An ever-increasing usage of armor and self-propelled guns had been noted. The 8th Infantry launched a coordinated attack at 0830 and progressed during the day against constant opposition from Blehou. The 12th Infantry launched a coordinated attack in conjunction with the 8th Infantry, from the vicinity of Les Forges and encountered heavy resistance. The 22nd also launched a coordinated attack from the vicinity of Les Forges, seized and secured positions.

11 JULY 1944—D+35: The enemy continued to offer strong resistance by occupying hasty defenses and well placed machine gun positions. Defensive employment of small units of armor continued. The 8th Infantry attacked at 0900 and occupied the towns of Les Aubrees and Blehou with no enemy opposition. Patrols crossed the Sèves river and occupied the area. The 12th Infantry attacked at 1000 and mopped up the area between Longueville-La Maugerie. The mission was completed at 1600. The 22nd Infantry attacked at 0900 and heavy enemy resistance was encountered throughout the day.

12 JULY 1944—D+36: The 22nd Infantry launched its attack at 0915 to capture the objectives east of Périers and encountered stiff enemy resistance. Enemy's strong resistance and extremely accurate artillery concentrations continued. The 8th Infantry supported the attack of the 22nd Infantry with all available firepower. The regiment remained in its former position and patrols were initiated across the Molerotte river. The 12th Infantry, in division reserve, assembled and moved to follow the advance of the 22nd Infantry and to protect the left flank and rear of the division. At 2145, the regiment started relieving the 22nd Infantry. Brigadier General Theodore Roosevelt, Jr. died of a heart attack. (To see a video clip of his funeral/burial the next day: **https://www.youtube.com/watch?v=y0XTcp-R1sk**

13 JULY 1944—D+37: Enemy tanks and troops appeared to be attempting to create the impression that they were in greater strength. The 8th Infantry, as on the preceding day, supported the attack of the 12th Infantry by fire from its positions. The 12th Infantry completed the relief of the 22nd Infantry and launched an attack at 0930. After a short advance to the southwest, the attack was halted by small arms and artillery fire. It was resumed at 1930 but little progress was made. The 22nd Infantry moved to an assembly area and prepared to follow the advance of the 12th Infantry.

14 JULY 1944—D+38: There was no active contact with the enemy except for a slight increase of artillery fire in rear areas. The 8th Infantry remained in positions formerly occupied. The 12th Infantry remained in position and prepared to attack to the south awaiting favorable weather conditions for air support. The 22nd Infantry remained in its assembly area.

Fit to Fight

From the *History of the 22nd Infantry Regiment in World War II* by *Chaplain Bill Boice:*
PERIERS – CORRIDOR OF DEATH

In spite of the irritation of training, the relaxation was wonderful! It was a good feeling to sleep without being shot at! The first hot meals since England were served, and never had food tasted so good! Hot showers and the first change of clothing did much to raise morale. The first mail since the invasion was delivered, and the joy of word from home was dulled by the number of letters that had to be returned marked WIA or KIA (wounded in action or killed in action).

On July 7th, the regiment prepared for an attack on the town of Periers. Assembled at Amfreville, the command was warned that fighting would be bitter and opposition severe, since the main German line partially blocked the American forces in Normandy. Feeling was strong the enemy would attempt a break-through to the sea, thus cutting the Americans off from their base of supply.

The fighting began on the morning of July 8th and soon became one of the bitterest battles of the war. French farmland was divided into sections by hedgerows, grown up many feet and providing excellent cover and concealment for the enemy.

The mission of the Second Battalion was the breaching of the enemy line south of Culot with La Maugerie as their objective. Neuville was the objective of the First Battalion.

The Second Battalion, after passing through lines of the 83rd Division in the morning, had been advancing against stubborn German delaying action all day. In the late afternoon, they had been stopped by strong resistance about 500 yards southwest of the creek at Culot. About 2100 hours they were ordered to secure lines for the night.

About 2130, three German tanks accompanied by infantry came up the road against the Second Battalion's position. The leading tank continued up the road between Companies F and G toward the rear of the battalion. At the road junction a few hundred yards in the rear stood an American tank which had been knocked out and was blocking the road.

Lt. Colonel Wellburn, CO 70th Tank Bn., had just come up to examine this tank when he heard the German tank approaching. At the same moment, Colonel Wellburn saw an American half-track towing a 57mm. gun coming down the road behind him. He stopped the half-track and said, "Uncouple that gun. Here comes a Kraut tank." The driver immediately pulled in the farm yard just behind the wrecked tank and the gun in a few seconds was uncoupled just at the corner of the gate, covering the road.

As the German tank came around the bend in the road, he saw the American tank a bare hundred yards in front of him. The German stopped and opened fire. His first round set the American tank on fire, and he moved forward slightly and continued firing. Several rounds went through both sides of the turret of the American tank, and one went all the way through the tank and knocked the door off the back.

Meanwhile, the 57mm. antitank gun was loaded and ready to fire. As the side of the tank came into view, the sergeant said, "Pour it in." The first shot hit the most vulnerable point and knocked the German tank out. The 57 put five more shots in the same place. When this encounter ended, the two tanks, German and American, were facing each other 50 yards apart, both riddled with holes and their crews wounded or dead.

A second German tank, accompanied by infantry, had swung west into the orchard in front of Company F, opening fire on the company. At the same time, the Germans put down a heavy artillery barrage on the orchard. Another German tank had swung east into the orchard in front of Company G. Private Hicks, with a bazooka, stood at the corner of a small house near the left flank of Company G and fired at the approaching tank. He got four hits, and on the fourth the German tank blew up. The turret was blown off, and the tank tipped over.

With two of the German tanks knocked out, the third withdrew. Company F was immediately ordered to retake the field from which they had withdrawn, and Captain Tommy Harrison, Battalion S-3, moved up to tie in the lines and prevent gaps from forming. The 44th Field Artillery, in direct support, laid down such a heavy barrage on this field and the enemy positions behind it that the smoke completely obscured the scene.

Company F attacked just before dark but was stopped by heavy German fire. About 0230 the next morning, Lt. Clark and six men who had been in the disputed field throughout our bombardment, succeeded in returning to our lines.

Meanwhile, the First Battalion moved through the gap effected in the enemy lines by the Second Battalion and before dark was on its objective.

It was well after midnight before all the troops were situated and dug in. Sleep was difficult. It was rumored throughout the command that the Germans had forty tanks in Periers which they intended to commit some place on the line. Tank traps were constructed in every conceivable approach and these traps covered with bazooka teams. The battle had only begun but the replacements knew what to expect.

Darkness on the front was always a time of discomfort and tension. Water seeped into the foxholes and clothing was clammy.

With the dawn, radios and field phones hummed with pre-attack conversations and last minute orders. The regiment was facing continued stiff resistance. Once again, Division HQ was unhappy with the failure of the regiment to attain its objectives and to break the German resistance. Accordingly, Colonel Robert Foster was relieved of his command, and quite unknowingly, the Double Deucers were about to begin a shot-gun association with a colorful figure who was to change the destiny of a regiment.

A field phone rang. A Captain answered and heard, "I am Colonel Charles T. Lanham. I have just assumed command of this regiment, and I want you to know that if you ever yield one foot of ground without my direct order, I will court-martial you."

It was a proper introduction to "Buck" Lanham. The regiment began to fight with a skill, imagination, and daring it would not have attempted before.

The 83rd Infantry Division was on the left flank. The usual rivalry between units became apparent when the Second Battalion of the Twenty-Second, moving into the attack found their left flank exposed through the failure of elements of the 83rd to move forward simultaneously with them.

"Continue the attack" was the order on the 10th with the First and Second Battalions in the assault. As the attack moved ahead, the Germans fell back to successive hedgerows, intending to fight a delaying action until they could get their lines organized well enough to smash the oncoming assaults.

About midday, the Third Battalion was committed on the east (left) of the Second Battalion, with orders to seize that portion of the Regimental objective east of La Maugerie. Shortly before dark, the Third Battalion's movement across the front of the Second Battalion masked the fires of that unit, and the Second Battalion reverted to regimental reserve. The First Battalion advanced to the outskirts of La Maugerie and held that position for the night, with the Third Battalion on their left.

It was during the bloody La Maugerie battle that the mortar barrage fell in the Company F area, wounding Lt. Jim Beam, the company commander, when a mortar shell landed almost between his feet. This was the same Jim Beam who, a couple of days earlier, upon receiving a radio message from Major Edwards as to his situation, replied, "The enemy has broken through on our left flank. They are infiltrating and attacking with tanks on our front; our right flank is exposed. The situation is well in hand."

Now with a right foot almost severed and with a left foot badly broken, Lt. Beam calmly lighted a cigarette and assisted Captain Humm, the Bn. Medical Officer, in completing the amputation of his foot. Having given himself a morphine surrette, he refused to be evacuated until he had completed his orders, reorganizing his company to withstand the fierce German attack. Such were the men of the Twenty-Second Infantry.

Again, on this day, Private Hicks, who was then known as the "human tank-destroyer," got his third tank from the corner of a hedgerow behind a tree. He got three bazooka shots into the German tank at less than five yards. He was so-close that the explosion scorched his face.

Lt. J. O. Jackson, tired of the constant harassing and dangerous fire from an enemy machine gun, climbed out of his foxhole and, before the eyes of his astonished G Company, crawled quietly around the edge of a field, over a hedgerow, pulled a pin from a hand grenade with his teeth, threw the grenade at the machine gun nest, and immediately after its explosion, rushed in to polish off the Germans with his bayonet, and then climbed back calmly over the hedgerow and back into his foxhole as he remarked succinctly, "That's the way to do it."

On the 11th of July, the attack was resumed. The Third Battalion was directed to seize the high ground in the vicinity of Raids by envelopment from the east. This battalion struck a strong defensive position and was delayed. The Second was employed to their left, and Company C mopped up La Maugerie to the southeast.

The attack on the 12th was to prove extremely costly in lives of both the officers and enlisted men. The Germans were waiting and well prepared. The first attack gained about three hundred yards following a heavy artillery preparation. Forward observers from the 44th Field Artillery Battalion moved well out in front of the lines in order to obtain good observation posts to better direct the fire of their units. It was an example of bravery doubly appreciated by soldiers who knew the effectiveness of artillery fire. The attack had only begun when Captain James B. Burnside, Second Battalion Executive Officer, was wounded, leaving the Second Battalion with only seventeen officers. The fighting became fierce hand-to-hand conflict.

Casualties mounted rapidly; the rifle companies did not have over seventy effective fighting men. Though the number was small, individual courage and initiative were everywhere apparent. First Sergeant Kenyon, of G Company, gathered together fifteen men and took over a section of the front normally held by a platoon. He said in a rather calm undisturbed manner, "I've taken over this part of the front and I'm going to hold it. You don't need to worry about it."

The Battalion Commander, Lt. Colonel Earl W. Edwards, was inspecting his battalion following one of the fiercest bits of fighting on the 10th of July, re-organizing and tying in. While crossing a field from one hedgerow to another he came upon a medic, a private first class, who had been on the front lines every single hour since the battalion had landed. His Company Commander swore by him, and everybody talked of his courage. But he had had about as much as he could take. When the colonel approached, he was doing his best to aid one of those impossible tragedies of the war, a man whose skull had been laid open and who had sustained such a severe brain injury that he could not possibly live, and yet he would not die.

The medic had done everything he knew how to do. He had been alone on this field for so long and the strain had been so great, and yet a devotion to duty and to a wounded member of his company was so great that he would not leave.

When he saw the Colonel, his reserve broke and he cried, "Sir, he won't die, He ought to die, but he won't. I have done everything I can for him, but he won't die. Why won't he die?" The Colonel led the aid man away, giving instructions for much needed rest and care for the boy. This was war at its lowest, purest hell.

By the morning of 13 July, the corridor of death had taken its toll. Little was left of a proud fighting regiment that had faced a determined enemy. The battle had been almost as costly as the beachhead assault. One thousand forty-four enlisted men were wounded and 263 were killed. Fifty-six officers were wounded and 16 were killed, for a total casualty list of 1,379 in less than one week of fighting. Total casualties for the five weeks now stood at 3,439, more than the total strength of the regiment at D Day.

In the Battle of Periers, even though the regiment did not succeed in capturing the city, they did help to break the back of the German defense of this sector in the bitterest hand-to-hand combat of the war.

During this period, Chaplain William S. Boice, Corporal Otto Oehring, and American Red Cross Field Director David Mitchell drove to Cherbourg to obtain flowers and wreaths. These flowers were placed on the graves of all known Twenty-Second men in the St. Mere Eglise cemetery. It was a sad task, done out of regard and genuine affection for fine men of a great regiment! But the crosses and Stars of David were many and presaged many more to come in the bitter fighting ahead.

Fit to Fight

From the **History of the Twelfth Infantry Regiment in WWII** *by* COL Gerden Johnson:

…Perhaps the agony of those ten days can best be realized when one examines the picture along the 4th Division front that morning of July 6. The breakthrough by the 4th Infantry Division was to be made in a sector south of Carentan. This meant clearing rugged terrain full of marshy swamps and rivers—ground ideal for the defenders. To reach firm ground where armored units could operate it was necessary for the infantry to fight inch by inch through that swampy country. The 4th was in the star role. Opposing the division were known to be the 17th SS Panzer Division and the 6th Parachute Regiment—both topnotch outfits.

For the next ten days, the 4th experienced hedgerow fighting at its worst. A hundred yard gain on a three hundred yard front often meant a whole day's work for a battalion. Enemy lurked behind every hedgerow. German gunners were dug in every few yards. Forward movement brought certain fire. Yet the 12th doughs, alongside their teammates in the 8th and 22nd, went into this new grim battle with the same unbeatable determination they had shown in storming the Atlantic Wall and in capturing Cherbourg.

In a narrow bottleneck, the 12th Infantry opened the division attack. The 2nd Battalion hurled nine separate attacks in two days, producing space no larger than a backyard garden. When the 12th eventually ripped out the whole enemy line, the 8th and 22nd swung into action.

On the main line of resistance the 8th struggled for three days before finally surrounding and annihilating an enemy regiment. On the other flank, the 22nd Infantry plunged ahead against large numbers of Panther tanks, proving that men can beat tanks—if they are the right men. The 22nd knocked out 20 Panthers in four days.

The Germans fell back to a new defensive line along a sunken road between two swamps. When the 4th took the position after four days of battling, it was relieved and sent to the St. Lo front for its next mission.

During this period of intense fighting, several incidents occurred which, when taken together, form the pattern that enabled us to engage two of the enemy's crack units long enough to enable adjacent friendly units to launch large scale attacks on our flanks. Formerly, the 12th Infantry had at least numerical superiority. But now the enemy not only outnumbered us, but his superior tactical dispositions gave him an even greater advantage.

The 3rd Battalion was attacking alongside the 2nd on July 6, with the 1st Battalion in Regimental reserve. At 1500, a gap developed between the two front line battalions and Col. Luckett promptly ordered Co. C to fill the breach. By 2000 hours, the regiment, having advanced 300 painful yards in five hours, dug in for the night, only to be subjected to relentless artillery and mortar fire. When Company F dug in for the night, it was only four fields away from an important crossroad. The Germans plastered the company area with mortar fire and Staff Sergeant McConnell shot an azimuth with his compass and calculated the time of flight of the shells. He gave the data to the forward observer of the 42nd Field Artillery which promptly knocked out the enemy guns. In Co. G, Capt. Jason Hardee of Loris, S.C. was mortally wounded…

From War Stories Volume I: Utah Beach to Liberation of Paris:
STORIES ABOUT BG TEDDY ROOSEVELT, JR.

Bill Parfitt, Elmira, NY
Company G, 22nd Infantry Regiment and HQ, 4th Infantry Division
Hogwash!

Bill Parfitt was an aide and bodyguard for BG Teddy Roosevelt. He accompanied General Roosevelt ashore on D-Day. Bill sent an article from the March 1999 American Legion magazine, which said that General Roosevelt was unarmed as he moved about on Utah beach. The article stated: "Armed only with a cane…" Bill clarifies General Roosevelt's armaments in his reply. –Bob Babcock

I note the clipping says that General Roosevelt carried nothing but a cane. That is hogwash. I know because I cleaned and oiled every weapon that was on the jeep every night. I wanted to be sure that they worked. The general had a Model 1911 .45-caliber pistol, usually in a shoulder holster. I know. I kicked my butt many times for not keeping the general's .45. I was also informed that when the general's stock of cognac was below a half case, I was to get more — anything I had to do to get it. When opportunity would prevail, I would get two cases and hide one in the jeep trailer.

I did the same thing with cases of canned premium tuna and anchovies that we had liberated in Cherbourg. I remember the day on the beach that the general was knocked down by some artillery, or he tripped and fell. This was when the helmet he was wearing, which was unusual in itself, came down on his nose as he hit the deck, and it busted his nose. He had a beautiful swollen nose, and I do not know who, but someone put him in for a Purple Heart for it. You know, he was all over the place from D-Day on, but I think this happened on the beach. I have the picture taken on the seawall, at the first CP that he had with General Barton.

I can also remember General Collins chewing his ass but good for failure to wear his helmet. I also remember that as Collins walked away, General Teddy tossed the helmet into the jeep. He hated the helmet and wanted to wear the little knit caps we all were issued. I also remember meeting General Roosevelt's son. He was an officer in the artillery and was some place on the Cherbourg Peninsula at the time of the general's death. I have read accounts that vary like the devil on this. The story that he carried no weapon was one, and that he was buried with no family present is another. Incidentally, General Roosevelt was buried next to an enlisted man.

Harold Blackwell, Mesa, AZ
Battery A, 377th Anti-Aircraft Artillery (AAA) Battalion
377th AAA Bn and BG Teddy Roosevelt Support of 22nd Infantry in the Hedgerows

The following is a brief account of my contact with Brigadier General Teddy

Roosevelt Jr., during the days before he received orders to take command of the 90th Infantry Division. At that time, I was CO of Battery A of the 377th AAA Battalion, directly attached to the 4th Infantry Division.

The 4th Infantry Division was having a difficult time making progress through the hedgerows of Normandy. General Roosevelt, the Assistant Division Commander of the 4th Infantry Division, was assigned the task of figuring out a way to take the hedgerows where the Germans were dug in. He got the idea of using antiaircraft weapons to assist the infantry, since it was almost impossible to get them out with the arms normally available to them.

I was assigned to work with the General, and in addition to my battery, I was given one platoon of four gun sections from Battery D of the 377th. From the very beginning, General Roosevelt and I hit it off really well. He was an outgoing, imaginative, enthusiastic commander. As I recall, we worked directly with Lieutenant Colonel Arthur Teague and his 3rd Battalion of the 22nd Infantry Regiment.

The tactics developed were to shell the hedgerows for about ten minutes with 40mm antiaircraft and .50-caliber machine guns. Under this intensive fire, the infantry advanced in a crawling position across the field. I had at my command twelve 40mm guns, shooting two rounds per second, and six quad .50 machine guns with power mounts on half-tracks. We also mounted two of the 40mm guns on half-tracks. That way, we could pull up into position, fire immediately, and withdraw when no longer needed.

These tactics worked very well as our antiaircraft fire kept the Germans pinned down in their honeycombed hedgerows as our infantry advanced. When the infantry got close enough to use flamethrowers, hand grenades, and rifle power, they would shoot off a red signal and we would lift our AA fire and pull back until we were ready to get in place for the next hedgerow. This operation was successful, and we moved from hedgerow to hedgerow.

During this entire operation, in early July 1944, General Roosevelt was very much in command and provided the enthusiastic coordination necessary for the overall success of the operation.

Fit to Fight

I remember on one occasion, General Roosevelt came roaring up to my command post and called out to me, "God, Blackie, what are you trying to do, kill the whole German Army at one time?" Our AA firepower was more than General Roosevelt, or the infantrymen were used to. They didn't realize we had such capability.

One afternoon, General Roosevelt made a special point of visiting my command post and told me that in the very near future, it looked like his next assignment was as Commanding General of an infantry division. The next day, he told me the orders had come through, that the CG of the 90th Infantry Division had been relieved and that he was going to their HQ that afternoon to meet the staff in preparation for taking over as CG. This was a promotion to Major General and an assignment he wanted very much. It was the last time I saw him.

Brigadier General Teddy Roosevelt Jr. was an inspirational leader. The next day, I heard that General Roosevelt died of a heart attack while at the 90th Division HQ. He was very common and always made you feel important. In the field, he usually wore only his green fatigues and the regulation knit stocking cap without his helmet on. Seldom did I ever even see his star of rank displayed other than a muddy red star on the front of his jeep. In my opinion, he was a great man, and one that I will always be proud to have served under, albeit for only a short time.

One outstanding remembrance of Brigadier General Roosevelt was when he told me about getting authorization to land with the first wave on D-Day. He said he was turned down by Major General Barton, 4th Infantry Division CG; Lieutenant General Collins, 7th Corps CG; and General Bradley, 1st Army CG, so he said, "I went to see Ike (General Eisenhower) at his headquarters and was told by him that General Officers just didn't land with the first wave. "In disgust," he said, "I told Ike to let me use the phone, I'll call my cousin (President Franklin D. Roosevelt)."

Ike smiled and said, "OK, Teddy. You win."

Brigadier General Teddy Roosevelt Jr. did land with the first wave on D-Day, June 6, 1944, and was a great inspiration to the assault troops on that stormy morning on Utah Beach. The rest is history.

Joel F. "Tommy" Thomason (Deceased), Fort Belvoir, VA
CO, 29th Field Artillery Battalion
Who's the Wise Guy? (Submitted by Irving Smolens)

It was either D-Day or D plus one. General Roosevelt was coming out of the 8th Infantry Regiment command post in either a farmhouse or a barn. There was a Signal Corps photographer standing by to take his picture as he emerged from the command post. Tommy said that when it came to his uniform, the general was the worst looking soldier he had ever seen. If he had on leggings, one pant leg would be inside and the other hanging on the outside of the legging. Tommy went to the photographer and told him not to take the general's picture as he emerged from the building, but to ask him to stand in front of a compost pile. The photographer did that and took the general's picture there.

The general soon realized what had been done and demanded to know, "Who was the wise guy who thought, I looked like a pile of horse sh-t." Tommy said that he didn't want anybody else to get in trouble for what he had done, so he had admitted that it was he who was responsible. The general then went over to Tommy and put his arm around him and said, "That's OK, Tommy."

I think the entire story deserves to be in the book that you are preparing because it demonstrates the spirit and camaraderie among the officers of the 4th Infantry Division, which transmitted itself down to the enlisted men and contributed to our success as a fighting unit.

THEODORE ROOSEVELT JR. MEDAL OF HONOR CITATION

For his conspicuous gallantry and leadership on D-Day, Brigadier General Theodore Roosevelt, Jr. earned the Medal of Honor. Following is the citation.

ROOSEVELT, THEODORE, JR.

RANK AND ORGANIZATION: Brigadier General, U.S. Army, 4th Infantry Division.

PLACE AND DATE: Normandy Invasion, 6 June 1944.

ENTERED SERVICE AT: Oyster Bay, New York BORN: Oyster Bay, New York

G.O. # 77, 28 September 1944

CITATION: For gallantry and intrepidity at the risk of his life above and beyond the call of duty on 6 June 1944, in France. After two verbal requests to accompany the leading assault elements in the Normandy invasion had been denied, Brigadier General Roosevelt's written request for this mission was approved and he landed with the first wave of the forces assaulting the enemy held beaches. He repeatedly led groups from the beach, over the sea wall and established them inland. His valor, courage, and presence in the very front of the attack and his complete unconcern at being under heavy fire inspired the troops to heights of enthusiasm and self-sacrifice. Although the enemy had the beach under constant direct fire, Brigadier General Roosevelt moved from one locality to another, rallying men around him, directed and personally led them against the enemy. Under his seasoned, precise, calm, and unfaltering leadership, assault troops reduced beach strong points and rapidly moved inland with minimum casualties. He thus contributed substantially to the successful establishment of the beachhead in France.

A BRIEF BIOGRAPHY OF BRIGADIER GENERAL TEDDY ROOSEVELT, JR.

Since he holds such a strong position in the history of the 4th Infantry Division, it is only appropriate that I take a little space here to give a short biography of "General Teddy". More can be found by Googling him. He is a key part of our 4ID legacy...(this is extracted from Wikipedia...)

Ted was the eldest son of President Theodore Roosevelt and First Lady Edith Kermit Carow. He was born at the family estate in Cove Neck, Oyster Bay, New York, when his father was just starting his political career. As a son of President Theodore Roosevelt, he has been referred to as "Jr", but he was actually Theodore III and one of his own sons was Theodore IV. His siblings were brothers Kermit, Archie, and Quentin; sister Ethel; and half-sister Alice...

WORLD WAR I

All the Roosevelt sons, except Kermit, had some military training prior to World War I. With the outbreak of World War I in Europe in August 1914, American leaders had heightened concern about their nation's readiness for military engagement. Only the month before, Congress had authorized the creation of an Aviation Section in the Signal Corps. In 1915, Major General Leonard Wood, President Roosevelt's former commanding officer during the Spanish–American War, organized a summer camp at Plattsburgh, New York, to provide military training for business and professional men, at their own expense.

This summer training program provided the base of a greatly expanded junior officers' corps when the country entered World War I. During that summer, many well-heeled young men from some of the finest east coast schools, including three of the four Roosevelt sons, attended the military camp. When the United States entered the war, in April 1917, the armed forces offered commissions to the graduates of these schools based on their performance. The National Defense Act of 1916 continued the student military training and the businessmen's summer camps. It placed them on a firmer legal basis by authorizing an Officers' Reserve Corps and a Reserve Officers' Training Corps (ROTC).

After the declaration of war, when the American Expeditionary Force (AEF) was organizing, Theodore Roosevelt wired Major General John

"Black Jack" Pershing asking if his sons could accompany him to Europe as privates. Pershing accepted, but based on their training at Plattsburgh, Archie was offered a commission with rank of second lieutenant, while Ted was offered a commission and the rank of major. Quentin had already been accepted into the Army Air Service. Kermit volunteered with the British in the area of present-day Iraq.

With a reserve commission in the army (like Quentin and Archibald), soon after World War I started, Ted was called up. When the United States declared war on Germany, Ted volunteered to be one of the first soldiers to go to France. There he was recognized as the best battalion commander in his division, according to the division commander. Roosevelt braved hostile fire and gas and led his battalion in combat. So concerned was he for his men's welfare that he purchased combat boots for the entire battalion with his own money. He eventually commanded the 26th Regiment in the 1st Division as a lieutenant colonel. He fought in several major battles, including America's first victory at Cantigny.

Ted was gassed and wounded at Soissons during the summer of 1918. In July of that year, his youngest brother Quentin was killed in combat. Ted received the Distinguished Service Cross for his actions during the war, which ended on November 11, 1918 at 11:00am. France conferred upon him the Chevalier Légion d'honneur on March 16, 1919. Before the troops came home from France, Ted was one of the founders of the soldiers' organization that developed as the American Legion. The American Legion's *Post Officers Guide* recounts Ted's part in the organization's founding:

A group of twenty officers who served in the American Expeditionary Forces (A.E.F.) in France in World War I is credited with planning the Legion. A.E.F. Headquarters asked these officers to suggest ideas on how to improve troop morale. One officer, Lieutenant Colonel Theodore Roosevelt, Jr., proposed an organization of veterans. In February 1919, this group formed a temporary committee and selected several hundred officers who had the confidence and respect of the whole army. When the first organization meeting took place in Paris in March 1919, about 1,000 officers and enlisted men attended. The meeting, known as the Paris Caucus, adopted a temporary constitution and the name The American Legion. It also elected an executive committee to complete the organization's work. It considered each soldier of the A.E.F. a member of the Legion. The executive committee named a subcommittee to organize veterans at home in the U.S. The Legion held a second organizing caucus in St. Louis, Missouri, in May 1919. It completed the constitution and made plans for a permanent organization. It set up temporary headquarters in New York City, and began its relief, employment, and Americanism programs. Congress granted the Legion a national charter in September 1919.

When the American Legion met in New York City, Roosevelt was nominated as its first national commander, but he declined, not wanting to be thought of as simply using it for political gain. In his view, acceptance under such circumstances could have discredited the nascent organization and himself and harmed his chances for a future in politics.

Ted resumed his reserve service between the wars. He attended the annual summer camps at Pine Camp and completed both the Infantry Officer's Basic and Advanced Courses, and the Command and General Staff College. By the beginning of World War II, in September 1939, he was eligible for senior commissioned service…

…In September 1929, President Herbert Hoover appointed Roosevelt as Governor of Puerto Rico, and he served until 1932…Impressed with his work in Puerto Rico, President Hoover appointed Roosevelt as Governor-General of the Philippines in 1932. During his time in office, Roosevelt acquired the nickname "One Shot Teddy" among the Filipino population, in reference to his marksmanship during a hunt for tamaraw (wild pygmy water buffalo)…

WORLD WAR II SERVICE

In 1940, during World War II…Roosevelt attended a military refresher course offered to many businessmen as an advanced student and was promoted to colonel in the Army of the United States. He returned to duty in April 1941 and was given command of the 26th Infantry Regiment, part of the 1st Infantry Division, the same unit he fought with in World War I. Late in 1941, he was promoted to the one-star general rank of brigadier general.

NORTH AFRICA CAMPAIGN

Upon his arrival in North Africa, Roosevelt became known as a general who often visited the front lines. He had always preferred the heat of the battle to the comfort of the command post, and this attitude would culminate in his actions in France on D-Day.

Roosevelt led the 26th Infantry in an attack on Oran, Algeria, on November 8, 1942 as part of Operation Torch, the Allies' invasion of North Africa. During 1943, he was the Assistant Division Commander (ADC) of the 1st Infantry Division in the campaign in North Africa under Major General Terry Allen. He was cited for the Croix de guerre by the military commander of French Africa, General Alphonse Juin.

As commander of a Franco-American detachment on the Ousseltia plain in the region of Pichon, in the face of a very aggressive enemy, he showed the finest qualities of decision and determination in the defense of his sector.

Showing complete contempt for personal danger, he never ceased during the period of Jan 28 — Feb 21, visiting troops in the front lines, making vital decisions on the spot, winning the esteem and admiration of the units under his command, and developing throughout his detachment the finest fraternity of arms.

CLASHES WITH PATTON

Roosevelt's collaboration and friendship with his commander, the hard-fighting, hard-drinking Major General Terry Allen, and their unorthodox approach to warfare did not escape the attention of Lieutenant General George S. Patton, the Seventh Army commander in Sicily, and formerly the II Corps commander, who disapproved of such officers who "dressed down" and were seldom seen in regulation field uniforms, and who placed little value in Patton's spit-shined ways in the field. Patton thought them both un-soldierly for it and wasted no opportunity to send derogatory reports on Allen to General Dwight D. Eisenhower, the Supreme Allied Commander in the Mediterranean Theater of Operations (MTO). Roosevelt was also treated by Patton as "guilty by association" for his friendship and collaboration with the highly unorthodox Allen. When Allen was relieved of command of the 1st Division and reassigned, so was Roosevelt.

After criticizing Allen in his diary on July 31, 1943, Patton noted that he had asked permission of Eisenhower "to relieve both Allen and Roosevelt on the same terms, on the theory of rotation of command", and added, concerning Roosevelt, "there will be a kick over Teddy, but he has to go, brave but otherwise, no soldier." Later, however, upon hearing of the death of Roosevelt, Patton wrote in his diary that Roosevelt was "one of the bravest men I've ever known," and a few days later served as a pallbearer at his funeral.

Roosevelt was also criticized by Lieutenant General Omar Bradley, the II Corps commander, who ultimately relieved both Roosevelt and Allen. In both of his autobiographies—*A Soldier's Story (1951)* and *A General's Life*—Bradley claimed that relieving the two generals was one of his most unpleasant duties of the war. Bradley felt that Allen and Roosevelt were guilty of «loving their division too much» and that their relationship with their soldiers was having a generally bad effect on the discipline of both the commanders and the men of the division.

Roosevelt was assistant commander of the 1st Infantry Division at Gela during the Allied invasion of Sicily, code named Operation Husky, commanded Allied Forces in Sardinia, and fought on the Italian mainland. He was the chief liaison officer to the French Army in Italy for General Eisenhower, and repeatedly made requests of Eisenhower for combat command.

D-DAY

In February 1944, Roosevelt was assigned to England to help lead the Normandy invasion and appointed Deputy Division Commander of the 4th Infantry Division. After several verbal requests to the division's Commanding General (CG), Major General Raymond "Tubby" Barton, to go ashore on D-Day with the Division were denied, Roosevelt sent a written petition:

"The force and skill with which the first elements hit the beach and proceed may determine the ultimate success of the operation...With troops engaged for the first time, the behavior pattern of all is apt to be set by those first engagements. [It is] considered that accurate information of the existing situation should be available for each succeeding element as it lands. You should have when you get to shore an overall picture in which you can place confidence. I believe I can contribute materially on all of the above by going in with the assault companies. Furthermore, I personally know both officers and men of these advance units and believe that it will steady them to know that I am with them."

Barton approved Roosevelt's written request with much misgiving, stating that he did not expect Roosevelt to return alive.

Roosevelt was the only general on D-Day to land by sea with the first wave of troops. At 56, he was the oldest man in the invasion, and the only one whose son also landed that day; Captain Quentin Roosevelt II was among the first wave of soldiers at Omaha Beach.

Brigadier General Roosevelt was one of the first soldiers, along with Captain Leonard T. Schroeder Jr., off his landing craft as he led the 8th Infantry Regiment and 70th Tank Battalion landing at Utah Beach. Roosevelt was soon informed that the landing craft had drifted south of their objective, and the first wave of men was a mile off course. Walking with the aid of a cane and carrying a pistol, he personally made a reconnaissance of the area immediately to the rear of the beach to locate the causeways that were to be used for the advance inland. He returned to the point of landing and contacted the commanders of the two battalions, Lieutenant Colonels Conrad C. Simmons and Carlton O. MacNeely, and coordinated the attack on the enemy positions confronting them. Opting to fight from where they had landed rather than trying to move to their assigned positions, Roosevelt's famous words were, "We'll start the war from right here!"

These impromptu plans worked with complete success and little confusion. With artillery landing close by, each follow-on regiment was personally welcomed on the beach by a cool, calm, and collected Roosevelt, who inspired all with humor and confidence, reciting poetry and telling anecdotes of his father to steady the nerves of his men. Roosevelt pointed almost every regiment to its changed objective. Sometimes he worked under fire as a self-appointed traffic cop, untangling traffic jams of trucks and tanks all struggling to get inland and off the beach. One GI later reported that seeing the general walking around, apparently unaffected by the enemy fire, even when clods of earth fell down on him, gave him the courage to get on with the job, saying if the general is like that it can't be that bad.

When Major General Barton, the commander of the 4th Infantry Division, came ashore, he met Roosevelt not far from the beach. He later wrote: "While I was mentally framing [orders], Ted Roosevelt came up. He had landed with the first wave, had put my troops across the beach, and had a perfect picture (just as Roosevelt had earlier promised if allowed to go ashore with the first wave) of the entire situation. I loved Ted. When I finally agreed to his landing with the first wave, I felt sure he would be killed. When I had bade him goodbye, I never expected to see him alive. You can imagine then the emotion with which I greeted him when he came out to meet me [near La Grande Dune]. He was bursting with information."

By modifying his division's original plan on the beach, Roosevelt enabled its troops to achieve their mission objectives by coming ashore and attacking north behind the beach toward its original objective. Years later, Omar Bradley was asked to name the single most heroic action he had ever seen in combat. He replied, "Ted Roosevelt on Utah Beach."

Following the landing, Roosevelt utilized a Jeep named "Rough Rider" which was the nickname of his father's regiment raised during the

Spanish-American War. Before his death, Roosevelt was appointed as Military Governor of Cherbourg.

DEATH

Throughout World War II, Roosevelt suffered from health problems. He had arthritis, mostly from old World War I injuries, and walked with a cane. He also had heart trouble, which he kept secret from army doctors and his superiors.

On July 12, 1944, a little over one month after the landing at Utah Beach, Roosevelt died of a heart attack in France. He was living at the time in a converted sleeping truck, captured a few days before from the Germans. He had spent part of the day in a long conversation with his son, Captain Quentin Roosevelt II, who had also landed at Normandy on D-Day. He was stricken at about 10:00 PM, attended by medical help, and died at about midnight. He was fifty-six years old. On the day of his death, he had been selected by Lieutenant General Omar Bradley, now commanding the U.S. First Army, for promotion to the two-star rank of major general and command of the 90th Infantry Division. These recommendations were sent to General Eisenhower, now the Supreme Allied Commander in Europe. Eisenhower approved the assignment, but Roosevelt died before it could be put into effect.

Roosevelt was initially buried at Sainte-Mère-Église. Photographs show that his pallbearers were generals, including Omar N. Bradley, George S. Patton, Raymond O. Barton, Clarence R. Huebner, Courtney Hicks Hodges, and J. Lawton Collins, the VII Corps commander. Later, Roosevelt was buried at the American cemetery in Normandy, initially created for the Americans killed in Normandy during the invasion. His younger brother, Second Lieutenant Quentin Roosevelt, had been killed in action as a pilot in France during World War I and was initially buried near where he had been shot down in that war. In 1955, his family had his body exhumed and moved to the Normandy cemetery, where he was re-interred beside his brother. Ted also has a cenotaph near the grave of his parents at Youngs Memorial Cemetery in Oyster Bay, while Quentin's original gravestone was moved to Sagamore Hill.

BG Teddy Roosevelt Jr. Grave in Normandy, France

LAST HALF OF JULY 1944

OPERATION COBRA

15 JULY 1944—D+39: The 17th SS Panzer Division withdrew under the covering of the 6th Parachute Regiment. Considerable shelling of the rear areas and increasing numbers of mines found which had been hastily laid by the retreating enemy. The 8th Infantry launched an attack at 1015 in conjunction with the 12th Infantry. Upon reaching the objective at 1800, the regiment organized positions for defense. The 12th Infantry did the same at 2100. The 22nd Infantry remained in assembly area as division reserve.

16 JULY 1944—D+40: Contact with enemy consisted mainly of artillery barrages. Enemy seemed to be fighting a stiff delaying action preparatory to withdraw to high ground around Périers. The 8th Infantry held and improved defensive positions gained during the preceding period. The 12th Infantry did the same until it was relieved at 2230. The 22nd Infantry moved to an assembly area in the vicinity of Mont Martin en Graines, closing there at 1430.

17 JULY 1944—D+41: Enemy contacts consisted of security patrols. The 8th Infantry held defensive positions until relief was completed by the 4th Armored Division at 2300. It moved to an assembly area near

Meautis. The 12th Infantry also moved to this assembly area (at 0115) and then moved to its final assembly area in the vicinity of Mont Martin en Graines (closed at 1045). The 22nd Infantry remained in the assembly area and proceeded to conduct training to correct deficiencies noted in combat.

18-23 JULY 1944—D+42 TO D+47: No contact with the enemy. The 4th Infantry Division was in the process of moving into position preparatory to attacking south with the mission of securing the gap Marigny-St Gilles. All divisional and attached units had been assembled within the division assembly area and were to remain there for several days to conduct care and cleaning of equipment, training to correct deficiencies, and take advantage of lessons learned. Hot showers were provided by First Army shower units.

21 JULY 1944—D+45: The 8th Infantry Regiment carried out reconnaissance to forward positions in the 39th Infantry sector and made further preparations to pass through this unit when operation Cobra was launched. The 12th Infantry Regiment moved by foot and motor to new assembly area and constituted a part of the division reserve. Movement of the Division and attachments to new assembly areas was now complete.

* * * * *

And don't believe for a minute that it was ever safe for troops of the 4ID from the time they landed on D-Day until the Germans surrendered on VE Day. Following is a gripping account of the death of a highly respected leader in the 12th Infantry Regiment who was killed by a German sniper on 16 July 1944.

Fit to Fight

Stories from **War Stories Volume I: Utah Beach to Liberation of Paris:**

Clyde R. Stodghill, Cuyahoga Falls, OH
Company G, 2nd Battalion, 12th Infantry Regiment
The "Iron" Major

On the fairly quiet Sunday morning of July 16, 1944, Major Richard J. O'Malley, commanding officer of the 2nd Battalion, 12th Infantry Regiment was killed by an enemy rifleman. Major O'Malley's worth can hardly be measured. His every action had been stamped by fearlessness, and he was undoubtedly one of the foremost combat officers of the Regiment. His men worshipped him. He had given them the inspiration that had carried the 2nd Battalion to its great successes, and, in turn, the welfare of his men was always uppermost in his mind. General Barton paid a final tribute to this gallant leader by ordering three volleys to be fired into the enemy lines by the massed artillery and mortars of the 4th Infantry Division—the only such occasion of the entire war. (Credited to the History of the 12th Infantry Regiment.)

The word that Major O'Malley had been killed was passed from man to man in disbelieving whispers, as if by repeating the words quietly they might turn into just another false rumor. The "Iron Major" dead—could it be true? Although death was all around us, it had seemed that the major was somehow immune, a man apart from the norm. To know that he had died left each of us more vulnerable. Words could not make it real to some of us—we had to see for ourselves. A friend and I were drawn to the place where he had fallen in Company E's sector as surely as metal shavings are drawn by a magnetic force. Neither of us cared that we had left our position without authority.

A medical jeep with racks for holding a litter had come up to the front. It was the first and only time I saw that happen. The United States Army was slow in removing the dead from a battlefield, but the corpse of a major could not be left lying on the ground for all to see.

Major O'Malley's body rested on a litter covered by an olive drab blanket. We arrived as the litter was placed on the racks of the jeep. The medics returned to a group of officers standing silently ten feet away. It was then that the only unexplainable incident of a long lifetime occurred. Although no one was close by and the wind was not blowing, the side of the blanket fluttered upward, remaining that way for a few seconds without support.

My friend said, "Look! The major's trying to get up." Knowing the kind of man Major O'Malley had been, his words seemed perfectly natural at the time, so I nodded in agreement. The only logical explanation that comes to mind is that the exhaust from the jeep's motor, which was running, had been responsible.

During my later years as a newspaperman, I came in contact with many men of stature: leading politicians, industrialists, entertainers, famous athletes, and coaches. Major O'Malley stands alone among them as a figure bigger than life, a man who towered above the pack.

Richard J. O'Malley was a ruggedly handsome man with a voice that could crack timber, a man whose every movement was brisk, decisive, and authoritative. He was not the sort of leader who had a word of encouragement or kindly comment for everyone, nor did he lead by fear. It was his presence alone that inspired, and unlike many battalion commanders, he was always present or somewhere close by. He did not lead from a command post in the rear; he led from the Line of Departure. Many were the times when he could be heard calling, "Up and at 'em, 2nd Battalion, follow me!" We did so with apprehension, but without hesitation.

While we didn't fear Major O'Malley as a bully, we did fear committing an act that would arouse his anger, or above all, his contempt. Proving unworthy of his respect was unthinkable. To an eighteen-year old rifleman, he was an awesome figure, a giant of a man. He was, as stated in the regimental history, a man worthy of worship.

O'Malley was a captain when he assumed command of the 2nd Battalion on the day in June when Lieutenant Colonel Dominick Montelbano was killed near Montebourg. He should have led a regiment, division, or corps. Many far less capable men did so. He had been our commander for only 33 days. In Normandy, that was the equivalent of a lifetime. Just as it came to seem that you had been there forever, it seemed that he had always been your leader and would continue to lead the battalion long after you were gone.

But now he was dead. Memories were alive, however, and would always remain fresh in my mind: the day when I didn't know what to do and was stammering on the radio so he came on and ordered me, an eighteen-year old private, to appoint a company commander; a dark afternoon when he grabbed canteens to find out if they held wine or cognac; the expression on his face as he looked down at a lieutenant who had shot himself in the foot; hearing him call, "Follow Me!" as he led an attack. Although he was a deadly serious man, I recall two occasions when he made us laugh.

The first came when we were lying in the sun on a slope that rose gently to where the major was attempting to interrogate a German. The man listened in bewilderment as the major grew louder and angrier. A GI I had not seen before and never saw again came walking over to them from our left. He wasn't wearing a helmet and was armed with only a pistol. He put a .45-caliber pistol to the man's head and shot him. After that, he went unhurriedly back to wherever it was he had come from.

Major O'Malley was speechless. He looked from one to another of us as if someone might be able to explain this extraordinary occurrence. Then, his expression changed to one of fury. He stalked off to the right saying, "I'll be damned! A man can't even interrogate a prisoner without some GI walking up and shooting him!" It required great effort to contain our laughter until the major was out of hearing range.

On another day, we were spread out along both sides of a shady back road, waiting to go forward to where E or F Company was engaged in a desultory firefight. Sunlight filtered through the trees, and we sat there enjoying the short rest amid pleasant surroundings. Suddenly a German bounded over the hedgerow about twenty feet to my right, ran across the road without looking in either direction, and peered over the opposite hedgerow, apparently hoping to see friends.

The incident came to mind eight years later as my Company sat along another back road in Louisiana. A gray fox, oblivious of our presence, ran among a hundred armed men to investigate the noise being made by cooks loading metal cans onto a truck at the far end of a field across the road. He suddenly became aware of us. Like a cartoon character, he leaped high in the air, completed a full turn before coming down, and then took off at full speed.

The German was less fortunate, although we just sat there watching until from thirty yards to our left Major O'Malley cried, "Shoot that man! Shoot that man!" He began firing his pistol, but his wild shots were scattered all along the road, so we dived for cover. Realizing his mistake, the German ran back to the center of the road, then stood there in amazed desperation as the major ran toward him, continuing to fire, still shouting, "Shoot that man!"

A BAR man, probably in self-defense from the wild shooting, rose up and fired a burst that sent the luckless German sprawling on his back. After Major O'Malley turned and went back to the place where he had been, we started laughing. A rifle squad leader, Curly Walsh, sat shaking his head, and still laughing a little said, "I'll tell you what, I was a helluva lot more scared of the major with his .45 than I ever was of any Jerry."

In later years, at Ivy Division reunions, those of us from the 2nd Battalion often talked of the major. Cliff Burke, who served under him when O'Malley was commander of Company H in the States, told how he would drive around various camps and nearby towns in a red Packard convertible—an automobile well suited to the major.

Half a century after he died, I talked with Major O'Malley's grandson, Richard Roy of Atlanta, who was seeking information on his grandfather's death. I told him about an E Company private I knew who had been shot by the same sniper just before he killed the major. During a reunion, the man explained how he shifted position just as the sniper squeezed the trigger. As a result, he was hit in the shoulder, not the head or throat. After the major was killed by the second shot, the wounded man watched from the ground as other men killed the young sniper concealed in a tree.

Richard Roy said the major's brother, a captain with the 2nd Armored Division's advanced party, was killed on D-Day. Forty-one years after the Normandy campaign, my wife and I walked along the rows of white crosses and Stars of David in the cemetery above Omaha Beach. We were looking for graves of 4th Infantry Division men so when she said, "Here's one," I went over to where she was standing.

For a moment I remained there unmoving, stunned at reading the inscription: "Richard J. O'Malley, Major, 12th Infantry Regiment." We had found the Iron Major.

An hour later, we stopped at a German cemetery a few miles away. Two busloads of German students were renewing the gold lettering on crosses of black. We paused at the first we came to and read the brief inscription:

George Drost, 19, July 16, 1944

Too much of a coincidence of course, that this could have been the German sniper. And yet, as the regimental history states, it was a fairly quiet day on the Sainteny front.

Patricia O'Malley, Dallas, Georgia
Daughter of Major Richard James O'Malley, USA.

In December 2000, Patrica O'Malley posted the following note to the 4th Infantry Division Association web page at **www.4thinfantry.org**

— *Bob Babcock*

My father, Major Richard James O'Malley, was Commander of the 2nd Battalion, 12th Infantry Regiment, 4th Infantry Division in WWII. He was killed among the hedgerows in France on July 16, 1944. I was one year old. I have tried to learn all about him that I can and would like to hear from anyone who knew him.

Recently, I made my first visit to his grave in France at the American Cemetery. It was a very emotional experience for me. I wrote my feelings about the trip and would like to share it with anyone who identifies with my feelings. May God bless you all for your service to our great nation and for all the sacrifices that have been made.

I arrived at the American Cemetery at Normandy, France, with excitement and eager anticipation. All my life I had waited for this moment. And here I was. I could scarcely believe it. I entered the office at the cemetery and asked the location of my father's grave. When the director found that I was the next of kin, she closed the office and escorted me. After a short walk, we stood before my father's grave. At last, I was there. I fought to contain my tears. Then, as if by magic, I heard broadcast over the loudspeakers, taps being played, followed by "volleys" being fired. The sounds echoed loudly across the ten thousand graves and out across the sea.

I could no longer contain my tears, and I cried. The woman left me so I could have time alone. I cried deeply for many reasons. I cried for the joy of being there and the sadness of my father's death. I cried for all the times I needed a father and never had one. I cried for all the words I had wanted to say and wanted to hear but had not. I cried and cried. And, when I was through, I just stayed there. I talked to my father and told him I loved him. I talked to him as if he were alive. I put my hand on the cold marble cross and held onto it as if it would make me somehow be holding onto him. And I knew that under the grass and dirt lay my father's bones. Part of my father was really here. He was real.

I spent the afternoon at the cemetery walking around and looking at the monuments and all the other graves. All the men had their own stories, their own wives, and children. I sat on a bench and looked out over the ocean. I heard the cry of the gulls and the sounds of the wind. Normandy Beach looked so peaceful now. But it was holy ground. Though I couldn't see the bodies or the blood of the battle, they were there. And though I couldn't hear the cries of the wounded or the sounds of the battle, they were there, too. And they will always be there. And so, we have erected monuments and constructed museums and historical placards all along the battle zones. These sites will forever be hallowed.

I had always wondered why my family left my father so far across the sea. Previous to my visit, I thought that was a wrong decision. But now that I have been there, it seems right. It seems right that my father, who always led his men in battle, would not desert them even in death. As I walked through the cemetery, I saw his men buried all around him. I knew that he was where he should be. He lay a fallen hero in a foreign land, high atop the cliffs of Normandy. I said good-bye to my father, and I thanked God that I was able to come. I said a prayer for him and for all the men who gave their lives that we might be free.

— Patricia O'Malley,
Daughter of Major Richard James O'Malley, USA

Note from Bob: *I've said it many times before and will say it many times again. We must never forget:* **Freedom Is Not Free.** *It has been paid for throughout our history, and continues to be paid for today, by the lives of America's military. Don't ever forget that…*

Clyde R. Stodghill, Cuyahoga Falls, OH
Company G, 2nd Battalion, 12th Infantry Regiment
Unclaimed Bed Rolls

They were stacked high along a stone wall, across a side street from the Pasteur Hospital, an even one hundred-fifty of them resembling oversized, khaki-colored sausages. These were the casualty rolls, a mute testament to the savage fighting on the road to Cherbourg.

No one had returned to claim them when the rest of us walked along the rows of blanket rolls laid out in military precision on the ground, each man seeking his own among the many that in appearance were markedly similar. When everyone had picked up a roll containing all his possessions other than those on his back, we stood off to one side waiting to be told what to do.

Then, as was always the case, those remaining on the ground underwent a transformation. They had been blanket rolls; now they were casualty rolls. With the new name came a new look, one that spoke of infinite loneliness, lost hope, shattered dreams.

Someone had to open these pathetic reminders of lives that a short time before had been robust. The GI equipment had to be separated from the personal belongings and then formed into piles: shoes here, pants there; a different stack for every item issued by the army. Small cardboard boxes awaited what was left. Bundles of letters in feminine handwriting, photographs of smiling girls, sometimes ones of young children could be found in these personal stacks of belongings. A fallen man's memories of another time and another world. Shaving gear, a candy bar, a paperback book, a spare pair of eyeglasses, a harmonica, the sparse possessions that made every roll unique, gave it the stamp of individuality, the mark of the man who had not returned to claim it.

The last thing a rifleman did before starting back down the road to the battle was make up his blanket roll. He laid his shelter-half (buttoned together with another, it made a pup tent) on the ground and then placed his two wool blankets on top, folded so as to leave a foot of canvas exposed on each side. Then came personal belongings, spare clothing, an extra pair of boots, tent pole and pegs, mess kit, minus the spoon that went with him to the front.

Once everything was in place, the exposed sides of the shelter half were folded over then rolled up tightly and one end was secured by making a loop of his tent rope. Then the rope was tied near the other end, leaving enough slack so the finished blanket roll was ready to be tossed onto a pile near the kitchen truck where it would stay until he returned...or it became a casualty roll.

The routine was the same regardless of weather. If a roll was made up in the rain, everything inside was still damp when it was picked up again. A man's blanket roll soon took on the musty smell of a long-neglected gym bag.

The cooks were responsible for the rolls until the company came off the line for a night or even an hour during a move from one sector to another. When the cooks heated up a meal of 10-in-1 rations on one of those brief pauses, retrieving a mess kit from a blanket roll hardly seemed worth the effort.

Before our arrival, the cooks laid out the rolls in long rows. Room was left for walking between them, and the names were facing upward. Weary and silent, we would amble along, each man searching for his own roll. Now and then, someone would call out the name of a friend. That man would walk over, retrieve his roll, and then help the friend find his own. It was a strange feeling, seeing the names of men in your own company displayed that way and finding the majority of them unfamiliar. At the beginning, it hadn't been that way for the company's original men, but it quickly became an organization of men who, for the most part, were strangers to one another.

In Normandy, the unclaimed rolls more often than not outnumbered those that had been picked up. At times, the neat rows were hardly disturbed, just a gap here and another there. I often looked at the haggard faces around me and wondered how many would be there the next time. Or how many times any man could hope to be among those taking part in the grim ritual. My thoughts would drift back to the day when I had last tossed my roll on the pile at the kitchen truck and watched as others did the same. Where were they now, all those men who had not returned to claim their rolls? At times, I knew. More often, I did not, because so many were merely a face without a name to accompany it, or just names I had never heard and sometimes faces I had never seen.

In Cherbourg, the unpleasant job of opening the one hundred-fifty casualty rolls fell to Mike Spinelli and me, a pair of eighteen-year old riflemen from Northeastern Ohio. It was a job no one wanted, one that would spoil an otherwise sunny and pleasant day of two young soldiers who would rather have been doing almost anything else.

This was not the first time that Company G casualty rolls had been opened. Near Montebourg, about seventy-five others had been processed—roughly two hundred twenty-five in three weeks of combat, more than the number of Company G men in the third wave to hit Utah Beach on D-Day.

Donald Lewis, the weapons platoon sergeant, was in charge of the detail. He handed Mike a clipboard with several sheets of paper containing typewritten names and serial numbers. Following each name was one of three sets of letters: KIA, WIA, MIA...killed, wounded, or missing in action. The many names followed by KIA told how bitter those three weeks of battle had been for the 12th Infantry Regiment. Numerous others were listed as MIA—men buried under the dirt, hurled by exploding shells and as yet unfound, a few vaporized when a shell hit at their feet.

After giving us the few instructions we needed, Sergeant Lewis said he would be in a small room opening off an alley at the far end of the wall. He told us to bring the roll of a man he named back to him without opening it.

So, we set to work, Mike and I. Each of us took a roll, put a check beside the name on the list and then sorted the contents. It proved to be a time-consuming job that lasted most of the day.

Mike was a small man with a serious face that seldom changed expression. He wasn't much of a talker. When he did make a comment, it usually was a sardonic one pertaining to the situation. His type was never seen in any of the inane war movies that always seemed to feature a noisy Italian. Aside from ancestry, Mike was the antithesis of that sort.

On the stock of his rifle, he had carved "Lillian," an act that anywhere but in combat would have earned him a trip to the stockade. Knowing his taciturn nature, I felt certain that somewhere back in Cleveland was a girl called Lillian who was completely unaware that she had captured Mike's heart.

He had a voracious appetite, but I never heard him complain when food was scarce. One day the cook who doubled as baker made doughnuts that were sent up to us at the front. The man had baked enough for a full company, and we were far short of being that. A great many were left over so Mike ate more than twenty of them. One day while in the rear, we were served canned pears, a treat beyond imagining for men starving for fruit and vegetables. A vat full of juice remained, so both Mike and I drank one canteen cupful of it after another. During the coming hours, a price had to be paid for our indulgence. It was worth it.

We had been working a short time when Mike came over to me with a sick expression on his face. "Look at this," he said, holding out a pocket-sized Bible open at the flyleaf. On it was written: "To Alton C. Bright from Mother. Read it and be good."

This was too much for Mike's sensitive nature. It didn't do a lot for my morale, either.

The advice had not been heeded; the gilt-edged pages had never been separated. I called to Eddie Wolfe, our platoon sergeant who was passing by, and showed it to him. He told us that Al Bright had been a staff sergeant, a rifle squad leader from Paris, Tennessee. He was the first man killed in Company G. Eddie said that as the ramp dropped on his landing craft and he was preparing to lead his men ashore, a bullet caught him in the forehead.

When we were told that it was time for a lunch of 10-in-1 rations, Mike said he wasn't hungry. That was unheard of for him. I didn't have much appetite myself, so we went on working.

Sergeant Lewis came by to check on us. We had placed personal items for shipment home in a number of the little boxes so Lewis looked them over. He was not happy. From one he took a bundle of letters and tossed them at my feet. "Look at the return addresses," he said. All were from girls in England or living in towns near camps where the 4th Infantry Division had been stationed in the States.

"Going to send those back to his wife, are you?" said Lewis. "That should make her feel damn good." From another box, he took a pair of eyeglasses, holding them out to me by a thumb and one finger. "Do you think his mother and father will want these for something to remember him by? Anyway, they're GI issue."

He had a few more caustic comments before going back to the alley. His message was received. When the job was finished, there wasn't a single item in any of the boxes. As the day wore on, French civilians gathered to watch. After years of having to do without, seeing all those shoes and the piles of clothing was a moving experience for them. A man of fifty-five or sixty approached me, smiling and holding out a black fountain pen. Pointing to the word "Berlin" stamped on it, he kept repeating, "Boche, Boche." He wanted me to take the pen, hoping that in return I would give him something from the stacks that had accumulated along the wall. As far as I was concerned, the people could have had it all, but I had no say in the matter. Reluctantly, I took the pen, feeling guilty about doing so, and more than fifty years later I still have it.

The crowd kept growing until men and women were almost on top of us and we had little room to work. I went to the room in the alley and explained the situation to Sergeant Lewis. He came out and waved them back, but they soon were pressing forward again so he sent word for one of his machine gun squads to set up their gun at the corner. Most of the crowd dispersed then, but a few civilians remained watching us from the other side of the street, including the man who had given me the pen, and his wife.

The pair slowly moved closer, finally halting at the center of the narrow street. A few minutes later four GIs from some newly arrived rear echelon outfit came by. They were a crude lot, the coarse type of men who were far too plentiful and gave all Americans a bad name.

The most repulsive of the group stopped beside the French man and his wife, grinning, and making lewd remarks that the man could not understand. He believed they were being friendly, so he and his wife kept smiling and nodding as the GI said, "Who's the old whore with you?" and other things of that sort.

His companions thought this was hilarious. What they didn't know was that Nick Scala, the machine gun section sergeant, was approaching from behind to check on his men. When he took in what was going on, he scared them out of their skins by shouting, "Ten shun!" from a foot away.

Scala shooed off the remaining civilians, then ordered the men to line up against the wall across the street. Turning to his machine gunner, he called, "Load!"

A .30-caliber light machine gun did not have a safety, so when not firing, the gun was kept on half load. This was done by feeding the belt of ammunition into the gun while pulling back on the operating handle a single time. This did not line up a round for firing, which was accomplished by pulling the operating handle back a second time to the "load" position.

Fit to Fight

The worthless foursome lined up against the wall, shaking with terror. I was anticipating the command "Fire!" with pleasure. Instead of giving it, Scala ordered the interlopers out of the Company G area and told them never to return because the next time he saw them they would die.

They took off on the dead run. More than one, I would have bet, had to go back to wherever they came from to change shorts. It was the one bright moment of a bleak, depressing day.

When in late afternoon we came to the roll that Sergeant Lewis wanted to open himself, I took it back to him. A little later a question came up, and I returned to the alley. When I opened the door of the small room I saw the contents of his friend's roll spread out on the floor. Lewis sat bent over them, hands covering his face. I quietly closed the door and went back to where Mike was working. The question, whatever it had been, no longer seemed important.

* * * * *

The above stories are real and depressing. The next stories won't be such downers. I include these to remind us all, once again, that **"Freedom Isn't Free."** As we continue to follow our beloved 4ID through the next highs and lows of their eleven-month fight across Europe between 6 June 1944 and 8 May 1945, let us never forget that.

22 TO 28 JULY 1944 — D+46 TO D+52: The 4ID participated in several key historic events during WWII. The first was D-Day on 6 June 1944; second was the liberation of Cherbourg (the first port liberated) on 25 June 1944; third was the St. Lo breakout (Operation Cobra) on 25 July 1944, fourth was the liberation of Paris on 25 August 1944 (there were others, I'll cover them later). In this section, we cover Operation Cobra — the St. Lo breakout where the 4ID led the attack to breakout of the hedgerows into the open parts of France.

22 & 23 JULY 1944 — D+46 AND D+47: Reconnaissance of forward positions, road repairs and reconnaissance for all supporting fire weapons was conducted by all units. (Not a lot reported as the 4ID prepared to jump off on Operation Cobra on 25 July 1944).

24 JULY 1944—D+48: Enemy started defensive fires using mortars, machine guns, and interdictory artillery barrages. The 8th Infantry (with other units among which were the 70th Tank Bn and the 634th TD Bn) attacked at 1300 in columns of battalions. The 2nd Battalion succeeded in advancing against heavy artillery and mortar fire to a line north of St Lô—Périers highway. Upon division order, the battalion withdrew to streamline and consolidated positions. The 12th Infantry and 4th Reconnaissance Troop remained in reserve and were prepared to follow the advance of the 8th Infantry. The divisional Artillery and attached units supported the advance, 29th FA and 42nd FA in direct support, the 20th in general support with harassing and interdiction missions.

25 JULY 1944—D+49: Today is a very key event in our division›s history. July 25, 1944 was when the St. Lo breakout started. Our 4ID has three dates, one month apart, that are key successes for us in the Normandy campaign—June 25 was the liberation of Cherbourg, July 25 was the St. Lo breakout (to get out of the hedgerow country), and August 25 was when the 4ID entered Paris. By September 25, we were fighting in the Siegfried line on the German border, November 25 had us locked in the fiercest battle of our history in the Hurtgen Forest, and December 25 had us in the Battle of the Bulge. (October 25 was relatively quiet and uneventful for the 4ID).

The enemy was forced to withdraw from its well-prepared emplacements north of the St-Lô—Périers road. The 8th Regiment and attached units attacked at 1100 and its 1st Battalion succeeded in advancing to La Chapelle-en-Juger. Then it outposted its area in preparation for continuation of the attack. The 12th Infantry remained in reserve and moved to vicinity of La Petite Grandière. (Editor's note: 22nd Infantry was detached from 4ID and was part of Task Force Rose of the 2nd Armored Division for this timeframe—their actions were not included in the 4ID AAR, they came back to 4ID in early August. I have covered the 22nd

Infantry actions in detail in this section, just not in 4ID After Action Reports now).

26 JULY 1944—D+50: The enemy fought a poorly organized delaying action from hastily prepared positions constructed during the hours of darkness. The 8th Infantry attacked at 0800. A considerable amount of resistance was encountered generally consisting of small arms, automatic weapons, and scattered artillery fires. Progress was slow until 1800 at which time the enemy resistance lessened.

27 JULY 1944—D+51: Enemy fought a disorganized delaying action which consisted of pockets of resistance supported by a few tanks and antitank guns. The 8th Infantry continued the attack to seize and hold the high ground on a line from Carantilly to Quibou along the Joigne river. Stiff resistance was encountered until early afternoon. The 12th Infantry attacked from Le Mesnil-Amey to clear the woods (1st Bn) and to take St Benoît (2nd Bn). The Artillery fired supporting mission for the advance of the 3rd Armored Division.

28 JULY 1944—D+52: The enemy withdrew in great haste and confusion, which was apparent from the great quantity of materiel left behind. The enemy's action consisted mainly of trying to break through the gap formed by the US VII and VIII Corps. The 8th Infantry attacked at 0700 to clear the road of enemy resistance. The objective was reached at 1100. Orders were issued to move south to an area near Notre-Dame de Cenilly. The 12th Infantry attacked to finish the clearing of the woods and were ordered to move by specified route.

*****

Fighting under the command of the 2nd Armored Division, the 22nd Infantry Regiment was teamed with 66th Armor Regiment to make up Task Force Rose. They were the spearhead of the St. Lo breakout. Since 1995, when 2nd Armored Division was deactivated and their Armor

Regiments were moved into the 4th Infantry Division (66th, 67th and 68th Armor Regiments), those former 2AD units have proudly worn the 4ID patch, and proudly look back at the fight in WWII where they (66th Armor) earned the Presidential Unit Citation with the 22nd Infantry Regiment.

You may or may not know that the major Infantry and Armor units of the 4th Infantry Division from 1995 to 2014 were made up of the Infantry units of the 4ID (8th, 12th, 22nd) and the Armor units of the 2nd Armored Division (66th, 67th, 68th) plus, of course, all the very important other units of the division. That merger was made at a ref-lagging ceremony on December 15, 1995 as the Army downsized to 10 active duty divisions (I participated in that ceremony, my first ever trip to Fort Hood). Over the years, other units have been moved into the 4ID and they are now a proud part of our current history—but this is about WWII, so let's focus on that…

That was not the first time the 4ID and 2AD had worked closely together. During the St. Lo Breakout in late July/early August 1944, the two divisions worked as a team. Most significantly, the 22nd Infantry Regiment was attached to the 66th Armored Regiment under the command of the 2nd Armored Division to form "Task Force Rose". They provided the spearhead for the breakthrough at St. Lo which got the American forces out of the intense hedgerow fighting they had been involved in since landing on the Normandy beaches on June 6, 1944. As a result of their actions and teamwork, the 66th Armor and 22nd Infantry Regiments earned the Presidential Unit Citation (PUC)—which reads as follows:

UNIT CITATION – PRESIDENTIAL UNIT CITATION (PUC) – ST. LO BREAKOUT

The 22nd Infantry Regiment is cited for extraordinary heroism and outstanding performance of duty in action in Normandy, France, during the period 26 July to 1 August 1944. The 22nd Infantry Regiment was the infantry element of an armored-infantry combat command (66th Armor Regiment was Armor unit) which successfully effected a breakthrough of the German line of resistance west of St. Lo, forming the St. Gillis-Marigny gap through which the armored-infantry column surged deep into German-held territory. Operating against hardened infantry, artillery, and panzer units, this Regiment, often riding its accompanying tanks, met and overcame the stiffest German resistance in desperate engagements at St. Gillis, Canisy, le Mesnil Herman, Villebaudon, Moyen, Percy, and Tessy-sur-Vire.

The 22nd Infantry Regiment, in its first action with an armored division, after a short period of indoctrination, assumed the role of armored infantry with unparalleled success. Throughout the swiftly moving, seven-day operation, the infantry teams kept pace with the tanks, only resting briefly at night, relentlessly to press the attack at dawn. Rear echelons fought with enemy groups bypassed in the assault. There was little protection from the heavy artillery which the Germans brought to bear on the American armor. Enemy bombers continually harassed the American troops at night, but in an outstanding performance of duty, the 22nd Infantry Regiment perfected an infantry-tank team which, by the power of its determined fighting spirit became an irresistible force on the battlefield. (I think it is safe to assume that the 66th Armored Regiment's PUC reads very much like this one—as a 22nd guy, I have a copy of our PUC).

So—it is not a coincidence that elements of the 22nd Infantry Regiment and 66th Armored Regiment were teamed up again, in late 1995, to show their might against an enemy of America.

1-22 Infantry and 1-66 Armor were two of the three maneuver battalions of the 1st BCT of 4ID and worked together, along with 3-66 Armor, during the first deployment to Iraq in 2003-2004 and in two additional Iraq deployments and one in Afghanistan. Sadly, 1-22 Infantry was deactivated in 2014, as was 3-66 Armor earlier. 1-66 Armor continues as an integral part of 4ID as of this writing.

From *War Stories Volume I: Utah Beach to Liberation of Paris:*

Clarence Brown, Buchanan, NY
4th Signal Company
Spearhead Division

On July 25, 1944, our 4th Infantry Division spearheaded the breakthrough at St. Lô for Patton's Armor. Just two weeks before, we had handled the calls to try to get oxygen for Brigadier General Teddy Roosevelt Jr., who later died in the field next to where our switchboards were set up. He died of a heart attack.

John C. Clark, Spring Hope, NC
HQ, 29th Field Artillery Battalion
Trapped

One day in the St. Lô area, McGrady and I were looking for an observation post when we came upon a stream with an old mill. I went over to the mill where I could climb up and see. I left McGrady the 610 radio and I took the walkie-talkie.

I was headed to the fourth floor of the mill when McGrady called and told me he could hear vehicles. I could see German trucks in the distance by that time, so I rushed down and used old bags to cover any tracks I had made in the flour. I also closed the trap door that I'd left open. Then I crawled up a ladder to the top of a wooden flour bin, where I stayed for three days.

I had one D-chocolate bar and some water in my canteen. I tried not to drink much water, for I didn't want to urinate much, and when I did, I spread it around as much as possible so it would not run down where they could see it.

There were about twenty-five or thirty Germans there; I figured a whole platoon. They checked out the mill. I was glad I had covered my tracks. I was almost afraid to move, and I was afraid to sleep for fear I would snore. I was on the third floor, and they stayed on the first floor or outside, but I didn't want to take any chances that they would hear me.

They left about dark on the third day, so I walked across the stream and headed back to the infantry's headquarters. I called ahead so I would not be shot as an enemy and found that I had already been turned in as missing-in-action, and Mom and Dad had already been sent a telegram.

This is just another of the many times that the Lord looked after me.

John C. Clark, Spring Hope, NC
HQ, 29th Field Artillery Battalion
Disaster at St. Lô

I will never forget our landing on Utah Red Beach on June 6, 1944. The smell of everything was unforgettable. I remember the difficulty in breathing as a result of all the burned powder from the bombing and the shelling. As impressive as that was, I remember more about our St. Lô experiences on the morning of July 25. Maybe I was too high strung to really appreciate what was happening on the beach.

We 29th Field Artillery forward observers were on point with Company B of the 8th Infantry Regiment that morning. Our objective was to lay a line of smoke shells along the St. Lô-Periers road as a marker to guide the planes on their bombing run. If memory serves me, it was a little after 0900 hours that we called for the smoke shells, and it was just a few minutes until we heard the sound of incoming planes.

There must have been several hundred fighter bombers that hit the smoke line from every direction for about a half hour. It looked as if they did a good job, but we wondered if this was all we were getting to soften up the line for the break out. Then we heard what sounded like a swarm of bees, but as the sound became louder, we realized it was hundreds of planes. It was one group of planes after another; they stretched as far as we could see. I had never seen so many planes at one time.

As the first bombers flew over us, the German 88's started to shoot at them. They got two or three before the Piper Cubs could report where they saw the gun flashes. After our artillery opened up, the 88's became quiet. I have no way of knowing how many planes were up there that day, but it was an impressive sight.

As we watched them coming, we began to hear the bombing getting louder. Then we realized it was getting closer. The wind had come from the south and was blowing the smoke back over us. The planes were dropping their bombs on our positions. My driver, Jones, and I crawled under a tank and hoped we didn't get a direct hit. The bombs were so loud that all we could think to do was wrap our field jackets around our heads to help stop the noise. We put our arms up over our ears and found it helped to open our mouths when we heard some close ones coming in. We were in as safe a place as we could find so all we could do was sweat it out and hope they missed us. The bombing lasted maybe a half hour, but it seemed like forever.

After the bombing stopped, Jones and I came out from under the tank into an eerie quiet. The ground was covered with craters. The raw earth was everywhere. As we started to regroup, we were very fortunate to find our jeep would run, but the radios were out.

When we looked around for our squad, we found that our two new replacements, McGrady and McLeroy, had completely lost it. We tied their shoelaces together, wrapped their gun belts around their arms, and took them back to the command post. As for Jones and me, it was several days before we could even talk in a normal voice, rather than shouting at each other.

After we picked up some radios, we went back up to B Company, which was regrouping. A lot of them were wounded or in shock, so it was not a good situation. We heard later that we had over six hundred "friendly fire" casualties, including Lt. General Leslie McNair. As I look back over my war years, St. Lô stands out as the worst incident among many traumatic experiences.

Don Warner, Jr.

Pharr, TX
Company A, 1st Battalion, 22nd Infantry Regiment
British Order of the Bath

According to records that I cannot put my finger on, members of the 22nd Infantry received twenty-five foreign decorations in WWII. There is still one pending for Lieutenant Colonel Lum Edwards: The British Order of the Bath. I was most fortunate to "liberate" a rough draft copy of the citation during my regimental tour serving under Colonel Edwards. You will notice that I removed the following inscriptions: TOP SECRET and FOR YOUR EYES ONLY from this draft. If awarded, total foreign decorations will hit twenty-six, not including the Belgian Fourragier, which is both an individual as well as a unit award. The copy reads as follows:

> "During the St. Lô breakthrough in late July 1944, Lum Edwards inherited a man by the name of Stone as his driver. As part of the combined Infantry-tank team spearheading the breakout through the German lines, Edwards, as Regimental S-3, had very little to do and was assigned to the staff of General Rose of the 2nd Armored Division. He was to act as liaison between the 22nd Infantry and the 2nd Armored as needed. He had no idea that General Rose always acted as his own scout and was always where the action was the greatest. Lum had no choice but to accompany General Rose wherever he went on the battlefield. This meant that his driver, Stone, followed Lum Edwards.
>
> "In so doing, in an open space in a barnyard, Stone noticed a horse or cow watering trough full of water. Stone then told Colonel Edwards that he thought the Colonel really needed a bath! Edwards was momentarily shocked to think that an enlisted man would make such a suggestion but knew that Stone was right. Edwards was also quick to point out that he religiously followed

Colonel Buck Lanham's instructions on field hygiene, in that he shaved each day, washed his feet, his family jewels, and under his arms. Stone still insisted that the Colonel needed a bath and needed it real bad.

"Lum was shown the water trough out in the open barnyard. Lum told Stone that he didn't want to strip down in front of all the soldiers who had set up defensive positions in the stone buildings surrounding his bath trough and were watching his every move. Stone told Lum to go ahead, strip down, get in, soak, relax, and enjoy his bath because he really needed it. Lum, at last, followed Stone's instructions, stripped, and entered the green moss-filled water trough to enjoy the luxury of a bath. Stone told the others to look the other way while Lum reverted to his birthday suit and took the plunge. The men cheered and clapped. Stone told Lum to stay in, soak, and enjoy the bath—he and the other men would be on the lookout for Germans.

"About this time, the Germans came out of a draw, in force, and attacked this location. Small arms fire covered the entire area, and it was nip and tuck for thirty minutes, with Lum pinned down inside the water trough. All during the period, Stone kept calling to Lum to keep his head down and enjoy his soak, and that he was trying to arrange a counterattack to get him out. Throughout the counterattack, Lum could constantly hear Stone's voice telling him to enjoy his bath; they would get him out.

"When the water trough was recaptured and Lum surfaced, he was blue from exposure, covered with moss and trembling from cold, although it was a hot July day. Stone spoke the first words following Lum's rescue, "Colonel, I know you enjoyed your soak, you really needed it."

Perhaps Lum Edwards should be recommended for the British Order of the Bath with moss cluster.

B.P. "Hank" Henderson, Knoxville, TN
Medic, 22nd Infantry Regiment
Crazy French Women

During the St. Lô breakthrough, we were attached to the 2nd Armored Division. The men not riding the tanks were riding with a trucking outfit to keep up with the Regiment. The 22nd got into an area that they proclaimed a rest stop for us. One of our medics went on a scouting mission and came back and told us there was a large, clear stream of water not far away. A bunch of us grabbed soap and towels and took off to the stream. There were two foot bridges across the stream about seventy-five or eighty feet apart. After we all got in, naked as jay birds, some French women were coming down to the upper bridge, but instead of crossing it, they came down to where we were to cross and stood on the bridge watching us swimming in the water without any clothes on. Crazy French women.

Marvin A. Simpson (Deceased), Baton Rouge, LA
Company D, 4th Medical Battalion
Gas Attack

In late July 1944, we were stationed near St. Lô when all hell broke loose. A gas attack, the last thing expected, occurred during the night, and we scrambled for our gas masks. After about one hour, the all clear was given—it had been a false alarm. What a relief. Early that morning, wave after wave of Allied aircraft flew directly overhead, which was the start of the St. Lô breakthrough. They were so low we could see the bomb bay doors open and the bombs falling. Unfortunately, some of the bombs were released too soon, killing and maiming some of our own troops. The Germans surrendered or retreated, and we were on our way, almost nonstop, to Paris.

Francis W. Glaze Jr., Clearwater, FL
HQ, 8th Infantry Regiment

Jack Capell, Portland, OR
HQ, 8th Infantry Regiment
A Near Miss on the CP

The following comes from an e-mail exchange between these two veterans.

Frank Glaze: Let's start with the bombings and subsequent breakthrough at St. Lô on July 24 and 25, 1944. To set the stage, the assault was to be made by three U.S. Divisions. From left to right, the 30th, 4th, and 9th Infantry Divisions. The 8th Infantry was the assault regiment for the 4th Infantry Division. The St. Lô Periers road was the front line between the Germans and the "Amis." For safety, we pulled the assault companies back five hundred yards to avoid "friendly bombs." On July 24, the bombing started on schedule, but after about thirty minutes or so, it was stopped. We found out later that bombs had fallen on the Regimental HQ to our left (30th Division), and Lt. General McNair had been killed.

I had established liaison with the adjacent Regiment of the 30th Infantry and the lieutenant, the driver, and jeep came back an hour or two later, still in shock and useless. But they were survivors of that mass U.S. Air Corps bombing. It took me a week to get their attention. As a result of this incident, we withdrew the assault companies another five hundred yards after dark. The incident you described occurred the next morning, before the "big" bombing started.

The Regimental CP was in an apple orchard, and about two hundred yards behind a low ridgeline that paralleled the St. Lô Periers road. Apparently, a German tank had fired an 88 toward something on our side and missed. The shell cleared the ridgeline and "trajectored" down at about the same rate as the slope of the orchard. The shell "moaned" in through an open window of the CP, hit the floor next to Sisk's foot, took off the heel of his shoe, and then the leg of an officer—I don't remember his name—and then up through the wall, about four feet from the floor.

In the back room, a liaison officer was asleep on a cot against that same wall. The shell used up all its momentum getting through the wall, so it came to rest on the officer's chest. The noise and the weight and warmth of the shell brought the poor soul wide awake and put him in instant shock! I was about three minutes late in getting to the scene, so I missed Colonel Rodwell's reaction, the fainting spell, and the first few minutes of "God d---!" I did get there in time to make sure both officers got medical attention and were evacuated. It was bad for morale to keep them around any longer than necessary. I remember sending Sisk over to Supply Sergeant Stein to get a new pair of shoes. I figured he'd earned them.

As I remember, the rest of the day got even more exciting. The bombing by three thousand Allied planes started about an hour later, using the St. Lô road as the dividing line between "them" and us. That was fine for the first few waves of planes, but then the dust rose so high it obscured the road and the wind was toward us. The 2nd Battalion was to make the assault (I think), and the forward Regimental CP was immediately behind the battalion CP.

To make the story short, the last half of the bombing was on the 8th Infantry Regiment assault companies, the rest of the 2nd Battalion, the Regimental CP, and the units stretched out five hundred yards behind us.

That was one time that the 8th did not "jump off" on time. It was a real effort getting those shell-shocked GIs (and officers) moving. The only good thing that day was that the Germans were worse off than we were. We moved forward on July 25 and 26, and got through the major obstacles, but it wasn't until July 27 that we picked up any speed.

Jack Capell: I was very pleased to get your recollections of July 24-25, 1944. My memory coincides almost precisely with yours. You spoke of the ridge about two hundred yards ahead of the CP. My foxhole was on the summit of the ridge. The 88 shell came directly over my head, so close that I was jolted by the shock wave. I looked back to the CP to see a cloud of dust rising over it, but there was no explosion. I headed toward it, being concerned about anyone being hit. I was sure that Horace Sisk had been in the building. He saw me coming and came out to meet me. He showed me his shoe and told me he had been sitting on a chair cross-legged when the shell came through the open window and clipped off the edge of his heel. The shell hit the leg of an officer and went through the wall. He told how it came to rest on the chest of a sleeping officer who awoke and promptly fainted.

COL Rodwell, 8th Infantry Regiment CO, was just arriving back at the CP. The officer was revived but was in a severe state of shock. Sisk told me the name of the officer who lost his leg was "Mabry," a brother of George Mabry of our Regiment.

I remember being told that the attack was postponed because of our casualties from the bombing. Shortly afterward, the word came that we were going forward. According to Ernie Pyle in Brave Men, our Company B did not get the word to postpone, so moved forward. When Rodwell discovered this, he ordered everyone forward.

P.S. Ernie Pyle was with the 4th Infantry Division before, during, and after St. Lô. He walked with the "dogfaces" of all three Regiments. He was the only correspondent that walked with the line companies that we knew of.

From Chaplain Bill Boice's **History of the 22nd Infantry Regiment in WWII**:

By 25 July, the beachhead of the Allied Armies in Normandy had been secured, and enough men and material landed to begin a large-scale offensive to liberate France.

The military plan was to shift from the hedgerow, hand-to-hand fighting of the beachhead to a new phase which would use the full and coordinated power of air, artillery, infantry, and armor.

The enemy had drawn its forces on a line from Coutances to St. Lo. To affect a break-through of this line was essential and it was to this task the Second Armored Division with the Twenty-Second Infantry providing the infantry support was set.

The men had been rapidly and well trained in the intervening days in coordinated fighting. Each platoon of infantry drilled with the platoon of tanks with which it was to fight, learning how to protect the tank while using the fire power and cover of the tank as supporting fire power for their advance. The performance of the infantry during the battle for St. Lo proved the effectiveness of this training and concept of fighting.

The Allied Command had ordered saturation bombing of the area to be attacked prior to the attempted breakthrough. On 25 July, the weather cleared, and the bombing began. It was deep enough and wide enough to shatter enemy resistance to the armored spear we were to send through their lines. Double Deucers counted as many as sixteen bomb craters per acre. Houses swayed as if made of some macabre papier-mache. Mark V tanks were turned on their backs like toys, with the occupants killed or stunned by the concussion.

German soldiers walked dazedly, unresisting, and unknowing, their eyes glassy and mouths gaping. More planes flew overhead, and enemy soldiers tried to hide from the death from the skies, but in vain!

Combat Command A (CC A) was waiting behind the 30th Infantry Division to go through the gap as soon as it was made and exploit the break-through. No advance was made by the 30th Division on that day, however, and the break-through had not been completed. Therefore CC A was ordered to pass through the 30th Division on 26 July to complete the break-through in conjunction with the balance of the 4th Infantry Division and 1st Infantry Division and then to continue the exploitation.

Fifty-three minutes past midnight on the morning of 26 July, the regiment, as part of CC A, began leaving its rest area in the vicinity of La Mine to begin its break-through operation in the direction of St. Gilles and Canisy. Originally, the CC was to attack in two columns, with the First Battalion in the left column and the Second and Third Battalions in the right or north column. The Third Battalion, in reserve behind the First, was to move by bounds with the special units. However, during the night of the 25th, plans were revised by the VII Corps, and the attacking force was changed to a single column with all elements on the north route.

The CC moved to a forward assembly area two miles north of Pont Hebert and attacked to the south at 0930 hours, with the First Battalion, Twenty-Second Infantry, on the tanks of the Second Battalion, 66th Armored. Initially, the movement was via hedge rowed fields and followed the following tactics: A tank platoon and a platoon of infantry would work together as a team. The five tanks deployed, with two going ahead as scouts and three following as a covering force. Upon entering a field, the two forward tanks would spray the hedgerow on their open flank and then would fire a 75 mm. round into the far corner of the field.

At the same time that they crossed the field, they fired their machine guns at the hedge to the front. The covering force tanks followed and drew up on line with the others and the doughboys trotted past to reconnoiter the hedge in front of the tanks for German bazooka-men and for the best places to break through the hedge. After this reconnaissance, the doughboys ran back behind the tanks and the two "scout" tanks would start the process again.

The advance was slow at first, due to unexpectedly heavy resistance from enemy positions which were still holding out. The Command encountered considerable high velocity and artillery shelling but very little small arms fire. Nevertheless, the effectiveness of the great aerial bombardment on the preceding day was clear. The Germans were still shaky, and the prisoners seen going to the rear looked beaten and stunned.

As the day progressed, the advance was accelerated, the CC having cleared the bombed area and apparently most of the German resistance as well. Late in the afternoon, CC A was directed to revert to the two column plan and to continue its advance on roads in order to accelerate the advance. Owing to the great length of the column, the disposition then in effect, and badly cratered roads, this split was not completed until St. Gilles was secured.

It was approximately 2100 hours when the CC passed through St. Gilles. Normally it is considered that tanks cannot operate successfully at night, but General Rose, Commanding CC A, was determined to take the objective regardless of time and the cost in men and tanks, since the whole operation depended upon the success of that mission. The advance continued down the main road to Canisy in complete darkness. As the CC passed through Canisy, the whole west side of the town was burning fiercely, and the long tank columns going through silhouetted against the blaze made a memorable scene.

The Air Corps had functioned superbly throughout this advance, working just ahead of the CC with perfect coordination all the way. They were very careful to be sure of identification before they bombed vehicles on the road. On one occasion, dive bombers came down twice for a close look at enemy vehicles and then the squadron leader himself dove down to be positive that they were German before attacking them.

A break-through had been affected despite German infantry and armor. St. Gilles and Canisy had been taken! During the remainder of the night, the head of the column occasionally stopped for some resistance, but it was never held up long. There is an amusing incident connected with this stage of the advance. Just north of Canisy, a German half-track with a trailer pulled into the column near the head and passed several tanks without being detected before making the mistake of passing the leading tank. The furious tank commander exclaimed, "Hell, I'm supposed to be leading this column," whereupon he recognized the vehicle as enemy and opened fire, knocking it out.

By dawn of 27 July, CC A was on its objective, the key terrain in the vicinity of Le Mesnil Herman. These positions, including Hill 183, Le Mesnil Herman, and St. Samson De Bon Fosse, had been secured by 1800 hours on the second day. Approximately 300 prisoners were taken, and the advance had gained 10 1/2 miles. As the regiment dug in for all-around defense, reconnaissance teams were pushed to the south. Infantry patrols combed the area. Late that afternoon two task forces, each consisting of a company of tanks and a company of infantry, were dispatched to reconnoiter in force to the south. Company K, in the western force, drove as far south as Villebaudon, where it was picked up the next day by the remainder of the Third Battalion attacking south to Percy.

During the morning of 28 July, the regiment consolidated its position and maintained enemy contact with patrols. That afternoon the CC issued orders for a three-column attack. In compliance with these orders, the Third Battalion was attached to the Third Battalion of the 66th Armored Regiment and pushed south along the Le Mesnil Herman-Percy Road. The First Battalion with the attached armor, attacked south in the direction of Moyen; the Second Battalion on their left (east) moved toward Tessy Sur Vire. The CC encountered a regimental combat command of the 30th Division delayed by a determined enemy. One effort to break the position was thwarted by a large stream, and the task force dug in. At the close of the day, CC A had halted with the Third Battalion near Percy, the Second Battalion 1 1/2 miles south of Le Mesnil Herman, and the First Battalion occupying Moyen.

Two men of the First Battalion, Captain Frank B. Reid, CO, Company C, and Pvt. Sharkey, also of Company C, merit special attention for their heroic actions during the Battalion's attack on Moyen on 28 July. Undoubtedly there were many other similar performances deserving of equal praise, but the story of Captain Reid and Pvt. Sharkey is indicative of all the fighting men who distinguished themselves so remarkably in the face of almost insurmountable obstacles. After penetrating the northern part of the city of Moyen on the 28th, the Battalion discovered that the enemy had strong tank forces south of the town along with other entrenchments and antitank guns.

Captain Reid led a patrol of twelve men south to a crossroads just east of the church to get a German antitank gun. The crew of the gun was dispersed by rifle fire and grenades, but immediately the patrol received heavy machine gun fire from a German tank in the distance. Captain Reid moved his patrol by circuit to the north and east and came up on the right flank of the tank. The ammunition carriers for the bazooka had been lost by this time and the patrol had only two rounds of bazooka ammunition. Pvt. Sharkey, known as a "bazooka hound," fired at the tank just across the hedgerow and, hitting it in the turret, knocked it out. A second enemy tank now came up directly behind the one destroyed and started blazing away from a distance of from 75 to 100 yards, whereupon Captain Reid leaned over the hedgerow just above the tank and dropped two WP grenades, one down the air vent on top of the tank and the other under the tank, setting it afire.

A column of German tanks, accompanied by infantry, was now coming along the road towards the town, and they opened a terrific volume of fire on the patrol. Pvt. Sharkey stood on top of the hedgerow and fired the last bazooka round at the leading tank, hitting it at the base of the turret and knocking it out. "Let's clear out of here before they zero in on us," Captain Reid shouted to his men. But Pvt. Sharkey remained standing on top of the hedgerow and fired at the approaching infantrymen with his carbine until a burst of machine gun fire from the tanks took off the whole side of his face. It missed the bones of the jaw but left the flesh hanging down over his chest. Pvt. Sharkey got up from the ground and walked away with the retreating patrol. The rest were crawling across the field under the heavy fire from the German tank column while Sharkey made the whole trip walking upright.

As they reached the road running east from Moyen, they found that another column of German tanks had moved up that road toward the town, and the leading tank was barring their way across the road. The patrol now had no ammunition other than two WP grenades, one fragmentation grenade, and small arms ammunition. Captain Reid threw the two WP grenades, one under the tank and one behind it. The tank backed up, but it was already on fire.

Meanwhile, the smoke from the grenades formed a screen across the road and under this cover the patrol got across and rejoined the company, without Sharkey and two other men whom Captain Reid had left to take care of Sharkey while he got the remainder of his patrol to safety. By this time, Sharkey had practically collapsed, and in the brief duration of the smoke screen, the other men were unable to lift him over the hedgerow. However, the German tanks had apparently been successfully frightened away; a little later the three men moved down the road into town, Sharkey again walking and holding up his finger in the victory sign. "Sharkey made the greatest display of guts I've ever seen," was Captain Reid's comment on the incident.

This is a long issue, but this is a key event in 4ID history. I had to give it the space it deserves. Thanks to those of you still with me. A month from this week, we will be liberating Paris.

29 JULY 1944—D+53: Combat Team 8 completed the move and at 0600, company I supported the attack of the 41st Infantry (2nd Armored Division) on Pont Brocard. The 1st and 2nd Bn took up defensive positions along the road Notre Dame de Cenilly to prevent the enemy from retreating from the northwest. Small enemy groups were encountered within the area, prisoners were captured, and other enemy forces contained. CT 12 completed its movement and attacked at 0900 to secure the road between Le Bourg and Maupertuis. Objectives were reached at 1100 without opposition. The 2nd Bn cleaned out opposition in Le Bourg during the late afternoon. The 4th Cavalry Reconnaissance Sqn was attached to the 4th Division and conducted reconnaissance in the late afternoon to the south. Crossings over the Sienne river were made before dark.

30 JULY 1944—D+54: The enemy continued to withdraw to the south by defending hastily constructed defensive positions. Enemy aircraft dropped numerous flares and antipersonnel mines. CT 8 protected the flanks of the Division. CT 12 attacked at 1100 to seize the high ground in the vicinity of Mancellière. The resistance, moderate at first, increased. CT 26 of 1st Infantry Division was attached to the 4th Division and attacked at 1100 to seize the high ground in the vicinity of Mesnil Bonant. At 2000, it reached its objective and initiated mopping up operations northward to the Sienne river.

31 JULY 1944—D+55: Enemy offered almost no resistance. CT 8 was in assembly area southeast of Hambye at 0001. At 1200, it was ordered to move to an assembly area northwest of Percy to protect the left flank of the Division. CT 12 attacked to seize objective Villedieu-les-Poêles.

Rapid progress was made by the 1st and 2nd Bn with comparatively little or no resistance. The 3rd Bn however met strong resistance in the vicinity southeast of Percy and failed to advance beyond this point during the day. The Division was still energetically pressing the attack toward the south against a disorganized enemy force.

CASUALTIES FOR JULY 1944

Killed or died of injuries: 42 Officers, 664 Enlisted Men

Missing: 5 Officers, 107 Enlisted Men

Seriously wounded or injured: 94 Officers, 1,733 Enlisted Men

Slightly wounded or injured: 38 Officers, 749 Enlisted Men

Total casualties: 3,432.

Cumulative Casualties for 55 days of combat since D-Day June 6, 1944:

Killed or died of injuries: 133 Officers, 1,699 Enlisted Men

Total casualties: 8,846 (this equals over 50% of 4ID strength on D-Day)

4ID troops passing through French village on August 1, 1944

AUGUST 1944

BREAKOUT IN FRANCE

1 AUGUST 1944—D+56: Small pockets of resistance by-passed by the assaulting armored units were encountered by the 4th Infantry Division. Small arms, antitank guns, and tanks were used defensively, taking advantage of favorable terrain and erecting road blocks on key arteries. From positions in the vicinity east of Percy, the 8th moved to the south and then continued the attack on Villedieu-les-Poêles. At 2200, the 3rd Battalion had occupied the town.

2 AUGUST 1944—D+57: It was apparent that the enemy had developed a policy of laying low and allowing the spearhead of armor to pass, and then rallying again to delay the advance of our infantry. Usually the resistance was built around a machine gun or an antitank gun. The 8th Infantry protected the left flank of the Division until passed through by elements of the 9th Infantry Division. The 12th Infantry continued the attack at 1000 while the 1st Battalion maintained defenses to the north, northeast, and east of Villedieu-les-Poêles. The 3rd Battalion cleared enemy pockets of resistance that were hindering transportation along the main route leading to the town. The 22nd Infantry was now reverted to control of the 4th Infantry Division and moved by motor to assembly areas north of Villedieu-les-Poêles. The 1st Battalion relieved the 1st Battalion, 12th Infantry, in the city. The 4th Infantry Division had succeeded in maintaining an active defense in its zone of action against enemy forces attempting to escape to the northeast.

3 AUGUST 1944—D+58: It was apparent that the enemy contemplated falling back to the high ground surrounding St Pois and thence to the Forest of Saint Sever where it appeared that the enemy would attempt a determined rear guard action while a general withdrawal was affected. Artillery fire was slightly heavier along the front lines. The 8th Infantry attacked at 0800 in the right half of the Division zone of action. During the afternoon, the task force was dissolved, and CT 8 assigned the mission to block the roads. The 12th Infantry resumed the attack at 0800 to clear the enemy from the Division zone of action and in the late afternoon was assigned the mission of containing St Pois and securing the left flank. The 22nd Infantry was ordered in the late afternoon to maintain contact with the 12th Infantry to the south and to block roads to the east and northeast. Movement to assembly area in the vicinity of Villedieu was completed.

4 AUGUST 1944—D+59: The ridge line parallel to the highway from Coulouvray-Boisbenâtre-St Pois was held by the enemy. The roads into St Pois were defended with tanks, machine guns, mines, and small groups of infantry. Heavy artillery fire was also encountered. The 8th Infantry attacked from positions in the vicinity of La Gautière to seize Hill 211 at 1020. The advance was slow due to heavy enemy resistance with small arms, machine guns, and artillery fires. Four battalions of the Division Artillery supported the attack, and two air attacks were made on the Hill. The 12th Infantry attacked at 1045 from positions along the road La Bruyère to clear out pockets of enemy resistance and to seize Hill 232. After repeated efforts to advance, the Division Commander ordered this unit to remain in its present positions. Heavy enemy fires were encountered on the left flank from the woods and high ground in the 9th Division zone of action. The 22nd Infantry moved from bivouac areas to an assembly area south of La Marcellière and attacked to the southeast to seize St Pois. The attack progressed satisfactorily with light opposition until two battalions were within 500 yards of St Pois. There heavy enemy resistance was met from the town and the high ground to the east.

*****

I'm sure you remember the story about the Iron Major. We start with a story from the same Soldier who in civilian life was a successful newspaper reporter. His writing lets you understand how good a reporter he was.

From *War Stories Volume I: Utah Beach to Liberation of Paris*:

Clyde R. Stodghill, Cuyahoga Falls, OH
Company G, 2nd Battalion, 12th Infantry Regiment
The Liberation of Hambye

Following the bombing and breakthrough at St. Lô, our battalion, perhaps the entire 12th Infantry Regiment, was assigned the job of cleaning out pockets of Germans left behind during the rapid advance. We hiked from place to place, frequently covering the same ground two or more times. Sometimes there were Germans waiting and a firefight ensued, but as often as not, they had either departed or had not been there in the first place.

It was a grueling assignment that allowed little time for rest or sleep and left us in a state of weariness beyond mere exhaustion. We kept going only because we did not want to fall out and let others down. There was little energy for talking, and I was among the many who repeated over and over to myself, "Just one more step, just one more step…"

I don't know how long commanders in the rear felt we could keep on that way. Certainly, we were past the point of being an effective fighting force. One day we passed a crossroad where military policemen held out candy bars for us to take, but no one within my range of vision had enough spare energy to take one.

After one entire night of hiking in circles, we dug in to take turns sleeping. Some had two hours; the lucky ones had three. In the afternoon we formed up on a road, but not the one we had arrived on. This one sloped gently downward to a little town about a mile ahead. Had the sun been shining, we would have been shaded by the many large trees where we had assembled, but the sky was dark and threatening, bringing thoughts of yet another soaking.

As we awaited the word to move out, one of the newer men in Bob Everidge's platoon suddenly keeled over and lay writhing on the ground. No one knew what to do for someone in the throes of an epileptic seizure, so we just stood watching. An aid man came forward, but seizures had not been covered in his training.

The lone comment came from Everidge, "I wonder if I could get out of here if I rolled around on the ground like that?"

The words were shockingly out of character. Not because they lacked sensitivity—very little of that could be found in any of us—but because it was the first time I had heard anything to indicate that Bob would have gotten out if he could. He never allowed any sign of fear to show in either his words or actions, always walking ramrod straight without bending in a "hedgerow stoop" as the rest of us did for protection. Was he nearing the end of his tether? No, I decided, not Bob Everidge. It was just that he was so damned tired.

Free of carrying the radio for a while, I went with Everidge's platoon when we moved out. One squad was on the point and the rest of us trailed about fifty yards behind as the advance party. The remainder of the company followed.

We were still some distance from the first buildings when a few civilians came out on the street ahead. This was unusual and therefore disconcerting. Germans were supposed to be in the town, and the presence of civilians was no guarantee that we wouldn't come under fire. If so, having non-combatants wandering about would complicate the situation. It was even possible that the Germans had driven them out on the street for that purpose.

As the minutes ticked away, more people poured forth from buildings. Others were hurrying along the street from the opposite direction, seemingly intent on greeting us. By the time the point squad reached the built-up area, the street was lined with people dressed in their Sunday best. Boys in black suits and young girls in white dresses carried flowers in their hands.

We passed a city limit sign reading "Hambye." Everidge and his squad leaders began the familiar, quiet chant: "Watch the windows, watch the windows. Observe to the left and the right, watch the windows." Over and over it was repeated, a reminder to men who knew what to do, but might forget for one fatal second.

Men on the left watched the points of danger on the right, and vice versa. It was done by looking more to the center of the street than directly at the buildings themselves, as peripheral vision would pick up movement that might go undetected if viewed from straight on.

The drill was forgotten, though, as we met the excited throng of smiling people, many of whom were clapping their hands and calling out a welcome. How could you watch the windows when small children were tugging at your clothes so you would bend down to let them entwine the stems of flowers in the camouflage netting on your helmet? Could anyone ignore the friendly overtures of freshly scrubbed, laughing girls and boys? A few could, but not many.

What, I was wondering, must they think of this unsavory group of filthy, unshaven, odiferous men with hollow cheeks and glazed eyes sunk deep into their sockets? As best as I could tell, they didn't mind how we looked or smelled.

Soon, we were having to push our way through a solid mass of humanity. A young woman I passed just to my right said, "So, you've finally come!" I nodded my head, but by the time I realized she had been speaking English and turned to say more, she was lost in the crowd.

When we reached the cobblestone town square with buildings on all four sides, every foot of space was occupied. It was impossible to continue on. Everyone was facing a building with a tiny balcony on which an ancient record player with a flared horn had been set up. The balcony seemed too small to hold anyone until a man stepped out and stood beside the record player.

Another followed him—a small and very old man I felt must be the town's last surviving veteran of the Franco-Prussian war three-quarters of a century earlier. He held a folded flag, which he shakily fastened to a staff. Then, as the red, white, and blue French Tricolor was unfurled in Hambye for the first time in more than four years, the strains of "Le Marseillaise" blared forth from the record player.

Every civilian, the majority with tears streaming down their cheeks, joined in singing what must surely be the most stirring of all anthems. In seven adventurous decades, I have experienced nothing quite so moving, so emotional, as those few minutes on the town square in Hambye. Several weeks later, we joined the French 2nd Armored Division in being the first troops to fight their way into Paris. It was exciting, of course, but failed to match the deep emotional impact of the liberation of Hambye.

Soon after the ceremony ended, a unit of the 2nd Armored Division, living up to its "Hell on Wheels" name, roared through Hambye on a road with a sign pointing to Villebaudon. Later, the sound of a major battle became audible in the distance.

We spent the night on the outskirts of Hambye, overjoyed at not having to spend another on the move. But as the night wore on, the sound of battle grew steadily nearer, and brilliant flashes lit the sky to the east. We did not know it, but the Germans were beginning to form a new line of defense that in the coming days would involve us in brutal battles at St. Pois and Mortain.

We left Hambye as the crisp night air was giving way to Sunday morning sunshine. A church bell sounded the call for early mass, but except for the presence of an elderly woman dressed in black, the streets were empty. I wondered if the fighting would reach the town, making the previous day's celebration meaningless. We could contribute little to a major tank battle of course, yet at least some of us felt guilty about leaving in the way that we were after having received such a joyous welcome.

From the *History of the 12th Infantry Regiment in World War II* by Gerden Johnson:

The breakthrough itself might be divided into two phases, close together. The first, west of St. Lo, was followed in ten days by the fall of Coutances on the west coast of the peninsula. The battle for Coutances to the northwest of our positions near Hambye was more of the same—more hedgerows, more flooded rivers, more German snipers, more suffering and weariness. After that, the complexion of the war seemed to change. But our part in this campaign is best made clear by these two actions: First, VII Corps punched the hole in the German lines west of St. Lo on July 25th. Through this, reserves sliced westward to the coast, getting behind and destroying enemy lines of communication and opening the way for the U.S. Third Army to roll. Then Corps was set to drive straight south through Villedieu and St. Pois to block out the Germans while the Third Army swept southward into open country. The 12th Infantry Regiment played a vital role in both phases of this plan. The second phase centered around the bottleneck between Villedieu and Avranches through which the Third Army had to pass. To guard this vital ground, VII Corps was ordered to seize a north-south line extending through Villedieu, St. Pois, and Mortain. In this operation, the 12th Infantry was destined to play an exciting and vital role...

From Chaplain Bill Boice's *History of the 22nd Infantry Regiment in WWII*:

All units advanced at daylight on the 29th. The left and center columns renewed their attacks but without success. At Moyen, the tank commander of the Second Battalion, 66th Armored, attempted to plunge through the town, but German fire knocked out one tank on the road to the southeast and another on the road to the south, thus blocking both roads. The Germans had tanks dug in south of the town as well as a strong force of mobile tanks; a prisoner subsequently stated that they had eight

Panzer companies in that sector. When the armored attack had failed, the tank commander decided to withdraw from the town and shell it. The withdrawal of the infantry was already under way when Major Latimer, the First Battalion Commander, discovered it and persuaded the tank commander to countermand the withdrawal, the tank commander failing to understand the harmful effects of infantry withdrawing from ground once won. The battalion tried to move back into the town, but the Germans had followed closely behind them as they withdrew, and they never succeeded in regaining all the ground given up.

The Germans now brought up strong tank forces just south of the town in addition to those that were dug in there, and a duel developed between the opposing tank forces, with the infantry in between. It was a terrible experience, and losses ran very high. Our forces were also under a great deal of artillery fire. In addition to the heavy physical casualties, both infantry and armor had a number of men who cracked up under the strain. One German tank which came up on the southwest caught the right flank platoon of Company A under very heavy fire and wiped out all but eleven of its men.

The Second Battalion, which was teamed up with the First Battalion of the 66th Armor, encountered strong resistance around Bessinerie and was stopped in a position abreast of the First Battalion on the road leading south to Tessy Sur Vire. When the Third Battalion fought its way to the high ground 1200 yards north of Percy, it was seven miles to the south of the remainder of the CC, and thus partially isolated.

At 1700 hours the three battalions of the Twenty-Second were attached to the armored battalions with which they were fighting and so passed from direct control of the regiment. Later in the day, this task force was relieved at Moyen by the 116th Infantry, and they withdrew just in time to escape a bombing by the Luftwaffe in which the Germans hit their own lines as well as ours. The Combat Command might have gone unobserved had not a machine gunner in one company cut loose with his gun at the planes. This was unfortunate, for the planes began circling and dropping flares which lighted up the landscape "bright as day." These flares were followed by bombs, but most of the "heavies" fell on the Germans who were a few fields away, due probably to the fact that the flares had drifted back over the German lines, thus causing the bombing error. The German infantry began frantically shooting up green flares to stop the bombing. The incident pleased the troops of the Command a great deal, and as Major Latimer, First Battalion Commander, later re-marked, "We were glad to see that the Germans could make mistakes too."

Because of this bombing and the shelling, which was still going on at frequent intervals, the relief was not entirely completed until after midnight. At that time, an attempt was made to move out on the road running west from Moyen, but the Germans were also entrenched there with dug-in tanks and this move failed. The entire task force withdrew to the northwest and bivouacked for the night a mile or so south of Le Mesnil Herman.

Meanwhile, the right task force, including the Third Battalion, had resumed its advance at 0700 that morning, Company L riding the tanks, and Company I following on foot. Company K was still holding east of Villebaudon. Company L got as far as La Tilandiere where they were stopped by a strong enemy position along the sunken road. Company K had been relieved at Villebaudon by a battalion of the 175th Infantry and had rejoined the Battalion. Later in the day, Company I was relieved by two companies of the 29th Division, while Company L continued to contain the enemy at La Tilandiere until the next day. The rest of the task force withdrew to Mesnil Ceron, where they bivouacked for the night.

* * * * *

Hopefully you still remember **PFC Helen Denton, the Army WAC who typed the D-Day orders for Ike in England,** whose story I told in the pre D-Day time period. Following is more of her story, from her book **World War II WAC** which I wrote for her:

…Toward the end of July, our hotel was hit with a bomb, and it was decided we would be safer in France. The morning we were notified that we would be leaving for France, I went across the street to the Telegraph office to send a telegram to my folks to hold up my mail, we would be moving again. While I was writing my telegram, a V2 bomb hit the building. When I woke up, I was laying on the floor, covered with glass and very upset. The officers in the building picked me up and after looking me over told me I wasn't hurt, and I could quit crying. I did, but I was still scared and shaken. (In fact, that sensation of the bomb exploding so close stayed with me even after I returned home. If someone slammed a door, I would go into the shakes. It happened a few days after I was home. I was so upset my parents took me to the hospital, about 25 miles away, the closest one to Woonsocket. The doctor put me to sleep with a sedative after my parents told him what happened, and after a good night's sleep, I was much better. They were very careful about making a sudden noise after that). Back to the V2 bomb — I was ready to leave London, and we did that night, July 27, 1944.

The following undated order was given to Helen and the WACs, explaining what they were to take with them...

NOTICE

MONEY: Lt Clarke will exchange your English money for French money. You may take with you only 20 shillings in English money. The amount of French money you take is up to your own judgment. Personal checks are OK to take, also American Express checks are OK.

PACKING: We are spot inspecting all those who are leaving two days prior to the day you are supposed to leave. Your actual day of departure may and in some instances has been pushed ahead. We will spot inspect nevertheless two days previous to the original date of departure. The actual final packing will be up to you and should be determined when you get definite word from your section when you will leave. Keep out one (1) class A uniform to wear until the last moment.

Pack in your DUFFLE BAG necessary items such as one (1) class A uniform, your blankets, your shelter half, your arctics. Put in your BARRACKS BAG excess items. Pack in your MUSETTE BAG enough personal things to last you for a few days in case you are separated from your baggage, such as toilet articles, wool shirts, etc.

HELMET AND LINER: Mark your steel helmet and liner with the prescribed marking—a white strip across the back parallel with the bottom of the helmet. Paint, brush, and stencil may be obtained in the orderly room. Do this immediately (NCO only)

RATIONS: Two (2) weeks PX rations may be obtained from WAC PX at any time.

(Signed)
MARGARET A. CLARKE
1st Lt., WAC
Company Commander

Our group of WACs was bused to Southampton and, after dark, boarded a troop ship and crossed the English Channel, destination Utah Beach…

UTAH BEACH IN NORMANDY, FRANCE – JULY/AUGUST 1944

After an uneventful trip across the English Channel, we arrived off the shore around midnight. Told to shoulder our packs, we were then told to disembark by climbing onto a rope ladder, down the side of the ship, to a landing craft that bounced in the water below us. Having never dreamed we would be doing that, it was with quite a bit of trepidation that we climbed over the side, holding on for dear life to the rope ladder, and welcoming the sailor who grabbed our leg to guide us down the final short jump into the landing craft.

Once we were all safely in the landing craft, it pulled away from the mother ship and headed toward the beach, just as it had done many times since the original landings on June 6. I bet the sailors on this small landing craft could have told us a lot of stories from previous landings they had made. We were pleased that our landing was not under hostile fire, the beaches were secure by the time we got there on July 28, 1944. Just like the men before us, we had to wade ashore through waist deep water and wait until morning so we could be picked up and carried to our holding area. Inland from the beach, an enclosed holding area was awaiting us. Small tents had two cots, without mattresses, and a special tent was marked as a female bathing facility.

We were starved, so we happily grabbed our mess kits and headed for the mess tent as daylight started to light the area. Just like the GIs with us, we lined up with our mess kits ready to hold whatever they were serving for breakfast, quite a change from our more civilized eating facilities back in London. I mentioned to my friend in front of me how happy I would be to get out of our wet clothes. A soldier behind us asked where our clothes were. We told him we hoped they were piled up back on the beach by now. We were promised before we left the ship that our duffel bags would be offloaded, brought all the way to the shore so they wouldn't get wet, and be available for us to pick up by daylight. He said he would get his jeep and take us back there to find them.

Little did I know at the time, but that soldier, Staff Sergeant Noel Denton, later was to become my husband.

The front lines were several miles ahead of us. Troops and supplies continued to pour in around the clock. A constant flow of soldiers and supplies moved in from the Channel and up toward the front lines each day. St. Lo had just been taken and the final breakout from the hedgerows in Normandy was not too far away. Fighting continued and movement was slow as the remnants of the German forces tried to slow the Allied thrust. We lived in tents and ate our meals with the troops.

Utah Beach was my first experience living this close to the front line, and seeing the devastation left after a battle. It was different from the V-2 and aerial bombings in London. There we saw buildings destroyed and had air raid warnings to take cover. Here we were in the countryside and never knew what type of devastation we would see—dead cattle, homes damaged, church steeples blown down by tanks or artillery firing at a sniper, trees strewn around the area, temporary cemeteries for burying our fallen soldiers, etc.

This is the area where the 4th Infantry Division and the 90th Infantry Division had landed on D-Day, and where the 101st Airborne Division and 82nd Airborne Division had made their parachute landings the night before D-Day. By the time we got there, thousands more troops had landed across that same beach and crossed through the small villages and farmland. Had we gotten there just three days sooner, we would have seen the thousands of bombers flying over as they did the saturation bombing of the German defenses around St. Lo, the beginning of the significant Allied breakout in Operation Cobra, later called the St. Lo Breakout. Sadly, we later found out that over 800 American troops had been killed when bombs fell off target into the American lines.

There was one office building on Utah Beach that was called Headquarters. We stopped by for information or direction, but as far as working at a project, there were none assigned. We were waiting for Paris to be liberated so we could move in there. Our time was free to come and go within our area. It gave me more time with Noel. Most of the time, we stayed close to the beach. The weather was beautiful, and we enjoyed watching the soldiers play ball or whatever they were doing to keep active in their time off.

Noel and I were able to visit Ste. Mere Eglise and see what was left of that town. We also found a farm with two older French people (husband and wife), their daughter and her small children. They had moved their cow into their house during the battle when it surrounded them, but their field had been destroyed and they were having a difficult time finding food. Several times Noel and I drove out there and left them food and supplies that the mess hall had given us. We also found parachutes left behind by the airborne troopers.

My relationship with Noel was very platonic because it was not time to get serious. Neither of us knew what was ahead and I did not want to experience heartache at a time like this. Not knowing what the future held, we just enjoyed the time we had and hoped for the best. I kept remembering the promise I made my dad to come home for my wedding—he planned to walk me down the aisle. We talked about the future, but Noel was concerned about his future when and if he returned, and whether he would still have a job with a future.

We had freedom to walk around on the beach as long as we didn't venture away from our assigned area limits. This gave me time to get to know Noel. He was a staff sergeant in the Signal Corps and had a group of men under his command. Their job was to support General Eisenhower's headquarters and to ensure communications were established in French villages as the front lines moved closer and closer to Paris.

Other than time spent with Noel, a highlight was the afternoon when Bing Crosby, Bob Hope, and a singer (whose name I don't recall) came to perform for us on the beach.

Note from Bob: You will hear more from PFC Helen Denton when the 4ID liberates Paris, and a few more times during the remainder of the war, including on VE Day.

* * * * *

The St. Lo breakout was successful, but the fighting was far from over. August was another tough month for 4ID as they broke out of the hedgerows of Normandy and started chasing the Germans toward Paris. The 12th Infantry Regiment fought what GEN Omar Bradley called "the most critical decision he made in WWII"—the battle for Mortain. And it is a chapter in the History of the Twelfth Infantry Regiment in WWII that is called "Bloody Mortain". I will focus primarily on that major strategic battle in the next chapter.

5 TO 11 AUGUST 1944 – D+60 TO D+66

In the pictures accompanying this section, the first map is the overall route of the 4ID in both WWI and WWII—dark blue line is WWI, Orange line is WWII. Second map is a closer view, showing Utah Beach to Paris only. You will note that Mortain, where this week's fighting was focused, is closer by about 2/3 to Utah Beach than it is to Paris—and in another three weeks, the 4ID will have liberated Paris. The other pictures are self-explanatory.

5 AUGUST 1944—D+60: The enemy launched a counterattack early. The enemy occupied and defended the critical terrain around St Pois until about 1725 hours when a general withdrawal to the southeast was affected. Another counterattack foreseen for 1200 was disorganized by our artillery. The 8th Infantry consolidated positions on Hill 211. A counterattack at 1000 by the enemy resulted in the temporary loss of three anti-tank guns and three half-tracks which were regained by counterattack. Three German tanks were destroyed in this action. The 2nd Battalion attacked to capture Le Mesnil-Gilbert and La Houssardière. The 12th Infantry continued to consolidate and clean up pockets of resistance. The 1st Battalion seized Hill 329. The 3rd Battalion supported by fire the attack of the 22nd Infantry in the seizure of Hill 232. The 3rd Battalion supported the attack of the 47th Infantry (9th Infantry Division) in the seizure of the hill in the vicinity of La Cobière. The 22nd Infantry attacked at 0900 to capture Hill 232 which after heavy resistance was taken at 1700. The 1st Battalion attacked at 0900 to seize the woods after by-passing St Pois from the south. Throughout the day, the 1st and 2nd Battalion received determined resistance from the high ground east of St Pois. The Division had seized key terrain features, eliminated isolated points of resistance, and destroyed numerous motor vehicles and foot troops retreating along roads northeast and southeast from St Pois.

6 AUGUST 1944—D+61: Enemy front lines did not exist as such. Isolated pockets were to be mopped up in the vicinity of St Pois. Armored movement was heard during the hours of darkness but seemed to indicate a withdrawal rather than an attack. The 8th Infantry mopped up small pockets of enemy resistance. Little opposition was met. The 12th Infantry did the same within its zone of action. The 22nd Infantry occupied the division outpost line to protect the division from enemy attack from the east.

A DIFFERENT WAR AND DIFFERENT TIME

AUGUST 6, 1966: Exactly 22 years and two months to the day after the 4ID stormed ashore on D-Day against a hostile enemy in Normandy, France, the 4ID again landed in a foreign country to fight for our nation. This time, the place was Qui Nhon, Vietnam on the morning of August 6, 1966. It was 2nd Brigade, 4th Infantry Division which led the way for the 4ID into the four and one half year deployment to Vietnam. I was a young lieutenant on that hot day in 1966 when 1-22 and 1-12 Infantry went ashore from the USNS Nelson M. Walker, with no hostile fire coming our way. 2-8 Infantry and 4-42 Artillery were two days behind, slowed by engine trouble on their ship, the USNS Pope. 4th Engineers and our advance party were already in country starting preparations on our base camp south of Pleiku.

By nightfall, we were manning the base camp perimeter south of Pleiku—ready for anything that came our way. And it did—rain and rain and more rain. We were in the middle of the monsoon season—miserable first days in Vietnam. Unforgettable memories came from those days when "we were Soldiers once, and young..." And our 4ID Soldiers of today's generation have come home from Iraq, Afghanistan, Europe, South Korea, and other hot spots with their own unforgettable memories that will last them a lifetime. For over 107 years, the 4ID has been ready to respond to whatever our nation needs from us.

Steadfast and Loyal, we're fit to fight, our Nation's finest Soldiers, keep liberty's light, Our Soldiers ROAR for Freedom, we're fit for any test ... the Mighty 4th Division, America's Best! (4ID Song)

7 AUGUST 1944—D+62: The enemy defended from hastily prepared positions with a concentration of resistance on Hill 230 (vicinity of Lingéard). The chief defensive fire came from automatic and direct fire heavy weapons. The enemy attempted to move east across our sector at 1630 but was immediately destroyed by artillery fire.

The 8th Infantry closed in bivouac area at 0000 to the south and southwest of Hill 211. As a result of the breakthrough by enemy forces in the 30th Division sector, the 2nd Battalion was notified at 0345 to dispatch patrols to Sursée and the 3rd Battalion between Les Fontaines-La Roussel. This movement was canceled at 0530 when it was found that the enemy was not attempting to go north of the river. At 0820 the 2nd Battalion was ordered to move to defensive positions in the vicinity of La Roussel. It was completed at 1215. The 1st Battalion remained in bivouac area (Hill 211) and the 3rd Battalion established a bridgehead at Sursée to allow the passage of the 2nd Armored Division over the Sée river.

The 12th Infantry was in assembly area 2000 yards northeast of Brécey at 0000. Upon notice of the threat of counterattack, they were ordered to establish a bridgehead across the Sée river. At 1515, CT 12 was created and attached to the 30th Infantry Division.

The 22nd Infantry was outposting a line extending from Lingéard Château to Hill 232. At 1200, Hill 230 was captured by Company C.

The 4th Division Artillery fired a concentration in support of Company C 22nd Infantry and fired on an enemy vehicle column consisting of approximatively 30 vehicles which had been spotted from the air.

Task Force Welborn consisting of 70th Tank Bn, 4th Engineer Combat Battalion, 4th Reconnaissance Troop, and 801st Tank Destroyer Battalion established an outpost line which extended from Fontière to Brécey to Le Besnerie.

8 AUGUST 1944—D+63: The enemy concentrated its armor at Le Mesnil Tôve for a second attempt to cut our lines of communication and to anchor its left flank at Avranches. This breakthrough was to have been exploited by elements of Adolph Hitler, Das Reich, and Deutschland divisions. This attempt and several subsequent attempts were disorganized and put to route by our artillery fire before they could gain any momentum. CT 8 maintained defensive positions and prevented enemy infiltrations from the southeast. CT 12 remained attached to the 30th Infantry Division. The 22nd Infantry maintained defensive positions until 1100 when the unit entrucked and moved to an assembly area. Task Force Welborn maintained an outpost line and patrolled routes and road blocks.

9 AUGUST 1944—D+64: The enemy defended from positions in the vicinity of La Mardelle. This position had been obtained after a night attack down the draw La Laucherie, Lingéard, La Mardelle. Three times the supporting artillery fired concentrations to repel the aggressive enemy counterattacks. The 4th Infantry Division still continued to maintain a perimeter of defense.

10 AUGUST 1944—D+65: No contact with the enemy. CT 8 remained in positions in the vicinity of La Roussel. At 2230 it was attached to the 9th Division. CT 22 remained in same positions until 1600 when it was ordered to move to new positions in the vicinity of Le Teilleul.

11 AUGUST 1944—D+66: Enemy patrols contacted our patrols along the Varenne river. Small arms and automatic weapons fire were exchanged. CT 8 was detached from the 9th Division at 1400 and was alerted for movement by truck to an assembly area in the vicinity of Désertines as division reserve. CT 22 initiated vigorous patrols at dawn to reconnoiter area east of La Varenne river. The Division established road blocks wherever necessary.

From Chaplain Bill Boice's **History of the 22nd Infantry Regiment in WWII:**

The First and Second Battalions patrolled the regimental zone of action during the night of 5-6 August with negative results. At 1000 hours the Second Battalion attacked in approach march formation, meeting only slight resistance. By 1300 hours the entire assigned area, from Hill 232 as far south as Chateau Lingeard, was cleared of enemy troops. Units of the Twenty-Second then moved to an assigned rest area, north of Cuves. A composite battalion, under command of Major Glenn Walker, Commanding Officer of the Second Battalion, consisting of Companies E, F, and K, re-enforced by heavy machine guns and one platoon of antitank guns, remained in positions to outpost the high ground from Hill 232 southeast to Chateau Lingeard.

In this connection, special tribute should be paid to the 44th Field Artillery and to the mortars of Company F for outstanding performances in the action around Chateau Lingeard on 6 August. The 44th F. A. from positions west of St. Pois was prepared to fire concentrations on Lingeard, La Cheminee, and on a stream junction east of Hill 230. No rounds were fired to sight the howitzers in, but all fires were plotted by coordinates. Later, when another company entered Lingeard, they found 90 dead Germans and captured 60. A number of these men had been killed by perfect artillery fire on the prepared concentration. At Lingeard, the Germans had had an assembly area, perhaps for a battalion. "That artillery fire was beautiful, " remarked Lt. Gerald J. Claing. The first rounds were perfect hits, despite the fact that the concentrations had only been plotted by coordinates.

As for the mortars, it seems that at a meeting the day before, the battalion commander had made a strong recommendation to his men to use their mortars more, since everyone had noted the neglect in using the 60's since D-Day. Apparently, the advice was taken seriously, for on the following day the mortars of Company F were used extensively and to great advantage. During the advance on the morning of the 6th, movement was held up on two occasions by two enemy machine guns, both of which were eventually knocked out by 60mm mortars. About noon when the company was setting up defensive positions, another machine gun opened up on the platoon which was on the lower slope of the hill. The same mortarman who already had two machine guns to his credit came to the fore once more to make his total three.

About 0200 hours the Germans threw their first counterattack, and coming from Lingeard, they moved right up into the creek bed below the hill. One of the outposts reported back to the platoon leader who passed the word on to the weapons platoon leader. The company order had been that if a counterattack should come from the little valley, all small arms fire would be withheld while the mortars would knock out the attack. The weapons platoon leader then got Sgt. John Prettyman, mortar squad leader, to lay down a barrage on the creek bed. There were 70 rounds of ammunition on the position. Lt. Claing, who had been called at his CP back off the road, ordered the jeep to carry up its load of an additional 70 rounds.

Ammunition was going so fast that it was finally necessary to send back to battalion supply at St. Pois for more. That night the Germans probed against F Company's position, approximately one patrol each hour. Everyone was repulsed by this one mortar alone which fired a total of 370 rounds with only two misfires. All night long, Sgt. Prettyman rained 60mm mortar hell down on the Germans. The German attack began with a 50mm mortar barrage which crept horribly right around the little road on top of Company F's hill. They attacked with machine guns and "burp" guns but could do nothing against the one mortar. The Americans fired not one single round of small arms fire that whole night and suffered only one casualty (one man was shot accidentally earlier in the evening). The mortars had proved themselves!

Before dawn the 7th of August, Company 'F' deployed on the high ground in the vicinity of Chateau Lingeard, repulsed two enemy counterattacks. Company 'C', re-enforced with one platoon of heavy machine guns, one platoon of antitank guns, one company of the 70th Tank Battalion, and one platoon of tank destroyers, was alerted to seize and hold Hill 230 north of Chateau Lingeard, the objective of the 47th Infantry of the 9th Division. The attack moved out late at daylight, but the objective was secured by 1045 hours. During the early morning hours an enemy attack broke through the 39th Infantry area and penetrated through to the area held by the 22nd Infantry. Company 'B' and Antitank Company, less two platoons, moved south of Cuves to construct road blocks on all roads and trails from the south and east. Company 'A' was moved from the rest area to a position south of Chateau Lingeard to add greater strength to the outpost line in that sector. Company 'K' was relieved by elements of the Forty-Seventh Infantry and moved from Hill 232 to the rest area, reverting to Third Battalion control.

From Gerden Johnson's *History of the Twelfth Infantry Regiment in WWII*: **BLOODY MORTAIN**

When General Omar N. Bradley stepped off the ship in New York upon his return from Europe after the end of hostilities, he was asked by reporters what he considered to be the most critical decision he had to make during the entire war. He replied that it was at Mortain. Following the breakout from the beachhead on July 25, the Third Army had sent six divisions racing toward Brittany. These divisions had to be funneled through a narrow corridor east of Avranches, from when the Germans flooded an area as large as Rhode Island.

According to testimony of the German High Command, the Battle of Mortain was the decisive battle of the entire hedgerow campaign. Not the operation beginning on July 25, but the Battle of Mortain a fortnight later, convinced the enemy that he had lost the Battle of France and there was no alternative to precipitate flight all the way back to the Westwall (Siegfried Line on the German border). One trio of German generals went so far as to declare the Battle of Mortain was one of the two critical operations leading to the defeat of Germany in the West. (The other was the loss of the Remagen Bridge across the Rhine). The German High Command, the Nazis said, was astonished that the attack of their four divisions failed to reach Avranches to cut off the American Third Army. Mortain was Old Hickory's (30th Infantry Division) epic battle. But this is primarily the story of the 12th Infantry's contribution to Old Hickory's great victory.

Against the narrow corridor through which the Third Army was pouring, Hitler personally ordered a counterattack with the mission of severing the thin American column and thereby cutting off the forces in Brittany from those in Normandy. This corridor through which Patton was racing, would enable him to either strike westward into Brittany or eastward, in the rear of the enemy, to Paris, or both.

The attack was spearheaded by four panzer divisions and was hurled against the 30th Infantry Division at Mortain. The Germans reeled the 30th back, trying to smash to Avranches and the sea. In this situation, General Bradley had to make a decision, and make it fast. His alternatives were (1) to call back through the bottleneck the six divisions then racing south or (2) take the calculated risk that the units guarding the Avranches corridor could stem the attack and keep the route open.

If he chose the first, the whole purpose of the great July breakthrough would be defeated, and it would be many bloody weeks before the hard-won advantage could be renewed. In this critical situation, General Bradley's decision was to recall one of the six divisions (the 35th Infantry), a task force of 3rd Armored Division, and to permit the remainder of the main forces to proceed on their original mission. To assist the units being sent to assist the 30th Division was added the 12th Regimental Combat Team.

The German Army made its first concentrated counterattack at 0400 hours, August 7. It was a supreme all-out effort to redeem the failure to stem the Allied invasion. The full force of the blow struck the 30th Division at Mortain. Almost immediately, that division committed its reserve regiment. Despite the dominance of German armor and the ferocity of the attack, the 30th did not break, but rolled back with the punch, slowing down the momentum of the attack and making the Germans pay dearly for their gains…

At 0400 on August 7 the 12th Infantry Regiment, just beginning to look forward to its first real rest from combat, was placed on a two-hour alert movement status. At 1450, orders were received to send one battalion combat team to Montigny as fast as possible and then to follow with the regimental combat team without delay. The rest period was over even before it started. The 12th Infantry Regiment was now attached to the 30th Infantry Division. The 3rd Battalion, in trucks, was on the road south of Brecey by 1830 hours. The rest of the 12th started to roll at 2000 hours.

The road march made by the 12th that night was a veritable nightmare. Vehicles of the armored divisions racing south jammed the only route and when darkness fell, control of our motor columns was almost impossible. Other units wedged in among our own and almost succeeded in diverting some of our vehicles to wrong routes...At 0150 hours on August 8, German bombers flew over the column and scored a direct hit on a halftrack of the Cannon Company, knocking out both the vehicle and the gun and killing the occupants. The halftrack, loaded with 105mm ammunition, burst into flames and the exploding shells made the route seem like the road to Hell. It effectively blocked the long line of vehicles until alternate routes could be found in the dark...

Expecting to be initially used as 30th Division reserve, the 12th quickly learned upon its arrival east of Juvigny that the tactical situation was so grave that commitment of our forces without a moment's delay was imperative. The events of August 7 had brought the 30th Infantry Division to the brink of disintegration...

A gap of 8,000 meters existed between two of the 30th Infantry Division's regiments on the south, facing Mortain. The 12th Infantry (less the 3rd Battalion) was assigned the mission of driving through the gap to seize the important road junction on the high ground north of Mortain, then drive south to relieve the pressure on the beleaguered 2nd Battalion of the 120th...

Colonel Luckett decided to move in march column to the east with the 2nd Battalion leading, until the vital RJ278 (Road Junction) could be secured. The 1st Battalion would then be sent to Mortain. This called for a ten-mile march, four miles of which were across open marsh country exposed to observed enemy artillery and mortar fire...

At 1600 it became apparent that the objective could not be reached without a fight. Lt. Col. Johnson, commanding the 2nd Battalion (Note from Bob: This is the same Gerden Johnson who wrote this great history of the 12th Infantry Regiment after the war was over), was forced to halt the column in order to investigate on his right flank to the south. At this time, Colonel Luckett decided to send the 1st Battalion directly to Mortain and to have the 2nd Battalion continue on its original mission.

Before the 1st Battalion had moved 2,000 yards, it was pinned down by mortar and small arms fire coming from an enemy occupied hill west of Mortain…The 2nd Battalion continued to attack to the east. It succeeded in gaining the hill and seized the west fork of the Mortain-St. Barthelmy highway. It had one company within 100 yards of the vital RJ278 when darkness fell amid a crashing artillery barrage and the battalion was forced to dig in for the night. The battalion commander placed three companies east of the highway and two on the west side and covered the road on both flanks with bazookas…

The 2nd Battalion had driven a salient into the German position. Both of its flanks were dangerously exposed, as the 3rd Battalion of the 12th was echeloned to the left rear and under control of the 117th Infantry. It could not establish contact with the left flank of the 2nd Battalion. The gap had been partially mined and during the night the enemy was able to operate between our two units. On the right, the 1st Battalion was dug in to the rear and there was no contact there either. Behind the 2nd Battalion, the swamp reduced the problems of supply and evacuation to arduous hand carry. It also prevented the forward movement of any vehicle and consequently the 2nd Battalion had no anti-tank guns, tanks, or tank destroyers to support it…

(*Space does not allow me to cover all this epic battle of the 12th Infantry Regiment, but the entire history of the 12th Infantry Regiment in WWII is available in the 12th Infantry Regiment book by Gerden Johnson, available from www.deedspublishing.com, click on the Bookstore button. This chapter, Bloody Mortain, starts on page 151 and ends on page 167—seventeen pages describing a battle that tested the strength of a 4ID Regiment, and our Soldiers of the Greatest Generation*).

I will summarize the next few days…The next four days (August 9-12) marked what was probably the fiercest, bloodiest contest in the history of the 12th Infantry (and remember they fought on Little Round top at Gettysburg during the Civil War). The enemy represented the best of Hitler's most fanatical troops…They had tanks and a reputed 20 battalions of artillery at their disposal, plus perfect observation…Although the 12th was still unable to get supporting weapons across the boggy country, *they continued to carry the attack to the enemy for four successive days*. Tremendous losses were sustained during this black period of bitter hedgerow combat.

I will stop now on this excerpt from Gerden Johnson's history…but be aware that later this month, on 25 August, we'll read a lot more about the 12th Infantry Regiment as they became one of the first Allied units to enter Paris.

Another note from Bob: Today's 4th Infantry Division has two battalions of the 12th Infantry Regiment active, 1-12 Infantry and 2-12 Infantry. Hopefully those of you with a Soldier in that unit will pass this account on to them so they can read with pride what their Regiment accomplished in August 1944. And, for those 8th Infantry Regiment Soldiers, Veterans, and Family members following this walk through 4ID history in WWII, I'm not ignoring your Regiment, but nobody took the time to write their history like LTC Gerden Johnson did for the 12th and Chaplain Bill Boice did for the 22nd. I can only work from the material I have available to me.

12 TO 18 AUGUST 1944 – D+67 TO D+73

While the fighting never stopped, this was a slower week for the 4ID than normal. Read on, there are some very interesting personal stories included.

12 AUGUST 1944—D+67: It appeared as though the enemy patrols along the Varenne river to Domfront were acting as a screening force while larger forces withdrew to the east or dug in on the high ground east of Domfront. Several rounds of large caliber artillery fell in the 4th sector. The 8th Infantry closed in assembly area at 0045. Roadblocks and outposts were immediately established, and reconnaissance initiated eastward. CT 22 continued reconnaissance to the east, conducted vigorous patrolling, and extended outpost lines to the northeast to include the town of Barenton.

13 AUGUST 1944—D+68: A ceremony was held at the 8th Infantry CP to award Distinguished Unit Citation Badges. The same took place in the afternoon for the 3rd Battalion of the 22nd Infantry. The 3rd platoon of Companies A and C of the 4th Engineer Combat Battalion received the same citation badge. These Presidential Unit Citations were awarded for the assault on Utah Beach. The enemy continued to outpost the Varenne river west of Domfront. Small fire fights were experienced between patrols. The 8th Infantry initiated reconnaissance eastward to La Varenne river, established road blocks and outposts. CT 12 was detached from the 30th Division and moved to assembly area. CT 22 continued reconnaissance east to La Varenne river.

14 AUGUST 1944—D+69: The enemy continued to leave listening posts and security detachments for the purpose of defending road blocks and mine fields. In all cases, these units dispersed when our reconnaissance elements closed in. CT 8 continued patrols as far east as La Mayenne river. At 1900, the regiment discontinued extensive patrols and closed into assembly areas. The 12th Infantry remained in assembly areas. The 22nd Infantry maintained road blocks and outposted lines till 1900.

15 AUGUST 1944—D+70: No contact with the enemy. CT 8 remained in assembly area, conducted maintenance and training plus small patrols as far east as La Mayenne river. The 12th Infantry remained in assembly area and conducted care and cleaning of equipment and rest. The 22nd Infantry and attached units conducted motorized patrols as far as La Varenne river within their sector.

16 AUGUST 1944—D+71: In front of a formation made of one enlisted man of each company, battery, troop and detachment of the Division, Lieutenant General Courtney Hodges, Commanding General First Army, awarded the Distinguished Service Medal to Major General Raymond Barton. MG Barton was awarded the Silver Star Medal by Major General Collins, Commanding General VII Corps. LTG Hodges awarded the Distinguished Service Cross (DSC) to LTC Arthur Teague

22nd Infantry, LTC John Welborn 70th Tank Battalion and MAJ George Mabry 8th Infantry (Editor's Note: Mabry later earned the Medal of Honor in the Hurtgen Forest). 45 officers and enlisted men received the Silver Star. Among them were BG Harold Blakeley, COL James Luckett 12th Infantry CO, and COL Charles Lanham 22nd Infantry CO. Combat Infantry Badges (CIB) were also awarded. All units remained in assembly areas, conducting necessary training (scouting, patrolling, and familiarization firing) and maintenance.

(By the way, the Normandy campaign ended on 24 July 1944 and the Northern France campaign started with the St. Lo breakout on 25 July 1944 and will run through 14 September).

17 AUGUST 1944—D+72: The 4th Infantry Division completed movement from vicinity of Le Teilleul to the vicinity of Carrouges.

18 AUGUST 1944—D+73: The Division remained in assembly areas. 8th near Carrouges, 12th near Les Villettes, and 22nd near L'Oisonnière. The 4th Reconnaissance Troop reconnoitered routes for possible movement to the vicinity of Alençon.

*****

A rather slow week for 4ID, not to last long. At the end of next week, we liberate Paris. But in the meantime, read the following...

*From **Swede Henley's Diary**... 22nd Infantry Regiment*
(used with permission of his daughters)

6 AUGUST 1944: Bn. pulled back for rest. Jerry counterattack breaks thru near Mortain and gains success but finally stopped. Air Corps and 3rd Army trapped German column and annihilated all vehicles. Bn. alerted to assist but never moved out.

NOTE: G-2 poop on Jerry—Morale low, Ammo low, Hungry.

Jerry don't want to fight.

GI's Poop -

Watch the Free French because somebody is shooting the hell out of us.

- FFI using plain gas to kill krauts
- Good stuff—it kills krauts

7 AUGUST: 3rd Bn. moved and occupied position of 2nd Bn. on high ground south of St. Pois (Lingeard). Bn. CP located in Lingeard Chateau.

8-10 AUGUST: Still in position. On night of August 9 our CP took one helluva shelling. The Jerry was trying his best to get us, but he didn't. We sweated him out. This is supposed to be a rest period—still sweating it out.

- P-47 shot down near (300 yds) our Bn. CP.
- Pilot bailed out and landed safely.

Received orders at 1600 to be on road at 1730 for south of Mortain via Brecly—St. Hiliare du Harcourt—Buais, Le Teilleul—St. Marc d'Egrenne.

Relieved 137 Inf. Dug in and waited for German counterattack. G-2 report jerries have 500 tanks in woods east of Domfront. Plenty of tank destroyers. Tanks and anti-tank guns ready.

11 AUGUST: Started patrolling across river to confront French underground joining up with our troops. German patrols trying to get thru our lines were shot. No artillery falling and it is a very quiet front. If this is war, we like it this way.

12 AUGUST: Still in position waiting for threat—heavy patrolling—just resting easy and hoping General Patton's in Paris.

Night raiders sent out for recon across river towards Domfront. Returned with location of German machine gun positions and CP—artillery placed on them.

13 AUGUST: Awaiting jerry to counterattack—weather clear and bright—extensive patrolling "I" Co. patrol captured 10 krauts. Free French wanting to sign up and fight with "L" Co. Captain Blazzard has 28 on his roll.

14 AUGUST: 83rd Recon attacking Domfront. Patrol sent to high ground north of Domfront. Still resting and taking it easy. If this is war, we like it. No artillery for 7 days now, and this place is paradise.

15 AUGUST, HAPPY BIRTHDAY: Counting our change. Drew $15 from Finance Officer. Captain Samuels goes to 2nd Bn. as Exec. Officer. Air Corps active again today. 3rd Bn received citation ribbons. Allied Armies landing in Southern France.

16 AUGUST: Still counting our change. (Editor's note: an old time saying meaning 'hanging around and doing nothing.')

17 AUGUST: Received orders to move out at 0800 to 2 mi. NW of Carrouges. IP at Passais. Route taken—Passais, St. Fraimbault Sur Pisse, Ceauce, Sept. Forges, Couterne, La Ferte Mace, Carrouges.

Arrived at assembly area at 1800 hours—outposted area.

18 AUGUST: Still counting our change—listening to good news of Patton's army heading for Paris—landing of American Army in Southern France.

From Chaplain Bill Boice's **History of the 22nd Infantry Regiment in WWII...**

On August 8th, separated elements of the 9th Division joined southeast of St. Pois and pinched out the Twenty-Second Infantry. To meet this situation, the Regiment realigned in a defensive position along the line Chateau Lingeard--St. Pois, backing up the 9th Division. The units comprising the composite battalions were relieved and joined their battalions. There was no direct contact with the enemy that day or the next, and the Regiment remained stabilized. But this turned out to be the calm before a storm, and about 2100 hours, the Regimental CP was sprayed with artillery and mortar barrages which wounded the Regimental Commander, the Regimental Executive Officer, the Headquarters Commandant, killed Mr. Harvey, the Assistant Adjutant, and killed or wounded some fifteen additional men in the area. The First Battalion was placed on an alert status at 2255 hours for possible movement to aid the 30th Division.

Again, on August 10th, the situation was quiet in the Regimental area except for some artillery fire. At 1500, an order was issued for early movement south to the vicinity of Le Teilleu on a defensive mission. The Regiment started moving at 1730 via St. Pois, Brecey, St. Hilaire de Harcout, Buais, to Le Teilleu, with the leading company on tanks and the balance by motor convoy. The thirty-five mile movement, completed at 2330, was rapid and without enemy contact. To thwart any possible enemy thrust, a defensive position was established from Passais north along the west bank of the La Varenne River to the vicinity of La Bourdonierre.

At daylight on August 11th, vigorous patrols moved east toward the La Varenne River to ascertain the enemy's disposition. Patrolling continued throughout the day and confirmed reports that the enemy positions were along the east bank of that river. Enemy patrols were encountered on the west bank of the river, and some prisoners were taken. The day was used to improve defensive positions, with particular emphasis on blocking roads that might be used by enemy armored columns.

The main defensive positions were quiet on the 12th, but active reconnaissance patrols made several contacts with the enemy forces on the La Varenne River. Regimental patrols reconnoitered to a depth of 5,000 yards inside the German lines, despite considerable numbers of the enemy armed with rifles and machine guns who were laying for the patrols. Later in the day, the defensive sector was increased, and Company 'E', re-enforced with one platoon of heavy machine guns, and Antitank Company, less one platoon, was shifted to Barenton with the mission of establishing a defense around the town.

Possibility of an enemy offensive seemed remote by the 13th, and there were definite signs of enemy retrograde. That afternoon a combat patrol from the First Battalion established a small bridgehead across the La Varenne River and, after a light skirmish, occupied Torchamp. That same afternoon friendly troops passed through the lines moving east and this, in conjunction with the movement of the 2nd Armored and 1st Infantry Division elements across the front of the Regiment, again pinched out the lines of Combat Team 22.

Activity during August 14th was confined to reconnaissance patrols to the east, which reported indications of an enemy withdrawal to the northeast. In accordance with new boundaries and in view of friendly troops between the enemy and the Twenty-Second Regiment, the rifle battalions were assembled in battalion bivouac areas, and a much needed and well-deserved rest-training period commenced.

The Twenty-Second Infantry had participated in the campaign of the break-through from the 26th of July 1944 to the 14th of August 1944, a total of twenty days. During that time, the Regiment travelled ninety-seven miles, and Allied territory in France was increased approximately twelvefold. In the latter part of their campaign, the Twenty-Second Infantry Regiment became part of the force containing the enemy, pending completion of the envelopment move south and east by the Third Army.

The results of the successful break-through of CC 'A' were far-reaching in their effects. Thousands of Allied troops poured through the gap made in the German lines and the entire western German position was upset, greatly aiding the attack of the Third Army along the west coast of the Cotentin Peninsula to Brittany. The Allies finally had sufficient ground and front to maneuver large units. As the situation developed, the Allied Command was able to move powerful armored columns to the enemy flank and rear, and the German withdrawal became a major retreat from Western France.

This campaign, after its initial stages, was characterized by its fluidity and movement, as contrasted to the position warfare of the earlier Sainteny campaign. In place of advancing from hedgerow to hedgerow, there were leap-frogging movements of many miles.

Our losses for the entire campaign were as follows: Six officers and 109 enlisted men killed; thirty officers and 561 enlisted men wounded; and 43 enlisted men missing in action. In another column, 386 German prisoners were captured and processed by the Twenty-Second Infantry. This figure, however, does not accurately indicate the number actually captured, as the rapid movement of the action necessitated that many others be turned over immediately to other units.

The campaign was filled with many notable incidents that will never be forgotten by the men who were there; the all-night move through St. Gilles and burning Canisy shortly after midnight; Captain Reid, Private Sharkey, and the close-in fighting with tanks near Moyen; August 1st, the day on which the last remaining tank of a tank company pushed on with infantry to its objective at Tessy Sur Vire; and the taking of Hills 232 and 230 on August 5th and 6th by the Third Battalion and Company 'C', respectively.

In its first action with elements of a regular Armored Division, the Twenty-Second Infantry Regiment assumed the role of Armored Infantry with unparalleled distinction. General MAURICE ROSE, Commanding General of Combat Command 'A', stated that he never operated with finer infantry than the Twenty-Second.

Now that the gap had been opened and troops were able to maneuver, it was known that the next move would be to Paris. It was obvious that the St. Lo break-through had actually broken the main German defenses and commanders believed the next actual encounter with strong hostile forces would not come until the units reached Paris and the Seine River Line. If this was true, the German forces must be kept on the run and not given a chance to form any intermediate lines.

On the 17th of August, after several days' rest, an oral order came down from Division HQ directing CT 22 to move to an assembly area in the proximity of Carrouges, starting at 0800 hours on the 17th, the mission being to re-enforce the French 2nd Armored Division. The Combat Team closed in the new area at 1700 hours and set up the outpost line of resistance.

From the 18th to the 22nd of August, the Regiment remained in place but continued the needed training. During this period, the 4th Infantry Division passed from the VII Corps to the V Corps, and CT 22 prepared to move tactically by motor convoy to the south of Paris. Shortly before dark on the 23rd of August, the Regimental Combat Team began a motor march to assembly areas near Ablis with the mission of establishing a bridgehead across the Seine River south of Paris. Advance during the night was quick and steady despite a torrential rain. Company 'A', 377th Antiaircraft Artillery Battalion, furnished the column with mobile protection from enemy aircraft.

*From **War Stories Volume I: Utah Beach to Liberation of Paris**:*

Paul Brunelle, Avon, MA
Company G, 2nd Battalion, 8th Infantry Regiment
Good Advice

*From the book **Company G, 2nd Battalion, 8th Infantry Regiment, 4th Infantry Division** by Shirley Devine. Used with her permission.*

In early August 1944, I was assigned to the 4th Infantry Division. When I joined the Division, I was fresh out of training and one of the things they told us was that you never volunteer for anything. Well, I remember that when I was going to Company G, I was told that they needed some machine gunners and some mortar men—I guess to fill the companies that had received casualties at St. Lô. So, instead of listening to the advice that I was given in training, when they asked for mortar men, I immediately put up my hand. I didn't know one bubble from the other, but I was glad to say that I was a mortar man and had been trained to be a mortar man. Since most of what I did for the next few months entailed carrying ammunition, the fact that I didn't know much about mortars was no detriment at all.

We were at a place called St. Pois, out in the fields. We never really got to go inside of a city or town unless there was some "mopping up" to do.

I remember that hill at St. Pois. We were dug in along a hedgerow. Some of the fellows were dug into the hedgerow, which was about six feet below the level of the field. Sergeant Conway came along as I was digging a slit trench and he told me that I had better dig a foxhole because they had reports that there were German tanks operating in the area. That advice proved to be very beneficial to me. It was just a little while later that some German soldiers in front of us and down the hill, started waving a white flag. I guess the American soldiers just threw caution to the winds and started exposing themselves. As they did, a white flare went up and we started getting shelled very heavily.

During that action, some German tanks did come up. The place that I was dug in was right on the edge of a wheat field. A couple of the shells landed very close to my foxhole. One of them exploded about twenty feet away. I had been having lunch when they approached. I ducked into the foxhole quickly and left my canteen and dish on top of the foxhole.

The nearness of the explosion threw dirt in my canteen and down on top of me. Thanks to the advice that I had received, I was not injured. Shrapnel from the same shot that exploded just a few feet from my foxhole went in between the two hedgerows where some of the guys were dug in. A young fellow who came in the day I did (his name was Whitehead,) was killed by a direct hit. There were others who were wounded too because I could hear screams for help. The shelling didn't last all that long, but when it was over, we had received some casualties. I don't recall very many incidents like that.

I also recall another time when we were advancing, and we had some American fighters over us. They were bombing and strafing the enemy. One or two of the bombs from a fighter broke loose and landed within our lines. I don't think we had any casualties from it, but it was unnerving to have our own fighter bombers dropping bombs within our own ranks.

Editor's Note: Paul Brunelle was president of the 4IDA during the 50th anniversary year of D-Day and the liberation of Paris (in 1994) and represented all the 4ID veterans during the ceremonies in Paris 50 years before. Paul and I became great friends, sadly he is now deceased.

Robert Gast, Warsaw, IN
Companies B and C, 1st Battalion, 12th Infantry Regiment
Welcome Aboard

I joined the 4th Infantry Division, 12th Infantry Regiment as a replacement officer just prior to the St. Lô breakthrough and the dash for Paris. The Commanding officer of Company B walked me to my new platoon, the 2nd rifle platoon of Company B. They sure looked like a rough bunch. They were sitting around drinking from a bottle, something I later learned to be Calvados. One of the men took a big swig, filled his cigarette lighter, lit a cigarette, and then handed the bottle to me. I knew I had to take a drink, and I wasn't much of a drinker. I raised the bottle to my lips and took a big slug. Well, I coughed and choked until my helmet fell off. The men really got a big laugh, and it did kind of break the ice. I learned that they were really glad to have me aboard.

John K. Lester, Stone Ridge, NY
Battery B, 29th Field Artillery Battalion
"Still Had a War to Win"

Just outside Paris, France, in August 1944, my Forward Observer party (three of us), had our first home-cooked meal. The area was under intermittent fire—nothing serious, just annoying. A boy of about twelve yelled at us to come into his home. We were a little apprehensive, but we parked the vehicle under cover and went in. What I saw amazed me. This boy knew more about the war than we did. He had large maps hanging on the wall and was trying to keep track of what was going on. The maps didn't help us, but he sure was proud of them.

While he was telling us about his maps, his mother was fixing a meal. They didn't have much food, but wanted to share what they did have with us. I remember having chicken, potatoes, and green beans. It was a feast and of course, we had wine. It was an enjoyable hour or so, and a small reprieve from the war. For a change, I had something good to remember. When we left, we gave them whatever rations we could spare. All we had were K-rations and limited C-rations. The little chocolate bars were a big hit with the boy. I can still see him standing proudly by the maps he had made. They were happy people; the war was over for them.

We went on from there to be among the first Americans to enter the city of Paris on August 25. We may have been there first, but we didn't get to stay in Paris very long. We moved out the very next morning, heading for Belgium and the road to Germany. I believe it was the 28th Infantry Division who got to parade and enjoy Paris. I know it wasn't us. We didn't have the proper dress for parades and celebrations. They needed fresh troops for that—not dirty, tired, out of place combat troops. Besides, we had to go on. We still had a war to win.

Peter Triolo, Pueblo, CO
HQ, 1st Battalion, 12th Infantry Regiment
Five War Stories

The following stories and events took place after the Battle of Mortain, on the road to Paris. My duties were basically to patrol and set up outposts. However, early each evening I would go back and locate Regimental Headquarters in order to make the Colonel's late evening trip to get combat orders for the next day. During the French operations, most of our combat took place from sunrise to sunset. My days were continuous activity: Daily patrols, scouting for the Colonel's meeting, and attending the operations meetings. We would finish the cycle at about 0200 or 0300 hours, just in time for the next day's officers' meeting. I kept this cycle going with limited opportunities for sleep.

1. Millionaire for a day: This morning we jumped off in the attack. The Germans had our front lines zeroed in. We received between fifty and sixty casualties in the first half hour. We pulled back to reorganize. The colonel called for me and several other officers. He said there must be a German outpost directing fire because the shots were too accurate. Looking out over the front, we spotted a French farmhouse and buildings about a mile off our right front. Colonel Jackson said, "I bet that is what we are looking for."

With a two-jeep patrol, we drove down to the farmyard. We talked to the French farmer and his wife. We could see they were nervous and scared. While checking out the barn in the hayloft we found a map and a radio. We had found our problem. We also found a small footlocker full of brand new French francs. We estimated it had to be close to a million dollars in thousand dollar packages. Corporal Shanks took a package of French francs and stuck it in the cushion on the driver's side of the jeep. The jeep cushions had a cheap zipper pocket where you could store things. When we arrived at headquarters, there was an officer from Regiment waiting for us.

He said, "Pete, give me the money."

"I don't have any money," I replied.

He said, "Yes, you do." They had captured the two German officers. These two not only admitted to directing the artillery fire, but also continued to tell about the money that was in the barn. So, I was a millionaire only for the day.

2. The orange panels — a close call: This time, I was in the advanced CP with Colonel Jackson. The advanced CP was located about fifty feet behind the advanced fighting troops. We had Air Corps coverage. Two planes would fly overhead waiting for target assignments. All of a sudden, we heard one of the planes start to dive down on a target assignment. About a thousand feet above the ground the plane released a five-hundred pound bomb and took off. Of course we all hit the ground, and I am sure we were all praying. The bomb hit about one hundred fifty feet from our location. Thank God, it was a dud. Colonel Jackson called the pilot on the radio to find out what was going on.

"We are friendly troops," he said.

The pilot said, "You are in front of the orange panels, so we took you for the enemy."

In the early days of the war, all the troops had orange panels that they would lay out so our pilots would know we were friendly troops. What had happened was the artillery unit about five thousand yards behind us had laid out their orange panels. As a result, the Air Corps thought we were the enemy out in front. This was a problem with many of the troops in the early days of the fighting. Finally a decision was made, I am sure by Eisenhower, that only infantry troops would have the orange panels. All other troops turned in their panels, which eliminated the problem.

3. Tank Support: Another day in the advanced CP with Colonel Jackson, we were coming out of a wooded area ready to cross an open area. We received heavy machine gun and mortar fire from a wooded area about five hundred yards to our right front. As a rule, we had two tanks assigned to us every day to help us in combat. The tanks were about eight hundred yards behind us, with the reserve units. When I arrived there, I talked with the tank commander and informed him what the missions may be.

To get to the front lines, we had to go through about two hundred feet of a trail between two hedgerows. I told the tank commander that if the tank draws fire while we're on the trail to let me get into the tank for protection. Sure enough, about half way through the trail, German mortars started to fire on the tanks from that wooded area. I jumped on the tank to get in, but the commander had already closed up and wouldn't let me in. The only place left for me was under the tank. Well, to get out of the fire zone, the tank started to back up. To move backwards, the tank had to wiggle left and right as it moved back. Now I had to get out from under the tank or be crushed. I was left with the front lines being the safest place to go. I informed Colonel Jackson of what happened and that no tanks were coming up. Returning to the CP that night, we were informed the tanks did not stop at our CP but returned to their tank company area. We never saw that tank commander again, and that was lucky for him.

4. Ernie Pyle, here I come: On this day, Colonel Jackson requested I set up an outpost with an antitank gun, a machine gun, and about ten men to protect the left flank. There was a main crossroad there, and we wanted to make sure that a German attack could not happen from those roads. Upon reaching the site, we found that there were three main roads, not two. On the top of the hill, about two hundred yards away, was a small village. I told my driver, Shanks, to take us up there and check it out.

To get to the village we had to take a sharp right turn. Our normal routine would be to get out and check before we made such a sharp turn. We hadn't seen German troops for a day or two, so I told Shanks to just go on in. Sure enough, sitting on the stoop of the first house were two Germans with their guns across their lap pointed in our direction. Even in their surprise at seeing us, they managed to fire a few rounds in our direction. Shanks and I went over the jeep backwards, leaving it as we took off back around the curve.

About half an hour later we took a small patrol up there and retrieved the jeep.

The Germans were gone. The two Germans ran straight into one of our companies and were captured. They told the officers interviewing them about the incident between them and two Americans on a jeep. Because of our stupidity, we were the joke of the area for the next few days. On returning home, I was told that this story was written by Ernie Pyle and was in the Minneapolis newspaper.

5. An especially memorable patrol: The morning before jumping off on the attack, Colonel Jackson asked me if I would fly over a bridge about two miles ahead of us in the artillery Piper Cub airplane to see if the bridge was safe. I didn't think that was the proper way to investigate the bridge, as I sure didn't want to fly in the Piper Cub. They could be shot down by a rifle. I'd rather take a patrol out there.

On the way back, the German patrol had set up a trap about a thousand yards before we reached our lines. They pinned down my patrol and me in about a five-acre, hedgerow-fenced field. When the Germans set up a trap like this, they would usually set up two machine guns on separate corners of the hedgerows. They would set up the machine guns so one would fire shells as tracers about five feet off the ground, and the other gun would fire ammunition about three feet off the ground. One of my men said, "Lieutenant, I can see the guns, I can get them." Knowing their tactics, I told him to stay down. Being a young kid of eighteen or nineteen years old, he wanted to be a hero. He jumped up and was shot through the stomach.

I had to get my men out of this field quick. I told them to work their way back to one corner. Then I would count from one to five, and one man would jump out of the field and out of the trap. That left me with the young boy shot through the stomach. He died in my arms, so I left him there and got myself out of the trap. We went back to the CP and informed the Colonel that the bridge was OK.

19 TO 24 AUGUST 1944 – D+74 TO D+79

I am only covering six days here. 25 August 1944 is such a special date in 4ID history that it warrants its own special section. That is the day that 4ID, led by the 12th Infantry Regiment, liberated Paris from Nazi occupation. There will be pictures and many personal stories from 4ID veterans of their memories of their time in Paris in the Liberation of Paris special issue.

19 AUGUST 1944—D+74: The Division remained in assembly areas and conducted tactical and technical training, maintenance of vehicles, and cleaning of personnel, clothing, and equipment.

20 AUGUST 1944—D+75: No change in the activities. (But stay tuned—in five more days, the 4ID will do something that will always be one of the key events of our history).

21 AUGUST 1944—D+76: The Division prepared for possible movement.

22 AUGUST 1944—D+77: The Division was alerted and prepared for movement east to Chartres. The 4th Division Artillery and 377th Antiaircraft Artillery moved at 1350 to the vicinity of Châteauneuf en Thymerais and were alerted to rejoin the Division on its route to Chartres.

23 AUGUST 1944—D+78: The Division started movement east to the vicinity of Ablis. The 102nd Cavalry Reconnaissance Group was attached at 0315 hours and ordered to screen the advance of the Division.

24 AUGUST 1944—D+79: The 4th Infantry Division completed motor movement of approximately 145 miles without serious mishap and closed in a new assembly area in the vicinity of Arpajon. The 8th Infantry closed at 2130 in the vicinity of Courson-Monteloup. The 12th Infantry was ordered to push farther to Nozay. The 22nd Infantry was also ordered to push farther, to Erougny-sur-Orge (at 1953 hours).

From **War Stories Volume I: Utah Beach to Liberation of Paris.**

Jack Cunningham, Manteca, CA
Battery C, 29th Field Artillery Battalion
France: A Unique Way to a Chicken Dinner for the Battery

Somewhere in France, the battery had a three or four-day rest period. Captain Jim Hurst, CO of Charlie Battery, 29th Field Artillery, told me to get Sergeant Brown, our mess sergeant, and the two of us were to take his command car and go to some of the farms in the area. We were to get some chickens so the battery could have a good meal.

For trade, we took cigarettes, chocolate ration bars, (which had a lot of stuff added to the chocolate), naphtha soap, and miscellaneous items. A piece of the chocolate bar took an hour to melt in your mouth, and the soap produced no suds but did a good job of cleaning. Naturally, the farmer and his wife were happy to see us. He wanted cigarettes—and time to have a few drinks. His wife wanted the chocolate, soap, and some of the knickknacks. He brought out a bottle of cognac or Calvados, and we negotiated.

When this was complete, the wife and the children went out and collected the chickens and we sat there and had a few drinks. We put the curtains up on the command car, tied the legs of two or three chickens together and put them in the back seat.

During the day, we visited four or five farms, and at each the trading and sipping was about the same. We returned to the battery after dark with a load of chickens. Hurst came out and unhooked the curtains to look in the back seat. He was very unhappy. There were chicken droppings smeared all over the rear seat, along with a mass of feathers. I wandered off and he told Sergeant Brown to get some men, remove the chickens, and clean up the car. The next day, Hurst had calmed down, and the dinner was good—or at least better than C-rations.

*****

Meanwhile, back on Utah Beach waiting for Paris to be liberated, our PFC WAC friend, Helen Denton, described her experiences in her book: *World War II WAC*.

Despite what started as a platonic relationship, it was during this time when I fell in love with Noel, my future husband. He and his men would go into towns after they had been taken by the Allied forces and set up telephone wires, then come back to the base camp at night. They also were waiting to go to Paris to set up lines in General Eisenhower's office so they could talk to London and Washington.

Dating on a Normandy beach soon after the invasion was not easy, but we figured out a way. We would walk out to a little farm that had apple juice and Cognac. We'd sit on a log and drink and talk.

On 14 August 1944, the following order was given to all WACs on Utah Beach. I wonder if Helen and Noel had any part in causing this to be written...

DETACHMENT A, WAC DETACHMENT
HEADQUARTERS COMMUNICATIONS ZONE (FORWARD)
APO 886
14 August 44

INSTRUCTIONS TO NEW MEMBERS

WELCOME TO FRANCE! In the time that the WACs have been here they have made an enviable record both in efficiency on the job, and the ease with which they have accepted and adapted themselves to local conditions.

The following points are taken from various Memorandums, Daily Bulletins and the experience of other WACs and will help you to follow the regulations of the camp and avoid difficulties. Read them carefully—know what is expected of you—and continue the high standards of the WACs in Normandy.

1. UNIFORM For duty hours:

Trousers (outer)

Jacket, field (optional). If worn, all buttons except first will be buttoned. Shirt, wool OD (first button open—sleeves may not be rolled)

Leggings (at all times outside of WAC area)

Field shoes and wool socks

Helmet liner (worn at all times outside of WAC area—straight on head—never carried in hands or under arm)

In off duty hours, uniform is same, except trousers, inner liner, may be worn. When leaving camp, steel helmet will be worn. Fatigues may be worn when doing fatigue work, or on day off around WAC area and going to and from Mess.

2. REVILLE

First call—0600 hours

Five minute warning — 0610 hours

Reveille — 0615 hours. Members will fall in at attention and at normal interval. Within 3 minutes, 1st Sgt will give command "Fall In", and take reports. Any member joining formation after "Fall In" is given is late and will be so reported by Squad Leader. Uniform will be field shoes, trousers, jacket (buttoned) and helmet liner. Leggings are optional. All members will stand Reveille except the following:

Sick in Quarters

Working late (after 2000 hours)

Day Off

3. INSPECTION Lt. General Lee requires uniformity of living quarters for inspection. All members will follow the SOP prescribed by this office for arrangement of tents. Tents will be ready for inspection from 0830 to 1630 hrs daily, except Sunday. Members may sleep on day off, but must have area neat and orderly.

4. POLICING AREA Each member must be responsible for policing

her own area and picking up papers around the WAC area. This is especially important due to tendency to throw things on grass, thus detracting from general appearance of camp.

5. MAIL The address to be used is:

WAC Detachment, Detachment A
　　　　　Section, Hq Com Z (Fwd)
APO 887, c/o P.M., N.Y.

Mail will be left in sections for censoring and will be delivered to all personnel in the Sections.

6. CAMP RESTRICTIONS Until such time as passes, leaves, and

furloughs are granted, no member may leave the camp except on official business. Members will be informed of off-limits areas in each camp.

7. MESS Members will sterilize mess kits before each meal. They will take only as much food as they can eat, and no food will be wasted. The mess hours will be posted for each camp.

8. BED CHECK Call to Quarters at 2245 hrs, and all members will be in the immediate vicinity of the WAC area. Bed check is at 2300 hrs; at which time, all members will be ready for bed and in bed. Quiet will be maintained in all tents after 2300 hrs.

9. BLACKOUT See Bulletin Board for schedule of blackout. This is a very serious matter and no member will light cigarettes, have fires, or expose any lights after blackout time. It is a court-martial offense to violate blackout regulations.

10. CAMOUFLAGE Wire paths indicate restricted areas. Members will not go in these areas. White clothes will not be exposed at any time.

11. VEHICLES Members will not ride in vehicles except on official business. Helmets will be worn, and members will not sit on sides of jeeps, radiators, or running boards.

12. OFF-LIMITS The living quarters of EM, WAC officers, and Army Officers are off limits at all times to WAC personnel.

13. DAILY BULLETIN A Daily Bulletin from this office is posted every day. All members are responsible for reading this Bulletin, initialing names when they appear on Bulletin Board and reading other notices. Any changes to these instructions will be posted on the Bulletin Board.

KEEP UP THE NAME—OF THE WACS IN FRANCE

(Signed)
ISABEL B. KANE
Capt., WAC
Commanding

WACs

25 AUGUST 1944

LIBERATION OF PARIS

"One of the proudest days in the storied history of the 4th Infantry Division came on 25 August 1944 when the division was one of the first Allied forces to enter Paris. History gives credit for the liberation to the French 2nd Armored Division. The 12th Infantry Regiment led the way into the eastern part of Paris, followed by the rest of the 4th Infantry Division.

(D-Day (6 June 1944) and the capture of Saddam Hussein (13 December 2003) are probably the other most memorable single days in our history)."

— *Bob Babcock*

On August 25, 1944, Paris was liberated. Although the French 2nd Armored Division has taken credit for the liberation, those who were there, including General Omar Bradley, know that the 12th Infantry Regiment of the 4th Infantry Division had a key part in the liberation, along with other American troops who followed closely in their footsteps.

General Bradley wrote in his book, *A Soldier's Story*: "To hell with prestige," I finally told Allen, "tell the 4th (Infantry Division) to slam in (to Paris) and take the liberation." Learning of these orders and fearing an affront to France, Leclerc's French 2nd Armored Division mounted their tanks and burned up their treads on the brick roads to enter Paris.

As it was throughout the war in Europe, the Allies worked together to accomplish the mission. Both the French Second Armored Division and America's 4th Infantry Division take great pride in liberating Paris.

*****

In Colonel Gerden Johnson's book, *History of the 12th Infantry Regiment in WWII*, originally published in 1947, he wrote:…The significant date flashed through the minds of the men and brought home with startling impact how much battle had been crowded into two short months of the 12th Infantry's drive—June 6, D-Day; June 25, Cherbourg; July 25, the (St. Lo) breakthrough; and now August 25—Paris!

At 1230, Colonel James S. Luckett, commander of the 12th Infantry Regiment, contacted Colonel Billotte of General Leclerc's French Army Staff, and the Police Prefect Captain Edgard Pisani, at the Prefecture of Police located opposite Notre Dame Cathedral. The colonel was informed of a show of resistance in a German barracks near the Palais Bourbon (National Assembly = Lower House) and also at the Place de la Republique.

Colonel Luckett, Major Lindner, and four enlisted men armed with tommy guns hopped into their jeeps and proceeded with some difficulty to the Palais Bourbon. French Second Armored Division forces were firing at the bullet spattered barracks nearby. A short truce was arranged. Terms were discussed with the besieged German commander, General von Cholitz. The Nazi would not surrender without a show of arms—a matter of honor. Thereupon both parties retired to their cover and fired their weapons. At 1300, the German general surrendered and was taken into custody by the French. He was returned under heavy guard to the Prefecture of Police. Colonel Luckett then returned to the Montparnasse railroad station where General Leclerc and the American V Corps commander, General Leonard T. Gerow, were located. He was told by General Gerow just what sectors of Paris to clear.

It was evident that had it not been for the timely arrival of the men and the supporting weapons of the 12th Regimental Combat Team, some of the small, isolated pockets of German resistance would have developed into a strong threat to vital bridges and communication links in the city. However, Paris, the capital city, belongs to the French. Hence the capitulation of Nazi officials to General Leclerc in Montparnasse at 1700 hours...

From the After Action Report of the 4ID:
25 AUGUST 1944 – D+80

The enemy opposed our attempts to cross the Seine in the vicinity of Corbeil by bringing small arms, including automatic weapon fire, and 20-40 mm antiaircraft fire. Toward the end of the day, the enemy withdrew, and a crossing was made without determined resistance. The defense of the city of Paris was very light, chiefly snipers were encountered within the streets. The main obstacle to the rapid advance was the frenzied zeal of the populace itself.

The 8th Infantry 1st Battalion secured bridges and established a bridgehead on the east bank of the Seine river. The 2nd Battalion completed movement at 2230 to positions west and northwest of Longjumeau to protect the flank against the enemy pocket at Palaiseau. The 3rd Battalion completed at 1100 occupation of airports.

The 12th Infantry moved by motor from assembly areas at 0600 via Longjumeau—Villejuif and entered Paris at 1220, proceeded to Hotel de Ville at 1315 and mopped up southeast Paris of scattered snipers.

The 22nd Infantry moved by truck to the vicinity of Corbeil to establish a bridgehead across the Seine river and protect the construction of a treadway bridge. At 0900, Company L attempted an assault but was forced to return after suffering casualties of two boats and fifteen men. At 1000, Company G attempting to secure a position for a treadway bridge received heavy 20 mm and 40 mm flak from woods on east bank of the Seine river. The 2nd Battalion brought heavy small arms and mortar fires into German positions and made observations for heavy artillery concentration. At 1030, patrols were conducted along the Seine toward Company G. At 1520, small German forces surrendered to the 2nd Battalion and Company G effected a crossing in rubber boats. At 1800, the 1st Battalion effected the crossing, established a bridgehead and held to enable a treadway bridge which was under construction at the end of the day. The 377th Antiaircraft Artillery fired missions in support of the 2nd Battalion 22nd Infantry and materially aided in the crossing.

The 102nd Cavalry Reconnaissance Group plus 4th Reconnaissance Troop (mechanized) had screened the entire south of Paris and entered rue de Fontainebleau at 1115. It proceeded to Notre Dame Cathedral at 1145, met slight resistance in cemetery, and secured bridges across the Seine.

Following are stories from **War Stories Volume I: D-Day to the Liberation of Paris:**

Peter Triolo, Pueblo, CO
HQ Company, 1st Battalion, 12th Infantry Regiment
Capturing Paris

Paris was declared an open city. That meant neither the Germans nor the Americans could bomb or destroy the city on the way in or on the way out. At the time, we did not know it, but it was estimated that 10,000 German soldiers were in civilian clothes in Paris to escape the war at the time we arrived there.

The 4th Infantry Division, upon arriving in an area about ten miles outside of Paris, was told to park along the road and hold our position. The 12th Infantry Regiment was leading the 4th Infantry Division. We arrived in this position about August 22, 1944. We were told to wait there because the French troops were going to pass through in order to take the honor of capturing Paris. However, at every farmhouse along the road, the French soldiers stopped and partied. This went on for two or three days.

The problem was every night the Germans would send over one or two German aircraft to machine gun the 4th Infantry Division parked along the road.

The commanding officer of the 4th Infantry Division requested permission from General Bradley to go in and capture Paris. It was stupid for the 4th Infantry Division to sit there and be shot up by Germans every night. Evidently, General Eisenhower agreed. On the morning of August 25, he gave permission for the 4th Infantry Division to go into Paris. Since the 12th Regiment was the head of the 4th Infantry Division column, and the 1st Battalion of the 12th was leading the column, I was up front. I was told by Colonel Jackson to take my French-speaking sergeant and a two-jeep patrol and lead the 4th Infantry Division into Paris. We stayed about four hundred feet in front of the column the whole time. So, I was unofficially the first American officer to enter Paris.

Peter Triolo, Pueblo, CO
HQ Company, 1st Battalion, 12th Infantry Regiment
Events in Paris Worth Talking About

1. Party Pooper: After entering Paris, we were stationed in a large city park about three or four blocks square. In one corner was a little shopping center. We took over a large building that was like a meeting hall for battalion headquarters. On the second morning, Colonel Jackson called me into his office. He wanted me to find out what all the activity going on across the street was about. I walked into the building and entered a room. On one side, there was a long bar with tables and chairs out in the open area. But overhead, above the bar, there was a balcony with stairs on both ends leading to five or six rooms. As it turned out, it was a whorehouse. The men, of course, were going in and out of there. Colonel Jackson closed it up and made it off limits. A lot of men were unhappy.

2. Feed the Children: At meal times, we had a real serious problem. When the men would go to eat, fifty to one hundred children would stand around and watch the soldiers eat. This would embarrass the men, and they would give their food to the kids. Colonel Jackson put a guard around the kitchen. He gave the mess sergeant orders to feed the men first and whatever was left was to be given to the children. That solved part of the problem.

3. The Daily Routine: My duty for the five days I was in Paris was to maintain a motorized patrol around the area for security. It was reported that there were over ten thousand German soldiers in civilian clothes still in Paris. They gave us no trouble—they were glad to get out of the war.

4. The Missed Parade, or My soul for a Bath: On the fourth day, we had a big parade for the capture of Paris, strictly for publicity. I was supposed to march in it, but one of my officers talked to me. He said, "Pete, I got acquainted with the manager of the hotel. He gave me a room for two days so the officers could take showers and clean up." Well, you know where I was. I was up showering while everybody else was parading. (Only very few 4ID Soldiers were in the parade, if any—the 4ID was chasing the Germans toward Germany).

Carlton Stauffer, Charlton, NY
Company G, 2nd Battalion, 12th Infantry Regiment
Liberation of Paris

At 1900 hours, August 23, 1944, our 12th Regimental Combat Team consisting of the 12th Infantry Regiment, the 38th Cavalry Reconnaissance Squadron, the 42nd Field Artillery Battalion, Company B of the 634th Tank Destroyer Battalion, and Companies B and D of the 70th Tank Battalion, started a motor march, which was to be the most exciting experience I would have during my army career. The mission of our combat team was to seize and hold the bridges over the Seine River in the vicinity of Corbeil, which is approximately twenty-five miles southeast of Paris.

As it seemed to be in our usual pattern of things, the weather was dark and stormy. It was another night of skidding off the road into ditches with the usual few Nazi planes overhead. This motor march was in 6x6 trucks with as many fellows as could possibly fit into the cargo area jammed in. There were fold-down seats along each side, but most of us sat on the floor. To say we were miserable is a gross understatement, with the rain coming down in buckets all night long.

Every few hours we stopped to let the men stretch their legs and make the necessary nature calls. I remember one guy in the front part of the cargo space who had very little control and had to relieve himself several times during the night. Naturally, he used his helmet, the all-purpose accessory of the infantryman. As we were moving forward, he had to pass it back to have someone in the rear empty it so as not to blow into the side of the truck body. By morning, all of us were losing patience with the guy and about the only thing to relieve the tension was to curse at him.

As dawn appeared, matters became more tolerable. The rain finally subsided, and we saw a new world—gently rolling terrain—the kind we felt would be tank country. Gone were the hedgerows of Normandy. War had moved quickly over this terrain, and there was less evidence of its devastation. As we passed through the small French towns, the townspeople lined the streets and greeted us with enthusiasm, holding flowers and wine up to us. It was only a taste of the celebration that awaited us in Paris.

We stopped at a little town named Orphin at about 1030 hours on the morning of August 24. We let ourselves dry out as we stretched our legs and got some rations. The vehicles were gassed up. We got the word that it would be the honor of the 12th Regimental Combat Team to be the first U.S. troops to enter Paris. We were to support the 2nd French Armored Division, which was given the political role of liberating Paris.

To ensure that nothing went awry, the Supreme Headquarters, Allied Expeditionary Forces assigned the responsibility to the 12th Infantry to insure a smooth liberation. We resumed our motor march sometime during the afternoon of the 24th, and since we were in the suburbs of Paris, the celebrating was getting into high gear even then. Madly cheering

French people wanted our convoy to slow down to give their hands, their flowers, their wine, and their sincere thanks to their liberators.

About 0800 hours on the morning of August 25, we began to move into the city of Paris. The details of an acceptable surrender with the Nazis are a matter of history, but we in our six-by-six's knew nothing of the plans. We all felt an exhilaration that would not be surpassed in the lives of any of us infantrymen. As we entered the Rue d'Italie, our tactical motor march became a huge victory parade, and our vehicles became covered with flowers. The pent-up emotions of four bitter years under the Nazi yoke suddenly burst into wild celebration, and the great French citizens made us feel that each of us was personally responsible for the liberation of these grateful people. We felt wonderful!

The men, women, and children surged against our trucks on all sides, making a four-mile travel to our positions hours long. There were cries of, "Merci! Merci! S'ank you, S'ank you Vive la Amerique!" Hands reached out just to touch the hands of an American soldier. Babies were held up to be kissed. Young girls were everywhere hugging and kissing the GIs. Old French men saluted. Young men vigorously shook hands and patted the GIs on the back.

Finally, late in the afternoon we took up our position for the night. I had the good fortune to be assigned to a chemistry building at a university on the west side of the Seine. We walked into the building and were met by a lady who was determined to make life just wonderful for us.

Captain Tallie Crocker, who was our company commander at that time, spread his blanket on the floor. Being an infantryman, he was always getting as close to the ground as possible. The lady immediately took his blankets and spread them out on a sort of couch that looked like an operating table. It was easier to let her do that than to explain anything. When she left, Captain Crocker put his blanket on the floor. At about this same time, we all heard loud machine gun fire outside the building. I went out with the captain to see what all the noise was about. In the courtyard outside our building, a Frenchman of their 2nd Armored Division was in a jeep with a .50 caliber machine gun firing away at the corner of a building in the court.

Captain Crocker approached the Frenchman and asked what he was firing at. The Frenchman told him there were "Boche" in the building. Captain Crocker tried to convince him there were no Boche in the building. There was no meeting of minds. Finally, the Captain took the Frenchman on a "Boche hunt" through the building, proving once and for all—no Boche. Situation resolved! The girls came back to the jeep, and we did more wild riding around Paris. When we went back into the chemistry building, Captain Crocker's blanket was back on the table.

That evening some of us went for a walk around town, hitting a few places for a celebration drink. The best part of the evening was to return to our chemistry building with its indoor plumbing.

At 0930 hours on the morning of August 26, Father Fries, our regimental chaplain, held Mass in the famous Notre Dame Cathedral, the first mass said after the liberation. Joe Dailey and I attended. It was a strange sight for Notre Dame to see us doughboys sitting at Mass with our rifles and battle gear. The problem confronting us at Mass and afterwards was to keep civilians away. There were ten civilians to one soldier. At last, the company commanders told the crowds that the soldiers were tired and needed sleep. Immediately, and with apologies, the civilians left our positions.

That evening we were abruptly brought back to the reality of war when at 2330 hours, the Germans launched a heavy aerial bombing. Fortunately, all we encountered were the flashes and the booms—someone else at the distant part of Paris took it all.

Robert Gast, Warsaw, IN
Companies B and C, 1st Battalion, 12th Infantry Regiment
Fond Memories

Stories of our entry and stay in Paris are plentiful. I still have a hard time convincing people that women brought their babies to me—a twenty-one year old second lieutenant—to be blessed and kissed. There are four things that I remember the most about Paris: One, the children watching us eat, and we were not allowed to feed them. Two, the rumor that the 4th Infantry Division would stay in Paris and guard the bridges. Three, the day they bombed Paris I was officer of the day and riding about in a jeep.

When the siren sounded, the driver headed into a tunnel. It turned out to be a command post for the Free French Army. It was quite an experience. Four, the day we left Paris on foot. All of my men had stashed bottles of wine, loaves of bread, and jars of jam under their shirts. It was a very hot and humid day. The farther we walked, the hotter it got, and the more bread, jam, and wine ended up on the road.

George Knapp, Westchester, IL
Chaplain HQ, 12th Infantry Regiment
Always First

One of the thrilling experiences was General Eisenhower selecting the 12th Infantry Regiment to be the only American unit to help in the liberation of Paris. Another "Top 25" experience was Cherbourg. As we entered, the Parisians came out to greet us by the hundreds. We were surrounded on the Champs Elysees. As chaplain, I had cigarettes from the Red Cross to give out to our men. I was passing them out to the Parisians, one at a time, when I accidentally showed an entire pack. Well, the people tore at the pack like a bunch of chickens, and all the cigarettes were torn to shreds.

After one night in Paris, we had to move on towards Germany. Our Catholic Regimental Chaplain had the privilege of saying Mass to our Catholic men in Notre Dame Cathedral. The 4th Infantry Division was always the first—first on the beach; first into Paris; first into Germany.

Jim Roan, Fenton, MI
Company H, 12th Infantry Regiment
One Day in Paris

Regimental Headquarters was set up in a combination residential and business area in Paris. I rode shotgun with Lieutenant Ragland, and we entered the city the early morning of August 26, the day after the troops entered the city. There was a huge American flag flying under the Arc de Triomphe and more American flags flying throughout the city. The French civilian population used bicycles for transportation, and the street was full of them. The civilians were throwing kisses, trying to catch up with our jeep, and wanting to give us bottles of booze. Apparently, they were saving it for such a day. A very large French woman was standing on the curb of the Arc de Triomphe yelling, "Where the hell have you guys been? We have been waiting for you!"

In the city we noted a number of French women getting their heads shaved by groups of Frenchmen with FFI arm bands. German troops were being marched as prisoners of war with a few GIs guarding them. We stopped at Notre Dame Cathedral, and an old man ushered us around. I stopped at a small souvenir shop nearby and purchased a ring that had the outline of the Eifel Tower engraved on its face. It immediately turned my finger green. We drove slowly among groups of civilians and turned down many bottles of various brands of booze. Ragland tried to follow a map, and we wound up on a side street close to the Arc De Triomphe in the city proper.

We parked the jeep at the curb and noted a young couple exiting an apartment building on the opposite side of the street, carrying a small child. They looked at us with a weird expression on their faces and walked over to where we were parked. You have probably seen a number of newsreels of jeeps with large white stars printed on their hood and a small white star on each side, apparently a strange sight to Paris civilians. They walked over to us very cautiously and noted that we were speaking English and asked us, in broken English, who we were. We responded by saying that we are Americans. They started to cry and hugged and kissed us. We noted that a number of apartment dwellers started to exit various places, so we left before we were mobbed.

Lieutenant Ragland had to pick up and drop off various reports that only took a few minutes. We returned by driving close to the Eifel Tower, stopped, and tried to get the elevator ride to the top, but it was all locked up. We found our way back to the outfit. The Division was ordered to continue the war and only stayed in Paris one night, camped in a large park in tents. The civilians mobbed the area, and the GIs could not get any sleep. The Germans were regrouping in the suburban area and had to be dislodged before they could make a stand.

Paul Brunelle, Avon, MA
Company G, 2nd Battalion, 8th Infantry Regiment
The Tricolor Flies

From the book **Company G, 2nd Battalion, 8th Infantry Regiment, 4th Infantry Division** *by Shirley Devine. Used here with her permission.*

Entering Paris, I remember this little town of Longjumeau. I remember seeing the Eifel Tower in the distance. I had a pair of binoculars that somebody had loaned to me. I took the binoculars and looked up at the Eiffel Tower, and there was the tricolor flying. The people in this little village had not seen the tricolor on top of the Eiffel Tower since the occupation. As I handed the binoculars to the people, one by one, the emotion that they expressed was something that a person would never forget. They were just dumbfounded, and so happy that Paris was liberated. At least the area of the Eiffel Tower had been liberated because there it was — the tricolor flying.

We were brought into Paris on two-and-a-half-ton-trucks and driven along a wooded park. I remember the people greeting us, and how happy they were to see us and to know that we were among the liberating troops.

One of the little things that I remember was going into a tiny French town one night. We were the first troops to enter, and the people were all outside singing the national anthem. It was quite moving. I was very young, and I had never had a drink in my life. I think the first drink I ever had in my life was that green liqueur, Pernod. I had some, and said, "Well, I guess maybe I'm a man now, because I can drink something if I want to." However, I did not drink much of anything, even for the next few months of the war.

Bill Riiska, Winsted, CT
4th Reconnaissance Troop (Mechanized)
My Mustache for a Memory

To the best of my recollection I joined the 4th Infantry Division on D+2 near St. Mère l'Eglise. We moved into Arpajon, south of Paris and spent the night of August 23 there.

While in Arpajon, a Frenchman, Lladislaw (Woidek) Francuz, asked to join with us in fighting the Germans. He stayed with us more than three months when orders came that civilians could no longer stay with us. He came from Bretigny and rode in my jeep.

We moved into Paris some time before noon. I saw a shadow down at the corner and started to depress the trigger when a girl in short shorts and a blouse came waltzing around the corner.

August 25, from the south. I don't recall meeting any Germans at that time. I was fairly fluent in French by then, and when the captain's interpreter was busy and someone who spoke French was needed, I was often sent out.

We moved into Paris on the 25th and I recall meeting a French girl by the name of Audrey Cremer. I remember making two very exciting trips across Paris in a one-jeep parade with thousands of Parisians waving and cheering.

One trip was to deliver a message to the French Army, I'm sure that it was to General Leclerc and the French 2nd Armored Division. We found the tank outfit, and the message was delivered to the first ranking officer we found. I don't recall who was in my jeep, but I believe it was our platoon leader, Lieutenant George Gillon.

After we delivered the message, we found our way back to where the recon troop was located. It was like a parade when we were working our way back. I do remember that some of the Parisians were exacting retribution on the girls who were consorting with the Germans.

The second trip that I took was to bring up ammunition to one of our platoons. I also remember being posted near a park, observing a side street to the east and being told that no one but Germans would be coming up that street.

There was a .50 caliber machine gun mounted on our jeep, and I sat and watched down that street. Either it was extremely hot, or I was very tense. I had my thumbs on the triggers of the machine gun ready to fire at anything I saw down the street.

I remember sitting on a corner under a street light, which I believe was lit, talking with Audrey Cremer. I made a date with her for the next night. She said, "Yes, but only under one condition." I had to shave off my mustache. I had a big handlebar mustache that I had been raising since we left the States in April.

We were sleeping that night in what seemed to be a garden house in back of a large estate. When we got up that morning, I shaved off my mustache. No sooner had I done that when our sergeant came by and yelled, "Pack up, mount up, and move out." We left by the northeast, heading for Belgium, and I never returned to Paris.

As usual, those Americans most deserving of seeing Paris will be the last ones to see it...if they ever do. By that, I mean the fighting soldiers. Only one infantry regiment and one reconnaissance outfit of Americans actually liberated Paris, and they passed on through the city quickly and went on with the war.

Chester Frydryck, North Versailles, PA
Company M, 3rd Battalion, 22nd Infantry Regiment
Kisses from the Mademoiselles

From Utah Beach to St. Lô the landscape was devastation. Towns and villages were in flames and total destruction. Bodies, animal carcasses, and equipment destruction were everywhere. After the St. Lô breakthrough, the front advances were swifter. More destruction and bodies were encountered and columns of prisoners in greater numbers. Our outfit was in a sweep around the Falaise Pocket, heading for Paris.

As we were approaching Paris, there was a sense that the war may be ending. An airfield in the distant right was fully intact—destruction or annihilation wasn't evident. As we approached the suburbs, throngs of people lined the streets, cheering, waving French and U.S. flags, at times impeding our convoy, offering drinks as our convoy slowed. Many of our guys were greeted with kisses from the mademoiselles. Our convoy came to a halt in the Paris suburbs for several hours, offering an opportunity to mix with the French.

Some of our guys were quick to find the bars and gals. The excitement and activities were virtual pandemonium, an unforgettable event. I vividly recall a parade of dump trucks driven through the streets with French freedom fighters holding pistols to shaven heads of women who were supposedly German fraternizers.

Some French customs became evident to us when we had need for outdoor city rest rooms. They were unisex. As the celebrations continued, we began to move out to an area in town adjacent to a circus setup where we spent the night. We moved out the next day leaving behind a brief moment of civilization and the hopes and sense of the war ending. Continuing through France to Belgium, we had a beautiful view of the Swiss Alps, and on to the Siegfried Line. But the war and the devastation were far from over.

Lester Steele, Lexington, KY
Medical Detachment, 22nd Infantry Regiment
Wish I Could Have Spoken French

I do remember the day we went into Paris. Part of the time we were riding, and some of it in the outskirts was on foot. I remember a funny looking little Frenchman running up to me with a big hug and a kiss on the cheek that drew a lot of laughs from my fellow soldiers. I talked with a beautiful French girl on the edge of Paris. She gave me a glossy photo that I still have. Sure wish I could have spoken French!

I got a pretty good look at the Eiffel Tower, and I think I can remember the Champs Elysees columns. We also made it into one bar, and I had a shot or two of some kind of cognac. While we were riding, I remember that we were warned to still be on the lookout for snipers.

"Big Hawk" Hawkins, Motor Officer
22nd Infantry Regiment
A Paris Liberation Story

After the Fourth Infantry Division entered Paris, Colonel "Buck" Lanham received word that his friend, "Ernie" Hemingway was living at the Ritz Hotel. So Colonel Lanham sent one of his officers, one John E. Minnach, to Paris with a cache of enemy weapons and some ammo. Consequently, Captain Minnach found "Ernie" Hemingway at the Ritz Hotel and gave him his gifts. Later, it was reported that Hemingway and friends were shooting pigeons from the balcony attached to his room.

Oscar Romero, San Diego, CA
Company I, 3rd Battalion, 22nd Infantry Regiment
People Were Celebrating

Two things happened that day when we entered Paris that I still remember. Company I, 3rd Battalion, 22nd Infantry Regiment was in reserve, so we were riding two-and-a-half-ton-trucks, and our job was to clean up pockets of resistance by-passed by the spearheading troops. We had stopped because of a firefight ahead of us. We were ordered to dismount (what a mistake that was). People were celebrating and giving us wine, fruit, flowers, etc. We were short of officers after all the fighting since the breakthrough at St. Lô, so I was the platoon sergeant in charge of the first platoon. There weren't too many of us left, but when the word came to mount up to go, I had a hell of a time rounding up my men because everyone had joined in the celebration.

Anyhow, I finally rounded them all up except one. His squad leader and I went looking and found him in a bar, drunker than hell and waving his rifle in the air with a grenade launcher on the end of his barrel. He was singing the French national anthem when I hollered at him, "Let's go!" He accidentally pulled the trigger on his rifle and the sh-t hit the fan.

There were screams from the women, and everybody was covered with plaster and wood. We dragged him out, put him on the truck, and were on our way.

The next heroic thing we did that day was to liberate a bunch of women from a hotel that they told us was being used by the Germans as a prison. To this day, I still say this was a "cat-house" because among all these women were four American GIs who had been shot down over France and were being hidden by four of the ladies as their husbands—French berets and all. One of them came up to me and told me how glad they were to see us.

I said, "Are you ready to get back to your outfit?"

He said, "I think I'll wait for them to catch up with me." I said to myself, "What a beautiful way to fight a war!"

The next time I saw the real downtown Paris was in October 1944 when another sergeant and I were given a three-day pass from the Front before going into the Hürtgen Forest.

George Wilson, Grand Ledge, MI
Companies E and F, 2nd Battalion, 22nd Infantry Regiment
Friendly Smiles Were Everywhere

I was with the first U.S. troops to enter Paris. At the beginning, we were following tanks of the French 2nd Armored Division. They were feeling pretty excited about coming home. Some of the drivers should have been arrested for drunk driving. The tanks seemed to disappear as we reached the Champs Elysees. I was thrilled to see the huge crowds of excited people who jammed the streets from wall to wall. They gave us flowers, bread, cookies, wine, and anything you can imagine. My arm ached from handshakes. Friendly smiles were everywhere. Women threw us kisses, and some even climbed on trucks to give a few men a thrill.

Our next stop was at a suburb on the northeast edge of Paris. We didn't see any more French or German soldiers, only some very excited FFI groups hanging from cars and hanging guns from every window. We camped in the backyards and seemed to be welcome. We were told there were Germans in the area and one of our men was shot by a German. The next day, the French held a "kangaroo court" where five women were convicted of collaboration with the Germans. All five were found guilty. Shorn of all hair, they had to march down the street while the crowd threw eggs, tomatoes, and paper sacks filled with human waste at them. Shorn of all dignity, they were marked for a long time.

John F. Ruggles (Deceased), Phoenix, AZ
Executive Officer, and Regimental Commander, 22nd Infantry Regiment
Those of Us Riding in Jeeps Were Really Mobbed

> Major General (Retired) John F. Ruggles died on January 15, 1999. He was an Honorary President of the National 4th Infantry Division Association and Honorary Colonel of the 22nd Infantry Regiment. He also served as a former president of the 22nd Infantry Regiment Society. He also became a good friend of mine

during the last years of his life. He was a big factor in getting me involved in 4ID WWII history.

— Bob Babcock

Bert Pokol was a very young soldier of Hungarian descent assigned as my jeep driver. He was a handsome young man with an eternal smile and eyes that danced. He never spoke of his father. His mother, if still living, was in Budapest. Hungarian-American friends back home in Perth Amboy, New Jersey, were the only ones to share his military burden with him. His English was very limited. As our acquaintance widened, our relationship become something approaching a father/son relationship. Duties as jeep driver became secondary to Pokol's attention to my safety, welfare, and comfort. Food packages Pokol received from "home" were shared with me and others to augment our field rations. Pokol foraged vegetables from gardens all across France and Belgium to meet our needs. He did well, cooking on a small gasoline burner.

Thanks to the 12th Infantry Regiment's liberation effort, the 22nd Infantry Regiment moved through Paris motorized. It was a start-and-stop move as the streets were jammed with celebrating French citizens hugging and kissing soldiers they could reach. Those of us riding in jeeps were really mobbed. Steel helmets were not designed for wear in this kind of an encounter.

Pokol, that handsome devil (with helmet abandoned), was having a hard time driving. He turned to me during a short break in the assault from beautiful French women and said, "Sir, you will get some of this if you get rid of that cigar," then he added, "and the helmet, too." He was right.

Bill Boice, Phoenix, AZ
Chaplain, 22nd Infantry Regiment
The Tomb of the Invalides

Shortly after midnight on August 25, 1944, Combat Team 22 was ordered to cross the Seine River. By noon the next day, the entire team was across the river and the liberation of Paris was accomplished—not by the French—as the news reported, but by the 4th Infantry Division. After the cheering and the impromptu parade was finished, David Mitchell, our Regimental American Red Cross Field Director, and I determined we would like to see the Tomb of the Invalides, better known as Napoleon's Tomb.

We tried to enter wrought iron gates at the front of the building, but they were securely locked. Occasional shots could still be heard from German sharpshooters isolated in buildings. We walked around the right of the building when a door opened in the heavy stone wall. An aged Frenchman in the uniform of a prior war stepped out of the building, saluted us as Americans, and asked, in halting English, if we would like to enter the building.

"Indeed, we would," we said.

Thus, Mitch and I were the first Americans to enter Napoleon's Tomb as the "City of Light" was being liberated. We stood by the great Rotunda, and our eyes went to the right where our guide pointed out the bronze tomb of Marshall Foch of World War I fame. His sarcophagus rests on the shoulders of six French soldiers. Then we looked across the rotunda and saw a huge mirror in front of which hung a great crucifix. But in a moment, we saw that it was not a mirror, but was a window through which we could see into a long chapel from whose ramparts hung the tattered and faded flags of the Napoleonic campaigns.

"Which is Napoleon's Tomb?" we asked. "Look down," instructed our guide.

We looked down. One full level beneath us, in the center of a mosaic circle, rested the imposing, bronze colored granite tomb of the Emperor.

Our guide continued, "When the memorial was being planned, the officials called for designs to be submitted. This was the one they preferred."

But a question was raised by some of the officials. "Why," they asked, "do you have visitors standing above the tomb around the rotunda and looking down on the Emperor?"

Napoleon's Tomb rests one full level beneath the rotunda. "I designed it," said the architect, "so that no one can stand in the presence of the Emperor without his head bowed." It was a lesson of history that David Mitchell and I have not forgotten.

Tommy Harrison, Vero Beach, FL
HQ, 2nd Battalion, 22nd Infantry Regiment
The Day Paris Fell

The night before we were to take over and fight for the rest of Paris that was still in German hands, Colonel Lanham took about six of us to a cafe that Ernest Hemingway used to visit. Here it was night, and the six of us go to this cafe—and quite a place it was. Hemingway had left word that we would be there that night. The owner treated us like heroes and even opened up a wine cellar that he had hidden from the Germans. We had a great dinner and great wine. The owner said the Germans had been there the night before. We were the first Americans he had seen in years. Hemingway's French troops had opened up the area, clearing the Germans out.

The next day we were alerted to drive through the rest of Paris. We had a "point" out to warn us when and if we ran into any Germans. I remembered riding through Paris in a jeep. Parisians lined the streets, waving and yelling at us. It was like a ticker-tape parade down Wall Street. They told us the Germans had pulled out the night before. We were to go to a point where the suburbs started, set up a position and start cleaning out the area. Just as we set up in position, we were told to pack up and move out—the Germans apparently had flown the coop. We alerted our troops and moved out. We got about ten miles outside of Paris when we sat up and sent out guards to keep us apprised of the German positions.

That was Paris. We (all except six of us) didn't get a chance to really get involved in Paris. As you know, we all are very proud that we were there, "the day that Paris fell."

David Rothbart, Pittsburgh, PA
Company E, 2nd Battalion, 22nd Infantry Regiment
Paris Jews in Hiding

I re-read what I had written in my World War II Army Journal. In the entry dated September 1, 1944, I wrote about Jews I spoke to in Yiddish who had just come out of hiding in Paris. Leo Gorelick and I visited them in the quarters that they still occupied—hideous rooms, with secret chambers in dilapidated tenements in the slums and back alleys of the city. There were quite a number of them.

It just occurred to me now, fifty-four years later, that many French Christians had to know they were there and did not report them to the German authorities or their French agents. From time to time, I still hear a few Americans cynically question the integrity of the French while they were under German occupation. My observation today, that the Jews in hiding were not given away, convinces me that the French people, on the whole, other than the notorious Vichy French, truly knew and did what was right.

Weldon Frye, Columbia, SC
HQ, 22nd Infantry Regiment
Kissing Babies

Watching on television the thousands of happy, French citizens celebrating the World's Cup Soccer Championship in Paris brought back memories of when we entered that city in August 1944. The day that the 22nd Infantry Regiment entered Paris by way of the Champs Elysees, we were greeted by what I remember to be thousands of beautiful women in colorful dresses and different colored hair, riding bicycles.

Words cannot describe the happiness and appreciation shown by the people in Paris that day. They were crying; they were trying to hug, kiss, and love the 22nd Infantry to death. After being in hard and continuous fighting from D-Day until then, I can assure you that we loved and appreciated the way we were welcomed by these happy people.

As we moved slowly forward, we were surrounded by more and more people who just wanted to touch, hug, kiss, or share a toast. At times, we were picked up bodily and passed over the crowd so everyone could share in the excitement. We were passed into houses and offices full of people who just wanted to be part of the celebration. Of course, this meant kissing what seemed like thousands of babies. This scenario continued until late afternoon. I can't remember details (too many toasts) other than we were not allowed to remain in the city overnight. We moved on through and formed a defensive position outside the city in position to repel a counterattack if one occurred. If I remember correctly, the next morning, the famous 22nd Infantry members jumped off in their normal attack in pursuit of the enemy. As you know, we still had many more hard battles ahead.

B.P. "Hank" Henderson, Knoxville, TN
Medic, 22nd Infantry Regiment
Someone Found a Case of Champagne

We rode all night in a pouring rain. When we reached Paris the next morning we were quite wet, and we dried out in the hot sunshine. When we got into Paris we were stopped by huge crowds of people. They were hanging out of their windows, and the crowd was so thick that we could not get off our trucks to urinate. We had to take our liners out of our helmets and use it for a pot and pour it over the side of the truck.

Service Company pulled into a garage that was fenced in, and we were restricted to that area. Some of the men climbed up the gutters of a house that boxed the garage in. We stayed there two days. The second day some of us went about three or four blocks and visited a beautiful church. We moved out to the outskirts of Paris and stayed there two nights.

The first night someone found a case of champagne, and First Sergeant Hoit Chandler invited me to the champagne party. The next morning, we could hardly hold our heads up. After two days there, we moved a little farther out of Paris. That day I patched up three different men who had shot themselves in the hand with a German P-38 pistol. Not any of them were serious enough for them to be evacuated back to Paris. From there, we headed for the Belgium border.

Bill Parfitt, Elmira, NY
HQ, 4th Infantry Division
(Bill had been BG Roosevelt's bodyguard before Roosevelt died in early July, then stayed in 4ID HQ)
Seeing General De Gaulle

We traveled in convoy along with the Free French and some of their tanks. It was amazing how often we stopped and, of course, the "ladies" would scramble up the sides of the tanks and disappear. We did remark that they must be packed pretty solid inside. I saw the first bikini I ever saw on a gal standing on the top of a high wooden fence surrounding a swimming pool. Along the way, we were greeted by crowds of people offering bottles of wine and bundles of fresh vegetables. Even ripe tomatoes were "tossed" into our reach. Some were immediately eaten, and some were saved.

We had an Italian lad with us by the name of Bennie Bertoline from Peekskill, New York, who was saving these vegetables like mad. As the convoy lurched along, some of the Free French tanks took on more passengers, and others just pulled off the road and stopped. We ended up at the Bois de Vincennes as the CP of the 4th Infantry Division HQ for the night. It was some kind of a public park that soon became a tent city with pup tents appearing all over the place.

Some of us were able to take a walk and ended up in crowds of people; all of them seemed to have a bottle of something with them. There is nothing to remind me of when we returned to Division HQ. I heard Bennie Bertoline call me and went over to his command car where he handed me his helmet. Inside was the most beautiful salad I think I have ever seen. He had added salt and pepper to the wine and had made a dressing that was poured over the vegetables the French had tossed us. Cucumbers were sliced, tomatoes were sliced, some carrots were added, and for lettuce, he used the leaves from maybe beets or greens. We sat and ate the helmet full and drank wine and he made a second helmet full of "salad."

I remember little until the next morning when we were busy informing the entire unit Headquarters as to where we were going to set up our next CP. It was funny to see strange heads emerge from some of the pup tents or get out of trucks, etc. They were not in uniform and were evidently female; they would look around and then start walking away.

This was also where we informed all the units that we were moving on and that another "clean" division was going to march in the victory parade for General De Gaulle. We were too dirty, it seemed, and they all had clean new uniforms. Somewhere in a book I have is the story on De Gaulle insisting that President Roosevelt send his "best" troops to enter Paris with the Free French, so the 4th Infantry Division was chosen. When we appeared and were dirty, unshaven, and not looking like fresh new troops, they substituted the 28th Infantry Division that had all clean new uniforms.

I think the greatest memory of this was in seeing General De Gaulle among the frenzied French people as we came to a blocked street where his parade was passing by. The funniest sight was the young "ladies" climbing up and into the French tanks and the tanks pulling off the road. The next funniest was seeing them getting out of GI pup tents just after daylight and slowly walking away. Undoubtedly, they had become tired and had just stopped to take a nap!

David Roderick, Carlsbad, CA
Company H, 2nd Battalion, 22nd Infantry Regiment
Across the Seine in Three Hours

The breakthrough at St. Lô had been successful. We were proud we could say that we had spearheaded the "breakthrough at St. Lô" for the units poised to make the run for Paris. But the 4th Infantry Division never rested. We were ordered on the 23rd of August to make the 100-mile motor march to Ablis, France. The objective was to establish a bridgehead over the Seine River, south of Paris. Our movement was fast in spite of a torrential rainstorm throughout the night and all through the next day.

We assembled near Corbeil to make the assault in small rubber boats at 0300 hours on August 25. The first elements of the 3rd Battalion were sunk by small arms fire and antiaircraft guns. The 2nd Battalion laid down a fierce artillery barrage and a platoon of Germans on the opposite shore surrendered. The battalion was across the Seine in three hours. The 1st and 3rd Battalions got a company across, and the combined forces made quick work of the Germans, but we were not without casualties. George Cole of Company C, 4th Engineers, remembers lying on the ground after recovering from his boat being sunk. Bob Stockman came running by, and he told him to sit down with him. As he sat down, a German bullet went through his leg. George's good friend, William Bates, was killed there.

Combat Team 22 completed our part of the liberation by moving in jeeps and trucks into Paris. It was a joyous sight with the throngs of cheering people. Hugs, kisses, and wine were exchanged. This was the first and only time that the line troops had any time to mingle with the people of France. They yelled constantly, "Merci! Merci! Vive la Amerique!"

When I finally rode into the bivouac area, the city dump, at 1300 hours, I looked forward to acquainting myself with some rest and the gaiety of Paris. I was there less than an hour when I got word that my section of mortars would be a part of a scouting party to move out and make contact with the withdrawing Germans. On the way in, I passed the Arc de Triomphe and on the way out, I passed the Notre Dame Cathedral. Good-bye Paris!

Tom Reid, Marietta, GA
Cannon Company, 22nd Infantry Regiment and Company I, 3rd Battalion, 22nd Infantry Regiment
Overall, a Glorious Day

Paris, "Gay Paree," "City of Light…" By whatever name it is known, it has an inexorable pull on the human spirit, the traveler, the wanderer in us all.

After the bitter fighting in Normandy and the decisive breakout late in July, the 4th Infantry Division was in the vicinity of Chartres, southwest of Paris. When the word came that the 4th would be the first to enter Paris, there was joy mixed with apprehension. Joy that the 22nd Infantry Regiment would soon be in Paris and apprehension that it might be denied us. In any event, it had a tremendous effect. No one wanted to leave the Regiment for any reason while this was contemplated. Word spread beyond the division and there were cases of men leaving the hospital without orders and making their way back to the Regiment. No one wanted to miss this once-in-a-lifetime opportunity.

The 22nd Infantry moved to positions at Corbeil, some twenty-five miles south of Paris, ready to move in, but no orders came. Instead, it was decided at higher echelons to let the French 2nd Armored Division be the first to enter Paris. There was no fighting in Paris; it had been declared an 'open city' in order to save it. For twenty-four hours, we watched the French limping along, towing some disabled vehicles, transporting others, and on the morning of August 25 they passed us and went into Paris to a joyful citizenry.

Soon the 22nd Infantry Regiment, motorized by the attachment of several quartermaster trucking companies, slowly wound its way through Paris. The only restraining order given was that no one could leave the vehicles. The day was glorious, the sun shined brightly, and crowds pushed forward until it seemed that all of France was welcoming us that day. People thrust bottles of wine into outstretched hands, threw flowers and notes at the troops, and crowded into the trucks. All in all, it was a most memorable experience. Soon, however, with the extra consumption of the wine, the order to remain in the vehicles was becoming harder to observe. This was where the steel helmet was given one more task to perform.

Still, the experience was unforgettable and lives with me to this day. The people lining the streets, the generosity of the French people, the noise, the excitement of being present at the Liberation of Paris—all of this was indelibly imprinted on a first lieutenant whose only command up to this time was an infantry platoon. The route through Paris was terminated by our arrival at a bivouac for the night at a walled enclosure. It was somewhere on the northern outskirts of Paris. The Regimental Commander had sent an advance party ahead to locate this compound. I've heard it said that, in fact, this was an insane asylum, and we merely used the grounds for the night. This I will leave for the historians to verify. The next morning, we were off in hot pursuit of the retreating Wehrmacht, and soon found ourselves in Belgium. On September 11, 1944, the 22nd Infantry Regiment became the first U.S. (and Allied) unit to enter German soil. But that is another story.

One final word. Whenever you see the oft printed picture of American troops massed fifty abreast marching down the Champs Elysees in Paris with the Arc de Triomphe in the background and billed as the liberation of Paris, brand it as a phony. That is the 28th Infantry Division some three or four days after the 4th Infantry Division had rolled through Paris that bright August day. Indeed, when this picture was published in the Stars and Stripes, the 22nd Infantry Regiment had already shaken the dust of France from its boots and would soon be in Germany.

Overall, a glorious day.

*****

If you enjoyed reading the stories of these 4th Infantry Division veterans, there are plenty more, equally as gripping, in the second volume of this two-book series, **War Stories: Paris to V-E Day**. While the two books of this series are focused exclusively on the 4th Infantry Division's experiences in WWII, the stories could just as easily have come from any of the dozens of divisions who fought to liberate Europe.

War Stories: Paris to V-E Day, available in both paperback and e-book from **www.deedspublishing.com** and from Amazon, continues the fight after Paris was liberated. While others celebrated the liberation in Paris, the 4ID continued the hot pursuit of the Germans across France, into Belgium, and were the first Allied force to breach the famed Siegfried Line and fight into Germany on September 11, 1944.

After their fight against the pillboxes and bunkers of the Siegfried Line, the 4ID found itself in the bloodiest battle in their history—before or since. November and early December 1944 found them fighting through Germany's Hürtgen Forest, a battle that has been all but forgotten after it was overshadowed by the Battle of the Bulge. But the 4ID Soldiers who fought there will never forget it—a typical rifle company suffered 150% casualties in the Hürtgen Forest, yet the division's objective was accomplished.

In early December, a tired division, desperately needing rest and refitting, moved to the relative quiet of Luxembourg, only to be thrown into the largest battle of WWII—the Battle of the Bulge. General George Patton praised the division's performance for holding the southern shoulder of the Bulge and securing the capitol city of Luxembourg and the major supply lines running back into France.

Once the German surge into the Bulge was stopped, the 4ID was part of the counter-attack in January 1945, going back through the Siegfried Line, often using foxholes the 4ID Soldiers had dug in September 1944. Slugging it out through the coldest winter Europe had experienced in years, the 4ID fought through Prum and many other German towns as they continued pushing the Germans back across the Rhine River. By the time the war ended on May 8, 1945, the 4ID had suffered more casualties than any other American division in Europe yet had accomplished every mission assigned to them.

To read more of the personal stories of those members of the "Greatest Generation," order your copy of ***War Stories: Paris to V-E Day***, available now from Amazon or an autographed copy from **www.deedspublishing.com**.

Or…continue to read selected stories from that and other sources in this book as the 4th Infantry Division continues our eleven month fight across Europe, culminating with complete victory on VE Day.

As always, please share these stories with your circle of influence. We want as many people as possible to know the great job our 4ID vets did between 6 June 1944 and 8 May 1945 to destroy the Nazi threat to the world.

*****

As you'll see further below, the 4ID did not stay in Paris, we continued the hot pursuit of the Germans across northeastern France, Belgium, and into their homeland. Though it is not 4ID related, I though you would enjoy reading an American WACs memories of her time stationed in Paris as part of General Eisenhower's headquarters…

From her book, **World War II WAC,** *published by Deeds Publishing.*
Soon after Paris was liberated, Helen Kogel Denton and her fellow WACs entered Paris, as shown in this article from a South Dakota newspaper:
JERAULD COUNTY WAC AMONG FIRST IN PARIS

Paris, France—(Delayed)—Laden with full packs, bed roll, and gas masks, the first WACs arrived here by truck just a week after the capital had been liberated. French men and women lined the sidewalks, cheering, waving, and shaking hands with the WACs at every opportunity.

Gazing wistfully at the gay clothes of the French women, one travel-weary WAC remarked, "I'd always dreamed of going to Paris someday, but I never thought that I'd look like this when I arrived."

The WACs will serve as telephone operators, jeep drivers, statisticians, draftsmen, secretaries, and interpreters.

Among the first WACs to arrive were three South Dakotans. They were Pvt. Ruby Nicholl and S/Sgt. Ruth Herdman, both of Custer, and Pfc. Helen Kogel, of Wessington Springs.

Fit to Fight

HELEN CONTINUES WITH HER STORY...

Soon after Paris was liberated, we were flown into Paris on a cargo plane, landing at the main airport. We traveled by bus to our hotel in Paris. There was still sporadic fighting in the streets, so we were confined to our quarters for three days. There was no food available for us, so we all pooled our K-rations and made do until the truck arrived from the mess hall. Noel happened to drive the supply truck that brought us our food. His unit was assigned to Paris to ensure the central telephone office was not booby trapped by the Germans on their way out. Paris streets were still filled with Parisians of all ages celebrating their freedom.

The room I was assigned to had a surprise in it: a German officer's clothes were still in the closet. It didn't take long for me to call the hotel manager to come and clear out those uniforms. I didn't want him to come back and find me there.

As soon as we were settled, we were able to open up our office and meet the group we would be working for. We set about getting General Eisenhower's headquarters set up and went back to work.

Our first hotel was very rundown. We stayed there a month and then moved to another upscale hotel, just off the Champs Elysees. That was a very good place to stay, an excellent hotel where we stayed until the end of the war.

Working in Paris was different. All of us girls were put into one room, an office pool, where an officer could request any of us to work for him. I wouldn't say it was Top Secret work, but I do remember one of the officers was tracking a submarine and we were fascinated to watch how he was able to have a warship sink it.

We were allowed to use our spare time, especially on the weekends, to visit all the great museums and places of interest. Seeing places I had read about in my history books at school made me realize what a wonderful opportunity I had been given. Seeing the Louvre, the Eiffel Tower, the Arc de Triomphe, Notre Dame, the Versailles Palace, the whole city was something to see.

Noel was with the Signal Corps and stayed in Paris for about four weeks, making sure all communications were set up and working properly. We had time to meet after work and get better acquainted. His outfit would follow a unit that would clear a town and then they would make sure there was telephone service back to the headquarters in Paris. Even after he went on to the front lines, he would call me late at night, usually at midnight, when the lines were clear of other traffic. We both knew girls in the central telephone office that would pass his calls through. It was our way of keeping in touch. He would tell me where he was and what happened each day, so I could write his mother for him. His letters were always censored, and I could keep her informed without letting his exact location be known.

Noel was good looking and a great cook. He was also a nice gentleman. I was attracted to his manners and the way he cared for his mother. A man who respects his mother respects his wife.

Noel and I had a great dating experience. We went to dances on the weekends and to the movies. There was a lot of entertainment to choose from once Paris became the hub of the Allied headquarters. The only things lacking in the city were the restaurants. Paris didn't have any food at that time. The USO provided food though, and we were grateful. We did have a favorite meeting place, at one of Paris' famous outdoor corner cafes.

Liberated Paris was a wonderful experience. It was the main place for the military to send troops for rest and relaxation (R&R). The USO provided very large living and eating quarters for all of them to use. There were plenty of activities, including the latest movies and a canteen for dancing, especially on the weekends. Tickets to all the special shows were available. We took in the Follies and other dancing programs. I missed a great opportunity—shopping in the large department stores. It was because I didn't need anything. The Army forced us to wear our uniform at all times and I was not good in their money exchange and did not understand the French language, so I stayed away from the department stores. I did use the hair salons and perfume shops of Paris, so I didn't miss out on everything.

I did buy a hat and sent it to my mother on her birthday. After I returned home, I asked her how she liked the hat. I thought she would wear it to some of her meetings, but she said it was so unusual, compared to what they wore during the rationing days of the war, that she gave it to my sister to redesign into something not as flamboyant.

I had very little contact with troops coming into Paris, other than meeting them at USO dances. I did associate with those that I worked with. We often used the bicycles available at our hotel to visit parks and interesting places not available by the Metro. Their transportation was great to most places. Several of us visited Versailles, where the armistice ending WWI was signed. We also took a boat trip down the Seine River.

I loved to dance at the USO. The jitter bug was the dance we all enjoyed. I wore a pair of shoes out and had to have them replaced.

One of the highlights in Paris was when we were informed that the hotel where the officers were billeted had invited the Glenn Miller Orchestra to play, and we girls were invited to join them. Tex Benike brought the band over from London and was directing them. We kept asking when Glenn Miller was going to arrive. We didn't learn until the next morning that his plane disappeared over the Channel and was never recovered.

Other than the Glenn Miller band, I didn't meet any famous people, not even General Eisenhower other than seeing him at a distance as he entered the headquarters. I did not know or hear about Kaye Summersby, his driver, until she wrote her book. I did read in another book that the General's adjutant wrote saying she was part of his office, but she was more involved with an officer on the front lines. I can't speculate about the often-quoted story linking General Eisenhower and his driver together romantically. I've also been asked if I had my picture taken with General Eisenhower. Of course I didn't — corporals don't go up to generals asking to have their picture taken with them.

I met a Parisian girl, Nicole, who became a good friend. She was having a hard time, and I would meet her and give her my chocolate candy and cigarettes to barter for food. One day she invited me to her apartment (one room with kitchenette and bath) for lunch. She had picked some mushrooms from an underground field. We had steamed mushrooms,

French bread, and a glass of wine. That's the way a lot of the people survived.

* * * * *

Two last bits of history and I'll stop this liberation of Paris history lesson on the 4ID. First, **Ernest Hemingway**, who had attached himself to the 4ID soon after D-Day, entered Paris the night before the liberation, leading a ragtag band of French Freedom fighters. There is a very interesting story about his dealings with French MG Leclerc and how his actions that day had a big part in the 4ID being the only one of the original five D-Day assault divisions to **not** be awarded the French Croix de Guerre. That's a story to be told another day.

Second, this was not the first time the 4ID had marched through Paris. On July 4, 1918, two battalions of the 4ID, from the 39th and 58th Infantry Regiments, were sent to Paris to participate in the parade and tribute to American independence. While this was going on, the rest of the 4ID was celebrating with games and field events outside Paris. The next day, they moved forward to enter the battles of WWI. For that short day in 1918, the 4ID was the clean and fresh ceremonial troops worthy of a parade.

Now back to the 4ID and our pursuit of the Germans…Here is the After Action Report covering the remainder of August:

* * * * *

26 AUGUST 1944—D+81: The enemy attempted to delay our clearing of Paris by fighting a delaying action using small groups of infantry and tanks sheltered in buildings or behind walls. Armored action was limited to the "shoot and run" tactics. The 8th Infantry Regiment maintained road blocks to prevent enemy from advancing southeast from Palaiseau, established patrols to the northwest and west. The 3rd Battalion continued outposts of airfields occupied the previous day with addition of another one. The 12th Infantry continued to mop up enemy resistance and at 0830 initiated movement to new assembly areas in the vicinity of Bois de Vincennes, closing at 1230. Active patrolling was initiated to the east and northeast. The 22nd Infantry continued to protect the bridgehead in the vicinity of Orangis. At 1345 after completion of the bridge, the regiment was ordered to withdraw all units. The 4th Engineer Combat Battalion completed the construction of treadway bridges by 1200, cleared mines, prepared charges, and disposed of road blocks in the city of Paris.

27 AUGUST 1944—D+82: Numerous encounters between the enemy and FFI forces were reported in the area Neuilly Plaisance—Neuily sur Marne. The enemy continued to delay our advance by forming pockets of resistance along our route. The 8th Infantry moved to the assembly area in the vicinity of Bois de Vincennes, closing at 1130. At 1400, the Regiment attacked in a northeasterly direction against sporadic enemy resistance and independent action of tanks. Stiff resistance was encountered from a fort located on Hill 108. Additional resistance was encountered from Neuilly. At the end of the day, the 3rd Battalion closed in assembly area in woods vicinity of Montfermeil. The 12th Infantry remained in assembly area in the vicinity of Bois de Vincennes as division reserve. The 22nd Infantry closed at 1230 in the assembly area vicinity of Bois de Vincennes and pushed forward against slight resistance.

28 AUGUST 1944—D+83: Scattered small arms and antitank fire from dug in positions and buildings continued. The 8th Infantry moved forward with no resistance. Some long range artillery fire was received at 1950. The 12th Infantry moved to the northeast, meeting sporadic resistance. The 22nd Infantry attacked across canal at 1505 and moved to objective after meeting moderate resistance.

29 AUGUST 1944—D+84: Representative from G1 Section accompanied the Commanding General to Paris to attend ceremony officially marking the liberation of the city. Again enemy front lines did not exist as such. Our units were as far as Le Mesnil Amelot—Dammartin and

Montgé. The defensive positions used by the enemy were mostly dug in to permit good fields of fire along the main routes to the north and northeast. Enemy tanks continued to operate in small groups.

The 8th Infantry conducted vigorous patrolling during the night covering the area along Canal de l'Ourcq. The 1st Battalion moved and closed in vicinity of Courtrey at 0915 and again moved. The 2nd Battalion and 3rd Battalion attacked at 1000 and moved forward. At 1400, both 1st and 2nd Battalions met strong resistance in the vicinity of Mitry-Mory, overcame resistance, and reached objectives at 2230.

The 12th Infantry conducted vigorous patrolling around Claye Souilly during the night. The 3rd Battalion reached Messy at 1315 reporting enemy retreating. The 2nd Battalion met light resistance at Charny. The 22nd Infantry reached Villepinte at 1700, consolidated and outposted around the town. The 3rd Battalion mopped up opposition and moved to Tremblay les Germease (?) arriving at 1430. The 4th Reconnaissance Troop moved at 0700 to the east, encountered enemy and fighting resulted in the killing of many enemy and the capture of a large number of prisoners. Troop went into bivouac in the vicinity of Belleville at 2130.

30 AUGUST 1944—D+85: Our troops advanced with little opposition to the general line La Montagne—Ormoy—Villers—Levignen. The enemy depended on blown bridges to delay our pursuit. The 8th Infantry conducted vigorous patrols during the night and at 0900 continued the attack to the northeast. At 2010 all elements had closed without opposition in the vicinity of La Montagne. The 12th Infantry conducted vigorous patrolling during the night and at 0900 attacked to the northeast. At 2000, it closed in the vicinity of Bois du Roy, having made no contact with the enemy. The 22nd Infantry did the same and at the close of the day it occupied positions in the vicinity of Ermenonville. (Editor's note from Bob: this was my first birthday, you can see that I don't remember WWII, just love to study our history).

31 AUGUST 1944—D+86: Our troops met steady delaying action by scattered infantry, antitank, and artillery fire. Considerable fire was received late in the day from the woods southwest of Pierrefonds-Les-Rains. Our forward elements reached the general line Palesne—Villers-Cotterêts. Intermittent 75 mm artillery fire was reported. The 8th Infantry continued its advance behind the 5th Armored Division and was engaged on the left by the enemy well prepared in the woods. CT 8 dug in for the night at 2100. The 12th Infantry continued behind armor without resistance and stopped at 1715. The 22nd Infantry remained first in assembly area and entrucked at 1800, the plan being to advance after the 5th Armored Division and to secure bridgehead along the Aisne river. Due to limited progress of armor, the Regiment closed in assembly area at 2110. The 4th Engineer Combat Battalion moved bridging material forward.

Notes about logistics: The shortage of gasoline had become critical by the end of the month. Replacement of vehicular losses became increasingly difficult. The evacuation of casualties was handled in a most expeditious manner.

CASUALTIES FOR AUGUST 1944

Killed or died of injuries: 20 Officers, 257 Enlisted Men

Missing: 1 Officer, 51 Enlisted Men

Seriously wounded or injured: 34 Officers, 623 Enlisted Men

Slightly wounded or injured: 34 Officers, 575 Enlisted Men

Total casualties: 1,595

Prisoners captured: 1,236.

CUMULATIVE CASUALTIES SINCE D-DAY JUNE 6, 1944

Killed or died of injuries: 153 Officers, 1,956 Enlisted Men

Total casualties: 10,441 (this equals approximately 65% of 4ID strength on D-Day)

From **War Stories Volume II: Paris to VE Day**:

Robert Gast, Warsaw, IN
Companies B and C, 1st Battalion, 12th Infantry Regiment
The Tankers Shared

The so-called mad dash from Paris to the Siegfried Line was really not a dash. It was a combination of walking, riding trucks, and riding tanks. I thought that riding tanks was one of the most memorable experiences of the war. The officers and men of the armored unit attached to us were great people. They got a big kick out of waving good-bye to us when they closed the hatch. They were always willing to share some of the things they had that seemed like luxuries to us — things like their rations, a razor, and even a tooth brush.

From **History of the 22nd Infantry Regiment in WWII** *by Chaplain Bill Boice:*

We knew that beyond the borders of France and across Belgium there lay the West Wall, Siegfried, mighty warrior, symbol of the hope and armed might of a determined enemy who had first battled for a world and was now at bay, fighting for his own existence.

Thus the Fourth Infantry Division was among the first in Paris. It was disconcerting to see newsreels released for American viewing of the French Second Armored Division under General Leclerc given credit for the liberation of Paris. We understood the political and propaganda value, but it still rankled Double Deucers to know the Famous Fourth had been part of the first in Paris, fighting for the liberation of that proud city, only to have it credited to French troops.

Immediately upon arrival at the assembly area, powerful reconnaissance patrols were sent out to the northeast, and the First and Second Battalions prepared to attack abreast. The patrols ascertained that further resistance to the objective was slight.

The scheme of attack was for one company from each of the assault battalions to travel motorized to the vicinity of their respective battalion objectives, then to detruck and continue afoot. By midnight the objectives were secured. The remainder of the regiment quickly staged forward with the Third Battalion in position to assist either battalion.

Combat in the northeast Paris environ near St. Germain continued the next day with CT 22 securing a suitable 'jump-off' line for the attack on the 28th of August. Early morning patrols reported that there was indicated enemy activity all along the regimental front. The First Battalion consolidated its positions and tied in with the Second Battalion on its right. Contact with the enemy was general throughout the day. Heavy artillery and mortar concentrations were fired upon located enemy positions. The Third Battalion remained in reserve, so located that it might aid either of the other battalions or Combat Team 8 on the right. During the night, extensive patrolling was carried out.

In compliance with orders, the Combat Team attacked on the left flank of the Fourth Division on the 29th. The Second and Third Battalions moved abreast, the Second Battalion on the right. The First Battalion formed the Combat Team reserve. A highly coordinated attack was made, and the objective, Le Mesnil Amelot, was secured by dark. To carry out this five mile advance, the Regimental Commander previously established a series of intermediate objectives and echeloned the attacking forces to the right.

Negative results were obtained from reconnaissance patrols the night of the 29-30th of August. During the day, CT 22 reverted to Division reserve and followed to the left rear of CT 8, protecting the Division left flank.

On the 31st of August, the regiment was to move via Nanteuil Le Haudouin--Ormoy Villers and to relieve elements of the Fifth Armored Division in securing a bridgehead across the Aisne River. CT 22 completed the motor march of almost nineteen miles without enemy contact, closing in an assembly area in the vicinity of Vez by nightfall.

From **Diary of Swede Henley**—*used with permission of his daughters:*

28 AUGUST: In position near Gargan. Received orders for one Company to clean out woods going into town of Villepinte and town also at 1800. 2 tanks attached. Attack jumped off and after good fight was started, the Colonel sent 2 SP TDs guns into action to knock down house when MG was firing. K Co. reached objective at 2200. Rescued 4 U.S. pilots who were shot down 3 weeks before.

29 AUGUST: Ordered to continue attack at 1000. Vintepinte fell at 1100 and attack on toward Tremble des Genessu. I Co. passed thru K Co. and captured town at 1430 (152 prisoners). L Co. passed thru I Co. to take high ground NE of Trembley and then on to town of Le Mesnil Amelot. Heavy rain slowed down operations. L Co. attack on town slowed down by MG fire. K Co. thrown in on left flank now with platoon of TDs. Town in our hands at dark.
- Bn CP set up in home where German headquarters were the night before. Clean sheets—running water with Johnnie.

30 AUGUST: Received orders at 1800 to move to new location at Ermenonville. Bn closed in by dark.

31 AUGUST: Left Ermenonville and moved into Ossy area at Bonnevil

Chaplain Knapp

Flag waving

Soldier with girl

4ID Troops Riding With Lady Through Paris

SEPTEMBER 1944

4ID IN BELGIUM AND GERMANY FIRST — ALLIES TO PENETRATE SIEGFRIED LINE

This week is characterized by the 4ID in hot pursuit of the Germans as they withdrew from France, into Belgium, and on back to their own homeland to stand and defend at the vaunted Siegfried Line, just inside the German border. Next, we will see that the 4ID attains another first in WWII — the first Allied unit to reach German soil.

Stay tuned, the war is, sadly, far from over. We have eight months of hard fighting ahead of us.

1 SEPTEMBER 1944 — D+87: Enemy withdrew rapidly, and advance was so rapid that front lines did not exist. The 4th Infantry Division continued to advance to the northeast. The 8th Infantry with the 29th FA attacked to clear the woods along the road Morienbal-Berneuil-s-Aisne, seize crossings over the Aisne river, build a class 40 bridge and continue to advance. Task Force Taylor consisting of Task Force Burton (CC "A" 5th Armored Division), CT 22, 747th Tank Battalion and 4th Reconnaissance Troop attacked and met resistance of small arms and mortar fire at crossroads west of Coucy-le-Chauffrique and just south of Chauny. As a result of these two engagements, column was held up 2 1/2 hours. At 1530, leading elements consisting of Reconnaissance Troop, TF B and 1st Bn 22nd Infantry reduced resistance and continued on original route while remaining elements reversed their direction and used a parallel route. Task Force Regnier consisting of CC "A" 5th Armored Division, CT 12 and 70th Tank Battalion (less Co A) attacked but due to troubles encountered in traffic control and preparation and securing river crossings, the task force was dissolved at 1400 and elements broken in two parts. CT 12 secured crossings of the Aisne river and continued its advance.

2 SEPTEMBER 1944—D+88: Enemy front lines still did not exist. The enemy resisted our advance with road blocks, demolished bridges, and strong points occupied by infantry, generally organized in the outskirts of key towns. The 4th Infantry Division (reinforced) continued its advance to the north. The advance was halted at 1800 by order of the CG V Corps. The 8th Infantry and attached companies en-trucked at 0700 and followed the CC A 5th Armored Division at 0805. Good progress was made until 1205 when leading elements were held up by a destroyed bridge. Construction was started at 1500 and head of column crossed at 1745. Progress was fair thereafter. The 12th Infantry with attached units continued its advance at 0730. At 1030 these units were delayed due to a destroyed bridge and trouble experienced bringing up bridging materials. The bridge was made crossable at 1600 and thereafter good progress was made with no resistance reported. Task Force Taylor made good progress throughout the day against moderate resistance. At 1735 Task Force was ordered to halt the advance vicinity of Landrecies and protect the right flank. The 377th AA Artillery engaged eleven flying bombs at 0530 and one of them was heard to explode.

3 SEPTEMBER 1944—D+89: The enemy occupied and defended hastily constructed strong points with groups of disorganized personnel withdrawing into Belgium. Although the enemy was poorly organized and equipped, the resistance was steady and determined. The 4th Infantry Division secured crossings of the Saint Quentin Canal and Canal de la Sambre. The 8th Infantry proceeded to Wassigny by motor to open main supply route for TF Taylor, moved at 1030, advanced rapidly and seized objective at 1545 after meeting only slight scattered enemy resistance. The 12th Infantry, on orders, halted further advance, secured river crossings and at 2050 was alerted to move to the south and east. TF Taylor in two columns continued the advance against enemy resistance and made contact at 1800 with the 8th Infantry vicinity Wassigny.

4 SEPTEMBER 1944—D+90: Scattered groups of enemy attempted to prevent our forces from advancing across the Meuse river. However the 102nd Cavalry operating in conjunction with the 4th Infantry Division held the bridges at Vireux, Haybes and Montherne. Small, disorganized detachments of enemy were mopped up in the vicinity of Landrecies. Considerable confusion caused most groups of enemy to surrender after offering very little or no resistance. The 4th Infantry Division remained in position, conducted patrols, and prepared for movement east. The 8th and 12th Infantry conducted patrolling on their flanks and cleared area of enemy. The 2nd Battalion 22nd Infantry attached to 102nd Cavalry Group, began movement at 0730 and contact was completed at 1400 at Brunehamel. Remainder of the Combat Team remained in position to prevent enemy infiltration and completed mop-up of Foret d'Hormal.

5 SEPTEMBER 1944—D+91: The enemy continued to collect stragglers and remnants of retreating units to occupy hasty defensive positions. Enemy tanks were reported but no action was initiated by them. The 4th Infantry Division moved by motor to vicinity Foret d'Ardennes and secured crossings of the Meuse river. CT 8 moved by motor commencing 0730 by way of Arreux to seize and secure crossings of the Meuse river. At 1630 bridge over the Meuse had been secured. CT 12 moved by motor commencing 0800 by way of Roccroi and by 1730 crossings were secured. CT 22 remained on previous mission of cleaning up small pockets of resistance in area north and northwest of Wassigny.

6 SEPTEMBER 1944—D+92: Increasing resistance was encountered in the vicinity of Willerzie and Rienne, Belgium. The enemy took advantage of the rugged terrain which was extremely favorable for fighting a delaying action. Felled trees across the roads combined with booby traps and teller mines were numerous. An infantry force mounted on eleven half-tracks supported by five light tanks fought a rear guard action along the highways running east and west through Willerzie, Rienne, and Godinne. This force utilized towns in settling up its defense and withdrew when our troops attacked in force. The 4th Infantry Division continued its advance to the east, meeting and overcoming pockets of enemy resistance, and maintaining contact with VII Corps on the left and the 5th Armored Division on the right. Shortage of gasoline and unfavorable terrain hampered the advance. The 3rd Battalion 8th Infantry met heavy resistance at 1520. The 12th Infantry crossed Hanille river by foot bridges. The 22nd Infantry remained in area to protect VII Corps boundary from enemy infiltration and its 1st Battalion cleared the Bois de Hazelles.

7 SEPTEMBER 1944—D+93: Strong delaying forces at all road centers and towns defended road blocks, strong points, and destroyed bridges, employing rear guard patrols mounted in tanks and armored cars together with infantry armed with small arms and antitank guns. Characteristic of enemy action was the attempted defense of Wellin. The greatest obstacles to a speedy advance remained unfavorable terrain, destroyed bridges, and shortage of gasoline. CT 8 moved consistently forward throughout the day, meeting scattered resistance. CT 12 continued the attack at 0800 and its 1st Battalion reached Chanly at 1935. CT 22 released from prior mission, began movement east at 1000, closed in new area in the vicinity of Graide and was assigned as division reserve.

*This story comes from Volume II of my War Stories series — **War Stories Volume II: Paris to VE Day:***

Morris L. Harvey (Deceased), Benton, KY
Company M, 3rd Battalion, 22nd Infantry Regiment
A Story Worth Preserving — As told to his son, Kerry Harvey

This is the story of my father's World War II combat experiences, told mostly in his own words. It is a story worth preserving. In those days, he was known as Private First Class Morris L. Harvey.

Morris: After we left Paris, we started chasing the German Army again the rest of the way through France and most of Belgium. When we finally caught up with them, we couldn't let them go.

Kerry: Were there any battles during that time?

Morris: Like I said, there were one-day or two-day actions at a time. Then you would move again. My job was machine gunner on a lead jeep. My jeep was out front all the time to make sure nobody was ambushed. We were there to draw fire. If anybody was going to be ambushed it was going to be our jeep. It was kind of a nervous time. A time or two we got too far ahead and ran into Germans with nobody close enough to help. We would just have to turn tail and run and hope we got out all right. Finally, one day in September, our lieutenant said, "Hey Y'all, come up here, I want to show you something." I wasn't really interested in anything he had to show to me, but I didn't have much choice. I went up the hill, and he handed me his field glasses. I couldn't see anything but trees and the like for a while. Then I saw a lot of German pillboxes in a fortified line. That kind of made your heart drop. That was the Siegfried Line.

Kerry: What was the Siegfried Line?

Morris: That was a defensive line along the German border that was supposed to be impregnable. It was built out of concrete block, reinforced pillboxes, and they were about half buried in the ground. They were painted green like the woods, and they were hard to see. The 4th Infantry Division made the first breach in the Siegfried Line. We were on German soil, and we were the first American troops across the German frontier...

From Swede Henley's Diary—used with permission from his daughters...

1 SEPTEMBER 1944: Plans changed. Orders received to move out for Southern Belgium. Bn crossed IP 0830 following 1st Bn. After moving about 25 miles, found enemy in force. 1st Bn committed the remainder of RCT—moved over to Lan and then north. Bridge blown at Lan. Held column up for night. Bn coiled up for night. Rain set in again.
- Saw buzz bombs in flight. They really lit up whole sky and sounded
- like 2 cylinder outboard motors skipping.
- Col. Lanham wants to win the war all by himself. *
- Tommy Harrison still stuttering—smoking—and has the crud.

2 SEPTEMBER: Attached jumped off again 0930 and advanced and established bridge head across canal at Lancerie (K Co. and Bn of tanks). Orders received to hold up advance.
- Kraut hunting was really good—loot was awful good.

3 SEPTEMBER: Bn crossed river and started the attack on woods west of Lancer ie—I Co. on left and L Co. on right. Ran into MG and mortar fire. We poured mortar, artillery on them. Called for air support—80 minutes Air Corps came in and annihilated horse and wagon train. The worst scene yet...the dead horses, wagons and equipment scattered all over the road for about a mile. Jerry took off across fields, woods and everywhere. Mounted "L" Co. on tanks and took off after them. Rounded up approximately 350 prisoners. Called it "quits" for the day and looked for a place to sleep.

- Champagne supply still in good shape.
- Looting good.
- Kraut hunting at its best.

4 SEPTEMBER: Ordered to patrol from Lancerie north to Jenlain. Took off in 2 columns 5 miles apart and returned at 1600 with 77 prisoners. Mostly rift-raft left behind. Alerted for 90 mile move in the morning.

5 SEPTEMBER: Possible move called off and extensive patrolling started again to the north. Captured more prisoners. Received alert order for possible move to the east at 0800 in the morning.

6 SEPTEMBER: Orders cancelled at 0700. Received warning order for move at 1000 tomorrow morning.

7 SEPTEMBER: Moved out at 1030. Route: Pommerevil, Catillion, Le Nouvoir, La Capelle, Hirson, Bellevoe, Tarzy, Rocroi, Fumay, Hargnie, Cross border into Belgium, Willerzie, Gedinne, Bievre, Graioe, Our bivouac for further orders.

From Chaplain Bill Boice's **History of the 22nd Infantry Regiment in World War II:**
THE RACE TO THE SIEGFRIED LINE – THROUGH FRANCE

With the fall of Paris, it was evident the major portion of the German army would move hastily out of France, organizing its defense behind the vaunted Siegfried Line.

Much Nazi propaganda centered around the Siegfried Line. It was termed "formidable," "impregnable" and careful preparations were made by the Allied Command as their armies moved through France toward the German fatherland.

Time was a vital factor, and American troops moved swiftly to keep heavy pressure against the German army.

Before dawn on 1 September, the 22nd Combat Team was alerted for a move and shortly thereafter Brig. General George A. Taylor, Assistant Division Commander, arrived at the Regimental Command Post at Chateau Vez.

In two short hours, Task Force 'Taylor' was formed, plans originated, and attachments effected. The missions of the Task Force were to move northward with all possible speed through a designated zone of action, by-passing all points of resistance if possible, and to reach the Corps objective in Belgium east of Valenciennes by dark, 3 September. This distance approximated ninety miles. Because the main bridge at Soissons which was in VII Corps sector had to be cleared by 1200, the Task Force was forced to move initially with great rapidity.

The first element crossed the IP at 0800 hours on the 1st to follow the route Soissons, Crecy, Guise, Landrecies, to the vicinity of Valencience. A rapid, uncontested march placed Task Force 'Taylor' in Soissons by 1100.

Just north of Soissons a deviation was made in the original route so that Combat Command 'Burton' could join the Task Force from a position near Epagny. The First Battalion, led by Major Latimer, Bn. Commander, crossed the highway bridge and then turned left on a dirt trail along the north bank of the river to Pommiers, then turned north to Epahny. General Taylor had prescribed this route with the intention of putting CT 22 in behind Task Force 'Burton' which he knew to be in the general vicinity of Epagny. As a result of this movement, the use of the Pommiers bridge by any other column was effectively blocked.

At 1615, the head of the column met enemy resistance just north of Folembray. Because here there was a narrow road through the woods between banks, the tanks were unable to maneuver. Shortly afterward, Colonel Lanham came to the front and, seeing the situation, immediately returned to the CP at Bonne Maison farm (2 miles northeast of Epagny) and obtained General Taylor's approval of a plan to break the Task Force into two columns. Task Force 'Burton,' the Fourth Recon Troops, and First Battalion, Twenty-Second, would be left under the command of Lt. Colonel Ruggles, Executive Officer of the Twenty-Second, and would proceed to the north by the best available route.

Fit to Fight

The remainder of the force would move by better roads farther east. Due to the confused disposition of the column, which was spread over the various roads between Epagny and Soissons, it was a difficult problem to get underway. Colonel Lanham immediately gave orders to break the column just south of Epagny and just off the highway running north from Soissons at the point where it turned into the secondary road to Epagny; then to have the 747th Tank Bn., which at that time was on the road south of Pont. St. Mard, take the lead and coil the column in the fields to the east until they had cleared the road south to Epagny and the secondary road running east from Epagny.

When this was accomplished, the 747th Tank Bn. then led the march back down the road to Epagny and the secondary road through Bagnaeus and Juvigny to the highway, thence north up the highway, (the highway bridge over the canal was intact), and to la Fere. The 747th Tank Bn. was followed in order by 2nd Bn. of the Twenty-Second, Third Battalion of the Twenty-Second, and the rest of the Combat Team.

This maneuver proceeded rapidly and without a hitch, and by about 1900 the head of the column had reached the bank of the Oise River of la Fere. There was one point on the road to la Fere where the road went through an archway which was too narrow for the M-10's to pass. This was the only difficulty encountered between Epagny and la Fere, but it caused no delay since the M-10's were immediately run off the road and the column continued.

At la Fere the bridge was out, causing the column to turn southeast to Laon thence north to Crecy. A reconnaissance detachment which had been sent ahead to investigate the bridge at Crecy came under fire from the far bank, by a small enemy force, which was disbursed by 2300. However, the bridge was blown, and no other crossing could be found nearby. The column coiled in the fields and waited for the engineers to construct a new bridge.

By dark the west column had eliminated the resistance north of Folembray, taking about 30 prisoners. This column then continued to the Oise River but found the bridge at Chauny out. Col. Ruggles then turned east along the south bank of the river seeking a crossing. As all bridge crossings to the north were destroyed, the column proceeded in the dark through St. Gobain, Danizy, Reinies, and Pouilly. This column joined the East column just south of Crecy at dawn, the 2nd of September.

By about 0830, September 2nd, the new bridge had been constructed by the engineers, and Task Force resumed the advance to the north in a single column. Only occasional slight contact with the enemy occurred until the Sambre River was reached there was a brief halt near Foucouxy while Tank Destroyers were brought up to knock out a German Mark V tank; several German vehicles were destroyed at le Herie; and a wagon column was destroyed a mile north of Guise. At Iron River, the column again split, Col. Ruggles taking Task Force "Burton" and the 1st Battalion, 22nd and turning west on the road to le Cateau. This column had a skirmish at Hannapes where they secured the Sambre Canal bridge before it could be destroyed, even though it had been prepared for demolition. This force met other small enemy forces near Wassigny and Ribeauville.

The east column continued to Landrecies meeting only occasional small groups of the enemy. At Landrecies the column found the main bridge over the Sambre River destroyed. (The bridge had been completely blown up with unusually heavy charges). Within 30 minutes an old railroad bridge (trestle) was improved sufficiently to be used. The head of the two columns crossed and continued several miles north of Landrecies and surprised an enemy column, inflicting extremely heavy losses.

Early in the evening on September the 2nd, orders were received to halt the advance. The east column was to bivouac on the south side of the canal, excepting the 747th Tank Bn., Company K, Twenty-Second Infantry, and the 4th Recon. Troop, which had already crossed. These latter units held a defensive position around Landrecies to protect the crossing. This position was outposted by the 4th Recon. Troop which, during the night, contacted the enemy, apparently trying to move to the east. The Recon. outpost knocked out two German sedans and a self-propelled gun. The west column bivouacked for the night around the crossroad just north of Ribeauville.

During the advance on 2 September, the Task Force had been moving on one of the main routes of retreat of the enemy. In addition to occasional German vehicles overtaken and destroyed on the road, many small groups of German soldiers fled into the fields as our column came by. In some cases, these groups fired on the column, in others the Germans surrendered. A considerable number of prisoners were picked up in this manner during the day and were turned over to the Free French of the Interior.

During the night, an order was received to move the Task Force into an assembly area in the vicinity of Pommereuil, between Landrecies and la Cateau. At 0800 3 September, the east column moved toward Pommereuil. Our planes could be seen attacking something on the road not far ahead. When the column reached it, this proved to be a German column consisting of many more assorted motor vehicles and at least 40 horse-drawn vehicles, with infantry of about a regiment strength. Many of the vehicles had already been destroyed by the air attack; the remainder were knocked out by the Task Force. The German infantry of the column had deployed and put up a fight which was not finished until sometime in the afternoon. When it was over, some 200 or 300 prisoners had been taken and the rest of the enemy killed. There was so much destroyed enemy equipment on the road that it was necessary to use a bulldozer to clear it.

Meantime, the west column had not received the order to assemble until about noon. They then moved to Pommereuil, passing southeast of la Cateau. By 1700 the entire Task Force had closed in the assembly area. The area Landrecies --le Cateau--Poix was mopped up during that night and the next two days. The Recon Troop was given the mission of cleaning out the western portion of Foret de Normal. Several hundred prisoners were taken during the night and still more were taken throughout the next two days. The Task Force processed 1300 prisoners taken in the le Cateau-Landrecies area in addition to several hundred which had been taken on the march and turned over then to the FFI. The enemy was evidently greatly confused in the le Cateau--Landrecies area and during the night of 3 September there were cases in which Germans started digging in close by our units.

General Taylor had a bullet pass through the side of his jacket, just grazing his skin, while he was standing on the railroad bridge at Landrecies. This same bullet had first passed through Colonel Lanham's sleeve.

At la Groise when the column halted, a gasoline truck, methodically keeping his 50-yard distance, came to a stop in the middle of a road junction. Within a few minutes an enemy gun, a considerable distance away on a side road fired one round which hit the truck squarely and blew it up, killing the driver and another man. A few minutes later, while the remains of the gasoline truck were burning fiercely, a terrific explosion occurred; the 22nd Infantry had blown up a German ammunition dump nearby, but on the explosion, everyone ducked for cover. A few minutes later a Frenchman dashed out of a house near the road junction, snatched the tri-color which was stuck in the fence, and disappeared into the house with it.

At 0300 hours the 4th of September, a warning order was received from Headquarters 4th Infantry Division to alert a reinforced battalion to move at daylight to Brunehamel and there report to the 102nd Cavalry Group, to which it was to become attached upon arrival. The 1st Battalion was the designated unit and they moved out in the early dawn. Later that morning, the Task Force was disbanded. The balance of the Regiment continued mopping up operations that day and through the night.

Following up the northward drive, which had driven the Germans well back, the units prepared to push on through Belgium and into the Siegfried Line. Everyone believed that now it would be only a matter of a few weeks before the retreating German armies would be forced to surrender. Things were going well for the 22nd Regiment—remarkable gains had been made since Paris, and casualties were almost nil.

At night, it was still possible for artillery flashes to be seen from the positions of the 44th Field Artillery Battalion supporting the 22nd. Since leaving Paris, however, the 44th had fired only fifty rounds of ammunition.

On the morning of September 7th, movement orders were received from 4th Infantry Division Headquarters for the Combat Team to rejoin the Division in Belgium. Leading elements crossed the IP south of Pommereuil before noon. In accordance with orders, the Combat Team proceeded to Graide, Belgium, some eighty-five miles, closing in before dark. Upon arrival, the Combat Team was placed in Division reserve to secure the flanks of the Division with patrols. These past few days had been relatively easy, and the officers and men were enjoying a period of appreciated relaxation.

8 SEP 1944 TO 14 SEP 1944 – D+94 TO D+100

8 SEPTEMBER 1944—D+94: Showing improvement in its coordination of defense of road blocks and strong points, the enemy continued to resist the advance of the 4th Infantry Division. Armored patrols were maintained between these points and strategically emplaced antitank guns continually harassed the advance of our armor. As previously, resistance from these points ceased when our units pressed the attack in force. The 4th Infantry Division continued its advance, secured assigned objectives, and prepared to resume the attack to the Luxembourg-German border. CT 8 advanced throughout the day against a stubborn rear guard action. CT 12 met moderate enemy resistance and by 1917 its 2nd Battalion was approaching its objective in the vicinity of Saint Hubert. CT 22 protected the flanks of the division by patrols and screening for enemy pockets of resistance behind the two other CTs and moved in the late afternoon to vicinity of Paliseul. A superior job was accomplished by the 102nd Cavalry Reconnaissance Group.

9 SEPTEMBER 1944—D+95: Enemy delaying forces were fighting a stiff rear guard action with elite troops. Enemy tanks continued to operate in small groups as contact patrols between the various defense installations along our axis of advance. CT 8 resumed the attack at 0900, reached the first objective at 1200 and moved to second objective to secure important road junctions by seizing and organizing commanding terrain. This was done at the end of the day. CT 12 attacked at 0900, continuing to advance slowly against rear guard action including numerous road blocks and a destroyed bridge. CT 22 moved by motor at 1200 to pass through the 8th Infantry.

10 SEPTEMBER 1944—D+96: Enemy continued its stubborn delaying action. Enemy artillery showed a sharp increase during the period. The 4th Infantry Division continued the advance preparatory to assembling before launching a coordinated attack on the West Wall.

11 SEPTEMBER 1944—D+97: The enemy continued its determined defense. **A 22nd Infantry Regiment patrol crossed the German border, vicinity of Elcherath at 2120 and procured among other things, a package of German soil prior to returning.** The 8th Infantry with same attachments as before, resumed the attack at 0900 and by 1200, reached the intermediate objective. The Combat Team (motorized) moved out at 1320 to its final objective south of Bovigny and reached it by 1800. The 2nd Bn moved to the high ground to protect the right flank of the division and at the end of the day, was still en-route. The 12th Infantry with its same attachments continued the advance and at 0900, removing unmanned roadblock en-route, had encountered the enemy. By 2000, all battalions were forcing crossings of the Salm river against enemy opposition. The 22nd Infantry continued its advance at 0900 and by 1800, the entire Combat Team had closed in its assigned area after having overcome the enemy but still maintaining contact with it by dispatching patrols to the German border.

On September 11, 1944, elements of the 4th Infantry Division (22nd Infantry Regiment) became the first Allied troops to move into Germany—a proud moment among many in our long and distinguished history.

12 SEPTEMBER 1944—D+98: Abandoning for the most part the practice of installing road blocks, the enemy resorted to a delaying action and its major part was hurriedly withdrawing to the security of the Siegfried defenses. Enemy was engaged at St Vith. The 4th Infantry Division dispatched reconnaissance and combat patrols across the German border and subsequently continued its advance. CT 8 closed in assembly area vicinity of Hill 520 at 0125 and remained there throughout the day. CT 12 continued the advance at 0800 to the east. Intermediate objectives were secured by the 1st and 2nd Bn at 2045 and the 3rd Bn at 2115 vicinity of St Vith. CT 22 conducted vigorous patrolling during the night and at 1400 initiated movement, securing objectives in the vicinity of Elcherath by 2030.

13 SEPTEMBER 1944—D+99: A considerable increase in the size and amount of artillery supported the delaying action of enemy troops occupying hastily built dug-in positions. Enemy planes were again over the 4th Infantry Division sector, but as usual no aggressive action was taken by them. The 8th Infantry in division reserve moved forward behind CT 12 and 22. The 12th Infantry sent patrols at 0800 with the main body following at 1000. The CT continued the advance throughout the afternoon against light rear guard action of the enemy and by 1800 reached its objectives. The 22nd Infantry proceeded the same way and objectives were secured and consolidated prior to dark against light resistance.

14 SEPTEMBER 1944—D+100: The enemy dug in and occupied hasty emplacements west of the Siegfried Line. Permanent installations of reinforced concrete were manned. Many additional emplacements were encountered in addition of the pillboxes, bunkers, and guns emplacements mentioned on the defense overprint. Heavy concentration of fires of all calibers were brought to bear on our assaulting forces.

The 4th Infantry Division continued against mounting resistance, successfully penetrated the defenses of the Siegfried Line in four localities and prepared to exploit those gains. The 2nd Battalion CT 8 was ordered to move by motor to the vicinity of Scheenberg to relieve the 3rd Bn 12th Infantry. At 1530 the remainder of the CT commenced movement to the vicinity of Radscheid, closing at 1930. Positions were then secured for the night. The 12th Infantry dispatched patrols of platoon strength to the east during the night. The 1st and 2nd Battalion moved out at 1010 and intermittent artillery and mortar fire was encountered. Vehicular movement was hampered by a virtually impassable and meager network of muddy roads. Cross country movement was impeded by the heavily wooded terrain. Complete penetration of the Siegfried Line was made by 1300. The 22nd Infantry sent reconnaissance patrols during the night and penetrated the Siegfried Line at two points. The penetration was made by heavy fighting against small arms fire, mortar fire, antiaircraft fire, and 88's. Many more pillboxes were encountered than foreseen and the enemy, SS troops included, refused to surrender until wounded or blasted from its forts.

From **War Stories Volume II: Paris to VE Day…**

Morris L. Harvey (Deceased), Benton, KY
Company M, 3rd Battalion, 22nd Infantry Regiment

This is a continuation of the story I started above…
A Story Worth Preserving—As told to his son, Kerry Harvey

Kerry: How did you manage to get across the Siegfried Line?

Morris: It was just a matter of taking one pillbox at a time. We soon found out you couldn't take them from the front. They all had a crossfire in front of them and we had to get through that.

Kerry: What do you mean crossfire?

Morris: One covered the other one. In front, you got fire from that pillbox, and then there was one on each side of you shooting at you from both sides. My job was to fire into that pillbox. (In and around it to keep any Germans pinned down and to keep their heads down while riflemen went in.) We first tried blowing the steel doors off them with bangalore torpedoes. Sometimes that would work and sometimes it would not. We used satchel charges and everything. We would get around behind them and either kill them, run them off, or take prisoners. The riflemen got on top of the pillboxes. They couldn't hurt us when we were on top of them, and we could throw hand grenades in the gun slits. We could eventually find something to blow the door off, but usually after a few hand grenades and a couple of explosions on the door, they would come out with their hands up.

Kerry: So, you were not on the jeep when doing that?

Morris: No. That was strictly on foot, packing that gun on your back.

Kerry: How was your gun set up? How many people did it take to serve the gun?

Morris: There were seven men in a machine gun squad. There was a first gunner, a second gunner, and five ammunition bearers. Their job was to keep ammunition to the gun. A belt of ammunition had 250 rounds, and every fourth round was a tracer. In my case—I don't know about other gunners—I never did use a sight. I used the tracer, and I had good depth perception. I could tell where I was shooting.

Kerry: You were the first gunner?

Morris: I was the first gunner.

Kerry: Do you remember who your second gunner was?

Morris: Some of them I never did even know by name; some of them didn't last long. I had several. I couldn't exactly say how many. I remember the first one because he was the first gunner when I joined the squad. When I joined the squad, he moved to second gunner, and I moved in as first gunner. He had been an ammunition bearer, and he didn't know much about shooting the gun; I had been trained for that. He was from New York City, New York. He was hit and I got another one.

Kerry: So the second gunner would be the guy in the hole with you?

Morris: Yes. He was the guy who fed the belt into the gun. Ammunition bearers brought the ammunition up, and I think each one of them carried maybe four boxes, which was 1000 rounds. I could burn a belt in about a minute.

Kerry: How many second gunners did you have?

Morris: One kid I remember joined me on the Siegfried Line. We had stopped because we had run out of food and ammunition. Everything was in short supply, and we had to stop. We were down to about half-strength. About half of our battalion had been killed or wounded and we weren't getting replacements.

We weren't getting any kind of supplies. We just dug in there for a couple of weeks. We dug a good hole and put logs and dirt on top of it and just sort of set up housekeeping. Some of the guys got out behind the lines, and we killed some deer. That was the first venison I ever ate. We sent it back to the kitchen, and they cleaned them and made hot venison sandwiches and sent them up. That was in the Ardennes Forest. They decided they wanted us to take an "armored" town called Brandscheid, and we had to pour fire into that town. I didn't know the name of most of the towns, but I knew the name of that one because it was an armored town, and we had a pretty good little fight over it.

Kerry: What does that mean, an armored town?

Morris: Well, it was just surrounded by pillboxes. There were pillboxes in it. We used chemical ordnance and dropped some phosphorous shells in there. A few months later, after the American Army was kicked out of Brandscheid, I came back and helped take it a second time. It was still glowing from the phosphorous they had dropped. I imagine the Germans got a hot seat over that."

Harold Blackwell, Mesa, AZ
Battery A, 377th Anti-Aircraft Artillery Battalion
We Got Real Brave

My first battery CP in Germany was near Bleialf—actually we were in an abandoned pillbox complex. I had a Lieutenant Campbell, who was fluent in German, and the German phone line was still working. We were surprised to realize that we were on a party line and hearing German troop movement information. Lieutenant Campbell, who passed away at age 88, listened carefully to the German orders and interjected counter commands at frequent intervals. This was typical GI sport, but it only lasted about fifteen minutes until the line went dead.

My jeep driver and I were on a short reconnaissance just north of Bleialf and heard noises like singing coming from a pillbox. We got real brave (or foolhardy) and crept up to the pillbox and tossed a grenade into an opening. We were doubly surprised to see about seven SS soldiers come tumbling out with their hands up. All seven had had a generous amount of Calvados or whatever. We covered them, disarmed them, and marched them in front of the jeep to the nearest prisoner of war compound. To this day, I still have a picture of the SS Lieutenant and kept his Luger and SS dagger.

P.S. I also was pleased to find my battery mentioned in Dr. Boice's history. Yes, we were attached to the 22nd Combat Team for eleven months. We got official credit for thirteen German planes shot down in the 22nd Infantry zone of operation. Of course, we thought we shot down a lot more. Ho-hum.

Emmett G. Ryan (Deceased), Apache Junction, AZ
Company B, 1st Battalion, 12th Infantry Regiment
Wounded in Action
As told to his daughter, Janice Bryson, Tolleson, Arizona

I was wounded twice during the European Campaign. The first time was at Mortain in August 1944. My wife has an article from the Arizona Republic in which I am quoted as saying to a reporter, "The Mortain fighting was the toughest part of the campaign. Large German Panzer Divisions were trying to split the Allied Armies by throwing everything at us."

I made the mistake of having the rear of my anatomy exposed to gunfire as I wasn't lying flat enough. Fortunately for me, my field glasses were in the way and the wound was not serious as the bullet was deflected. After resting about five days, I went back into the action. The medics weren't doing anything with the wound, and I couldn't sit down anyway. I figured I might as well be fighting.

The second time was a little more serious. Our unit was one of the first to smash into the Siegfried Line. I was leading my platoon through pillboxes and anti-tank obstacles when I was struck in the left shoulder with shrapnel. I walked back to the aid station, about a mile back. When I arrived, an officer asked for any wounded men who could sit up, to go as guards while taking the more seriously wounded back to a field hospital in a jeep. The Germans were trying to get back to Germany and would attack jeeps and steal them to drive back. I thought I was also going to the hospital, just acting as a guard along the way. It turned out we were going to another aid station. Patients were then being sent on to the hospital.

When we arrived at the camp, everyone was eating. One of the drivers from our Division recognized me and got me something to eat. I was really hurting by then and only wanted to rest. I looked for a tent and found one with no one else in there. I had no bed and no blankets. I was hurting so bad, and it was so bitter cold. I just lay down in the empty tent. I should have found a tent with other people for warmth. I woke up the next day and went to eat breakfast. An officer came up to me and asked why I had blood all over me. I explained to him how I happened to be there at the camp.

The officer told the MP to put me on the first ambulance going back to Bar Le Duc. A number of the wounded were being taken there. We stopped at a barracks somewhere along the way. There were about fifteen or twenty of us guys. We were given towels and told to go in and clean up. There was a pilot with us that had bad burns on one arm and shoulder from his plane catching fire. I had blood all over my back.

The pilot said, "If you wash my back, I'll wash yours."

It felt good to be clean for a change. For the seriously wounded guys, it was a true statement: If you made it to the aid stations, you would usually make it. The people there were really good.

I was operated on at Bar Le Duc and flown to England. Planes were dropping paratroopers and supplies into Holland. They would then land in other areas and take the wounded back. It wasn't a pleasant flight; I've never flown since. I was strapped onto a stretcher, and there were holes in the plane from anti-aircraft fire.

I spent three months in the hospital in Frome, England. When the Battle of the Bulge started, it wasn't long before all the NCOs and officers were sent back into action. I sure hated to go back. It hadn't bothered me on D-Day, but now I knew what it was really like. As we were heading into the battle area, I was afraid I wouldn't be assigned back to the 12th Infantry Regiment, so I hitched a ride over to them and rejoined the outfit.

Conrad "Frenchy" Adams, Gulfport, MS
Company E, 2nd Battalion, 8th Infantry Regiment
A Miracle in the Siegfried Line

As we went on towards Germany, we entered the Siegfried Line. One night, we were told to dig our foxhole near a fence. We started to dig and hit rocks. So my buddy and I backed up around ten feet and dug our foxhole. During the night, a German 88 hit exactly in the middle where we had been digging our foxhole. (Remember, I believe in miracles—that's another one.)

Robert Gast, Warsaw, IN
Companies B and C, 1st Battalion, 12th Infantry Regiment
An Unusual Thing Happened

My platoon was the second platoon from our battalion to enter the Siegfried Line. I was to contact the first platoon that had gone earlier and had not been heard from. We were very fortunate and stumbled onto a bunch of German soldiers that were caught completely by surprise. They surrendered without a shot being fired. This gave us the wrong idea as to what to expect from the enemy.

One very unusual thing happened. We were dug in and tied down and here comes another battalion attacking through us. I thought, my God, what are they doing? It wasn't long before they came running back to us. Another strategic withdrawal. A young lieutenant jumped into my hole with me. It was Bud Reed, a guy I knew at Indiana University and a good friend of my sister and brother-in-law.

NEWSPAPER ARTICLE – SIEGFRIED LINE – SEPTEMBER 24, 1944

An interesting article found in the archives is the following story, written by Henry T. Gorrell. The title, "Atlantan on First Patrol in Germany," indicates it may be from an Atlanta paper.
— *Bob Babcock*

WITH THE FOURTH INFANTRY DIVISION IN THE SCHNEE EIFEL, SEPT 24 (DELAYED) (UP)

The US Fourth Infantry Division, first American Army outfit to crack the Hindenburg Line at Meuse-Argonne in the last war and first to enter Paris in this one, also was first to penetrate Germany through the Siegfried Line in force, it was disclosed today.

Lieutenant C. M. Shugart, of Sioux City, IA, was the first United States infantry officer to lead a patrol in Nazi Germany, and three days later, the door to Germany was opened when Colonel Charles T. Lanham, a West Pointer from Washington, DC, led his 22nd Infantry Regiment in a gallant, daring charge through lines which had been considered impregnable.

Shugart's patrol crossed into Germany on September 11; Lanham's charge came on September 14. The men of the 4th Infantry Division might still be fighting hand-to-hand to breach the Siegfried Line had it not been for the tall, slim colonel's heroic dash.

PINNED DOWN

The 22nd Regiment had spearheaded a frontal attack against the formidable, six-foot-thick Siegfried pillboxes, but they soon found themselves on top of the fortifications with only rifles, while Germans inside had machine guns. At his command post, Lanham received a report over his field telephone: "We are pinned down by heavy fire…tank destroyers are unable to make any progress."

Later came an even gloomier report. "I'm afraid the men are falling…"

This last report had followed direct hits on our infantry tanks and tank destroyers, leaving the foremost Doughboys temporarily unsupported. Then, the field telephone went dead.

Lanham dropped the telephone and rushed forward as far as he could in his staff car. Accompanied by four men, one a French volunteer, he left the car and ran up the wooded hillside with bullets and shrapnel clipping the ground around his feet.

HOLLYWOOD SPECTACLE

Soon Lanham was among the invading infantrymen, shouting and singing at the top of his lungs, waving his .45 in the air and calling out his men by name as he waved them forward. The reaction was instantaneous. If the colonel could wade into the Germans, so could all the rest of them, and there followed a Hollywood spectacle of troops rushing forward to battle, singing and shouting as they passed the colonel.

Bypassing their colonel, the men of the 22nd Infantry stormed through the last Nazi bunkers and were shortly masters of the topmost heights of Schnee Eifel. The Siegfried Line had been breached.

It now was the colonel's duty to rejoin the main body of his troops, and he retraced his steps, followed by the Frenchman and the three members of his staff. They were fired upon from a bypassed bunker at a range of twelve feet. The colonel was unhurt, but the young Frenchman fell, mortally wounded in the stomach. Lanham bent over the youth and the youth whispered, "I'm dying, sir, but I'm glad to be dying here within the Siegfried Line after fighting the Germans on the soil of Germany."

He died as five German Storm Troopers exited the nearby pillbox by a secret door and again fired on the little group. The Americans opened fire, killed three of them, and wounded two others as they attempted to flee. Then a tank destroyer moved up and blasted away the steel doors of the pillbox and twenty Germans marched out with their hands up.

Lanham returned to his command post. With him on the gallant dash were Captain Howard C. Blazzard of Phoenix, Arizona; Captain Robert C. McLean, of Shelbyville, Tennessee; and Sergeant James C. Smith, of Tullahoma, Tennessee. Lanham is a native of Washington, where his wife lives and where his father is commissioner of the District of Columbia.

Lanham's charge was preceded by the patrol penetration into Germany of Shugart, who led his eight men across the frontier early on the night of September 11.

ATLANTAN ON PATROL

With Shugart were Sergeant Wallace W. Morton, of Indianapolis; Sergeant Paul C. Mercher of Kurtztown, Pennsylvania; Private First Class James C. Carney, of Taunton, MA; Private First Class Dennis O. Cain of 754 West Echo St NW, Atlanta; Private First Class Edward Reinert of St. Paul, Minnesota; Private First Class Arthur Peters, of Thoorp, Pennsylvania; Private First Class Joe A. Pachecosanto, of Domingo, New Mexico; and Private First Class Henry Weber, also of New Mexico.

The patrol's mission was to find a fording place across a river over which larger elements of the Fourth Infantry Division might follow.

Shugart beat a hasty retreat, but not before grabbing souvenirs, including a button off a German's coat and a helmet full of "sacred" Nazi soil, which he delivered to Major General Raymond O. Barton, of Ada, Oklahoma, commander of the Division.

Since the initial penetration, forward battalions of the Fourth, including one commanded by Lieutenant Colonel Charles Jackson, of Bell, California, have repelled successive German counterattacks aimed at recapturing Siegfried Line pillboxes in the Schnee Eifel where the Division opened the door to Germany proper about a week ago.

WITH HEMINGWAY

This correspondent hit the Normandy Beach with the Fourth Infantry Division on D-Day and was one of three correspondents with it on the entry into Germany, after it had blazed the path of the First Army from Paris through Northern France and Belgium. Among the three correspondents was author Ernest Hemingway, who is believed to be the first correspondent to enter Germany. I compared notes with him, and he convinced me that, with the Fourth Infantry Division, he entered Germany a full hour before tanks of an American armored division crossed the frontier at Rotgen in the vicinity of Aachen.

Among those who led the Fourth's assault troops into Germany were company commanders Lieutenant W. Wittkopf, of East St. Louis, IL, and Captain Glenn W. Thorne, of Morgantown, WV. The two were lead company commanders in Jackson's battalion, which effected the first complete breakthrough in the Siegfried Line where it was considered strongest, in the wooded heights of Schnee Eifel.

Tom Reid, Marietta, GA,
Cannon Company, 22nd Infantry Regiment and
Company I, 3rd Battalion, 22nd Infantry Regiment
First Troops on German Soil

Editor's Note from Bob: *I became good friends with Tom Reid during the last years of his life. I had the honor to be the speaker at his funeral when he died—a great American who served in WWII, Korea, and Vietnam, and retired as a Colonel.*

August 1944 for the 22nd Infantry ended with the triumphant entry into Paris on the 25th, followed by a rapid chase of the retreating German Army through Northern France and into Belgium.

The 22nd Infantry entered Belgium early in September and pursued the Wehrmacht relentlessly. The advance was on the order of ten to twenty miles per day. Some days we were motorized for the larger part of the trip. Towns and villages became a blur as the Germans chose to retreat, hindering our advance by roadblocks such as fallen trees and blown bridges, rather than making a stand.

All of this took a toll on the normal order of things. Rations were K-rations—three boxes, each of a different outer color for breakfast, lunch, and dinner. The "heat" was on the supply echelons to get food, ammo, water, and supplies forward. They did it through prodigious effort and teamwork by all.

On September 11, the 22nd Infantry Regiment entered Germany, the first troops on German soil, and on September 14 we penetrated the Siegfried Line of pillboxes and dragons' teeth in the vicinity of Bleialf and Brandscheid, just over the German border.

I was a first lieutenant at the time, serving as a forward observer for Cannon Company. In the Regiment at that time there was a Cannon Company equipped with six 105mm short-barreled howitzers with a maximum range of 6500 yards. This gave the Regiment immediate access to some firepower in addition to the artillery which was in direct support.

During this attack on the Siegfried Line, I was mostly with Company

I, 22nd Infantry, commanded by Captain Joe Samuels. He was still commanding the company after bringing it ashore on D-Day in Normandy some three months earlier.

Naturally, we had been moving much too fast for the bath units to catch up, and now that we were in the Siegfried Line, we were spread too thinly for units to rotate to the rear for baths or anything else.

September moved along, and in early October the 22nd moved northward to new positions. Thus, the month had come and gone, and my bath story for September 1944 is easy to tell—I didn't get one.

Peter Triolo, Pueblo, CO
HQ, 1st Battalion, 12th Infantry Regiment
You Won't Believe What We See

Large concrete underground bunkers and gun emplacements fortified the Siegfried Line. The bunkers were about twenty feet in diameter and ten feet deep in the ground. Only about two feet of concrete were above ground. They had one problem: they vented the bathrooms with a four-inch cast iron pipe. Rather than trying to capture them, we brought tanks up with steel blades and moved dirt over the top of the pillbox, covering it completely. Then we threw a string of dynamite down the pipe; that took care of the pillbox.

The second day we were on the Siegfried line, we got a call from one of our rifle companies on the radio. The message was, "Colonel Jackson, you won't believe what we see." There was a German officer with about fifty men marching up the road singing. They were a reserve unit that didn't even know we were there. Colonel Jackson ordered that we set a trap and capture them. When they brought the officer to headquarters, he demanded to know what we were doing in Germany. I'm sure we all laughed. They were sent back as prisoners.

Robert O. Babcock

From **Swede Henley Diary—used with permission of his daughters…**

8 SEPTEMBER: In position at Our—patrolling to east and northeast, just hunting Krauts. Bridge blown but we found a bypass. (Stayed in ex-German headquarters.) Received orders to move to Smuids. Moved by motor to Smuids. Saw electric lights for 1st time.

9 SEPTEMBER: Received orders to move out at 1530 to pass thru 8th Inf. and take Houffalize. Moved out with 7 TDs (tank destroyers) at 1530. Found bridge blown but bypassed it. Then ran into road block and bypassed it. Moved out again. Jeep patrol shot up—lost three jeeps. Stopped for night.

10 SEPTEMBER: Moved out again at 0730 for Houffalize. Moved along nicely after moving several road blocks. Found bridge blown—civilians rebuilt bridge in about 90 minutes. Jerry artillery gave us hell. Stayed in house about 3 miles north of Houffalize.

- The TDs and tanks spotted German convoy 2500 yards to north and gave them the fits.

11 SEPTEMBER: Moved out again at 0900 for German border. Caught jerry napping at Courtil. Kraut hunting good. He gave us artillery barrage—2nd to none. Took high ground east of Maldange (inside of German border of 1940).

12 SEPTEMBER: Jumped off at 1130 AM for action. German border. Crossed river into actual German border at 1730. Forded river as bridge was blown. Entered Hemmeres and Elcherath—my what a cold reception the civilians gave us. No more liberating towns—it's conquering now.

13 SEPTEMBER: Jumped off again at 0900 for high ground and cross road (Hill 557) one mile north of Bleialf. Move "L" Co. into Buchet at 2300.

14 SEPTEMBER: Attack Siegfried line at 1000 and penetrated it. 3rd Bn turned right and 1st Bn turned left. 2nd Bn in reserve. Fought pillbox after pillbox — took lots of prisoners (SS troopers).
- The German West Wall
- pill boxes galore and tank traps — dragon teeth — mines. Lived in jerry pillboxes in West Wall for 3 days. Our Bn covering
- 2000 yd front — something for the tactics expert to write about. Casualties heavy — 88 the 1st day — 58 the 2nd day — approx. 50 the next day.

This wraps up another key event in 4ID history. **D-Day, liberation of Cherbourg, St. Lo breakout, liberation of Paris, and now first Allied unit to cross into Germany.** You can see why we who have the honor to wear the 4ID patch (and our Family members who have always supported us) are so proud of the accomplishments of the veterans of this great division, from WWI through today.

We've got a long way to go, and the fighting in the Siegfried Line through the rest of the month of September is fierce. Stay tuned. And, as always, please share this with those of your circle of influence who would be interested in it.

Steadfast and Loyal,

Bob Babcock, Past President, Historian/Archivist, National 4th Infantry Division Assn

15 SEP 1944 TO 21 SEP 1944 – D+101 TO D+107

Fighting in the Siegfried Line continues…and it is fierce as the Germans are determined not to let the Allies invade their homeland…

15 SEPTEMBER 1944 — D+101: Several enemy counterattacks, at least one of which was of battalion strength, were launched in an attempt to regain pillboxes occupied by our forces in the Siegfried Line.

In other places where the enemy still held the concrete emplacements, a determined resistance was met. The 2nd Battalion CT 8 moved out at 0800 and by 1300 was stopped in the vicinity of Losheim by heavy artillery, small arms, and machine gun fire. The 3rd Battalion was stopped by strongly fortified positions and heavy enemy fires. At the end of the day, the two battalions disengaged from the enemy under cover of the darkness and moved to assembly area in the vicinity of Rabscheid in preparation for an attack.

CT 12 attacked at 0800 to secure the crossing of Kyll river. Immediate contact was made with the enemy and, due to strong resistance in thick woods, the advance was slow and was continued with many casualties resulting from heavy artillery, mortar, and small arms fire.

CT 22, prior to the attack at 0800, received a counterattack on the left flank which was repelled but the enemy continued to infiltrate all day. The 3rd Battalion continued its attack on the heavily fortified town of Brandscheid, but progress was slow due to the very heavy enemy resistance. The advance of the 1st and 2nd Bn was slow and impeded by heavy enemy resistance, thick woods, and poor visibility. Throughout the day, the CT received heavy artillery, machine gun, mortar, and small arm fire from emplacements and surroundings.

16 SEPTEMBER 1944—D+102: The enemy defended from well dug in and camouflaged positions and from concrete emplacements housing machine guns and antitank guns. Artillery which was employed constantly consisted of heavy barrages of 88, 105, 150 and 170 mm. The enemy engaged in strong active patrolling and counterattacked with up to company strength. Tanks and assault guns were employed in support. Among the units in contact were SS Division Hitler Jugend, 2 SS Division Das Reich, and 9 SS Division. The 4th Infantry Division continued its attack on the Siegfried line fortifications and had succeeded against stubborn enemy resistance and constant artillery fire in securing objectives well to the east of the outer line of defense.

The 8th Infantry attacked to the northeast between CT 22 and CT 12. The 12th Infantry continued its attack in column of battalions. Company E, 2nd Battalion, was surrounded by 1100 by a pocket of enemy infiltrated at 0900, and after a fire fight of increased intensity, contact was re-established by 1610. The advance of the battalion continued until 1800, time for consolidation and preparation of the attack on the following day. The 22nd Infantry continued its attack with the mission of capturing the town of Brandscheid. Despite heavy opposition around the road net, elements of the 3rd Battalion succeeded in reaching the edge of the town. At the close of the day, two companies in column were entering the town from the north. Elements from the south were held up by enemy resistance, fortifications, and extensive mine fields.

17 SEPTEMBER 1944—D+103: The enemy continued to defend its well prepared and concealed earthen emplacements and dug-outs in addition to concrete pillboxes and bunkers. The positions were the base for determined concentrations of fire. Strong patrols invaded our lines, and several determined counterattacks were attempted to regain lost pillboxes. The 4th advanced at 0900 to cleanup enemy resistance and pillboxes against heavy enemy resistance, particularly increased intensity of artillery fire which was estimated as having doubled from the previous 24 hours, with the additional handicap of dense woods and inclement weather.

The 8th Infantry moved off at 0900 to secure favorable ground and to clean up enemy and destroy pillboxes. This advance was hindered by inclement weather, lack of road net, poor visibility, and thick woods but the CT continued to mop up. The 12th Infantry did the same in its area. The 22nd Infantry attacked at 0900 to seize the town of Brandscheid and to continue to the east to secure high ground east of Sellerich, and to protect the south flank of the Division.

18 SEPTEMBER 1944—D+104: The enemy continued to employ the same effective tactics in defending its excellent positions. The 4th Infantry Division continued to exert aggressive pressure against the enemy. Combat Teams secured favorable ground and assigned objectives prior to dark. Artillery fire decreased in intensity, but the 1st Battalion 8th Infantry was still engaged in a fire fight with approximately 300 of the enemy which it had succeeded in surrounding by 1600, prior to darkness.

The 8th Infantry continued to clear the enemy from and secure favorable ground. The 2nd Battalion moved 2000 yards west, mopping up as it advanced. The 1st Battalion had surrounded the enemy and was still engaged with them at darkness. The 12th Infantry 1st and 2nd Battalions moved a short distance to an assembly area, cleaning up all resistance by the end of the day. The 3rd Battalion engaged the enemy in a heavy fire fight during the day but eliminated them by 1800. The 22nd Infantry, 1st Battalion moved approximately 1000 yards to the north, mopping up as it advanced. The 2nd Battalion remained in its position and was engaged by the enemy to the east. The 3rd Battalion sent patrols to the southwest into the town of Brandscheid and met enemy resistance (mortar and artillery fire throughout the day).

19 SEPTEMBER 1944—D+105: The enemy counterattacked with forces ranging from a company to that of a battalion reinforced. All counterattacks were preceded by artillery preparations which lasted about ten minutes. It was apparent that the aim in each case was to retake the pillboxes and bunkers lost to our forces. Very heavy concentrations of rockets were received. The 4th Infantry Division successfully repelled four coordinated counterattacks, maintained its positions, and continued to exert pressure upon the enemy.

The 8th Infantry 3rd Battalion was subjected at 0600 to a counterattack by an enemy force estimated as one battalion composed of various elements of SS Elite troops. This attack was repulsed after the 3rd Battalion returned a great volume of small arms, automatic weapons, mortar, and artillery fires. The 1st Battalion continued the attack against small pockets of enemy and by 1400, this attack developed into a heavy fire fight. At 1530 a second counterattack made of an estimated two companies of the enemy was received by the 3rd Battalion. Elements of the 2nd Battalion initiated movement in encirclement of this force and the battle continued until dark.

The 12th Infantry received a counterattack at 0830 from elements later identified as some six different companies, mostly SS troops. The enemy attack was supported by artillery fire and fire from tracked vehicles which effected surprise and drove the 3rd Battalion back 400 to 500 yards. The 2nd Battalion initiated movement to secure more favorable terrain and at 1030, the 3rd Battalion counterattacked to recover lost ground. At 1430, elements of the 1st Battalion became engaged with part of the same enemy force.

The 22nd Infantry received a counterattack from the direction of Hontheim against the 1st Battalion. Heavy artillery fire was exchanged and the fire fight continued until 1430 at which time pressure began to slacken. Toward the close of the day, enemy activity had ceased, and the Regiment remained in previous positions, no ground having been yielded.

A WWII vet, commander in 377th Anti-Aircraft Artillery, sent the following note: *Bob—In reading the account of WW II days Sept. 15—17, it brought back memories of the first time I saw flame-throwers in action, it was exciting watching the flames aimed at the front of the Pill-boxes and seeing the Krauts running out the back. I also remember well the action around and in Brandscheid. As far as I know, the 22 CT was the first unit in Germany and the Siegfried Line. Thanks for the memories. HRB—Seattle (Note from Bob—he is now deceased, as are most of our WWII vets).*

20 SEPTEMBER 1944—D+106: After an attack in the vicinity of Wascheid, the 1st and 3rd companies of the Deutschland Regiment withdrew and reorganized for a second attack. This attack, like the first, was also repulsed with many losses being inflicted upon the enemy. The 2nd Company of the Deutschland Regiment succeeded in infiltrating our lines and later withdrew under the cover of darkness. The 4th Infantry Division continued to mop up enemy pockets and destroy captured pillboxes in the gap made in the Siegfried Line, readjusting, and improving its positions. The 2nd Battalion 22nd Infantry continued a fire fight with an enemy pocket throughout the day.

21 SEPTEMBER 1944—D+107: Enemy, estimated at 300 to 400 troops, at 0700 attacked against the right flank of the 8th Infantry. At 1000, CT 8 in coordination with elements of CT 22, counterattacked and by 1725, reports from prisoners of war stated that one-half of the enemy had been eliminated. Thick underbrush, well protected with machine guns and riflemen, prevented the entire annihilation of this force. At 1830, the commanding officer of CT 8 suspended action and consolidated for the night. The 12th Infantry continued to secure and consolidate more favorable positions. Vigorous patrolling was continued to the east. The 22nd Infantry sent patrols from the 3rd Battalion toward Brandscheid. The 1st and 2nd Battalions coordinated with CT 8 to eliminate the enemy groups.

From **Swede Henley's Diary—used with permission of his daughters…**

15 SEPTEMBER: Attack jumped off at 1915 to take cross roads on road to Brandscheid. Took cross roads.
- The "Wamp Guns" (76 mm on TDs) really blasted pillboxes—
- made Christians out of the SS troops.

16 SEPTEMBER: Attack jumped off at 1315 for pillboxes between cross road and Brandscheid. Cleaned out everything to edge of town.

17 SEPTEMBER: Still in position in the German west wall about 2 miles north of Brandscheid. Ordered to continue mopping up of pillboxes in immediate vicinity and continue on to clean out pillboxes to Brandscheid. Moved on town itself with tanks and TDs and was ordered to withdraw and move at once to help 1st Bn who were cut off by counterattack. Jerry artillery and mortar fire heavy—enemy sniper active. We called on Corps artillery for counter battery. Artillery dueled all day and night.

18 SEPTEMBER: Still in position and ordered to be ready to move out on short notice with tanks and TDs. Lt. Col. John Dowdy killed by jerry artillery at Sellerich. Returned to Brandscheid to cover up pillboxes with bull dozer.
- Rode in tank as assistant gunner. Set 6 houses on fire
- blew up 4 haystacks and put long range tank fire on herd of cows and a flock of chickens.

19 SEPTEMBER: Transferred to the 1st Bn as Executive Officer. Reported for duty at 1030 just as the jerries were counterattacking. Things were hot for the rest of the day. Stopped attack and took a lot of prisoners. 12th Inf. counterattacked by Infantry and tanks — lost some ground. Still shacking up in the Siegfried line.

20 SEPTEMBER: Still here counting our change. Jerry still throwing artillery and mortar. Major Latimer relieved of Bn and I took command of it. Capt. Tommie Harrison came over as Ex. Off. — Capt. Eggleston S-3.
- The surprise of my life when Col. Lanham called on the phone and said, "You are Bn CO — start functioning."

21-22-23 SEPTEMBER: Still shacking up in the Siegfried line — patrolling — hunting krauts sweating out what is coming up. Everything too damn quiet. Jerry artillery stopped.

A short piece from COL Gerden Johnson's ***History of the Twelfth Infantry Regiment in WWII:***

This shows that it was a vicious fight all across the 4ID front as the Germans were determined to regain what we had taken since September 11, 1944.

All during the night of September 15-16, and the greater part of the next day, the men of Co. E engaged the enemy with every available weapon, thereby succeeding in inflicting many casualties, including approximately 30 killed, 50 wounded, and 75 prisoners. Each and every member of the company performed his assigned task in a most courageous and outstanding manner.

The 1st Battalion had cleared resistance in its sector and had made contact with the main body of the 2nd Battalion.

For September 16, the mission was the same, but moving forward, it was necessary for the 2nd Battalion to reach Co. E, with Co. F leading off. It was foggy when Co. F jumped off shortly after dawn. The 1st Platoon on the right of the road and the 3rd on the left advanced 400 yards through the woods before drawing enemy fire. They were then within 100 yards of their objective (Point E), an enemy pillbox, and a house at a crossroads around which German trenches were known to be dug.

A sharp fire fight developed, and both platoons build up good lines. The Germans launched a frontal attack, but when Staff Sergeant Leonard L. Pitman of Pueblo, Colo., killed the enemy leader, they withdrew. But they hastily reorganized and attacked the right flank of the 1st Platoon. Again, Pitman singled out the German leader and killed him, and again the Germans withdrew. This pattern was repeated with increasing violence as the day wore on.

The enemy tried to hit both assault platoons with artillery and mortar fire, but failed because they were so close to our lines. However, they did hit the 2nd Platoon and company headquarters in the rear and inflicted several casualties. At 1600, when the entire Co. F had only two clips of ammunition left, T/Sgt. George Sahershuk of Elkhorn, W. Va., managed to break through from company headquarters loaded down with bandoleers of ammunition. Then Co. C with one platoon of Co. D, 70th Tank Battalion attached, attacked on the left flank of Co. F and the Germans were soon waving a white bedsheet and yelling, "Kamerad!"

They marched into our line in a column of fours with their hands clasped on top of their heads. There were about 150 of them, some wounded, all badly beaten.

Co. E, having now been contacted, Co. F advanced to the crossroad (objective at Point E) where they found nearly 100 dead Germans, two 88mm guns, and several automatic weapons. There they dug in for the night.

In the meantime, the 1st Battalion had been committed on the left (west) flank to relieve the pressure on the 2nd Battalion. Again, heavy fog, lack of roads to guide on, and thick woods made progress difficult.

16 SEPTEMBER 1944 – SPECIAL EDITION 4ID IN WWII – LTC JOHN DOWDY

Of all the Americans I have heard about in WWII; John Dowdy is one of several I would have loved to have met in person. It was not to be, he was killed in action less than a month after my first birthday. I will take my editor's prerogative and put in this special chapter about John Dowdy. It was just a few days ago when I learned that he had graduated from the University of Georgia in Athens, GA—the place where I live now. But that has nothing to do with John Dowdy's story—it was his Deeds not Words way of leading Soldiers in combat that warrants this special chapter on the anniversary of the day he was killed.

John Dowdy, like Major Richard O'Malley, CO of 2nd Battalion, 12th Infantry Regiment—the Iron Major I included in July, stood out among all the leaders that our 4ID WWII veterans always remembered and always mourned their loss.

While all losses were tragic, it is important to me to pay this special tribute to LTC John Dowdy, while going above and beyond the call of duty of looking out for his men. (In November, I will cover our 4ID WWII Medal of Honor recipients in detail—another five 4ID special people who deserve a Special Issue—four of them earned the MOH in the Hurtgen Forest, and BG Teddy Roosevelt, Jr. on D-Day).

John Dowdy
CO, 1-22 Infantry—1944
A Tribute to One of America's Finest Combat Leaders—Killed in Action in the Siegfried Line on 16 September 1944

"He was a fountain of strength at which all men might drink."

In the over two hundred year history of the 22nd Infantry Regiment, John Dowdy was one of the most aggressive, yet charismatic, commanders that 1st Battalion and the 22nd Infantry Regiment has ever seen. He led his men always from the front, never expecting them to do anything he was not prepared to do himself. He inspired courage in his Battalion, motivating his Soldiers to continue pressing on in the face of extreme hardships, regrouping them after costly setbacks from the enemy, and instilling in them the dedication to ultimate victory which was the essence of his fighting spirit.

Thanks to the efforts of his cousin, Karen Scott, and to 1-22 Infantry's webmaster, Michael Belis, his story has come to light to ensure that he will never be forgotten.

Karen wrote: "Such an American story—who would guess that a little kid growing up in the boonies, with his overalls hanging down, would someday rally his troops on a ridge in France, turn the tide of the battle, take the objective, and clear the way to Cherbourg?"

John Dowdy served his entire military career with the 22nd Infantry Regiment. Though details of that career are sketchy and incomplete, the following is an historical sketch of one of the most dynamic leaders the Regiment has ever seen. In thirty-eight total days of combat, John Dowdy received the Distinguished Service Cross, two Silver Star Medals, two Purple Heart Medals, and the Combat Infantryman's Badge.

John Dowdy entered the US Army from the University of Georgia on June 15, 1939 as a 2nd Lieutenant in the 22nd Infantry Regiment. On February 25, 1941, he was promoted to 1st Lieutenant. On February

1, 1942, he received a promotion to Captain, becoming, at the age of 23, one of the youngest Captains and Company Commanders in the Army at that time. On August 16, 1943, he was promoted to Major and served on the Regimental Staff of the 22nd Infantry's Commander, Colonel Hervey Tribolet.

Sometime in late 1943, prior to the Regiment sailing overseas in January of 1944, Dowdy was made Executive Officer of the 2nd Battalion. On D-Day he came ashore on Utah Beach with 2nd Battalion in the second wave of the landings. On June 8, 1944 (D-Day plus two), he was given command of 1st Battalion, relieving LTC Sewell Brumby, who had been wounded. (Brumby lived a long life and is buried in a cemetery near the University of Georgia football stadium in Athens, GA).

Dowdy took 1st Battalion inland from the beach area, as the 22nd Infantry became the right flank of the 4th Infantry Division's point of attack. The Regiment's mission was to reduce the enemy strongpoints along the beaches and destroy the heavily fortified batteries several miles inland. Positioned on the high ground between Dodainville and Azeville were two German battery forts, one at Azeville and the other at Crisbecq. Each fort consisted of four massive concrete blockhouses containing the artillery batteries, the guns at Crisbecq being 210mm long barreled monsters. The Crisbecq battery was one of the most powerful coastal battery forts of the entire German Atlantic Wall. Both forts were protected by interconnected trenches, pillboxes, barbed wire, and automatic weapons.

For four days, the Regiment battled fierce German resistance in the attempt to take these forts, while suffering heavy casualties in the process. Azeville and Crisbecq were taken, as were Ste. Marcouf and Ozeville. The last major strongpoint on the way to Cherbourg was the heavily fortified high ground of the Quineville ridge. On June 14, the 22nd Infantry and one Battalion of the 39th Infantry attacked this high ground with tank support. Dowdy took 1st Battalion, with its supporting tanks of the 70th Tank Battalion, and captured the eastern part of the ridge, and another hill to the east of that. For his actions that day he was awarded the Distinguished Service Cross. The citation for that award read:

"For extraordinary heroism in action against the enemy on June 15,

1944 (sic). Fierce artillery, machinegun, mortar, and small arms fire inflicted heavy casualties upon Lt. Col. Dowdy's command as it attacked high ground. One assault company, having lost all its officers and most of its key non-commissioned officers, became completely demoralized; withdrawal was imminent. Friendly tanks operating in support of the attack began to retreat. Realizing that his entire command was threatened with annihilation, Lt. Col. Dowdy, disregarding completely his own safety, moved afoot through a hail of fire and personally directed the fire of the tanks upon the enemy. Courageously he proceeded forward unfalteringly to the forward elements of his command. While under fire, he organized them for an attack. Lt. Col. Dowdy's exemplary actions spearheaded a devastating assault, which resulted in the capture of the strongly fortified position and more than 100 prisoners."

For the next several days, the Regiment assembled and received replacements, and on June 19 began the drive toward Cherbourg. By June 22, 1st Battalion was holding high ground near Gonneville, on the extreme right flank of a three Division assault upon the fortress city. For six days, the Regiment held the flank and prevented German forces from linking up with the city.

On the last day of continuous action, June 27, while leading his Battalion, Dowdy suffered serious shrapnel wounds to his right leg from enemy artillery. Refusing to be evacuated, he remained in command for 18 hours after being wounded, most likely until the surrender of all German forces east of Cherbourg, at 1330 hours on June 28. For his actions that day John Dowdy received the Silver Star and Purple Heart.

Dowdy spent the months of July and August in a hospital in England recovering from his wounds and was promoted to Lieutenant Colonel on July 21, 1944. He rejoined the Regiment on September 1, 1944. Colonel Charles "Buck" Lanham was then in command of the 22nd, and Dowdy became part of Lanham's staff. During the three days of September 1-3, Dowdy became Lanham's "right-hand-man." In those three days, the Regiment fought its way across more than 100 miles of France and Belgium, with Lanham and Dowdy directing its movements and operations.

On September 4, Dowdy resumed command of 1st Battalion. Lanham wrote of Dowdy:

"When this fight was over I gave John back his battalion (1st Battalion) which had suffered heavily in his absence. Within twenty-four hours, it was like a new outfit. John was everywhere and his courage, his strength, his spirit, and his personality ran like flame through the command. I think he was the greatest leader of men that I have ever seen, and I have spent a lifetime in the Army. And certainly no man has ever been more deeply loved by those he led and by those who had the high privilege of serving with him as fellow officers.

John was with us when we broke the Siegfried line on (Sept) 14th. The blow that he and his battalion struck that day will never be forgotten by our enemy. We ruptured the line on September 14th and on September 15th we continued the attack to widen the breach and to improve our positions. The fighting was bitter, and the enemy was fanatical. The troops that opposed us were largely SS formations, the elite of the German Army, with orders from Hitler in person to fight to the death. And in large measure this is what they did.

On September 16th, John and his battalion again took their objective—a critical hill in our zone. The enemy reaction was violent. He made repeated efforts to throw John from his hard-won position, but these were beaten off. He then resorted to violent artillery and mortar fire—this was probably the heaviest series of concentrations we have ever received. John ordered his battalion to dig in on the high ground for the night. He then began circulating among his troops, adjusting their positions, correcting their dispositions, placing his weapons in the most advantageous locations, joking with the men, reassuring them, seeing to their safety. He walked through the storm of shellfire as if he were walking down a street in his home town—calm, cool, completely composed, and without the slightest trace of hurry or excitement. He was a fountain of strength at which all men might drink.

He made two complete circuits of his position, and still not satisfied that his men were adequately cared for, he began a third trip. He was perhaps halfway through when the fatal shell landed. He was killed instantly, and though it might well have been otherwise, his body was not mutilated. Only a fragment of the shell did the deadly work."

Charles B. MacDonald, in the book "The Siegfried Line Campaign" described the above action thus: "The only bright development on this part of the front came in the afternoon of 16 September when the 1st Battalion pushed out of the Pruem State Forest to seize a hill that commanded the Bleialf-Pruem highway a few hundred yards west of the German-held village of Sellerich. Even this achievement was marred by the loss from German shelling of some thirty-five men wounded and eight killed, including the battalion commander, Lt. Col. John Dowdy." (p. 53)

For his leadership and bravery under fire, at the cost of his life on that September day, John Dowdy was awarded his second Silver Star and second Purple Heart. He was 26 years old when he died.

Regimental Chaplain Bill Boice wrote of Dowdy: "One of the finest officers of the regiment, Lt. Colonel John Dowdy had proved himself an able officer in combat again and again. His personal care for the troops under his command, his knowledge of military tactics, had saved lives and boosted morale."

Perhaps the best tribute to John Dowdy was written by Colonel "Buck" Lanham, in a personal letter to John's mother, Eva, when he wrote:

"...I have seen many officers, and many men go down. Each one, no matter how humble, has been a blow and a personal loss to me. But I say truthfully that never has a death so stunned me as that of John. And the Regiment shared that grief with me. John was worshipped by his battalion; it was a form of hero worship, and

John was a hero and died a hero, in the true sense of that much abused word."

LTC John Dowdy was buried in the US Military Cemetery at Fosse, Belgium. For several years, a Belgian family adopted the grave and kept it well looked after, making sure it always had fresh flowers. On April 8, 1949, LTC Dowdy's body was returned to the US, and he now rests in the Dowdy plot in Tifton, Georgia.

Karen Scott's (John's cousin) dedication to preserving the memory of her ancestor insures that LTC Dowdy's legacy will always be remembered. Thanks to her, this important chapter has been written in the history of the 4th Infantry Division and the history of 1-22 Infantry. We also thank Michael Belis, 4ID Vietnam vet of C/1-22 Infantry, for preserving this story, plus more, including pictures, in the website he runs for 1-22 Infantry, www.1-22infantry.org.

22 SEP 1944 TO 30 SEP 1944 – D+108 TO D+116

22 SEPTEMBER 1944—D+108: The 8th Infantry resumed the attack with 1st and 2nd Battalions to eliminate a small enemy salient and by 0945 were meeting strong resistance. Enemy had strongly entrenched during the night, succeeded in bringing up small reinforcements and used heavy caliber rocket fire and 40 mm AA weapons to resist our advance. Vigorous patrolling was conducted throughout the day by other elements of the CT.

The 12th Infantry placed interdictory fires upon enemy observation posts and installations located during its continuous patrolling.

The 22nd encountered increased enemy patrol activity in the early hours. Aggressive patrolling was continued with use of mortar and machine gun fires to disperse enemy patrols.

23 SEPTEMBER 1944—D+109: The enemy employed strong patrols in an attempt to probe our lines at various points. The 4th Infantry Division dispatched strong combat patrols, eliminating the small pocket of resistance in CT 8's zone of action and at the end of the day was fully consolidated on its main line of resistance.

24 SEPTEMBER 1944—D+110: The enemy remained for the most part on the defensive and there was a notable decline in aggressiveness and patrol activity. Considerable enemy movement noted in the vicinity of Hontheim. Strong combat patrols were sent to reconnoiter roads, dispositions, and activities to prevent enemy infiltration and if possible to direct artillery fire on enemy installations.

25 SEPTEMBER 1944—D+111: The enemy continued to patrol towards our right and left flanks, while in the center of the line it continued to improve its defensive positions. On the whole, enemy activity showed considerable decline. The 4th Infantry Division maintained and improved its positions within the outer defenses of the Siegfried Line, aggressively patrolled to the front and prepared to continue the advance to the east.

26 SEPTEMBER 1944—D+112: The enemy remained on the defensive. Strong points along the enemy front appeared to be mutually supporting and tied in with patrols. Extensive and aggressive patrolling for all the units continued.

27 SEPTEMBER 1944—D+113: The enemy devoted considerable attention to improving its defenses and living conditions. No change: active patrolling and artillery fires on enemy targets.

28 SEPTEMBER 1944—D+114: Constant preparations were made with a view to a coordinated attack to the northeast.

29 SEPTEMBER 1944—D+115: A number of unidentified planes flew over and it was believed that propaganda leaflets were dropped by them. The 4th Infantry Division readjusted present positions, maintained pressure by patrolling aggressively, and at the end of the day, prepared to move to the north to designated assembly area before making another thrust at the Siegfried Line.

30 SEPTEMBER 1944—D+116: The 8th Infantry continued to send patrols east and southeast. Except for an enemy patrol repulsed, very little enemy activity.

The 12th Infantry 1st Battalion moved at 0715 by companies to assembly area to the west, closing at 1020. The 2nd Battalion took over defensive positions of the 1st Battalion. The 3rd Battalion continued to improve its outpost positions protecting the north flank of the division.

The 22nd Infantry continued aggressive patrolling to the south and southeast. At 1800, a patrol moving east to Hontheim was involved in a fire fight and was not disengaged until approximately 2200. The latter patrol estimated 80 Germans in Hontheim.

(You will want to read the following logistics report—it shows how our supply lines were being severely tested and the Soldiers on the front lines were suffering as a result).

Notes about logistics: On 3 September, the gasoline shortage became critical. At this time only 15 miles of gasoline were in the tanks of vehicles and in reserve. Receipt of gasoline increased on 12 September, end of the movement to the east, and by 20 September sufficient gasoline was on hand to fill all tanks and cans. Very few cigarettes were received, and the shortage continued throughout the month. Heavy rains occurred during this period. The service shoes issued the men absorbed water. Despite the definite need for overshoes, none were received. The treatment of venereal disease (gonorrhea and syphilis) with penicillin is now in effect. The evacuation of prisoners of war was a difficult problem. Returning supply vehicles were utilized to bring back prisoners and V Corps furnished an escort guard.

SUMMARY FOR SEPTEMBER 1944

Killed or died of injuries: 22 Officers, 200 Enlisted Men

Missing: 3 Officers, 63 Enlisted Men

Seriously wounded or injured: 25 Officers, 420 Enlisted Men

Slightly wounded or injured: 20 Officers, 717 Enlisted Men

Total casualties: 1,270

Prisoners captured: 5,000

CUMULATIVE TOTAL OF CASUALTIES TREATED FROM 6 JUNE 1944 TO 30 SEPT 1944

8th Infantry: 3,930

12th Infantry: 4,227

22nd Infantry: 4,274

Total casualties for 4ID from 6 June 1944 to 30 Sept 1944:

Killed or died of injuries: 175 Officers and 2,156 Enlisted Men

Between now and early November, I don't have any personal stories from my War Stories book. We are going into the slowest month of the war (October 1944) for the 4ID. Thus, when I asked for stories from our WWII vets in 1998, their most prominent stories were not about October 1944. But don't despair, we have plenty of stories coming up from the remainder of the war.

Fit to Fight

From **History of the 22nd Infantry Regiment in WWII by Chaplain Bill Boice:**

From the 18th of September to the 3rd of October, the Combat Team remained in a static position. Lines were secured and adjusted. Enemy counterattacks were numerous but always repulsed. The Regiment sent out vigorous patrols day and night to keep in continual contact with enemy activities. Enemy movement was reported to be extensive around Hontheim, but never materialized. The 44th F. A. Bn. in the days of the holding action had fired over 15, 000 rounds in support of Combat Team 22.

The assault and penetration of the Siegfried Line revealed several important facts.

In the assault of the line of fortifications, the best method was found to be an attack in strength on a relatively narrow front. Once the line was pierced and the pillbox system of mutual support disrupted, it was fairly simple to roll back the line, hitting the boxes from the flanks or rear. At this stage of the operation, the greatest difficulty was fending off attacks by small enemy groups issuing forth from rear positions or by-passed emplacements. The excellent camouflage of the pillboxes and presence of more than shown on G-2 maps caused numerous emplacements to be by-passed, and it was necessary to form patrols to search them out.

The majority of pillboxes (estimated at 75%) were destroyed by the coordinated attack of direct fire weapons: a tank, a tank destroyer, and infantry. This method was used whenever terrain permitted. Supporting fires from any other available direct fire weapons, including 50 cal. machine-guns and 57mm antitank guns, were used to chase the enemy into the pillbox and force the closing of the firing embrasures or door. Under this cover, a tank destroyer with close-in infantry protection would move to within 15 or 20 yards of the box. From this close range, the tank destroyer would preferably blow out an embrasure or door. If these could not be reached, the three-inch guns would pierce the concrete sidewall itself. The infantry then moved in, mopping up with fragmentation and white phosphorous grenades, or if necessary, with demolition charges and flame-throwers. Flame throwers were very effective when fired through holes blown by the tank destroyers. Experience proved that best results were obtained by first squirting some of the liquid, not ignited, into the hole, and following that immediately with a burning blast.

When terrain and trees would not permit the close approach to a pill-box by a tank destroyer, tank-infantry tactics were used. Tank fire, together with any other available direct fire weapons, forced the enemy into the box. If fire could be brought to bear on the embrasures, they were of necessity closed. At least the enemy's field of fire was greatly restricted by the embrasures. The infantry then closed in, and with flame-throwers and demolition charges cleaned out the fortifications. Pack charges effectively blew out embrasures or doors, and the concussion either killed or stunned the occupants. The pillbox could then be mopped up with grenades or flame-throwers. An infantry combination of one assault (demolition) squad and one support (rifle) squad, worked well. Lack of men trained in demolitions and flame-throwers handicapped this method. In an infantry assault on a pillbox, captured German bazookas (hand-panzer) were very effective. These weapons would knock a hole through the concrete, and the concussion and blast effect killed the occupants. Our bazookas were not effective.

In some instances, a tank dozer was used to seal pillboxes. Sunken doorways were easily blocked in a similar manner, although this was more difficult, the embrasures being above ground level. This method will prevent occupants from escaping as the doors, which swing out, are blocked. However, several boxes so buried were excavated from the outside and reoccupied by the Germans.

THE SIEGFRIED RESTS

The Twenty-Second Infantry had spent slightly less than three weeks inside the Siegfried Line. Though the regiment had not actually breached the Line, they had penetrated it to a depth of several miles. Had the necessary supplies, ammunition, and equipment been available, it is believed that the Line could have been breached and the Allied forces driven well into Germany. At this time, the German armies were staggering and confused to such an extent that weeks would have been required before they could have organized a defensive line.

On October 4th the Combat Team was ordered to move to a new area.

From **Swede Henley's Diary—used with permission of his daughters:**

24-26 SEPTEMBER: Still at jerry pillbox CP. Extensive patrolling to front. Shot hell out of Homthein again. Raining again—everything muddy as hell. Received orders for reg: attack. 3rd Bn taking Brandscheid tomorrow at 1300. Orders cancelled at 1600. Sweatin' out the winter season coming on and hoping war is over before it starts.
• Issue of Scotch whiskey (White Horse) came in handy. Paid off in Kraut money.

26-30 SEPTEMBER: Same thing—raining every day—mud a foot deep. Patrolling heavy. Tied in everybody including the jerries. Secure stove for pillbox CP. Heated things up. New replacements and officers arrived—sure glad to see them. Sun came out for part of the day on September 29th.

30 SEPTEMBER:
• Sweating out American baseball results
• Received orders that we might be relieved tomorrow and move north to punch new hole in Siegfried line.

1 OCTOBER 1944 SUNDAY: Listening to radio news and music from good ole U.S.A. Having a few drinks of gin—just wishing we were home.
• Drinking rum wishing we were at a good football game

2 OCTOBER: Counting our change. Raining like hell.

From the 4ID Yearbook, covering the narrative of our fight across Europe: This summarizes our fight in the Siegfried Line in September…

Following a 4th Infantry Division patrol which had crossed the German border on the evening of the 11th, and which was the first Infantry division unit to enter Germany, the remainder of the Division crossed in force on September 12th. Two days later, the great assault began, and within two or three hours two entire combat teams had driven through the "impenetrable" line and had fanned out on top of the Schnee Eifel, key terrain feature of this line. With ever-increasing strength, the hostile forces fought off our attacks until, by about September 18th, it became clear that we could not make and sustain a penetration through the enemy. At this time there were only six divisions and a few hundred cavalry troops along the entire First Army sector of the line, from Aachen to the southern tip of Luxembourg, and these forces were spread out (as in the case of the 4th, with its 15-mile front) that exploitation was not possible. Not only was our front wide, but a gap of ten kilometers existed on the right flank and 40 kilometers on the left.

On September 17th, Major General Leonard Gerow, on occasion of his temporary relief from command of the V Corps at that time, in a commendation said of the 4th: "The aggressive courage, unselfish devotion, tenacity of purpose, and outstanding leadership of all ranks is evidenced by the fact that the 4th Infantry Division has never failed to capture its assigned objectives and has never lost ground to the enemy. You are battle-tested, battle-wise, and a first line combat division with an outstanding record and reputation. I am proud to have had the opportunity of commanding you in battle, and I shall watch your future successes with the greatest of interest, with the knowledge that victory is assured."

Let me tell you now, October is going to be slower reading than what I've covered up to now. We had our only month (out of 11 months fighting in Europe in WWII) where we were holding in place rather than continuously attacking the Germans and driving them back into their homeland.

Don't abandon me, I will continue to report on what happened to 4ID in October 1944. And, come the first week of November, we are going into the toughest fight in the history of the 4th Infantry Division—the hell in Hurtgen Forest. That will be followed, less than two weeks later, by the Battle of the Bulge and our holding the southern shoulder of the Bulge in Luxembourg.

Thus, be patient—don't abandon this history lesson—and I will guarantee you that you'll be happy you stayed with me.

No division accomplished more than did our beloved 4ID.

MG Barton (driving jeep) and COL Lanham (standing) — first Allied officers to cross Siegfried Line

Siegfried obstacles

OCTOBER 1944

4ID IN GERMANY

1 OCT 1944 TO 6 OCT 1944 – D+117 TO D+122

1 OCT 1944—D+117: Occupying the bunkers and pillboxes line and improving its defensive position by digging foxholes and trenches, the enemy continued to send forth small patrols to probe our lines to establish the disposition of our troops.

The 4th Infantry Division continued outposting and patrolling to the east within the Division zone of action, preparatory to being relieved and moving into new assembly areas to the north.

At 1600, Company E CT 8 was counterattacked by a reinforced enemy platoon supported by mortars, artillery, bazookas, and hand grenades. This thrust succeeded in dislodging our troops before the enemy was routed by 1900.

The 12th had its 1st Battalion acting as division mobile reserve, its 2nd Battalion consolidating and patrolling to the east and northeast, on the division main line of resistance while its 3rd Battalion was outposting the division left (north) flank.

The 22nd continued patrols to the southeast and south. Small arms fire was exchanged with enemy forces in Brandscheid at 0900.

2 OCTOBER 1944—D+118: The enemy continued to improve its defensive positions: digging activities and camouflage. A few patrols were contacted but they showed little desire to assault our forces and were soon dispersed.

Preparations to being relieved and moving to the north in the vicinity of Hunningen were completed.

The 8th continued active patrolling to the east and southeast.

The 12th and 22nd activities were the same as the previous day.

3 OCTOBER 1944—D+119: The enemy continued its work and additional fields of fire were cleared.

The 8th Infantry prepared to be relieved by the 9th Infantry Regiment and prepared for move. The 1st Battalion was relieved and moved to an assembly area at Wisheid.

The 12th Infantry continued vigorous patrolling and prepared to be relieved.

The 22nd Infantry continued patrolling and plans were formulated for move.

4 OCTOBER 1944—D+120: The 4th Infantry Division was relieved by elements of the 2nd Infantry Division by 1800. It occupied two sectors. In the old sector the enemy front lines remained the same while in the new sector, there was no contact. As in previous periods, considerable effort was made by the Germans to improve their positions.

The 8th Infantry having been relieved, moved to the north.

The 2nd and 3rd Battalions of the 12th Infantry Division, having been relieved, moved by foot to a new assembly area in the vicinity of Holzheim, closing therein at 1930 and 1845 respectively.

The 1st Battalion of the 22nd Infantry, having been relieved, moved by motor at 1330 to the north in the vicinity of Honsfeld. The 2nd and 3rd Battalions moved by foot to temporary assembly areas in the vicinity of Buchet and prepared to move by motor.

The 4th Engineer Combat Battalion supported the movement of division units by improving roads and preparing unit assembly areas to the north.

5 OCTOBER 1944—D+121: In the new sector, enemy troops were encountered protecting a road block. Its force was estimated of about a company strength, and it employed small arms and machine guns in dug in emplacements. The enemy offered little resistance and hastily withdrew immediately upon being engaged by our forces. An increasing usage of land mines was noted.

The 4th Infantry Division moved remaining units to the north, improved areas, sent reconnaissance patrols to seek information, and continued preparations for future operations.

6 OCTOBER 1944—D+122: The enemy used an outpost line as an intermediate line of defense which was employed with the objective of holding out as long as possible and then falling quickly back to the permanent installations of the Siegfried line. The outpost positions in all cases had at least one machine gun well dug in and defended roads and trails leading east into West wall. Numerous mine fields indicated that the enemy had spent considerable time in preparing the defense of the arteries leading into the Siegfried Line.

The 4th Infantry Division patrolled vigorously and maintained contact with the 112th Infantry Regiment on the north and the 2nd Infantry Division on the south. At the end of the day, plans were formulated to attack to the east on 7 October.

*From the **4ID Yearbook**, covering the narrative of our fight across Europe:*

A period of readjustment and waiting set in, characterized by vigorous patrolling, sometimes even flaring up into company battles. The morale of the Division began to ebb as the weather grew worse. Infernal mud, continuous rain, and damp fog made this, the first stable front since D-Day, completely miserable. We were given a new sector to which we moved on October 5th, just north of the one we had held. Everyone prepared for an attack on October 8th. But none came. Throughout all of October, the Division sat, enduring hardships of weather and especially the German artillery. Toward the latter part of the month, Jerry amused himself by sending his "buzz" bombs roaring over the heads of the troops. These flying bombs were aimed at Liege and other big cities, but occasionally one fell short. No Division casualties were reported as having resulted from the terrific explosions of these gadgets.

From the **Diary of Swede Henley—used with permission of his daughters…**
(he served with the 22nd Infantry Regiment throughout the war)…

3 OCTOBER: Major Drake took over command of Bn. Capt. Henley Ex. O—Capt. Harrison transferred to 2nd Bn as S-3.

4 OCTOBER: Relieved by 2nd Division 38th Inf. 3rd Bn and received orders to move to the north. Route—Bucket—Schonberg—St. U. Th—Bullingen—Hons Feld. Reconnoitered for outpost line in vicinity of Murringen, Belgium.

5 OCTOBER: Moved Bn to Murringen. CP closed in at 1200 in a beer joint. A very nice CP but out of whiskey. Patrolling roads to Siegfried line.

6 OCTOBER: Still in Murringen—still patrolling. Received orders to secure LD 1500 yds of the big line, starting 1000 on October 7.
  • One of the girls had a boyfriend who was a PW in the U.S.—lucky rascal *

From the **History of the 22nd Infantry Regiment in WWII** *by Chaplain Bill Boice…*

THE SIEGFRIED RESTS

The Twenty-Second Infantry had spent slightly less than three weeks inside the Siegfried Line. Though the regiment had not actually breached the Line, they had penetrated it to a depth of several miles. Had the necessary supplies, ammunition, and equipment been available, it is believed that the Line could have been breached and the Allied forces driven well into Germany. At this time, the German armies were staggering and confused to such an extent that weeks would have been required before they could have organized a defensive line.

On October 4th the Combat Team was ordered to move to a new area near Bullingen. Elements of the Second Infantry Division began relieving the Twenty-Second Infantry on October 3rd, and it was completed on the 4th without enemy interference. The First Battalion and special units, immediately upon completion of their relief, moved to an assembly area near Honsfeld.

Early on the morning of the 5th, the First Battalion initiated reconnaissance to affect the relief of the 102nd Cavalry Reconnaissance Squadron in the Combat Team's new zone of action. This completed, the battalion moved into position immediately to the rear of the cavalry outpost line. That part of Combat Team 22 which remained in assembly areas near Buchet moved north by motor convoy on the 5th and arrived in the new area at Honsfeld that afternoon.

Strong security patrols were maintained on the 6th in order to protect the relief and aid the oncoming attack. The attack moved out in an approach march formation before noon that day, and by 1400 hours the leading elements of the First and Second Battalions were 1700 yards beyond the line of departure. The Third Battalion, following up in reserve, moved into the vicinity of Murringen. Contact was continuously maintained with Combat Team 112 on the left and Combat Team 8 on the right. Combat and reconnaissance patrol from the two forward battalions which were sent out short distances east of our lines that night reported that they had seen entrenched enemy within sight of our positions.

Even though the Combat Team had shifted its zone of action to the north, it was still located in the Schnee Eifel and Monschau Forest area. There was in reality very little aggressive action aside from the skirmishes encountered by the combat patrols.

This is shorter than normal, as most of October will likely be. Finally, after 6 June through September slugging it out with the Germans non-stop, we got a slight break. Yes, we had to conduct daily combat patrols. Yes, we dealt with semi-regular artillery barrages from the Germans. But compared to the past four months, October was relatively easy (none of us would volunteer to put up with what our 4ID forefathers dealt with in October 1944).

7 OCT 1944 TO 13 OCT 1944 – D+123 TO D+129

7 OCTOBER 1944—D+123: The 4th Infantry Division advanced to the east and secured preliminary objectives and line of departure to attack the Siegfried Line in the vicinity of Udenbreth.

The 8th Infantry secured by 1245 objectives across the main north-south road. It encountered the enemy defending its dug in positions.

In front of CT 12 the enemy defended the crossroads in the vicinity of Losheimer Graben using heavy machine guns, 80 mm mortars and small arms; the enemy utilized dug in emplacements and cellars of buildings to stubbornly defend this crossroad. Finally after being shelled by artillery from Cannon Company and 81 mm mortars, the estimated force of 200 enemy was dislodged with bazookas and tank support, and by 1730 was driven from the position. Mopping up operations were begun.

The 22nd Infantry advanced to the east in a steady advance. First contact with the enemy was at 1305, consisting of sniper fire and a little mortar and artillery fire. Around 1340, the objectives were reached. Except for some slight offensive action by a few patrols, the enemy remained defensive.

8 OCTOBER 1944—D+124: The enemy launched four counterattacks. They were made by forces of about 50-70 men, and they occurred at 0630, 0745, 0800 and 1030. Two of the attempts were preceded by heavy artillery and mortar barrages. In all cases the counterattacks were repulsed and in at least one instance, the enemy received heavy casualties. In addition usual interdictory and harassing fires on roadways and junctions were experienced.

The 4th Infantry Division maintained and improved positions, dispatched patrols, and continued plans for the coordinated attack.

9 October 1944—D+125

The enemy remained on the defensive except for a few small patrols, mainly in the 8th Infantry sector.

The 4th Infantry Division sent out strong patrols to report enemy dispositions.

10 OCTOBER 1944—D+126: The enemy was still improving its positions and fields of fire. The area about Neuhof was particularly active.

The 8th Infantry improved positions secured in preparation for the attack and conducted vigorous patrolling.

The 3rd Battalion (reinforced) of the 12th Infantry attacked at 0900 to seize favorable terrain from which it could support the planned assault. Leading elements reached objective by 1030 and consolidated positions throughout the balance of the day.

The 22nd Infantry conducted reconnaissance for emplacing direct fire weapons to support the attack and patrolled aggressively with two patrols reaching enemy line of concrete emplacements.

11 OCTOBER 1944—D+127: Considerable heavy mortar fire fell on our front line elements, but enemy artillery was not particularly heavy.

The 8th Infantry improved its positions and conducted training in assault of fortified positions.

The 12th Infantry sent vigorous patrols to the east and conducted training.

The 22nd Infantry patrolled aggressively with one patrol reaching the outskirts of Udenbreth with little activity of the enemy being noted. It also conducted training in assault of fortified positions.

The 70th Tank Battalion moved to vicinity of Hunningen, closing at 1200.

12 OCTOBER 1944—D+128: Combat teams sent out strong patrols to the east to determine enemy disposition and strength.

CT 8 and CT 12 kept minimum of troops in line with remainder to the rear for rest, cleanup, and training.

CT 22 reported small arms fire coming from the vicinity of Miescheid and it was reported that two enemy assault guns were firing from the vicinity of Giescheid. The enemy was observed placing mines in the shell craters leading up to the West wall defenses. As in previous periods, no evidence of enemy armor was reported. The results of our propaganda dissemination were further proven by the fact that all prisoners of war surrendered with "Safe Conduct" passes.

13 OCTOBER 1944—D+129: The enemy improved its defensive position with renewed vigor. More mine fields were layed, even during the night in areas which had previously been swept and cleared.

The 4th Infantry Division continued active patrolling, and under battalion rotation policy, instituted training program with emphasis on tactics in assault of fortified positions, tactics of tank-infantry coordination, use of flame-throwing tanks, and schools for determination of hostile mortar positions.

From the **History of the 22nd Infantry Regiment in WWII** *by Chaplain Bill Boice:*

From October 8th to the 10th, patrol activity continued in an effort to keep in close contact with enemy plans and movements. A coordinated plan was drawn up for the attack on the Siegfried Line. The plan was never put into effect since orders were rescinded, and the mission of the Division was changed.

Before the official delay of plans arrived, the field artillery battalions in support of CT 22 opened fire on the afternoon of the 11th and fired a number of heavy concentrations. Additional support was given by the IX Tactical Air Command, which dive-bombed and strafed enemy positions in the vicinity of Udenbreth. As a result, partial withdrawal of enemy troops in the forward positions was observed. When information was received to delay the attack, plans were set up at once for outposting the Combat Team with one battalion—two battalions to be in reserve.

From the 12th of October until the 22nd of October, the Combat Team remained relatively static. Patrols were constantly on the move reconnoitering to the east to include the towns of Miescheid and Udenbreth. Only slight casualties were sustained. The weather increased in severity, and the countryside was under an oppressive overcast of drizzling rain and penetrating cold. Every advantage was taken of the comforts that could be enjoyed. Showers, movies, Red Cross facilities, USO shows were setup in Murringen, and daily, quotas of men were sent back from the reserve units to enjoy them while they were available.

From **Swede Henley's Diary, used with permission of his daughters:**

7 OCTOBER: Bn moved across LD at 1000 with B and A abreast, C securing LD in woods. Sweating out what is coming up. On objective at 1400 and dug in with overhead shelter. Rained again, as usual.
- G-2 states it is just a thin crust—the 1st line has only 2200 jerries in it—the 2nd line only 2200 jerries in it, and only 2200 jerries in-between. This fight should be a push-over.

8-11 OCTOBER: In position in woods along hard road 1700 yards south of Edenbreth. Heavy patrolling to front to find out where mines and dragons teeth in defenses (Siegfried Line around the strong point at Neuhof and Edenbreth. Enemy counterattacked several times but to no success. Prisoners captured were soldiers who had chronic stomach ailments.
- Captured prisoner who gave us information about defenses—number of pill-boxes, etc. Bn CO of garrison at Edenbreth was a Major living in the First Aid tent—the dirty bastard.
- Studied aerial photo showing pillboxes. Orders issued on the 11th

to attack on the 12th. 1st Bn in the lead. (Rained every day). Orders cancelled on afternoon of the 11th.

12 OCTOBER: 1st Bn relieved by 3rd Bn and 1st Bn moved into area 1500 yds in rear of present position (raining).
- P-47 dive bombed Edenbreth. A beautiful sight to see those jerries take it.
- One plane shot down just in front of our lines. Pilot bailed out and landed
- OK and went in wrong direction and walked into Edenbreth and was captured.
- Poor devil.

13 OCTOBER FRIDAY (D + 129): Bn getting washed and clean clothes. USO show for 400 men at Murringen, Belgium (2 miles back). Raining again in the morning.

Even with the slowness of October, you can see where our troops are staying engaged and keeping the Germans off balance.

14 OCT 1944 TO 20 OCT 1944 – D+130 TO D+136

14 OCTOBER 1944—D+130: No changes in the activities of strong combat patrols and rotation of the battalions for training.

15 OCTOBER 1944—D+131: Our patrols observed considerable activity in the vicinity of the Siegfried defenses and at 1600 a group of about 200 enemy were observed moving east across country southeast of Neuhof. It was learned that enemy troops had been warned to stay away from felled trees because they were all mined. It was learned that the 3d Panzer Grenadier Division which had been reported crossing the front opposite the 4th Infantry Division during the previous two days had been committed in the 1st Infantry Division zone of action.

Same activities for the 4th Infantry Division with periods being devoted to care and cleaning of equipment, rest and recreation, cleanliness of personnel and clothing, and training.

16 OCTOBER 1944—D+132: There was little activity on the part of the enemy except for a considerable increase in mortar shelling, principally in the CT 8 and CT 22 sectors. The 4th Infantry Division dispatched strong combat patrols to the east, harassed the enemy and continued training programs for the units not actively engaged on the front line.

17 OCTOBER 1944—D+133: The enemy was observed engaged in such activities as washing clothes, cutting trees, and generally moving about in Ulenbreth. One of our patrols that reached Miescheid received high-velocity fire from an antitank weapon in a pillbox and heavy machine gun fire from pillboxes located in the northern end of Uldenbreth. The 4th Infantry Division continued patrolling, maintained main line of resistance, and conducted training.

18 OCTOBER 1944—D+134: At 0725 the enemy using an amplifying system directed music from phonograph records towards our front line troops. No changes in the activities with rotation battalion policy.

19 OCTOBER 1944—D+135: Enemy patrols were not active. An increase in enemy mortar fire was noted by CT 8 and CT 22; in some cases, the enemy fired smoke, probably to cover its activities in these areas. Several prisoners of war surrendered as a result of our propaganda broadcast delivered from the CT 8 area between 1200 and 1245. CT 12 continued normal patrol activity and rotation policy of battalions. The 4th Division Artillery continued firing registration, close support, harassing, interdiction, counter battery, and propaganda missions. Engineers continued to improve roads, remove mines etc.

20 OCTOBER 1944—D+136: Smoke was again used by the enemy, apparently to conceal its activities in and around the Siegfried emplacements. Mine fields were again encountered in strength.

From Swede Henley's WWII Diary—used with permission of his daughters:

14—15 OCTOBER: Raining again as usual. Mud getting deeper. Held school for regiment on locating enemy mortars.

16 OCTOBER: Still counting our change. Still raining. Mud getting deeper. My morale is low.

Wave after wave of heavy bombers went over to give ole Adolph's cities hell!

17 OCTOBER: Visited Spa Belgium—the bath center. Got good bath and massage.

18—21 OCTOBER: Rotated with 2nd Bn on screening the regimental front. Still raining and everything is wet. Heard news of Oct. 20th that Philippine Island invaded—news of 21st that Aachen fell—Good News.
- Used the "Daddy Whamp Guns" 155mm SP rifles against German pillboxes.
- Muzzle blast set off 6 mines 12 yards away.

From Chaplain Bill Boice's History of the 22nd Infantry Regiment in WWII:

From the 12th of October until the 22nd of October, the Combat Team remained relatively static. Patrols were constantly on the move reconnoitering to the east to include the towns of Miescheid and Udenbreth. Only slight casualties were sustained. The weather increased in severity, and the countryside was under an oppressive overcast of drizzling rain and penetrating cold. Every advantage was taken of the comforts that could be enjoyed. Showers, movies, Red Cross facilities, USO shows were set up in Murringen, and daily quotas of men were sent back from the reserve units to enjoy them while they were available.

From COL Gerden Johnson's **History of the Twelfth Infantry Regiment in WWII:**

The rest of the month was spent in comparative quiet. The only contact with the enemy was by daily patrols. The constant threat of enemy booby traps and mines made this very difficult, and several casualties resulted, among them being Capt. Bill Mills who was wounded by a shu-mine, and Lt. Piper who was injured by a booby trap during a patrol action. Otherwise, the month was put to good advantage in necessary weapons training, mortar shell report schools, woods fighting technique, and demonstrations of pillbox fighting with the aid of flame throwing tanks.

With the large number of replacements in the regiment, the problem arose of indoctrinating the new members with the priceless spirit and tradition of the 12th Infantry. To this end, when the tactical situation permitted, the Regimental Colors were brought under guard as far forward as the battalion command posts where the history of the regiment was imparted to members of reserve companies. The inspiration by the knowledge of the history and traditions of the old 12th paid dividends in battle, for our troops upheld with honor the fighting reputation of the regiment. This inspiring incident is now being related to the cadets at West Point in their leadership course.

The 12th Infantry newspaper, "The Big Picture," was published almost daily and movies were shown in an old barn at Holzheim. In between patrol missions, the men rested, little realizing that the fiercest fighting of the war lay just ahead.

Many words have been written by correspondents in an effort to bring home to the American people that true feeling of gratitude which the people of France and Belgium felt towards the American soldiers who liberated their homelands, but the following letter written by a Belgian girl to the parents of a 12th Infantryman who was killed in action tells the story in a manner which all will understand. Its simplicity so clearly plumbs the depths of heartfelt thanks that it will always remain among the treasures of the 12th Infantry as a reminder that its sacrifices were not in vain:

Rue De La Conver
Saint Hubert
Ardenne, Belgique
21st October 1944

To Family Bill,

I know just a few words of English and it is from a very little Belgium town, they will start for to express our grateful to you Americans for the liberation of our Country by your Sons (the 8th September).

My thanks to you in particular because we have been happy that Bill to be our liberator. He is first American soldier we have seen. We will always remember this nice and lofty fighter, may God keep him throughout the future years and words can never say how in our gratitude towards you and yours.

When you write to Bill said to him I will always think very much to him and if he can come in Saint Hubert, I shall be very happy to see him again.

Said to him also, I am always waiting him, and he writes with me when that is possible and you also.

Excuse my English. I can explain me very well, but I hope you understand me.

Sincerely yours,

October was our quietest month of the war for the 4ID and all our regiments. As the history of the 12th explains above, they were not aware that the toughest fighting of the war was ahead of them in November and December.

21 OCT 1944 TO 28 OCT 1944 – D+137 TO D+143

We are still in our October 1944 lull for the 4ID.

21 OCTOBER 1944—D+137: Some enemy patrolling activity took place. The shelling of our front lines with fairly heavy mortar fire continued. The 8th Infantry prepared to relieve the 22nd Infantry on main line of resistance to be affected on October 22 and the 22nd Infantry prepared to relieve the 28th Infantry Division.

22 OCTOBER 1944—D+138: The enemy increased its patrol activity and established more outposts. It increased also the number of mine fields.

The 1st Battalion 8th Infantry maintained positions on the main line of defense, the 2nd Battalion continued their training program, and the 3rd Battalion relieved the 22nd Infantry. The 12th Infantry continued aggressive patrolling to the east and southeast to establish ambushes and harass the enemy. The 22nd Infantry moved to a temporary assembly area prior to affecting relief of the 28th Infantry Division in their zone of action to the north.

23 OCTOBER 1944—D+139: Several rounds of artillery, estimated to be 105 mm, fell in the CT 22 area from 1200 to 1800 hours. The 8th Infantry consolidated and improved positions extended to the north, sent out patrols, one of which engaged an enemy outpost during the afternoon and captured three prisoners. The 12th Infantry with 4th Reconnaissance Troop (Mechanized) continued aggressive patrolling. The 22nd Infantry moved to the northwest and completed the relief by 1330 with regimental CP opening at Rocherath.

24 OCTOBER 1944—D+140: The enemy line in the newly defined northern sector of the 4th Infantry Division was vague. Small enemy forces were employed forward of the pillbox line. About thirty-two rounds of rockets containing enemy propaganda leaflets were received in the CT 8 area at about 1015. The 4th Infantry Division maintained positions to the immediate west of Siegfried line fortifications, and continued patrols and training.

25 OCTOBER 1944—D+141: 4th Infantry Division had skirmishes with enemy small reconnaissance patrols during combat, security, and contact patrolling.

26 OCTOBER 1944—D+142: The enemy continued to employ small patrols. No changes in the activities of the 4th Infantry Division.

27 OCTOBER 1944—D+143: There was less enemy activity. Small patrols did operate, especially in the wooded area, while strong outposts were maintained over most of the sector. Mortar and artillery fires continued to harass our front line elements.

From **Swede Henley's WWII Diary—used with permission of his daughters:**

22-24 OCTOBER: Relieved by 8th Inf. and we relieved the 28th Div. Still just holding. Buzz bombs have been going over regularly.

25-31 OCTOBER: Still in position—sweating out the jerry and what is to come next. Buzz bombs just clearing trees and make awful noise. Our Air Corps in force every night. Nights and days cold as the devil.

28 OCTOBER: 4th Wedding Anniversary

31 OCTOBER: Halloween Night—bo-daddys were out in force.

I found a War Story from October that I haven't used before. This comes from my **War Stories: Paris to VE Day** *book…*

Earl Slater, Hendersonville, TN
Companies E and G, 2nd Battalion, 22nd Infantry Regiment
A Chilling Affair — Combat Bath — As told to his daughter, Anita Slater Capps

Most Americans consider a hot bath a necessity. It rates right up there with our daily bread. Compared to much of the world, we are bath obsessive. It is the prime directive of war that a hot bath is the first casualty of the civilized world. Therefore, to an American infantryman in combat, a hot bath is the ultimate luxury.

It is the second unwritten law of battle that infantrymen seldom know their exact location in relation to the rest of the planet. One foxhole with five inches of water in the bottom looks pretty much like the last one you crawled out of. I can only testify that this incident occurred in the European Theater of Operations, somewhere between Eupen and St. Vith, Belgium.

One chilly October day, word came around that bath facilities were available. All I knew was that somewhere about ten miles behind our lines lay the possibility of a hot bath and clean clothes. As supply sergeant for Company G, 2nd Battalion, 22nd Infantry Regiment, I had a jeep at my disposal. (It was our outfit's only motorized vehicle). Three of us ultimately piled into the jeep, and off we went. Eventually we located a huge tent set up in a big field right next to a stream. Wisps of steam wafted from every opening. Just inside, a hot bath awaited! We were jubilant at our good fortune.

I, for one, had seen my last real shave and shower before I'd landed on Utah Beach on D-Day. The best I'd been able to do since then was a bit of a sponge bath at a creek. Most often, all that was available was a helmet full of cold water and a very bad razor. All attempts at cleanliness were pitiful indeed. Anyway, there was seldom time on the battlefront for such delicate considerations. And clean clothes? I had been in my uniform so long that I could scarcely remember how to get out of it, much less what it looked like when it was clean.

We eagerly ducked under the tent flap and were instantly enveloped in a heavenly vapor. We could scarcely see each other through the mist. The outside temperature was only 35 or 40 degrees, so all of that wonderful hot water was putting off enormous clouds of steam. This was scarcely a luxury accommodation. Plumbing was one big pipe that ran the length of the tent. It was studded with about forty closely spaced showerheads. The temperature of the water was set somewhere else. There were no controls for personal preference, but it seemed like the Hilton to us.

After being issued soap, razors, and the first real towels that we had seen in months, we quickly stripped off our overripe uniforms and dashed into that glorious flow of heated water.

Everything was going great. We got all soaped up from head to foot and then jumped back under the shower to rinse off. The hot water was gone! The water was being pumped directly from the stream behind the tent into some kind of boiler system, and either the fire went out or we had simply used up the heated water supply.

Some of the men were stunned speechless at the unexpected icy shock of cold water, and, of course, some of them heated the air with an assortment of colorful language. There was a tent full of soapy men dashing in and out of one huge freezing shower bath. Myself, I ran under the water about six times before I got rid of the soap.

Once we were dry, things were really looking up again. We climbed into fresh uniforms. Then, somewhat reluctantly, we donned our still nasty field jackets and combat boots. This unexpected treat didn't extend quite as far as clean jackets and boots, but that was OK. We took that little setback in stride and headed for the jeep.

Jeep? Where was the jeep? Gone! Somebody stole our damned jeep! Now, those jeeps didn't have ignition keys, just a switch that you turned off and on. We stumbled around there for a while arguing about what to do. At last, I said, "I'm going to steal us another jeep!"

We appropriated an unoccupied vehicle and returned to our unit. After that experience I swore that I wasn't going to take another damned bath before I left Europe! No matter—there was never another opportunity.

From Chaplain Bill Boice's **History of the 22nd Infantry Regiment in WWII:**

Relief of the 28th Infantry Division began at 0700 hours on the 23rd of October. The rifle battalions side-slipped to the north in the order 1st, 3rd, and then the 2nd. The 1st and 3rd Battalions, Combat Team 22, occupied that front previously held by Combat Teams 109 and 112, 28th Division. The relief was completed by early afternoon, and the battalions established and improved the positions to the northeast and coordinated their defensive fires. This new position placed the defending battalions on a front previously covered by an entire division.

Through the remainder of October and until the 5th of November, the Regiment occupied a position with its front paralleling the Siegfried Line fortifications in the proximity of Krinkelt, Belgium. With no indication of an order for an attack, the Combat Team confined its combat activity to harassing fires and patrolling. The period was highlighted by sharp patrol clashes, considerable harassing and interdicting artillery and mortar fire, and harassing long-range machine-gun 57mm antitank, and self-propelled weapons fire, The battalions, whenever in reserve, conducted training on demolitions and mines, and physical training.

28 OCT 1944 TO 3 NOV 1944 – D+145 TO D+151

28 OCTOBER 1944—D+145: Enemy artillery and mortar fires were lighter than previously.

The 4th Infantry Division continued patrolling and rotation of units to rest and training. It continued planning for future operations..

29 OCTOBER 1944—D+146: The same method of employing patrols and outposts while its main body occupied the pillbox line. Harassing fires were continued by the enemy.

30 OCTOBER 1944—D+147: The 4th Infantry Division sent out combat patrols who reported enemy contacts and installations, plus continued training and preparation for future operations.

31 OCTOBER 1944—D+148: Some activity was seen amongst the enemy forces in the pillbox line. The 8th Infantry sent out patrols from its 2nd and 3rd Battalions to locate and destroy enemy outposts, locate enemy installations, and harass enemy OPL (Out Post Line).

The 12th Infantry continued combat, security, and contact patrolling by the 2nd and 3rd Battalions. Company A remained attached as V Corps CP guard.

The 22nd Infantry sent out patrols from the 1st Battalion. Enemy positions, including Hellenthal and Hollerath, were harassed by indirect fire from 57 mm antitank guns and from caliber .50 machine guns. Training was conducted for units not employed, with emphasis on woods fighting and infantry-tank coordination.

Casualties for October 1944:

Notes about logistics: During the period, emphasis was placed on securing winter supplies. Additional blankets (a total of four per man), woolen underwear (two suits per man), and overcoats were issued. Difficulty was experienced in securing sufficient overshoes (larger than size 9 not available) and sleeping bags (only 5,000 for the division). Sufficient anti-freeze solution was obtained to protect only 10% of the vehicles of the division.

Killed or died of injuries: 2 officers, 49 EM

Missing: 1 officer, 14 EM

Seriously wounded or injured: 5 officers, 21 EM

Slightly wounded or injured: 16 officers, 222 EM

Total casualties: 330

Prisoners captured: 207

Total casualties for 4ID from 6 June 1944 to 31 Oct 1944:

Killed or died of injuries: 177 Officers and 2,205 Enlisted Men

A total of 18,691 prisoners have been taken since D-Day.

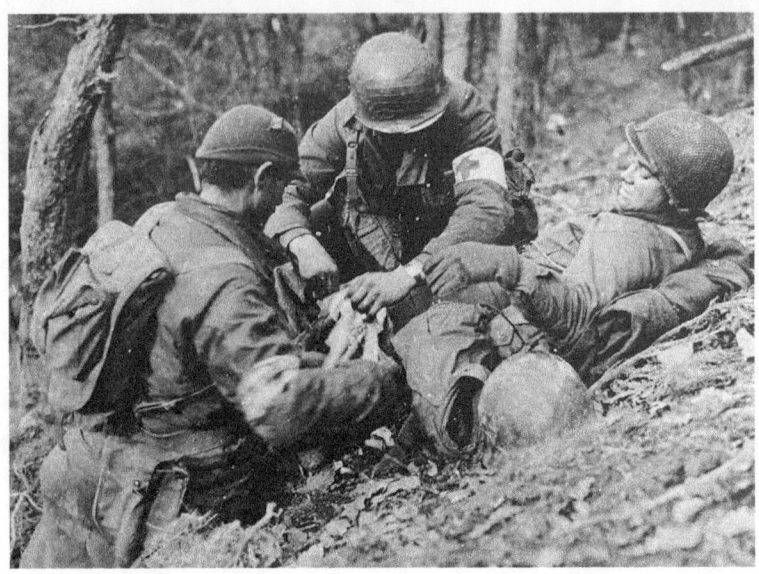

Epic of stark Infantry combat — virtually every 4ID Soldier who fought in the Hurtgen Forest from early November to early December 1944 said the Hurtgen Forest was their toughest fight. Casualties were worse here than any other time in their eleven month fight across Europe. Four of the five Medals of Honor earned in WWII came from the Hurtgen Forest.

NOVEMBER 1944

4ID IN GERMANY
BLOODY HURTGEN FOREST BATTLE

1 NOVEMBER 1944—D+149: The 4th Infantry Division remained in its position in the vicinity of Bullingen, Belgium. During the first days of November, a portion of the Infantry was sent on pass to Paris and to the Corps Recreation Center at Eupen, Belgium. It meant baths, shaves, clean clothes, good rest, and various leisure activities, and also church services.

Enemy patrol activity was relatively light. Mortar fire, however, showed an increase, and small arms fire was directed at our front lines. About 24 shellings, mostly 75 mm and 105 mm were reported.

The 4th Infantry Division maintained its present main line of resistance, continued combat, contact and security patrolling, harassed the enemy positions with artillery, anti-tank weapons, and machine guns. The 8th Infantry sent patrols into no man's land with the mission of capturing prisoners but failed to encounter the enemy. The 1st Battalion supported by light tanks conducted company attack problems in the woods. The 12th Infantry continued combat and contact patrolling without encountering the enemy. The 1st Battalion conducted training in woods fighting and coordination of tanks with infantry. The 22nd Infantry did the same things as the two other regiments with the same results.

2 NOVEMBER 1944—D+150: The enemy defended its Siegfried defenses by employing patrols and dug in outposts. An increase in mortar fire and continued harassing fire from small arms and automatic weapons was in evidence.

The 8th continued combat patrolling, contacted enemy patrols, harassed them, and captured two prisoners. The 1st Battalion relieved the 2nd Battalion, and the training continued. The 12th Infantry continued combat and security patrolling. Companies were rotated to conduct training with emphasis on small unit problems, flame thrower, mine detection, scouting and patrolling. The 22nd Infantry continued security and contact patrolling but limited by our own artillery fires. Company A encountered a stronger enemy patrol and after a short skirmish, returned without suffering casualties. Long range caliber .50 machine gun fire and artillery was used to harass enemy positions. Training continued with personnel not actively engaged with emphasis on platoon attack problems, woods fighting, and mine detection. The 4th Division Artillery fired a diversion mission in conjunction with the attack of the 28th Infantry Division.

3 NOVEMBER 1944—D+151: In addition to the harassing fire, the enemy increased its patrol activity sharply.

Company I, 8th Infantry, was attacked by an enemy patrol of twelve men but dispersed them. The 2nd Battalion conducted training with emphasis on the attack of a river line. The 3rd Battalion, 12th Infantry, repulsed an enemy patrol of six men at 0400. Non employed personnel conducted training with emphasis on enemy mines, coordination of tanks-infantry, and log exercises. Patrols of the 1st Battalion, 22nd Infantry, were engaged in skirmishes with the enemy, captured one prisoner, and withdrew without casualties. Reserve elements received additional training in woods fighting, automatic weapons, and demolitions.

From Swede Henley's WWII Diary—used with permission of his daughters:

1-2 NOVEMBER 1944: Counting our change in these dam woods just short of the Siegfried Line. Buzz bombs going over regularly. Cold as the devil. Buzz bomb fell about 1000 yds from CP on November 1—exploded—scared hell out of us.

3-4 NOVEMBER: Same place doing same thing.

Stay with me—November will be full of the toughest fight in the 107+ year history of the 4th Infantry Division, including four of the five Medals of Honor from WWII being earned in November in the "Hell in the Hurtgen Forest."

4 NOV 1944 TO 10 NOV 1944 – D+152 TO D+158

Fasten your chin straps, we will soon be going into the worst battle of the war for 4ID. Led by the 12th Infantry Regiment on 7 Nov 1944, the entire division was engaged from 16 Nov 1944 into early December. Most of you have never heard of the Hurtgen Forest. It was not covered much in the news when the Battle of the Bulge hit soon after it was over. The 4ID was in both, with no rest in November or December 1944—and the winter weather had set in…

4 NOVEMBER 1944—D+152: Only two small enemy patrols were reported. Harassing small arms fire was again directed at our front line troops.

The 8th and 12th Infantry continued the same activities. The 22nd Infantry continued patrolling, placed harassing fire, long-range fire from machine guns, and a 57 mm antitank gun on enemy positions. It made plans for relief on 5 November by elements of CT 39, 9th Infantry Division. Reconnaissance was made of the area in the vicinity of Krinkelt for contemplated new assembly area.

5 NOVEMBER 1944: Scattered harassing small arms fire and minor patrol activity constituted the enemy action.

The 8th Infantry was relieved by elements of the 39th and 60th Regiments, 9th Infantry Division, beginning at 0955 and completed at 1400. The 12th Infantry was relieved by CT 60, beginning at 1130 and completed by 1200. The 22nd Infantry was relieved by CT 39, beginning at 0900 and completed by 1330. Then the three Regiments moved to temporary assembly areas occupied prior to the move to the north. The 4th Reconnaissance Troop moved to an assembly area in the vicinity of Holzheim.

6 NOVEMBER 1944—D+154: The 4th Division prepared for and initiated movement of some of its elements to assembly areas in the vicinity of Zweifall. The CT 12 crossed the IP at 1810 and was still en route at the end of the day.

7 NOVEMBER 1944—D+155: The 8th Infantry sent 50 vehicles with reconnaissance personnel to the new assembly area. They closed at 1920. The remainder of the 8th Infantry remained in the vicinity of Hunningen until 2200 at which time movement was initiated. The 12th Infantry completed movement and closed in assembly area in the vicinity of Zweifall. Upon arrival, it was attached to the 28th Infantry Division and completed relief of the 109th Infantry Regiment at 1300. The 22nd Infantry sent 50 vehicles with reconnaissance personnel to the new assembly area and the remainder, still assembled in the vicinity of Krinkelt, continued preparation for movement on 8 November. Division HQ moved at 0900 and opened the new CP in Zweifall at 1300.

November 8, 1944: *marks the beginning of the most epic battle in the long and proud history of the 4th Infantry Division. Read this history lesson closely.*

Fit to Fight

The toughest battle ever fought by the 4th Infantry Division was waged in the Hurtgen Forest in November and the first few days of December of 1944. I'll cover that in detail—and you'll see why our 4ID vets from WWII always talked about the "Hell in the Hurtgen Forest" when talking about their toughest days in combat.

8 NOVEMBER 1944—D+156: The 4th Infantry Division was relieved from attachment to V Corps and attached to VII Corps.

The 8th Infantry closed in its new assembly area in the vicinity of Zweifall at 0730 and started tactical reconnaissance. The 1st Battalion of the 12th Infantry attacked at 1230 to take a limited objective. Companies B and C were stopped by machine gun and small arms fire at 1442. The enemy was well dug in and had put in tactical wire covered by its machine guns. Positions were consolidated for the night. The 22nd Infantry remained in the vicinity of Krinkelt until 2200 at which time movement was initiated.

9 NOVEMBER 1944—D+157: The 8th Infantry remained in assembly areas and continued tactical reconnaissance.

The 12th Infantry remained attached to the 28th Infantry Division. Company K of the 3rd Battalion attacked at 1100, advanced 250 yards and received machine gun fire at 1110. A fire fight occurred at 1144, 400 yards across the line of departure. A counterattack was also repulsed at 1305 and several men from the 109th Infantry Regiment were rescued. Company I moved forward at 1305 on the left, and elements of Company K that passed across the enemy tactical wire at 1630 were stopped by heavy enemy fires.

The 22nd Infantry closed in the new assembly area by 0930 and reconnaissance was conducted in areas of projected operations. The 801st Tank Destroyer Battalion, less Company A, which has been a permanent attachment since D-Day, was relieved by the 803rd Tank Destroyer Battalion at 0800.

10 NOVEMBER 1944—D+158: The 8th Infantry continued active reconnaissance, and in anticipation of the projected attack, various attachments were affected.

The 12th Infantry remained attached to the 28th Infantry Division until 1900. New attachments were affected. The 1st Battalion moved out at 0630 and attacked at 0700. It advanced 100 to 200 yards when Company F hit a mine field and was forced to withdraw to reorganize. The 3rd Battalion was counterattacked at 1220 by enemy using flame throwers. The 2nd Battalion was also counterattacked at 1300. In both cases, the enemy employed one company. The enemy was repulsed, and 38 prisoners were taken. The 22nd Infantry, still assembled, made extensive reconnaissance and preparations for impending operations. Attachments were affected.

*From **War Stories II: Paris to VE Day**, we have these stories from 12th Infantry Regiment vets about the early days in the Hurtgen Forest…*

Tallie Crocker (Deceased), Mt. Pleasant, SC
HQ, 2nd Battalion, 12th Infantry Regiment
Hürtgen Forest

On November 6, 1944, the 12th Infantry Regiment was attached to the 28th Infantry Division, which was having a rough time in the Hurtgen Forest. The Germans had driven a salient in their lines and had essentially split their defense in half.

The 12th Infantry left for this assignment at 1745 hours for the 45-mile motor march to the location of the 28th Infantry Division. The weather was miserable with a cold rain falling. The original plan was for the regiment to go into a bivouac area and wait until morning for the relief of the 28th.

Colonel Luckett, the Regimental Commander and his staff, along with Lt. Colonel Montelbano and the staff of the 2nd Battalion of the 12th Infantry, went ahead to meet with the staff of the 28th to get more information on the relief. I was S-3 (Operations Officer) of the 2nd Battalion.

When we reached the headquarters of the 28th, we were informed that the relief was to take place immediately, rather than the next morning, so there was no time for reconnaissance. Since we were operating with radios silenced, a messenger was sent to inform the column that they were not to go into bivouac. At 4 A.M. on November 7, the relief began—in pouring rain, total darkness—and was not completed until midmorning.

The positions that were occupied by the 109th Infantry Regiment were along a salient that the Germans had driven into the 28th lines and were not always in the best place for fighting. The positions that were occupied by the 2nd Battalion of the 12th were along a firebreak and not passable by vehicles, so everything had to be hand carried.

There were dead bodies of the 109th all over the area. Since we had replacements who had not done any fighting, we had some of our troops who had combat experience move the frozen bodies, pile them in several spots, and hide them with boughs broken from the trees by artillery fire.

On November 10, there was a 500-yard gap between Company E and Companies F and G. The plan was for the 1st Battalion to attack at the deepest part of the German salient; Company E was to attack the edge of the salient, and Companies F and G were to attack their fronts. Shortly after the attacks began, the Germans got behind F and G Companies. With Companies F and G were the Battalion CO, the S-3 (me), and an artillery observer with his radio operator. When we tried to send wounded people out, we discovered that we were surrounded by the Germans.

Every day we were subjected to an attack by the Germans. After each attack, we took stock of the .30 caliber ammo on hand for the machine guns, as well as for rifles. If we felt we didn't have enough machine gun ammo for the next attack, we took ammo from the M-1 eight round clips and hand-inserted it into the wet cloth machine gun belts or vice versa. We withstood an attack each day, with two attacks on one day.

On one occasion, the Germans brought tanks within one hundred yards of our positions and yelled for us to surrender since they had us surrounded. The men yelled back, "F**k you," and we requested the artillery forward observer to request artillery fire, high explosive as well as white phosphorus in the area of the tanks. The artillery officer at the guns requested a repeat of the coordinates because of the nearness to our troops. I took the handset from the observer, told the officer to fire, and assured him that we knew what we were doing. When those tanks saw the white phosphorus, they left the area in a hurry.

The lack of food was quite a problem. We searched the packs of the dead 28th Infantry Division troops for food and retrieved from the ground the "dog biscuits" and cheese that had been discarded by the troops. Our first-aid station, which was in large, log-covered holes, had a number of casualties to handle. We had a medic sergeant and aid men manning the aid station, and they really did an excellent job.

By the morning of the third day, November 12, only two of our radios had batteries with a little life left. Fortunately, the artillery radio worked until noon. We were finally left with our battalion radio, which couldn't reach our Battalion HQ. I knew that the 1st Battalion was closer to us than our Battalion CP. I remembered the channel number of their radio net because of a firefight we had taken part in with them in the Siegfried Line. When in a stagnant or offensive operation, we used call signs of Red, White, and Blue for the battalions. Also, when in a defensive situation, we used a three-day prearranged code. That code expired on our first day of isolation. I switched our radio to the 1st Battalion's channel and called, "Red from White," twice, with no response. I then called, "Red from White, come in Chuck." (Chuck Jackson, the 1st Battalion CO and my brother-in-law).

His reply was, "Love from ____." (I don't remember his code name now). But I still remember ours. His message was, "Bring all your loves to me."

We interpreted that to mean, "withdraw," but we wanted to make certain, so I replied, "I think I know what you mean, but want to be certain."

His reply was, "What do you do when you meet a girl with more than you have?" I later told Chuck that the reply should have been, "Attack!"

There was very little daylight left, so we assembled the two company commanders and discussed a withdrawal plan. We decided to withdraw to the location of the 3rd Battalion since it was a shorter distance (about six hundred yards). We also prayed for a foggy morning, but while we slept it snowed all night. When we got up it was to a bright sunny morning. For some reason, the Germans had left during the night. We lost only two men to mines during our withdrawal.

When Chuck Jackson greeted me, he said, "I'm so glad to see you—I wondered what Mary would say if she found out we were so close, and you didn't make it."

When we reached our Battalion Headquarters, Major General R. O. Barton, Division Commander was standing outside to welcome us and to inform us that we were again in the 4th Infantry Division.

When I returned to the CP, I learned that I had trench foot and was evacuated two days later. I didn't return to the 12th Infantry Regiment until early February 1945, so I missed the German breakthrough. We had been told nothing about trench foot or its prevention, but when more casualties were being sustained from that problem than from the Germans, prevention was really enforced. Trench foot was encountered in WWI also—guess that's where the word "trench" came from.

Robert Gast (Deceased), Warsaw, IN
Companies B and C, 1st Battalion, 12th Infantry Regiment
All Hell Broke Loose

I will never forget the first day that we entered the Hürtgen Forest. My platoon guide said to me, "Lieutenant, I don't like the smell of this." Those were his exact words. He went back to an aid station, and I never saw him again. In less than two weeks my platoon was gone, along with most of the line officers and men of the entire regiment. I only remember one day that we seemed to temporarily get the better of the enemy.

One afternoon we were getting nowhere trying to work our way forward in that treacherous forest. One of my men came to me and informed me that there was a road and a break in the forest on our left flank. We decided to deploy down the road, off to the side, and to keep complete silence. I sent two scouts out ahead, and my runner and I followed by about fifty yards. We had not gone very far when one of the scouts gave us the "down sign" and motioned me to come forward. I could not believe what I saw—a machine gun sticking out from a camouflaged foxhole. We walked quietly over and knocked the camouflage from the top of the hole. There at the bottom sat two German soldiers eating their rations. We not only took them prisoner, but we also captured a number of their platoon that we caught by surprise.

Captain Witkoff, our company commander, came forward and established his CP. A forward observer came up to direct fire on the enemy. Unfortunately for all of us, he came up short, and the 105s came pouring in on us. At the same time, the Germans had zeroed in on our position and 88s began bursting in the trees above us. The casualties were terrible.

In Colonel Johnson's book, *The History of the 12th Infantry Regiment in WWII*, he devotes a number of paragraphs on the attempt to get to and relieve Companies F and G. I was the only line officer left in Company C when that final attempt was made. We had been almost wiped out by the constant shelling and had made a withdrawal to regroup. I was in a hole with a group of soldiers when a voice called out, "Anyone in there?" Of course, we all came out. It was another lieutenant who was trying to round up enough men to open up a way to Companies F and G. We could locate maybe forty or fifty men. I'm not sure. I do know that he and I were the only officers. To make a long story short, we did manage to fight our way to Companies F and G. A lot of us were wounded, however, including myself, and ended up trapped along with the two companies of the 2nd Battalion.

I ended up in an "aid" hole with six or seven badly wounded men. Most of them were too bad to try to leave with the ill-fated attempt to evacuate the wounded. The next morning, at the crack of dawn, Colonel Sibert, about six or eight soldiers, twelve wounded men, and a number of German prisoners started the ill-fated escape. We walked right into a bunch of German soldiers. I was the first of the wounded, just behind a blinded GI. All hell broke loose. The mad dash back to where we started from is impossible to describe. I don't know how any of us made it. The next morning we left single file and used a different route. It was successful. We had only a few casualties from "Bouncing Betties."

Robert Williamson (Deceased), Lakeland, FL
Company F, 2nd Battalion, 12th Infantry Regiment
Three Days and Three Nights

We went at night by truck convoy and moved up and around Aachen. We stayed in a big forest called the "Hürtgen Forest," and got into the foxholes, which weren't very deep and weren't covered with logs when we got there. We had no blankets, and it was extremely cold. The next morning those Germans started sending over barrages and made it kind of hot for us all morning. Around 1000 hours we moved out farther into the forest where we relieved the 28th Infantry Division. When we relieved them, they had the men that had been killed piled up like cords of wood. The next morning, the artillery started again and lasted through the day. The following morning we took off through the forest and hadn't gone more than three or four hundred yards when some of the men stepped on some "shoe mines" and "Bouncing Betties," which blew their legs off. There were so many in our paths that we couldn't get through the forest to the Germans, which were about one hundred fifty yards on the other side of this minefield. We all had to turn back to our foxholes again.

We had just got back to our foxholes when the artillery started again. Off on the left flank the Germans started to move in. You should have seen us stop them in their tracks. We fought them off for three days and three nights. After the three days and three nights without food or water and with ammunition running low, the fourth morning came with "relief " and got us out of the forest. It had snowed on the third night, and that was what we ate to keep alive. When we got down to the valley, we took off our helmets, dipped them in the creek, and drank our fill.

Most of us were wounded and when we got back off the lines, they set up a first aid station. They put us through the first aid station, and then we were sent to the rear in ambulances. I was wounded with shrapnel in my neck the first day. At the first aid stations, the doctors tried to remove the shrapnel from my neck without any anesthetic. It hurt so much that I told them to leave it alone. I went to the 189th General Hospital outside of Paris. There they were afraid to remove the shrapnel because it could paralyze me.

Most of us were shipped back to Germany in January of 1945, sent through replacement pool camps, and then shipped back to our outfits. When we got back to our outfits, they were across the Rhine River, and we had some hard fighting ahead.

11 NOV 1944 TO 18 NOV 1944 – D+159 TO D+16

11 NOVEMBER 1944—D+159: Our advances were contested stubbornly; the enemy was even counterattacking at every opportunity in strength varying from platoon to company. At least three such counterattacks were preceded by heavy artillery preparation. In addition to the formal counterattacks, the enemy aggressively attempted to infiltrate our line and attack our forces from the rear. Shelling by enemy artillery was constant throughout the period. Tanks and self-propelled guns were seen mostly in the vicinity of Hurtgen.

The 2nd Battalion of the 8th Infantry moved to a forward assembly area, dug in, and secured itself for the night. The 12th Infantry improved positions beginning at 0800 and efforts were made to clean enemy resistance in the rear areas of the 2nd Battalion. Enemy pressure in this area continued throughout the day and resulted in Companies E and G being isolated. The 1st Battalion attacked to reach isolated companies but was stopped by heavy machine guns, small arms, and 88 mm fire. The 22nd Infantry continued reconnaissance, planning, and coordination for next operations.

12 NOVEMBER 1944—D+160: By holding our attempts to advance practically to a standstill, and his thorough employment of mines of all kinds, barbed wire, and blocks of various nature, the enemy found little difficulty in counterattacking fiercely with infantry supported by armor. Continuous shelling by three to four batteries, ranging in caliber from light to medium, made it difficult for our forces to organize a thrust against the enemy.

No changes for the 8th and 22nd Infantry. The 12th Infantry repulsed enemy counterattacks at 0841, 0846, 1020 and 1413. The enemy attack at 1020 consisted of approximately 150 infantrymen and some tanks but was forced to retreat toward Hurtgen at 1203, leaving about 90 men isolated behind companies F and G, and the 1st Battalion which had previously attacked and broken through to relieve F and G companies. At the end of the day, the enemy had cut communications and contacts between the CT 12 and 1st Bn and F and G companies.

13 NOVEMBER 1944—D+161: The 12th Infantry was engaged in fierce fighting in the Hurtgen Forest. Casualties were high and it was necessary to unify all efforts to obtain necessary replacements.

The enemy remained relatively inactive. Its defense was organized along the same front lines from which patrols operated to probe our positions and to determine our strength. Twenty-one shellings were reported by the 4th Infantry Division units. It was estimated that there were three battalions of enemy artillery capable of firing into the sector held by CT 12. All battalions of the 8th and 22nd Infantry conducted instructions for all officers in adjustment of artillery fire. Beginning at 0730, isolated companies A, C, F, and G, 12th Infantry, initiated a short withdrawal to reestablish contact. By mid-afternoon, while being harassed by small arms and artillery fire, the operation had been completed successfully.

14 NOVEMBER 1944—D+162: The Assistant G-1 First Army visited the division to check on casualties and replacements. The hazards of fighting were intensified by the dense forest and the lack of roads. Medical aid men found it necessary to carry litter cases up to two miles over rough terrain and through extensive mine fields. The casualty rate among aid men and litter bearers was extremely high and replacements were difficult to obtain. It was necessary to use other means for this purpose and to utilize personnel from rear installations.

The enemy defended its same front line with heavy artillery and mortar barrages. Only one other action, a single patrol which withdrew hastily upon engagement with the 298 Engineer Combat Battalion was reported. No change of activities for the 8th and 22nd Infantry. The 1st Battalion, 12th Infantry relieved the 2nd Battalion on the main line of resistance and the 2nd Battalion moved to an assembly area, closing therein by 1700.

15 NOVEMBER 1944—D+163: The Division obtained 27 Medical Department enlisted men. This was the last large shipment of medical personnel received during the month. This was only about half the number of men needed to fill existing vacancies. Throughout the month, the problem remained acute.

The enemy defended its same front line with heavy artillery and mortar fire. A total of 35 shellings were reported by division units. The largest weapon employed was 210 mm. It appeared that most of the shellings were directed just behind our front lines and in the division rear areas (among them, the CP of the Division but without casualties), using this means to prevent our organizing an attack while the enemy probed our lines with patrols.

Troops of the 8th Infantry continued construction and improvement of shelters and protective covering. The 12th Infantry continued to improve positions, fields of fire, and main supply road. Installations of mines and booby traps were completed. The 22nd Infantry put emphasis on discussion and studying of maps and aerial photographs and coordination of all attached and supporting units.

(Between now and early December 1944, you're going to be reading about the fiercest fighting the 4ID has ever been engaged in—in a place called the Hurtgen Forest in Germany in November 1944.)

16 NOVEMBER 1944—D+164: The enemy fiercely resisted our advance by employing well located machine guns, small arms, and concentrated barrages of 80 and 120 mm mortars. Several log pillboxes with excellent fields of fire were encountered. The advances to each enemy position were well supplied with mines, both anti-vehicular and antipersonnel. In addition, barbed wire, sometimes consisting of three row concertinas, made any attempt to take the positions almost futile. 28 enemy artillery shellings were reported.

The 4th Infantry Division launched a coordinated attack to the northeast beginning at 1245 in the direction of Duren with three regimental combat teams abreast. Prior to 1800, they had succeeded in advancing through heavily wooded terrain approximately 1500 meters.

The 8th Infantry began movement at 0830 with the 2nd Battalion. The 1st Battalion moved forward to occupy the positions previously occupied by the 2nd Battalion at 0830 and closed at 1050. The attack was preceded by an aerial bombardment at 1115 and H-Hour was set for 1245. The 2nd Battalion jumped off following the artillery preparation and under heavy mortar fire, advanced slowly, Companies F and G abreast, until they reached a band of triple concertina wire covered by small arms and mortar fires. Due to the failure of the Bangalore torpedoes to function, the battalion was ordered to prepare its defense for the night. At 1355 the 1st Battalion received orders to move two companies forward to a hill previously occupied by two assault companies of the 2nd Battalion. This attack was initiated at 1540 but had to be terminated by 1625 and coordination affected for the night.

The 2nd Battalion, 12th Infantry left its assembly area at 1145 and together with the 3rd Battalion attacked one hour later. Small arms, mortar, machine gun, and artillery fires were received immediately, and the advances of both battalions were impeded by extensive mine fields. Heavy opposition continued throughout the day. Only the 2nd Battalion successfully negotiated the mine field confronting it and continued its advance to within 400 yards of its objective.

The 22nd Infantry attacked at 1245 and the main opposition encountered was in the form of heavy mortar concentration. Prior to the end of the day, considerable gains had been made over rough terrain.

* * * * *

This will be the longest history lesson that you'll read in this book. Not only was the battle in the Hurtgen Forest raging during 1944, the Battle of Dak To was going on in Vietnam in November 1967, and President Kennedy was killed in 1963. For those of you who, like me, love history—read on.

17 NOVEMBER 1944—D+165: The primary problem was the requisition and delivery of replacements to the regiments. The fighting was so intense and deadly that daily requisitions were necessary. The replacement system could not supply an adequate number of new men and the result was that the strength of all three regiments decreased steadily until at the end of the month the three regiments were very low in fighting strength. Both battle and non-battle casualties were extremely high. The thick woods, the continuous rain, plus the fact that the majority of replacements were not furnished with overshoes, caused a great number of cases of trench foot. Battle casualties were high due to the great number of mines and booby traps, and to the tree bursts from German artillery and mortar fire. No one was spared. The infantry Soldiers of the 4th Infantry Division will always remember the hell of the Hurtgen Forest.

The highest percentage of casualties suffered was among the leaders. A good Soldier might start an attack as a rifleman and by the time the objective was taken find himself acting squad leader. In order to control and employ his squad he must move about among his men and the result was that he became a casualty himself in a short time. At this rate of attrition, the most capable men in some companies were soon gone. This critical situation was alleviated to some extent by a small shipment of squad leaders, platoon sergeants, and 1st sergeants.

The enemy employed a well dug in position which covered the approaches through the woods along the firebreak and the few poor roads. Thickly concentrated barbed wire and mines were noted. The enemy probed our lines with patrols and in at least three instances counterattacks were received by our forces, the largest consisting of a force of 80 men.

The 8th Infantry attacked in a column of battalions at 0800 with the 2nd Battalion in the assault. Due to the heavy mortar fires received at H-Hour, and the heavy casualties suffered in the previous day's operations, this battalion was unable to advance beyond the concertina wire previously mentioned. An attack of the 1st Battalion was ordered but never initiated. Before the troops could begin passing through the gap, the enemy launched a counterattack. This attack was repulsed, and fifteen prisoners taken. The 1st Battalion was ordered to consolidate on its old position for the night.

The 12th Infantry attacked with the 2nd Battalion at 0840 and shortly encountered machine gun fire covering the mine fields. Work was continued under fire with an effort to clear the mines and booby traps while numerous patrols sought alternative routes. No gains were in evidence at the end of the day.

The 22nd Infantry was subjected during the early hours of the morning to extremely heavy artillery concentrations, casualties included the 1st and 3rd Battalion commanders. (For you Vietnam 4ID vets reading this, one of the wounded battalion commanders was Glenn Walker—who commanded 4ID in Vietnam as our Commanding General from Nov 1969 to Jun 1970). This resulted in a delay, but the attack was initiated at 0945 against heavy mortar, machine gun, and small arms fire. Two light tanks were knocked out by mines and those remaining were unable to proceed because of the denseness of the woods. However, by 1300 the 3rd Battalion had advanced and formed a defensive flank to the north. At this time, the 1st and 2nd Battalions were again ordered to attack. The virtually impassable terrain and the enemy infiltration in the rear of the 2nd Battalion hampered the advance. After reaching dominating positions on the main north-south road, the advance was halted, and positions consolidated for the night.

From the **Diary of Swede Henley—used with permission of his daughters:**

11 NOVEMBER: Armistice Day in U.S.A. but a day of hell over here. Rain fell most of the day. Attack delayed until tomorrow. We are hoping that this next attack is one that breaks Adolph's back...the sorry bastard. I'm after him.

12-14 NOVEMBER: Still counting our change waiting for the weather to get right so we can knock the jerry wide open. Plans have been delayed 3 days now. Snowing and sleet has been falling every day. Jerry shells our CP area daily. AT Platoon man hurt this PM.

15 NOVEMBER: Same place just counting our change. Jerry shelling hell out of us. Orders were cancelled until the 16th now and will go off on the 17th regardless of weather. 7th and 9th Air forces and the RAF in direct support of VII Corps. Received orders that attack would start at 1245 tomorrow. Mass bombing to start at 1115 and artillery to start at 1145 until 1245.

16 NOVEMBER D-DAY H-HOUR 1245: Wave after wave of heavy bombers came over and bombed. Artillery started at 1145 and blasted until H-Hour. 2nd Bn crossed LD on time and gained objective. 1st Bn passed thru E Co. and advanced about 500 yards before dark. Buttoned up for the night. Casualties extremely light—not artillery as expected.

17 NOVEMBER D-1: All hell broke loose. Jerry artillery and mortars cutting us to pieces. Major Drake killed—Capt. Henley took over Bn and fought it until they had secured objective and turned it over to Major Goforth who came up. Jerry artillery and mortars still cutting us to pieces. Casualties high—between 70 and 100 men hit. Evacuation extremely difficult. Had to hand carry wounded about 1 mile. All supplies hand carried over extremely hard conditions.

18 NOVEMBER D-2: Bn reorganized and jumped across main road and advanced about 500 yards, held up because 2nd Bn hadn't moved. Col. Walker, Major Samuels, Capt. Kerr, the S-6-5-3 hit and evacuated (Editor's note: that is battalion commander, executive officer, and operations officer—three main command guys in the battalion). Major Blazzard took over and 2nd Bn advanced up to the 1st Bn and tied in. Jerry still shelling everything. Casualties still high. Capt. Martin C Co. CO hit. Lt. Kersey, MacCracken killed. Roads mined so everything had to be hand carried. Hurtgen Forest—it lacked a long way from being a lovers lane.

From **War Stories Volume II: Paris to VE Day…**

Henry "Hank" Strecker (Deceased)
Company C, 1-12 Infantry
Siegfried Line Experiences

Submitted by his daughter, Leslie Strecker Weisner

The third time I was hit was about the time Ward Means got wounded. C Company, First Battalion, 12th Regiment, with one platoon from A Company were attacking the Germans in the Hurtgen Forest. Snow was falling on the morning of November 11, 1944. F and G Companies,

Second Battalion, 12th Regiment, were surrounded by Germans for about three days without food or medical supplies. It was do or die.

Heavy weapons D Company set up two water-cooled .30 caliber machine guns and opened fire as we charged the Germans. We ran at them yelling, "Let 'em have it," as we fired our rifles. The Germans were completely caught off guard. I took one German prisoner out of a foxhole; the rest ran off into the woods.

I started telling the boys from F Company, lying in their foxholes, that we had broken through the German lines. They were overjoyed and some began to cry with extreme relief. I was out of water, so I started scooping up hands full of water out of holes torn in the ground by shell fragments.

I felt like I owned that forest. The Germans started firing .88 mm armor piercing shells at us from a tank. The shells would hit the three to four inch thick pine tree trunks, snapping them off like toothpicks, three or four at a time. The tree trunks would snap in a cloud of steam-like vapor. I walked around like nothing could kill me. That feeling is very rare. Most of the time, you're groveling for a hole and praying you don't get hit. Also—shaking like a leaf.

It started getting dark and orders came up that we had to spend the night there. I started looking for a foxhole to crawl into. There was a dead German in a hole, and I grabbed him by the boots and started to pull him out, but the cloying smell stopped me. I did not think I could cope with that odor all night.

Ray Litterst occupied the next hole I came to, and Ray invited me to spend the night there. In the middle of the night, I woke up. Ice water was dripping down my neck and my feet were ice cold. I raised my head to look down at my feet. During the night it started to snow again, and my boots were covered with snow. The elements were taking their turn at giving us the works. At dawn, we awoke with nothing to eat. Ray had an extra bittersweet chocolate bar which he offered me. I appreciated this tremendously.

After about three hours, we received orders to withdraw from these positions. In the meantime, the Germans dropped a small mortar round on us. It hit in the pine trees overhead, sending a shower of snow down on us. The shrapnel hit no one. I thought to myself, this does not look good. They are probably zeroing in on us. As we moved on out, I saw a new BAR used as a support to hold up the front of a foxhole. I was tempted to change it for my old one, but second thoughts stopped me. Mine was tried and true.

As we moved on out, we had to pass through some cleared ground. As we suspected, we had given them four hours to set up their artillery. The German artillery gunners were second to none. All hell broke loose. By this time in my fighting career, I became an old hand at finding the nearest hole or whatever to crawl into. I found a hole with four other fellows in it. We were in there like sardines.

November 13th, suddenly I heard someone calling, "Help me fellow!" I immediately recognized the voice of Ward "Brownie" Means. I hesitated momentarily, thinking I'm relatively safe in this hole. But then you think, if that was me out there, I would want someone to help me. I scrambled out of the hole and ran over to where Brownie was lying in the snow. There was an aid lieutenant with Ward, but that lieutenant wasn't much bigger than me. I only weighed about 135 pounds, but the good Lord turned our bodies into steel. I put Ward's left arm over my shoulder and the lieutenant took his right. Ward was hit in the back and couldn't walk. His left hand had the forefinger tip and thumb blown off. Blood was running down the front of my raincoat. If someone saw you dragging someone at home here with a back injury like that, they would swear you were crazy. But the time was NOW.

Smoke was curling up out of the shell holes around us. We had to drag Ward over 200 yards of shell-ploughed ground with rounds falling all around us. Only by the grace of God did we make it. We put Ward on a litter and the aid men carried him back. The Germans shelled us for over an hour before they quit. They used zonal fire on us, not changing the settings on their guns.

I crawled into another hole with two aid men in it. The one aid man asked if I was hit. Ward's blood was on my coat and there were two holes in it. I said no. I opened my raincoat and fatigue shirt. I was wearing a German pistol I found in a farmyard back in Normandy. I had made a shoulder holster for it. A piece of shrapnel went through my coat and shirt, hit the pistol, tearing the holster, and gouging the steel butt, and bounced out leaving two holes, two inches apart. I still have the pocket material out of the shirt, with the holes in it, which means nothing to anyone but my family and me. God had his hand over me again.

Lloyd Crotteau, Wisconsin Rapids, WI
Company C, 1st Battalion, 22nd Infantry Regiment
Don't Bathe in the Woods

You want stories? As Jimmy Durante would say, "I got a million of them." I made the D-Day invasion. I was hit at Monteberg, St. Lo, and the Hürtgen Forest. In the Hürtgen Forest, on November 19, 1944, we were ordered to hold until afternoon. I was on C Company's right

flank when I spotted three officers heading straight into the German lines. I tried to motion to them, but they were looking at a map and didn't see me. I jumped the road and a small creek and ran along the edge of the creek until they saw me. They were trying to locate Company C. I showed them where we were and ran back to my foxhole.

On the way back, I filled my helmet with water and when it looked safe, I took off my shirt and started to bathe. I heard the gun go off and the whine of the shell. I dove for my foxhole, but it was too late. It was a tree burst, and I got a piece of it through my left arm, paralyzing it. I had a young friend help me back to the jump-off spot where I ran into a medical jeep, and they took me back. I've often wondered who those officers were and if they knew I was hit. Lesson learned — don't take baths in the woods.

David Roderick, Carlsbad, CA
Company H, 2nd Battalion, 22nd Infantry Regiment
Twenty-first Birthday

Back at my 81mm mortar section placement, I became aware of the usual "over and below" target landing of mortar shells near my position. What followed was the first barrage of firing for effect. I knew we were in trouble. I crawled from my hole next to the mortar placement into a ravine that ran in from my guns. Then, as shells burst around me, I scrambled along a ravine for seventy-five yards to our platoon CP, informed my platoon leader, and requested to move the men from the position. With permission, I hurried back up the ravine under fire and ordered all of the men out of their holes and into the ravine. I led them to safety and placed them into holes with our men from the other squads. A tremendous mortar barrage continued for some time.

Later, I went back to observe the situation and found direct hits on one gun emplacement and direct hits on two foxholes that would have been occupied by four men, including my own. Seven lives had been saved from serious injury or death. I received my second Bronze Star medal for my efforts. That night while discussing it with my close friend Sergeant Bert Smith, I remembered that it was November 18, my 21st birthday.

Paul Brunelle, Avon, MA
Company G, 2nd Battalion, 8th Infantry Regiment
German Artillery All Around Us

From the book Company G, 2nd Battalion, 8th Infantry Regiment, 4th Infantry Division by Shirley Devine. Reprinted with permission.

Well, I guess we moved through the Siegfried Line, and then into the Hürtgen Forest. The Hürtgen Forest, as we all know, was a terrible slaughter. Wonderful men were killed all around us. It was an experience that nobody who was there could ever forget. I can remember hearing about the big breakthrough that was going to take place. They moved us into the edge of the forest, had us dig foxholes, and prepare a jumping off spot to push through the Hürtgen.

Immediately upon the resumption of the attack, tremendous German artillery came in all around us. A great number of American casualties occurred in those very first couple of days. I remember Joe Regario received a battlefield commission and Lieutenant Bernard Ray (who earned the Medal of Honor) was killed during those first couple of days, as were many other people.

I dug in with a fellow from Oklahoma who was an Indian. I never really knew what his name was, but everybody called him Chief. I guess every Indian who served in the armed forces was assumed to be an Indian chief, so we always called him Chief. We had not only battlefield

casualties there, but we had a number of people who went back because of battlefield fatigue, shock, and one thing or another. It was truly a terrible experience.

After a few days, we were moved out of that position and attempted a penetration at another point. I recall seeing the tanks they brought in to clear a minefield. We had a number of casualties when the minefield was penetrated. People didn't know it was mined, and by the time the first person hit a mine, the troops were killed at that point. I also remember seeing a stream of German prisoners coming out of the forest. One poor soul was bleeding from the mouth and pleading for help. There was nothing that a poor PFC could do to help him, but I did have a great deal of compassion for him. I heard later on that he had died. It didn't surprise me, because when I saw him he was losing a great deal of blood.

Well, they moved us back again to that operation. The battle went on for some time and the casualties were great. The surviving troops were very few. Just about every day a whole new group of replacements would be sent up, and by nightfall we would be calling for more. This happened day after day. The casualty rate was high—very high—and the situation was gloomy. Everyone was depressed and expecting that he would be the next one to go.

In the Hürtgen Forest, I do remember how our company cooks strived to bring us hot meals whenever they could. They were always encouraging and really did the best that they could do to try to build up our morale. I can remember being served Thanksgiving dinner and just not being able to believe that all the traditional things that we knew of at home were served to us on that occasion. It was quite an achievement for the cooks in our company to have been able to prepare a meal for us like that.

Some of us survived, and we were then moved down to Luxembourg to regroup. When we were in Luxembourg, we were billeted in small towns. I recall staying in a farmhouse. Being a PFC, I didn't have any special privileges. So, instead of being inside of a house, I slept in the hayloft of the barn. But even that was a luxury after having slept in the cold frigid woods of the forest, so I didn't object. I considered myself very fortunate.

One night in the Hürtgen Forest or the Siegfried Line, they brought us up some wet blankets. As I said, our cooks and our rear echelon staff did the very best they could to try to help us. The blankets weren't really wet, they were damp, and when you rolled up in them at least you were warm. It was a rainy, cold night, and there was no way of digging a foxhole. There was mortar fire in the vicinity, but we just stretched out under the pine trees. We said if the mortars come tonight, there is no way we can protect ourselves, we'll just have to take it as it comes. But fortunately, they didn't drop mortars in on us. The next day we moved out, and we all made it safely.

I remember the corrugated roads. The engineers would come up and chop down these small trees and create wooden corduroy roads in the places that were just about a quagmire. Nobody could have gotten through them unless the engineers had been there and done this. I can remember the big trees and how the shells would land in the trees and scatter the shrapnel around.

This wraps this week's look back to the worst battle of 4ID history, and it has just begun. It will continue until early December. Four of the five Medals of Honor awarded to 4ID Soldiers in WWII were earned in the Hurtgen Forest. The first was earned by LT Bernard Ray on 17 November 1944. I'll have his and the other three citations later in the book.

18 NOV 1944 TO 24 NOV 1944 – D+166 TO D+172

18 NOVEMBER 1944—D+166: The same well prepared positions, protected by mines and wire entanglements, were utilized by the enemy in its slow withdrawal in front of our forces. In each case, the withdrawal was protected by heavy mortars and artillery preparations which enabled the enemy to abandon one position and then fall back to another previously prepared. A total of 35 shellings were reported, mostly with 105 mm.

The 4th Infantry Division continued its attack to the east and northeast.

The 1st Battalion, 8th Infantry crossed its line of departure at 0915 with Company C supported by one platoon of medium tanks. The tanks led the way, ran down the concertina wire, destroying anti-personnel mines and the attacking troops followed in the tanks' tracks, without casualties, to the main road. Being unable to continue across the road due to steep banks, the tanks were brought under enemy fire. The attacking infantry, however, continued its attack under cover of tank fire until they were ordered to consolidate positions for the night. During this time, the 2nd Battalion continued its reorganization without advancing and the 3rd Battalion staged two companies forward to high ground.

The 2nd Battalion, 12th Infantry, moved out at 0830 and passed through the line held by elements of the 1st Battalion at 1051 hours. The advance was continued slowly by company G for another hour and, without contact with the enemy, difficulties were experienced in negotiating the many mine fields encountered. These mine fields consisted mostly of teller and box mines in the roadways, S and Schu mines in the wooded areas. Companies E and F encountered small arms and machine gun fire shortly after 1600 and were unable to bring up tank support because of the nature of the terrain. At 1607, they were stopped by the hostile fires. Positions were consolidated at this time, the biggest advance having been made by Company G.

The 22nd Infantry attacked at 0830 with the 1st and 2nd Battalions abreast, across the main north-south road toward the high ground. The 2nd Battalion immediately encountered heavy machine gun and small arms fire and was held up. The 1st Battalion advanced slowly against heavy mortar and artillery fire but at 1013, Companies A and C were astride the road where the artillery and small arms fire was becoming intense. As the situation developed, the 3rd Battalion moved to protect the flank and to maintain contact between the attacking battalions. By 1345, the 1st Battalion had progressed 500 yards beyond the roadway and had secured its objective. The 2nd Battalion resumed its attack at 1430 and within an hour and a half, had pressed forward some 500 yards. By 1650, it was upon its objective.

Serious difficulties of supply and evacuation greatly handicapped the advance. The few roads were in poor shape (weather conditions) and were heavily mined as well as almost constantly interdicted with artillery, with as a result, the loss of important armored support.

19 NOVEMBER 1944—D+167: The enemy fought from well-fortified and well protected dug in emplacements, wooden bunkers, and pillboxes in an attempt to frustrate our advance. Several small counterattacks were launched against CT 22. Although well planned and supported by strong artillery, they did not penetrate our lines.

The 1st Battalion, 8th Infantry, was unable to advance because of heavy enemy small arms, mortar, and tank fire. The 3rd Battalion began movement at 0930 in the trace of the 1st Battalion. Companies K and L turned to the south and seized a limited objective.

The 2nd Battalion, 12th Infantry, initiated an attack at 0845. Continuous mortar fire was heavy and accurate enough to make mine removal and work on the necessary stream crossings a slow and tedious process for both the infantry and the supporting engineers. Interlocking bands of heavy machine gun fire covered the continuous mine fields installed in every firebreak. Numerous efforts were made but little gains were reported.

The 2nd Battalion, 22nd Infantry, was not re-supplied which necessitated postponement of the operation planned for this date. Hand carrying parties were organized and throughout the day, continuous progress was made in clearing forward routes. Positions were consolidated and patrols operated with occurrence of several skirmishes.

*****

In WWII, there were five 4ID Soldiers who were awarded the Medal of Honor. Four of those were earned in the Hurtgen Forest (other one was to BG Teddy Roosevelt, Jr. for his actions on D-Day). The first one was earned on 17 Nov 44 by LT Bernard Ray—here is the citation for his award:

RAY, BERNARD J. (POSTHUMOUSLY)

Rank And Organization: First Lieutenant, U.S. Army, Company F, 8th Infantry, 4th Infantry Division.

Place And Date: Hurtgen Forest near Schevenhutte, Germany, 17 November 1944.

Entered Service At: Baldwin, New York

Born: Brooklyn, New York, G.O. # 115, 8 December 1945

Citation: He was platoon leader with Company F, 8th Infantry, on 17 November 1944, during the drive through the Hurtgen Forest near Schevenhutte, Germany. The American forces attacked in wet, bitterly cold weather over rough, wooded terrain, meeting brutal resistance from positions spaced throughout the forest behind mine fields and wire obstacles. Small arms, machine gun, mortar, and artillery fire caused heavy casualties in the ranks when Company F was halted by a concertina type wire barrier. Under heavy fire, 1st Lt. Ray reorganized his men and prepared to blow a path through the entanglement, a task which appeared impossible of accomplishment and from which others tried to dissuade him. With implacable determination to clear the way, he placed explosive caps in his pockets, obtained several bangalore torpedoes, and then wrapped a length of highly explosive primer cord about his body. He dashed forward under direct fire, reached the barbed wire, and prepared his demolition charge as mortar shells, which were being aimed at him alone, came steadily nearer his completely exposed position. He had placed a torpedo under the wire and was connecting it to a charge he carried when he was severely wounded by a bursting mortar shell. Apparently realizing that he would fail in his self-imposed mission unless he completed it in a few moments, he made a supremely gallant decision. With the primer cord still wound about his body and the explosive caps in his pocket, he completed a hasty wiring system and unhesitatingly thrust down on the handle of the charger, destroying himself with the wire barricade in the resulting blast. By the deliberate sacrifice of his life, 1st Lt. Ray enabled his company to continue its attack, resumption of which was of positive significance in gaining the approaches to the Cologne Plain.

20 NOVEMBER 1944—D+168: The enemy continued its determined resistance from well camouflaged and thoroughly dug in positions. Antitank and antipersonnel mine fields as well as thick wire entanglements were encountered throughout the 4th Infantry Division's zone of advance.

The 8th Infantry attacked with the 2nd and 3rd Battalions at 1000. The 1st Battalion attack was again impeded by heavy artillery, mortar, and flat trajectory tank fire. The 1st Battalion covered 250 yards before heavy fires stopped it. Due to an anti-personnel mine field, the 2nd Battalion was forced to maneuver to the north and its advance was slow until it received the order to consolidate for the night. Heavy artillery and mortar fire prevented the 3rd Battalion from continuing to the south to establish contact with the 22nd Infantry.

Elements of the attacking 1st Battalion, 12th Infantry, were able to advance 100 yards but by 1250, were forced back by extremely heavy and accurate fire. By 1300, elements of the 3rd Battalion lost what little ground they had stubbornly fought for and were forced back. The only gain secured was the one of Company E (450 yards) and it can be attributed in part to the availability of three tanks.

Front line elements of the 22nd Infantry were subjected to heavy concentrations of both 120 mm mortars and 150 mm artillery fire during the night. The 2nd Battalion attacked at 0850 to take a limited objective approximately 600 yards astride the main road of Grosshau. Heavy opposition was encountered immediately. It was subsequently discovered that the enemy had launched an attack at the same time. The battalion forced its way forward slowly and at 1000 had company G on its objective. At 1050, a counterattack of an enemy force which included six tanks or self-propelled guns was repulsed with the reinforcement of Company L. The 1st Battalion, delayed, attacked at 0920 and progressed rapidly (300 yards) and by 1017, it had completed its mission. Roads were immediately blocked with mines and bazooka teams. A counterattack was launched by the enemy at 1037 but the 1st Battalion had completed consolidating and the enemy was allowed to come within very close range before being repulsed with heavy casualties. By 1420, the 1st and 2nd Battalions were firmly established upon their objective, but heavy artillery and mortar fire continued upon them. The essential bridge had been completely demolished and the almost constant shelling made engineer work extremely difficult.

The second Medal of Honor earned in the Hurtgen Forest was earned on 11-20-44:
MABRY, GEORGE L., JR.

Rank And Organization: Lieutenant Colonel, U.S. Army, 2nd Battalion, 8th Infantry, 4th Infantry Division.

Place And Date: Hurtgen Forest near Schevenhutte, Germany, 20 November 1944.

Entered Service At: Sumter, South Carolina

Born: Sumter, South Carolina G.O. # 77 September 1945

Citation: He was commanding the 2nd Battalion, 8th Infantry, in an attack through the Hurtgen Forest near Schevenhutte, Germany, on 20 November 1944. During the early phases of the assault, the leading elements of his battalion were halted by a minefield and immobilized by heavy hostile fire. Advancing alone into the mined area, Col. Mabry established a safe route of passage. He then moved ahead of the foremost scouts, personally leading the attack, until confronted by a booby trapped double concertina obstacle. With the assistance of the scouts, he disconnected the explosives and cut a path through the wire. Upon moving through the opening, he observed three enemy in foxholes whom he captured at bayonet point. Driving steadily forward, he paced the assault against three log bunkers which housed mutually supported automatic weapons. Racing up a slope ahead of his men, he found the initial bunker deserted, then pushed on to the second where he was suddenly confronted by nine onrushing enemy. Using the butt of his rifle, he felled one adversary and bayoneted a second, before his scouts came to his aid and assisted him in overcoming the others in hand-to-hand combat. Accompanied by the riflemen, he charged the third bunker under pointblank small-arms fire and led the way into the fortification from which he prodded six enemy at bayonet point. Following the consolidation of this area, he led his battalion across 300 yards of fire-swept terrain to seize elevated ground upon which he established a defensive position which menaced the enemy on both flanks and provided his regiment a firm foothold on the approach to the Cologne Plain. Col. Mabry's superlative courage, daring, and leadership in an operation of major importance exemplify the finest characteristics of the military service. (George Mabry later advanced to the rank of Major General. His uniform and Medal of Honor are in the collection at the National Infantry Museum at Fort Moore (former name was Fort Benning), Georgia.)

21 NOVEMBER 1944—D+169: Other than one counterattack of company size against CT 8, the enemy was satisfied to defend its line by sending forth patrols and shelling our front line elements. Either tanks or self-propelled guns were active against CT 8.

The 1st and 2nd Battalions, 8th Infantry, continued to maintain their positions while the 3rd Battalion moved out at 0830 on its mission to destroy all enemy forces east and west of the road. The terrain cleared of the enemy during the day was outposted by elements of the 24th Cavalry Reconnaissance Squadron.

The 121st Infantry Regiment of the 8th Infantry Division moved out at 0900 to attack through and relieve elements of the 12th Infantry. The relief of the 1st and 3rd Battalions was completed by 1500 and the 2nd Battalion by 1700, but the withdrawal of the 12th Infantry was not initiated.

Because of the supply and evacuation difficulties and the necessity of cleaning out by-passed enemy pockets, the day of the 22nd Infantry was utilized in consolidating positions and opening a motor route. The engineers worked continuously under fire. The heavy rains hindered their work by decreasing the efficiency of their mine detectors. At 1155, the critical bridge and main supply road were finally cleared; at 1555 Company I supported by tanks and tank destroyers moved to the north and established contact by 1655 with elements of the 8th Infantry Regiment.

22 NOVEMBER 1944—D+170: The enemy continued to resist fiercely and to fall back slowly from one line of fortified positions to the next. Enemy armor of a defensive nature, i.e. dug in with a prepared field of fire, was encountered.

The attack of the 8th Infantry was delayed in an effort to bring up the supporting armor; this failing, the attack was initiated at 0930 by the 1st Battalion. Supporting fires were furnished by the 2nd Battalion. The 1st Battalion fought its way stubbornly forward against strong resistance and succeeded in reaching the edge of its objective, Jagerhaus. At 1120, the 3rd Battalion started moving along the axis of advance of the 1st Battalion, then worked back to the southeast, effecting a partial encirclement of the enemy, and resulting in the annihilation and capture of large numbers. The area to the southeast was then considered clear.

The 12th Infantry moved to assembly areas to the north of the new division right (south) boundary. It closed there by 1215 as division reserve.

The 22nd Infantry had as its objective the road junction just short of Grosshau. The 1st Battalion feinted several false attacks after 0800 and, it seemed, accomplished its mission of detracting the enemy from the attack of the 3rd Battalion further to the north. The 3rd Battalion moved shortly after daylight. Enemy mortar, artillery, and small arms fire were encountered but the advance continued and several machine gun positions were overrun. By 1335, the attack had carried to a point from which the road junction was under direct fire. The battalion consolidated its positions to cut the roads. Direct artillery fire was received from the western edge of Grosshau which was within sight. A small enemy attack was repulsed by the 2nd Battalion at 0905. At 0950 the 2nd Battalion attacked to the east and immediately encountered stubborn resistance, including fire from two dug in self-propelled guns. Slow progress was made and despite numerous casualties, the battalion continued to advance until the left flank was approximately 500 yards to the southwest of the 1st Battalion. There positions were consolidated.

23 NOVEMBER 1944—D+171: The enemy continued to stubbornly resist our advance by covering its numerous mine fields, wire entanglements, and road blocks with effective fires. Once our advance showed signs of slowing down, the enemy counterattacked viciously with approximately reinforced platoon strength. At least four such counterattacks were repulsed.

The 4th Infantry Division continued the attack to the northeast in the direction of Duren and despite strong resistance of small arms, machine guns, artillery, mortars, mines, booby traps and well defended bunkers, secured important terrain.

The 8th Infantry attacked at 0840 with the 2nd Battalion. After the capture of a number of unarmed prisoners, it was able to move toward its objective. Again supply problems delayed the attack, and the 3rd Battalion was unable to move before 0900. A slow advance was continued, and good progress was made. Due to extremely heavy enemy fire, the 1st Battalion was unable to move forward throughout the day.

The 12th Infantry moved its 1st Battalion to a forward assembly area starting at 0945. At 1045, the 2nd Battalion initiated an attack to the east. A mine field was encountered at 1118 but the battalion crossed the main north-south road at 1351. In the late afternoon, the battalion was stopped short of its objective by additional mines and enemy resistance, and positions were consolidated for the night.

The orders provided to the 22nd Infantry were to consolidate positions, to clear the rear areas and routes forward, and to secure four key trail and road junctions. A small task force organized by the 1st Battalion moved eastward at 0850 to clear the road and it was completed by 1350 under artillery and mortar fire. Enemy pressure on the northern flank of the 3rd Battalion increased during the morning, but no ground was gained by the Germans. Enemy mortar and artillery fire continued to pound the battalion area. By 1145, the 2nd Battalion had readjusted its lines and controlled the trail junction by fire. Very heavy enemy artillery fire was received in the battalion sector.

NOVEMBER 22, 1963: All who were alive and of school age or older on that fateful day remember exactly what he or she was doing when they heard about the assassination of President John F. Kennedy. It is said, and I agree, that it was on this date in history that America lost its innocence. Where was I? I was laying on my bed in my dorm room in college in Pittsburg, Kansas, ready to head out for my 1:00 PM class — I never made it to class that afternoon...

VIETNAM — NOVEMBER 1967

(an insert because of its importance in 4ID history)

Many of you know that the 173rd Airborne Brigade was part of Task Force Ironhorse during Operation Iraqi Freedom 1 in Iraq in 2003-2004. That was not the first time the 173rd has fought alongside the 4th Infantry Division.

During the month of November 1967, the 4ID and 173rd Airborne Brigade were engaged in one of the biggest and bloodiest battles of the Vietnam War — the Battle of Dak To. Nine infantry battalions (plus supporting artillery and other units) of American Soldiers from 4ID (1-8 IN, 3-8 IN, 3-12 IN, 1-12 IN), 173rd Airborne Brigade (1-503 IN, 2-503 IN, 4-503 IN), and 1st Cavalry Division (2-8 CAV, 1-12 CAV), fought the 1st PAVN division in the rugged mountains and jungles of the western central highlands along the Cambodian border. The battle started on 1 November 1967 and escalated in intensity to its peak in the 19-23 November period before all contact was broken by 1 December.

On November 15, the NVA shelled the Dak To support base and demolished two C-130 aircraft, damaged another one, and blew up eleven hundred tons of ammunitions, including 30,000 artillery shells, destroyed a number of 10,000 gallon bladders filled with aviation fuel and gasoline, and littered the ground with jagged shrapnel which posed a constant threat of blowouts to wheeled vehicles.

The last fierce battle was taking Hill 875, which started on 19 November and was finally accomplished about noon on Thanksgiving Day, 23 November 1967.

In that battle, places like Dak To, Hill 875, Ben Het, Hill 1338, and Hill 1262 became part of the history of our units. Enemy casualties totaled 1,644 by body count. American casualties were 283 killed, 1,188 wounded, and 18 missing. Of the killed, 192 were from the 173rd Airborne Brigade with about 70 of those killed by 'friendly' fire from errant air strikes and artillery fire.

These words can't begin to describe the struggle that our Soldiers of 4ID and 173rd Airborne Brigade went through during the Battle of Dak To. You'll have to talk to the veterans who fought the battle to get a glimpse of that special brand of hell. But, as our predecessors in WWI and WWII did, they answered the call and successfully completed the mission given to them. And our Soldiers continue to answer the call today…

…and finally for our Vietnam history lesson today…

NOVEMBER 20, 1966: On a personal note, it was November 20, 1966 that PFC David Mendez, radio operator for 2nd platoon, Company B, 1st Battalion, 22nd Infantry Regiment was killed by 'friendly fire' during Operation Paul Revere IV in the jungles along the Cambodian border of the central highlands of Vietnam. Our company was in a blocking position to help troops of the 3rd Brigade, 25th Infantry Division who were under attack by the NVA when a 4.2" mortar round fired by them fell into our position. Along with Mendez being killed, ten more of our B/1-22 Soldiers were wounded. I'll never forget that afternoon and night for as long as I live—I was the first one to him after he was hit. David Mendez' Family will always be in my thoughts and prayers.

CONTINUING...4ID IN GERMANY›S HURTGEN FOREST:

24 NOVEMBER 1944—D+172: After using the hours of darkness for the purpose of laying more mines, constructing blocks, and digging defenses, the enemy defended its new position until forced slowly to fall back to each successively prepared line of defenses. It was also evident that under the cover of darkness, the enemy was bringing up replacements, probably consisting of remnants of units almost totally wiped out, which would serve to absorb the smash of our first attack during the day.

CT 12 on the right and CT 8 on the left advanced slowly throughout the day against a stubborn enemy in heavily wooded terrain made more adverse due to the ever consistent intermittent rain.

The 8th Infantry was ordered to continue the attack in the direction of Duren by 0830. Company B, 1st Battalion, was unable to continue forward movement until 1000 due to heavy artillery and mortar fire, as well as extremely heavy small arms fire from a well dug in enemy. But after 1000, Companies B and C, 1st Battalion, reached the objective, and were relieved by the 3rd Battalion. The 2nd Battalion advanced slowly, meeting extremely heavy machine gun and small arms fire as well as artillery and mortar fire. At the end of the day, it had captured considerable enemy personnel, weapons, and equipment and by 1800 was ordered to continue its attack on the following day.

The 12th Infantry continued the attack at 0900 with the 3rd Battalion passing through the 1st Battalion. It advanced rapidly and by 1102 was moving onto its objective. The 2nd Battalion reached its objective at 1030 and by 1215 was firmly established. By 1400, it had gained contact with the 121st Infantry (8th Infantry Division). The 1st Battalion mopped enemy groups in the rear areas and established contact with the 24th Cavalry Reconnaissance Squadron.

The 22nd Infantry received heavy artillery fire, including direct fire, on forward units. The day was used to regroup, adjust, and consolidate. Patrols moved and engineers with infantry support rushed to open all roads and trails.

From the Diary of Swede Henley—used with permission of his daughters:

18 NOVEMBER D-2: Bn reorganized and jumped across main road and advanced about 500 yards, held up because 2nd Bn hadn't moved. Col. Walker, Major Samuels, Capt. Kerr, the S-6-5-3 hit and evacuated. Major Blazzard took over and 2nd Bn advanced up to the 1st Bn and tied in. Jerry still shelling everything. Casualties still high. Capt. Martin C Co. CO hit. Lts. Kersey, MacCracken killed. Roads mined so everything had to be hand carried.

Hurtgen Forest—it lacked a long way from being a lovers lane.

19 NOVEMBER D-3: Same position, reorganizing—re-supplying—trying to get road opened. Capt. Eggleston transferred to 2nd Bn as Bn Ex. Officer. Capt. McLane made Bn S-3.
- Another close call. Lt. Hall hit in the ribs standing right beside me.
- I applied first aid and went for aid. These 5 days so far (Nov. 16-21) the roughest and bloodiest I have seen.
- It was a nightmare.

20 NOVEMBER D-4: Jumped off and went to objective 500 yds off. Jerry counterattacked and we threw everything we had at them. Counterattack stopped. 2nd Bn bit hard but held. Few men wounded.
- CP now located in Jerry log shelter. Jerry shelled area at about 15 minute intervals...too damn hot for my old chassis.

21 NOVEMBER D-5: Held in place—reorganized—fed 80 replacements into line. Raining and everything wet.

22 NOVEMBER D-6: 1st Bn held tight. 3rd and 2nd Bn advanced up about 1000 yds—2nd Bn had a hard time. Captain Whaley killed. 3rd Bn held up at dark 800 yds from Grubhan. Jerry mortars and artillery still raising hell. Jerry counterattacked but got their ears pinned back.
FAMOUS WORDS:
- "That jerry has been shooting at me personally for 3 days now. I'm getting damn tired of it."
- Hope we break that bastard's back (Hitler) by Christmas."
- "That bastard just adds up a lot of figures and puts them on that RR (railroad) gun sights and he ain't far off."
- "Call Berlin 6 and tell Adolph if he's shooting at that RJ he is off—and adjust it for him as it is falling on my foxhole."

23 NOVEMBER D-7 THANKSGIVING DAY: Still fighting to get out of these damn woods and get in the wide open spaces. Jerry artillery still giving us hell. Fixed turkey for front line troops. Lt. Bolyard hit this AM.

24 NOVEMBER D-8: Still in the woods—hoping to come out tomorrow and run the krauts crazy with our armor. Jerry still shooting that damn railroad gun. Received 7 new officers today. To jump again tomorrow morning at 0715. Need a bath bad all over. Casualties light.
- Listen to those 81 mortars…"They are coughing like a man with consumption."
- (During Hurtgen, 15550 rounds + 2000 on train + 2 truckloads of Jerry ammo

Robert S. Rush, Ph. D.
Quotes from the Hürtgen Forest

From his book, *Hell in Hürtgen Forest: The Ordeal and triumph of an American*

Infantry Regiment, written about the 22nd Infantry Regiment—I highly recommend this for a blow by blow account of the actions of the 22nd Infantry Regiment in the Hurtgen Forest. Available from Amazon.com, or a local bookstore can order it for you.

Quote from Technician 5th Grade George Morgan: "The forest up there was a helluva eerie place to fight. Show me a man who went through the battle of the Hürtgen Forest and who says he never had a feeling of fear and I'll show you a liar… You can't get protection. You can't see. You can't get fields of fire. The trees are slashed like a scythe by artillery. Everything is tangled. You can scarcely walk. Everybody is cold and wet, and the mixture of cold rain and sleet keeps falling. They jump off again and there is only a handful of the old men left."

Quote from Colonel Buck Lanham, Regimental Commander, in a letter to Carlos Baker, Ernest Hemingway's biographer: "At this time my mental anguish was beyond description. My magnificent command had virtually ceased to exist…these men had accomplished miracles…my admiration and respect for them was…transcendental."

Chaplain Bill Boice wrote: "Perhaps in the final analysis, the sacrifice demanded in the Hürtgen will be deemed worthwhile; we wouldn't know that… We are only the men who fought the battles…who lay in the slime and mud night after night…who did not come out of a foxhole long enough to eat Thanksgiving dinner, for life was more precious than food… A part of us died in the forest, and there is a part of our mind and heart and soul left there."

Captain Donald Faulkner in his diary recorded: "Company E had 79 men and six officers before Grosshau (when he took command of the company.)…received about 160 new men and now only a little over 80 with three officers are going back. It had better be worth it."

George Wilson, last commander of Fox Company, wrote in his book,

If You Survive: "The objective lay only four-and-a-half miles away, but it took eighteen terrible days to reach… It was an awful beating—a terrible price for that damned patch of ground."

Ernest Hemingway, war correspondent with the 22nd throughout the battle, penned the following: "Well, anyway, this Regiment was rebuilt as American regiments always are by the replacement system… It boils down, or distills, to the fact you stay in until you are hit badly or killed or go crazy and get section 'eighted'…We got a certain amount of replacements, but I can remember thinking that it would be simpler, and more effective, to shoot them in the area where they detrucked, than to have to try to bring them back from where they would be killed and bury them…"

These quotes are reprinted here with permission from Dr. Robert S. Rush, author of Paschendale with Tree Bursts, re-titled as Hell in Hürtgen Forest: The Ordeal and Triumph of an American Infantry Regiment.—Bob Babcock—again, I HIGHLY recommend this book, day by day and blow by blow account of the 22nd Infantry Regiment in the Hürtgen Forest.

25 NOV 1944 TO 30 NOV 1944 – D+173 TO D+178

This is another long section, but I think you will learn from the daily details and the personal memories of some of those who lived this time in the "Hell in Hurtgen Forest". Read on…

25 NOVEMBER 1944—D+173: Against CT 8 and CT 22, the enemy's resistance was stubborn and effective. Small arms, mortars, and artillery were utilized to maximum advantage. A number of self-propelled assault guns were employed with good results against CT 22. The enemy was overrun by CT 12 in its zone of advance. The resulting confusion and ineffectiveness on the part of the Germans made it apparent that once the main line of resistance could be reached and rapidly crossed, lack of leadership, poor contact, and incompetent troops made the enemy a "pushover". Companies and platoons that knew their flanks had been enveloped failed to withdraw before they were cut off.

The intermittent rain rendered the few roads and trails into a mass of mud, which did much to hinder the advance. It was almost impossible for the tanks and tank destroyers to keep up with the advancing infantry.

The 2nd Battalion, 8th Infantry, attacked at 1130 to the southeast. At 1330, it repulsed a small counterattack by 40 to 50 enemy infantry. 2-8 Infantry continued the advance and by 1410, had succeeded in capturing its objective. The 3rd Battalion strengthened its previous positions and patrolled.

The 12th Infantry attacked at 0800 and made good progress through the difficult wooded, hilly terrain against light resistance of disorganized enemy. It succeeded in seizing its objective and from that position was able to assist by fire the attack of the 5th Armored Division on Hurtgen. The three battalions then mopped up small pockets of by-passed enemy.

The plan of the 22nd Infantry was to attack with 2nd and 3rd Battalions, without artillery preparation in hope of surprising the enemy. The 3rd Battalion was to envelope Grosshau to the north, and the 2nd to reach the edge of the woods at the southwest. The 2nd Battalion, delayed by the attached armor unable to negotiate the poor roads, attacked at 0820 and the 3rd Battalion at 0745. Both battalions encountered heavy resistance immediately. The advance of the 2nd Battalion was bitterly contested but by 1030 they were on their objective, the edge of the woods overlooking Grosshau. By 0845, the 3rd Battalion onto the high ground paused for reorganization (and moving of the armor) before assaulting the town of Grosshau. At 1145, it attacked across the open field leading to the town. The enemy reacted immediately by placing very heavy fire and stopped the attack, destroying four tanks and two tank destroyers. Further attempts were repulsed and by 1500, the battalion dug in north after suffering heavy casualties. The 1st Battalion, in reserve, moved out at 1300 and dug in at the road junction west of Grosshau.

26 NOVEMBER 1944—D+174: The enemy centered its defense

around well dug in tanks and assault guns. Utilizing the fire power of those weapons and supplementing this with small arms, mortar, and artillery, the enemy presented a formidable defense.

The 4th Infantry Division maintained its previous positions throughout the day. The period was used to straighten the lines, clear the rear areas and secure favorable terrain in preparation for the impending attack in conjunction with the 8th Infantry Division and the 5th Armored Division to take Kleinhau.

The 1st Battalion, 8th Infantry, moved forward at 1300 to relieve the 2nd Battalion, that was completed at 1445.

The 3rd Battalion, 12th Infantry, had to attack at 0800 in order to straighten the main line and establish contact between all elements. The advance was made under extremely adverse conditions, heavy woods, steep slopes, icy streams, and great distances to carry supplies by hand, but the Battalion reached its objective by 1630 and began consolidation to assist by fire the 8th Infantry Division. The battalion took numerous prisoners.

No major attack was made by the 22nd Infantry. Grosshau was pounded by 81 mm mortar high explosive shells as well as by our artillery fire. Company C, 1st Battalion, attacked to clear the woods just west of Grosshau and stubborn resistance was encountered. By late afternoon, it had reached its objective but just before dusk an enemy counterattack with 75-100 men and four tanks hit Company C. The attack was determined and was preceded by a heavy artillery and mortar barrage. The Company was driven back to its positions of the night before and sustained heavy casualties. A patrol of the 3rd Battalion moved out after dark to investigate Grosshau. The first attempt was hit by heavy concentrations of mortar but on the second attempt, they reached the outskirts where they remained in observation and listening.

27 NOVEMBER 1944—D+175: The enemy continued to build its defense around assault guns and tanks well dug in. Its fields of fire for these weapons were improved and all the approaches were found to be thoroughly mined, booby trapped, and protected by wire blocks. Considerable movement on the road between Kleinhau and Grosshau was carried on behind smoke screens. A counterattacking force composed of the 3d Parachute Division might be expected against our forces.

The 8th Infantry maintained captured positions and patrolled aggressively to clear rear areas and flanks, and to seek information on enemy lines.

The 2nd Battalion of the 12th Infantry were passed by units of the 8th Infantry Division and so the battalion moved to a new assembly area from 0900 to 1500. The 3rd Battalion continued to mop up areas and directed fire on the town of Kleinhau.

Company B, 22nd Infantry, attacked at 0900 to retake the ground west of Grosshau and the enemy resisted bitterly. By late morning, the attack had come to a standstill and Company E was ordered to aid the attack. By 1440, companies B and E were on the edge of the town and the position was organized. At 1800, led by antitank guns, supporting weapons, tanks and tank destroyers reached this forward area. After dark, a patrol moved into Grosshau but encountered enemy small arms fire and was driven back. The town of Grosshau proved to be heavily defended.

And it was on November 27, 1944 that Macario Garcia of Company B, 22nd Infantry Regiment earned the fourth (of five) Medal of Honor that was awarded to 4ID Soldiers in WWII:

Rank And Organization: Macario Garcia—Staff Sergeant (then Pvt), U.S. Army, B/1-22, 4th Infantry Division.

Place And Date: Near Grosshau, Germany, 27 November 1944.

Entered Service At: Sugarland, Texas.

Born: 20 January 1920, Villa de Castano, Mexico. G.O. # 74, 1 September 1954.

Citation: Staff Sergeant Macario Garcia, Company B, 22nd Infantry, in action involving actual conflict with the enemy in the vicinity of Grosshau, Germany, 27 November 1944. While an acting squad leader, he single-handedly assaulted two enemy machine gun emplacements. Attacking prepared positions on a wooded hill, which could be approached only through meager cover, his company was pinned down by intense machine-gun fire and subjected to a concentrated artillery and mortar barrage. Although painfully wounded, he refused to be evacuated and on his own initiative crawled forward alone until he reached a position near an enemy emplacement. Hurling grenades, he boldly assaulted the position, destroyed the gun, and with his rifle killed three of the enemy who attempted to escape. When he rejoined his company, a second machine-gun opened fire and again the intrepid Soldier went forward, utterly disregarding his own safety. He stormed the position and destroyed the gun, killed three more Germans, and captured four prisoners. He fought on with his unit until the objective was taken and only then did he permit himself to be removed for medical care. S/Sgt. (then Pvt.) Garcia's conspicuous heroism, his inspiring, courageous conduct, and his complete disregard for his personal safety wiped out two enemy placements and enabled his company to advance and secure its objective.

28 NOVEMBER 1944—D+176: The 8th Infantry improved its previous positions and conducted vigorous patrolling to the northeast and south to seek information. Cleaning of the area was continuous.

The 12th had to fill the large gap existing between the 8th and 22nd Regiments. The 1st Battalion attacked at 0910, with the 2nd Battalion in support, and became engaged immediately in a fire fight. This resistance was eliminated by the aggressive action of the battalion that advanced north along the road. No resistance was encountered until late in the afternoon when a strong point was engaged. The 1st Battalion held up there for the night. The 3rd Battalion continued to support by fire the attack of the 22nd Infantry and the 5th Armored Division.

The 22nd Infantry sent a small task force of the 3rd Battalion to seize the high ground to the east. By 1350, the task force (composed of two platoons) reached the objective and cleaned out small, scattered pockets of enemy. Any movement in the 1st Battalion sector was followed by a mortar barrage. Plans were made to seize the high ground northeast of Grosshau. The enemy resistance in the Grosshau area continued to be extremely heavy.

29 NOVEMBER 1944—D+177: The enemy continued its defense of advantageous ground and earthen emplacements by employing small arms and direct firing assault guns set up on high ground. In addition, considerable mortar fire and artillery impeded the advance of our troops. Plus the usual mines, booby traps and wire entanglements on the most opportune avenues of approach.

After the relief of the 1st Battalion, 8th Infantry, at 0830 by the 24th Cavalry Reconnaissance Squadron, the 1st and 2nd Battalion attacked at 1000 through the lines held by the 3rd Battalion. The 1st Battalion met heavy small arms and machine gun fires shortly after beginning its advance. It withdrew for the purpose of heavily shelling the enemy positions confronting it and after, the advance was resumed. The 2nd Battalion in the face of small arms, machine gun, artillery and mortar continued its slow but steady advance. Resistance became more determined at all points at the end of daylight.

The 12th Infantry attacked at 0830 and met no resistance. The objective was reached by 0950. Combat patrols were sent to the east and the south. The 3rd Battalion moved to an assembly area.

During the night, the 22nd Infantry was submitted to moderate enemy artillery and mortar harassing fire. A night patrol from the 3rd Battalion penetrated the enemy outpost line. Ordered to attack at 1100, the 3rd Battalion was delayed by heavy enemy artillery fire and moved out at 1200. The battalion pushed to the northeast against heavy fire and determined resistance. At 1830, the battalion had reached its objective, Hill 92 northeast of Grosshau, and it was secured by 2050. The 1st Battalion followed and by 1445 occupied the original positions of the 3rd Battalion, prepared to assist in the capture of Grosshau. The 2nd Battalion attacked at 1250 to take Grosshau. The attacking force consisted of Companies E and F with armored support. Immediately upon jumping off, Company F received a counterattack which it repulsed. Company E advanced slowly under heavy German machine gun fire. Fighting was intense and Company E had advanced only 75 yards beyond the first house in town by 1635. At dusk, the battalion was ordered to continue the attack. By 1843, three houses remained in enemy hands. Resistance in the houses and cellars finally ended at 1915.

30 NOVEMBER 1944—D+178: In the northern sector, our forces advanced against fox holes and bunkers constructed and reinforced with logs and earth. In the center, a more hastily constructed type of emplacement was defended by the enemy. In the southern sector, the enemy defense was based on strategically located assault guns and considerable mortar and artillery fire. As always, avenues of approach were heavily mined and obstructed with wire and fallen trees.

The 4th Infantry Division continued the coordinated attack to the east and northeast.

The 8th Infantry attacked with the 1st Battalion at 0845 and the 2nd Battalion at 0900. The enemy resistance was heavy throughout the day. The enemy used many automatic weapons firing along the mined and booby trapped firebreaks and trails in the eastern edge of the Hurtgen Forest. Heavy mortar and artillery fire was also encountered. A small counterattack was repulsed by the 1st Battalion and by 1200 both battalions succeeded in capturing the positions occupied by the enemy during the night. At 0930 the 3rd Battalion moved forward and became involved in a fire fight. After several attempts to overcome it, the battalion was ordered to consolidate their positions for the night.

The 12th Infantry attacked with the 2nd Battalion at 0800 and the 1st Battalion at 0830. Initially the advance was slow due to the constant danger of mines and booby traps. At 1030, the 2nd Battalion encountered an extensive deceptive mine field, and the 1st Battalion became involved in a fire fight with an enemy strong point. By the end of the day, the two battalions had succeeded in capturing the high ground overlooking the town of Gey.

Heavy enemy mortar and artillery concentrations fell in the 22nd sector during the night. After an artillery preparation, the 2nd and 3rd Battalions attacked at approximately 1130. The 3rd Battalion moved against relatively light resistance until 1500 when it was 300 yards short of its objective. The opposition stiffened and in accordance with orders, the 3rd Battalion secured for the night at 1630. The 2nd Battalion, attacking east from Grosshau, encountered machine gun fire, and increasing mortar and artillery fire. At 1335 the battalion was 300 yards beyond its line of departure and moving slowly. Even with the arrival of an armored support unit, the 2nd Battalion was unable to continue and dug in for the night shortly after 1630. The enemy fire on the forward positions (200 yards west of the woods) was intense.

Notes about logistics: Extreme difficulties were encountered in the delivery of rations, water, and ammunition and in the recovery of vehicles, weapons, and other equipment (considerable combat losses) because of the mass of trees and branches brought down by mortar and artillery fire, plus all the mines and traps.

With the troops continuously exposed to rain and mud, trench foot broke out and evacuation of these cases was heavy. Issue of overshoes and additional socks was expedited and reduced appreciably the trench foot cases.

November 1944 Casualties:
- KIA Officers = 42, Enlisted Men = 390
- MIA Officers = 10, Enlisted Men = 245 (Many of these were later listed as KIA)
- SWA Officers = 20, Enlisted Men = 318 (Seriously Wounded in Action)
- LWA Officers = 133, Enlisted Men = 2,895 (Lightly Wounded in Action)
- Total Officers = 205, Enlisted Men = 3,848
- Prisoners Captured: 1,757

From the **Diary of Swede Henley**—*used with permission of his daughters:*

25 NOVEMBER D-9: 3rd Bn jumped off to take Groshau but didn't accomplish mission. 1st Bn moved up to take 3rd Bn position. "C" Co given mission to clean up between 3rd and 2nd Bn. Groshau full of SP guns. Jerry artillery still heavy and accurate. Men are tired and sleepy, and their nerves are about shot. Too much of anything is too much.

Capt. Eggleston killed by burp gun on afternoon of November 25, 1944.

26 NOVEMBER D-10: 1st Bn given orders to take and clean out pocket between 2nd & 3rd Bn. C Co attacked it and after losing approx. 50 men, took objective at 1600. The Jerry counter attacked with tanks and drove them back.

27 NOVEMBER D-11: B Co given same mission and after losing 70 men, took objective and dug in for night in edge of Groshau.
- The most Jerry artillery and mortar I have ever seen or heard of.
- The railroad gun has just about cleaned out this draw.
- Damn—what a shell that thing throws.

28 NOVEMBER D-12: Held ground and consolidated position. Jerry shelled us steady for the 4th straight day.

29 NOVEMBER D-13: "B" Co withdrawn, and new men sent to Co. 3rd readjusted lines. Capt. Surratt evacuated for concussion.

Ernest Hemmingway—Bill Walton visited CP today…says "War will be over by Christmas." Seems like wishful thinking.

3rd Bn attacked NE to cut main road between Groshau and Gey. E Co with tanks to clean out town. CP located in German CP dugout. Casualties have been about 500 so far. Groshau fell with 100 prisoners.

The RJ 1000 yards west of Grosshau to edge of town cost us 200 men…B Co went with 125—came back with 31…C Co went with 115—came back with 21.

30 NOVEMBER D-14: Sniper fighting broke out in Groshau again. 3 Co sent in to clean out town. 3rd Bn to move forward to phase line in edge of woods south of Gey. 17 more prisoners taken out of Groshau. Sun is shining for change. Air Corps out giving Jerry hell. More replacements came in—over 500 used in 1st Bn—1500 in Regiment.

Personal memories from ***War Stories, Volume II: Paris to VE Day…***

Patrick L. O'Dea, Grapevine, TX
Company F, 2nd Battalion, 22nd Infantry Regiment
Attacking the Hurtgen…

The afternoon was rather mild, and I took the opportunity to clean my rifle since it was getting downright rusty in lots of places, and I began to doubt if it would work when I needed it. After I got it a little cleaner and oiled it, I felt more like a soldier. I was making plans to get a good night's rest with the blankets when the word was passed down that we were going to attack that night. This was really bad news since I hated the thought of fighting in the dark of night. So, we ate our evening meal with a great deal of somber thoughts about what might come later.

At dusk, we gathered into squads and prepared for the advance to our objective. I was in the third squad, and I remember the company commander flying into a rage and whispering furious curses, calling for the third squad. Actually, we were in the right place all the time, but Dan, the squad leader, had not spoken up when the CO called for him. There were only six or seven of us in each squad, so we looked more like a couple of squads than a platoon. No wonder the CO got confused. He was in a vile mood when we started out. Incidentally, that was the first time I ever saw him. I never did learn his name.

We started out walking in a single file, following the perimeter of the forest religiously. It was a grueling march. The ground was soft and thick with mud. I had a pair of galoshes on, and these made walking difficult, and with my bad feet I was in no shape for easy walking, much less this kind of hike. We were supposed to keep five yards distance between us, and this was not easy. When we walked through patches of the forest it was impossible to keep five yards and still maintain contact with the man in front of you. And, if there was one thing I didn't want to do, it was to lose contact with the man in front of me. I had horrible visions of doing this and thus leading the scores of troops who followed me into some kind of a terrible trap or ambush.

To say that this march was tiring would be a miracle of understatement. It was a march through forest and bush, up slimy hills where roots and low brush tripped your feet and sent you crashing to the ground. It meant walking through forests, straining your eyes to see the man you were following, only to have a pine bough set in motion by the man in front come springing back to lash you across the eyes or in the mouth. It meant having strong branches reach out and try to knock the rifle from your shoulders. It meant plodding along gullies and stream bottoms where the soft mud allowed your feet to sink six or eight inches, and then closed over them like an earthen vise from which you struggled, cursing, to release your foot with a squishing gurgle. Every now and then, we would come to a flat area where, to our right, a large plain lay quiet and foreboding in the soft light of the newly risen moon. Occasionally we would stumble over a body. I hoped they were all Germans.

At one time we were moving along the side of a hill with as much stealth as possible when a young, clear, American voice rang out from higher on the hill, "Who's that walking along there?"

We were startled to hear the voice from what I thought was a "no man's island." No one answered. The voice came again, more insistent.

"Are you guys GIs?"

Still no one answered him, and I glanced around impatiently to see if the sergeant was nearby and whether he was going to answer. I didn't want to answer myself, but I was scared that the young soldier might start firing at us. I told the man behind me what I thought, and I could hear whispers along the line. The boy's voice came again, and I could still hear whispers. The boy's voice called once more, this time almost pleading, "If you guys don't answer me, I'm going to open up with this machine gun."

That was the final straw. Since the sergeant didn't seem to know what to say, a whole chorus of voices went up telling him, "Shut up—we're GIs."

I don't know how long we walked, but it was something more than an hour, maybe an hour and a half. We stopped once for a rest and then moved out again.

The second time that we stopped, I sat on the muddy ground, pretty well exhausted. After a few minutes I revived a little and started looking around.

I was surprised to see a house about one hundred yards away, faintly outlined in the moonlight. A few seconds later I heard the sound of many approaching footsteps. A group of German prisoners appeared, being herded by some GIs on their way to the rear. I realized then that we must be near our objective. This was the first time all evening that I had any idea of what we were supposed to do that night. Since there were no sounds of a battle nearby, I guessed that there was a village close by that some other company had already taken and that we would be used as reinforcements to hold the village. Sure enough, the sergeant came back soon and told us we were lucky because the village had been taken, and we wouldn't have to do any fighting that night. This news made me a bit happier, for I was very tired, and my feet pained me considerably.

At a signal from the sergeant we started out again, and in a short time we emerged from the forest into a small village that had been destroyed by the war. All the houses had been severely damaged: some were burned out shells; others had huge holes in them. It was a typical German village, the first I had ever seen. None of the houses was more than three stories, and most of them appeared to be well built. A couple of the houses were still burning, and we ran past them as fast as possible because our silhouettes made fine targets against a background of flame. I saw a number of GIs throughout the village, but not one German civilian. I assumed that they all had fled the area long before the battle started. Other groups of German soldiers were being returned to our rear. Most of them looked dirty and exhausted.

We continued through the village and were ordered to take up positions on the outskirts, at a point from which we had a clear view of several hundred yards of bare ground. It was a good place to set up a line against possible German counterattack. At this point, the sergeant learned that several of our platoon had become separated and he got mad and went back through the town yelling for them.

Having found most of them, he came back and started assigning us spots to dig in. We were still tired from our hike, and none of us wanted to spend three hours or so digging a foxhole. But the thought of a possible German attack in the morning made up my mind for me. Our platoon started digging in about fifteen yards from a road that separated us from the village, which was probably called Grosshau. After we had been digging about twenty minutes, I realized that a tree only a few feet away might be a source of danger, because a shell hitting it would send a deadly shower of shrapnel into our hole. I remarked about this to Steve, my 21-year-old foxhole buddy. We were halfheartedly considering digging in at some less dangerous place, but I hated to have all that work on the present hole go to waste. The dilemma was solved from an unexpected quarter when the sergeant came over and ordered the whole platoon to fall back about forty yards to the other side of the road and dig in there instead.

There was the usual grumbling, but I was willing enough. The area was pockmarked with shell holes, and most pairs of men selected a shell hole for conversion to a foxhole because it meant less digging. The hole that my partner and I got was sort of deceiving because we had to do a lot more digging than I estimated. The ground was rocky, and our entrenching tools would only go an inch before they hit a rock. We both dug silently for a while. It was only about 2030 hours, and we had been in Grosshau for less than an hour.

I suppose it took the enemy a little time to dispatch messages to his rear echelon informing them of his withdrawal from Grosshau. They, in turn, would instruct their artillery to blast the town before we had a chance to dig in. The German artillery did just that, and soon the first salvo of 88s came screaming in. We dived for our half-completed holes and huddled in terror as the great shells exploded near us. In a few minutes the barrage was over, and we jumped up and resumed digging with increased fervor. I wondered anxiously when the next barrage would be hurled at us. The time between barrages would be a good index of how frequently we would be blasted for the rest of the night.

As daylight came, it was time for the attack. To my surprise about a dozen GIs lined up on the road and headed as a skirmish line toward the enemy. I supposed they were another platoon of our company. One fell wounded before they had advanced a dozen yards. Our sergeant gave the order to move out and we followed about fifty yards behind the other platoon. Enemy shells began to fall, and small arms fire began. Two German soldiers jumped up and surrendered about forty yards in front of us; they were manning a machine gun. I was amazed that the enemy had been that close to us all night.

In a few minutes the enemy shells had disrupted our formation so that we and the other platoon were all mixed up together. Our own heavy weapons platoon observers were with us, and they passed back orders to raise or lower our mortar fire. It seemed to me that their orders were being garbled, as they were being passed back orally, and I expected our own mortars to fall on us. I don't know whether they did, but we were brought to a halt just a few hundred yards from the town. The artillery shells and mortars fell on us in such numbers that the men hugged the ground for safety. Most of us were able to find shell holes that were shallow and dish like, but they did afford some protection. Small arms fire would frequently come our way, but it was not as dangerous as the shellfire.

At one point during a heavy shelling, I noticed large lumps of what I thought were clods of dirt falling around me. A few of them hit me although they did not hurt me. One that fell looked like a potato, but on closer inspection, it turned out to be a turnip. I must have been lying in somebody's turnip field. It occurred to me that the army might have to send my mother a telegram saying, "Your son was killed by a large turnip." I still had my sense of humor.

Our platoon became more and more scattered. We were mixed in with people from other platoons. It was hard for our sergeant to pass orders along to his platoon. During a short lull, after we had endured a long artillery bombardment, the sergeant crawled over to me and some of the other platoon members and said he wanted us to move forward about a hundred and fifty yards because the enemy seemed to have his guns zeroed in on this spot.

A few minutes later, the sergeant yelled out the command to get started. Several of us jumped up and followed him, dodging shell holes and changing direction every few steps to prevent a sniper from getting a bead on us. When artillery shells exploded near us, we would hit the ground. Some people say it's too late to hit the ground when you hear the shell explode, but that's what we did.

I was able to keep the sergeant in view and tried to follow him closely. In a few more minutes, it seemed to me, the sergeant and I were the only men who were moving forward. The others seemed to be lost. Finally, the sergeant stopped running, hit the ground, and motioned me to join him.

"Stay here," he said, "I'm going back to get the other men. I'll be back in a few minutes." All I could say was "OK," but I wasn't happy about it because it seemed to me that the sergeant and I had made the deepest penetration of the German lines in that sector. I could imagine a squad of Germans rushing up to me, blasting away with their burp guns. I fired at where I thought the Germans were likely to be dug in, but I could see no action there.

Sure enough, the sergeant returned in a little while with other men from our platoon. My foxhole buddy from the night before, Steve, dropped into a shell hole not far from mine, close enough so that we could talk. After each nearby heavy shelling, we would rise up to see if the other had been hit. The shelling continued to be heavy, and I was convinced that the Germans had us under direct observation. Surprisingly, I did not see any of our tanks. I thought that this terrain would be excellent for tank support of an infantry advance. The tanks could smash machine gun emplacements and even bunkers that were holding us up. Off in the distance, to the north, I thought I could see GIs from other companies also trying to advance in the face of withering artillery.

Finally, during a severe bombardment by 88mm shells, I felt a sharp blow on my arm as if someone had hit me with his fist. I was lying in a shallow shell hole holding my helmet on with my hands when it happened. As usual, I was praying for protection from the shells. I was pretty sure that a shell fragment had hit me. I could still wiggle my fingers and move my arm, so I thought I was not in immediate danger from the wound. After a while, I could feel blood running down my arm and I stuck my other hand inside my shirt. I raised my head and asked my buddy if he had been hit. Sure enough, he had. The shelling continued, and I decided it was too dangerous to try to go back to the village and look for a medic. My buddy agreed, so we remained.

Our attack was probably part of a general advance by a battalion or two in our sector, but it seemed clear that our attack had stalled. None of the men near me were trying to advance. We were all pinned down by artillery. Small arms fire swept over us at times, but the artillery was causing the casualties. As far as I could see, no American units were making any progress as the afternoon dragged on. The last time I saw the sergeant, he was about twenty yards to my left in a shell hole. I debated whether to wait until dark and then try to return to the village or whether it would be smarter to start back right away. But the artillery shells bursting around us made me postpone any attempt to go back to the village.

The hours dragged by. I felt sure that the wound was not bad and that I would not bleed to death. As evening approached, my buddy and I agreed that we should start back for the village and try to stick together. We waited for a lull in the shelling and then jumped up and headed for the village. It was a long run. We would hit the ground every hundred feet or so, sooner if shells fell nearby. It was hard to maintain contact with each other. I left my rifle in a shell hole. While running, I noticed that my web belt with an entrenching tool hanging on it and a canteen and several clips of ammunition was slowing me down. I had already discarded my bandoleers of ammo.

At one point, I jumped up and looked for my buddy to do the same, but I couldn't see him. I hesitated for a few seconds and resumed running toward the village. I met a GI who was lying on the ground, badly wounded and promised to get a medic for him. As I reached the village edge, a mortar shell seemed to explode a few yards away from me. I was running at the time and couldn't believe that I wasn't wounded. I saw a red cross and headed for it. The officer in charge, a doctor I suppose, made me take off my jacket and open my shirt so that he could see the wound. He then told me to wait for transportation back. I told him about the wounded man out on the field. Here in the village, there was a semblance of normality; jeeps and trucks came and went, and men walked around…but carefully.

After a while, a jeep drove up to the aid station, and I was sent back to another aid station about a quarter mile back. The medic examined me, and since my wound was not life threatening he offered me a cup of coffee and told me to sit down and wait for the truck going back to the next aid station. The coffee was hot and revived my spirit. Eventually a truck drove up.

By now it was dark, and several wounded men were helped into the truck. We drove in the darkness for what seemed to be a long time and were taken, finally, to a building where our names and other information was taken. We were given more coffee and some doughnuts, I think. Then we took another truck ride in the darkness and ended up in town, probably in Belgium, and were taken to a field hospital.

About one hundred wounded men were there waiting for some kind of treatment. Most were American, but a few were German. One German soldier sat on a chair with his chest bare and a neat bullet hole where his heart was supposed to be. A lot of us wondered how he could still be alive. He sat up straight and never whimpered. Before long, he was taken by a medic to the operating room.

My feet were hurting, and I thought the warmth of the building had something to do with it. At least I knew that sooner or later somebody would treat my feet as well as my wound.

Eventually my name was called, and I was led to an operating room. I got to see my wound in the bright light. A shell fragment had entered my right arm near the shoulder. It missed the bone and had partly exited on the other side of the arm. I could see the metal fragment sticking out of the arm. The doctor told me that he would put me to sleep and would remove the shell fragment and dress the wound. He and his helpers gave me sodium pentothal, and I drifted to sleep almost immediately.

I woke up the following morning in a ward with about two dozen other GI patients. Someone was shaking me and telling me to wake up. Someone else was handing me a cup of coffee telling me that it would wake me up. Someone was holding me in a sitting position, but I kept going back to sleep. They kept talking to me and asking me questions and trying to make me wake up. One nurse was being helped by the GI patients from nearby beds who were trying to awaken me.

After I was wide awake, they asked me my name, where I was from, and what outfit I was with. One man, who I later found out was a sergeant from the 29th Infantry Division, asked me where I was when I was wounded. All I could say was that I was in "the woods."

He then told me that it was the Hürtgen Forest, and that it was a major German defensive point that protected Cologne.

So, for the first time, I learned where my adventure had taken place. I was very dirty, and a ward man brought me a towel, soap, and water. I cleaned myself as best I could and felt a lot better. Shaving was next, and that turned out to be a painful process. My face had been caked with mud for ten days, and it had been ground into the skin. The razor was army issue and not very sharp to begin with. The ward man helped me all he could, and after a painful hour, my face looked a lot better. That ten-day growth of beard was tougher than I had ever dreamed it could be.

John K. Lester, Stone Ridge, NY
Battery B, 29th Field Artillery Battalion
No Regrets — Just Memories

As a member of Battery B, 29th Field Artillery (part of a forward observer party), I sometimes think about the mud and cold of the Hürtgen Forest. I remember at times having chains on all four wheels of my jeep and worrying about whether the enemy would hear the clink of them when I was driving from point to point. I didn't have them on any longer than was necessary. When I did have them on, Technician 4th Class George Doolittle, our motor mechanic, adjusted them so they would be as noiseless as possible. I owe a lot to George. He installed a vertical bar on the front of my jeep to protect me from cables strung across roads. He put extensions on the pedals so he could put sandbags on the front floor, hoping they would protect me if I happened to run over a mine. If there was anything he could do to my vehicle to make my job safer, he did it.

I remember the crossroads that were zeroed in by the enemy artillery, the dreadful tree bursts from which there was little protection, and the mines, both antitank and antipersonnel. When the infantry was in a holding position, between attacks, the trip between their position and the artillery battery of 105s, was always a nerve-wracking experience. We used the jeep to run communication wire between the positions. We had a reel of wire mounted on the rear of the vehicle for this operation. Sometimes the enemy would infiltrate and plant mines in the so-called roads we used that had previously been cleared by the engineers. I remember one time when the radio operator and I were bracketed by German artillery while we were returning to our unit. We were caught in the open. We had been through that area four or five times before without any problems at all. It was a miracle that we got to cover. That's just an example of how fast situations could change.

A number of the casualties I saw in the Hürtgen Forest were the result of antipersonnel mines. One incident I'll never forget was when a GI stepped on a mine, lost, or mangled his foot—and two other GIs trying to help him were injured by the same mine. I sure am glad I wasn't a medic. They had a real rough job. I can't imagine what must have gone through their minds at a time like that. It must have been awful.

One thing that has, and still does, haunt me is wondering how many enemy soldiers and civilians were killed or crippled for life due to the artillery fire that my observers directed on enemy positions. I have had mixed feelings about that over the years. The only consoling thought is that, at the time, it had to be done. It was our job, and we did it well. I have no regrets—just memories.

Bill Parfitt, Elmira, NY
Company G, 22nd Infantry Regiment and HQ, 4th Infantry Division
Little Laughter in Those Terrible Days

During the Hürtgen Forest battle, I was in Zweifall, Germany, with the 4th Infantry Division HQ. During one of those terrible seventeen or eighteen days, we had a call from a guard outpost that needed a medic and a jeep to evacuate a wounded man. I was the only one available, so I grabbed the jeep and headed to the bridge on the edge of town where these guys were.

Arriving there, I could hear the guy hollering and found him in a hurry. He was lying face down and refused to roll over. After some minutes of persuasion, we got him turned over, and then he wanted us to check him out as he thought he had lost his "manhood," shall we say. It turned out he had climbed out of his hole to relieve himself and just then a shell dropped near him, and a fragment hit him. He was sure he was a loser! When I informed him this was not so, that he had just lost part of his thumb and a cut in a finger, he jumped to his feet and laughed and laughed as if he was nuts.

We got him into the jeep, and I took him to a hospital a mile or so from Zweifall. The last I heard was something about a million-dollar wound and his continuing to laugh like he had really gone nuts. There was little laughter in those terrible days, but this was the one that really took the cake.

I had another strange one there in Zweifall as well. The cooks had set up to do business in an old barroom. Someone had been able to get one of those gray-looking rolls of meat that came in one of those cold storage packs. It didn't look like hamburger, but we were looking forward to having it hot. Suddenly, there were shells coming in. One or two came through the roof and filled the room with shrapnel. The loaves of meat lying on the bar were shredded. After the shelling was over, the cooks went at it and desperately tried to find the bits of steel, wood, and such but had to toss the stuff out. We ended up eating either K or C rations that night. The only ones getting hot food that night was the General Staff.

Billy Cater, Cambridge, OH
Service Company, 22nd Infantry Regiment
Thanksgiving in the Hurtgen Forest

During the Hürtgen Forest campaign, I was Services Company commander. The HQ company commander was killed, and I was assigned as Headquarters CO. The personnel wanted to take a patrol to recover his body. I did not approve it and so was not in very good with the troops.

The cooks were trying to prepare turkeys for Thanksgiving dinner. We were under artillery fire from the Krauts—they carved our turkey.

The last available men from our Regiment (I think about 135 cooks, clerks, and truck drivers) were assembled, and we were assigned a sector of the front line with me in charge. We established a line of defense in previously dug foxholes. I was checking positions toward a concrete pillbox with a door, where my company clerk (probably seventeen years old) and a recently decorated truck driver (who was still badly shook up from moving a truck load of ammo that was on fire from a congested area) were standing. The pillbox and our sector came under a heavy shelling with a direct hit. Both men were standing in the door; the company clerk in front was critically wounded and died in the hospital.

DECEMBER 1944

4ID IN HURTGEN FOREST AND LUXEMBOURG BATTLE OF BULGE

1 DEC 1944 TO 7 DEC 1944—D+179 TO D+185: This is the week in 1944 when the 4ID left the Hell in Hurtgen Forest and moved to what was thought would be a period of refit, rest, bringing in replacements, and some much needed short passes to get back to civilization. It was a good idea, but the Germans had other ideas.

1 DECEMBER 1944—D+179: The enemy continued to employ well dug in defensive positions with increased infiltration tactics. Fairly large groups of Germans lay concealed until our attack by-passed them.

The 4th Infantry Division took important terrain during the day's operations, the high ground west of Gey along the edge of the woods.

The 8th Infantry attacked at 0815 with the 1st and 2nd Battalion abreast. By 1015, both battalions had encountered enemy mine fields, both antipersonnel and antitank, and small arms fire within the regimental sector was described as the worst that had been encountered on this front. At 1200 the 3rd Battalion was committed between the 1st and 2nd Battalions. By 1445, the 1st and 2nd Battalions had cleared most of the mine fields and reported that the enemy now seemed to be softening up somewhat. Nevertheless, further advances were not made by nightfall.

The 12th Infantry moved out at 0900 to attack. The progress of the 1st and 2nd Battalions was very slow throughout the day; the attacking battalions encountering many strong points and heavy artillery fire. By 1500, they succeeded in reaching the high ground overlooking Gey and were bringing up supporting weapons after eliminating several enemy strong points.

The 22nd Infantry with the 46th Armored Infantry Battalion (5th Armored Division) moved in the attack at 0835. By 1000, the 3rd Battalion reached its objective and was proceeding to dig in. In the interim, the 2nd Battalion with the 46th Armored Battalion was making very slow progress against heavy resistance consisting of small arms, machine gun, mortar, and artillery fire. At 1100, the 46th Armored was ordered to withdraw to the hill they had occupied on the previous night. The 1st Battalion had been committed between the 2nd and 3rd Battalions with the mission of advancing and attacking southeast. The general advance made by the regiment was slow throughout the day and the resistance encountered was considered extremely heavy, especially on the right flank, but the 1st and 3rd Battalions had reached positions from which they could support by fire the attack on Gey and Stras.

2 DECEMBER 1944—D+180: The enemy received reinforcements during the night so that our advances were vigorously contested by comparatively fresh troops.

The 4th Infantry Division once again continued its attack and made considerable advances in the northern part of its sector, but our advance was both slow and costly.

The 8th Infantry attacked with the 2nd Battalion at 0830 and with the 1st and 3rd Battalions at 0900. All battalions moved forward slowly throughout the day against heavy resistance consisting of many well dug in automatic weapons, small arms, and mortars. All roads and trails were reported as being thoroughly mined. The terrain was thickly wooded and rough but by 1300, Companies A, C, and K had affected a penetration of the enemy's defenses which was immediately exploited. At 1600 it was necessary to consolidate all gains in preparation for continuation of the attack on 3 December.

The 12th Infantry reported at 0830 a counterattack by enemy infantry against Company D. At 0845, the enemy had been completely stopped. At 1000, the CT was ordered to attack with the 2nd Battalion to reach the edge of the woods and to make contact with the 22nd Infantry. By 1315, the 2nd Battalion had reached its objective and was consolidating. By 1700, the 1st and 2nd Battalions were consolidated and had cleaned out all infiltrating enemy from their rear areas.

The 22nd Infantry reported at 0655 that it was receiving a fairly strong counterattack between the 1st and 3rd Battalions. By 0845, the enemy had succeeded in lightly penetrating the front line positions and had reached the rear areas at which time the regimental reserve was committed. By 1010, Companies K and L had reestablished contact and were mopping up. The situation was reported to be well in hand and by 1300 the counterattack was considered to have been repulsed. Before darkness fell, contact had been re-established between all units and with the 12th Infantry on the left. All enemy had been cleared from the rear areas and units were consolidating for the night.

3 DECEMBER 1944—D+181: Against CT 12, the enemy situation was extremely fluid inasmuch as the entire period was characterized by numerous counterattacks of varying size. Against CT 22, the enemy line remained the same. The enemy defended from camouflaged strong points in the northern sector. In the center and along the southern part, the enemy continued to counterattack in approximately the same places and about the same time as previously. One of these attacks, against CT 8 was made up of men of the 8th Parachute Regiment. The attack was vigorous and was only thrown back after a lively fight.

The supporting antiaircraft within the division zone of action brought down a large number of enemy aircraft.

The 8th Infantry suffered extremely heavy concentrations of artillery fire just prior to the time scheduled for the attack (0900) and it was apparent that the enemy likewise had planned an attack. Numerous small infantry actions took place, preventing us from gaining much terrain. The 8th Infantry was ordered to consolidate its present position on the most favorable terrain and to mop up the enemy forces which had infiltrated around its right flank.

The 12th Infantry remained on the defense throughout the day. At 0830, it was reported that enemy was infiltrating around the west flank of Company B and caused the withdrawing of Company G. The lost ground was regained with the support of one platoon of Company L. Numerous prisoners of war were taken during the day.

The 22nd Infantry remained in its defensive positions until 1130 at which time elements of the 330th Infantry Regiment (83rd Infantry Division) initiated their relief. In the interim, the 1st Battalion successfully repulsed a counterattack which had been launched at 0930. By 1900, the entire relief had been affected and the regiment moved to its new assembly area.

4 DECEMBER 1944—D+182: The 8th Infantry attacked to the south at 1030 with elements of the 1st and 2nd Battalions to clear enemy pockets of resistance between their present positions and the right boundary of the regiment. Contact was made with the enemy at 1130 and a small arms fire fight ensued. The attack progressed and the enemy pocket was successfully liquidated. The attacking units returned to positions formerly held and the new cleared area was outposted by the 24th Cavalry Reconnaissance Squadron.

The 12th Infantry launched an attack with the 3rd Battalion to the northeast to clear enemy pockets of resistance between its positions and the regimental left boundary. The attack progressed and by mid-afternoon, the objectives had been reached. Then the battalion withdrew, and the terrain covered during the fight was outposted by the 24th Cav Sqn. In the interim, the 1st and 2nd Battalions adjusted their positions on the main line of resistance. Between 1600 and 1800, Company B was subjected to extremely intense artillery barrages which caused heavy casualties. This company was withdrawn.

The 22nd Infantry began the movement at 0945 at which time it passed the IP at Zweifall, en route to new assembly areas in the vicinity of Luxembourg. The three battalions closed there at 2200 but the remainder of the Combat Team was still en route at the close of the day.

CT 330 (83rd Inf Div) remained attached to the 4th Infantry Division and improved and readjusted the former front line positions. Sporadic artillery fire was received but no encounter with the enemy was reported.

5 DECEMBER 1944—D+183: The enemy remained for the most part on the defensive, being content to harass our front lines with heavy artillery and mortar fire.

The 8th Infantry consolidated its front line positions and maintained contact with the 4th Cavalry Reconnaissance Squadron on its left (north) flank and the 24th Cavalry Reconnaissance Squadron on its right.

The 12th Infantry adjusted its positions and prepared for relief.

The 22nd Infantry completed its movement to the new division zone of action and passed to the control of the 83rd Infantry Division.

The CT 330 improved its front line positions. A counterattack by an estimated 47 enemy infantry was launched shortly after first light after a heavy mortar and artillery preparation had been laid down. The assault was repulsed after inflicting heavy casualties on the enemy and a total of 20 prisoners of war were taken.

6 DECEMBER 1944—D+184: The 4th Infantry Division continued to defend its main line of resistance while plans were continued for the relief of the remainder of the division by the 83rd Infantry Division.

7 DECEMBER 1944—D+185: The 8th Infantry Regiment continued to defend its main line of resistance with its 1st and 3rd Battalions on line. Patrols were sent to locate all the enemy defenses, but no enemy was observed.

The 12th Infantry was relieved by the 331st Infantry Regiment beginning at 0800. The battalions moved to a temporary assembly area. By 1800, the entire relief was completed, the regiment was assembled and prepared to move the following day to a new area in the vicinity of the City of Luxembourg. The Commanding General of the 83rd Division assumed the responsibility for this zone of action while the Commanding General of the 4th Infantry Division assumed responsibility for the new zone of action fronting the Sauer and Moselle rivers in the vicinity of the City of Luxembourg.

The 22nd Infantry passed to the control of the 4th Infantry Division and continued to defend its sector while other elements of the Division moved during the day to their new assembly areas.

And never forget... it was on 7 December 1941, that the Japanese attacked Pearl Harbor "A Day That Will Live in Infamy" and America declared war on Japan and Germany.

From **Swede Henley's Diary—used with permission of his daughters...**

1 DECEMBER 1944 D-15: 1st Bn ordered to swing from behind 3rd Bn across open ground to help 2nd Bn advance. Jerry artillery—mortar and rockets—worst seen yet. Attack jumped off at 1000 hours. Objective taken at 1400 and area cleared of Krauts. Plans to be made to move CP in town of Groshau this afternoon.

- 2 yanks bringing 5 Krauts 1 officer back to CP when Jerry artillery killed all the Germans and wounded one yank—6 less to feed.
- CP in cellar in Groshau. Jerry shelling the top floor out. The armorer is supposed to roll day after tomorrow.
- P-51 airplane shot down over our CP and pilot bailed out and floated into German lines—the poor bastard.

2 DECEMBER 1944 D-16: Jerry counterattacked 3rd Bn and overran I Co. Alerted our outfit and called on cooks and KPs and supply personnel and put them in line.

- Everything under control again at 1100. Jerry still shelling us continuously. Our CP still in Groshau in cellar.
- Found German woman in Jerry uniform

3 DECEMBER: Good news—83 Div. 330 Inf 1st Bn relieving us today. Moving back to new area to reorganize. Jerry air corps out in force—50 planes strafed and bombed us. We shot down 6 in short order.

4 DECEMBER: Ordered move at 0915 for area near Luxembourg via Zweifall, Monschau—Eupen -Verviers—Pepinster—Theux—Louveigne—Remouchamps—Aywaille—Staumont—Trois Ponts—Salmchateau—Bovigny—Luxembourg Canach. Relieved 331st Regiment 1st Bn on outpost along Mosel River.

5 DECEMBER: Relief completed at 1600. CP in Canach in house. Took first bath and changed clothes for first time in 20 days.

6 DECEMBER: Moved CP to Gostengin. Really have nice CP with accessories. A Co located Wormeldange. B Co in Gostengin. C Co in Hiederdonven.

7 DECEMBER: Raining, but we are warm and comfortable in our CP. Planning complete reorganization of Bn as losses in last fight were 100% in combat troops.
- Casualties during Hurtgen Forest fight were 2800 men and 145 officers from Nov. 16 to Dec. 3, 1944. 1st Bn lost 750 men—
- *28 officers.

It was on 2 and 3 December 1944 that our 5th and final 4ID Medal of Honor was earned in WWII. Private Pedro Cano of Company C, 8th Infantry Regiment's Medal of Honor citation reads as follows:

For conspicuous gallantry and intrepidity at the risk of his life above and beyond the call of duty:

Private Pedro Cano distinguished himself by acts of gallantry and intrepidity above and beyond the call of duty while serving with Company C, 8th Infantry Regiment, 4th Infantry Division during combat operations against an armed enemy in Schevenhutte, Germany on December 2 and 3, 1944. On the afternoon of the 2nd, American infantrymen launched an attack against German emplacements but were repulsed by enemy machine gun fire. Armed with a rocket launcher, Private Cano crawled through a densely mined area under heavy enemy fire and successfully reached a point within ten yards of the nearest emplacement. He quickly fired a rocket into the position, killing the two gunners and five supporting riflemen. Without hesitating, he fired into a second position, killing two more gunners, and proceeded to assault the position with hand grenades, killing several others and dispersing the rest. Then, when an adjacent company encountered heavy fire, Private Cano crossed his company front, crept to within fifteen yards of the nearest enemy emplacement and killed the two machine gunners with a rocket. With another round he killed two more gunners and destroyed a second gun. On the following day, his company renewed the attack and again encountered heavy machine gun fire. Private Cano, armed with his rocket launcher, again moved across fire-swept terrain, and destroyed three enemy machine guns in succession, killing the six gunners. Private Cano's extraordinary heroism and selflessness above and beyond the call of duty are in keeping with the highest traditions of military service and reflect great credit upon himself, his unit, and the United States Army.

Citation represents Soldier's rank at time of action.

From Chaplain Bill Boice's *History of the 22nd Infantry Regiment in WWII:*
THE 22ND SEES LIGHT THROUGH THE TREES

"Now the focus of battle shifted to the 22nd Regiment whose commander, Colonel Buck Lanham, could see light ahead through the trees. His battalions were spread like two fans on either side of the ravine. Muddy trails from the rear brought up replacements to fill out his riddled lines, fresh-faced second lieutenants still untried by enemy fire, privates in clean overcoats standing in the trucks with grave expressions, not scared but very serious as the sound of shelling echoed through the trees.

In his wooden trailer, Colonel Lanham was talking on a field phone: "Tell 'C' Company to get in there with bazookas and grenades and take that high ground. Hill 90. We've got to have that high ground. Hill 92 doesn't do us any good until we've gotten 90, too. And Blue can't advance until the Krauts are knocked off those hills. Tell them to fight like hell."

He hung up and turned tensely to the map on his small folding table. Prematurely gray, with black eyes bright behind his spectacles, the colonel seemed too absorbed in the map's crayon hieroglyphics to notice the stocky, wide-faced captain waiting across the table. Without looking up he said, "You didn't know it was me you had on the phone last night, did you, Swede?"

"No, sir, " said the captain, shifting nervously. When the colonel looked up he smiled. Swede smiled too, with relief.

"That's all right, Swede," the colonel said in a voice softened by understanding. "I know how it is when you see a lot of your friends knocked off. But you've got to treat your superior officers with more respect."

Swede was silent a moment, then he said quietly, "Colonel, sir, I don't care if you break me for it. I meant what I said last night, even though I didn't know it was you on the line. That little patch of woods we're fighting for ain't any good to anybody. No good to the Germans. No good to us. It's the bloodiest damn ground in all Europe, and you make us keep fighting for it. That ain't right."

Now it was the colonel's time to be silent. Two men sitting across the table looking at one another in silence. The colonel, slight of build, keen-faced, intense. The blond captain, bulky, mud-spattered, a two-day growth of beard on his wide face, a face designed for grinning but dead serious now and pale with fatigue.

"There's nothing in the world," said the colonel deliberately, "that I'd like to do better than tell all you boys to call it off and go home. You know that, Swede. But it can't be done. The only way we can get this thing over is by killing Krauts. To kill them you've got to get to them."

Swede grunted.

"Look here on the map. You know they're dug in all through these woods you're talking about. Once we've got those two hills then we'll be able to pour so much stuff into that patch of woods that not a Kraut will be left. Then we can push on to where the woods end and fight in daylight like little gentlemen again. Wherever there are Krauts we've got to kill 'em. I know they've killed lots of our boys in that patch, but we've killed even more of them, and that's what counts."

Swede sighed. "I know you're right, Colonel. Knew it all the time. I just have to get things off my chest once in a while."

"Pour yourself a slug of good Heinie cognac," said the colonel. When Swede left he was smiling again. The phone buzzed.

"Charcoal speaking," said the colonel. "Yes, wild man. Got up on top the hill, did they? That's the stuff. Keep 'em going and let me know so we can start concentrating on that wooded patch."

No sooner had he hung up on his G-2 officer than the phone buzzed again.

"Charcoal speaking. Oh, hello, General. Yes, Blue is going to jump off soon. Just as soon as Hill 90 is cleared. Yes, sir. That's right. You can count on us, but I wish you'd get that damn task-force armor to start moving south of us. You know how armor is, wants every foxhole cleared out before they'll move…Well, I suppose so…Yes, sir."

During the dreary afternoon, Lanham's 'C' Company fought up to the top of Hill 90 and started firing down into German positions before the early winter twilight made them button up for the night.

A colorless dawn brought more artillery, but by 8 o'clock the gray sky had broken sufficiently for fighter-bombers to lay on a mission. Tobogganing out of the western sky they came down over Grosshau, the tiny village just beyond the eastern edge of the forest. Each cracking explosion fountained smoke and debris into the still air. In foxholes scooped from rotting pine needles, the foot soldiers watched approvingly. "Give it to the bastards." "Now we're getting somewhere." "Lookit those houses go whammo."

In the thunder heaped on Grosshau, it seemed impossible for any living thing to survive. Cautiously, riflemen and Tommy gunners hunched down the hill from tree to tree, firing whenever a shadow moved unnaturally in the woods ahead. Now they were fighting in Swede's bloody patch of woods, where every tree was shattered into a naked spear of white ugliness against the dark earth, where weather-soaked corpses had lain so long the stench was unbearable.

As the day advanced, the dirty brown uniforms drove the dirty gray uniforms out of the last woodland west of Grosshau. Emerging onto treeless ground, the Americans felt as naked as strip-teasers at a Sunday-school picnic. The forest which had been hateful seemed friendly and protective now that they had only tiny hillocks and shell craters to shield them.

Artillery hidden in the woods across the barren plain intensified their thunder when the Americans appeared. From crater to crater Lanham's men dodged, fired over rims, ducked to another crater farther ahead. From Grosshau, which had seemed completely uninhabitable, the machine gun and small arms fire grew intense.

Time after time the 22nd pushed forward, stumbled, took cover. Six Sherman tanks were knocked out. The lines regrouped to try again. But too many men were falling. The plague of shells grew even thicker.

Back in the forest, a major talked to Colonel Lanham by phone. When the major had explained, Lanham said, "All right. Have your boys dig into the best positions possible. Just hold on. We'll have to try it another way."

The other way was to keep to the woods and circle northward around Grosshau and the plain. Already Major George Goforth's battalion was pushing over a series of wooded hills that bulged like a ripple of muscle along the forest rim. That was on Monday, the 27th. For two days they fought through those hills, with casualties bad on both sides.

In his gloomy CP, a lantern-lit log dugout, Major Goforth talked over the situation with his exec, Swede Henley. A company commander had just come in to report.

"We're hunting for officers," said the new arrival, slumping onto a battered tin water can. "G Company's got only two officers left. Lost three this afternoon. We can't go on like this, Major."

Goforth shook his head. "I know, boy, but where am I going to get them? Division says we can commission any good man right here in the field. But who?" He looked around a circle of dirty, unshaven faces watching him in the sputtering light, faces drained of color like those of drowned men.

"There's McDermott," said Swede. "Can't spare him. He practically runs G-2."

"He's the last available sergeant. We've already commissioned six. Guess we'll have to depend on replacements," said Goforth. "The trouble with replacements is that they don't last long enough," observed the company commander. "Trucks brought up 30 for me this morning; 18 were hit even before they could get into the line. No percentage in that."

As he spoke, the blanket covering the dugout doorway was pushed aside and three young lieutenants entered, saluted, and said they were reporting for duty. "There you are, Jack," said Goforth. "Replacements for you. Take 'em with you when you go back."

Bill Boice continues in his **History of the 22nd Infantry Regiment in WWII …**
FROM HURTGEN FOREST TO LUXEMBOURG – 4 DECEMBER 1944

It was a full day's trip south through Belgium to the Duchy of Luxembourg and the men were very, very tired but relaxed when the convoys pulled in, in the dark, to the little towns along the Moselle River to take over the patrol of the Moselle. The 83rd Division was relieved that night and the CT was on its own in a strange land where all was quiet; too quiet to the battered squads, platoons, and companies that holed up in the little towns like Manternach, Grovenmacher, and Flaxweiler.

This was "Chocolate Soldier" -"Prince Rupert of Hentzau"— "Beverly of Graustark" land. It was fantastic and unbelievable. All the people were gone, just as though the Pied Piper had passed this way once again. The houses had REAL beds, the bins were full of apples and potatoes, the deserted cafes were full of wine, a few billy goats and chickens disconsolately poked their way around town—and the Germans were just across the river.

Hurtgen Forest had been a grim tale in many ways. The regiment had taken more casualties in this one battle than many regiments had taken in the entire war. No one, least of all our own command, could logically explain how, day after day, decimated, disorganized, cut to pieces, and under the most adverse conditions the regiment had still fought against over-whelming odds and had still functioned as a fighting machine. As casualties mounted, morale dropped, for as every shell thudded into the earth, there shuddered too into the mind of the disillusioned GI the inescapable fact that the German Army still existed and that the war was far from over.

When at last the regiment had been pulled from Hurtgen and ordered to Luxembourg, the men were stupefied to know that after the heaviest casualties of the war, they were not to be withdrawn from the area and given a rest, but were to be sent down to the Luxembourg front, which even though static, still represented work to be done, patrols' to run, and the constant, unceasing vigil which the GI had to maintain under battle conditions.

When the men had moved into Hurtgen, they had gone proudly as members of a great combat team. They had been given the best available benefit of clean clothing and hot food. Now they came out, after 18 days of fighting, unshaven, unbelievably weary, with eyes that were partially vacant. They were really "fed up with the set-up." The sick, sweet odor of death was never far away from any man. Vehicles were in as bad shape as the men. Jeeps were frequently telescoped in front and rear because while moving in convoy the vehicle had no brakes and no one was able to stop on short notice. It was a haggard, whipped, abysmally unhappy, utterly disillusioned remnant of a great combat team that made its heartbreaking move from Hurtgen, Germany, to Luxembourg.

Not even the warmth of the welcome of Luxembourg, nor its undamaged homes and bright modern shops, which might well have been a street from any modern city in America, could interest those GIs. There was still fighting to be done and they had come to the inevitable conclusion that they were the ones who would have to do it.

And yet, not a soldier present, from the high command to the lowest private, so much as dreamed that within a matter of days this same group of men would be forced to face all of the power and might of a great Von Rundstedt offensive whose plan had largely been based upon the German knowledge that the Fourth Infantry Division, as a fighting organization, should, by all rights, have ceased to exist. Indeed, this was so utterly true that on Christmas Eve, 1944, Drew Pearson announced from information picked up from a German broadcast that the Fourth Infantry Division had been completely annihilated.

Early on the morning of 4 December, Combat Team 22 had begun its motor march into Luxembourg, a distance of 130 miles. The column proceeded via Zweifall, Eupen, Veriers, Pepinster, Theux, Louveigne, Remouchamps, Auwaille, Houffalize, Bastogne, Arlon, Steinfort, and Luxembourg City. Combat Team 22 was to relieve CT 331, 83rd Infantry Division, along the Moselle River line by the 5th of December. Thus, each of the rifle companies moved directly to the area held by a similar company of CT 331. Special units moved into bivouac areas in the neighborhood of Moutfort.

Shortly after daylight the 5th of December, the actual relief of front line units had all taken place. By dark the operation in the entire area was completed without enemy interference. In its new sector, CT 22 occupied defensive positions on a twenty mile front paralleling the Moselle River in Luxembourg. The usual wide front in the area had been further increased in order to free one regiment to participate in the regiment-by-regiment shuttle switch of the 4th and 83rd Infantry Divisions. When the transfer of the divisions was complete eight days later, the front was reduced by one-third. Three rifle battalions occupied the front with outposts varying in size from half squads (4 to 6 men) to platoons (20 to 40 men). The entire sector was passive and the only aggressive action between forces was occasional harassing artillery or mortar fire and an occasional patrol.

From the 6th to the 15th of December 1944, the regiment continued the outposting and patrolling along the Moselle River and worked to regain the combat efficiency it had lost. Clean-up of personnel, equipment, and vehicles began at once, A small amount of training was carried on daily, but the Division was in no condition to fight. Nobody expected it to have to fight. The Combat Team frontage was reduced to about thirteen miles on the 13th. When elements of the 8th Infantry relieved the Second Battalion, it allowed that battalion to move to the area, Schrassig Moutfort, as CT reserve. Six to eight weeks were planned to rehabilitate and strengthen the units. *(But that was not to be…)*

8 DEC 1944 TO 14 DEC 1944 – D+186 TO D+192

I have included a map of the beginning of the Battle of the Bulge, even though it isn't until later when we start reading details about it. This map came from Wikipedia. For those who want to read ahead, there is a lot of Battle of the Bulge information on the internet. To stay focused on the 4ID's role in the Bulge, stay focused on the southern shoulder of the Bulge and the fighting in Luxembourg.

8 DECEMBER 1944—D+186: The enemy front lines existed generally along the east bank of the Sauer and Moselle rivers. The area in and around Wasserbillig was occupied by enemy troops. The enemy defended its line by utilizing concrete emplacements and strategically emplaced dug in strong points. Most emplacements were mutually supporting. Vehicular activity was detected moving south on the Bitburg-Trier road.

The 8th Infantry remained attached to the 83rd Infantry Division in the vicinity of Zweifall.

The 12th Infantry initiated movement at 0705 from the vicinity of Gressnich to its new assembly area, closing therein at 2130. Company E relieved Company G of the 329th Infantry Regiment on the positions held in the vicinity of Echternach. This was completed at 2000 while the remainder of the Regiment was conducting preparations to relieve the remainder of the CT 329 on the morning of 9 December.

The 22nd Infantry conducted active patrolling and its troop dispositions remained unchanged.

The Artillery HQ arrived at 1425 in the vicinity of Neudorf and the 4th Reconnaissance Troop in the vicinity of Monsdorf.

(This begins a very slight lull in action for the 4ID before the Battle of the Bulge started on 16 December 1944. You can see there was very little rest for the weary Soldiers of the 4ID after they came out of the Bloody Hurtgen Forest).

9 DECEMBER 1944—D+187: The enemy activity was restricted to fifteen rounds of artillery which fell at various times.

The 4th Infantry Division continued its defense and active patrolling. The relief of the 329th Infantry was completed at 1420 without incident.

10 DECEMBER 1944—D+188: The 12th Infantry maintained and readjusted its positions, dispatching reconnaissance, security, and contact patrols.

The 22nd Infantry moved its CP from Senningen to the vicinity of Mondorf. Enemy activity was negligible.

11 DECEMBER 1944—D+189: Small exchanges of artillery were experienced as the enemy continued to improve its defensive line.

The 12th Infantry maintained its positions and conducted vigorous patrolling within its sector facing the Sauer River. Between 1400 and 1500, Company E in the vicinity of Echternach received some small arms fire and upon retaliating with a concentration of 81 mm mortar fire, our garrison received about 50 rounds of 120 mm mortar fire and several rounds of 150 mm artillery fire.

The 22nd Infantry improved its positions and conducted patrolling. Little or no enemy activity was reported.

CT 8, still in the vicinity of Zweifall, prepared to move on 12 December to rejoin the 4th Infantry Division.

12 DECEMBER 1944—D+190: The 8th Infantry was detached from the 83rd Division and moved at 0800. The final elements reached the City of Luxembourg at 1935. The Combat Team closed within its new assembly area by 1950, the 1st Battalion in the vicinity of Flaxveiler, the 2nd of Uebersyern, the 3rd of Wecker and the 29th FA Battalion in the vicinity of Flaxweiler.

The 12th Infantry maintained its positions. Enemy activity was negligible except several exchanges of machine gun and mortar fires across the Moselle river.

The 22nd continued active patrolling along its front.

13 DECEMBER 1944—D+191: The enemy remained defensive as a small amount of harassing artillery was employed by him against road intersections and likely train supply roads.

The relief of elements of the 12th and 22nd Infantry Regiments was effected by CT 8.

In the sector of the 12th Infantry, 42 propaganda shells containing three types of leaflets were fired by the enemy in the town of Burschdoy at 1600.

(Keep in mind, this is the lull before the next battle hits—the Battle of the Bulge began on December 16, 1944…)

14 DECEMBER—D+192: The 8th Infantry maintained its positions and reported to have received a few rounds of light artillery in the 1st Battalion area during the night.

The 12th Infantry conducted patrolling within its sector. The regiment had been charged with the defense of Radio Luxembourg in the vicinity of Junglinster and this installation was outposted accordingly.

The 22nd Infantry conducted active patrolling. Very light sporadic artillery fire consisting of one round every one half hour constituted the only enemy activity.

From **Swede Henley's Diary—used with permission of his daughters…**

8 DECEMBER: Still in Gostengin. I was granted a 3 day trip to Paris—to see the sights.

9 DECEMBER: Took off for Paris. Drove 100 miles to Reims and spent the night.

10 DECEMBER SATURDAY: Left Reims and arrived in Paris at 1300 to see the sights of Gay Paree.

11 DECEMBER: In Paris. Meal for 4 of us cost $89.00. 4 cups of coffee $4.00. Ask Kemp about it.

12 DECEMBER: Left Paris at 1545 for Reims.

13 DECEMBER: Arrived back at Gostengin at 1800. Tired, but glad to be back.

14-15 DECEMBER: Still in Gostengin, living like kings.

Individual Stories from—**War Stories Volume II: Paris to VE Day:**

John E. Kunkel, Springfield, OH
Company L, 3rd Battalion, 22nd Infantry Regiment
Smelled Like Billy Goats

I would like to relate something that took place a day or two after we were relieved in the Hürtgen and pulled back to what I recall was an old German training camp. A short time after we got there, we were all given a bunk and a gray German army blanket. Well, about midnight it happened—we all started to itch all over. My buddy said he felt something crawling on his neck. I took my pen flashlight out and, sure enough, there they were—body lice.

Now the problem was getting rid of the lice. About daylight we found an old kerosene lantern. We poured the kerosene into a steel helmet and with an old dirty sock, we all took a sponge bath. It was hard on the skin, but we got rid of the lice. It was some time until we could take a real bath with good old water. We started to smell to the point we all smelled like Billy goats—it got to where we could not live with one another.

I am now 75 and still love to hear stories about the 22nd Infantry Regiment and the 4th Infantry Division. (Editor's note: This was written in 1999 or so, thus, if he were still alive, he would be about 100 now, but I doubt he is still alive—thank goodness he shared his story when he did).

Donald Faulkner, Winter Park, FL
Company E, 2nd Battalion, 22nd Infantry Regiment
First Bath, *Excerpts from his diary*

When Company E pulled into Manternach, Luxembourg, from the Hürtgen Forest, we were dirty, muddy, pooped, bashed, and dead tired. It was December 8, 1944. The next morning, two or three of my men arrived at our CP and shouted, "Come with us for a bath!"

So, down the street we went to a bombed-out house and up to the second floor. It was all shelled out, but visible to us all was a tub and a small wood stove above it, filled with burning kindling, making hot water. I took off my boots and jumped into the tub, muddy clothes and all.

As my men applauded, I disrobed and had the first bath since leaving the USA on September 15, 1944. Wow!

Donald Faulkner continues with another of his diary excerpts, this one titled: **Talking in Tongues**

December 9, 1944: Company E sent its first platoon eighteen men, from

Manternach, Luxembourg up to the Mosell River to guard and observe from a wine distillery. Next morning, the phone check sounded like blabbering idiots. Someone was "talking in tongues!" A relieving squad revealed the mystery when they found they had all drunk the green wine from the fall crop of grapes and were simply "stewed."

Tom Reid, Marietta, GA
Cannon Company, 22nd Infantry Regiment and Company I, 3rd Battalion, 22nd Infantry Regiment
Battle of the Bulge Begins

Early in December 1944, the 22nd Infantry Regiment moved to Luxembourg after a bitter three weeks of fighting in the Hürtgen Forest. It was supposed to be a quiet area and a much-needed time to rest, receive replacements, and refit. However, such would not be the case. In the redisposition of the troops in Luxembourg, Service Company of the Regiment, commanded by Captain Billy Cater and Captain Clarence Hawkins (known as "Big Hawk"), the regimental motor officer, managed to set up shop at the Luxembourg Country Club. This was an elaborate facility complete with hot water, showers, real beds, and the comforts of home.

Captain Cater and Big Hawk invited anyone in the regiment to come by and take a hot shower, and many availed themselves of that privilege. I just didn't have the opportunity until that fateful Saturday, December 16. I say fateful, because just as I finished the first hot shower I had enjoyed in over a month, I received word that my company had been alerted to move to northern Luxembourg immediately. The Battle of the Bulge had begun, and the 22nd Infantry would help stop the advance of the Germans on the southern shoulder of this penetration.

I got into my jeep, hurried back to my company, and by dark we were in position north of Luxembourg City.

Nothing was unusual about the alerting of the Regiment and its hurried move that day, but after the first hot shower in weeks, I was a prime candidate on that cold move to catch pneumonia.

Luckily, I did not get sick. The Regiment performed at its usual peak efficiency; eventually the Germans were driven back, and the war was ultimately shortened by the last great fling of the Germans that December. I will always remember my only December 1944 bath.

Although Billy Cater is still with us, Big Hawk has gone on to that great motor pool in the sky. Deeds not words!

(Editor's Note: Billy Cater is now deceased, as is Tom Reid, but the sons of Big Hawk and Billy are both regular readers of my blogs. I had the great honor of being the speaker at Tom Reid's funeral service and was able to relate some of his stories from WWII, Korea, and Vietnam (a three-war veteran. Also, for any who have an interest and time to listen to a 92 minute interview I did with Tom Reid in September 2002 for the Veterans History Project, it discusses Tom Reid's complete experiences in WWII. You can Google Veterans History Project and then search for Tom Reid in Army in WWII).

Jack Capell, Portland, OR
HQ, 8th Infantry Regiment
From Paradise Back Into Hell

The date is March 7, 1997. This is an oral history contribution on the Battle of the Bulge to the Eisenhower Center, New Orleans, Louisiana, attention Dr. Stephen Ambrose. This is from John C. Capell. I am known as Jack Capell.

I was a member of the 4th Infantry Division, 8th Infantry Regiment, Headquarters Company from D-Day until the end of the war, including the Battle of the Bulge. I was a combat infantryman. I am arranging these recollections in a series, rather than giving continuous narration, because I think it is a matter of record as to what the 4th Infantry Division did during the Battle of the Bulge, and I see no reason I should go over that or include many numerous details. I will give you some of the memories that I have of that period.

The first recollection begins just prior to the outbreak of the battle.

When we arrived in Luxembourg on December 12, 1944 we had been fighting in the Hürtgen Forest and had been severely battered, were battle weary, exhausted, had suffered terrible casualties, and were seriously depleted in manpower and much in need of replacements. We were removed from the Hürtgen Forest and sent to the Luxembourg front in the Ardennes Forest.

The 28th Infantry Division had a similar experience. They also were among those divisions that were spread out alongside of us. We were, at the time, near the town of Senningen, Luxembourg, just to the west of the Moselle River near the Luxembourg/German border. Supposedly, we were facing a rather weak German unit. It was considered to be a quiet front. Some of the veterans of the Hürtgen Forest, especially those who had been in for the full time, were allowed forty-eight hours at a hospital rest camp in Arlon, Belgium. I was one of the first to be able to go and was to leave on December 15. There were about ten of us loaded on a two-and-a-half ton truck early in the morning to head back to Arlon.

The camp was in a large stone building, and there were cots complete with sheets, blankets, and mattresses; hot water showers; and a supply of clean-laundered clothing. Good hot food was served in a mess hall, and it was pure luxury.

We spent December 15 with great pleasure and looked forward to a full night's sleep. We expected to have another enjoyable day on the 16th. However, early in the morning on the 16th we were ordered to get ready to go back. We were shocked and thought there must be a mistake. We loudly proclaimed that we had one more day to stay in Arlon. The officer who gave the order insisted there was no mistake; we were to go back. We protested loudly, and a major then came on the scene and ordered us to get ready to go out and to be ready to leave in a very short while. He said there was a problem at the front, and if we didn't go and follow orders we would be charged with refusing duty, so we reluctantly complied, but complained bitterly.

We were loaded onto a two-and-a-half ton truck and headed back. The weather had turned cold that day, and there was a biting wind that blew through the back of the truck. We were not only extremely angry, but miserable from the cold. After a time we stopped to refuel. While waiting, we went inside the fuel dump shack to get warm for a few minutes and heard an English language broadcast on a radio the men had there. Suddenly, we forgot how cold we were when we heard about a German counterattack and specific mention of the fact that the 4th Infantry Division had been annihilated in the fighting. We were stunned, since we were all from the Headquarters Company of the 8th Infantry Regiment, 4th Infantry Division. We frantically interrogated the driver, who was from division headquarters, and asked him where he was taking us. He said he knew nothing about it except that he was to take us to division headquarters for instructions. From then on, there was no further concern about the cold, but there was great anxiety.

At division headquarters, the driver was instructed to take us to the town of Senningen. Then we left. My foxhole, or shelter trench, had been half a mile forward from Senningen. When we returned, we came right back to the town and found that members of our company were in the cellar of a stone building in the center of Senningen. Immediately upon arriving, we were issued TNT and dynamite caps, or blasting caps, to set off the TNT in order to blast foxholes in frozen ground. We were also issued more grenades that we strapped around our belts and were ordered to check our M-1 rifles. If there were any malfunctions, there were a few replacement rifles for which we could exchange them.

Immediately we were marched to a position near Senningen on the front and ordered to hold the position. By this time we had learned about the German counterattack and about how our division had survived. We found there were few, if any, casualties in our company, but those who were around the town of Echternach, Luxembourg, were in serious trouble and probably were all killed or captured. That seemed to be the area where the 4th Infantry Division had suffered the worst losses. Otherwise, except for some minor withdrawals, the line was being held.

Artillery, mortar, and small arms fire were intense. We had begun hearing heavy artillery fire even before we reached Division Headquarters when we were coming back. The Germans had broken through just to the north of us but had failed to penetrate very far into the 4th Infantry

Division sector. The 4th Infantry Division was now forming the southern border of the new front. Our division had lost Echternach and the area around it, but we fought very hard to keep from yielding any more ground. We apparently did prevent the Germans from breaking through to Luxembourg City. In just a twenty-four hour period, we had gone from paradise back into hell again. This concludes my recollection of how I first learned about the Battle of the Bulge.

Full-blown chaos broke loose on 16 December 1944 as the Battle of the Bulge started…I have lots of 4ID stories from that time period. Keep reading…

15 DEC 1944 TO 21 DEC 1944 – D+193 TO D+199 BATTLE OF THE BULGE BEGINS…

16 December 1944 is start of the Battle of the Bulge. When you hear about the Battle of the Bulge, you most likely think of the 101st Airborne and their stand at Bastogne or of General Patton coming to their rescue with his Third Army. You most likely know very little about the key role the 4th Infantry Division served during that key turning point battle of WWII. Read on to learn the key role that 4ID played in that most famous of all battles of WWII. And in the 4ID battles, the key player was the 12th Infantry Regiment. They earned the Presidential Unit Citation for their actions holding the southern shoulder of the Bulge during those historic days in the last half of December 1944.

Here are the first days of the Battle of the Bulge:

15 DECEMBER 1944—D+193: Some long range machine gun fire combined with the usual amount of harassing artillery fire was employed by the enemy while he continued to remain on the defensive.

The 4th Infantry Division maintained its defenses. Outposts and searching parties were continued throughout the rear areas.

Enemy activity was negligible except for the fact that the 1st Battalion 22nd Infantry reported receiving 10 rounds of heavy artillery fire during the night.

First Days of Battle of the Bulge follow here…

16 DECEMBER 1944—D+194: Against CT 8 and CT 22, the enemy remained defensive. In the CT 12's sector, the enemy crossed the Sauer river in strength after a very heavy artillery preparation. The enemy attacked Berdof, Lauterborn, Dickweiller, Osweiler, and Echternach.

The situation in general that existed throughout the 4th Infantry Division on the morning of 16 December when the German Commander in the west, Von Runstedt, launched his large scale counteroffensive, was far from favorable. The division had been relieved after a period of hard fighting in the Hurtgen Forest and was considerably under strength in all infantry battalions. At this time, three regimental combat teams were holding a front of approximately 35 miles along the west bank of the Sauer and Moselle rivers in the Grand Duché of Luxembourg. Communications because of the shortage of equipment and the large division sector were strained to the utmost. The attached 70th Tank Battalion which likewise had taken severe punishment in the Hurtgen Forest, was at this time engaged in maintenance and clean-up of vehicles. Parts were virtually unobtainable, resulting in a number of tanks being actually non-operational.

All three regiments were contacted prior to 0600 and reports revealed that there had been some light enemy patrol activity in the sector of the 12th Infantry which was defending on the north portion of the Division zone of action. The usual small amounts of artillery fire had been received during the night but shortly after first light (0630) approximately 40 rounds of artillery of an estimated 150 or 170 mm fell in the 1st Battalion sector.

The towns of Berdof, Lauterborn, Alttier, Osweiler, and Dickweiler received heavy artillery preparations, but the largest concentration fell in the town of Echternach. This heavy fire continued for several hours and was directed accurately in the immediate vicinities of the command posts, which resulted in the complete loss of wire communication to all units below battalion level. Shortly after 0900, the enemy began to penetrate our forward positions with strong reconnaissance forces and later stronger formations of infantry. Three notable efforts were evidenced in the early hours in the vicinities of Berdorf, Echternach and the towns of Osweiler and Dickweiler. Reports covering this early period, because of the lack of wire communication and the initial failure of radios, were few and the situation remained obscure for several hours. Only in the late afternoon was the situation beginning to clear. Company I was reported as being surrounded in Dickweiler.

At 1100, an alert order was issued to tank companies of the 70th Tank Battalion and initially some elements were ordered to move to the 12th Infantry Regimental CP. By the time this supporting armor had reached forward battalion areas, Company F, 12th Infantry, had been completely surrounded in Berdorf and plans were being formulated to rescue them by mounting Company B, 12th Infantry, on the tanks. A fire fight ensued on the southern outskirts of the town. This continued until dark with a small measure of success as the enemy was driven out of part of the town but contact with Company F had not been restored.

Concurrent with this attempt, similar operations were started to drive through to Company E which had been encircled in Echternach, and Company G which was reported isolated in Lauterborn. Company A, 12th Infantry, mounted on light tanks reached Lauterborn after a light skirmish and the Company G supply route was opened. Strong resistance was met 500 yards northeast of Lauterborn. The enemy was driven back, but darkness quickly set in and forced the conclusion of this effort.

In the interim, the town of Osweiler continued to be occupied by Company L and Dickweiler by Company I. Elements of Company K mounted on tanks of the 70th Tank Battalion broke into Osweiler first and then Dickweiler, just in time to frustrate an enemy attack. Thereafter Companies I and L and this small task force were isolated due to an enemy penetration moving to the southwest against Herborn shortly after dark.

At the close of the day, plans were being made to reinforce the regiment on 17 December and to resume efforts to reestablish contact with all units.

The 8th Infantry Regiment continued outposting its positions next to the 12th Infantry's zone of action. Little enemy activity was noted, except for 160 rounds of artillery fire at 1930 hours. All units were alerted for a possible enemy thrust.

The 22nd Infantry Regiment continued to maintain its positions and reported no enemy activity. During the early afternoon, the 2nd Battalion was furnished transportation and alerted to be prepared to move motorized upon one hour's notice for the zone of action of the 12th Infantry.

17 DECEMBER 1944—D+195: Due to a drastic change in the tactical situation, notice was received from higher HQ that all passes would be suspended indefinitely.

The great German counteroffensive continued with the full weight of the 212 VolksGrenadier Division being thrown against the 12th Infantry. The dogged determination of the Combat Team and all supporting units was the greatest contributing factor in saving the City of Luxembourg and its many important installations, both political (Radio Luxembourg) and military (HQ XII Army Group) from being overrun by the enemy. During the day, the enemy was able to extend its advance on Berdorf to the southwest as far as Mullerthal, and from Echternach southwest as far as Scheidgen, but its third penetration in the Osweiler-Dickweiler area was checked and heavy losses inflicted upon him.

The 12th Infantry resumed operations at an early hour to contact all isolated elements and to reestablish former outpost lines. All troops held in spite of mass German infiltrations up to battalion strength, as deep into our lines as four kilometers. All units, however small, continued to stave off the enemy and harass him to the limit of their capacity.

During the night 16-17 December, patrol efforts to reach Companies E (Echternach), F (Berdorf) and I (Dickweiler) had failed. All communications with the 3rd Battalion's garrison in Osweiler and Dickweiler and also the three tanks were completely cut off.

Elements of Company B, reinforced by two tank platoons, resumed their counterattack on Berdorf. The attack was pushed, and the medium tanks drove into the town, firing at enemy in the buildings. The leading tank fired several rounds into a large hotel which had formerly been the CP of Company F when suddenly one tank commander noted a large American flag being unfurled on the roof. At least sixty Soldiers still occupied the hotel. The counterattack through the balance of the town was resumed but the enemy attacked with bazookas and knocked out one tank. With darkness beginning to set in, the position was consolidated. Heavy artillery, mortar, and rocket concentrations continued upon our forces throughout the night *(Note from Bob: The March 1945 Saturday Evening Post article about the battle at the Parke Hotel in Berdorf is very interesting. You may find it online or in your local library.*

In the interim, Companies A and G consolidated their positions in Lauterborn to the southwest of Echternach and were unable to effect contact with Company E which continued to hold out against tremendous odds in the heart of Echternach. The enemy had established outposts on the ridges surrounding our positions in Lauterborn and laid down continuous mortar and artillery barrages.

Meanwhile the 2nd Battalion of the 22nd Infantry had moved in the early morning to an assembly area in the vicinity of Bech. Supported by Company A of the 12th Tank Battalion (9th Armored Division) they advanced in the direction of Osweiler. Contact was established with Companies I and L. Company C of the 12th Infantry, in greatly reduced strength, had pushed from the vicinity of Herborn and had nearly succeeded in closing the Osweiler-Dickweiler area prior to dark. It halted and consolidated its positions on favorable terrain to the south of the two towns, which aided materially in the attempt to stabilize our lines.

On the extreme left of the 12th Infantry's zone of action, the enemy advance from Berdorf up the Schwaise-Ernz River valley had been anticipated by the Commanding General of the 4th Infantry Division. The 4th Engineer Combat Battalion with the 4th Reconnaissance Troop attached was ordered into the line on the high ground immediately to the south of Mullerthal. A task force under the command of Colonel James S. Luckett was constituted with these units, plus the 2nd Battalion of the 8th

Infantry Regiment and Companies A and C of 70th Tank Battalion. The enemy moved up the draw toward Mullerthal where they were engaged by reconnaissance elements of the 803rd Tank Destroyer Battalion after which they turned to the west and were engaged by the 60th Armored Infantry Battalion (9th Armored Division).

Late in the afternoon, enemy were noted approaching Consdorf along a drive northwest of the town. A handful of infantrymen and the tank from Company C were quickly thrown in to stem the tide. At dusk, after considerable firing, the attack subsided.

Against CT 8 and CT 22, the enemy remained on the defensive east of the Sauer and Moselle rivers.

18 DECEMBER 1944—D+196: Once again the enemy was aided by the weather, a thick fog preventing any use of the air forces.

The enemy's actions opposite CT 22 and CT 8 remained wholly defensive. Active patrolling was conducted, and defensive positions were improved. There was continuous harassing fire in the areas of Mompach and Lellig.

Against CT 12, the penetrations of the enemy were all met and contained, and in several places, the enemy was driven back. The only new threat came from an estimated company of enemy moving on Dickweiler from Girst. This attack was repulsed, and the enemy forced to withdraw. Then the enemy contented himself by harassing the defenders at long range. The 3rd Battalion of the 12th Infantry with two tanks moved to Herborn. With doughboys of Company K they succeeded in reaching a point about 200 yards south of Dickweiler before driving back to Herborn. The mission was a complete success as supplies were carried. In the interim, the 2nd Battalion 22nd Infantry with Companies E and G continued its attack against an estimated enemy battalion. Company F with Company A, 19th Tank Battalion attacked from the direction of Osweiler to the west against the same force.

In the central part of the 12th Infantry's sector, generally from Echternach through Scheidgen, Company E continued to hold out in Echternach. Companies A and G were still firmly entrenched in the vicinity of Lauterborn and made futile attempts to make physical contact with Company E. Task Force Riley from Combat Command A of the 10th Armored Division assisted our forces in this sector by initiating an attack at 0800. They advanced to Michelshof thence to Scheidgen where they encountered heavy enemy resistance. Leaving a force to contain this town, they continued on and passed through Lauterborn, establishing a line approximately 300 yards southwest of Echternach. Supplies were sent to Company E in Echternach.

Concurrent with these operations, Task Force Standish of CC A 10th Armored Division advanced at 0800 through Consdorf to our infantry and tanks in Berdorf. In conjunction with Companies B and F, 12th Infantry, they attacked to the southeast toward Hill 329 against heavy resistance. Little progress was made.

Task Force Luckett, still holding its positions on the high ground to the south of Mullerthal against a strong enemy force, consolidated its defense but it was apparent that better terrain would have to be secured. At 1515, the Task Force attacked with the 2nd Battalion of the 8th Infantry Regiment and the 4th Engineer Combat Battalion in conjunction with the attack launched by Task Force Chamberlain of CC A, 10th Armored Division. This task force reached Mullerthal but stopped because the steep ravine might easily prove a tank trap. Meanwhile elements of the 2nd Battalion 8th Infantry and the 4th Engineer Combat Battalion reached their objectives on the high ground overlooking Mullerthal, which was invaluable.

19 DECEMBER 1944—D+197: Throughout the northern part of the Division's zone of action, the enemy continued aggressively, although no notable progress was made by him except in the vicinity of Consdorf where the road to Berdorf was cut by patrols. The heaviest fighting was from Hill 329 where the enemy estimated as one battalion were reported to be well dug in. Throughout the period, enemy troops were reported moving across the Sauer river from Minden to Steinheim, reinforcing its forces in and around Echternach.

The day dawned cold and foggy with visibility limited to a very few yards. During the early morning hours, the enemy pounded our positions with heavy artillery fire and seemed to be reinforcing its troops on the bridgehead. Throughout the division sector, the situation was confusing, but an intelligence summary seemed to reveal that the enemy was regrouping and generally hiding out in wooded areas, mostly draws. The enemy was having considerable difficulty in maintaining communications and our constant artillery interdictions of its stream crossings prevented him from reinforcing its units with as much supporting armor as planned. The situation was also confusing to the enemy.

The 12th Infantry succeeded in gaining contact with some isolated units, in many cases only temporary. Nevertheless armor and infantry teams were successful in carrying sorely needed supplies to them. Local counterattacks were continued with systematic elimination of small infiltrating groups of enemies.

As our lines were becoming more stable, better communications resulted and prompt supporting fires were delivered, by both artillery and armor, resulting in heavy casualties upon the enemy.

By nightfall, the enemy was decidedly failing in its attempts to force back this shoulder of its counteroffensive.

Company I, reinforced, maintained its positions at Dickweiler and continued contact with Company L in Osweiler. Small enemy patrols constantly harassed their positions and at 1300, Company I repulsed a small attack. At 1500, Company C 70th Tank Battalion moved to Osweiler and took up defensive positions north of the town. The enemy laid many concentrations of artillery and mortar fire, notably at night. In the interim, the 2nd Battalion 22nd Infantry moved into Osweiler against light opposition, made contact with Company L, and both units consolidated their positions to defend the town.

Company E, still firmly entrenched in Echternach, even though a part of the town was held by an enemy force much larger than its own, was given permission to withdraw but the commanding officer elected to remain. An order to evacuate was issued by the CO 12th Infantry by 1800.

Companies A and G maintained their positions in the vicinity of Lauterborn and continued to prevent enemy infiltration. Task Force Riley re-supplied Company E in Echternach in the early morning. Another team of this Task Force had secured Hill 313 by 1300 against stiff resistance.

The road from Consdorf to Berdorf had been cut by enemy patrols and three of our tanks were immobilized by bazooka fire. Task Force Standish continued its attack to the east from Berdorf and closed upon Hill 329 at 1110. Meanwhile the 159th Engineer Combat Battalion maintained its positions in the vicinity of Scheidgen. In the afternoon, they proceeded to rout pockets of enemy.

At 1000, Task Force Luckett launched a coordinated attack with Task Force Chamberlain of CC A 10th Armored Division and the heaviest resistance was encountered by Company E of the 8th Infantry. Then the CO of Task Force Luckett received orders that his mission merely consisted of denying the enemy the use of the road net in the vicinity of Mullerthal and Company E was withdrawn. In the interim, Task Force Chamberlain was ordered withdrawn to the vicinity of Consdorf. By the close of the day, it began to appear that the main force of the enemy attack had been spent, unless he could improve his stream crossings and bring up substantial reserves.

The 8th Infantry continued to improve its positions and despite the conflagration on the immediate left flank, training was continued. Enemy activity consisted of several small reconnaissance patrols. Harassing artillery fire and moderate concentrations of mortar and artillery fire were received by front line elements.

The 22nd Infantry reported that there was no direct enemy contact, just some enemy artillery fire. By 1635, the 3rd Battalion was relieved by the 4th Reconnaissance Troop and moved to an assembly area in the Schrassig-Montfort area, closing therein at 1800. The Battalion passed to Division reserve.

20 DECEMBER 1944—D+198: The 4th Infantry Division was relieved from First Army and VIII Corps and assigned to Third Army and XII Corps.

Due to the seriousness of the tactical situation and the under-strength of the Combat Teams, sixty-one men from the Divisional HQ were sent into the line of the CT 12 sector to aid in holding the positions.

The weather had not improved and the fog was dense. Tenacious defense was continued throughout the day and elements of the 80th Infantry Division moved into reserve battle positions to the rear of the 12th Infantry. Most of the daylight hours were spent in small engagements, numerous enemy patrols searching for soft spots.

The 12th Infantry maintained its positions in the Osweiler-Dickweiler area where enemy patrol activity was especially notable. In the late afternoon, the 2nd Battalion of the 22nd Infantry with two tanks of the 70th Tank Battalion, made an attack west of Osweiler toward the high ground against an enemy force estimated to be about 400 strong. After an advance of about 500 to 700 yards, contact was made. Positions formerly held by the enemy in the wooded draw were taken but the engagement did not continue after darkness. The artillery and mortar fire steadily increased in the town of Osweiler, and buildings fell under the barrages, forcing the supporting tanks to take up new positions.

In the Echternach area, all reports previously made that Company E had attempted to infiltrate back to our lines had proven incorrect. Before withdrawing from this sector, Task Force Riley was unable to get through to help Company E.

Companies B and F and several tanks of the 70th Tank Battalion, together with Task Force Standish, successfully repulsed another enemy attack in the vicinity of Berdorf and brought artillery fire to bear on a force of ten enemy tanks, causing them to pull back. Late in the period, orders were issued to withdraw to the south in the direction of Consdorf. At 1800, the movement was initiated and then completed after an ambush from the enemy.

Task Force Luckett continued to defend its sector in the vicinity of Mullerthal. Much time was spent in the construction of effective road blocks and the laying of mine fields. The artillery and mortar support were utilized to the fullest extent.

Late in the day, the 9th Armored Division, on the left, reported that a penetration of their lines had been effected and that the town of Waldbillig had fallen to the enemy.

No changes in the situation of the 8th Infantry and 22nd Infantry.

From a WWII Vet of 4ID: Hi "Old Soldiers"

DECEMBER 20, 1944: ..."Ah, yes, I remember it well!"...from musical "*GiGi*". This was the day 12 Infantry "B" & "F" Companies, plus 10th Armored Division CCA...saved the asses of the surrounded members of "F" Company, in the Parc Hotel, Berdorf, Luxemburg. We had been there since December 16, FIRST day of the big "Battle of the Bulge"...Germans blew a hole in the hotel wine cellar, but we were too frightened to drink! Thus, I have been SOBER ever since, and why I am STILL HERE! Some other people were playing (prevent) "Capture the Flag" game with the Germans over our Regimental Colors...

21 DECEMBER 1944—D+199: Every effort was made to obtain much needed reinforcements to bring combat teams up to fighting strength.

In front of the CT 8 and CT 22, the enemy continued to remain on the defensive. In the CT 12's sector, the enemy made several attacks in strength. At 1545 an estimated 350 enemy attacked in the vicinity of Scheidgen. This attack was contained, and the enemy appeared to fan out north of the town..

The enemy again became more aggressive, especially in the vicinity of Consdorf and Scheidgen. It attacked with limited armor support and employed heavy artillery fire during the afternoon.

At 0800, the 2nd Battalion of the 22nd Infantry continued its attack west of Osweiler against very heavy resistance. At 0830, this enemy force launched a counterattack which was beaten back by our battalion, and by 1030 we had advanced about 400 yards. Numerous counterattacks with enemy infantry supported by small groups of tanks were hurled against this battalion throughout the afternoon, but no ground was yielded. In the interim, Companies I and L had received extremely heavy artillery fire for two hours in Osweiler and Dickweiler and Company L had been attacked at 1330 from the north and northwest. Strong enemy pressure was still prevailing at the end of the day.

Companies A and G were withdrawn from their positions in the vicinity of Lauterborn during the hours of darkness to an assembly area in the vicinity of Scheidgen with the view of establishing a new main line of resistance.

The 2nd Battalion of the 12th Infantry began early in the day making local attacks on its left flank and gained some desirable terrain, although any sizable advance was halted when at 1530 the enemy launched an attack to take the town of Consdorf with at least two companies. Our tanks and the few infantrymen left waited until they were well up the hill and out into the open before they commenced fire. At least sixty enemy were claimed to have been killed. By 1700, the situation was well in hand and the enemy had withdrawn into a wooded area.

The 159th Engineer Combat Battalion remained in its positions on the high ground and in the town of Scheidgen. This force was attacked several times during the day and two tanks of the 70th Tank Battalion were sent to support the engineers. The enemy was driven out just as darkness fell. During the action, the artillery and mortar fire on our troops was especially heavy.

Task Force Luckett continued to deny the road net in the vicinity of Mullerthal and to prevent any enemy penetration. The slight readjustment of positions due to the capture of Waldbillig was continued. The enemy was unable to make the maximum use of this area due to our strong left flank positions.

The 8th Infantry continued maintenance of the defensive positions within its sector and, at 1430 assumed responsibility for the former zone of combat of CT 22.

The 22nd Infantry maintained defensive positions and continued to conduct active patrolling. At 1430, the 22nd turned over control of its sector to the CT 8 and prepared to move and relieve elements of the 3rd Battalion 12th Infantry in the Osweiler-Dickweiler area. At 1515, the 3rd

Battalion of the 22nd Infantry had initiated its movement and closed in the vicinity of Bech by 1730. The remainder of the Combat Team moved to the vicinity of Rodenbourg.

At the close of the period, the 22nd was in reserve positions prepared to relieve elements of the 12th Infantry and to counterattack in conjunction with the 10th Infantry of the 5th Infantry Division.

(Are you still thinking that only the 101st Airborne and LTG George Patton were key in the Battle of the Bulge? You can see our 4ID Soldiers did a fantastic job in stopping the German thrust into Luxembourg—as did many other fine units all along the line).

From Swede Henley's Diary—used with permission of his daughters…

14-15 DECEMBER 1944: Still in Gostengin living like kings.

16 DECEMBER 1944: Gostengin, Luxembourg still on outpost duty on Moselle River. Krauts on one side—Yanks on the other. Krauts in northern sector (12 Inf. area) started attack across river this morning on 40 mile front. The 12 Inf. is catching the devil. We have been alerted and may have to help them. Col. Lanham had a small party at Mondorff for officers and invited a few girls from Luxembourg. Everybody had a good time until we got orders to report back to our outpost as Jerry is about to overrun the 12th Infantry. Damn Jerry won't let us have any fun at all. Let them come—we'll open the Kraut hunting season again.

17 DECEMBER 1944: Got big Christmas package from Lila and it was so good. She is such a thoughtful person, but Xmas this year won't ever come for me because she won't be with me.

18 DECEMBER 1944: Got alert order tonight for possible move to the north to stop German counterattack near St. Vith tomorrow. Sure will hate to leave Gostengin in good ole Luxembourg.

19 DECEMBER (ONLY 6 MORE DAYS UNTIL XMAS): Ordered to stay in place until further orders. Jerry counterattack is going to town. They have recaptured Krinkelt—St. Vith and now on the Bastogne Road.

20 DECEMBER: Received orders that we would remain in place and if regiment and 3rd Bn moved we would be attached to 8 Inf. Jerry counterattack being slowed down.

21 DECEMBER: Living like kings in Gostengin. Attached to 8 Inf. as 22 Inf. moved north to assist 12 Inf. Jerry counterattack still doing fair. A lot of U.S. Divisions are being called up and put in action.

From Bill Boice's **History of the 22nd Infantry Regiment in WWII …**
THE BATTLE OF THE BULGE – LUXEMBOURG

The German offensive struck with lightning speed and in great force early on the morning of the 16th of December. Initially, enemy pressure was felt north of the Division area and on Combat Team 12. Because enemy pressure was increasing rapidly in the area of CT 12, all units of the Twenty-Second Regiment were alerted for enemy activity and movement plans. The Second Battalion was completely motorized and was to assist the 12th Infantry the following morning. Plans were also instituted whereby the Fourth Reconnaissance Troop would patrol the Third Battalion sector, should it become necessary for that Battalion to move to the assistance of CT 12.

Hitler and his staff knew without a doubt that the Hurtgen Forest Battle had weakened the units which had been engaged. They also knew that the American defensive lines in Luxembourg were thin. German forces were massed for a counter-offensive. The best remaining German strategist, Von Rundstedt, was placed in command. On 16 December 1944, these forces struck the Allied Armies in the Ardennes and started their drive through toward the coast. As the hours passed, it became clear that what Von Rundstedt primarily intended to do was this: In the quick thrust his armies were to penetrate and capture the First Army supply points, demolish communications, and destroy the Americans en route. As rapidly as this was completed, they were to drive northward toward Antwerp, thereby splitting the Allied forces into two commands, a northern and a southern. When this was complete, the third successive mission was to defend the southern flank and crush the northern Allied command. This planned area of penetration was into the First Army sector in which the Fourth Infantry Division was defending the southern shoulder.

At dawn 17 December, the Second Battalion moved out from its reserve position at Oetrange, some 15 miles northeast, to an assembly area 300 yards south of Bech, Luxembourg. It was now attached to CT 12 to aid in the defense of the Osweiler-Dickweiler sector. Before noon Company F, with Lt. Wilson and Lt. Loyd, entrucked and moved to Berbourg, where they mounted the tanks of Company A, 19th Tank Battalion of the 9th Armored Division, to go to the aid of Company L, 12th Infantry at Osweiler.

Company F, with the tanks, moved on east into Osweiler, arriving there in the middle of the afternoon. As they neared the town, an American plane attacked the column and knocked out one tank. Identification panels were immediately displayed, and the attack from American planes ceased. By nightfall, the situation was well under control after a very exciting afternoon. Company F remained within the town, while the tanks withdrew to Berbourg.

While Company F had been moving to Osweiler, the rest of the battalion marched on foot northeast from Bech, with companies in column G, E, H. One section of heavy machine guns and a section of mortars were with Company G and a section of machine guns with Company E which left four machine guns, four mortars, 48 men, and four officers with Company H at the tail of the column. The Battalion Command Group was between Companies G and E. At a road junction a thousand yards south of Michelshof, the column turned right on the trail which leads to the eastern part of the woods. About 800 yards beyond the road junction, just beyond the point where the trail crosses the small road to Geyershof, the column encountered a mudhole at least knee deep. They were never able to get any vehicles through this obstacle and from there on the move was entirely by foot.

The advance continued, following the trail through the big woods around to the north along the crest of the ridge. It was just after this move started that the column was attacked. The Germans had evidently been moving south at the foot of the steep bank on the east edge of the woods. They came up this bank at several points, cutting and eventually passing through the American column. The first attack hit the head of Company 'H'. The Germans were apparently as much surprised at the first encounter as were the men of Company 'H'. The first enemy seen was a single scout who reached the top of the bank to find himself face to face with Americans. The German opened fire with a burp gun, but the radio operator of Company 'H' killed him with a carbine. Then more Germans came up attacking Company 'H' on the right flank and also passing across the front of their column and getting on the left flank. Practically all of the German troops had automatic weapons and they also opened fire with a 50 mm mortar. The men of Company 'H' had been caught flat-footed while carrying the machine guns and mortars. There was a dogfight for a while until Company 'H' succeeded in pulling back a few hundred yards to a draw where they formed a circular defense. There Company 'H' was surrounded for the rest of the afternoon, fighting off an enemy which considerably outnumbered them.

The machine gun section which was at the rear of Company 'E's column had also been involved in the first enemy attack. Several casualties occurred immediately, including the death of 1st Sgt. Willard of 'E' Company. As the Germans came up in force between them and the rest of Company 'H', they ran forward to catch up with Company 'E'. It was some minutes before the rest of the battalion knew that Company 'H' was in a fight. Battalion Headquarters heard the firing, but it sounded so distant that they did not suppose it to be in their battalions as they had been hearing considerable remote firing all afternoon. The first information that the battalion had of this attack was when the Executive Officer, L.t. Mason of Company 'E' ran up to the command group and said that Company 'H' was in a fight. About the same time, the radio operator of

Company 'H'—the same man who had killed the first German—got through with a message to the same effect.

Col. Kennan ordered Company 'E' under Capt. Faulkner to reverse its direction, move back astride the trail, and relieve 'H' Company. Company 'E' made little progress before they ran into strong German forces and were stopped. The enemy had evidently come up from the east in at least company strength between Companies 'E' and 'H'. At the same time they came up all around Company 'G' commanded by Capt. Jackson who was almost immediately wounded by mortar fire. For the rest of the afternoon those two companies were under heavy small arms and 50 mm mortar fire and for a while were separated from each other as well as from Company 'H'. The battalion suffered a number of casualties during the afternoon skirmish which turned into a dog fight on all sides.

That night contact was restored between 'E' and 'G', and they formed an all-around defense circle near the eastern edge of the woods, with the battalion command group and a section of machine guns completing the circle on the north. There was no contact with Company 'H', the last radio message having been received shortly after the attack started when the 'H' Company operator said, "Don't call me anymore; the enemy are too damned close."

Apparently there had been no enemy activity north of the positions of Companies 'E' and 'G' as during the afternoon it had been possible to move to the trail junction about 500 yards north of Company 'G' and back down the other trail to 'E' without encountering the enemy. After dark there was no contact and no firing throughout the night. Evidently the hostile force had gone on its way to the southwest. Company 'H' also was able to withdraw after dark and returned to Bech.

Communication was difficult and uncertain throughout December 17th and 18th. When the battalion advanced from Bech that first morning, a wire vehicle accompanied the command group in the usual way, but it was stopped at the mudhole north of Geyershof. The wire crew then removed the reel from the vehicle and tried to follow the advance on foot, but they were unable to keep up. Throughout the afternoon this crew was by itself in the woods doggedly laying wire, but they never succeeded in reaching the forward CP. Throughout the fight in the afternoon and the passage of the German battalion through the woods, the wire crew was never attacked, but the next day German wire was found tapped in our line. Apparently the enemy deliberately allowed our wiremen to go on with their work.

There was only intermittent wire communication from the CP at Geyershof to the rear. The line back to Bech was cut repeatedly by artillery fire and though repair was continuous, the line was out much of the time. During the night this line stayed in but just south of Bech the wire to the 12th Infantry CP was cut by shelling. Because of this difficulty with its wire, most of the communication to the rear during the late afternoon and night was transmitted through the artillery, which managed to keep in its line from Geyershof to the battery at Bech, which had a line to 42nd FA Battalion and thence to 12th Inf.

There was, however, little positive information to transmit to the Regiment that night. About all that was known at the CP about the situation was that the battalion was surrounded by enemy in unknown strength. There was no wire forward and little use could be made of the radio, partly because of poor reception in the Geyershof hollow and partly because Col. Kennan was unwilling to talk much on the radio for fear of informing the enemy of the situation. Again the artillery battery did an excellent job of maintaining communication in spite of the difficulties. When the artillery radio jeep was stopped at the mudhole, the radio operator showed excellent initiative in finding a way to operate in spite of being left behind. He brought his jeep back to Geyershof and parked it at the window of the switchboard room at the CP. He remained in contact with the forward observer by portable radio, and the next day successfully controlled fire by receiving radio messages from the FO and shouting them in the window at the telephone operator who transmitted them to the battery at Bech. (This man was killed the next day when a shell fragment hit him in his fox hole).

Supply was also a problem. The impossibility of getting vehicles through the mudhole on the route followed by the battalion and the fact that the enemy was putting observed fire on Michelshof, made it necessary to resort to carrying parties. Supply jeeps went as far forward as possible, which was about 200 yards east of Michelshof, and there they were met by the A and P Platoon, which hand-carried everything for the remaining mile and a half to the battalion. It was a source of amazement to the battalion officers that in spite of the enemy battalion, which was somewhere in the woods nearby, the A and P Platoons worked without interference all night and completed the carriage of supplies.

The lone tank destroyer which was in Michelshof was very uneasy about its exposed position and asked for infantry protection. This the battalion was unable to furnish, and the tank destroyer wanted to withdraw. With much persuasion they were induced to remain, Capt. McLean pointed out that members of the carrying party and the jeep drivers would be near their position most of the time. McLean was very anxious to keep the tank destroyer there to furnish a little protection for the sensitive transfer point on the supply line. After the last trip, the carrying party remained with the tank destroyer until morning, which led to their being cut off when the Germans advanced.

On the morning of 18 December, the Battalion up in the woods found itself free of any enemy contact. They moved south to a lateral trail, turned east, and marched toward Osweiler without any opposition from the Germans. But as they came out of the woods on the road, north of Fromburg Farm, they received heavy fire from American tanks, the same tanks that were with Company F. These tanks, which had spent the night at Herbon, had returned to Osweiler in the morning and had been sent eastward to assist the battalion. In view of the situation which had existed the previous night, it was not reasonable to expect that the battalion would march out of the woods unopposed, without the firing of a shot, and the assumption by the tanks that they were the enemy was natural. It was a difficult situation for nearly two hours with the infantry battalion pinned down and suffering several casualties. Eventually a patrol with a white flag made its way around through the draw on the right and made contact with our own tanks.

A little before noon, Companies E and G entered the battered streets of Osweiler and joined Company F. For the rest of that day and the 19th, they remained dug in at Osweiler under very heavy artillery fire and taking no action except the outposting of the town. Here the three rifle companies were reunited but were far separated from the battalion headquarters at Geyershof and the Service elements and the greater part of Company H at Bech. These elements were ordered to move to Herborn, but before the move could be made they became heavily involved with the German 316th Regiment.

On 20 December, patrols were sent out to Rodenhof and to the woods where the battalion had been surrounded on the 17th. The latter got well into the woods before meeting enemy and did not return until after dark. The other patrol found the enemy holding the high ground in front of Rodenhof strongly. This patrol got back to the battalion under cover of artillery fire which was directed by the forward observer who was with them.

The battalion organized an attack on this resistance, getting started in the late afternoon. They got just across the steep ravine which runs southwest from Rodenhof and were stopped by enemy strongly entrenched on the opposite bank. E and F organized their position in the dark for the night with the most forward holes only several yards from the German holes.

The rest of the CT was still down in Luxembourg and because there was no direct contact with the enemy from the 17th to the 20th, Combat Team 22, less the Second Battalion, carried out training whenever possible.

The Third Battalion was relieved of its positions by the Fourth Reconnaissance Troop on the 19th and moved up to reserve positions near Schrassig-Moutfort. The First Battalion was to remain in position attached to CT 8.

The Combat Team, less the detachments, continued its outposting of the Mosell River line until 1455 hours the 21st of December, at which time they were ordered to move to the vicinity of Bech with all possible speed; the 3rd Battalion arrived at the new area shortly before dark and immediately established a defense of the town.

In the meantime, the 2nd Battalion on December 21st had continued its pressure northeast of Osweiler and made slight gains. They were constantly harassed by enemy attempts to infiltrate, and often the advance completely stopped while mopping-up patrols cleared out the enemy groups behind the lines.

The Combat Team now occupied a sector between CT 8 (on the right) and CT 12 (on the left) with a front of 7, 500 yards. Upon arrival in its new zone of action, the Combat Team regained control of the 2nd Battalion defending Osweiler. The 3rd Battalion of CT 12, in a defensive position within the area of CT 22, was placed under control of CT 22. The 1st Battalion still remained in its positions along the Moselle River attached to CT 8. In this location a delaying action was to be initiated.

22 DEC 1944 TO 28 DEC 1944 – D+200 TO D+206

22 DECEMBER 1944—D+200: During this period, we were able not only to inflict severe casualties on the enemy while frustrating several of its attacks, but also started a coordinated attack to regain the terrain previously lost and clear the enemy from its bridgehead.

The 12th Infantry continued to defend until 1330 at which time and in conjunction with the 10th Infantry Regiment (5th Infantry Division) attacked to the north with the mission of destroying the enemy. Just prior to H-Hour, at approximately 1300, two battalions of the enemy (about 400 troops) launched an attack against the 1st Battalion in the vicinity of Scheidgen. Furious fighting continued all afternoon in the vicinity of the line of departure, making it impossible for any advance. At 1430, approximately 150 enemy infantrymen, in wedge formation, advanced to attack the 1st Battalion. All our fire, including supporting tanks and heavy weapons, were withheld until the enemy had closed to within 75 yards at which time the command "commence fire" was given. This force was virtually annihilated and thereafter 154 enemy dead were counted on the field.

The 10th Combat Team became attached to the 4th Infantry Division. Movement was initiated at 0800 to the vicinity of Hemstall and the CT prepared to attack to the northeast.

At 1330, the attack was begun with the 2nd Battalion on the right and the 1st on the left, and they passed through the 1st Battalion 12th Infantry. Heavy resistance of artillery and small arms fire was met almost immediately, and the 2nd Battalion was unable to advance beyond the line of departure where fierce fighting took place throughout the remainder of the day. In the interim, the 1st Battalion, meeting very little resistance, was able to advance but had to wait for the 2nd Battalion.

The 3rd Battalion of the 22nd Infantry with the 3rd Battalion of the 12th Infantry attached, started movement at 1015 and was assigned the mission of establishing contact with the 2nd Battalion near Osweiler (reverted to control of the 22nd Infantry), clearing the woods to the southwest of Dickweiler, and securing a line running from Osweiler to Dickweiler. By 1545, the 3rd Battalion had completed its mission.

Meanwhile the 2nd Battalion defended from positions generally around the town of Osweiler with the mission to hold present positions and to support the attack of the 10th Infantry Regiment. Heavy artillery and mortar fire was received on the positions and in Osweiler. Numerous attempts were made by the enemy to infiltrate small patrols into the town.

Task Force Luckett on the left of the division sector remained on its mission of denying the road net to the enemy in the vicinity of Mullerthal and the protection of the Division's left boundary. Having noticed no aggressive action nor any activity of the enemy, patrols were sent out at 1145 and they located various groups in positions. When our patrols had withdrawn, all enemy positions were taken under fire by our artillery and mortars.

For the first time in a week, the weather which was greatly improving by mid-afternoon permitted maximum use of air support.

The 8th Infantry with the 1st Battalion of the 22nd Infantry, the 4th Reconnaissance Troop, and other elements, maintained its positions fronting the rivers. Active patrolling was continued and no aggressive action by the enemy was reported except a few rounds of artillery.

23 DECEMBER 1944—D+201: The enemy's front lines extended generally from the vicinity Waldbillig, Mullerthal, Melickschech, Osweiler, Dickweiler, thence southeast to the vicinity of the Sauer and Moselle junction. The enemy employed its hastily constructed defenses to prevent our throwing back its penetration.

The weather was cold and clear. The attack by the 10th Infantry Regiment was continued, supported by elements of the 12th and 22nd Infantry Regiments. Aircraft from the XIX Tactical Air Command bombed and strafed enemy troop concentrations and succeeded in destroying a number of bridges the enemy had established across the Sauer river.

The 12th Infantry continued to defend and supported the attack of the 10th Infantry Regiment with fire. The enemy launched no attacks, but heavy concentrations of artillery and mortar fire continued throughout the sector. At 1100, the 2nd Battalion reported Nebelwerfer fire.

The situation in CT 22's zone of action remained static. Enemy activity consisted of moderate artillery fire on the 2nd Battalion's rifle companies and heavy mortar-rocket barrages on Osweiler.

Regimental Combat Team 10 resumed its attack at 0745 with two battalions abreast and stiff resistance was met immediately. The enemy defended from positions favorably situated and well dug in. Little progress was made.

The 8th Infantry reported little or no aggressive enemy action and only a few rounds of artillery fire.

24 DECEMBER 1944—D+202: Again visibility was excellent, and the skies were clear. All elements contained the enemy until 1100 at which time the 5th Infantry Division, in conjunction with the 10th Armored Division on its left, launched a coordinated attack to the north through our lines. They relieved elements of the 12th Infantry and Task Force Luckett. A new and greatly reduced sector was assigned the 4th Infantry Division.

The 12th Infantry supported by fire the attack of the 5th Infantry Division. At 1645, it was relieved, and its 1st and 2nd Battalions moved to new assembly areas, closing therein respectively at 2030 and 2230.

The 3rd Battalion made plans to be relieved by elements of the 22nd Infantry.

The 22nd Infantry assumed responsibility for its new zone of action at 1100. The 1st Battalion which reverted to regimental control at 1920, moved to its new assembly area in the vicinity of Herborn, closing therein at 2045.

The 10th Regimental Combat Team continued its attack in the direction of Echternach where prisoners of war reported that a strong American force still held out, and at 1000, reverted to the control of the 5th Infantry Division.

Task Force Luckett was passed through by elements of the 5th Division at 1200 and at 1645 was relieved of responsibility and dissolved.

25 DECEMBER 1944—D+203: The enemy showed little aggressive activity due to the pressure exerted by elements of the 5th Infantry Division attacking to the north.

The 8th Infantry readjusted its positions and conducted maintenance and care of equipment.

The 12th Infantry assembled its 1st and 2nd Battalions in the vicinity of Bourglinster and Schuttrange. The 3rd Battalion was relieved at 1030 by the 1st Battalion of the 22nd Infantry in the vicinity of Osweiler and Dickweiler and it moved to an assembly area in the vicinity of Munsbach, closing therein before the end of the day.

The 22nd Infantry adjusted its positions and at the end of the period, the 3rd Battalion was in the process of relieving the 2nd Battalion of the positions held in the vicinity of Osweiler.

26 DECEMBER 1944—D+204: The enemy continued its non-aggressive policy.

The 4th Infantry Division continued the adjustment of units on the outpost line, and maintenance and care of equipment for the units not actively employed.

Contact had still not been established with Company E, 12th Infantry, in Echternach.

The 2nd Battalion of the 22nd Infantry was relieved by the 3rd Battalion and moved to an assembly area at Berbourg where they carried on reorganization.

27 DECEMBER 1944—D+205: Major General R.O. Barton who had commanded the Division since July 1942, called a meeting of all officers and enlisted men in the CP and made known the fact he was leaving the Division. Brigadier General Harold W. Blakeley assumed command. (MG Barton left the 4ID due to health problems which he had been fighting since soon after D-Day).

No aggressive ground activity of the enemy except some patrols and light artillery. Several planes were over the area during darkness and Roodt was strafed.

The 8th Infantry continued reorganization and training, plus active patrolling to the east during daylight hours.

The 12th Infantry remained in assembly areas. A patrol was dispatched to Echternach during the daylight hours. They entered the town and found no sign of any human habitants.

Beginning at 1500, the 22nd Infantry effected the relief of elements of the 10th Infantry Regiment along the high ground to the south of Echternach. At 1800, the 3rd Battalion was relieved by the 1st Battalion in the vicinity of Osweiler because of an adjustment of boundaries.

28 DECEMBER 1944—D+206: At the direction of the Commanding General, action was initiated to obtain necessary information to recommend the 12th Infantry Regiment for the Presidential Unit Citation.

Friendly patrols entering Girsterklaus and Wasserbillig were engaged by enemy forces.

The 1st Battalion of the 12th Infantry Regiment was enroute to the vicinity of Echternach and Lautenborn and the 3rd Battalion was enroute to the vicinity of Berdorf to affect the relief of CT 10 during the hours of darkness.

Fit to Fight

From **Swede Henley's diary—used with permission of his daughters…**

22 DECEMBER: Still in Gostengin and liking it. The poor ole 2nd and 3rd Bn are in the fight north of us. The regimental CP located at Rodenbourg. Just hoping we can stay here for Xmas dinner.

23 DECEMBER: A beautiful day and the Air Corps is out in full blast giving the Krauts the fits. P-51 shot down about 40 yards from CP (captured) Capt. John H. Hoefker 0442148 15 TAC RCN 10 Photo Gp APO 141 U.S. Army. Received alert orders to move north tomorrow.

24 DECEMBER: Kraut in P-47 fired rockets at CP—dirty bastard—was poor shot—no casualty FA shot him down. Relieved by 2 Cavalry at 1800—moved north to Herborn. Christmas Eve night and no Santa Claus and then too, we moved north to Herborn to go in line to help stop Jerry rampage. It was a beautiful night—a real white Xmas.
- People in this country will always fight. All houses are reinforced with concrete and * always have embrasures. Even the toilets have firing ports.

25 DECEMBER—CHRISTMAS DAY: Relieved 3rd Bn 12 Inf. at 1045. A helluva way to be spending Christmas -hunting Krauts. CP set up in Herborn. A Co in line at Dickweiler. B Co at Burchdolf. Turkey dinner with C Company.
- Col. Lanham had bad case of crud. Situation is normal as he has had a case since joining us.
- Tommy Harrison—still has not been hit but I still love him.

26 DECEMBER: Krauts strafed CP this morning—no casualties. Turkey dinner with D Co and bourbon whiskey.

27-28-29 DECEMBER: Still in Herborn—patrolling vigorously to Moselle River. Krauts are in numbers on other side. Jerry counterattacked—stopped—and we have gone to killing Krauts wholesale. Gen. Barton relieved on December 27, 1944 (health reasons).

From *Chaplain Bill Boice's* History of the 22nd Infantry Regiment in WWII:

Orders for the Combat Team to counterattack to the north came down on the 22nd of December. The attack was to be made in conjunction with Combat Team 10, 5th Infantry Division (CT 10 was to take over the sector left, now west of the 22nd). That morning liaison contact was established with Combat Team 10, and co-ordination included the 2nd Battalion's helping the northward advance of that team by supporting fires.

H-hour for the attack was set at 1200 hours, but in order to gain more complete coordination, this was delayed almost an hour. The 3rd Battalion, the assault unit advanced northeast from Bech, sweeping the area to its objective, the dominating terrain south of Osweiler and Dickweiler. From this position the 3rd Battalion prepared to counterattack to the north.

Elements of Combat Team 12's Battalion were defending Dickweiler, and the 2nd Battalion of CT 22 was, with cooks, clerks, kitchen police, and one platoon of riflemen defending Osweiler. The 3rd Battalion re-enforced the Dickweiler defenses with one rifle platoon and sent Company 'L' to re-enforce Osweiler. The rest of the Combat Team front was covered by platoon strongpoints on dominating terrain, and by the 2nd Battalion's depleted rifle companies on line, facing west of the Combat Team's left boundary. The rest of that day and the next the situation remained static with minor skirmishes and patrol action, while the Combat Team waited for CT 10 to pull up abreast on the left.

At 1035 hours the 3rd Battalion was ordered to begin preparations for the relief of the 2nd Battalion, this relief to be effective when CT 10 of the 5th Division came abreast of the 2nd Battalion. The 1st Battalion, still attached to Combat Team 8 along the Moselle River, was relieved and they closed in at assembly areas near Herborn shortly after dark.

In the Echternach area, the line has been stabilized. The enemy has been checked in the areas of Dickweiler, Osweiler, and Berdorf. West and south of Echternach in the sector east of Sarregemund we have occupied Osweiler.

On the 25th and 26th of December there was only light artillery fire and some patrol activity. The 1st Battalion relieved the 3rd Battalion of CT 12, thereby occupying the defenses of Dickweiler and positions east of the Combat Team's right boundary. The 3rd Battalion, 22nd Inf. relieved the 2nd Battalion Christmas night.

Excerpts from the diary of **Capt. Faulkner, 'E' Company, 22nd Infantry Regiment**.

Note the actions of the first days of the "Bulge" as they affected the men of that unit.

"There is no rest for the weary. We were alerted on Saturday, December 16 to be ready to move in an hour. Got our march order at Bn. CP at midnight from Col. Kenan and made plans to move out at 0700, 17 December.

"We did and joined the motor column at 0730 at the IP. It was ticklish as an air warning was out, the Luftwaffe was active again. By 1100 we de-trucked at Beck, were oriented and moved out at once on foot behind 'G' Company—followed by 'H'—to go to the relief of some 12th Inf. troops in Osweiler and Dickweiler, this side of Echternach. The Krauts had started with patrols and were now crossing the Moselle in force. My Company strength close to 100 with 3 lieutenants, one old timer, Lt. Mason, and two new replacements, Lt. Moore, and Lt. Alderfer. We wondered what the Krauts were up to. No one it seemed knew yet for sure. Weather clear and cold with frost.

"Moved single file up the road and east into the big woods. Things didn't smell right. Too quiet. Moved east into a firebreak trail. Belt of big trees on the right for several hundred yards and the open valley beyond with Osweiler burning in the distance. Very close second growth pine on the left.

"Suddenly, burp gun, MG and M1 fire was heard to our rear. I asked on the SCR 536, "Is that fire on us?" Answer—"It is to our rear." We keep going several minutes until Lt. Mason dashes up. Says our Co. Hdq. and 'H' Company were ambushed and cut off from us. We notified Big 6 (Col. Kenan) at once. Both Companies 'G' and 'E' reversed direction and worked back through the woods to clean out and contact our people. Situation very tense. Wish Lt. Lloyd was with us.

"We contacted people all right, but not ours. Jerry MG fire cut across and into my front, stopping the lead platoon. 'G' Company on my left had a sharp attack. We got about 20 to 30 rounds of mortar which chopped up part of the 1st platoon, wounded the only aid man and almost got me. We got one PW, a wounded aid man, but armed. Sent him to Bn.

"Ordered 3rd Pl. to move right around through small pines to try to envelope the Krauts. 1st Pl. to assist by fire from its forward position, 2nd in reserve, 4th to set up only 60mm mortar we had. Just in the middle of this when S-2 crawled up with orders to dig in at once before it got totally dark. Called back 3rd Pl., set up defense and dug in. We had arrived at the ambush point and picked up several wounded from the Hdq. group and a few dead among whom was 1st. Sgt. Willard. A wonderful man, and I grieved in my heart for him. He had been a D-Day man, wounded twice, but always said, "It's not if you'll get it, but when and how bad." He was right.

"It was a weird night. Small arms fire and MG heard in the distance, criss-cross artillery fire coming from all ways, Krauts on our front and flanks, our rear exposed toward Echternach, yet not a round on our position.

"18 December. At first light we dropped in about 12 rounds of 60mm mortar we couldn't carry anymore. Put it where we thought Jerry was. One came out toward us. Nice, well-built, blonde S. O. B. with a MG. We took him, buried the gun, and sent him back to BN. Perhaps he was the one that killed my 1st. Sgt. The men and I wanted to shoot him—but didn't.

"So, we all withdrew back through the small pines in single file. Guess we had Jerry surrounded, only he had us surrounded more. 'G' Company lead out. Found that Capt. Jackson, just back for the second time since July, had been wounded by mortar fire. Tough luck again. I was only captain with a rifle company. We got news that our 'F' Company had ridden on tanks through artillery fire into the town the evening before and were holding until we got there. "Good going for Lts. Wilson and Lloyd. The column stopped as we heard MG fire ahead. Found that two of our tanks in the valley saw the head of our column start down from the woods and fired. They wounded several of 'G' Company before Lt. Greenlee ran down waving his maps and stopped them. Fate was being extra cruel.

"I really prayed and asked the Lord to get us the two miles across those turnip fields and open valley and into Osweiler without fire. He did. It might have been at the expense of several of our tanks who were moving southwest out of the valley, as we could see the gray splotches of Jerries artillery shells exploding around them as they passed out of sight over the hill. We went on through the mud and into town.

"Picked our houses in town none too quick, as some big stuff—real big smashed into the center of town, causing the remaining tanks to keep shuffling around. Jerry had a good OP somewhere. Got a direct hit on the house into which my 2nd Platoon had just disappeared. Sent a runner who reported back they were shaken, but all O. K. Thank the Lord.

"We rested and ate K rations. Went to Bn. CP in school house basement and got new part of town to defend. Back through artillery fire, got everyone on the move around burning buildings, set in position, sent OP out 500 yards to bare hill and settled down for the night. It had been a strenuous December 18th.

"That night and Tuesday were uneventful with spasmodic fire coming in. Sat all Tuesday afternoon in Bn. CP going over three attack plans, each one tougher and more suicidal than the next. Finally told to hold. Returned to a feast at my own CP. Lt. Mason and acting 1st Sgt. Hughes had got all the chickens cached away with six being fried up. Delicious soup, plenty of coffee, homemade jelly, preserved cherries, and a jar of sugared honey found in a closet upstairs. Our thanks to the good house fraus of Osweiler who really knew how to make jelly. Worked out route for our 22 man patrol with Lt. Alderfer to take before dawn next day, go five miles, observe, and return by dark. Patrol to be known as "Able Peter". Thus ended December 19th, my 8th wedding anniversary. What a helluva wedding anniversary!

"Wednesday the 20th, saw our "Able Peter" patrol off before first light and we used the rest of the day to perfect defenses, knock holes through stone barn walls for fields of fire, plan AT tank mine and platoon areas. All laid out perfect by 1500 and all changed at 1530 when ordered to move out to northwest at once to the woods, attack east to join 'F' Company who were now moving into the woods opposite Rodenhof, a small village about a mile to the northeast. Find the enemy and attack him! Ugh!

"Got everyone on the way by 1615 except Lt. Mason who could hardly walk with a case of bad swollen trench feet and my "Able Peter" patrol who had not returned. Saw we could hardly get out of the valley before dark, so pushed hard. No time for security patrols. Had to lead with Lt. Moore as scouts. Tough going uphill through muddy fields. To make things worse, two of our tanks pulled up on our right and started shelling the woods to the north to help 'F' Company. Anyone looking toward the tanks could see my men wending their way up. We were tired and weak.

"We saw Jerry as he saw us. He was dug in along a belt of bushes above us—150 yards away. We raced for a wooded draw to his right, got the lead platoon in and opened fire before he did, but his MG caught our 4th Pl. and heavy MG section attacked and cut them up badly. Just dusk now, and we had a <u>real</u> fire fight. Moon with our only LMG got in O. K. and did swell work.

"Our TD artillery forward observer got a battery of artillery on the Krauts. One of our first rounds landed only ten yards to our rear and shook all of us, but then the next volley was on Jerry, and really blew him up. We fired as we dug in. Rather crowded in our little draw and getting dark.

"The town was getting its worst shelling, very heavy artillery and screaming mimies (rockets) and burning like a bonfire. We cast long shadows if we stood up. Sent "Frenchie" and another runner to get a guide. They finally returned and we trudged through the mud, in the open, through the woods, uphill and down on the spookiest march I've ever had. Our new tank destroyer F. O. laughed so hard he got hysterics over our adventures of the past three hours, but this was getting to be S. O. P. for us.

"Found 'F' Company in the pitch black dark dug in in deep draws with Jerry only a few yards away. We got into some kind of position after midnight. Tried to dig in the rooty stony sides of the slopes. Quit at 4 A. M. and laid in the open holes to sleep. Exhausted!

"Able Peter" patrol with Lt. Alderfer arrived at 0725 on 21 December in the dark with orders for us to attack at 0800 with 'G' Company coming out from town. So — made a map reconnaissance and issued the order by flashlight under my trench coat. Rough!

"Did move out at 0815. Open draw on our right for 100 yards with wooded ridge beyond. Ridges and deep draws across our direction of attack. 'G' Company moving up on our left at top of ridges and ahead. My plan, 1st. Pl. on right, 3rd on left, 2nd to follow in support, but all hell broke loose again as we moved out. No enemy to our immediate front but heavy mortar fire and all sorts of MG and rifle fire from across the draw on our right flank. No way to get at them there except work around. We kept moving.

"Lt. Moore was shot in both legs. The Sgt. leading the 3rd platoon was lost, and I talked to 3rd platoon radio operator and put him in charge to bring the platoon up the ridges. Sgt. Emberson leading the 1st platoon was shot in arm and did he yell! I moved up to the crest of the next ridge and got blown to the bottom by a mortar round landing on top of the ridge. Radioed word for all platoons to get up to 'G' Company as fast as they could. Ran on along the heads of the ridges. Put command group in a hole and went on with 1st. Sgt. Hughes, Sussman, the 300 radio operator and Frenchie, our runner to get the lay of the land.

"We headed down into the next open draw as a burp gun opened up, making dirt bounce at our feet. Jumped high and hit the draw. Found Lt. Greenlee and a few of his command group of 'G' Company there — some wounded. Watch out! Six Krauts coming in counter-attacking over the ridge just over our heads and more following. Only two grenades left in our group, and I had 'em. Tossed one to Sgt. Hughes, we pulled pins and threw them on top of the ridge. Fired the carbine and Lt. Greenlee picked off two with his M1. Nipped that attack in the bud.

"Rest of our platoons came up just as we counted close to 80 or 90 Krauts running across the open into the woods on our left. Got our artillery right on the spot within a few minutes and that stopped that threat and made 'em sweat. The 2nd platoon killed 6 snipers in a draw on our left with a squad under Lt. Alderfer and two on our right.

"Issued orders to dig in at once. We dug deep. Sawed 8" logs to cover holes. Hard freeze that night and the dugouts were like cement pill boxes. Our feet too. Trench-foot hit us hard that night with several going out on stretchers, Lt. Alderfer went back with an infected arm, and I was the only officer left.

"Got a lieutenant the next day. Held hard the 22nd and 23rd with enemy holding the same way. Some patrol action.

"On Christmas Eve one of our month-old replacements crept 40 yards and tossed a hand grenade into the nearest Kraut slit trench. Finis.

"December 25, Christmas Day, our 6 man patrol under Sgt. Mitchell worked 130 yards through the woods to shoot two Krauts in their dugout and steal their MG 34. Swell going for our Christmas present. A light snow and all is quiet.

"Relieved by Company K starting 2200, 25 December 1944. Sneaked across the frozen fields back to Osweiler, hit the sack for two hours and started a foot march at 0415 back to Herborn and by truck from there to Berbourg. Approximately 50 men and 2 officers now left in Company E. Rest, it's wonderful!"

More from Chaplain Bill Boice's **History of the 22nd Infantry Regiment in WWII:**

No one can describe the loneliness of Christmas in combat. The regiment had endured Hurtgen, quite sure that nothing could be worse than this endless slaughter. But Luxembourg and the Battle of the Bulge was worse. The decimated rank of the regiment was forced to cover assigned fronts too large for a full strength division to defend.

The pressure against the regiment by the enemy was so constant as to keep the men at battle pitch for days on end without the necessary time to re-group and to release the tension absolutely vital if men are to endure.

During these vital days, men awoke to fight out of their fox holes; command posts were over run. Mail clerks and cooks joined the battle and fought valiantly for the life of the regiment. Incredibly, it held! The Twenty-Second never broke, even though overrun, or surrounded. It fought as it had never fought before, and it survived.

Christmas is cold in Luxembourg. The city of Luxembourg was beautiful and modern; the people were uniformly friendly and helpful. But on the front, men were dug into the snow, or existed in ruined buildings, never free from the chilling uncertainty and pressure of enemy attack. "Merry Christmas" was not merry. The men in the rifle companies 'E', 'F', and 'G' up in the woods were exhausted, on two-thirds rations, no blankets, short on overcoats, no winter boots, short on dry socks, but still long on morale.

Bits of bright tinfoil or gaily colored paper frequently decorated a foxhole. One insuppressible aid man attached a small Christmas tree to his helmet.

Christmas Eve was bright with a bomber's moon. A communications sergeant cut the switchboard into a radio broadcast and throughout the front, men listened in lonely misery as Dinah Shore sang hauntingly, "I'll Be Seeing You." The music was interrupted to order out a patrol which must cover an extended front to assure the enemy was not trying to move through. Sgt. Heavener led the patrol.

And in a Luxembourg home, Captain Clarence C. Hawkins and Chaplain Boice sat down to dinner as guests. Mother and Father, three children and Grandmother and Grandfather were their hosts. The dinner, excellent though it was, was second to the friendship and warmth of this family sharing its love with Americans far away from home.

And after dinner, the children watched excitedly while mother and father lighted each candle on a beautiful tree. Then, in the candle shine, the group sang "Silent Night, Holy Night, All is calm, All is bright."

Grandmother and Grandfather sang it in German. The children and the parents sang it in French. Captain Hawkins and Chaplain Boice sang it in English with voices choked a bit. In any language, it was understood. In any time or any place it was the hope of men who dreamed of their own homeland, their own fireside and loved ones. And as they went out into the night, only the great candle of God hung in the sky. And the memory of "Silent Night" slipped away as the sound of breaking artillery and machine gun fire made a mockery of "Peace on earth."

Returning to the regiment, Chaplain Boice was called to the aid station. Three of the men on the patrol had been wounded; one had been killed. It was Christmas.

A letter written from the hospital in England, 6 January 1945.

Dear Sir:

I'm writing you this note in all sincerity, and I pray you will give it your deepest consideration.

First I want you to know that I don't blame you that you didn't let me come back until we were relieved. I fully understood the situation we were in at the time I asked to be evacuated.

If those two days had even cost me my feet, I feel that Reconnaissance Patrol in which we captured the German machine gun was worth it.

I'll always feel we were a good outfit, and I would have followed your leadership anywhere.

Sir, since I had no chance to get my mail I would consider it a great favor and would appreciate it very much if you would personally see that my mail is forwarded to this address as soon as possible.

God bless you and Company E.

Sincerely yours,
Sgt. —--—-

THE STARS AND STRIPES — SATURDAY, DECEMBER 23, 1944
FOE 38 MILES FROM FRANCE

On the southern flank where the drive had been halted as early as Tuesday, fighting had stabilized, and all thrusts were checked in the areas of Dickweiler-Osweiler.

CHICAGO SUNDAY TRIBUNE — December 31, 1944.

With the U. S. 3rd Army on the western front, December 30 (AP)

High praise for the 4th Infantry Division for saving Luxembourg was expressedby Lt. Gen. Patton in a letter today to the divisions commander, Major General Raymond O. Barton of Ada, Okla.

"Your fight in the Hurtgen Forest was an epic of stark infantry combat" said Patton, "but in my opinion your most recent fight—from December 16 to December 26—when a tired division you halted the left shoulder of the German thrust into American lines and saved the City of Luxembourg, is the most outstanding accomplishment of yourself and your division."

The 12th Corps commander, Maj. Gen. Manton S. Eddy, also sent a letter of commendation to Barton, noting the division's record since D-day. "There are other divisions of the Third Army which can report the same sort of story of sudden moves, hungry mornings, cold and hard fighting—all of which spelled disaster for the German breakthrough attempt on the southern flank.

"The 5th "Red Diamond" Infantry division was fighting in the Saarlautern bridgehead when the order came for it to switch to the north.

"Twenty-four hours later the 5th had covered 70 miles to take up reserve positions north of Luxembourg City.

"Forty-eight hours later a combat team of the 5th launched an attack on Reinstedt's southern flank at Echternach and within another twelve hours the whole division was passing through the 4th Infantry Division which had borne the first shock of the Nazi offensive and was attacking as a unit."

The Combat Team's boundary was shifted almost 2,500 yards west on the 27th of December. In view of the change, the 3rd Battalion moved two rifle companies west, swept the intervening areas, and relieved elements of CT 10 at 1800 hours. The 1st Battalion moved Company 'C' to Osweiler and relieved the elements of the 3rd Battalion defending the town.

During the day, the 1st and 3rd Battalions established outposts to the north and northeast and sent vigorous patrols probing to the front. These patrols were able to reach the Sauer River and Echternach, which were enemy-occupied. The 2nd Battalion remained in mobile reserve in Berbourg.

While the Combat Team was defensively deployed near Echternach, Luxembourg, a very amusing incident occurred to several men of Company 'M'.

Overlooking Echternach from the south was an extremely high hill. Situated on the back slope of this hill was S/Sgt. Miller and his section of 81mm mortars. From the top of the hill and from the side of the western base it was possible to see the German fortifications and often slight movement. In this section was a rather new replacement, Pfc. Bryan, who had previously served with the 2nd Infantry Division. This man loved excitement in its most dangerous form. Sgt. Miller and Pfc. Bryan, while lying in their foxhole one cold snowy night, requested permission of their platoon leader to go down to the river the following morning and fire at the Heinies. Shortly after dawn, these two ambitious soldiers struck out across the snow. Behind them lay their wind-swept trail and the other men of the section, who were wondering if they would ever see these two again. This task was extremely hazardous, for these men were under enemy observation and fire for almost eight hundred yards. Taking advantage of all possible cover, they maneuvered into the first line of houses along the river bank.

Immediately they set their radio into operation and reported their position in code: "Tare-Item to Tare-Fox, Tare-Item to Tare-Fox, Over."

Fit to Fight

T/Sgt. Romeo Bolduc answered from the gun positions, "Tare-Fox to Tare-Item, Tare-Fox to Tare-Item. Send your message. Over."

The reception faded and became almost indistinct, but after several anxious minutes of waiting the message came through. "Tare-Item to Tare-Fox. Donkey men OK. We are going on to our position. We are now at Able seven-niner. Sugar one five. Over."

"Tare-Fox to Tare-Item. Roger. Out."

The two men had found in the first house a phonograph and several records. These they started playing, and they sampled the latest cognac before continuing.

After twenty or thirty minutes, the two men slipped from the house and went along a stone wall which paralleled the river and provided a means of partial defilade. When the wall terminated, they dashed across the open space to a railroad embankment which ran along the river bank. Proceeding south almost 200 yards, they located a culvert under the tracks and decided the CP was to be here.

Pfc. Bryan secured the radio and called the platoon CP: "Tare-Item to Tare-Fox, Tare-Item to Tare-Fox. Fire concentration six. Over."

Back at the command post the radio hummed and the message broke through. Gun crews quickly laid on the target, and in a few minutes the dull, unmistakable cough of the mortar was heard. Then the message, "Tare-Fox to Tare-Item. On the Way. Over."

As Sgt. Miller and Pfc. Bryan tensely awaited the explosion, they looked for another target. Suddenly black smoke drifted up 100 yards in front of them. That was perfect. Now to find a Kraut and let him have it. While they waited for enemy movement, they fixed numerous concentrations on located positions. After several hours, Sgt. Miller tapped Pfc. Bryan on the shoulder and pointed to one lonely German walking along the far edge of the river. They had to restrict their talking to mere whispers, as it was quite easy to hear several Germans talking in dugouts across the river.

Pfc. Bryan grabbed the radio and said, "Let's get that bastard before he knows what's up." The radio buzzed and the fire mission was delivered to the gun crews. All six guns laid on the target and, at a command from the platoon, fired one round. In a matter of seconds, the rounds hit, completely circling the German, wounding him slightly, for he took off like a streak of lightning for the nearest bunker.

Back at the CP, everyone waited nervously for the adjustment, but none came. Capt. Offt and the radio operator tried frantically to contact the two observers, but it proved impossible. Everyone tried to act unconcerned; then Sgt. "Juicy" Walters broke the silence saying, "They are probably just moving to a better CP and turned the radio off." The men tried hard to believe this, but as darkness fell and the radio still had not made a noise, the hopes for the observers' returning was about gone.

As soon as it was totally dark, when the waiting had become unbearable, a patrol was organized to search the river line for the two men. Just as the patrol moved out, the message came in to Pfc. Bowen, the radio operator with the patrol, "Donkey men returned to Charlie Peter. Everything O.K." The patrol returned to the platoon CP.

Later, in talking to the two observers, it was learned that they had purposely turned off the radio because the enemy had spotted them. Later, when they tried to re-establish contact, the aerial broke and the radio was put out of order. Sgt. Miller related the story that our own artillery shells had fallen both in front of and behind them as they lay in the culvert. As they left the CP, they said, "Well, Lieutenant, if you want us to do it again just say so and we're ready. It was a lot of fun, and boy, did we get a good phonograph."

This wraps up the Christmas week, 1944 part of the 4ID's fight across Europe. To everyone reading this, be especially thankful as we observe Christmas that our 4ID Soldiers and many other Allied divisions did not relax…they were holding back and defeating the last frantic German attempt to hold back the Allied force that was pushing them back into their homeland.

29 DEC 1944 TO 4 JAN 1945 – D+207 TO D+213

29 DECEMBER 1944—D+207: The enemy abandoned its defense of the Gisterklaus area, and our patrols moved quite freely in that area.

The 8th Infantry maintained its defensive positions and continued reorganization and training.

At 1045, the 12th Infantry assumed responsibility for its new sector and its 1st and 2nd Battalions adjusted their positions. The 2nd Battalion moved during the afternoon to an assembly area in the vicinity of Alurier, closing therein at 1705.

The 22nd Infantry sent combat and reconnaissance patrols and new outposts were established overlooking the Sauer river valley.

30 DECEMBER 1944—D+208: The enemy continued to maintain its defensive strength east of the Sauer and Moselle rivers. Artillery fire was scattered and harassing. Two enemy planes strafed south of Olingen at 1000.

Patrols of the 8th Infantry reconnoitered the western banks of the Sauer and Moselle rivers, both in daylight and during the hours of darkness. Enemy activity was negligible.

Reconnaissance patrols of the 12th Infantry reconnoitered the south bank of the Sauer river within their sector.

Two reconnaissance patrols of the 22nd Infantry were able to cross the Sauer river in the vicinity of Minden during the hours of darkness, 29-30 December, but two other patrols were frustrated in their attempt to cross in the vicinity of Rasport.

Units not actively engaged conducted training in demolitions and the use of flame throwers.

31 DECEMBER 1944—D+209: Enemy activity was almost nonexistent. Our patrols crossing the rivers reported the enemy defenses there quite formidable. They consisted of foxholes, dug in machine gun emplacements, double barbed wire fences, and numerous trenches dug into strategic ground.

At 1125, an unknown number and type of aircraft dropped high explosive and incendiary bombs in the vicinity of the 8th Infantry CP. Roads in the vicinity were badly cratered and two buildings set afire.

Patrols of the 12th Infantry continued to reconnoiter the south bank of the Sauer river.

Patrols of the 22nd Infantry were dispatched to determine enemy positions in the vicinity of Edingen and Goddendorf. Other patrols were sent to reconnoiter the west bank of the Sauer river. The 2nd Battalion was placed on an alert status and named as part of a counterattack force to be under the control of XII Corps.

Notes about logistics: The supply of Class I (rations) and III (gasoline) was normal.

Class II: the most serious shortage continued to be overshoes. It was created when large numbers of reinforcements arrived without overshoes. The Division was short 1,835 pairs. Other critical shortage were cups, canteens, and tent shelter-half. A requisition was placed for 7,640 snow camouflage suits, but at the end of the period, only 450 suits had been procured.

Sufficient quantities of Class V (ammunition) supplies were available except mines and all types of firing devices.

December 1944 casualties:
Officers — Enlisted
KIA 10 — 344
MIA 10 — 418
SWA 9 — 90 (Seriously Wounded in Action)
LWA 51 — 926 (Lightly Wounded in Action)
Total 80 — 1778
Prisoners: 684

Since landing on Utah Beach on 6 June 1944 through 31 December 1944, the 4ID lost 229 officers and 2,939 enlisted men (total of 3,168) KIA with over 17,000 additional who had been wounded in the 209 consecutive days of combat. Another 90 days of combat are ahead of the 4ID before they get their first relief since D-Day.

One of the 4ID's best friends and a real story teller visits the 12th Command Post to find out how the shoulder of the Bulge was held. Left to right: MG Raymond O. Barton, Ernest Hemingway, and COL R. H. Chance. Junglinster, Luxembourg, 12/27/44.

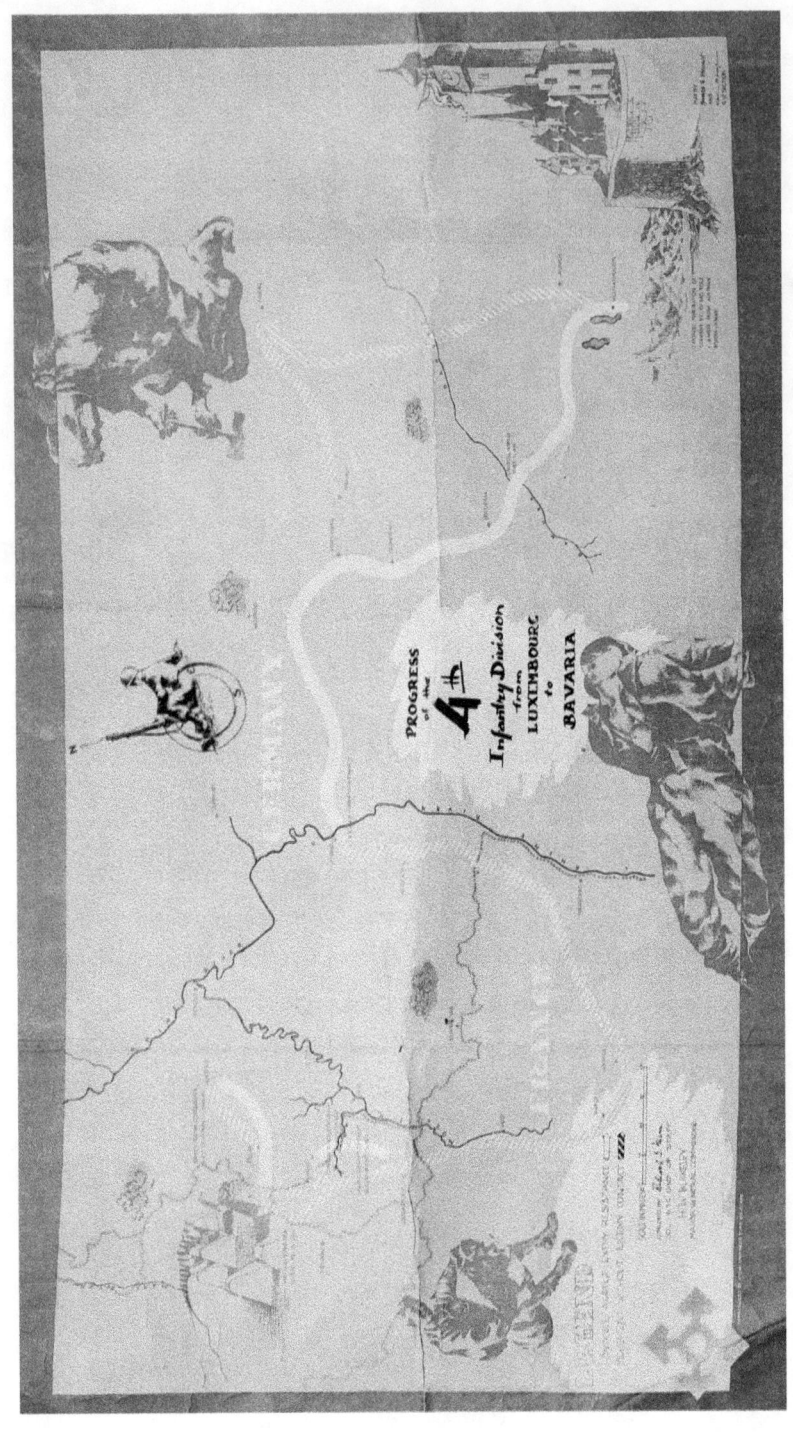

JANUARY 1945

4ID IN LUXEMBOURG, BELGIUM, GERMANY

1 JANUARY 1945—D+210: The enemy reacted sharply to our patrols which crossed the rivers and employed harassing artillery fire throughout the period.

OPERATIONS 1-14 January 1945—D+210-223: (The 4ID after action report for the next two weeks was consolidated into the following summary rather than daily updates as in the past—daily after action reports will resume as of January 15, 1945. Short daily reports are all we have for the next two weeks).

During the first two weeks of January, the 4th Infantry Division continued to defend along the west banks of the Sauer and Moselle rivers with three regiments abreast, the 12th, the 22nd and the 8th, from left to right. Each of the three regiments in turn defended their sector with two battalions abreast and one battalion in reserve.

A counterattack force under the command of the 17th Armored Group was constituted by the CG XII Corps in the event the enemy endeavored to launch another attack against the City of Luxembourg. Elements of the 70th Tank Battalion and one battalion of the 22nd Infantry Regiment were kept on an alert status as a part of this force.

In conjunction with the 4th Engineer Combat Battalion, all regiments continually improved their defensive positions and in addition to maintaining an outpost line, extensive work was done.

Throughout the period, extensive patrolling, both in daylight and during the hours of darkness, was carried on by all units. It succeeded also in effecting a crossing to probe enemy positions.

An effective plan was employed of rotating battalions on the outpost lines, together with carrying on an extensive training program within all units not actively engaged in the defense: instruction by engineer officers, technique of assaulting fortified positions, real firing of various weapons.

From **Swede Henley's Diary—used with permission of his daughters:**

27-28-29 DECEMBER: Still in Herborn—patrolling vigorously to Moselle River. Krauts are in numbers on other side. Jerry counterattacked—stopped—and we have gone to killing Krauts wholesale. Gen. Barton relieved (medical reasons) on December 28, 1944.

30 DECEMBER: (nothing written)

31 DECEMBER: New Year's Eve
It stinks as we are still hunting Krauts. Goforth went back for physical check-up. Krauts bombed us today and missed—the sorry bastards. THIS IS ALL FOR 1944.

1 JANUARY 1945: Still in Herborn, Luxembourg sweating out Krauts. Received orders for river crossing into Siegfried line—horrible—I fainted.

2 JANUARY: Relieved by 2nd Bn and we moved back to Berbourg. Snow started—cold as the devil.

3 JANUARY: Still in Berbourg—training—digging in—on the alert, etc. Snowing all night.

4-5-6-7 JANUARY: Berbourg, in good ole Luxembourg. Sweating out the Jerry and snow.

Some Christmas and New Year stories from, **War Stories Volume II: Paris to VE Day**

Jack Capell, Portland, OR
HQ, 8th Infantry Regiment
From Paradise Back Into Hell

The date is March 7, 1997. This is an oral history contribution on the Battle of the Bulge to the Eisenhower Center, New Orleans, Louisiana, attention Dr. Stephen Ambrose. This is from John C. Capell. I am known as Jack Capell.

I was a member of the 4th Infantry Division, 8th Infantry Regiment, Headquarters Company from D-Day until the end of the war, including the Battle of the Bulge. I was a combat infantryman. I am arranging these recollections in a series, rather than giving continuous narration, because I think it is a matter of record as to what the 4th Infantry Division did during the Battle of the Bulge, and I see no reason I should go over that or include many numerous details. I will give you some of the memories that I have of that period.

My second recollection concerns Christmas Day, 1944.

The weather had cleared somewhat, but it was still very cold with snow having come on or about December 20. I recollect the Christmas Day situation because of its irony. We were promised we would have hot Christmas dinners on Christmas Day, even though we were still holding the line at the front. I didn't know how this would be possible. On that day our kitchen truck came up to regimental headquarters about a quarter of a mile back from where I had chiseled a shelter trench out of the snow and ice.

One by one we were allowed to go back to the kitchen truck and get our Christmas dinners. I had the mess kit lid (I had discarded the rest of it) and my canteen cup. I walked back through the ice and snow and was given servings of turkey, reconstituted dehydrated potatoes, some cranberry sauce, and a cup of coffee. I was ordered to return to my hole and not to stay by the same truck and eat it there. So with my rifle over my shoulder, I precariously made my way back through the snow and ice, trying to keep from spilling my coffee and dinner until I finally arrived at my hole. When I sat down to eat it, I found the cranberry sauce had frozen to the mess kit and everything was ice cold, including the coffee. I chiseled out the cranberry sauce and had my Christmas dinner. It was the most unusual Christmas dinner I had ever had.

Another recollection occurred sometime during that period, but I am not quite sure what date. We had been warned about English-speaking Germans in American uniforms infiltrating our units. A rumor was circulating that our command post had been visited by mysterious strangers who left unidentified. My good friend, Horace Sisk, from Illinois, was the regimental clerk. I knew he could tell me what had happened if anything.

He told me that a jeep driven by one enlisted man and two men wearing uniforms of high-ranking American officers as passengers arrived at regimental headquarters. The party passed the guard without being questioned after stating they were from corps headquarters. While the driver stayed in the jeep, the two officers walked into the regimental headquarters building and immediately asked for Colonel McKee, who was the 8th Infantry Regiment Commander. They were told he was not there but was expected back soon. They expressed anger and said that he had told them he would be there to meet with them, and they demanded to see the next in command. They were quite irate. They were directed to Lieutenant Colonel Strickland, with whom they spoke briefly. They then preceded to lower ranking officers, particularly a captain who apologized for the fact that McKee was not there. The officers continued to express their anger, and to appease them, he answered their questions about 8th Infantry positions and strategy, as well as detailed information about the deployment of our troops. The officers quickly left.

Colonel Strickland finally became suspicious and went to the captain.

Fit to Fight

The captain said that since the officers had already talked to Strickland, he assumed that Strickland had identified them.

Strickland realized they had been duped. The officers were imposters. When Colonel McKee returned to the Regimental Headquarters, he became extremely upset and terrified because he had made no appointment. The imposters must have known that Colonel McKee was not at regimental headquarters. Possibly they had monitored radio transmissions from Division HQ and knew he was there.

The fourth recollection I have took place on December 31. By that time, we had moved to the town of Wecker, Luxembourg. The civilians had been evacuated. The German guns were quieter than usual. It was still cold, but it was a bright day, and I had gone into the lower floor of an evacuated two-story frame house to relax and get a bit warmer. Soon I heard bombs whistling, then suddenly a jarring explosion followed by one after another. I was struck with a terrible shock and deafening noise very close to the house. The air was filled with dust and debris, and I was aware of things falling on me. I quickly exited the house and returned to my foxhole. The bombing continued a while longer. Medics were coming to treat our wounded. I soon learned that one of my very good friends, a man from Pennsylvania by the name of Sepik, had been killed.

Some of the men said they had seen the aircraft through some high clouds. They identified them definitely as American heavy bombers—B-17s, as I recollect. We were completely puzzled because we were not on the front at the time. We were back in reserve and wondered why they would bomb so short. We concluded that somehow or another there had been some American heavy bombers captured by Germans, and these were actually being flown by Germans. We could not believe that American pilots could be that far off target. However, it had happened once before. Prior to the St. Lô breakthrough on July 25, it happened when the smoke line marking to the target on the German side drifted over us. We lost many men in that bombing.

On the following day, January 1, 1945, the weather was even brighter. We were still in and around the town of Wecker, and we were astounded to see American P-38 fighter planes swoop down over our area and begin strafing us. This was the second day in a row we were hit by American planes. We immediately laid out cloth panels showing the American insignia. They had to be visible to the aircraft, but the strafing continued. Our regimental history indicates that there were twelve P-38's involved in this raid. After the raid, according to my friend in Regimental HQ, Horace Sisk, a command car came up to visit. It was carrying American officers with no identifying insignia. We learned that they were American air corps officers investigating what had gone wrong. Their identification was kept secret because of concern over what some of our men might have done had they learned who they were. That concludes the fourth memorable recollection.

The fifth recollection is probably the most memorable of all. It took place during the cold, snowy, winter weather during the latter part of December and January. Some of us still had no overcoats, and although we had the new longer and heavier field jackets, they were not sufficient protection against the cold. We had wool gloves and the new combat boots. They had leather tops, which replaced the old leggings, but they were not any more protection against severe cold. We wore rubber overshoes to help insulate, but had a deadly fear that we might rip an overshoe such that snow could work its way in.

Once the snow melted from the body heat, and then one stopped to rest, the foot would quickly freeze. Trench foot was a serious problem. It may have caused more casualties than actual battle wounds during that particular period. We supplemented our clothing by cutting up burlap sacks found in farmhouses. We wrapped those around our heads, necks, and legs. The Germans did the same thing, and some of the prisoners we took were so wrapped up they looked like mummies.

At night many of the men, in groups of two or three, would make a shelter from trunks of trees. I carried a crosscut saw in one of our company vehicles for this purpose. We would huddle together and use body heat to help keep us warm. Sometimes we half-filled a C-Ration can with gasoline and lit it. It would burn slowly, giving off enough heat to help considerably. This, of course, could only be done if the low, steady flame could be obscured somehow by having it in a shelter, or at least in a pup tent with snow heaped around so that the enemy could not see the light.

Sometimes I would be sent on a mission and return after dark. Being unable to take adequate protection against the cold, I would find myself unprotected from the cold for the night. I would sometimes seek a manure pile. There were huge manure piles in front of the peasant houses. They were flattened on top, and by throwing some boards on top of the manure, one could crawl on top and keep warm as the manure fermented. It was so warm that the snow would melt off, and steam rose. There was strong methane gas being given off, and the pungent odor meant that one could survive only a short time without getting away for some fresh air. Then I would have to spend the rest of the night in the cold.

One cold and dark night, I was alone without protection. Searching for a building to get into, I found in the darkness a shed or a barn of some sort with an open door, and I sensed the feeling of warmth. I reached down to find a floor of concrete, which was warmer than would be expected. I felt around on the floor until it felt even warmer. At that spot, I lay down and immediately went to sleep.

Shortly afterward, I was awakened by something nudging me in the back. I reached over and felt a furry leg and a hoof. I realized I was sleeping by a cow that was resting on its side. I went back to sleep. When daylight came, I found I had spent the night sleeping between the cow's legs and considered that to be an excellent way to beat the cold.

The worst times in the cold were when we did sentry duty. There was little one could do to protect from the biting wind. More than once, after a seemingly endless session on sentry duty, I returned to my hole for shelter so cold and thoroughly fatigued that I was afraid to fall asleep for fear of freezing.

I was often assigned to take the weapons carrier to get back to division headquarters and pick up supplies and ammunition as well as a number of other miscellaneous missions. I often accidentally got into enemy territory. Sergeant Mike Camarote, who was wounded and being returned to the regiment, noticed what I was doing and volunteered to accompany me for some extra protection.

One time when Mike and I were together we were carrying a supply of TNT and dynamite caps for blowing foxholes. The explosives compartment was directly behind the driver's seat in the weapons carrier. As Mike and I were driving back on a narrow icy road, on top of a dike, we encountered a two-and-a-half ton GMC truck approaching from the other direction. It was impossible for both vehicles to come to a stop, and there was not room for both of us on top of the dike. We collided, and the weapons carrier went into a spin as the heavier GMC truck went on without stopping to see what happened.

We spun and slid off the edge of the dike, then dropped eight to ten feet. The vehicle was lying on the driver's side where the TNT was stored. When we hit, Mike bounced on top of me. I was not injured, and I asked Mike if he was OK. He was just shaken up a little bit. Then I said, "What do you think, Mike? Are we in another world now, or, if by some miracle that TNT and dynamite did not explode when we hit?"

Mike gasped. "My God, I had forgotten about that!" Then he laughed and said, "Well, must be the same old world. I'm just as cold as ever."

Another major recollection also has to do with events that occurred during the extremely cold weather. We were on a ridge with a valley going down to a creek bed. An American tank column was attempting to move along the steep slope on the other side of the draw. An infantry column was also moving up about the same time. The lead tank began to attempt to traverse the side of the hill. The commander was standing with his upper body extending out of the hatch. The tank slid sideways and rolled over. The tank commander was crushed. The other tanks following stopped before attempting to traverse the slope. I looked back to see a most entertaining sight. The next tank was traversing the slope with ropes extended out from the front and rear of the tank and at least fifty infantrymen holding on to ropes to keep the tank from sliding sideways.

It was like a tug of war with the tank in the middle. Suddenly, one infantryman lost his footing and slid downhill, toppling a dozen or so men. The same thing happened on the other rope, and this happened time and time again—the tank sliding sideways a few feet each time, but still making some progress forward. Eventually, all the tanks went across the slope. That would have been a great scene to capture on film as an example of sheer ingenuity and perseverance. There was an element of comedy as one man would lose his footing and topple a dozen or so, or more like dominoes. All of them would scramble to regain their feet and get going once more. Again, the foot soldier proved his worth.

During January, the 4th Infantry Division made a thrust into the territory the Germans had captured during the Bulge. We were transferred to General George Patton's 3rd Army on December 20, 1944, because we were closer to them than the 1st Army. Until then, we had been members of the 1st Army. At one time, we were apparently cut off because we received supplies by parachute. Our thrust was across the Saar River on January 18. When we reached Vianden, Germany, we captured many prisoners. We then withdrew to a more defensive location.

Conrad "Frenchy" Adams, Gulfport, MS
Company E, 2nd Battalion, 8th Infantry Regiment
Outpost in the Snow

Company E was very short of men as the Battle of the Bulge went on. Many men had been killed or wounded. As a machine gun assistant, I was told to go on a 24-hour stakeout. At that time, the snow was knee deep — and that was a lot of snow for a country boy from Louisiana, who had only seen snow once in his life — and I had to walk three quarters of a mile down a ravine to get to my post. As night fell, I started to expand the foxhole that someone before me hadn't finished. I hit rocks, and the German soldiers started firing 88s at the place where the sound was coming from. I had to stop digging and set up my shelter half. It started to snow harder during the night, and my shelter half fell on me. I couldn't move until the next night because the Germans would have seen me if I had moved.

With the snow on me all night, I became hoarse and could not talk for a month. Although I couldn't talk, I was never taken to the rear for a checkup. As I said, we were short of men, short of new replacements, and that was a hell of a feeling...but we kept on going.

Also, I remember one time the GIs were drinking cognac or schnapps, and I didn't drink. We hadn't taken off our shoes for a couple of months, so I put some of the liquor in my helmet, after removing the liner, took off my shoes and soaked my feet in the helmet—boy did that feel good.

Marvin A. Simpson, (Deceased) Baton Rouge, LA
Company D, 4th Medical Battalion
A Pretty Girl

I had my first taste of Calvados at a pub that catered to the American soldiers.

During late December and early January 1944, we were stationed in the wing of a hospital on the outskirts of Luxembourg, where we received many casualties from the Hürtgen Forest and the Battle of the Bulge. This was during the Christmas holidays, and I had my first taste of Calvados at a pub that catered to the American soldiers. I must admit, I was attracted to a very pretty girl and was a good dancer. Her father was a banker in downtown Luxembourg and the family invited me for dinner one Sunday, which I enjoyed very much.

Wayne Brown, Marshalltown, IA
Company F, 2nd Battalion, 12th Infantry Regiment
Back to Active Duty

I was wounded on July 12, 1944, in Normandy, so I missed the St. Lô breakthrough and the taking of Paris. My shoulder wound was so serious I was sent to a hospital in England for recovery, which took until early September. I was sent back to my original unit but didn't recognize anyone. Most had been killed or wounded. Some of the wounded returned later. We continued our push through the Siegfried Line and into Germany.

In November we encountered one of the worst battles of the war — in the Hürtgen Forest. We were down to three or four men to a squad before I was wounded a second time on November 30, 1944. A bullet struck me in the chest but must have struck a tree first and entered my chest sideways, just to the right of my breastbone. It didn't hit my lungs or any vital organs. I was sent to a Paris hospital where they removed the bullet.

I was in a convalescent hospital when the Battle of the Bulge breakthrough came. We were helping the nurses decorate the tent hospital for Christmas, which we assumed would include us. On December 24, a group of doctors came through the tent asking every man that could stand to do so. A doctor looked at my chart, and I told him that I still had stitches, which he quickly removed and said, "Back to active duty."

That afternoon, we were loaded on "forty and eight" railroad cars and sent back to our units in Luxembourg and Belgium. What a way to spend Christmas. I missed most of the battle Company F had at the Parc Hotel in Berdorf but knew a lot of the fellows who were there, such as Master Sergeant Ed Potts from Hudson Falls, New York, and others.

From that day on, the weather was horrible. I thought Iowa winters were bad, but when someone is trying to kill you, it is worse. I went days without taking off my combat boots, which were wet. No wonder so many men had trench foot. Walking through a foot or two of wet snow with a heavy army overcoat on was very tiring and also made us good targets against the white snow. We didn't receive any white camouflage suits until well into February, after most of the snow was gone.

I was wounded the third time when our own artillery shelled a house we had taken in Germany. We had lost our radioman so didn't know we were supposed to pull back before they shelled the town. A shell came through the roof of the house and exploded, wounding several of us as well as the eight Germans we had captured. I was hit with shrapnel at the belt line. It went through my army overcoat, field jacket, cartridge belt, web belt, and long johns. It embedded about one inch into my back, just right of my spine. If it had been an inch or two higher or lower, who knows what would have been the outcome. I still have the piece of shrapnel, the web belt, and the helmet with a bullet hole in it that cut the liner strap but didn't draw blood. This happened later in Germany in a forest battle.

Anyone who lived through the Battle of the Bulge should give thanks every day. Everyone thought that after the Battle of the Bulge the Germans were done, but a lot of soldiers were killed in February, March, and April 1945.

Ed Burgess, Las Vegas, NV
Company E, 2nd Battalion, 8th Infantry Regiment
Prisoner of War

I was at Fort Meade, Maryland, for Thanksgiving Day, 1944. Then on to Camp Shanks, New York. I embarked on the USS Marine Devil on December 12, 1944. We disembarked at Marsiller, France, on December 24, 1944. My first airplane ride (C-47) touched down at Lyon, France, landing at Air Base Relfa, France, between Nancy and Metz. We had Christmas Dinner on December 26, 1944.

We mounted large trucks that night, going by General Patton's Headquarters in Nancy, France. We arrived at Luxembourg City after midnight. We were lined up in the snow and deposited our extra-large, duffel bag-sized backpacks. Much foul language came from those who had purchased cartons of cigarettes and had to leave them in the snow. I joined Company E, 8th Infantry Regiment, 4th Infantry Division in Luxembourg City on December 27, 1944. I was wounded twice, captured, and taken as a prisoner of war by the German Wehrmacht at 0500 hours January 13, 1945. Our position was on the outskirts of Hinkle in the Rosport jurisdiction. We were captured near the Moselle River, which is the boundary between Luxembourg and Germany.

Marcus Dillard, Largo FL
Company M, 3rd Battalion, 12th Infantry Regiment
In God's Hands

I was assigned to Company M, 3rd Battalion, 12th Infantry Regiment, 81mm mortars. I served with them from the start to the finish—all five campaigns and the landing. With the help of God, I came through it all without ever being wounded. Three different times really stand out in my mind; I came so close to being a casualty in these particular events.

The first was in Normandy. We had our 81s dug in. It was a beautiful sunny afternoon, and you could not hear one shot being fired—like the war was over. We were by our guns doing nothing, and then we did what we were always taught never to do. We all ganged up around one gun pit and started talking. After a few minutes I said, "I am going back to my mortar."

I turned and had walked maybe fifty feet when all of a sudden, out of nowhere came an 88mm shell and hit the edge of the gun hole. It killed two of my buddies and wounded five others. All was quiet again.

The second time was in Germany. We had a salient into the German lines. Just like a finger sticking in there. We had to be on alert most of the night as the Germans sent patrols out, and they came to our area and planted mines and booby traps almost every night. This one night was my turn to go to the rear in our jeep to get hot chow. My buddy, Joe Peel, from Cleveland told them to let me sleep, that he would go in my place. They had gone about half a mile when the jeep ran over a mine that had been planted that night before. Joe was not killed, but he never came back.

The third time was during the Battle of the Bulge. We had been in Luxembourg supporting Company I. After fighting the Germans, we were out of Dickweiler and went back to Herborn where our company was.

As my buddy and I left the house we were in to go to the chow line for supper, I noticed I did not have my canteen cup. I told my buddy to go ahead, that I had to get my cup. While I was in the house, I heard a big boom like a railroad gun, and all of a sudden, the shell landed right where they were serving chow. My buddy was wounded, but not killed.

I believe in all cases that God was guiding me, and guiding all the battles, also.

George Knapp, Westchester, IL
Chaplain, HQ, 12th Infantry Regiment
The Three-Man Quartet

During the Battle of the Bulge when we were in Luxembourg, one of the first shells severely injured the first sergeant of our 3rd Battalion, 12th Infantry Regiment as he stood near me. I took off my belt, made a tourniquet for his leg, and he was sent at once to the hospital. We never saw each other until our National Association Reunion in Pittsburgh about twenty years later. He was OK, but it was hard for me to think of him as the same man. He had changed a lot.

On Christmas of '44, in a small town close to the river separating Luxembourg and Germany, I conducted a candlelight service in a barn alongside the road leading to the front line.

Candelabra and candles came from a bombed-out church in town. Men of all faiths attended. We only had a trio to sing as the other member of an intended quartet had been captured with others from Company K. Men from another outfit were going on the road past the barn, on the way to relieve our men up in the foxholes at the front. I was glad for my men, but sorry for the replacements getting into those frontline foxholes on Christmas Eve. The next morning, my Christmas Day Services were conducted in a two-lane bowling alley in another town a bit farther away from the front. Other services were held that Christmas Day of 1944.

When we eventually left Luxembourg, the officer in charge of a chateau in Luxembourg City said to me, "Chaplain, everything is cleaned up, but here is a set of golf clubs. Can you take them?"

He knew that I had a jeep and a trailer, so I did. I still have that set of golf clubs. We went on again into Germany into some of the same towns we had been before—this after the war passed through twice, leaving nothing but rubble—no streets visible, etc. Since the war was winding down, we were coming from the south into Munich and heading out east from the center of the city. As we were proceeding outside the city limits, all of a sudden, my assistant let out a yell, jumped out of the jeep from the driver's seat without putting it into neutral and ran on ahead faster than the column was moving. I slid over and brought the jeep to a halt.

Why had he jumped out? He had seen his buddy from Company K coming to us after he and others who had been captured at Echternach, Luxembourg, had been freed from a POW camp by another outfit up ahead. What a reunion! His buddy was the fourth member of the quartet that was to have sung at Christmas time.

5 JAN 1945 TO 11 JAN 1945 – D+214 TO D+220

Welcome to the New Year and 1945. As stated in the previous issue, the first half of January had only summarized daily After Action Reports, the daily detailed reports resume on 15 January.

I will include what we have about this time period and will also include some individual stories from 4ID Soldiers and four stories from wives of our WWII 4ID veterans (you'll want to read all these stories—you will surely see them as a great highlight to this series of stories).

This week's pictures lead with a map showing the route ahead of the 4ID from now through VE Day. Follow the orange line from Luxembourg to track them to early May 1945.

From the **Diary of Swede Henley—used with permission of his daughters:**

4-5-6-7 JANUARY: Berbourg, in good ole Luxembourg. Sweating out the Jerry and snow.

7-10 JANUARY: Berbourg—training like hell.

11 JANUARY: Relieved by 3rd Bn along Sauer River east of Ecternacher. Still cold as hell.

From **History of the 22nd Infantry Regiment in WWII** *by Chaplain Bill Boice*:

Combat Team 22 was defensively employed during the period, 1 January 1945 — 13 January 1945, and held part of the southern shoulder of the Bulge created by the German counter-offensive. It was responsible for the Osweiler-Dickweiler sector in Luxembourg, extending along the south bank of the Sauer River.

While the first Battalion was located in Osweiler, Lt. Col. George Goforth moved his forward CP to a village almost on the banks of the river, and almost certainly under the observation of the enemy. There were only three houses grouped together. In the basement of these three houses the CP took its stand. The Colonel, with his S3 and S2, were in one basement. Lt. George Kozmetzsky had the forward aid station in the second, and Capt. Reece (Daddy) Dampf, Adjutant of the First Battalion, had his Communications and I. and R. Section in the third basement. Every effort was made to keep any activity from being observed by the enemy, when along toward dusk, high in the lean-to next to Daddy Dampf's CP, in some mysterious manner, probably by a careless cigarette or a G.I. heating coffee, a fire started.

The consternation caused by the conflagration was great, especially in the face of approaching darkness and the fact that the burning buildings lighted the entire CP like a signal fire for miles around. The efforts of Daddy and his men to put the fire out were totally ineffective, but increasingly amusing to those who were observing from a distance. Not only was Daddy Dampf warm from the fire and from his personal exertion but was made considerably warmer by the caustic comments from Col. Goforth, whose vocabulary was certainly not limited. Thus, the CP of the First Battalion was moved, and it was not due to enemy action.

The greater part of the enemy had been forced to withdraw to the confines of the Siegfried Line fortifications on the northern side of the Sauer. Combat activity was confined to harassing and interdictory artillery and machine gun fire and patrols, combat, reconnaissance, security, and contact.

Because the enemy was able to cross the river during the hours of darkness and establish listening and observation posts, there were numerous patrol clashes and several ambushes. This could be done because of the wide frontage and the wooded, rugged terrain, but the Regiment worked continuously to improve its positions. The defense was prepared in depth, fires were better coordinated, protective wire was strung, road and bridge demolitions were prepared, mine fields were laid, and booby-traps set.

Whenever possible, training was carried on. Emphasis was placed on such topics as flame throwers, demolitions, mortar drill, and small unit assault training, to include the use of the assault beat. Re-organization and indoctrination of re-enforcements continued.

Stories from **War Stories Volume II: Paris to VE Day:**

Norm Chapin, Jenison, MI
Companies A and B, 1st Battalion, 22nd Infantry Regiment
German Soldiers, Loaded For Bear

I joined the 22nd Infantry after the Battle of the Bulge as a brand new Second Lieutenant coming from the 100th Division. My battalion commander, Lieutenant Colonel George Goforth, was a great officer. I was called into the CP one night and given orders to go to a town called Elligen and hold it until the battalion came in the next morning. Captain Claude Ecabert was my CO, and Captain Willis Williams was our S-3.

I felt—being called that late—that I would probably get my liquor ration. What else would we do at that time of night? I was given my mission and soon found out.

I selected one squad comprised of twelve men and took off down the road. On the way I heard a noise, so I stopped my squad. Here came two German soldiers on bicycles. I stopped them and determined that they were two snipers going down the road to shoot at our battalion in the morning as we advanced. I still have the compass one of them carried, plus a pair of field glasses and a sniper's rifle one of my squad leaders gave me.

As we proceeded down the road, we heard more noise. I still had part of my squad on both sides of the road. To my amazement, here came at least two squads of German soldiers, loaded for bear. Not knowing just what to do, I stepped out in front of them and indicated I had a lot of men with me. They surrendered, and then I had the problem of just what I would do with them. As luck would have it, a half-track came up behind me and took them off my hands.

The funny part of the whole escapade was the last incident. As we proceeded into the town of Effigen, we encountered another German soldier. He was riding a bicycle and headed in our direction. We stopped him and found out he was the squad leader of the squad ahead of him. Drunk and very belligerent, he became one of us.

Harper Coleman, Tucson, AZ
Company H, 2nd Battalion, 8th Infantry Regiment
(Harper Coleman is still with us at 102 years old—thanks for this great story, Harper).
London

While in England, I got to leave the hospital on occasion. The local people would give afternoon tea parties, and some of the hospital patients would be invited. We would go by truck to the homes. Also, there were several tours to town and one to a park with canoe rides.

On December 26, 1944, I was transferred to a replacement center near the hospital. I was there several days. While there, we were required to do guard duty at the POW camp in the area. I had several of these tours of duty during my stay.

From there, we went to Le Havre, France, where we were put on boxcars. We were on them four or five days going across France. It was winter time and very cold during this trip. There were a number of rest stops along the way with hot meals. Very soon in the trip someone came up with an old bucket of some kind. With a little coal from the engine and some wood along the tracks, we had a fire going in the middle of the car. We also burned a hole in the floor.

I was back with the 4th Infantry Division by the first week in January of 1945.

It did not seem like the unit I had left. Almost everyone was new, and I knew very few of them. The gun crew that I served with was gone. I was told that they took a direct hit on their position sometime during the Battle of the Bulge.

This time, the snow seemed to get deeper—several feet deep in most places. Roads were almost impassable with the mud, snow, and rain. This was during the time the division was pushing the Germans back after the Bulge. We were on line for more than a week in the rain and cold. We were issued "Snow Packs" (rubber bottom shoes with leather tops). I had gone for about a week without being able to change socks or to dry out my shoes. After about a week of this, and being so cold, I came down with a bad case of trench foot.

By the end of January 1945, I was back in the hospital in Paris, unable to walk, where I stayed for about a week. After this time, they decided to send me back to the rear. I was put on a hospital train and sent to England for the second time. This time I was in a hospital about an hour's ride by train north of London. I stayed there until after VE Day, May 8, 1945.

While in the hospital in England and after I was able to walk, some men were given passes to go into London on a number of occasions. We could be away from the hospital for three or four days if we wanted to. We would stay at the USO club in London for several days at a time. The hospital was located a mile or two from a small town and the railroad station.

Several things happened while at the hospital. On one occasion, on our way back to the hospital and on a very foggy night, we had to crawl in the ditch by the side of the road to find where to turn to get to the hospital. Another time, four or five of us decided to take a cab back. When the cab was within several blocks of our stop, someone said to stop here, and we all jumped out and ran. We still owe the driver. If I ever find him, I will pay up.

In London I was sad to see the destruction of the city. The air raids had done quite a bit of damage. During this time, they were being bombed by V-2 rockets and Buzz Bombs. I was very close to the V-2 rocket explosions on several occasions. There were bomb shelters all over the city, but you could not always get in when the sirens would sound. The buzz bombs started sometime in October or November while I was still on the front lines. We would hear them going over every night. However, they were going on past us, and we did not get too concerned about them at that time.

It was the policy at this time that if anyone had a given number of days stay in the hospital, they were automatically to go stateside. With a little help from several nurses, my records disappeared for several days. With the end of the war near, it did not make any difference. I was sent by hospital ship to the States. I entered the hospital at Camp Butner, North Carolina. After a thirty-day leave, I received a medical discharge on September 6, 1945.

Robert R. Gable, Upperco, MD
Company I, 3rd Battalion, 8th Infantry Regiment
Knoll's Raiders

Sometime after the Sauer and Our Rivers, Company I was coming out of a wooded area. The word was given to take cover in the woods. After some

Fit to Fight

time, someone came to the first platoon and called out for me to go see the Company Commander, just ahead of us in the woods.

I was told by the captain that I was to be part of Sergeant Knoll's Raiders along with Private First Class Owens, Raymond Lord, Crisfield, Winford Norris, Norman Fritz, and an artillery forward observer. The CO briefed us on our mission, which was to take an outpost on the hill.

Sometime later, we were all given white cloth to cover our uniforms, and we set out to take the high ground. We started out in the wooded area to keep cover—until we were about fifty to one hundred yards from the pillbox.

The artillery observer called for artillery fire on the area. At the same time, we would go out of the woods, into the clearing, with artillery going over our heads. Our observer was very good...the shells were landing just in front of us. It was now getting late in the day, and the Germans were all inside for safety from the shelling.

As we were able to get close to the pillbox, we could see two houses with Germans who were forming a triangular defense. We had to stop for more artillery. After the artillery barrage opened up on the final house and dazed the few remaining Germans, the patrol moved in to capture them. The Raiders captured forty-six prisoners, of which seventeen were captured without firing a shot. We had zero losses in the raid.

By nightfall the battalion was able to come up to the high ground, set up, and secure the hill. Sometime later, the account was in the Stars and Stripes service publication. Our battalion commanding officer sent each one the clipping describing the fight that Knoll's Raiders took part in.

And during this slight lull in other news to report, I will include four stories from my book that were written by ladies on the home front. We must never forget, the home front was an equally important part of WWII, just like the troops fighting the war.

STORIES FROM THE WORLD WAR II HOME FRONT

While our soldiers were training and fighting, their loved ones were anxiously waiting for them, and taking on the added responsibilities associated with being a serviceman's wife during war time. Although we do not have many home front stories, the accounts included here will give you an idea of the hardships of those who stayed at home and waited.

Ethel Frances Grimes Williamson, Lakeland, FL
Wife of Bob Williamson
Company F, 2nd Battalion, 12th Infantry Regiment
The Love We Shared

When the War broke out between England and Germany, I was eleven years old and living in Liverpool, England. I was at an age where the memories of the war remain etched in my mind and will forever be in my thoughts and dreams.

It was Sunday morning, September 3, 1939, that the war was declared. I was at church with my sister Patricia. She was only six years old at the time. When we got home from church our parents told us that we were at war with Germany. My sister didn't really comprehend what war was. It was not too long after that that my sister and I eventually began to realize what war was really all about.

We had an "Anderson Air-Raid" shelter in our backyard. It was made out of corrugated steel, with part of it being dug under the ground. The part of the shelter that was above the ground had grass growing on it so that the German planes couldn't spot it from the air. There also was no door on any of the Anderson Air Raid shelters because if there had been an explosion nearby, it would cause a concussion and the shelter would disintegrate. There was only a square hole in place of a door. This is how the water and cold air got in. Before my father knew about what concussions would do to a shelter, he had tried to put a door on ours, and the authorities came around to our houses and told him to take the door off.

For the next two years, my mom, dad, sister, and I slept in that air-raid shelter every night. The German planes seemed to fly right overhead around 1900 hours until 0700 hours. While we were in our shelter, we would hear the German planes going overhead and hear the bombs dropping around us. The sounds of the bombs were deafening. I lost my hearing in my left ear from the blasts of those bombs.

In the winter months, our air-raid shelter would get water in it. My father had made two bunk beds on each side of the shelter for each of us to lie on. The beds had no mattresses. In the dead of winter the water would flood the two bottom bunk beds on the floor, which would leave the four of us on the top bunks all night. We would all be hunched over with no room at all to hold our heads up…cold and scared. My parents never got much sleep while protecting my sister and me throughout the night. They would always throw their arms around us whenever they would hear the bombs falling close to our house. The bombs would fall so close to us that they would make our shelter shake.

Yet, through all the pain and hardships, the morale of the British people was marvelous. They would be in their air-raid shelters, and you would hear a family during a lull moment of the German planes passing overhead, singing songs like, "Roll out the Barrel," and "White Cliffs of Dover," and other songs of WWII.

In our neighborhood, all of the families had Anderson Air-Raid shelters. One night in the winter, while one family down the street was at home, the air-raid sirens went off. The family went directly to their shelter for protection from the bombs. That night they received a direct hit on their shelter from a German bomb. The entire family was killed.

As the war continued and worsened, my father had decided to evacuate my mother, sister, and me to the countryside. We had family living in Staleybridge, England. In Staleybridge they didn't get the bombings that Liverpool got.

During this time, people in England didn't have cars of their own. People rode bikes or walked. Most people used trains, buses, and ferries as a means of travel. Our family took a train to evacuate. Our train had no sooner left Liverpool and a German bomber was spotted following us. The plane followed our train until we were out of Liverpool and then started bombing the front section of the train. Some of the coaches had been hit; yet everyone still managed to get off the train. Then the German bomber came back. Some British troops were on the train at the time of the bombing and saw that all the people were off the train. Then they told everyone to get back onto the train. Everyone started scrambling to get back onto the train with women and children who were scared and crying.

A while after we were on the train, they told us to get out of the train and go to a public air-raid shelter. We ran all the way and stayed there for the rest of the night. The next day we got to see the damage the bombs had done to our train. There was no train to go back to. The railroad tracks had been demolished. There was broken glass everywhere. Most everyone started to walk. We walked past store fronts where the windows had been blown out and broken glass lay everywhere. We couldn't avoid walking through the broken glass. Some of the Brits that had cars or trucks would pick up people walking from the bombing. The vehicles would be packed full of people, like sardines. They would feel bad that they had no more room for the women and children walking. We finally got a ride from a young man. His vehicle was small, a sports car. He still stopped and picked our family up, all four of us.

We arrived in Staleybridge exhausted. We had been through a nightmare. We were relieved to be greeted by our family. We stayed with our family for about a week, relieved not to be sleeping in an air-raid shelter. We would still hear the German planes overhead on their way to bomb Liverpool. They had an indescribable sound—a heavy humming sound—a special sound that only the German planes made.

At a distance from our home in Liverpool, you could see the sky lit up in a bright orange color from the bombs. The Germans were bombing the Liverpool docks where all the big ships would come in with supplies, and also the ships with troops on them.

Upon our return back to Liverpool, the British government decided to have compulsory evacuation of all children in Liverpool.

This was truly a sad day in my life. My mother and father took my sister and me to the train station to be evacuated. I was scared, only eleven years old and having the responsibility of taking care of my sister during the war. All my sis and I had were our gas masks, which we took everywhere, and a small bag of clothing. My mother told me to hold on to my sister's hand and not let loose.

My sister and I cried at the thought of leaving our parents. My mother was crying, and my father was fighting not to. My sister and I evacuated to Whitchurch, a small country village. We stayed with a lovely young couple, but after three weeks apart from our parents, our parents decided they wanted us back in Liverpool with them. At this time, the bombings had slowed down a little in Liverpool. To this day, I can still smell the rubber of the gas masks.

In the early 1940s, I can remember the American troops arriving in England. This really helped boost the morale of the British people. Of course, the British called the American troops "Yanks," and also GIs.

It was 1945 that I met and fell in love with one of those Yanks. He was in the 4th Infantry Division. His name was Robert Williamson. He was at a hospital in Wrexham, England, recovering from a war wound. This was his third wound. I had grown up fast during the war. I was just sixteen years old, and Bob was nineteen. Bob and a buddy of his got what they called a furlough. I met Bob at a St. Patrick's Day dance. We had only known each other for nine days when Bob, my future husband, proposed to me.

But Bob still had to go back to that bloody war. A few months later, I got a letter written by a U.S. nurse in Paris at an American Hospital. She told me that Bob had been in a mine blast and had lost the sight in both of his eyes. I was devastated, even my parents told me how difficult it would be to be married to someone blind. It made no difference to me. I had promised him I would marry him someday. The war would not stop the love that we shared.

Bob was blind for three months without knowing if he would ever see again. He would have the U.S. nurses write to me while he was blind. An army doctor operated on his eyes but could only save the sight in his left eye.

In 1946, I kept the promise that I had made to Bob and came to the

United States to be his bride. I took a ship from Southampton to New York. It took me thirteen days to cross the Atlantic Ocean as we ran into storms at sea. I was seasick the whole way. My face had to be green. It sure felt like it. To this day, I'm afraid of being in a boat on the water.

Bob and I celebrated our 50th wedding anniversary in England. We went back to my home in Liverpool where I grew up, which brought back a lot of childhood memories. We stayed at a bed and breakfast in Chester, and visited some of my family while we were there. We just celebrated our 54th wedding anniversary. We now call Lakeland, Florida, our home.

We have two sons, four grandchildren, and six great grandchildren. At times, I look back to when our oldest son was eleven years old, and our youngest son was six years old; the same ages as my sister Pat and I were when the war broke out. Tears come to my eyes. I would think about a war parting us from them — to be evacuated not knowing if I would ever see them again. It was then that I would realize the actual horror that my parents had gone through.

A lot of the men from the 4th Infantry Division tell me they arrived in Liverpool before they were shipped to Europe. I look at these men who all have such a brotherly love for each other and I thank each one of them for saving my country from being invaded by the Germans. I say to myself, "Where would I be today if it wasn't for the bravery and courage of those very special men and women who gave up their freedom to fight for my country?"

I would like to dedicate my story to the memory of Sarah and Joseph Grimes, my mother and father. If not for their strength and courage, I would not be here today to write this story. I love you both with all of my heart.

Thelma Avery, Three Oaks, MI,
Wife of Walt Avery
Company B, 1st Battalion, 22nd Infantry Regiment
On the Home Front

(**Editor's Note:** *This was the same company I served with in Vietnam ... thus very interesting to me, as are all the stories I hear*).

When your grandchildren talk about reading in their history book about "That Guy Hitler," you know you're old. We lived through it and their Grandpa was there.

The year was 1941. After dating three months, we married. I was nineteen; Walt was twenty-two. My family predicted it wouldn't last six months. We celebrated our fifty-ninth anniversary in March 2000. By 1944, we had two children: a boy, two years old; and a girl, just past one year old. Walt had a good job in a defense plant making 75 dollars a week with lots of overtime. Life was wonderful. We thought that with two children and his job he wouldn't be drafted ... wrong.

In June of 1944, Uncle Sam called. We were in shock. How could we survive the separation? There is nothing like a war to make you grow up quickly. Walt left June 6, D-Day. My monthly allotment was one hundred dollars a month, not a great deal of money, even in 1944. Walt's parents invited me to move in with them, but I was determined to be independent. Besides, what could I do with the half dozen pieces of furniture we had acquired? These dear people drove forty miles round trip, with rationed gas, to check on me once a week, bringing groceries and clothes for the children.

I was better off than many wartime wives because we were living in my hometown where I had graduated from high school. At the time Walt left, we were living in a little house that we rented for fifteen dollars per month. A short time after Walt left, I learned the house had been sold. Affordable housing was nonexistent. My dad was a hard-working farmer who was still recovering from the depression but said if he could find something he could pay cash for (he did not want a mortgage) he would buy it and we could either buy it from him when Walt came home, or he would sell it.

Just a couple blocks from where we lived was a big, old, ugly, drafty house. Dad said, "It's good and solid" and he bought it for 3,500 dollars. I was so grateful I didn't care what it looked like. Before we were even settled I met the next-door neighbors: a wonderful, childless couple who immediately "adopted" us. They took down the old fashioned storm windows, put up screens, and did all the chores I couldn't manage. They also helped comfort and reassure me on bad days.

Walt and I wrote each other daily, but the mail was unreliable much of the time. Sometimes I would receive no mail for several weeks and then there would be a box full. One time I received a big heavy envelope. Walt couldn't find any paper, so my letter was written on pages from an old recipe book. He told me how much the boxes of goodies were appreciated, even if the cookies were often reduced to crumbs.

It is strange how clearly I remember funny little incidents. Now, I might not remember what I had for lunch yesterday, but I remember vividly the day in 1945 when I left my purse on a local bus and worried about losing twenty dollars. It was returned to me — the money was there — but the ration stamps were gone.

Or the time I walked with the children to the grocery store. On the return trip, our son saw the house where we used to live and broke away from me and ran down the middle of the street. I let go of the stroller that had a bag of groceries balanced on the back. The stroller tipped over, the baby was screaming, the grocery bag split and spilled groceries all over the sidewalk. A very kind lady heard all the commotion and helped me put everything back together again.

Most of all, I remember all the wonderful people that helped me cope: The country doctor who made a house call for two sick children and didn't charge because their daddy was in the Army. And the semi-retired electrician who installed wiring for an old electric stove I bought. I worried about not having enough money to pay him. He charged fifty cents.

And of course, my wonderful neighbors. How could I feel too bad for too long when I had these great people and wonderful little children that always had hugs and sticky kisses? I was grateful they were too small to realize what danger their daddy was in.

Walt was wounded February 14, 1945. I have never been so frightened. The dreaded telegram, which I still have, said, "slightly wounded," but how did I know? I soon received a letter from Walt, and he reassured me. He said because of his injury he would be discharged. He arrived back in the States in July. He didn't know where he lived, so in the middle of the night he found his home with the help of a flashlight. Today he would probably have been shot, but the 1940s were a kinder, gentler time.

We are still living in this "old ugly house." With a lot of blood, sweat, tears, and thousands of dollars, it is attractive and very comfortable. All our old neighbors are gone, replaced by younger ones, but they have been great.

I don't recommend starting a marriage this way, but I do know the experience gave us a deeper appreciation of each other and we know that if we could survive the war, we would never sweat the small stuff.

Lois (Jerry) Brown, Marshalltown, IA
wife of Wayne Brown
Company F, 2nd Battalion, 12th Infantry Regiment
Fifty-Five Year Honeymoon

Wayne and I met in June of 1943 outside an ice cream shop, introduced by a mutual friend. We talked for about an hour. Then my girlfriend and I were invited to ride along to take the mutual friend home, twelve miles away. Somehow, on the way back to town, Wayne and I ended up in the back seat while Lyle, Wayne's brother, drove. My girlfriend was up front with him. I thought, here we go again. But Wayne was so polite, quiet, and cute.

They asked us for dates to go to Des Moines on July 4. We accepted. We went to an amusement park and historical museum that day. We dated about twice a week until Wayne entered the army at Camp Dodge in

Des Moines, Iowa, in October of 1943. I was a senior in high school at that time.

I wrote to Wayne every day. He came home in February 1944 from Camp Roberts, California, where he took basic training. It was during the worst blizzard of the winter. The county plowed the road out to his folk's farm, three miles from town, but the wind drifted the snow back in so fast it was hard to keep it open for long, so he walked to town to see me. After that we knew we were meant for each other. We graduated early in April, so the boys in the class could help on the farms. That was a laugh as every one of them was taken into military service before the year was over.

I went to work at Fisher Governor Company, where they made valves and regulators for gas lines on oil wells, ships, and many other things. Fisher's Logo was: "If it flows through pipes, chances are it is controlled by Fisher." I worked in the "White Room" for a while, and we were making something secret for the war effort. They never let us know what it was for. But the whole plant received the "E" award, and we each got a pin with an E for Efficiency award in 1944 and 1945.

Wayne was wounded three times, and they never told us where or how bad, or where he was. I cried a lot but still wrote to Wayne every day. It was also hard on his mother, who kept a scrapbook of the war in Europe for him. After the war in Europe ended, he came home on July 16, for thirty days of rest and recuperation. We were married July 26, 1945. We went by train to Louisiana to visit his brother Lyle, who was to leave for the war in Japan after his basic training at Camp Claiborne, Louisiana. He did not get a leave to go home.

After that we were going on a honeymoon trip to Minnesota to visit his aunt and uncle in the same 1931 Model-A Ford we had dated in, back in 1943. When we got to Albert Lea, Minnesota, church bells were ringing, sirens were wailing, horns were honking, and people were dancing in the street. When we stopped to see what was going on, they told us Japan had surrendered. Were we happy! We honked our way through town. Wayne had told us they were going to train for the invasion of Japan after his leave was over.

Wayne went back to Camp Butner, North Carolina, and they had so many to discharge on the point system that they asked him if he wanted to go home for ten days. Of course, he said, "Yes." He returned to Camp Butner and then to Camp Croft, South Carolina, where he was discharged on the point system, October 21, 1945. He spent two years and one month in the Army with fourteen of those months overseas. From our marriage, we have two daughters, one son, four grandchildren, two great grandchildren, and had our 55th Anniversary on July 26, 2000.

(Editor's Note: Wayne and Jerry are both deceased now—and badly missed by all of us. Wayne was long time treasurer of the National 4ID Association and Jerry was always with him at reunions. Truly a Steadfast and Loyal couple).

Luella Mullen, Bradenton, FL
Wife of Orval H. Mullen
HQ Company, 1st Battalion, 8th Infantry Regiment
The Loneliness of a War Bride

I've been asked to write and tell how it was here in the United States as a war bride while our husbands were in the war. I think the worst thing, of course, was the loneliness of having my husband so far away, and the communications were so bad. Sometimes we would not hear from each other for a month or two—and me not knowing if he were dead or alive during the heat of battle. I know I wrote to him every day, and he'd write to me saying, "How are you and why don't you write to me?" Sometimes I would receive several letters at once (that I still keep in a trunk).

I think the only time he didn't get to write was during the fighting and sometimes when he couldn't find paper to write on.

It is still so hard for me even after so many years. It doesn't seem possible that it is 56 years ago because it is still so fresh in my mind. I'm sure it is in his, also. When he has shared some of his experiences, like laying on a raincoat covering (that we still have) with half of it and the snow covering him, I just want to hug him and try to make him forget some of the bad experiences. When I think of his being in the middle of the

Atlantic Ocean, seasick at the same time I was in the hospital having our first child (he was not aware of it for about a month, or whether it was a son or daughter), I still cry.

I lived with my mother in an apartment. We had a fire escape, and I'd go out there and hold my baby when it got warm, and I'd cry. This almost sounds terrible to tell sad things, but people need to know how horrible war is, and that it was horrible for us loved ones back here and other people that were hurt. My husband used to say, "Please send me pictures," and I did all the time, but it took so long for him to get them. With the way things are now and how things have changed, many things go so fast.

Orval was gone for twenty-one months. We did not see each other from the time I was five months pregnant, while he was still in the States, because at that time we had no money to do things. The only time he could call was one time from New York with someone listening, and all we could really say was that we loved each other. We did not see each other again until our son was almost two years old.

I remember Orval sent me hankies from France. Another thing I'll never forget: one time when he was wounded, he wrote a letter to me and said he would write another letter and send me a watch and for me to open the back of the watch and read a note in there. (Censorship didn't allow sending much information.) It told me where he was wounded and how he was doing—he was OK. I'll bet that's the first time a wife got a love letter in the back of a pocket watch. A few days later I got a "regret to inform you, your husband has been seriously wounded in combat," letter. Did I say communications were bad?

There are so many things to remember. One of the things I've always loved him for was that when he received approximately 21 dollars per month in pay, he got soap out of that and sent the rest to me and our son. (Our son became a doctor of immunology and died of a heart attack in 1988.)

When Orval got back to the States he called me and then took a bus home, arriving about 2300 hours. I didn't have a car, so I walked the two miles to the bus station and to this day, I can see him getting off that bus. He also saw I hadn't cut my hair as I'd promised him. We walked those two miles home stopping every little bit hugging and crying. When we got home I showed him his son. I'd left him naked (hoping nothing would happen) because I wanted him to see him as he came into the world. As most people then, we had a time adjusting to his being back, but it was wonderful. I got pregnant as soon as he came home. We didn't know whether he would go to Japan, but the war ended. Thank God, I didn't have to have another baby without him being there with us.

So many things pop into my mind. When he was wounded at St. Lô, he told me a little about things, but I didn't learn all about it until listening to him being interviewed in New Orleans at the National D-Day Museum grand opening in June 2000. We cried more tears, and I saw more people who experienced WWII crying than we've seen in years in those few days. I talked to other wives who said they were learning things about their husbands that had never been talked about before.

I must tell something funny after all this gloom. When we walked into the National D-Day Museum in New Orleans on June 4, 2000, I saw my husband's face when he saw the Higgins Boat, and I said, "Go over and let me take your picture by the boat."

He just walked on and ignored me. About a half hour later, he was showing me the coils of wire in a stack and telling me how he laid it out for communications. (Too bad we didn't have some of that communications for us sometimes.) A cute young gal came up and started to talk to us and asked if she could take his picture.

He said, "Sure," and posed like a newborn baby without the bare butt. Needless to say, I had no more problems with him posing for me for pictures, and I got my picture of him in front of the Higgins Boat.

I really believe WWII affected so many lives of "The Greatest Generation" (as Tom Brokaw calls us). The memories are so lasting for our lifetime. We have so much to praise God for to this day, and a hope of a great tomorrow.

(Editor's Note: I got to know Luella and Orval Mullins during the week of the grand opening of the National D-Day Museum, now the World War II Museum, in New Orleans in June 2000. They were a couple I very much enjoyed spending time with. I stayed in touch with them for several years but lost track, I'm assuming they are deceased now).

* * * * *

If you're sentimental like I am, you are sitting here now with tears running down your cheeks. I am truly amazed at the strength and resilience of those who have well earned the nickname of "The Greatest Generation." And it saddens me that we lost so many of them who did not write their stories to leave a legacy for future generations to learn from.

I encourage you to share this with your Family and friends and circle of influence. This is true history that needs to be read and passed on to a wide circle of patriots. And if you have a veteran of any war in your Family who hasn't told his/her stories, now is a great time to try once again to get them to tell you the stories they have been carrying for so many years.

Steadfast and Loyal,

Bob Babcock, Past President, Historian, and Archivist—National 4ID Association

12 JAN 1945 TO 18 JAN 1945 – D+221 TO D+227

No daily reports for 12-15 January 1945, but we do have daily reports from here on to the end of the war...

16 JANUARY 1945—D+225: Except for harassing fire from artillery and machine guns, the enemy remained wholly defensive.

The 8th Infantry was relieved by the 346th Infantry Regiment of the 87th Infantry Division. The 8th Infantry less the 3rd Battalion which remained attached to the 5th Infantry Division and less the 2nd Battalion which remained in an assembly area, vicinity of Wecker, moved to its new zone of action, closing therein at 1500, at which time the entire combat team reverted to the control of the 5th Infantry Division.

The 12th Infantry maintained the defense of its sector.

The 22nd Infantry maintained the defense of its sector and patrolled actively. Shortly after dawn, relief of the regiment by the 347th Infantry

Regiment of the 87th Infantry Division was initiated. By 2140, the entire relief was completed and movement of the regiment to the vicinity of Savelborn was begun.

17 JANUARY 1945—D+226: The enemy occupied hasty and permanent fortifications which were well camouflaged and had excellent fields of fire. Outposts and patrols covered the north bank of the Sauer river. Buildings in this sector were employed by the enemy to house troops and as shelters for machine gun positions.

The 4th Infantry Division assumed responsibility for its new sector facing the south banks of the Sure and Sauer rivers, Bettendorf to Bollendorf.

The 8th Infantry Regiment relieved the 10th Infantry Regiment of the 5th Infantry Division within its sector facing the Sure river, during the hours of darkness. At 0730, the 2nd Battalion began movement to its new assembly area vicinity of Ermsdorf, closing therein at 0930. The 8th Infantry reverted to control of the 4th Infantry Division at 0900. During the period, two patrols from the 8th Infantry succeeded in crossing the Sure river on a reconnaissance mission to secure information for the projected attack.

At 1000, the 345th Infantry Regiment of the 87th Infantry Division began the relief of the 12th Infantry. This was continued without incident until 2205. The 3rd Battalion meanwhile began movement at 1340 to a new assembly area in the vicinity of Schoenfels; closing therein at 1715. After their relief, the 1st and 2nd Battalions moved to an assembly area in the vicinity of Keispelt and were still enroute at the close of the period.

The 22nd Infantry continued movement to the vicinity of Savelborn, arriving in the new area by 1715. Relief of the 11th Infantry Regiment of the 5th Division was completed at 2100.

18 JANUARY 1945—D+227: After crossing the Sauer river during darkness, CT 8 by-passed enemy pockets of resistance. Opposite CT 22 the enemy continued to defend along the north bank of the Sauer river. At first the enemy's reaction to our crossing was slight, but when the situation became apparent, it attempted to halt our attack with all weapons and troops at hand. Considerable small arms and machine gun fire was placed on the river crossing sites and later, an increase in artillery and mortar fire was noted. At our approach, enemy forces in Bettendorf came out of the buildings and counterattacked. This action was repulsed by our advancing troops.

The 4th Infantry Division attacked with the 8th Infantry Regiment at 0300 in conjunction with the attack of the 5th Infantry Division on the left. The attack was launched down the steep snow covered slopes of the south bank of the Sure river to secure crossings and to seize the high ground fronting on the Our river and the Siegfried Line. The attack was launched without an artillery preparation in the hope of gaining the advantage of complete surprise. Before the enemy discovered our intentions, elements of the 1st Battalion, on the left, and the 3rd Battalion, on the right, had crossed the Sure river in two places, using assault boats, and were moving rapidly toward their objectives. It was later in the day before all elements of the two assault battalions were able to cross the river. The 2nd Battalion of the 8th Infantry Regiment was ordered to move forward to cross the Sure river but was unable to cross at the selected site because enemy artillery fire destroyed all boats that the battalion had planned to use. After Company K had succeeded in driving the enemy from the bridge area, this battalion crossed on the foot bridge.

During the day, the 4th Engineer Combat Battalion had labored continuously under adverse terrain (very rough with steep slopes) and weather conditions (ice and snow) and while under fire by the enemy. Their efforts resulted only in one foot bridge (an infantry support bridge and a treadway bridge had been expected as well).

The 12th Infantry completed movement to its new area in the vicinity of Keispelt, closing therein at 0220. Its 2nd Battalion initiated movement at 2000 to Eppildorf and was still enroute at the close of the day.

The 22nd Infantry maintained its defense in the right of the Division's zone of action.

Fit to Fight

From **Diary of Swede Henley—used with permission of his daughters...**

12-14 JANUARY: Still patrolling across Sauer River and trying to keep warm. Went back to Luxembourg and took a bath on Jan. 14th. Whiskey ration came in—drinking—awful.

Hay shed next to CP burned down. Capt. Dampf, Lt. Eidson fought fire like veterans. Hay shed burned down—Col. Goforth moved back to rear CP. Should have seen Dampf telling Colonel about fire.

15 JANUARY: No change.

16 JANUARY: Relieved by 87 Div 347 Inf 3rd Bn and moved into assembly area at Junglinster. Ordered to move out next morning at 0930. Closed into Junglinster at 0100.

17 JANUARY: Moved at 0930 to Beaufort and relieved 1st Bn 11 Inf. 5 Div. Relief completed at 1910.

18 JANUARY: Readjusting position. 8 Inf jumped off to cross river at 0300. 1st Bn faked attack with automatic fire. 8 Inf made nice gains and secured objective.

From **History of the 22nd Infantry Regiment in WWII** *by Chaplain Bill Boice*:

On the 13th of January, plans were formulated, and orders were issued for the 2nd Battalion to clean out the tongue of land formed by a bend in the Sauer River some 2,000 yards below Echternach. A deep wire entanglement covered by automatic fire protected the base of this peninsula, and further re-enforced the defenses of a strong enemy outpost believed to occupy the tongue. Company 'G' was assigned the mission.

By 0400 hours the following morning, January 14th, the Scouts and

Raiders of the 2nd Battalion had blown diversionary gaps in the enemy protective wires. As planned, Co. 'G' further gapped the wire by using bangalore torpedoes, and one platoon passed through the gap, turned southeast, overran several enemy bunkers, and swept almost all the peninsula. The mission complete, Co. 'G' returned to its former defensive positions.

Information was received the next day that CT 22 was to be relieved by Combat Team 347, 87th Infantry Division, then to move to the 5th Infantry Division area some 12 miles west and relieve Combat Team 11. Staff planning and coordination began at once. Liaison contact between relieving units had been established by dark and final preparations were made.

Combat Team 22 was relieved by Combat Team 347 on the 16th of January. The 3rd Battalion, first relieved, moved motorized from its reserve location in Berbourg to the village of Haller and there relieved the reserve battalion of CT 11. The relief of the 1st and 2nd Battalions, their move, and their assembly in the town of Junglinster were delayed. Trucks were late, roads were poor, and the forward positions received a heavy shelling during the relief. The relief was completed at 2200 hours, and CT 347 assumed the responsibility for the front.

The 1st and 2nd Battalions assembled in Junglinster, closing in shortly after midnight. At 0830 hours the complete relief of CT 11 was affected, and by 2100 hours that night it was complete. Because several outposts were forward and could not be relieved until after dark, the delay was necessary. The 22 CT occupied the same defensive positions as had been held by CT 11.

From **War Stories Volume II: Paris to VE Day...**

Frank Douglas, Janesville, WI
Company F, 2nd Battalion, 8th Infantry Regiment
Send Our Bodies Home

From January 17, 1945 on, we were basically in combat. Our rest and recovery was over and the one hundred new replacements were "baptized." We old timers felt sorry for them, but such are the ways of war. On the 18th we were attacking across the Sour and Our Rivers. Company F was going down a rather steep, wooded slope to the river. The engineers were to get us across in boats. Most of the company crossed, but we mortars were bringing up the rear when the Krauts sank the last boat. We moved back up the hillside a bit when the Krauts started working us over with screaming meemies rockets. One exploded in the top of a tree that I was under. I was knocked out cold, and my mortar barrel was cut in half by a big piece of steel. Everybody assumed I was dead. Eventually Chapman came over to get my wallet and watch to send home to the folks. Thank God he did—otherwise I'd have frozen to death during the night.

About this time, Lieutenant Bacon had fallen into the river and was soaked. He told us to hole up in some nearby foxholes, post guards, and wait for him to return from the Battalion CP, where he'd gone to get some dry clothes, if possible. Several hours later, the Germans really shelled the hillside. During the confusion, a tree burst really did a job on Moody. He was really bloody with a cut in his gut area. Bacon came back, found him and Theil, but claimed he couldn't rouse any more of us.

The next day we waited and waited, but there was no sign of Lieutenant Bacon. We stayed the night there again. The next morning Rene and I found a CP and were told how to get back to our company. Captain Reborchek was dumbfounded to see us. He'd been told we were dead. Our suggestion to send our "bodies" home got nowhere, so we went up the street and rejoined the rest of the weapons platoon that had originally gotten across the river.

* * * * *

This is the story of the soon to be husband of Ethel Frances Grimes Williamson, the British War Bride who wrote *"The Love We Shared"* story in the last section. You can see the other part of this story from Bob Williamson, her soon to be husband…

Robert Williamson, Lakeland, FL
Company F, 2nd Battalion, 12th Infantry Regiment
A Million-Dollar Wound?

Our first lieutenant of Company F phoned back and asked what our company was supposed to do. The CO said that we were supposed to take a town. Just the second squad of the second platoon was supposed to take this town.

This was madness, but orders are orders. We waited until dark, and then we moved up to the edge of this town where two of our Sherman tanks had moved up. These tanks left us as soon as we got there and we were left there by ourselves, just twelve men to hold off the Germans. The next morning it got awful hot. The Germans threw everything but the kitchen sink, and I think they threw that, too. The artillery came so close to the two houses we were in that the shrapnel was coming through the windows. Then to top it off, the Germans started attacking, and it really got hot. I was shot in the right wrist from a Burp gun. I had to fire my rifle from my left shoulder. The lieutenant wanted me to go back to the battalion first aid station, but I said I would stay and fight it out with the Germans. The men needed all the help they could get.

I was given orders that I was supposed to stay in this house with our medical man and a few other men. They sent the prisoners for us to take care of. They all came back after taking the town and that night at dusk, another fellow and I took the prisoners over to the MPs. Then this fellow and I went to the battalion aid station and got our wounds taken care of. We were then sent back to the rear, to the hospital in Whexham, England. When I got back to the outfit, the fighting was just about over.

I had been back to the outfit for about two weeks when I got an explosion in the face. I was blind in both eyes. I looked like I had been cut up with a knife. The ambulance took me to the battalion aid station, and they put me on a C-47 plane to Paris. I was put in the hospital, and they operated on my eyes. The doctors saved my left eye. Then I was put on a C-54 plane to the United States to Crile General Hospital in Cleveland, Ohio. This is where I stayed from June to October 12, 1945.

John K. Lester, Stone Ridge, NY
Battery B, 29th Field Artillery Battalion
A Dud 88

I can't remember names of the many small towns and villages that we overtook. Time and places didn't register. I had close calls, saw many of our soldiers, the enemy, and civilians that had been wounded or killed. It really bothered me at first, but after a few weeks it seems that you start to get used to it. You try not to let it bother you anymore. I was very fortunate that I was able to survive the 337 days of combat without injury. One time I thought I was hit bad by German artillery. I was seeking protection under my jeep during a German artillery barrage when I was jarred by a deafening explosion. My head (I was wearing my steel pot) and shoulders were splattered with what I instantly thought was shrapnel.

Thanks possibly to some of the forced labor that had to work in the German munitions factories, I was splattered with dirt and debris. The 88 shell had landed about five or six feet from my jeep. It was a dud and sprayed me with the dirt it had dug up when it landed. If that had been a live shell or had traveled a few feet farther…

I always had to be on the lookout for any signs of land mines. I had to be very cautious at crossroads because the Germans almost always had them zeroed in by artillery fire. Booby traps, open areas, artillery tree bursts, snipers, etc. kept you on the alert at all times.

A radio operator, a second lieutenant, and I comprised our observer party. We alternated with another similar group. When we were back from the infantry, if telephone communication lines were needed, I would use my jeep for running telephone lines from the artillery to the infantry. I had a large reel of wire mounted on the back of the jeep. I would also be involved in keeping the lines operating. One thing I want to mention is that I had a good buddy who was a member of one of the 105mm gun crews. He always had a foxhole ready for me if it was needed when I returned to the battery area. His name was Richard E. Showalter.

Another important member of my unit was William (Bill) R. Cook. He distributed one of the most important things that we looked forward to—mail, and occasionally a package from home. I still see Bill a couple of times a year.

* * * *

Action and stories pick up as we get out of January and into February 1945. Stay with us, we still have three and a half tough months ahead of us—fighting back through the Siegfried Line, Prum, and the pursuit across Germany are coming up.

19 JAN 1945 TO 25 JAN 1945 – D+228 TO D+234

19 JANUARY 1945—D+228: The enemy increased its resistance to our advance. Several pockets of resistance continued to hold out in rear of our forward line. Heavy shelling continued in the vicinity of our bridge sites.

The 4th Infantry Division continued its attack to the north with the 8th Infantry and the 2nd Battalion of the 12th Infantry, capturing the town of Bettendorf and the high ground overlooking the Our river. At 1830, supporting engineers completed a treadway bridge and at 1700, an infantry support bridge was completed in another place.

The 8th Infantry was endeavoring to construct bridges across the Sure river, the need for supporting weapons and tanks on the bridgehead was growing. During the hours of darkness, Company C was successful in reaching positions on its objective. Company B, in conjunction with Company A of the 10th Infantry, cleared all the town of Bettendorf by 0930. Company I was successful in reaching the 3rd Battalion objective. Company K remained in position to the rear along the river line where small pockets of resistance were eliminated. Meanwhile Companies E and F continued fighting in the town of Kleinreisdorf. This action continued throughout the day while Company G remained on the high ground to the north of the village to prevent any enemy reinforcements. In the afternoon, the 2nd Battalion of the 12th Infantry moved to positions preparatory to relieving the 3rd Battalion of the 10th Infantry south of Longsdorf.

The 12th Infantry less the 2nd Battalion, remained in division reserve. The 1st Battalion moved to an assembly area in the vicinity of Eppeldorf, closing therein at 1330. The 3rd Battalion remained in an assembly area at Helmdange.

The 22nd Infantry maintained the defense of its sector.

20 JANUARY 1945—D+229: The enemy resisted stubbornly from its strong points and pockets. In the town of Kleinreisdorf, resistance was determined until sometime during the night when an enemy force of about one company withdrew. At Longsdorf, resistance was also heavy and the town was still in enemy hands at the close of the period. Artillery fire was heavy and constant throughout the period.

The 8th Infantry continued its attack to the north and northeast to seize the high ground overlooking the Our river. The 1st Battalion maintained the positions secured on the previous day commanding the high ground within its sector. The 2nd Battalion succeeded in clearing the town of Kleinreisdorf and continued to advance to secure its objective. The 3rd Battalion sector remained quiet. At 2025 supporting engineers completed a Bailey bridge in the 8th Infantry sector. At 0830 the 2nd Battalion of the 12th Infantry reverted to the control of its parent unit.

The 1st Battalion of the 12th Infantry Regiment attacked at 0845, passing through the 2nd Battalion in the positions which it had just taken over from the 10th Infantry and subsequently the town of Longsdorf was cleared. Just north of the village, the 1st Battalion encountered strong resistance which continued throughout the day. In the interim, a strong combat patrol from the 2nd Battalion moved out at 1000, pushing north, reported the town of Tandel cleared, and continued for approximately 300 yards before meeting two platoons of enemy infantry dug in along the road Tandel-Fouhren. The 2nd Battalion then moved into position in the vicinity of Tandel. The 3rd Battalion moved from its assembly area to the town of Eppeldorf, closing therein at 1100.

The 22nd Infantry maintained the defense and conducted active patrolling.

21 JANUARY 1945—D+230: The enemy continued to occupy emplacements and strong points located on favorable terrain. Mines, booby traps and concentrations of artillery and mortar assisted the enemy in its defense. From the vicinity of Bettel, enemy tanks or assault guns fired on our troops.

The 8th Infantry resumed its attack. The 1st Battalion encountered stiffening resistance. The 3rd Battalion extended its sector and relieved the 2nd Battalion which moved to an assembly area in the vicinity of Bettendorf.

The 12th Infantry continued the attack to the north with the 1st and 2nd Battalions. Throughout the day, the 2nd Battalion encountered heavy artillery, small arms and tank fire. Many casualties were sustained by Companies F and G. Company E captured and cleared enemy from the town of Longsdorf.

The 22nd Infantry continued to defend. Enemy activity in the sector was negligible.

22 JANUARY 1945—D+231: Enemy small arms fire was heavy from the emplacements of the Siegfried Line. The defensive line Malsdorf—Fouhren offered considerable resistance. Tanks were observed in various places.

The 1st Battalion of the 8th Infantry attacked at 1030, utilizing supporting armor and made good progress, capturing some advantageous terrain. The 3rd Battalion continued to improve its defensive positions on the high ground facing the Our river while the 2nd Battalion remained in regimental reserve.

The 12th Infantry resumed the attack. The 1st Battalion began to push patrols down the draw to the northeast toward the Our river in the vicinity of Bettel. The 2nd Battalion in its advance encountered stiff resistance again in the vicinity of Fouhren. The 3rd Battalion advanced rapidly against little opposition. Company I captured and occupied the town of Walsdorf.

The 22nd Infantry continued to maintain defenses. At 1345, the 2nd Battalion was relieved by the 3rd Battalion and moved to an assembly area in the vicinity of Haller.

23 JANUARY 1945—D+232: A force of about 200 enemy and 4 tanks were driven from Fouhren. A counterattack against this town was launched later in the period and was repulsed.

Several counterattacks by enemy infantry were repulsed in the zone of action of the 12th Infantry in the afternoon.

(Sorry, no further information because a page is missing from the After Action Report).

24 JANUARY 1945—D+233: The enemy defended along the same general line as in the previous period. Enemy activity was slight except in the Fouhren and Bettel areas where patrol activity was in effect.

(Sorry, no further information because a page is missing from the After Action Report).

25 JANUARY 1945—D+234: The 2nd and 3rd Battalions of the 8th Infantry Regiment remained on regimental outpost line while the 1st Battalion remained in reserve in the vicinity of Bettendorf.

The 12th Infantry continued to readjust positions facing the Our river. Enemy activity consisted of skirmishes with our patrols during the hours of darkness.

The 22nd Infantry Regiment maintained the defense of its sector while its 2nd Battalion remained in reserve in the vicinity of Haller. During the hours of darkness, the enemy harassed our front line positions with long range machine gun fire and light artillery fire.

From **Swede Henley's Diary**—used with
permission of his daughters...

19 JANUARY: CP located in cellar at Beaufort, in good ole Luxembourg.

20-26 JANUARY: Still in Beaufort—snowing—cold.

From **War Stories Volume II: Paris to VE Day**...*compliments
of Robert Rush, PhD and retired CSM...*

19 JANUARAY: 4th Div gains heights overlooking the Our NE of Bettendorf; in conjunction with 5th Div clears Bettendorf but is unable to reduce strongpoint across the Sauer from Reisdorf.

20 JANUARY: 4th Div, committing RCT 12 on left of RCT 8, continues attack N of the Sauer, clearing angle formed by junction of Sauer and Our Rivers, bypassing Longsdorf to gain positions just N and occupying Tandel.

21 JANUARY: 4th Div captures Longsdorf but is unable to take Fuhren.

22 JANUARY: 4th Div gains ground along W bank of Our River and takes Walsdorf but is still unable to clear Fuhren.

23 JANUARY: Fuhren falls to 4th Div.

24 JANUARY: 4th Div consolidates along W bank of Our River from Vianden to confluence of Our and Sauer Rivers.

26 JANUARY: 4th Div withdrawn from XII Corps and line.

28 JANUARY: 4th Div attached to VIII Corps and enters line between 87th on N and 90th on S, occupying Burg Reuland-Maspelt sector.

From **War Stories Volume II: Paris to VE Day ...**

Sydney Krause, Kent, OH
Company K, 3rd Battalion, 12th Infantry Regiment
Remembrance of a River Crossing

I recall what it was like to be sniped at by an 88 and the reaction of Sergeant M, who shared the scare with me. He was a guy we looked up to as the most combat-savvy and gutsiest man in our Company, known to all as just plain "M," his nickname.

During the drive to push back the breakthrough, we were brought up to a jumping-off point just west of the Our River. Once off the six-by-sixes, we started our trek toward a hill just above the river. We had to trudge across a broad open slope, cursing the knee-deep snow that made it slow going, especially with us being such inviting targets. There we were, a string of lumpy black figures against that white background, minus so much as a sheet for cover. But as we'd drawn no fire half way to the wood ahead of us, we relaxed a bit and just concentrated on making it across. About ten feet in front of me was M, and walking along a fence in the draw below was another line of guys. In among them was the "Mad Russian," who had been hit some time before and was just back from the hospital. He was in high spirits, having put some Schnapps in his canteen so it wouldn't freeze up on him—not a thing we'd want to do going into the attack. Joker that he was, the Russian had spotted some of our light tanks on the road, and, noting their 37mm guns, he laughed, "What do they think they're going to shoot with them—mosquitoes?"

Carrying on the way he was, I thought he'd probably missed Hürtgen. For a long time, none of us had done any laughing.

Before I knew what was happening, I saw M suddenly throw himself down, and I did the same. In that instant the air was split by a familiar ripping sound from an explosion that hit just below us. The shrapnel was zinging inches over my head as I dived into the snow. As we all knew, the 88 was so lightning fast that by the time you heard the report, the darned shell was on you. Down by the fence, the Russian was strangely dancing around in pain, bleeding, his helmet blown off. He threw his M-1 away, and with his arms flailing and knees pumping he was starting to grope his way back when the second round came pounding in. M and I had crunched ourselves further down in the snow waiting for the third round we knew would be coming, after which we made a mad dash for the woods. It occurred to me afterwards that if the 88 rounds were point detonating, we might have been saved by the snow we had cursed.

Having reached the woods, we burrowed down into the snow as deep as we could get and waited, hearts beating in the back of our mouths. You could be vaporized by a direct hit from an 88; it had happened in the mud of Hürtgen. I could just picture that forward observer following us with his binoculars and in a foul German rage growling back to his gunner, "Du Arschloch! Zwei rechts, eins runder, und mach's schnell!" (You @$*=#!, two turns right and one down, and be quick!)

He evidently had something to show the first time around (our Russian probably wasn't the only one he'd snagged), but it must've burned him that we got away. I had the feeling he'd looked into our very faces, tight with fear, and said he had to get those gutless swine.

We didn't have to wait long for the damned things to come bearing down on us like so many banshees crashing through the trees. We shook with each boom as if it was right on us. Thanks to the observer's rage (half a turn down and he'd have had his wish) the shells landed just ahead of us. As we moved on up, M said something to me about how scary it was — an 88 coming after us like that. And, dammit, the way he followed us. This stuff was bad enough without them going for you personally. It made me feel a lot better to know how he took it.

We spent the rest of the day in place, sort of huddled against the snow, and broke out our K-ration while we waited for orders. The sunless air was getting icier by the minute. As luck would have it, I had the lunch ration and, already frosted to the bone, that meant eating a chunk of cold cheese with a lemonade chaser. But I was alive.

At dusk, we finally proceeded up a kind of winding trail and just off the trail at the top of the slope I came on a sight I hadn't seen before—a frozen mound of four GIs curled up on one another. They were the guys in Company I who had taken the 88s intended for M and me. How they got heaped that way, I didn't know. Would they have sort of clung together protectively when they heard the stuff coming in? It was one of those things you tried to put out of your head. I felt bad for them and bad that we had brought it in on them.

It wasn't long before we arrived at the top of the hill above the west bank of the Our. Somebody thought he heard some small arms fire in the distance (a patrol?), which didn't seem to make any sense. We knew where they were, and they us. A kid who had come up with the last batch of replacements said maybe it was guys from Company I wanting to get even. Oh, sure.

We finally made our way down to some well-dug foxholes, nicely built up—German style—with logs on the sides and top. Next morning, at first light, the stuff was hitting all around us. Some thought it might be coming from behind, our own artillery supposedly wanting to soften up the Germans over the river and falling short. Others thought it was the Germans wanting to take some casualties and hold us up. The runner stumbled into our hole, white in the face, holding his stomach. I got the medic, who gave him a morphine shot and put a bandage on him. A piece of shrapnel had made a hole about the size of a half-dollar in the middle of his gut. It scarcely bled. Maybe it was the cold. Anyway, it was the classic million dollar wound. As we moved out, he asked the medic to make sure somebody knew he was there.

When we started peppering the hill on the other side of the river, the most active fire was coming from one of our machine guns. The gunner, "E," a ruddy, hoarse-voiced kid from Minnesota (they liked to have a guy his size lugging the barrel), was about twenty paces to the right of me. The night before we got on trucks we were having a smoke together, and E had taken off his knit hat and was scratching his head with his trench knife. I didn't say anything, but I didn't like the looks of it. Jinxed for sure, I thought.

Anyway, just as we were getting the order to move on over the river, I heard a sharp metallic pop. E had stuffed his canteen inside his field jacket, and a sniper had hit him right in the canteen covering his heart. The red water gurgled out, and he fell face down on the ammo box. I thought I heard the chatter from M's angry grease gun, but it was more likely to be accurate at closer range. The kid said he'd seen a Jerry come out from behind a tree trunk and steady his rifle on a low branch...no telling. M had sprayed in that direction.

The snow was pretty deep on top of the frozen river and our haste only made us stumble all the more as shells started falling in among us, breaking holes in the ice. We stopped firing when we noticed it had become quiet on the bank. Once there, we found that the Germans who hadn't been killed or wounded had taken off. We yanked several of the wounded out of their holes—pathetic-looking guys—wet-faced and calling out in spasms, "Nicht schiessen! Bitte, nicht schiessen! Keine Gewehr." (Don't shoot. No weapons.)

They'd cast off their helmets and their gray uniforms were torn. One guy was bleeding down both sides of his face. Another had a bloody hand over his side, and the third was holding his thigh. I did a little scrounging in their hole. It was not above their comrades to leave a booby trap or two to reward the scrounger looking for a Luger. Next to the helmets and rifles was a half-eaten tin of Baltic sardines—Spruten. The image of it hit me as kind of sad. Nothing else to eat. Sure enough, life in the infantry was as lousy for them as for us. My father had told me he used to eat Spruten—poor man's caviar. Only he had them with black bread and beer.

M was about to march these guys around to the other side of the hill, but he paused as if he had second, second thoughts. He looked around for someone to take these guys back. I didn't want to be the one. That forward observer might get his wish. Besides, I had to be scouting out a hole or digging one, since the Germans were usually zeroed in on a position they'd just abandoned. I went looking for somebody to dig with me and found a lone guy who had apparently lost his buddy. I didn't especially like him, but no matter...He would be OK and besides, he happened to have a strong arm. I was thinking M had better get with it and do some digging of his own.

Later on, when I asked around, I got word that rather than being knocked off trying to take care of those whimpering clowns, he'd had second thoughts. At least that's what I heard. If that's what happened, M had probably considered it a necessity (him for them, potential victims of their own incoming anyway?)—for which it would be hard to fault him.

M was the soul of our Company. He was not a big guy—at most, five-nine, skinny, with a gimpy walk—far from imposing. But he had a forceful personality, and everybody saw him as a natural for his role as leader. Whenever a new second lieutenant came up—which was often enough—M would tell him what he had to know. Wanting to see to it that the Company made its objective and maybe a little more, M was a CO's dream. Eventually it would cost him.

Back in Normandy, he took a burst from a burp gun that got him up the side of the leg, and when the Company pulled back, M lay there in pain behind enemy lines, playing dead until the hedgerow was retaken. Sometime after crossing the Our, the Company had taken a certain town. But a remnant of Germans were holding out in a house at the far end. M and B, his right-hand man, a wiry little squad leader in M's platoon, went out to get rid of that remnant. At about the time M and B called back that they had flushed the Germans out and had taken the house, our artillery came in on it and killed the two of them. But that's another story.

Lon Murphy, Jr., Columbus, OH
Company L, 3rd Battalion, 12th Infantry Regiment
The Fight Goes On

As we advanced toward the Our River in early February, some companies adjacent to us had already crossed the river. They had advanced so rapidly that some German units were bypassed and remained on the west side of the river. We were proceeding down a draw toward a paved road just west of the river. I was at the front of the column with the lieutenant. The temperature was just below freezing, and there was a light snow on the ground. The sky was gray and overcast. The lieutenant, my BAR assistant, the radioman, the company runner, and I crossed the road to the cover of some trees on the other side.

The lieutenant shouted, "Heinies!" and jumped into the road firing his carbine. A German heavy weapons platoon was walking right down the side of the road with their weapons broken down and slung over their shoulders.

The remainder of our column was still coming down the draw. They fanned out to the right and formed a skirmish line coming down the hill. It was all over in a couple of minutes. Germans lay dead and dying in the road. Many were screaming or crying. They never had a chance to fire their weapons. They were taken completely by surprise.

We proceeded through the woods to the river bank. The Our River wasn't a very impressive river. It was narrow and not very deep. The water was murky. It was flowing swiftly with runoff from some melting snow. Ahead and to the right crossing the river was a one-lane bridge with wooden planking.

Our objective was to cross the river and take the large hill on the other side. The lieutenant called for smoke to cover our crossing but was told we had already used our daily smoke ration. Since we had just wiped out a German platoon, the lieutenant decided we should be clear to cross the bridge.

The lieutenant called for the radioman, Carter, and another GI to be the first to cross the bridge. Just as the radioman and the GI cleared the bridge and set foot on the east bank, a machine gun cut them down. The radioman fell to his knees and slumped forward. Carter spun around and ran back to us. The machine gun kicked up dirt around his feet as he ran, coming closer and closer. Carter dived through the air and rolled as he hit the ground with bullets ripping all around him. He rolled into the brush at the edge of the woods. He wasn't touched by any of the bullets. We knew the Germans had the hill defended and the bridge zeroed in.

The lieutenant called for other GIs, including Esposito and me, to go across the bridge next. The first man made it across. Splinters were flying from the wooden bridge as the machine gun raked across it. As I was running, I could see Esposito under the bridge, hanging onto it with his hands and his feet in the water. I decided running across the bridge would mean certain doom.

I ran full speed toward the river about twenty yards upstream from the bridge. When I got to the bank, I leaped as far as I could. I couldn't swim, but the river didn't look very deep. I hit the ice cold water and immediately sunk in over my head. I kept running under water. The current was swift, and I was swept downstream towards the bridge. I managed to get to the east bank about ten yards upstream from the bridge.

I was completely waterlogged. My boots, cartridge belts, bandoleers, pockets, and helmet were all filled with water. I found it very difficult to get up the river bank. I was water soaked and it was very muddy and snowy. I pulled myself up to discover there was an open area to cross to get to the cover of some trees.

I ran as fast as I could but felt like I was in slow motion. The extra weight of the water slowed me down a lot. I heard the machine gun open up. I could see dirt kicking up from the ground in front of me. I saw tracers pass eight inches in front of my eyes. If I had been dry and running one step faster, I would have been dead. I could hear guys from my company cheering for me as if it was a football game. They were shouting, "Run! Run! Run!"

As I ran for the trees, I noticed a four-foot tall wire fence topped with barbs stretched as a barrier between me and the safety of the trees. There was no way I was going to clear that fence as waterlogged as I was. Out of the corner of my eye, I noticed a spot where someone had dug a hole under the fence. I dived for it and made it through.

The machine gun couldn't shoot at me anymore. Due to the contour of the terrain, it couldn't sweep any further in my direction. While all of this was going on, some of our guys were able to set up a machine gun on the west side of the river and lay down some suppressing fire. The German gun fell silent. More GIs got across the river, and we assaulted the hill. By nightfall the hill was ours.

It was a dark, cold, winter night in Germany. I was soaking wet and had no change of clothes, and we were sleeping outside. The guys found a blanket and gave it to me. I wrapped myself up in the blanket and before long I was dry.

Rations had been brought up from the rear by truck but had been left on the other side of the bridge. There was a call for volunteers to follow a guide-wire through the dark, down the hill and back to the bridge to get rations and bring them forward. Each volunteer would get one extra ration. Esposito and Sergeant Roe went along with me.

As we approached the bridge we noticed some soldiers coming down the road. One of them shouted out, "Bist du Deutsches soldat?" (Are you a German soldier?)

"Hell no!" replied one of us, and a firefight broke out.

Apparently there were still some Germans around that we had by-passed in our advance. Sergeant Roe asked for some grenades. We gave him about four grenades, and he crawled off to the right. He tossed the grenades on them, and that ended the encounter. Esposito was badly wounded with two bullet wounds in the side. He was helped to the rear, and I never saw him again. We got the rations and returned to our foxholes.

We had taken the crest of the hill and began to dig in. As we were digging, the Germans counterattacked. They were coming through a hedgerow and then a small clearing. We killed several of them. Company K was on our right flank. I was the last man on the right of Company L and Sergeant Ramsey was the last man on the left of Company K. He was our point of contact. He was about ten feet away from me during the counterattack when he was shot in the head and killed. We walked by some of the German bodies the next morning. It was a gruesome sight. Their eyes were wide open and staring at us. Some of them had frozen with their hands stretched upward and fingers spread apart.

The next morning I was part of a patrol that was sent down the hill again. There was a railroad tunnel through the hill, and it was feared that the Germans would use this to get behind our positions. We were prepared for the worst as we crept into the tunnel.

We encountered no resistance, but we did find the remnants of an abandoned German machine shop. They had excavated rooms into the sides of the tunnel and installed machinery for the manufacture of small arms. Apparently the shop had been evacuated in a hurry. The only German found was a civilian. He was an old man and worked as a custodian in the shop. Some of my fellow soldiers held him at gunpoint and searched him. They went through his personal items and found a pocket watch that looked as old as he was. It was probably given to him by his father or grandfather. I could see the fear and sadness in his eyes and tried to talk the guys out of taking his watch. I was unsuccessful. My heart was filled with sympathy and compassion for the old man.

We made contact with the rest of the company at the east end of the tunnel and proceeded to press the Germans back. Three straight times we advanced against the Germans and were pressed back. Each time, we ended up at the same position we held at the crest of the hill. Sergeant Ramsey's body was still lying there.

26 JAN 1945 TO 1 FEB 1945 – D+235 TO D+241

26 JANUARY 1945—D+235: Small enemy patrols attempting to probe our lines were dispersed by artillery and small arms fire. There was no energetic attempt on the part of the enemy to regain lost ground.

Preparations were begun for movement of the entire division to assembly areas in the vicinity of Trois Vierges.

The relief of the 8th Infantry Regiment by the 319th Infantry of the 80th Infantry Division was initiated at 1800. The relief of the 3rd Battalion was completed at 2200 and of the 2nd Battalion at 2240. Upon completion, the 2nd and 3rd Battalions moved to assembly areas in the vicinity of Bettendorf and Moestroff respectively while the 1st Battalion closed within its assembly area in the vicinity of Medernach.

At 1845, the relief of the 12th Infantry Regiment by elements of the 2nd Infantry Regiment (5th Infantry Division) and elements of the 319th Infantry Regiment (80th Infantry Division) was initiated. Upon completion, the 1st and 2nd Battalions moved to assembly areas in the vicinity of Ernsdorf and Stegen respectively. Meanwhile the 3rd Battalion closed within its assembly area in the vicinity of Gilsdorf.

The 22nd Infantry maintained the defense and preparations were begun for relief.

27 JANUARY 1945—D+236: The 8th Infantry moved to the north to the assembly area in the vicinity of Hoffelt.

The 12th Infantry initiated movement early in the morning and closed in the vicinity of Monnet at 1515.

The relief of the 22nd Infantry by elements of the 317th and 318th Infantry began at 1500. The 1st, 2nd, and 3rd Battalions upon being relieved, moved to assembly areas in Medernach, Waldbillig, and Christnach respectively, and preparations were continued for movement to new assembly areas in the vicinity of Trois Vierges.

28 JANUARY 1945—D+237: The 8th Infantry Regiment began movement from assembly areas at 1200. The 1st Battalion closed in the vicinity of Alster by 2400, the 2nd Battalion in Maspelt and in the interim relieved the 3rd Battalion of the 347th Regiment (87th Infantry Division). The 3rd Battalion did not close until shortly after midnight.

The 12th Infantry initiated movement at 1300 to relieve the 1st and 2nd Battalions of the 347th Infantry Regiment in the vicinity of Burg Reuland. The 1st Battalion closed at 1045. The 2nd Battalion remained in the vicinity of Monnet. The 3rd Battalion closed in the vicinity of Bracht. Patrols were immediately sent forward.

The 22nd Infantry began movement from its assembly areas in the vicinity of Larochette early in the period. By 2215, the Combat Team had closed in the vicinity of Hautbellain.

29 JANUARY 1945—D+238: Enemy front lines during the period existed along the high ground east of the Our river. The enemy employed small delaying forces located near defiles and buildings. These forces were supported by automatic weapons and self-propelled artillery or tanks.

The 8th Infantry attacked at 0830 with the 2nd Battalion and the 1st Battalion echeloned to the right rear, while the 3rd Battalion remained in reserve. Opposition initially was light, and the 2nd Battalion advanced to the high ground southeast of Lommersweiler. The 1st Battalion fought its way into the town of Lommersweiler and at the close of the day, two companies were still fighting in the village. Before daylight, all resistance had been eliminated.

The 12th Infantry attacked in conjunction with CT 8 at 0830 in a column of battalions with the 3rd Battalion in the assault. Resistance was moderate and at the close of the day, the 3rd Battalion was in the newly captured town of Elcherath. The 1st Battalion had closed within the town of Bracht by nightfall. The 2nd Battalion's progress was retarded by heavy artillery fire.

The 22nd Infantry remained in division reserve.

30 JANUARY 1945—D+239: Small enemy forces holding high ground east of the Our river provided little resistance to our advance.

The 4th Infantry Division continued its attack, facing adverse weather and road conditions. Very little progress was made.

The 8th Infantry completed the mopping up of Lemmersweiler. During the morning, the 1st Battalion made little progress while progress of the 2nd Battalion was negligible. The 3rd Battalion remained in reserve.

The 12th Infantry continued the attack during the night of 29-30 January. Companies I and M continued to advance while Company L crossed the Our river and captured the town of Hemmerres by 1945. The 1st Battalion remained in the vicinity of Bracht and the 2nd Battalion in the vicinity of Burg Reuland.

The 22nd Infantry remained in reserve.

31 JANUARY 1945—D+240: In CT 12 sector, the enemy organized positions on the high ground and in the town of Ihrein. The enemy defended high ground and towns employing small arms, mortar, and artillery fire in an effort to delay our advance. Enemy forces after being forced from Elcherath, the high ground, and Einzelborn, withdrew to the east toward Ihrein and Winterscheid.

The 8th Infantry sent a strong combat patrol to the outskirts of the town of Urb. Shortly after first light, the 3rd Battalion passed through the 1st Battalion. Company K captured the town of Weppeler while Company I secured Hill 470. Plans were coordinated to move the 2nd Battalion, motorized, through the 87th Infantry Division's zone of action the following day.

The 12th Infantry cleared the town of Echerath with the 1st Battalion by 1005. Hill 491 was captured, and patrols sent to reconnoiter the next objective. They were repulsed by heavy fire and preparations were made to advance during the hours of darkness.

The 22nd Infantry stayed in reserve.

Notes about logistics: Snow suits could not be procured in sufficient quantities; 3,000 suits were received.

After the reception of 6,600 shoe pacs, all men were equipped with either overshoes or shoepacs.

Casualties in January 1945:
Off—EM
KIA 9—168 (Killed in Action)
MIA 6—74 (Missing in Action)
SWA 6—39 (Seriously Wounded in Action)
LWA 30—482 (Lightly Wounded in Action)
Total 51—763
Prisoners: 346

FEBRUARY 1945

4ID IN GERMANY
RETAKE SIEGFRIED LINE, BATTLE OF PRUM

February starts with our counterattack through the Siegfried Line into Germany. After the January lull, the 4ID is back into strong attack mode, hitting the Siegfried Line, Prum, and points east.

1 FEBRUARY 1945—D+241: Major General Troy Middleton, VIII Corps Commander, presented the DSC to Colonel C. T. Lanham, CO 22nd Infantry. Every third day throughout the month, a total of 16 officers and 55 enlisted men departed for Paris on 72 hour passes.

The enemy was unable to set up a defensive line as our troops continued to advance, meeting only light resistance.

The 4th Infantry Division continued to attack to the north and northeast, advancing approximately four miles during the day. The towns of Ihlren, Urb, Winterscheid, Mutzenich and Schmeiler were cleared of enemy. This advance was made in spite of a very poor road net which at times was almost non-existent. A cold intermittent rain fell during the entire period.

The 8th Infantry Regiment met considerably lighter resistance than during the previous period. Most of the enemy action consisted of small arms fire. The 3rd Battalion captured the town of Urb, continued the attack and captured Mutzenich at 2000. The 2nd Battalion moved motorized through the 87th Infantry Division's sector to their objective at 1640. Both 2nd and 3rd Battalion sent patrols out to the front in order to locate the enemy dispositions.

The 12th Infantry Regiment continued the attack. The 1st Battalion jumped off at 0800 to capture the town of Ihlren and then proceeded north. Company A proceeded on to the town of Schmeiler and then to their next objective. At the end of the period, the remainder of the 1st Battalion was closing on Company A. The 2nd Battalion also jumped off at 0800, following the 1st Battalion through Ihlren and then moved to capture Winterscheid. After Winterscheid was cleared of enemy, Company E moved to the northwest to secure a position along the road. The remainder of the 2nd Battalion closed on the position. Patrols from the 2nd Battalion were sent to Bleialf.

The 22nd Infantry remained in division reserve.

2 FEBRUARY 1945—D+242: The enemy manned hasty defenses and installations in the Siegfried Line and in the town of Bleialf. Direct fire was received from installations (31 pillboxes) in the vicinity of Brandscheid. Enemy resistance showed a sharp increase as our troops attempted to take high ground south of Radscheid.

The 4th Infantry Division was able to make good gains in spite of the weather and poor road conditions. It was very difficult to maintain supply and evacuation routes, and the infantry was obliged to move forward without supporting weapons.

The 2nd and 3rd Battalions of the 8th Infantry Regiment moved forward to the high ground west of Radscheid and Oberascheid. The enemy appeared to be very disorganized. Patrols were sent forward to determine the location and strength of the enemy in the Siegfried Line defenses.

The 2nd Battalion of the 12th Infantry Regiment met resistance at 0900 as they moved forward to the line of departure. The objective of the 2nd Battalion was Bleialf. At the close of the period, Company F had advanced into the northern part of the town against small arms and tank fire. Company E advanced to the southern outskirts of the town but did not enter because of the risk of confusion in the darkness.

The 22nd Infantry Regiment remained in division reserve.

3 FEBRUARY 1945—D+243: It was believed that the enemy had withdrawn into the Siegfried defenses. Enemy resistance continued in Bleiaf until 1020 when the town was taken. No opposition was met as the towns of Oberascheid, Hatenfeld, and Buchet were cleared.

The 8th Infantry continued the attack. The 3rd Battalion assaulted the town of Halenfeld shortly after first light. At 1400 the Battalion had secured the town with no resistance. Company K continued toward Buchet and by 1600, Buchet was cleared of enemy. Elements of the 3rd Battalion remaining in Halenfeld were relieved by the 1st Battalion of the 22nd Regiment and the entire 3rd Battalion was assembled in regimental reserve.

The 12th Infantry continued the assault against Bleialf with Companies E and F during the hours of darkness. Bleialf was entirely clear of enemy at 1015. Patrols advanced to the east and established contact with the 90th Infantry Division on the right and the 8th Infantry Regiment on the left.

The 22nd Infantry displaced forward to an assembly area in the vicinity of Ihrenbruck, closing at 1400. The 1st Battalion relieved elements of the 8th Infantry in Buchet. Reconnaissance and preparations were completed for the attack against the fortified town of Brandscheid.

4 FEBRUARY 1945—D+244: The attack of CT 8 surprised the enemy whose troops were thrown into confusion and forced to surrender after being surrounded and engaged by small arms fire. By the end of the period, most of the pillboxes in the CT 8 sector had been cleared. CT 22 at first advanced against light resistance which increased during the period. Direct fire from tanks was also received.

The enemy outer defense line was penetrated with elements of the 8th and 22nd Infantry Regiments at the same place that the 4th Infantry Division penetrated on 14 September 1944. (Many of our 4ID vets have told me they occupied the same Siegfried Line foxholes in February that they had dug in September).

The 1st Battalion of the 8th Infantry moved against the Siegfried Line fortifications during the hours of darkness. The attack was launched astride the road leading east from Hallenfeld and by first light, the Battalion had their leading elements through the line of pillboxes. A heavy snow storm covered the advance of our troops, resulting in complete surprise of the enemy. The advance was continued by the 2nd and 3rd Battalions passing through the 1st. Numerous small engagements took place as the fortifications were surrounded and overrun.

The 12th Infantry maintained and readjusted its positions in the vicinity of Bleialf and Winterscheid.

The 22nd Infantry advanced with its 1st Battalion in a coordinated attack with the 8th Infantry Regiment. By 2400 the 1st Battalion had consolidated its positions along the ridge line after having succeeded in cutting the northeast-southwest road against light resistance. The 2nd Battalion had closed in the vicinity of Buchet. The 3rd Battalion had passed through the 1st Battalion and attacked toward Brandscheid. It had advanced to within 200 yards of the main crossroads northeast of Brandscheid.

5 FEBRUARY 1945—D+245: The enemy resisted the advance of CT 8 to the northeast with intense small arms, mortar, artillery, and rocket fire which showed an increase towards the close of the period. The enemy displayed a poorly organized defense against CT 22. At about 1500, the town of Brandscheid was occupied by CT 22. Tanks and self-propelled guns were reported operating in the vicinity of Brandscheid.

The attack of the Division was renewed against the Siegfried Line fortifications. By the close of the period, the Siegfried Line had been breached on a front of approximately three kilometers.

The 8th Infantry continued the attack at 0830 to the northeast along the Schnee Eiffel. The 2nd Battalion advanced approximately 800 yards against light resistance. The 3rd Battalion was following after it had been relieved by the 1st Battalion of the 12th Regiment. The 3rd Battalion passed through the 2nd Battalion and continued the attack against increasing resistance of small arms and direct fire weapons. Positions were consolidated on favorable terrain.

The 12th Infantry, except its 1st Battalion, maintained and adjusted its positions.

The 22nd Infantry attacked at 0745 with its 3rd Battalion against Brandscheid. The enemy at a crossroad defended stubbornly in pillboxes and bunkers but during the afternoon, this resistance was cleared up and the attack continued into Brandscheid. Initially the fighting in town was very heavy but with the aid of supporting tanks and tank destroyers, the resistance was overcome. The 1st Battalion which was following turned to the east and secured the high ground west of Sellerich. After the capture of Brandscheid, the 90th Infantry Division was ordered to relieve the 22nd Infantry in the town in order that the 4th Infantry Division could continue the attack towards the important road center of Prum.

6 FEBRUARY 1945—D+246: Against CT 8, the enemy defended particularly from crossroads employing infantry weapons supported by self-propelled guns, rockets, and mortar fire. Shortly before first light, a counterattack of 400 enemy hit elements of CT 22 in Brandscheid. This attack was repulsed, and 160 prisoners of war were taken. CT 22 continued the attack to the east clearing Hontheim, Sellerich, and Herscheid against strong enemy delaying action.

The 8th Infantry Regiment maintained defensive positions with the 1st Battalion. The 2nd Battalion advanced without resistance approximately 1500 yards. The 3rd Battalion cleared all enemy in its zone and set up a defensive position at the crossroad.

The 12th Infantry remained in division reserve.

Before the relief of the 3rd Battalion of the 22nd Infantry Regiment could be affected; the enemy launched an attack against Brandscheid in an attempt to retake the town. The 3rd Battalion suffered heavy casualties but was successful in repulsing the enemy. It was finally relieved at 1430. The 2nd Battalion jumped off in the attack at 1205 against light resistance and captured Hontheim at 1745. The 1st Battalion jumped off in the attack at 1200 against light resistance and captured Sellerich, Herscheid, and the high ground.

7 FEBRUARY 1945—D+247: A special quota of one officer and four enlisted men was received from VIII Corps. This officer and enlisted men were to be returned to the United States on detached service for sixty days in the purpose of touring war materiel production plants and informing workers of the vital need for their continued all out efforts. LT Col Thomas A. Kenan, 22nd Infantry was selected. One of the four enlisted men selected from the 4th Division Artillery was a member of the 29th FA Battalion. **This soldier was the only remaining artilleryman who fought in WW I with the 4th Division.**

CT 8 encountered light resistance in attacking Warscheid. Resistance increased considerably in the vicinity of Gondenbrett. Enemy opposition to the advance of CT 22 was light, consisting of small arms, automatic weapons, artillery, and mortar. At 1440, three separate counterattacks were launched by the enemy. The first attack consisting of tanks and infantry came from the vicinity of Niedermehlen and advanced toward Hill 553. Initially, our troops were forced from the hill but regained it late in the period. The second attack occurred at 1450 when an unknown number of enemy attacked from Steinmehlen. This attack was repulsed by artillery. At 1610 an estimated company of infantry and three tanks attacked toward Obermehlen. At the close of the period, our troops in the town had been reinforced by armor and the counterattack had been repulsed.

The 8th Infantry Regiment jumped off in the attack with the 1st Battalion at 0330. Initially, only light resistance was encountered, and the battalion advanced toward the town of Gondenbrett. The stiff enemy resistance in the town held our troops in the outskirts at the close of the day's fighting. The 2nd Battalion moved off at 0430 and succeeded in capturing Warscheid without opposition. The 3rd Battalion remained in regimental reserve.

The 12th Infantry remained in division reserve.

The 22nd Infantry jumped off in the attack to the southeast at 0425. Company E captured the hill and at 1445 received a counterattack from the vicinity of Wiedermehlen which forced them to withdraw approximately 400 yards. Company F immediately counterattacked and drove the enemy from the hill. During the counterattack, Company G moved forward and captured Obermehlen. At 1500, Company G repulsed a counterattack. The 1st Battalion advanced against light resistance to capture the high ground and at 1500, it repulsed a counterattack coming from the vicinity of Steinmehlen.

8 FEBRUARY 1945—D+248: Brig Gen Blakeley presented the DSC (Distinguished Service Cross) to Major Howard C Blazzard, 22nd Infantry.

The enemy defended from hastily constructed field fortifications and from buildings. In the northern sector, the enemy offered slight resistance to the advance of CT 8, however, in the vicinity of Gondenbrett, a more determined stand was made. CT 22 received three counterattacks during the period. All three attacks were against our forces in Obermehlen. The first two which occurred at 0830 and 0910 consisted of an estimated company of infantry in each case. The third attack at 1030 was made up of tanks and infantry. All three attacks were repulsed without loss of ground. An unknown number of tanks were heard in the vicinity of Weindsheim at 1700.

The Division gained very little ground during the day, because of the increased amount of artillery, numerous small local counterattacks, and adverse weather conditions which resulted in very poor road conditions.

The 8th Infantry continued the attack with the 1st Battalion on the right and the 3rd on the left. The 1st Battalion fought for the town of Gondenbrett throughout the day and succeeded in clearing all the town except for a few houses. The 2nd Battalion continued the advance and was on its objective by dark. The 3rd Battalion relieved the 2nd Battalion which moved to Washeid to reorganize. An increased amount of enemy artillery was reported during the latter part of the day.

The 12th Infantry continued to hold favorable terrain on the right flank of the 8th Infantry before being relieved by the 8th Infantry. Then the 1st and 3rd Battalions of the 12th Infantry moved into position on the right flank of the Division. The 1st Battalion of the 22nd Infantry was relieved by this movement at 1915.

The attack of the 22nd Infantry Regiment with the 2nd and 3rd Battalions began at 1300. The 2nd Battalion after repulsing several small counterattacks cleared the town of Obermehlen.

From Swede Henley's Diary—used with permission of his daughters...

1 FEBRUARY 1945: Moved from Hullange to Oudler. Saw a lot of Jerry equipment knocked out by Air Corps. Snow melting and everything muddy and nasty. Planning to go back into Siegfried again at same place as before.
- Russian news sounds good—hope they break Kraut 6 back.
- The dirty bastard.

2 FEBRUARY: In Oudler—sweating out the move tomorrow. Ordered to move by truck for Bliealf.

3 FEBRUARY: Crossed IP at 0745. Route—Oudler—Grufflengen—St. Vith—Schonberg -Bliealf—arrived at 1200. Received orders to patrol and occupy Bucket tonight. Bn closed in Bucket at 0100. Patrolled into Siegfried line. Found Krauts disorganized. CP located in Bliealf.
- St. Vith is no more—a complete wreck.
- Kraut counterattack messed things up.

4 FEBRUARY: "A" Company assaulted line and was on objective at 1000. Bn got on objective by 1200. 3rd Bn passed thru and closed on part of objective by dark. Casualties extremely light. Captured or killed heaps of Krauts.
- Same methods, plans and tactics retook Siegfried Line.
- Regiment took same position in line on September 13, 1944.

5 FEBRUARY: 3rd Bn attacked and occupied Brandschied. 1st Bn covered left flank and they attacked pillboxes about 100 yds from Misert on road to Sellerich. CP in pillbox in Siegfried. Lt. Brooks killed by mortar shell.

6 FEBRUARY: 1st Bn jumped off on the attack for Sellerich, Herscheid, and high ground to east. On objective at 1600. 3rd Bn on being relieved in Brandschied were counterattacked and overrun. Position retaken and captured 200 prisoners. Jerry shooting a lot of 6 barrel mortar.
- Kraut Kate after big secret move we made — "Glad to see our friends the Green Hornets back with us again."

7 FEBRUARY: Ordered to continue the attack for objective Number 11 (1200 yds SW of Niedermehlen). Secured objective at 1500 — 2nd Bn on left flank was counterattacked from Niedermehlen and driven off of hill 553. Jerry tanks and infantry were in the attack. We counterattacked and retook hill. Jerry shooting 6 barrel mortars and tenie fire. Every place is hot as hell. Still raining. Captain Williams wounded, and Captain Martin took over. Lt. Gottschalk wounded. Communication so far stinks, except by radio.

8 FEBRUARY: Still catching hell from the Jerry. The dirty bastard is shooting artillery air burst at us and that dam 6 barrel mortar. Didn't gain much ground today.

From Chaplain Bill Boice's **History of the 22nd Infantry Regiment in WWII…**
REPEAT PERFORMANCE – SECOND PENETRATION OF THE SIEGFRIED LINE

The great German counter-offensive led by Von Rundstedt had been smashed in the past month of action. In reality, the Ardennes offensive had ended about the middle of January. Since then, the American forces had been reorganizing their lines and preparing to push the Germans back across the Rhine River. During the German drive, the enemy was able to again secure their Siegfried defenses. The Germans were now sending troops into the line and preparing to defend the Homeland. Because the Allied Armies had previously penetrated the Siegfried Line, the Germans found the deficiencies in the structure of the Line and were making every effort possible to correct these.

Even though there was snow on the ground on the 1st of February, spring was in the air. Days were longer and the sun shone brightly. Our aircraft were seen daily leaving their misty trails through the clear skies as they streaked for the German interior. It was a glorious sight; thousands of huge bombers, supported by fighter planes, roared continuously; bomb-run formations developed before one's eyes; and enemy ack-ack fire specked the sky. As the Combat Team moved eastward along the highways, it was possible to see the destroyed German vehicles, horses, and trains that the Air Corps had previously wiped out.

The defeat of the counter-offensive brought with it initiative, renewed courage, and a surge of power. The troops now realized that they could crush the enemy in spite of what he planned. On the eastern front, the mighty Russian war machine had begun to plow across the captured countries. It was becoming more apparent each day that Hitler had exerted his main potential reserves in the Ardennes strike and had suffered severely in this great loss.

On February 1st, Combat Team 22 was assembled near Hautbellain, Luxembourg, Combat Teams 8 and 12 were pushing on toward the Siegfried defenses near Bleialf to secure a jump-off line for an assault to be made on the Siegfried Line. Minor adjustments in assembly areas were made during the day; the 1st Battalion staged forward to Oudler, Belgium; the 3rd Battalion shifted its position slightly to within the town of Huldange; and the 2nd Battalion remained near the town of Hautebellain. For the remainder of this day and the next, all units of the Regiment remained in place.

The 44th Field Artillery was hurriedly repairing their gun tubes and mounts for the oncoming attack. They had fired well over 100,000 rounds by this time and the artillery wanted to give the best possible support to the infantrymen. The forward observers from the 44th were relaxing a bit from their strenuous jobs. In the field artillery it is the forward observer and his radio party who have the front line duty to accomplish, for they are continuously with the forward-most elements of the rifle companies so that they can direct effective artillery fire whenever called upon. Oftentimes the field artillery radios were the only sets in operation and all vital communications were transmitted through them.

During the night 2-3 February, reconnaissance parties checked the routes forward to new locations. The Combat Team moved out that day at 0745 hours in the order 1st Battalion, 3rd Battalion, Regimental Headquarters, and then the 2nd Battalion. The Regiment moved via Hautbellain, Oudler, St. Yith, Schonberg to forward assembly areas in the proximity of Schweiler, Germany.

Attacking elements of the Division (Combat Teams 8 and 12) made excellent progress, and Bleialf was captured that afternoon. In view of this, one company of the 1st Battalion, 22nd Regiment, moved eastward to secure Buchet, the proposed jump-off point for the Combat Team's attack on the Siegfried Line. By dark, word was received that patrols of the 8th Regiment had entered Buchet uncontested. The entire 1st Battalion, therefore, moved into Buchet before midnight. Combat Team 22's leading elements were now within a thousand yards of the first belt of Siegfried Line pillboxes. That night a strong 1st Battalion patrol moved out to investigate the Line.

Company C, 4th Engineer Battalion, Company C, 70th Tank Battalion (medium tanks), and Company B, 610th Tank Destroyer (90mm. self-propelled) Battalion were all attached to the Regiment at 1500 hours.

The decision was made, in planning the attack, to again assault the Siegfried Line from Buchet. From the eastern edge of town covered approaches led to within three hundred yards of the woods concealing the first Siegfried fortifications. This route of approach was north of the regimental boundary, but, upon request, Division provided a temporary north boundary to include this approach. The scheme of maneuver was almost identical to that used over the same ground the 14th of September 1944; an attack from Buchet in a column of battalions.

As D-Day was set for February 5th, the CT planned to use the 4th of February to complete last minute preparations, assemble the battalions well forward, open roads for the supporting armor, organize field artillery positions, and reconnoiter the Siegfried Line and its approaches. However, at 0003 hours information was received that CT 8 (north of CT 22) would continue their attack and push on into the Line before dawn; and, in addition to this, a First Battalion patrol from CT 22 reported that they had penetrated the Ormont-Brandscheid Road and had found the first line of bunkers unoccupied, the second line unoccupied. In order to take advantage of these unexpected developments, Col. Lanham, at 0505 hours, ordered the First Battalion to attack at dawn.

Little time remained to alert the troops. At once company officers awakened their commands and briefed the troops on the situation. The men arose from their wet foxholes in the misty fog to quickly eat a K ration and then meticulously checked their weapons. Those men who had been here before knew the Siegfried Line was going to be a tough fight. This time they had orders not to penetrate the Line, but to breach it and drive to the open plains that stretched west of the Rhine.

The 44th Field Artillery Battalion hastily alerted the remaining men of the gun crews and opened additional ammunition crates. Forward observers with the infantry companies hurriedly organized their parties and made preparations to move forward.

Then as the first rays of light broke over the wooded horizon came the command, "Let's go, men; this is it!" The First Battalion moved out in a column of companies proceeding along the corduroy road that led to the first line of bunkers. Contrary to the previous reports, all pillboxes were found occupied and defended, but resistance varied from moderate to light. Just before the assault on the first pillbox, the old veterans who had been here before saw, still hanging in a tree, the trousers of a man who had stepped on a mine in September and had been blown to pieces. It was an eerie feeling; this sudden remembrance of a comrade who in a matter of a split second had been annihilated. This might happen to anyone anytime now.

The Germans knew the war game and meant business. By noon this battalion had pierced the first line of fortifications and had cut the main northeast-southwest road into Brandscheid. One rifle company was in position forward with the other two companies echeloned to the right and left rear.

The 3rd Battalion assembled in Buchet and followed directly behind the 1st. As the column of men moved through Buchet, they were forced to step over a pool of blood and pieces of flesh left behind where a man had been sliced to ribbons by flying shell fragments. The Jerries were well zeroed in on Buchet and could lay down artillery and mortar barrages any place in the town. The 81mm mortar platoons, trying to dig in within Buchet, were continuously subjected to artillery fire and suffered heavily in casualties.

By the middle of the afternoon, the 3rd Battalion had passed through the 1st Battalion, turned south, and continued the attack along the main road. After severe fighting through the heavy woods, the battalion, without benefit of armored support, advanced and gained control of the crossroads at Meisert. It was now quite apparent that the Germans in their brief offensive had begun improvements on the Siegfried Line. There were to be found connecting trenches in front of each fortification, added camouflage, repaired embrasures, and foxholes intermittently spaced about each of the bunkers.

The 1st and 3rd Battalions dug in and secured for the night; the 1st Battalion outposted the ridgeline just east of the Ormont-Brandscheid Road; the 3rd Battalion remained at the Meisert crossroads. The initial penetration of the Siegfried Line had been successful, and casualties were comparatively light.

Before the 3rd Battalion could successfully capture Brandscheid the next day, the roads had to be repaired and supporting armor brought forward to the assault companies. That night the entire 2nd Battalion and the 4th Engineers worked to clear the road. Colonel KENAN and Captain BURNSIDE, the Battalion Commander, and Executive Officer respectively, worked knee-deep in the half-frozen mud alongside the men and officers in an effort to get the armor through. It had to be done and quickly. Before dawn February 5th, the road was clear.

Four hours later, the 3rd Battalion attacked Brandscheid with two platoons of 90mm self-propelled tank destroyers, and two medium tank platoons attached. Capt. Lee led Item Company and Capt. Roche led King Company in the assault. A dense fog had settled over the landscape, and confusion arose. In the midst of the confusion, the two companies were able to secure their assigned pillboxes. Col. Lanham came down shortly after the attack got underway in order to observe the operation. Capt. Roche said that he didn't have time to explain to the Colonel what was going on. The Colonel must have sensed this, as he remarked, "Captain, don't let me stop you."

As the Battalion moved across the crossroads at Meisert, fighting became intense and eleven supporting, protecting, pillboxes were nullified. By the middle of the afternoon, the strongly fortified town of Brandscheid had been taken, and mopping-up operations continued.

Before dark, Lt. Perkins, with his platoon from Co. 'K', moved to the left flank of the company sector to occupy several pillboxes in that area. By dark, he had deployed his squads into the vacated bunkers and his defense for the night was organized, Lt. Perkins and his platoon were in a very precarious position, as was learned the following day.

In the meantime, the 1st Battalion echeloned to the left rear and followed the attack of the 3rd Battalion. In order to establish a defensive left flank, the 1st Battalion moved approximately 2,000 yards to the southeast along the Bleialf-Sellerich Road. The 2nd Battalion moved from its reserve location in Buchet to occupy the 1st Battalion's former positions.

Late that day, CT 22's zone of action was shifted to the north, and the directions of attack shifted southeast toward Prum. Brandscheid was now in the sector of the 90th Infantry Division. Preparations were made immediately for the relief of the 3rd Battalion by elements of the 90th Division.

The relief of the 3rd Battalion in Brandscheid began at 0445 hours on February 6. As the relief was being made, a strong enemy counterattack, estimated to be five hundred men, hit Brandscheid from the southeast. Co, 'L' which had been completely relieved, immediately counterattacked. A close-in bitter struggle ensued as the enemy, in the confusion of the relief and the blackness of the night, infiltrated throughout the town. Casualties mounted, and the relief was becoming more confusing by the minute. The only usable road into Brandscheid was a mass of vehicles—some moving forward, some to the rear. By 0900 the situation was stabilizing. Lt. Perkins and his platoon had been completely surrounded and were fighting to drive the Germans back. By the middle of the afternoon the relief was complete, with the exception of the one platoon.

At 0845 hours, in spite of the situation in Brandscheid, the 1st and 2nd Battalions of CT 22 attacked abreast, 2nd Battalion on the left, along the axis of the Bleialf--Sellerich Road. The 1st Battalion captured Sellerich, Herscheid, and the high ground just east of the two towns by late afternoon. The 2nd Battalion met light resistance and by dark had taken Hontheim and the high ground just east thereof. The 3rd Battalion tied in to the right rear of the 1st.

Having taken the high ground east of Herscheid, Sellerich, and Hontheim, the Combat Team again attacked toward Prum on the 7th. The attack was to move through the three towns of Obermehlen, Niedermehlen, and Steinmehlen. In these three towns one of the war's hardest localized battles was to be fought.

A platoon size combat patrol from Company 'E' moved out before daylight to seize the dominating high ground west of and between Niedermehlen and Obermehlen, called Objective 11. The remainder of the company followed, and the objective was secure by 0830 hours. Co. 'G' by-passed Objective 11 to the north and, after eliminating machine gun and small arms resistance, took Obermehlen. Further advance by the 2nd Battalion was prevented by enemy counterattacks. Co. 'E', on Objective 11, was hit by an infantry tank attack from the direction of Niedermehlen and was forced to withdraw from the hill. A similar force hit Company 'G' in Obermehlen, but no ground was lost. Shortly before dark, Co. 'F' attacked through Company 'E' and recaptured Objective 11, from which they could re-enforce the fires of Co. 'G' in Obermehlen.

At 1000 hours the 1st Battalion moved out to seize the ridge line approximately 1,000 yards west of Niedermehlen, Objective 14. Favorable progress was made, and the ridge was secured by 1430 hours. At once preparations were made to attack Steinmehlen to the southwest. An enemy counterattack, even though repulsed, stopped any further advance of the 1st Battalion.

Because of the heavy enemy pressure on the 2nd Battalion, the 3rd Battalion moved two rifle companies behind the 2nd to secure and to serve as a counterattacking unit.

After dark that night, Lt. Perkins, who with his platoon was still isolated, sent out a two-man patrol to find out who held the town of Brandscheid. This patrol after many narrow escapes, found a CP of the 90th Division and returned to the platoon with this information. Before dawn the next day the platoon escaped back through the lines and later joined their company near Sellerich.

The terrain surrounding Prum, Germany, consisted of huge rolling hills which afforded long distance observation of troop movements. From the high ground just east of Sellerich, it was possible to look down into Niedermehlen and up to the hills surrounding Prum. All roads running into this area could be observed by the enemy for miles and as a result vehicle travel was greatly restricted. A vehicle driver in this type of terrain had to be a calm, collected individual. Oftentimes drivers were expected to travel alone to secure ammunition or rations and to return to the front lines. When sitting in a vehicle with the motor running, it is impossible to hear the deathly whistle of incoming artillery; mortar barrages creep down like a swarm of bees; direct fire weapons find no better target; and snipers easily pick off the occupants. There are no safe jobs in the infantry, only varying degrees of comparative safety.

On the 8th of February, the objective, the German communication center of Prum, still had not been taken. The 3rd Battalion was to relieve the 2nd Bn. on Objective 11, seize Niedermehlen, and be prepared to continue the attack to the high ground about three hundred yards west of Prum, known as Objective 8. The 2nd Battalion was to push out from Obermehlen and seize the high ground east of Niedermehlen, Objective 15. The 1st Battalion, from its position on the ridge line overlooking Niedermehlen, was to support the attack by fire.

Due to constant enemy counterattacks from the town of Niedermehlen, the 2nd and 3rd Battalions were not able to make an advance. The 1st Battalion was relieved of its objective, Steinmehlen, by elements of the 12th Regiment and reverted to regimental reserve in the rear of the 2nd Battalion.

A story from **War Stories Volume II: Paris to VE Day**…

Denver Sayre, Wildomar, CA
Battery C, 44th Field Artillery Battalion
100-Yard Dash

On February 5, 1945, the 3rd Battalion, 22nd Infantry Regiment, with tank destroyers and medium tanks attached, attacked Brandscheid. I was attached as a Forward Observer for the 44th Field Artillery Battalion. Pea-soup fog came in. As we advanced, a large number of pillboxes were taken, and by late afternoon Brandscheid had fallen. We were to be relieved by the 90th Infantry Division and move to a different sector early the next morning. That night we bedded down in a large stone house on an intersection in the center of town. Early the next morning, just before first light, my buddy, Forward Observer Robert Smith, and I took our sleeping bags out to a parked jeep about one hundred yards from the building. Just as we were throwing the bags in the back of the jeep, what seemed like a hundred Jerries came out screaming from behind other buildings and sheds.

They were yelling, "Surrender, surrender!"

We had left our carbines in the building and were standing there unarmed. I believe we broke the record for the hundred-yard dash without a shot being fired. Once inside, all hell broke loose. It seems about five hundred enemy troops had taken advantage of the dark foggy night and amid the confusion during the relief, they had infiltrated our lines. Bob and I wanted to get to one of the windows to help ward off the attack, but the lieutenant told us they already had too many riflemen at the windows. He sent us to the basement to assist in caring for the wounded. The firefight lasted for about three hours until the tank crews got enough cover to man the tanks. We almost immediately heard cries of "Comrade! Comrade!" from the ones ordering us to surrender. As we left, we observed the sickening sight of bodies strewn about, some run over by tanks. I give thanks to this day that we made that dash to safety.

9 FEB 1945 TO 15 FEB 1945 – D+249 TO D+255

This was the week that the 4ID fought the tough battle to take and hold Prum, Germany.

9 FEBRUARY 1945—D+249: At 0620 the enemy launched an attack of company size to capture the high ground in the vicinity of Walcherath. This attack was repulsed with heavy losses to the enemy. Hermespand was then taken by our troops against moderate resistance. Along the east bank of the Prum river, the enemy increased its resistance with strong dug in positions, supported by tanks. At 1305 the enemy counterattacked with two to three companies of infantry supported by five or six tanks. The enemy employed also heavy caliber antiaircraft fire and artillery in this effort. This engagement was still going on late in the period. Against CT 12 the enemy defended Steinmehlmen with an estimated two companies. At 1630 the enemy also counterattacked CT 12 with an estimated 200 troops. This attack was repulsed with heavy losses to the enemy.

The attack to the east to capture Prum and the bridges along the Prum river was continued at 0730.

The 8th Infantry repulsed a small counterattack against its 1st Battalion. The 3rd Battalion jumped off and captured Hermespand against light enemy resistance. The 3rd Battalion continued its advance and before dark had Companies I and L across the river on the high ground. Throughout the day, fighting continued in Gondenbrett but by dark all enemy had been cleared from the town.

The 12th Infantry continued its attack at 0730. The 1st Battalion objective was Steinmehlen which was not entirely cleared of enemy at the close of the period. The 3rd Battalion on the left received a counterattack against Company L which resulted in some hard fighting. The 2nd Battalion moved forward to Herscheid.

The 22nd Infantry was unable to advance forward because of a blown bridge. The 2nd Battalion assisted the engineers in building foot bridges. The attack began at 0835 with the 1st Battalion leading and the 3rd Battalion following in column. The 3rd Battalion in conjunction with the 2nd Battalion attacked Wiedermehlen which was eventually captured at 1800 after some hard fighting. The 3rd Battalion repulsed a counterattack made of tanks and infantry, from Taffel at 1300.

10 FEBRUARY 1945—D+250: The enemy opposed CT 12 from the east bank of the Prum river with some enemy troops still holding out in Niederprum. At 0900 the enemy launched a counterattack in an attempt to dislodge CT 8 from the high ground northeast of Hermespand. This attack was repulsed without loss of ground. Several counterattacks were launched against CT 22. In each case the enemy thrust was contained without loss of ground. At 0915 elements of CT 12 assisted CT 22 in throwing back a counterattack. At 1105, Company A CT 12 dislodged the enemy from Steinmehlen. At 1830 the enemy blew the bridge in the face of the advance of CT 12. The railroad opposite Niederprum was reached against small arms fire and direct fire from heavy weapons. Enemy armor, for the most part in a defensive role, was observed between Prum and Weinsheim. A total of fifteen to twenty tanks were operating in this sector.

There was very little ground gained by the division during the day. Enemy resistance stiffened in front of Prum. Low hanging clouds over Prum made dive bombing on the enemy tanks impossible.

During the early morning hours, the 1st Battalion of the 8th Infantry closed into the town of Hermespand and prepared to capture Dansfeld. The 3rd Battalion was counterattacked by enemy infantry and tanks during the morning. This counterattack was quickly repulsed. The 2nd Battalion cleared some houses in Walcherath.

The 12th Infantry continued its advance to seize the town of Ndr

Prum and the bridges in the vicinity. The 1st Battalion succeeded in clearing Steinmehlen of enemy at 1105. In the late afternoon, the 3rd Battalion was reported directly across the river from Ndr Prum.

The 1st and 3rd Battalions of the 22nd Infantry encountered stiff resistance and made only small gains during the day.

11 FEBRUARY 1945—D+251: At the close of the period the enemy defended along the line Kleinlangenfeld—Willverath—Dausfeld—thence along the east bank of the Prum river to Watzerath. Some enemy troops were still holding out in Prum at the end of the period. At 0815 the enemy counterattacked CT 8 in the vicinity of Willwerath, using two infantry companies supported by an initial artillery preparation, tanks, and assault guns. This attack was repulsed without loss of ground. The enemy was reported withdrawing from Prum, possibly to defend the high ground east of the town. Several armored vehicles were seen, and tank fire was received in the vicinity of Hermespand.

The 4th Infantry Division readjusted positions throughout the period and made preparations for a defensive line along the west bank of the Prum river from Watzerath to Olzheim.

The 8th Infantry Regiment withdrew all elements of the regiment east of the Prum river beginning at 0400.

The 12th Infantry Regiment initiated a withdrawal along the Prum river in the vicinity of Niederprum. The readjustment of positions was continued throughout the day.

The 22nd Infantry Regiment readjusted its positions by side slipping units to the left in order to assume responsibility of the new regimental sector. In the afternoon, the 3rd Battalion began its advance to the southeast into Prum and at the close of the period, all companies were in the western portion of the town conducting a systematic search of all the buildings.

12 FEBRUARY 1945—D+252: The enemy launched a counterattack consisting of at least three companies towards Olzheim at 2115. This attack was initially supported by heavy artillery barrages and subsequently strengthened by tank, mortar, and rocket fire. Until 1200 close contact was maintained with the enemy but our forces suffered no loss of ground. In consolidating the town of Prum, CT 22 met resistance from small, isolated groups emplaced in cellars and behind debris formed by demolished buildings. Direct fire from enemy tanks and assault guns was received in the vicinity of Hermespand and Olzheim.

The Division improved its defensive positions along the Prum river.

The 8th Infantry reported that the attack launched by the elements of the 9 Panzer Division was under control at 0500 and that the enemy made no penetration.

The 12th Infantry continued to readjust and improve positions, its 3rd Battalion being in reserve.

The 22nd Infantry continued mopping up operations in Prum and by 1320 it was reported that the town was clear of organized enemy resistance. Enemy artillery, mortar, and direct fire weapons continued to shell Prum throughout the day.

13 FEBRUARY 1945—D+253: Except for a ten man patrol which approached Hermespand at 0420, the enemy remained entirely defensive in CT 8's sector. Early in the period a small counterattack by 25 infantrymen approached Prum from the north but this force was repulsed with no loss of ground.

The 4th Infantry Division continued to improve the defensive positions and rotated battalions on the main line of resistance. Enemy activity was mainly made of harassing and interdictory fires.

The 3rd Battalion of the 22nd Infantry continued mopping up enemy resistance in and around Prum.

14 FEBRUARY 1945—D+254: The enemy defended along the same line and remained for the most part unaggressive, utilizing all available time in improving its defenses and fields of fire. A counterattack consisting of 150 men armed with bazookas, machine guns, and mortars was directed towards Prum from the north. This attack started at 0700 when the striking force crossed the Prum river and advanced south parallel to the Prum river. The mission of this force was to recapture the eastern part of Prum and establish a bridgehead there. The attack was repulsed with no loss of ground. Tank fire was received in Olzheim during the period.

15 FEBRUARY 1945—D+255: A letter was received from VIII Corps authorizing an allotment of British Awards and Decorations.

The enemy continued to defend the same line and sent patrols west of this line in order to probe our positions to determine strength and disposition.

The 4th Infantry Division continued to organize and defend within its sector. Forward elements received intermittent artillery fire throughout the period.

From **Swede Henley's Diary—used with permission of his daughters:**

9 FEBRUARY: 2nd Bn attacked hill 15 (E of Obe)—driven back by counterattack at night, 1st Bn held hill 10 but was relieved and went into reserve.

10 FEBRUARY: Col. Kenan relieved—Major Henley took over. 2nd Bn in Obermehlen. 1st Bn went for hill 15—got objective and fought off counterattack. 2nd Bn attacked south to take town Niedermehlen and get 3rd Bn rolling. Objective taken with infantry and tanks at 1750 after 10 minutes T.O.T. (time on target) artillery preparation—5 Bns of artillery.

11 FEBRUARY: 1st Bn attacked east for 5 points (1 mile NW of Prum)—secured 5 points but could not advance any further. 3rd Bn took hill 8, 2nd Bn secured left flank. Ordered to go into defense position. Casualties heavy—knocked out 11 Kraut tanks and SP guns. Killed a lot of Krauts.

12 February: Prepared defense position along Prum river—north of Prum—CP located in Gonderbrett.

13 February: In same position

14 FEBRUARY: In same position

15 FEBRUARY: Relieved 3rd Bn in Prum and went into defense along forward edge of Prum along river. Relief completed at 0200 on the 16th.

From Chaplain Bill Boice's **History of the 22nd Infantry Regiment in WWII** ...

Summary: In the nine days of offensive action, 4th through 12th of February, CT 22 had advanced approximately 10,000 yards through the Schnee Eifel; this advance included the breaching of the Siegfried Line, taking of Brandscheid, and moving over extremely rugged terrain to seize the Eifel focal point of Prum. Adverse weather conditions prevailed throughout the period; there was either snow or rain and sometimes both; and roads, either icy or muddy, were invariably mined. Initial enemy resistance was from the 326th and 340th Volksgrenadier Division, and 1082nd Security Battalion. However, after the Siegfried Line had been breached, the 2nd Panzer Division was rushed to this sector on February 7th and 8th. In the hard fight for Niedermehlen on the 9th of February, our Second and Third Battalions destroyed the First Battalion, 304th Panzer Grenadier Regiment of the Second Panzer Division. The CT took 12,373 prisoners during these operations; and approximately 150 Siegfried pillboxes and bunkers were reduced.

From the 13th to the 26th of February the Combat Team maintained defensive positions west of the Prum River. For the most part, combat activity was limited to consolidation of positions which overlooked the town of Prum and provided direct observation on the streets of the city. Consequently, movement in the town was restricted, and resupply had to be carried on during the hours of darkness.

This is a rather short, but tough and important part of our WWII history. There are no stories from this timeframe in my War Stories book, and the

12th Infantry Regiment history is very sketchy during this time period. Also, as a reminder, nobody ever wrote the history of the 8th Infantry Regiment in WWII, so I don't have history from the 8th to report. My guess is action was so tough through the Siegfried Line and taking Prum that our 4ID Soldiers were too busy to write it down, and or wanted to forget it.

Don't give up on me — the rest of February, March, and April 1945 are full of action. Those who have been with me since I started this when the 4ID was training in England in February 1944, I appreciate your interest in the accomplishments of our great Soldiers of the 4ID during the fight across Europe.

16 FEB 1945 TO 22 FEB 1945 – D+256 TO D+262

16 FEBRUARY 1945—D+256: At 1600 the enemy launched an attack of company strength towards Hermespand. One of our observation posts was surrounded and cut off at about 0430. A patrol sent to investigate found that the enemy had occupied the observation post.

The 4th Infantry Division continued to defend within its sector.

One attack of company strength against Company C of the 8th Infantry was repulsed at 1600.

The 2nd Battalion of the 22nd Infantry was in the process of relieving the 3rd Battalion in Prum at the close of the period.

17 FEBRUARY 1945—D+257: Brig. Gen. Blakeley presented one DSC and 26 Silver Stars to personnel of the division and attached units.

The enemy defended along the same line and except for a small arms demonstration in the vicinity of Prum between 1000 and 1045 confined its action to harassing small arms fire and interdictory mortar and artillery fire.

The 8th Infantry Regiment with the 1st and 2nd Battalions on the line made preparations to demonstrate by fire to divert attention from the attack of the 90th Infantry Division.

The 12th Infantry continued to occupy the defensive line with the 1st and 3rd Battalions.

The 22nd Infantry maintained defensive positions with the 1st and 2nd Battalions.

18 FEBRUARY 1945—D+258: Information was received from G-1 VIII Corps, requesting names of officers who desired to take infantry training or to attend a refresher course in infantry tactics at training camps. A negative report was submitted. (This is the funniest item I've seen yet in the After Action Report. Don't think they needed the extra training after what they'd been through for 258 days).

Light harassing and interdictory shelling by the enemy continued.

Each combat battalion sent a combat patrol out as a diversion from the attack of the 90th Infantry Division.

A new boundary between the 4th Infantry Division and the 90th Infantry Division became effective at 2000 and there was also a shifting of regimental boundaries due to the new right division boundary.

19 FEBRUARY 1945—D+259: The enemy continued to employ harassing small arms, artillery, and mortar fire. Noise of tracked vehicles was heard on the Weinsheim-Dausfeld road between 0300 and 0400.

The 4th Infantry Division continued on a defensive mission while the remainder of VIII Corps continued the attack against the Siegfried Line. Active patrolling was conducted by the infantry regiments and ambush patrols were established on the west bank of the Prum river.

20 FEBRUARY 1945—D+260: A small arms demonstration on the part of the enemy in the vicinity of Hermespand occurred during the early morning. Another fire demonstration was laid down by the enemy at 0600 opposite CT 22. The enemy in CT 12's area, although badly disorganized, put up a stubborn fight and were finally cleared from the woods southwest of Pittenbach.

The 8th Infantry improved its defensive positions along the Prum river on the left flank (north) of the Division. A very heavy concentration of artillery was received in Olzheim during the morning.

The 12th Infantry improved its defensive positions on the right (south) flank of the Division. The 2nd Battalion continued to mop up the area in the vicinity of Pronsfeld.

The 22nd Infantry established ambush patrols during the hours of darkness. It maintained and improved its defenses in the central sector of the Division.

21 FEBRUARY 1945—D+261: The enemy employed light patrol activity and light harassing artillery and mortar fire along the front lines.

The 4th Infantry Division remained on the defense. The three regiments continued to rehabilitate the personnel of the reserve battalions.

22 FEBRUARY 1945—D+262: Light patrol activity and light harassing rocket, mortar, and artillery fire constituted the enemy's main effort as it continued to defend east of the Prum river.

All regiments conducted patrolling within their sectors.

From **Swede Henley's Diary—used with permission of his daughters…**

16-20 FEBRUARY: Still in Prum. Jerry shelling hell out of us. Knocked down part of my CP. Shell knocked down rear end of CP—too close for comfort. Had to close Ladies Ready to wear Dept. to basement.

21 FEBRUARY: In Prum dodging Jerry's artillery.

22 FEBRUARY: Moved from 2nd Bn to 1st Bn as Ex. Officer. Maj. Kemp took over 2nd Bn CO.

Fit to Fight

From **War Stories Volume II: Paris to VE Day...**

Elmer Klaus, Columbus, OH
HQ, 22nd Infantry Regiment
Shangri La

As you know, not too many war stories were fun and games, especially if you were in a line company and would always be looking for ways to stay alive for another sunrise. The following incident has some humor and took place in the vicinity of Brandscheid, Germany in February 1945—just beyond the Siegfried Line, and the weather was terrible.

I wasn't feeling well while on guard duty, and the sergeant of the guard said we were short of men, and I had to continue on duty. Shortly thereafter, I doubled up in pain and was transported to an aid station, which was a huge barn that looked like Shangri La to me. It was away from the misery of the front lines, and I was hoping I could stay there for a few days. No such luck. I was diagnosed as having the GIs, given medicine that had a horrible taste, and, lo and behold, I was back at the front the next day—all cured. I found out the miracle drug was Kaopectate—'nuff said.

Milt Bremer, (Deceased) Sherman Oaks, CA
Company K, 3rd Battalion, 22nd Infantry Regiment
The Fly of Your Pants

In the early months of 1945, we were following a tank unit, making sure there were no pockets of the enemy hiding out where they could harass us. I was assigned a hill and the area on the other side. With my men spread across about seventy-five yards, we started up on what seemed an easy task. However, the hill was covered with wet leaves, and it was like climbing a sheet of ice. We had to dig in our heels and rifle butts to make any progress. Even though the weather was cool, we were soon drenched with sweat.

I kept saying, "Come on, let's keep moving. It's all downhill on the other side." I was hoping there was some level ground where we could catch our breath. Eventually we did reach the crest and discovered to our dismay that it dropped away as precipitously as the slope we had just climbed. To stand required that you use one foot, ankle bent, on each side of that knife-blade ridge. If there had been any enemy around, we could have been picked off like targets in a shooting gallery.

Finally I gave the order to start down. The descent was worse than the climb with men sliding into each other or sprawled on a sled of wet leaves. When we hit bottom we sat, breathing hard, while I decided to find an easier way to return to the company CP. One of the men scouting around came back with word of a railway tunnel. So, off we went. Near the exit at the other end, some of the men discovered a stack of wooden cases. It turned out to be a cache of beer. Of course, there was no way to keep the hot and thirsty men from sampling. There was one problem though: as one of the men put it, the beer was pretty good, but if you were going to drink it, you better do it with the fly of your pants open.

Merle P. Davies, New Baltimore, MI
Company F, 2nd Battalion, 12th Infantry Regiment
Christmas Hymns

Sometime after the battle for Nieder Prüm, Germany, I was 'vacationing' in an unremembered military hospital. Each morning the major commanding the nurse brigade would sneak into the wards, one by one, swagger stick under her arm. She was on the prowl for any erections among her male domain. Down the rows of beds she would proceed, smacking down all who "stood" in her way. After your first experience with this lady in the morning, it became our first activity of the day. One patient challenged her as to the purpose of this mission, to which she replied, "I do not want my young nurses to be embarrassed."

During a Christmas Eve service, the choir and parishioners were to join in the singing of the hymn, *"Silent Night, Holy Night."* As the first words of the selection were delivered, my mind flashed back to another evening many years ago. A group of "still alive" soldiers were singing those same words. In unison with that hymn was the delivery of a fire mission by a nearby artillery battery, interlaced by the sounds of a firefight off in the distance. What a contradiction of ideas and feelings in those times. That particular experience and many others were purposefully blocked from my mind for over fifty years. The singing of a Christmas hymn triggered a long-forgotten experience. The months of November and December have always produced at least one nightmare relating to those turbulent times. I was once called a "foxhole hero," but I consider myself only a survivor.

Stan Tarkenton, Virginia Beach, VA
Company M, 3rd Battalion, 22nd Infantry Regiment
Taking a Break

Battalion Reserve is a holiday with capital letters. In simple terms, that rare occasion means you and your guys may have ten or twelve or more hours off from the war. The adjoining battalions continue with the nasty war business while you may have the chance to catch up on some sleep. Sure! Or, you may even have the opportunity to sew a few stitches in the rags you are trying to keep together...sometimes, a shave.

There were not any quick trips to paradise to soak up a few rays, but there were some precious few hours away from the shooting war. I remember seeing the movie, *Meet Me in St. Louis*, in a barn in France while in reserve. It was a fair movie. Not really, but it was a diversion to escape from the reality of the times.

On one brief reserve, we were so far in the rear there were rear echelon-type people walking all around us in the town. These GIs looked like real soldiers compared to our ragtag crowd. Some even carried weapons, which I doubted they knew how to use. They wore nice, new, clean-looking uniforms; they shaved and probably took a bath every week or so. They were impressive looking. They seemed to act as though they thought they knew what they were doing. Our guys were wearing an assortment of tattered and torn clothes, muddy and cruddy looking. Our boots looked like they had been rejected by the Goodwill people. We were not only dirty to look at…we were dirty. Since shaving was an almost unknown luxury, everyone sported ugly beards which had the appearance of something thrown out of the Persian glue pots.

One of the rear echelon dandies approached us asking, "Hey, do you guys want to take a bath?"

"Bath?" was the response, "Hell, yes!" I could not remember the last time I had soap and water on my scroungy hide. "Where can we get this bath?"

Directions were given. Second invitations were not necessary. Even though my feet were worn and hurting, I hurried along with everyone else. On the way, I was thinking about how much I was going to lie back in the tub with plenty of hot water and soapsuds.

Since it was one of those blue-cold days without sunshine and with dreary winds blowing off the snow, I decided I just might spend the rest of the war reposing in that hot tub of water. I could almost feel the heat again, already. In our obvious eagerness, one would have thought someone was giving away free beer.

We arrived en masse at the park, but I did not see a bathhouse. What's this? Someone's idea of a joke? There were no bath facilities in this park. Some of those clean-uniformed jokers were prowling around in the park area. One of our men corralled one of the official-looking, clean-uniform types, with chevrons up and down his sleeves, saying, "Hey, Jack, where's the freaking showers?"

"This is it," he beamed proudly.

"Yeah? This is what?" demanded one fairly short-tempered individual.

"This is the shower," he said, pointing to a series of overhead pipes that had the appearance of an extended child's gym set—without the swings. One man assisted the clean-uniformed man by grasping him about his necktie, saying, "Listen to me, you smart ass. We came over here to take a shower. You start talking "perlite-like," or I may just kick your butt inside out."

"I told you," he says, "This is the shower."

"WHAAAAT?"

The sergeant-type goes on to explain they would heat the water via some kind of a heating contraption, and the warmed water would be pumped through the pipes while we washed under the flow. "Are you nuts! It's freezing out here!" shouted another man. It really was a blue-cold day.

"It will not be cold under the warm water," the sergeant-type allowed.

"What about our clothes?" someone said. "We sure as hell can't strip down in the buff here in the middle of this town. Them are Krauts walking all around out there. Some of them are women, too."

"They don't care, if you don't," Sarge said. "Heat up the water!" After about a half hour, the sergeant calls, "OK, boys, your shower is ready. Here's some soap and towels."

So about twelve of us pile our weapons in a heap and promptly shuck off our dirty rags down to our bare-assed skin. We soap up our beards and our hides under the warmed water flow while trying to see the color of our skin again. Some of the German females walking by the park smiled or outright laughed and pointed. We sure as hell did not care. "Eat your heart out."

(Editor's Note: Stan Tarkenton was one of my favorite WWII vets — we became good friends. He was happy to be a PFC assistant machine gunner. He told me he delivered ammo to the machine gun and then got as far away from it as he could since he knew it was a big target for the Krauts. He took more ammo to the gunner when it was needed. After WWII, he went into banking and became an Executive Vice President with the Bank of Boston.

One time at a 22nd Infantry Regiment Society reunion back in 1996, a retired Vietnam era one-star general, who had been a Lt. Colonel in Vietnam, took exception that I didn't treat him like a general. (In veterans' organizations — rank is left at the front door. We are all equal as veterans). I pointed to Stan Tarkenton, explained his assistant machine-gunner PFC job in WWII and his Executive VP job at Bank of Boston — probably equivalent to a three-star general — and said, "Who deserves more special attention, you or Stan."

He got my point — and never showed up at one of our reunions again.

Good riddance. And Stan was at each reunion religiously until just before he died, never pulling rank on anyone. I still miss him. I'll have another story or two from Stan Tarkenton before we finish this book).

23 FEB 1945 TO 28 FEB 1945 – D+263 TO D+268

23 FEBRUARY 1945—D+263: The defensive mission of the 4th Infantry Division remained the same and the engineers completed reconnaissance of the Prum river.

24 FEBRUARY 1945—D+264: No aggressive activity on the part of the enemy was reported, except light artillery and rocket fire.

The 4th Infantry Division Artillery with the 610th Tank Destroyer Bn and the 377th AA Artillery Bn fired interdiction and harassing fire on enemy front line positions and crossroads in the rear areas.

25 FEBRUARY 1945—D+265: Artillery, rocket and mortar fire was light, and no enemy patrols were reported. At 1020 a direct fire weapon was reported east of Prum firing into CT 22's sector.

Active patrolling was conducted by the 4th Infantry Division throughout the period.

26 FEBRUARY 1945—D+266: Opposite CT 12 and CT 22 the enemy remained wholly defensive. Stray aggressive enemy patrols operated in the central and southern part of CT 8's sector.

Considerable vehicular movement to the east tended to substantiate the belief that some elements opposite the 4th Infantry Division were being relieved.

The 12th and 22nd Infantry Regiments reported that the enemy was unusually quiet along the entire sector.

27 FEBRUARY 1945—D+267: The enemy continued to maintain its hastily prepared line of field fortifications with no aggressive action. At this time it was believed that the 5th Parachute Division with a total estimated strength of 1,000 men constituted the opposition in the 4th Infantry Division zone.

All three regiments sent out two patrols each at 0300 to contact the enemy as diversionary demonstration for the 87th Infantry Division attack (despite the fact that the attack had finally occurred at 1500 on February 26.)

During the day, the VIII Corps issued a field order which required the 4th Infantry Division to launch an attack to the east on February 28 at 0515.

The 8th and 22nd Regiments conducted extensive reconnaissance in preparation for the attack.

Elements of the 12th Infantry were relieved by the 6th Armored Division during the night of 27-28 February. The 12th Infantry in turn relieved the 2nd Battalion of the 22nd Infantry Regiment in the vicinity of Prum. As soon as the 6th Armored Division and the 22nd Infantry progressed sufficiently to cover the front of the present defensive position, the 12th Infantry was to assemble in division reserve.

28 FEBRUARY 1945—D+268: VIII Corps informed the Divisional HQ that the presentation ceremony for the award of the Distinguished Service Order (British Decoration) to Lieutenant Colonel Arthur S Teague, 22nd Infantry, would be in Spa, Belgium, 8 March 1945. Recommendation for this award was submitted in June 1944.

The attack of CT 8 met strong small arms fire in some areas, but the enemy was unable to prevent the penetration of its line and the capture of positions to the rear. Small groups of enemy by-passed during darkness continued to hold out throughout the period. Approximately five counterattacks were made against Company G commencing at 1100. All attacks were repulsed. CT 22 met determined resistance early in the period and several small counterattacks were reported in its sector. Resistance encountered by CT 8 and 22 consisted of heavy small arms, automatic weapons, hand grenades, artillery, rocket, and mortar fire.

The 8th Infantry attacked to the east at 0515 with the 3rd Battalion on the left and the 2nd Battalion on the right while the 1st Battalion remained in reserve. Initially good progress was made by the 3rd Battalion. Company I after reaching the high ground east of the town of Olzheim was pinned down by artillery fire and remained in this position throughout the daylight hours. Company K meanwhile captured the town of Kleinlangenfeld at 1550. The 2nd Battalion advanced slowly through the wooded area east of Hermespand and was counterattacked by an estimated company of infantry at 1125. This attack however was quickly repulsed. At the close of the period, the 2nd and 3rd Battalions continued preparations for resumption of the attack while the 1st Battalion was moving forward.

The 12th Infantry remained in reserve. The 1st Battalion moved to the town of Prum preparing to relieve Company I during the hours of darkness. The 2nd Battalion remained in Brandscheid. The 3rd Battalion initiated a firing demonstration at approximately 0800 in conjunction with the 22nd Infantry Regiment's attack.

The 22nd Infantry attacked at 0515 with the 3rd Battalion on the left and the 1st Battalion on the right. Both assault battalions met stiff resistance and encountered numerous mine fields. By 1540, Company I had succeeded in clearing the town of Dausfeld and the remainder of the Battalion consolidated on the high ground to the northeast of the town. In the interim, the 2nd Battalion established a bridgehead across the river due east of Prum and was counterattacked at 1600 but this attack was repulsed. During the afternoon, the 1st Battalion moved to the river line between the 2nd and 3rd Battalions, effecting contact with both units. By the close of the period, a bridgehead was secured by the regiment approximately 3 ½ kilometers in width and in some instances almost a kilometer in depth.

Notes about logistics: The road net within the division and VIII Corps sector continued to deteriorate rapidly because of the sudden thaw and because of extremely heavy traffic. As one road broke down, traffic was diverted to alternate roads which became progressively worse. In some cases it was necessary to remove the rails from railroad beds and utilize these roadbeds for vehicular traffic. Traffic was held to a minimum, only supply and other essential vehicles, and the speed limit was reduced to 15 miles per hour for all vehicles. To further reduce the burden of the road network and to facilitate the supply of the division units, service elements were moved forward rapidly.

Because of the rapid advance of the enemy in their breakthrough of December, great quantities of materiel of all types had been abandoned throughout the entire area. An extensive salvage program was initiated, and large quantities of ammunition and equipment were recovered.

Numerous dead, both friendly and enemy, which had been left by troops formerly in the area were also discovered.

Casualties for the month of February 1945:
Officers Enlisted
Killed in Action 15 255
Missing in Action 1 76
Seriously Wounded in Action 10 95
Lightly Wounded in Action 50 847
Total Casualties 76 1273
Prisoners: 2,401

Rather than including my normal stories here, I want to make this a special edition to prove the point of the black rubber bracelet I have worn since March 2005, given to me by the wife of the 4/4 Aviation Battalion Commander of 4ID when they were deployed to Iraq. It says simply…FREEDOM ISN'T FREE.

Since D-Day on 6 June 1944, we have read about hundreds (thousands) of 4ID Soldiers who have been killed or wounded during the nine month fight (thus far) across Europe. I am going to finish this month's history with the story of one specific Soldier who was killed in action on 28 February 1945. To his Family, including twin sons who were two years old when he deployed to Europe in November 1944, he was the light of their lives. To the statistics of WWII, he was another KIA.

Robert O. Babcock

IN MEMORY OF PFC ORVIS D. SENEAR

In 2012, I received an email from Jerry Senear, a former 4ID medic who served at Fort Lewis, WA in the early 1960s, before we deployed to Vietnam. He finished his Army service in 1965, shortly before I arrived at Fort Lewis to train for Vietnam. I have never met Jerry in person, but he and I have become great friends over email since his first contact with me. He was asking what information I, as 4ID historian and president, could provide him on 4ID actions on 28 February 1944, the day his father, PFC Orvis D. Senear, was killed in action while serving with Item Company, 3rd Battalion, 22nd Infantry Regiment of 4ID.

Interestingly, I knew Tom Reid, who was company commander of I/3-22 IN on that date. Tom had stayed in the Army, served in Korea and Vietnam, retired as a Colonel, and lived in Atlanta where he and I became good friends when I took over in 1995 as President of the 22nd Infantry Regiment Society. Tom was the first person I ever interviewed when I became a Founding Official Partner of the Veterans History Project, part of the Library of Congress. I also had the honor of speaking at Tom's funeral when he died.

To make a long story short, Jerry Senear and I did a lot of research about his father, Orvis Senear, and located a WWII historian in the Netherlands, Nick Trommelen, who helped us tremendously. Among the three of us, we pinpointed the place of his father's death down to an area the size of half a football field. Following is the story Nick Trommelen wrote in 2014...

ASN. 37594638
AUG. 23, 1916 / FEB. 28, 1945
Written by Nick Trommelen, a Netherlands Citizen

Orvis D. Senear was born on August 23, 1916 in Champlin, Minnesota (USA) and was married to Jeanette I. Senear. They had twin sons, Lawrence and Gerald, before Orvis was drafted in the Army in 1944. Something unusual for a married man and father of two children to be drafted into the Army, but in 1944 things were different due to the shortage of men in the US Army and therefore Orvis was one of many to answer the call.

On November 24, 1944, he was assigned to the 22nd Infantry Regiment, 4th Infantry Division — Item Company. At this time this division was active in the battle for the Hürtgen Forest near the town of Aachen, where a bloody fight was fought in the woods against a stubborn enemy. Despite the tremendous losses in his unit, Orvis D. Senear managed to get through alive, and in early December his outfit was send to Luxembourg for a period of rest. The time of well-earned rest was only short, on December 16th the Germans launched the Ardennes offensive, and the 4th Infantry Division was once again in the midst of all the action, the Battle of the Bulge…

With Pruem taken (in mid-February), the advance in the 4th Infantry Division's sector had come to a halt. The halt was mainly because of supply difficulties that were a result of the bad weather conditions which had turned the supply roads into mud. The period that was to follow has often been labeled as the "Prüm-Stellung"—or the "Pruem river line." During this period the 4th Infantry Division had taken up positions basically west of the Pruem river and the Germans did so as well on the east side. The sector of the 4th was roughly from the village of Olzheim in the north to the village of Niederpruem in the south. The northern sector was appointed to the 8th Regiment, the 22nd in the middle, and the 12th in the south. The 3rd Battalion / 22nd Regiment of Orvis D. Senear took up positions in the wooded area called Tettenbusch and Wolfsschlucht, directly north of Pruem and opposite the villages of Dausfeld and Weinsheim.

In the remaining days of February 1945, the supply roads were being improved, outposts were set, and the Pruem valley was being patrolled. Some enemy patrols were encountered as well, but most of them were observed in time and were chased away. By the end of February, a small enemy counterattack was received and repulsed in the 8th Infantry Regiment's sector, but everything was nonetheless quiet.

On the 27th of February, company commanders were being informed that a new attack was planned, as was Captain Tom Reid, company commander of I Co. His objective was to cross the Pruem river the next morning, take the village of Dausfeld, and proceed towards Weinsheim. He would advance together with L Company who had the objective of seizing the hill of Dausfelder Hardt. Engineers would work on the blown bridges over the river near Pruem itself so that the attack on Dausfeld and Weinsheim could be supported by tanks and armor.

In the early hours of the 28th, an artillery barrage on the expected enemy positions began in the 22nd and 12th Regiment's sector. The 8th Regiment's attack was scheduled an hour or so earlier without artillery preparation, this to surprise the enemy. When the artillery barrage in the 12th and 22nd Regiment's sector concentrated farther east, the men of I and L company descended from the Tettenbusch and Wolfsschlucht heights and advanced towards the mill of Dausfeld, north of the village itself. This objective was easily taken, and the first enemy POWs were captured. But meanwhile, the German troops were aware of what was going on.

As the mill of Dausfeld was secured, L company moved up the steep slope of the hill Dausfelder Hardt, where it encountered well dug in enemy forces. Hand grenades had to be used to drive the Germans out, and casualties were high. L Company's attack proceeded slowly and with many difficulties.

Meanwhile, I Company moved south to take Dausfeld itself, the approach towards the village was without cover, and the road leading from Hermespand was taken as a route to try to access the village. I company set in to attack the village but immediately ran into fierce opposition. Many casualties fell due to hand grenades and even rocket / mortar fire was received by the attacking men. The Germans who defended the village belonged to the 3rd Battalion of the 15th Fallschirmjäger Regiment under the command of Oberleutnant Sniers, which had every approach towards the village covered. After the first attack failed, a shock troop was sent along the road leading from Hermespand to try to access the village again. The shock troop was completely annihilated within minutes. Tanks and armor couldn't be brought up where the engineers were being prevented to work on the bridge due to sniper and rocket fire.

Meanwhile, the situation of I Company was getting critical, with the enemy well-fortified in the houses of the village and in the hills of Dausfelder Hardt and Huenert overlooking the entire Pruem valley. Two PFC's, Ervin Bupp and Donald Seger volunteered to silence a German machinegun nest at the edge of the Dausfelder Hardt but were killed while trying. Around 1130 hours, a tank made it through the Pruem river on a shallow spot and made its way to the village, and a half hour later, more were to follow.

Thanks to the aid of the tanks who made it through, a new attack on Dausfeld could be made. The remaining men of I Company used the cover of the tanks to get a foothold in the village, and not much later the first house in Dausfeld could be taken. With that, 14 Germans were captured, and four American prisoners were freed. At this time, the enemy forces were retreating from Dausfeld towards the hill of Huenert, and at 1550 hours, a message to the 3rd battalion came that the village was in American hands. Leaving many dead and wounded behind, one of them being PFC Orvis D. Senear. At Dausfeld on the 28th, his platoon by-passed some enemy forces without knowing, the enemy opened fire with small arms and ambushed the nearest man, who happened to be Orvis. He was hit in the left chest and died instantly.

In total, 10 men of I company were killed in action, and 7 were wounded on the 28th of February 1945 at Dausfeld.

The remains of Orvis D. Senear were found on the 1st of March 1945 by PFC Bricco. His body was brought to Foy, Belgium where he was buried on the 5th, together with a copy of the New Testament. In 1948, the graves in Foy were being relocated, and his last remains were sent back to the US and his wife. He was reburied with military honors on April 23, 1949 at the Fort Snelling National Cemetery: section C-6, site 8161.

Written July 11, 2014.

References used:

After action reports 4th Infantry Division, February 1945

Die Woche der Entscheidung, Klaus Ritter

Bis zum bitteren Ende, Johannes Nösbusch

KIA & WIA list I Company

US Army human resources command
Own knowledge & archives

Orvis Senear's sons hardly remembered him. His Family did not talk about him. One of the twins died before his brother Jerry started researching the death of their father. As a result of the intensive work done over several years, Jerry Senear, Nick Trommelear, and I (Bob Babcock) were able to find a lot of information about Orvis Senear's death, including narrowing his death site down to no more than half a football field.

Jerry hopes to visit Dausfield, Germany one of these days, as do I — it hasn't happened for either of us yet. There is much more to this story and how we learned what we have learned.

Every Soldier who died in the fight across Europe has a story similar to this one. He is not a statistic, he was a husband, son, father, uncle, grandson, friend. His death left a big hole in a Family, and the community he came from.

Let us never forget that **FREEDOM IS NOT FREE**—many Americans have died to preserve it for us, ever since the first shots were fired in 1775 at Lexington and Concord. Every day, America's military forces are ready to make the ultimate sacrifice to preserve our country, our way of life, and prove that **FREEDOM IS NOT FREE.**

* * * * *

As you would expect, I'm melancholy after going back and pulling up the notes and pictures from the research Jerry, Nick, and I did back in the 2012 through 2015 timeframe.

We will resume the attack across Germany and will go back to our normal first person stories that I have. Please share this with your sphere of influence.

Prisoners and guards duck heavy Nazi shelling, 28 February 1945

German Prisoners of the 5th Parachute Division at Dausfelder Mühle. Note how young the German prisoners look. This and the picture above were made on 28 Feb 1945. From this precise area (Dausfelder Mühle), Item Company, 3-22 Infantry attacked towards Dausfeld. PFC Orris Senear was probably KIA only 50 to 100 meters from this location.

PFC Orvis Senear with his twin sons prior to deployment to Germany in Fall 1944

MARCH 1945

4ID IN GERMANY
PURSUIT OF RETREATING GERMANS

1 MAR 1945 TO 7 MAR 1945 – D+269 TO D+275

It was on 2 March 1945, that Colonel John Ruggles took command of the 22nd Infantry Regiment. COL Ruggles joined the 22nd Infantry Regiment and 4ID in 1943 as CO of 1-22 Infantry. He moved up to Regimental XO (fought from D-Day to VE Day with the Regiment) then to Regimental CO until early 1946 when the 4ID and 22nd Infantry Regiment were temporarily inactivated after WWII. Ruggles was commander of troops at the ceremony at Camp Butner, NC when the 4th Infantry Division's colors were temporarily cased, to be reactivated in 1947 and to remain active without interruption until today and beyond.

    I asked MG (he retired as a Major General) Ruggles if I could have his helmet that he wore in WWII after he was gone. He quickly said yes. It is one of my proudest possessions and will one day be given to an Army or the 4ID museum to preserve. It was his helmet that was used to mix soil samples from all 4ID battlefields from WWI to today when we dedicated our 4ID monument at Arlington National Cemetery in Washington, DC in 2000. His helmet was present when we dedicated the 4ID monument at the National Infantry Museum at Fort Benning (now Fort Moore) in 2011. And the picture of me holding the helmet was taken at the Atlanta History Center on Memorial Day 2013 where we once again used it to mix soil from Army battlefields (along with the helmet of COL Rick Lester's dad, who landed on Omaha Beach) to spread across the Veterans Monument at the Atlanta History Center.

1 MARCH 1945—D+269: A directive was received from VIII Corps changing the Paris pass quota from 16 officers and 55 enlisted men to 15 officers and 70 enlisted men.

The enemy attempted to consolidate hasty positions along the best defensive ground. The enemy line ran generally along the east bank of the Prum river. In opposing the attack of CT 8, the enemy launched two counterattacks, one at 1110 and the other at 1130. Both attempts were weak and unsuccessful. Against CT 22, the enemy remained defensive with some increase in mortar and rocket fire. There was no aggressive action on the part of the enemy confronting CT 12. Enemy artillery fire continued to be heavy with especially heavy fire falling in the vicinity of front line positions around Olzheim, Hermespand, and Prum.

Several enemy tanks were observed in the vicinity of Weinsheim. Enemy units in contact were elements of the 5th Parachute Division.

The 4th Infantry Division continued the attack with the objective of securing a bridgehead at Willwerath-Gondelsheim-Fleringen-Remmersheim and Nieder Prum.

CT 8 continued the attack at 0645. The 1st Battalion sent Company B to mop up the town of Willwerath while the remainder of the battalion continued clearing up the woods east of Willwerath. The 3rd Battalion continued mopping up the woods in their sector. The 2nd Battalion was occupied throughout the day mopping up the woods, east of Hermespand. A very stubborn enemy was encountered, and infiltrations made it necessary to continuously move through the woods and apprehend the small groups.

CT 12 moved the 2nd Battalion from Brandsheid to Prum and across the river to a position in the woods northeast of Nieder Prum. Plans were made to attack on 2 March to clear Nieder Prum and the high ground surrounding the town. The 1st Battalion previously assembled in Prum, relieved at 1824 hours the 2nd Battalion of the 22nd Infantry after having cleared the woods east of the town of Prum. The 3rd Battalion continued to maintain defensive positions.

CT 22 continued the attack to the east at 0640. The 2nd Battalion was given the mission of clearing out the woods on the east bank of the river due east of Prum.

2 MARCH 1945—D+270: Colonel Charles T. "Buck" Lanham CO 22nd Infantry was relieved from assignment to the 4th Infantry Division and assigned to the 104th Infantry Division as Assistant Division Commander. Lieutenant Colonel John F. Ruggles assumed command of the 22nd Infantry Regiment.

The enemy achieved some success in organizing a new line of resistance before CT 8. The town of Weinsheim, on the south flank of this new line, presented a well-organized strong point supported by direct fire artillery. Willwerath was cleared by our troops during the period while Weinsheim continued to be stubbornly defended. The enemy's main weapon in opposing the advance of CT 22 was a series of well dug-in machine guns. Elements of CT 12 advanced against a determined delaying action on the part of the enemy.

The 4th Infantry Division continued the attack. The resistance by enemy troops throughout the day was fanatical and progress by the Division was limited.

CT 8 attacked at 0830 to capture the town of Weinsheim with the 2nd Battalion in the assault. It was impossible to employ the supporting tanks in this attack because of road conditions (blocks and craters). In the interim, the 1st Battalion moved to capture Gondelsehim and encountered heavy artillery, mortar, and rocket fire.

CT 12 initiated an attack at approximately 0500 with the 2nd Battalion to capture the town of Nieder Prum. The rifle companies did not directly assault the village but advanced and captured the high ground dominating it from the east and southeast.

CT 22 continued the attack at 0545 under heavy enemy artillery fire. Antitank fire within its zone of action was intense and accurate; five of the supporting tanks had been put out of action. The 1st Battalion's attack on the town of Bruhlborn met fanatical resistance and the enemy put up a house to house fight before the resistance broke. The 3rd Battalion remained in position awaiting the fall of Weinsheim.

3 MARCH 1945—D+271: Opposite CT 22 in the center of the Division's sector, the enemy did not defend along any clearly defined line. High ground and strong points amongst buildings and hasty fortifications were defended by the enemy in what appeared to be the beginning of a large scale rear guard action wherein the enemy seemed to be withdrawing the remnants of its forces toward the Rhine. In opposition to CT 12, in the southern zone of the Division's sector, the enemy presented a more determined defense. Open ground in the path of our advance was well covered by small arms, automatic weapons, and direct artillery fire.

The 4th Infantry Division resumed the attack to the east at 0600 to establish a bridgehead for Combat Command B of the 11th Armored Division. The towns of Nieder Prum, Rommersheim and Weindsheim were cleared during the advance, and elements of the 11th Armored Division began passing through our forward positions at 1315.

CT 8 resumed the attack at 0600 to clear enemy resistance in the wooded areas in the north of the Division sector and to capture the town of Gondelsheim. Stubborn resistance was encountered by all elements throughout the day. Antitank fire encountered was extremely heavy and severe tank losses were suffered. At the close of the day, elements of the 1st Battalion were closing upon their objective, the high ground north of Gondelsheim.

CT 12 resumed the attack prior to first light when patrols from the 2nd Battalion advanced towards Romersheim, and scouts and raiders from the 3rd Battalion advanced into the town of Nieder Prum. Resistance encountered in Nieder Prum was negligible and the town was cleared at an early hour. The attack of the 2nd Battalion towards Rommersheim progressed rapidly against sporadic resistance and by 1500 elements of the battalion were five hundred yards southwest of the town. Prior to the close of the period, Companies E and G advanced through the town against increasing resistance.

CT 22 resumed the attack at 0600 by the 2nd and 3rd Battalions. The 2nd Battalion advanced to the north into the wooded area west of the town of Weinsheim and screened this area to the northwest while the 3rd Battalion advanced into the town and reported it clear by 1030. The 1st Battalion advanced southeast towards its objective, the high ground west of Fleringen, and secured it.

4 MARCH 1945—D+272: Enemy front lines were fluid and at the close of the period could not be definitely established. CT 8 advancing towards Gondelsheim met stiff resistance early in the period. At about 0330 the enemy withdrew all but a few men from the town. As a result of continuous pressure by CT 8, the enemy was forced to withdraw slowly, fighting a determined rear guard action. Throughout the rest of the Division sector, the enemy continued its delaying action while withdrawing the bulk of its troops and equipment across the Kyll river. Enemy artillery fire was light, and the direct fire encountered during the previous day was absent. The enemy continued to hamper our advance by employing numerous types of antipersonnel and antitank mines, abatis and blown bridges.

CT 8 with elements of the 1st Battalion continued the attack throughout the night in an effort to clear the town of Gondelsheim but was unsuccessful until 1015 when, under cover of a heavy smoke screen laid on the town, Company B advanced into the village while the remainder of the battalion resumed its attack to the northeast along the edge of the wooded area. The 2nd Battalion resumed its attack to the northeast against an estimated force of three enemy companies. Opposition encountered throughout the day was extremely stiff and automatic weapons fire was heavy. Prior to the close of the period, the battalion was successful until forced to hold up in the face of extensive mine fields covered by fire.

CT 12, beginning at 0300, resumed its operations with the 2nd Battalion to clear the enemy from the high ground east and southeast of

Rommersheim, and at 0600 elements of the 1st Battalion initiated movement forward to Fleringen to relieve elements of the 11th Armored Division while the 3rd Battalion began movement forward to Rommersheim. The 1st Battalion outposted the town of Budhseim and the 3rd Battalion closed in Wallersheim in regimental reserve.

CT 22 continued the attack to the northeast with the 2nd and 3rd Battalions abreast after elements of the 8th Infantry had cleared the town of Gondelsheim. The 2nd Battalion cleared the town of Schwirzheim wherein the 1st Battalion in regimental reserve closed by 2200.

5 MARCH 1945—D+273: CT 8 advanced against light resistance. In opposing CT 22, the enemy presented a more formidable defense as strong delaying forces fought from key terrain features. In this sector, the enemy made liberal use of mines, booby traps, and abatis. CT 12 proceeded against stubborn resistance to the vicinity of Oos. Although fighting a determined delaying action at this point, the Germans were forced to withdraw to the east bank of the Oos river from where they defended fanatically.

CT 8 resumed the attack at 0700 with the 2nd Battalion. The only resistance encountered was enemy mine fields. By 0930 the battalion had successfully negotiated four mine fields and had encountered two more while elements of the 3rd Battalion on the left flank continued their advance toward limited regimental objectives.

CT 12 resumed the attack with its 1st Battalion at 0700 while the 2nd Battalion was relieved by elements of the 90th Infantry Division. Then the 2nd Battalion assembled in regimental reserve in the town of Budesheim. Company C advanced to assault the town of Oos and met more opposition than anticipated, so the remainder of the 1st Battalion had to be employed and by 1725, the village was cleared from enemy. The 3rd Battalion initiated an advance and then secured the high ground from which it sent patrols in the direction of Mullenborn. Upon Division order, the 1st Battalion continued its advance from Oos to secure a crossing of the Oos river. At the close of the period, this operation was in process with a fire fight near the stream.

CT 22 attacked at 0700 with the 2nd and 3rd Battalions to clear the enemy from the town of Duppach. At 1135, Company L had cleared the town while Companies K and I continued the attack to secure the high ground north and east. The attack of the 2nd Battalion proceeded with less speed and Companies F and E repulsed an enemy counterattack. The engagement continued throughout the later hours of the afternoon. By 1900, the situation was clarified, and positions were consolidated for the night.

6 MARCH 1945—D+274: Small delaying forces were encountered by our forces at road junctions and towns. At 1340, CT 12 received small arms fire from the vicinity of Mullenborn.

The 4th Infantry Division continued the attack, coordinating its movement with the 11th Armored Division.

The 8th Infantry assembled as division reserve in prearranged areas at 0920. The remainder of the period was used for rehabilitation of all troops and future plans were formulated for operating as a motorized task force as ordered by the Commanding General of the Division.

CT 12 continued the attack to the northeast. During the morning, the 1st Battalion captured the town of Roth and continued the advance to the northeast to affect a crossing of the Kyll river in the vicinity of Nieder Bettingen. The 2nd Battalion moved from its assembly area to the town of Roth and at the close of the period was also advancing to Nieder Bettingen to cross the Kyll river and coordinate a relief of the armored infantry of the 11th Armored Division. The 3rd Battalion moved also and at the close of the period, was reported to be along the river. Very little enemy opposition was encountered during the day as the movements were behind the 11th Armored Division.

The 1st Battalion of the 22nd Infantry was in regimental reserve in the town of Kellenborn while the 2nd Battalion was pushing to the northeast to exploit the bridgehead established by the 11th Armored Division. The 3rd Battalion moved to the town of Ober Bettingen and at the close of the period was preparing to cross the river.

7 MARCH 1945—D+275: There were no enemy lines established during the period. Our troops were opposed by rear guard elements. A determined resistance was put up by the enemy along the east bank of the Kyll river and it was not until late in the period that our troops were able to dislodge the opposition from these positions. CT 12, in advancing on Nieder Bettingen and Bewingen, received heavy mortar, machine gun, and small arms fire from across the river. The intensity of this fire prevented our troops from effecting a crossing until about 1700. CT 12 met resistance in the form of small forces employing numerous automatic weapons and small arms fire with an infrequent round of artillery.

Combat Command B of the 11th Armored Division, after operating within the 4th Infantry Division's zone, was ordered and withdrew to the south to continue the advance through the 90th Infantry Division sector. The 4th Infantry Division captured the towns of Dohn, Bolsdorf, Bewingen, and Killescheid. Progress was impeded by lack of adequate bridging facilities across the Kyll river. At the close of the period, Task Force Rhino consisting of the 8th Infantry Regiment and other elements of the Division was preparing to launch their attack early 8 March.

The 2nd Battalion of the 12th Infantry crossed the Kyll river in the vicinity of Nieder Bettingen during the night 6-7 March, relieving the armored infantry. During the day, the 2nd Battalion continued the attack and captured the towns of Bolsdorf and Dohn. The 1st Battalion moved rapidly across the river behind the 2nd Battalion. The 3rd Battalion in continuing its advance to cross the Kyll river, cleared the town of Bettingen. After crossing the river, the battalion fought its way to the high ground and occupied the woods.

The 3rd Battalion of the 22nd Infantry crossed, during the night 6-7 March, the Kyll river in the vicinity of Ober Bettingen and relieved elements of the 11th Armored Division. The battalion received a slight counterattack after completion of the relief but repulsed it quickly. The 1st Battalion and then the 2nd Battalion effected their crossing. During the hours of darkness, 7-8 March, Company E of the 2nd Battalion occupied the town of Hillesheim.

A treadway bridge was constructed within the 22nd Infantry sector.

Throughout the day, Bailey bridge equipment was being brought forward and arrived during the night 7-8 March. Every effort was being made by the 4th Engineer Combat Battalion to complete this bridge by first light of 8 March.

From **Swede Henley's Diary—used with permission of his daughters...**

23 FEBRUARY: In Gonderbrett counting my change.

24-25 FEBRUARY: In Gonderbrett—training—flew over Prum today in liaison plane.

26-27 FEBRUARY: In Gonderbrett—received orders to forge river crossing (Prum River) and gain footholds and take Danefeeld—Fleringen—Schwirzheim—Duppach.

28 FEBRUARY: Jumped off at 0530 and crossed river. Casualties heavy from booby traps and mines and machine gun fire. Still fighting 5th paratroops Div. They are mean bastards. Seized objectives. Attacked—lost 4 tanks fast by AT gun. Gained 1 half mile.
  • Once in a while—sometimes forever.

1 MARCH 1945: Transferred to 2nd Bn as CO—held up near Gondelsheim. CP in Weinsheim.

2 MARCH: Attacked from position and took Schertzheim. Krauts seem to be on run.

3 MARCH: Jumped off at 0400 for Duppach and high ground to East (Queen). Going was easy until we locked horns taking Queen. Finally took objective at 1800.

4 MARCH: Moved by foot to Scheuon, Kalenborn—went into assembly area on hill 23. Orders to move at 0120 (March 5) to Obr.

5 MARCH: Bettingen—jumped off attack at 1000 for "Dog" objective and Hillesheim. Took objective Dog at 1730 and Hillesheim fell at 2000.
- Charley Sunray to Easy Sunray
- Cannot go as I have run into Blue Baker
- ES to CS—Go in draw as planned
- CS to ES—Cannot go in draw as there are many obstacles
- There are snipers with MG

From Chaplain Bill Boice's **History of the 22nd Infantry Regiment in WWII:**

An order to attack across the Prum River came to the Combat Team on the 27th (Feb). Preparation for the attack continued that night, and at 0315 hours the 28th of February, the CT attacked to force a bridgehead across the Prum River and to seize the town of Dausfeld. Dausfeld was situated in-between two hills which had to be seized in order to gain control of the town. One hill was approximately 800 yards northeast, the other hill almost 1,000 yards to the southwest, the former to be Objective 3, the latter Objective 4. The 1st and 3rd Battalions attacked abreast, the 1st Battalion on the south at Prum.

The 3rd Battalion forced a crossing of the Prum River about 2,800 yards northeast of Prum and seized Objective 3. Part of Company 'I' entered Dausfeld and four men were captured, so the remainder of the company did not attempt to enter until armored support arrived. Before noon, some of the armor had managed to cross the river, and within three hours this armor, supporting the 3rd Battalion, drove into Dausfeld. Company 'L' had captured several prisoners, and Lt. Arthur, after brief questioning, determined that they were a part of Hitler's youth movement and possessed a cocky attitude. When later questioned by the I. P. W. teams, they continuously spoke of the new secret weapon which was going to later defeat the Allies. All of them were paratroopers, but a number had received no paratroop training. A few of these prisoners had even been brought down from Norway as replacements for the Westwall.

The 1st Battalion, meanwhile, in a column of companies crossed the river on improvised foot-bridges approximately 1,600 yards northeast of Prum. The 1st Battalion, suffering numerous casualties from mine fields, drove on and by noon had seized Objective 4, repulsed an enemy counterattack, and dug in.

Maj. Henley directed the 2nd Battalion across immediately behind the 1st and turned south to clear the ridge line opposite Prum. This action was only partially completed by dark, and the 2nd Battalion was forced to dig in for the night.

Enemy forces here were determined elements of the 5th German Paratroop Division and resisted fanatically.

Supply and evacuation of the wounded handicapped the CT as enemy fire delayed the bridging of the Prum River for vehicular traffic until after dark on the 1st of March. In spite of this hindrance, the attack was resumed the next morning by the 2nd Battalion. This battalion was to clean out the wooded slopes east of Prum. These hills were found to contain trenches five feet deep with built-up firing positions. Observation from these trenches was so clear that it was possible to see men moving about inside of the houses in Prum. This was obviously the reason the units in Prum suffered so heavily in casualties from sniper fire. Communication wires extended throughout the trenches and to listening posts on the Prum River. The Germans hadn't been caught by surprise; they had been well prepared. By mid-day the slope was clear, and the 2nd Battalion was relieved by elements of CT 12. The 1st and 3rd Battalions remained in position and did not attempt to advance.

Throughout this period, quotas of men were daily pulled back off of the front lines and given a three day pass to Paris. When the deserving men were selected to go back to Paris, they inwardly felt as if heaven had temporarily spared them the horrors of the battlefield and allowed them a bit of rest. These men loaded on two and one-half ton trucks and in a matter of hours were out of the combat zone. In Paris there were electric lights, music, and girls. It was like a slice of heaven brought to earth. For three days and three nights men were allowed to come and go as they desired. Paris was gay, the people were friendly, and everyone had a grand time. The night clubs, burlesques, movies, and sidewalk cafes catered to the combat soldier. After the three day period was over, the men returned again to the front. There was little complaining; no tears were shed; these battle-hardened veterans knew that their job was as yet unfinished and the sooner that they completed it, the sooner they would be able to return to the freedom of the United States.

On March 2nd, Colonel Charles T. Lanham was assigned to the One Hundred Fourth Division as the Assistant Commanding General. Thus ended a colorful association between a great fighting commander and a great fighting regiment. The relationship had sometimes been bitter; there was no easy way to lose lives. But there had come to be mutual respect.

Buck Lanham had led the regiment in every successful battle engagement of the war except the Normandy assault. He was driving, demanding, and aggressive. He was an able tactician, possessed a thorough knowledge of men, and commanded the respect of men who served under his command.

It was a brilliant and successful relationship and one the men of the regiment were destined to remember.

It was with genuine pleasure the regiment learned that Buck Lanham was to be succeeded by the regimental executive officer, Lt. Colonel John F. Ruggles, rather than by an officer from outside the regiment.

The 2nd day of March, the attack moved ahead, the First and Third Battalions fighting abreast. This terrain was fast becoming suitable for tank operations — the hills extended in long rolls, woods were scarce, and the bright sunshine was slowly drying out the mud. Before long the armored divisions would be able to smash ahead and rapidly crush the remaining German armies.

The 3rd Battalion advance was slowed initially by heavy enemy rocket fire and later by necessity of covering its left flank, which was now exposed due to the failure of CT 8 to take Weinsheim. The 44th Field Artillery Battalion laid down a perfect smoke screen between the town and the 3rd Battalion. The road leading southeast from Weinsheim was severed at 0808 hours. However, this drive was halted after penetrating approximately 1,000 yards east of the road; fire from both flanks covered all routes for further advance.

The 1st Battalion also received heavy enemy fire, and its attack eastward was temporarily delayed. But, by 0630 hours the attack was underway; the advance ceased when four supporting tanks were destroyed by direct fire from the enemy. Thereafter there was bitter indecisive fighting at Bruhlborn, but by dark the situation was favorable.

As leading elements were receiving effective fire from both flanks as well as the front, CT 22 adjusted its position and secured for the night by diffusing the left flank in the vicinity of Weinsheim and slightly withdrawing the most forward element to better defensive terrain. Orders received during late evening placed Weinsheim as an objective of the Regiment.

In an attempt to gain surprise, the 3rd Battalion, shortly before dawn on March 3rd, moved to positions from which it might assault Weinsheim. Before the attack got underway, white flags were seen in the town, and patrols verified the fact that the enemy had withdrawn from there. Immediately the CT pushed out and seized the high ground around the town. This was rapidly done as the 11th U. S. Armored Division had been waiting a suitable jump-off line; this was it. The 11th Armored moved through CT 22 and attacked east. At once, CT 22 received a new zone of action; the direction of attack was now northeast.

A coordinated attack by CT 22 and the 11th Armored Division on the 4th of March was delayed awaiting the seizure of Gondelsheim. At 1015 hours the attack got underway, and by dark the Team had advanced 6,000 yards to the high ground just east of Schwirzheim.

The following day, the 5th of March, Duppach was secured against only slight resistance. The 2nd Battalion, pushing out from Duppach, encountered very stiff resistance on a hill nearly 1,000 yards to the southeast thereof. By dark the hill had fallen. This hill formed the western edge of a saddle which had to be opened for the 11th Armored to pass through. The hill forming the eastern edge of the saddle fell to CT 12 shortly before dark that same day.

In agreement with orders, the 3rd Battalion relieved elements of the 11th Armored Division in Ober Bettingen and in the one-half mile bridgehead east of the Kyll River during the night of 6-7 March. At 0215 hours the relief was completed. The 2nd Battalion had moved into the right portion of the bridgehead, the 3rd Battalion in the left. Patrols of both the forward battalions from these positions moved into Hillesheim and encountered no organized resistance.

From **War Stories Volume II: Paris to VE Day…**

Bud Whelan, Silver Spring, MD
Company M, 3rd Battalion, 22nd Infantry Regiment
On the Job Training

I was inducted into the Army on October 3, 1944. Basic infantry training at Fort Blanding, Florida lasted thirteen weeks. "You will get more training up north," the Army advised.

I spent ten days at home, went to Fort Dix, New Jersey, and got all new uniforms and equipment. "You will get more training overseas," someone in charge said.

I went overseas on the Queen Mary. "You will get more training in England…" I got off the Queen and onto a train, which took me to a boat and then to France. We took a long hike up a steep hill—by this time, we were leaving three tracks.

At an old farmhouse, I was told I was now in Company M, 3rd Battalion, 22nd Infantry Regiment, 4th Infantry Division. "Pitch tents, set up guards—don't go into any other fields because they have not been cleared of mines," we were told.

The next morning we bitched because the GIs in the next field didn't pitch tents…until we saw some dead men in body bags. This was the start of my on-the-job training. We were sent into a town called Prüm, for "intensive training by foreign instructors."

I spent my nineteenth birthday in the small town of Hillshiem. While celebrating in the basement of a house, some of the uninvited instructors knocked the upper floors off the building. What a party—I will never forget it...*to be continued*...

Marvin A. Simpson, (Deceased) Baton Rouge, LA
Company D, 4th Medical Battalion
Afterward

In March 1945, stationed near Prüm, Germany, I was given a three-day pass back to Paris. This happened the day after I had won $300 in an all-night poker game. Wow! Was I ever excited and happy. I boarded a train with other comrades and arrived in Paris. Suddenly, I was in a different world. I took in all the sights, peed in an outdoor latrine on the sidewalks of Paris, rode in a two-seat taxi pulled by a bicycle and took in the shows and nightclubs. I had come a long way from the farm in Iowa to the streets of Paris. It was a tremendous 72-hour pass.

On VE Day our camp was near Starnburg, Germany. What a day to remember. We thought the war was over. A month later, however, we were on our way across the Atlantic for a thirty-day leave before going to the Pacific for the invasion of Japan. After arriving back in the States and traveling by train to Cedar Rapids, Iowa, I waited a long time for my wife to appear. It was there I realized I was getting a "Dear John" letter in a very subtle way. I was right—the marriage that began at the beginning of the war for me was over at the end. VJ Day came during my furlough, and I was discharged soon after with the rank of Staff Sergeant.

I went to Chicago and lived with my wartime buddy, Jim Saxton. I married the sweetest, most wonderful girl, Mary Fellmer. During our fifty-two years of marriage, I have experienced many breathtaking moments. Our first son, James, was born in 1949, then our second son, John, in 1953. My wife and I attended the 50th Anniversary of D-Day, lived with a French family in Normandy who called us "liberators," walked through the rows of white crosses at the Normandy American Cemetery, and, with tears in our eyes, we prayed.

Lon Murphy, Jr., Columbus, OH
Company L, 3rd Battalion, 12th Infantry Regiment
Keeping the Germans on the Run

By early March, we had been attacking for two months. We had to keep pressing the attack in order to keep the Germans on the run. If we slowed down or stopped to rest, it gave the Germans time to dig in and prepare defensive positions. We remembered what a well-prepared German defense had done in the Hürtgen Forest. The impact on the foot soldier was serious fatigue and nastiness. There was no time to sleep, bathe, shave, or change clothes. Our clothes were crusted and dirty and stank like garbage. Our hair was shaggy, and our beards were thick and scruffy. We lived in the holes in the ground through snow, sleet, rain, and cold. When it rained it streaked the dirt in our faces and made us look even dirtier.

As for me, my leather boots were cracked and split open. My shoulders were rubbed raw from the cartridge harness that carried clips full of ammo for my BAR. My feet were calloused and swollen from month after month of freezing, thawing, and walking through all kinds of terrain. I had been requesting new boots for weeks, but the army didn't care. The Army was interested in maps and objectives, not in the peripheral needs of a foot soldier.

After taking Prüm, we had to stop to set up defensive positions along the west bank of the Prüm River to allow our supply lines to catch up to us. Since I was a BAR man, I was part of the outpost rotation. The company was dug in about two hundred yards from the river. There were three advanced outposts placed along the river bank. Each outpost had three BARs and a bucket of grenades. Outpost personnel were rotated every twenty-four hours. It was dark by 1800 hours. The crew that was due for rotation would replace the previous crew each evening. Twenty-four hours later that crew would be relieved.

Our turn came, and it was time for Dwight Larrowe, Sam Carter, and me to pull outpost duty. It was a scary and lonely feeling. If the Germans attacked or a German patrol discovered us, there was no support within two hundred yards. With three BARs and a bucket of grenades, we knew we could hold out for a while and take a lot of Germans with us. We all hoped it wouldn't happen.

Larrowe was an excellent artist. He took an envelope out of his pocket. He sketched Carter and me in the dugout with our weapons and surroundings. I was impressed, and he gave me the picture. I sent it in a letter to my brother, Walter, who was on a destroyer in the Pacific. He carried it with him all the way through the war and gave it back to me in 1990 when I was visiting him.

The Germans were dug in on the other side of the river. We could hear the clanking of their mess kits as they ate, and some occasional chatter. We would even spot the top of a German helmet moving through their trenches once in a while. It was an eerie feeling to be closer to them than to our own lines. Even though we could see them once in a while, we would never snipe at them. There were two reasons for this: First, they weren't sniping at us, and second, it would give away our position.

We kept in touch with the company command post by phone. A wire was strung from each outpost back to headquarters. During the night the Germans would shell us sporadically to keep us from sleeping regularly. We did the same to them. Exploding shells would frequently cut the wire. One of us would have to leave the outpost, trace the wire to the point of disconnection, find the other end of the wire and splice them back together. This was extremely dangerous because you were outside of the safety of the dugout. Encountering a German patrol would mean certain doom.

One night we received word from the command post that the battalion raiders would be going on a raiding patrol that night. The patrol would cross the lines by one outpost and reenter by another outpost so as not to give away any positions. Their mission was to harass the enemy and keep them guessing about our intentions.

As they passed our outpost, I thought about how glad I was to be in a nice safe outpost instead of going with them behind enemy lines. Later we heard small arms fire and exploding grenades from behind the enemy lines. This was surely the work of the battalion raiders.

Later we caught sight of the patrol reentering our lines near the outpost to our left. I noticed one GI being helped by his buddies. His leg was missing from just below his knee. I was jealous. The war was over for him, and he would be going home alive while I remained in this frozen, muddy hell wondering if I had a future or not. I would have accepted the loss of a foot or leg to get out of my current situation. I heard a few days later that the soldier died because of blood loss.

After eight days of holding, the attack was called off. The Company Commander told me that this was my opportunity to get some new shoes from the quartermaster. The quartermaster was a few miles behind the lines, and I asked if I could have the jeep driver take me back. The commander said that wouldn't be necessary because we would remain in position for a few days, which gave me plenty of time to walk. I found it annoying that I had to walk three miles down a muddy mess of a road to get new shoes.

After I had been walking for a short time, along came a jeep with a major in it, and he offered me a ride. As I walked into the supply area it was obvious that I was out of place. The GIs in the rear had clean haircuts, clean shaves, and they were altogether clean. The quartermaster sergeant didn't even ask me what I was looking for. He took me to the supply room and made sure that I got two of everything. I received new uniforms, underwear, socks, boots, gloves, and an overcoat. He directed me to the showers. It was a wonderful feeling to take a nice hot shower. I was then showed to the mess tents where I had my first hot meal in three months. I was so grateful for those things. I never took anything for granted again for the rest of my life.

Our next objective was to take a town located in a valley. McCullough told me to keep an eye on the company and provide supporting fire if they got into trouble. At first, I felt good about not having to participate in the attack of the town, but after the rest of the company left, I wasn't so sure I liked the idea. There were just the three of us alone on this hill. I thought of all the times we had bypassed pockets of Germans and what would happen if a squad of them showed up. We couldn't see our column advancing from where we were, but we did notice when a German machine gun opened up about five hundred yards away from us. They must have seen some of our guys. I opened up with the BAR, and this gave the rest of the guys the opportunity to get into position and return fire themselves.

After the machine gun was silenced, Carter said he thought we should be moving since I had attracted attention to our position. About five minutes after we swung around to the other side of the hill, a mortar barrage peppered the area we had just left. I'm glad Carter was thinking. The idea had not crossed my mind.

* * * * *

You will recall from reading our special section on February 28 about the death of PFC Orvis Senear, I mentioned how much help Nick Trommelen, a WWII historian from The Netherlands, had given to Jerry Senear and me in finding details on Jerry's dad's death.

Nick Trommelen has launched a web site you all will want to visit, probably on multiple visits. His web page is focused on the fight around Prum in February and March 1945. It is a fabulous piece of work he has done, working at it over many months and years. I highly recommend you bookmark Nick's site and go back to it regularly. Many of the pictures I am including in this section of this book came from Nick's site — and he has many more besides the ones I used. Here is the note from Nick as he announced the site:

"Today marks the 75th anniversary of the Prüm River crossing in 1945. I have spent a decade researching this battle and it has resulted in an educative website which is online as of today. As you can see it almost turned into a "small" book, with a large photo database for the audience overseas and last but not least an extensive KIA list. Big thank you to Will Campbell, Jerry Senear, Bob Babcock, Danny van der Groen, and my girlfriend Evy for making this website possible.

PS. It is best to visit the website on your PC or Laptop. Because of the large contents." **www.imwesten.com**

I looked at Nick's series of "Then and Now" pictures, one of many superb features of this web page honoring those who fought in the Prum, Germany area in February and March 1945.

8 MAR 1945 TO 14 MAR 1945 — D+276 TO D+282

8 MARCH 1945—D+276: Our forces advancing rapidly along the entire front met practically no organized resistance. Road blocks, blown bridges, road craters, felled trees, and mines constituted the main resistance in the path of the 4th Infantry Division's attacks. While CT 12 and 22 advanced without contacting the enemy, Task Force Rhino swung quickly from across the Kyll river at Ober Bettingen along the northern flank overrunning the enemy to the town of Hoffeld from which point, at the close of the period, armored spearheads were continuing north to the Division's objective at Reifferscheid.

The 4th Infantry Division resumed the attack at 0825 when the 8th Infantry, motorized as part of Task Force Rhino under command of Brigadier General Rodwell, initiated the advance. Throughout the day, continuous progress was made against light opposition. The first resistance was encountered at 1305 in the vicinity of Kerpen where a barricade had been erected. This enemy force was eliminated in the short firefight that ensued and the advance continued. Prior to 2200, leading elements were in the vicinity of Honerath, a gain of fourteen miles.

The 12th Infantry echeloned forward in its zone of action and established outposts in the town of Zilsdorf and on the high ground to the northwest while the 22nd Infantry readjusted its positions in Hillesheim and on the high ground astride the road immediately to the north.

9 MARCH 1945—D+277: Task Force Rhino continued on to the east during the night and entered the town of Adenau where elements of the 70th Tank Battalion and the 1st Battalion of the 8th Infantry consolidated their positions. In the interim, elements of the 70th Tank Battalion followed by the 3rd Battalion of the 8th Infantry swung to the north in the direction of the Division objective and by 0715, the objective had been taken. During the night and early morning hours, the town of Honerath, Adenau, Rodder, and Reiffersheid had been cleared and little resistance was reported. During the entire operation, upwards of fifteen hundred prisoners of war had been counted while our losses were 2 KIA, 4 WIA, and one light tank.

By 1830, responsibility for the sector passed to the 6th Cavalry Group. All elements of the Task Force remained in positions and began preparations for assembly and movement.

The 12th and 22nd Infantry remained in positions on the high ground in the vicinity of Hillesheim and reorganized their positions prior to assembly.

With the exception of small bands of disorganized enemy still to be apprehended, there existed no further contact with the enemy at that time.

10 MARCH 1945—D+278: Major General Troy H. Middleton, VIII Corps Commander, presented the Legion of Merit to Brigadier General H.W. Blakeley, Commanding General, at an informal ceremony.

The 4th Infantry Division began assembling preparatory to departure from the Third Army sector to the VIII Corps area to the south in the vicinity of Luneville, France.

11—14 MARCH 1945—D+279 TO D+282: The 70th Tank Battalion, the 610th Tank Destroyer Battalion, and the 377th Antiaircraft Artillery Battalion moved by motor to new assembly areas in the vicinity of Gerbeviller, France.

The foot troops of the three regimental combat teams entrained at Bleialf, Germany and detrained at Bayon, France where they were shuttled by motor to their respective billets. The final elements were the foot troops of the 8th Infantry which detrained at Bayon at 1627 on 14 March.

All battalions of the 4th Infantry Division Artillery left positions in the vicinity of Schwirzheim, Germany, on 11 March between 0900 and 1300. After an uneventful motor march except for 508 flat tires, the 4th Infantry Division Artillery closed in the bivouac areas along Highway 7 in the vicinity of Mersch, Luxembourg, at 2145. The following day all units resumed the march, closing into assembly areas in the vicinity of Puttelandge, France, at 1745. Attached to XXI Corps Artillery with the mission of reinforcing the fire of the 63rd Division Artillery, reconnaissance was made during the daylight on 13 March and positions occupied during darkness of 13-14 March. All the battalions fired a preparation at 150300 March and continued firing normal harassing fire until approximately 1600 March 19.

The 4th Infantry Division Artillery fired 456 missions, expending 2764 rounds of 155 mm and 5850 rounds of 105 mm ammunition.

At 1200 March 19, the 4th Infantry Division Artillery was ordered to rejoin the 4th Infantry Division. They moved by motor, beginning at 1815, and closed into assembly areas in the vicinity of Gerbeviller at 0430 March 20.

Editor's Note: This marked the first time in 199 days (that's what the 4ID history says in our yearbooks, but to the best of my understanding, this is the first time since D-Day we have not been on the front lines. From me, I believe we were constantly in contact with the Germans for 279 days until we got this break. Except for these few days in March 1945, the 4ID was constantly on the front lines and in contact with the German forces from D-Day, June 6, 1944 through VE Day, May 8, 1945. And they'll resume their drive through Germany in a few days after this short break.

From **Swede Henley's Diary—used with permission of his daughters…**

6-7-8-9-10-11 MARCH: Hillesheim set up in a wonderful CP. Reorganizing—washing—clean clothes -paradise. Received order to prepare to move to south. God only knows what is in store for us.

12 MARCH: Moved from Bliealf by 40-8 train to Vieinitg Luneville, France for a rest period. An unbelievable thing.

13 MARCH: Set up CP (Charley Peter) in Domptail in Mayor's home. E & H companies in Xafferville—F & G in Menarmont.

Fit to Fight

14-19 MARCH: Still training—resting—reorganizing—weather has been beautiful.

From Chaplain Bill Boice's **History of the 22nd Infantry Regiment in WWII...**

Until the 12th of March, the Regiment held and consolidated its positions in the vicinity of Hillesheim. Patrols were sent out to the east and northeast to ensure security. Task Force 'Rhine' composed of Combat Team 8 and the 70th Tank Battalion, passed through the 22nd Regiment at 1100 hours on the 8th and moved rapidly eastward. In the ensuing days, the rifle battalions, assembled in Hillesheim, took advantage of the situation to repair and clean equipment, re-organize, and relax.

Late in the day of March 12th, in accordance with orders, preparations were made to move the Combat Team by rail and motor to the general area of Luneville, France. The move was made on the 13th and 14th of March. The two trains carrying the foot elements arrived in Bayon, France, in late afternoon of the 14th. From this point non-organic transportation carried the troops to their billets near Magnieres. The motor column moved through Prum, Bleialf, Dasburg, Luxembourg City, Metz, Toul, Bayon, to the respective billet areas. All elements of the Regiment closed in to the new location by midnight. Upon arrival, CT 22, as part of the 4th Infantry Division, became a reserve element of the Seventh U.S. Army.

After the move into France, the Combat Team, as a part of the 4th Infantry Division, had been engaged in continuous contact with enemy forces for 199 consecutive days. This well-deserved relief was fully enjoyed by each man. The climate in southern France was similar to that of Florida, and the men relaxed in the warm sun to take sun baths and swim in the nearby streams. It was unspeakably wonderful!

(Editor's Note—all the official 4ID records state 199 consecutive days of combat up to this point. As you can see from my daily After Action Reports, it has been 282 days since D-Day. I am perplexed at why the 4ID back in 1945 made the claim of 199 rather than 282 consecutive days of combat.)

From **War Stories Volume II: Paris to VE Day**

Albert Schantz, Reading, PA
Company A, 1st Battalion, 22nd Infantry Regiment
Pay Raise

On March 7, 1945, I arrived in Prüm, Germany, and was assigned to Company A, 22nd Infantry Regiment, as a replacement rifleman. The 4th Infantry Division was pulled back from the front line of battle to rest and take on replacement troops. The 4th Infantry Division had suffered many casualties after 199 consecutive days in combat and required a large replacement base.

We did some retraining and reorganizing; at which time I became the assistant 60mm mortar gunner in the 4th platoon.

After retraining, we boarded Army trucks and journeyed south through Luxembourg, on to Metz and Nancy, in France. Then east to Luneville, France, and north to Worms, Germany, where we crossed the Rhine River and engaged the enemy on the front line on March 29, 1945.

In school I had read about town criers. Well, for some reason we had to hold up in Luxembourg for a few days. There I saw the town crier. He walked through the town and cried out the news. All the people either opened their windows and listened or came outside to hear the news.

During our first battle, we were pursuing the Krauts when the 60mm mortar gunner collapsed from exhaustion, and I automatically became the gunner. That meant carrying a 60mm mortar and a .45 caliber pistol in place of the M-1 rifle. The mortar was heavy; it seemed to weigh about sixty pounds with the base plate.

The infantry motto was "Follow me!" I must have performed properly because I was promoted to Private First Class on April 1, 1945, just three days into battle.

The promotion and the Combat Infantryman Badge gave me a raise in pay. I can't remember exactly how much the promotion increase was, but I do remember that the private rating paid thirty dollars per month, and the Combat Infantryman Badge paid an additional ten dollars per month for the rest of my military career. I suppose the promotion raise was about five dollars per month, all of which raised my monthly pay to about forty-five dollars.

During one of our battles we encountered sniper fire. Our platoon leader, a field commissioned second lieutenant, spotted the sniper in the steeple of a church on top of the hill we were trying to take. He asked me to set up my mortar and knock the sniper out of the steeple. I set up and knocked the steeple and the sniper off the church on the first shot and saved a few American lives. The rest of my platoon cheered, but not loud, for fear of revealing our location. I don't remember whether this shot was the reason for earning my first stripe on April 1, 1945, but it may have been.

We were all scared of being shot at and terrified hearing the incoming German artillery shells, especially the screaming meemies. These were a special type of German artillery shell. They made screaming noises as they headed in our direction. I experienced anger, and my adrenaline made me want to fight harder when I saw my comrades receive a hit.

One of my comrades, Harry Campbell, was the most relaxed man I ever saw in the midst of a war. If we stopped for ten-minute rest, he would lean against a tree and fall asleep on his feet. We called him "Sleepy" Campbell. We couldn't depend on him to stay awake for guard duty.

George Peterman, Cinnaminson, NJ
Company B, 1st Battalion, 22nd Infantry Regiment
A World War II Infantry Replacement's Diary

On June 6, 1944, I was seventeen years old and a senior in high school. By the end of June, I had graduated, turned eighteen, and registered for the draft. In September of 1944, I was drafted. In October, I began the

16-week basic Infantry Replacement Training course at Camp Robinson, Arkansas. Upon completion, I took the usual route to Europe: a ten-day leave en route to Camp Meade, Maryland, then to Camp Shanks, New York—a five-day trip on the British liner, Aquitania, to Glasgow, Scotland—an express train to Southampton, England—Channel crossing by ship to LeHavre, France, a 40 & 8 boxcar ride, and finally to Metz, France. I was assigned to the 22nd Infantry Regiment, Company B, in Loonville, France.

The receiving officer told us that if we lasted the first day of combat we would be awarded the Combat Infantryman's Badge and made Private First Class. I didn't fully realize what he meant by "if you last the first day of combat." Nevertheless, I consider my Private First Class stripe a battlefield promotion.

I lasted five weeks in the light mortar section before I was caught in a screaming meemie tree-burst barrage. The concussion was terrifying and so was the shrapnel and my broken leg. The other three wounded in the platoon, though more seriously wounded than I, were able to leave the area on their own. My fractured leg was bleeding badly.

Fortunately, one of those courageous medics came to get me in a jeep. He gave me morphine and bent the vial needle around my dog tag chain. He also reduced the bleeding. Strange how we recall small details. From there it was to the battalion aid station; 11th Evac; 187th General Hospital in Rheims, France, then my first C-46 airplane ride, to England to the 188th General Hospital in Cirencester. As the war ended in May, I returned to the U.S. on the hospital ship Goethals in June. We were given a grand welcome home in Boston. I'll never forget that attention.

I finished my Army career of one year and twenty days at Camp Pickett, Virginia, on the 18th of October, 1945, with a deformed, scarred, and partially paralyzed leg. But I was only one of 1.2 million U.S. casualties of WWII. Over 300,000 of these were KIAs. Based on the cases I saw in the hospitals, I was very fortunate.

Fit to Fight

* * * * *

And, let me introduce you to Brigadier General James Rodwell, deputy commanding general of the 4ID.

He was a WWI cavalry veteran and joined the 4ID soon after they were reactivated at Fort Benning in June 1940. He trained with them, went to England as Chief of Staff of the 4ID, later commanded the 8th Infantry Regiment from early July through early October 1944 when he was promoted to deputy commanding general, a job he held until the 4ID was back at their new home at Camp Butner, NC after the war was over. As mentioned in the After Action Report above, he led Task Force Rhino 80 years ago, on 8 March 1945, and earned the Distinguished Service Cross for his actions that day (he should have also earned one for his actions at the St. Lo Breakout on 25 July 1944, but it was downgraded to his second Silver Star of WWII).

Below is the citation for his DSC:

Distinguished Service Cross

AWARDED FOR ACTIONS

DURING **World War II**
Service: **Army**
Rank: **Brigadier General**
Division: 4th Infantry Division
GENERAL ORDERS:
Headquarters, Third U.S. Army, General Orders No. 131 (June 4, 1945)

CITATION:

The President of the United States of America, authorized by Act of Congress, July 9, 1918, takes pleasure in presenting the Distinguished Service Cross to Brigadier General James S. Rodwell, United States Army, for extraordinary heroism in connection with military operations against an armed enemy while serving with the 4th Infantry Division, in action against enemy forces on 8 and 9 March 1945, in the vicinity of Adenau and Rifferscheid, Germany. A task force under the leadership of General Rodwell initiated an advance, crossing a river which had thwarted similar previous attempts, and penetrated swiftly and deeply into enemy territory. The force, animated by his vigorous leadership, eliminated each enemy point of resistance, and deftly surmounted each obstacle which the retreating Germans had left in their wake. He personally and on foot led his command group through an enemy occupied town at night while devoid of any support or assistance from combat troops. Brigadier General Rodwell's outstanding personal courage and aggressive leadership exemplify the highest traditions of the military forces of the United States and reflect great credit upon himself, the 4th Infantry Division, and the United States Army.

The next couple of weeks were slow—for the first time since D-Day, the 4ID was pulled back into France for rest, refitting, training, and taking a much needed and deserved break. But the war was far from over for us. We were back into action in later March, crossing the Rhine River, and pursuing the Germans until VE Day.

15 MAR 1945 TO 21 MAR 1945 – D+283 TO D+289

15 MARCH 1945—D+283: Lieutenant General A. M. Patch, Commanding General Seventh Army, visited the division command post.

A pass policy permitting members of this command to visit towns in the vicinity of their units during hours prior to curfew was approved by the Commanding General. The Division band was scheduled to tour the units to present concerts and to play at dances and presentation ceremonies.

16-19 MARCH 1945—D+284 TO 287: Report G 3 (operations branch): An extensive training program was conducted during four days.

This period afforded an excellent chance for rehabilitation for all personnel and for maintenance of weapons and equipment. Full advantage was taken during the time available.

16 MARCH 1945—D+284: Report G 1 (personnel branch): Brigadier General J.S. Rodwell, Assistant Division Commander, was awarded the Legion of Honor and the Croix de Guerre avec Palme by local French Royalty. Forty-five hundred Combat Infantry Badges were received and distributed equally among the three infantry regiments. The 8th Infantry was furnished with 1500 Presidential Unit Citation Badges and the 3rd Battalion of the 22nd Infantry with 500.

17 MARCH 1945—D+285: Report from G-1 (personnel branch): The Commanding General approved a division quota of twenty-five officers and 200 enlisted men to visit rest centers at Grenoble (officers) and Lyon (EM) for 5 days.

18 MARCH 1945—D+286: (Nothing reported)

19 MARCH 1945—D+287: Report G 1 (personnel branch): The 22nd Infantry Regiment was awarded the Presidential Unit Citation and the first badge was pinned on Lieutenant Colonel John F. Ruggles.

20 MARCH 1945—D+288: The 4th Infantry Division moved from the vicinity of Gerbeviller to the vicinity of Batzendorf, France, under the control of the VI Corps. Advance elements passed the initial point at 0500 and the entire division closed in the new assembly areas by 2030.

21 MARCH 1945—D+289: Because of the large number of officers and men away at other places of recreation, the Commanding General refused a quota to visit a rest center at Nancy.

From **Swede Henley's Diary—used with permission of his daughters:**

20 MARCH: Still in Domptail.

21-23 MARCH: Received orders to move out at 0830 – Baccaret – Domevre – Blamont – Sarre-bourg – Phalsboerg – Saverne – Hochfelden – Monnesheim and to Bernolsheim (6 miles from Haguenau). The weather is beautiful, and the rest is so good.

23—25 MARCH: Still in Bernolsheim. Orders to move on the 26th. Visited Strassbourg.

26 MARCH: Moved out at 1416 for Lambrech
Route – Haguenan – Neiderbrom – Setrhe – Walschbronn – Vinnegen – Permasens – Landan – Neustadt – Lambrech. Arrived 1950 hours (85 miles).
- Passed thru Siegfried defenses at Permasen and it looked nasty.
- Drive down thru the valley was beautiful and a good road. Air Corps had killed a lot of horses.
- War news sounds good—everybody is on the go.

27 MARCH: CP in Lambrech awaiting movement orders. As per usual it is raining again since we are back in Germany.

From Bill Boice's **History of the 22nd Infantry Regiment in WWII: THE ENEMY RESISTANCE CRUMBLES – BAVARIA**

"It is with the highest praise that I commend the officers and men who so gallantly fought the battles at Lauda, Konigshofen, and Bad Mergentheim. Words of praise could never express to each individual the sincere appreciation I hold within my heart for this great victory."

Fit to Fight

—Lt. Colonel John Ruggles—15 March 1945

This is a short report. 4ID is in reserve, resting, for the first time since D-Day. Next, we'll be back on the attack, crossing the Rhine River on 29 March 1945, and continuing to pursue the Germans across their homeland. Stay tuned for that action—the war isn't over yet..

22 MAR 1945 TO 28 MAR 1945 – D+290 TO D+296

22 MARCH 1945—D+290: Lieutenant Colonel Arthur S. Teague (22nd Infantry Regiment) was awarded the DSO (British Decoration).

21—25 MARCH 1945—D+289 TO 293: Report G 3 (operations): The 4th Infantry Division remained assembled, and until 1240 on 23 March, was kept on an alert status with the CT 12 motorized with trucks furnished by the VI Corps and prepared to move on three hours' notice.

After release from its alert status, the training program was continued, especially in the firing of individual and crew served weapons.

Effective at 1200 on 25 March, the Division passed to operational control of the XXI Corps.

26—27 MARCH 1945—D+294 TO 295: Report G 3 (operations): Movement was begun by motor at 0700. The 12th Infantry Regiment with the 42nd Field Artillery Battalion and companies from other units attached, closed into its new assembly area in the vicinity of Ellerstadt, Germany, by 1600.

The 22nd Infantry Regiment with the 44th Field Artillery Battalion and companies from other units attached, moved to the new assembly area in the vicinity of Lambrecht, Germany, closing there by 2100.

All other elements of the Division remained in the vicinity of Batzendorf until 27 March when movement of the 8th Infantry Regiment with the 29th Field Artillery Battalion and other companies from other units attached, was completed by 1545 to the vicinity of Bad Durkheim, Germany.

The 70th Tank Battalion and the 610th Tank Destroyer Battalion went into bivouac for the night in the vicinity of Hainfel, Germany, in order to release road priority for movement of the 12th Armored Division across the Rhine.

28 MARCH 1945—D+296: The Commanding General directed that the provisions of paragraph 2 Memorandum No 13, Looting and Fraternization in Occupied Territory, would be made known to all personnel of the Division and strictly adhered to.

The 4th Infantry Division remained in the vicinity of Neustadt, Germany, and conducted cleaning of vehicles and equipment. Movement of the tank and tank destroyer battalions to the Division area was completed.

* * * * *

This is the last week of WWII that the 4ID is not engaged with the enemy. Starting on 28 March 1945, we resumed our pursuit of the Germans and crossed the Rhine River on 29 March 1945. Thus, not a lot more to report from WWII in this report.

However, **21-22 March in 1967** was a very significant two days of action in the Vietnam War. On 21 March 1967, the 3rd Brigade of 4ID fought a significant battle at Soui Tre, also called Fire Support Base Gold, in the III Corps area of Vietnam, in a fight that started early in the morning and was over by 1100 hours. As a result, 647 NVA/VC enemy were killed.

For their actions in The Battle of Soui Tre, the 3rd Brigade, 4ID earned the Presidential Unit Citation and claimed the largest single day body count by a unit in the Vietnam War.

On 22 March 1967, Alpha Company of 1st Battalion, 8th Infantry Regiment of 4ID was attacked, their company commander was killed, and 1st Sergeant David McNerney took command and earned the Medal of Honor for his actions that day. Several years later, on 5 July 2001 at the dedication of the 4ID Monument on the road leading into Arlington National Cemetery, I met 1SG McNerney. We remained friends until his death in 2010. I was honored to preside over his burial at Houston National Cemetery.

Our lull is over next week — and we'll finish WWII in six more weeks. The fighting is not over and the daily pursuit of the Germans back into their homeland will be relentless until VE Day on 8 May 1945.

29 MAR 1945 TO 4 APR 1945 – D+297 TO D+303

29 MARCH 1945 — D+297: Orders were received for movement of the entire Division across the Rhine river. This movement was begun over the heavy pontoon bridge at Worms and the units were all enroute to the new Division sector in the vicinity of Heppenheim at the close of the period.

30 MARCH 1945 — D+298: The enemy continued to fall back in apparent confusion, keeping well ahead of our forces in order to contend with only a minimum of contact with our troops. Resistance in the form of scattered rifle shots and an occasional hand grenade thrown by soldiers in civilian clothes or by bona fide civilians in a burst of anti-Allied feeling characterized the period.

The 4th Infantry Division continued movement of all units and immediately attacked to the east within its zone, passing through elements of the 12th Armored Division and the 101st Cavalry Reconnaissance Group.

The 8th Infantry with the 29th Field Artillery Battalion and other companies, closed within its assembly area in the vicinity of Heppenheim after the motor march on the night of 29-30 March. From this assembly area movement was begun at 1040 to the east through its new zone of action. The only enemy resistance reported was a slight artillery barrage.

The 12th with the 42nd Field Artillery Battalion and other companies remained in Division reserve in the vicinity of Ellerstadt until shortly before the close of the period when movement was begun across the Rhine river.

The 22nd Infantry with the 44th Field Artillery Battalion and other companies, upon closing in the forward assembly area, moved as a motorized regiment, beginning at 1230. No enemy resistance and excellent progress was made toward securing the Seventh Army bridgehead line.

31 MARCH 1945—D+299: HQ 7th Army informed the HQ that the Company Commanders of D and M Companies, 8th Infantry, with one complete platoon from each of those companies, would report to Colonel Ladd, 12th Army Group at Fort Ehrenbreitstein, Coblenz, Germany, at 051200 April 1945, for the purpose of raising the flag which was lowered by these companies in 1923, signifying the departure of the last American occupational troops after the last war.

The enemy utilized hastily prepared road blocks, mines, and demolished bridges in an attempt to slow the advance of our forces. Light resistance in the form of small arms and automatic weapons fire was encountered as friendly troops entered several towns.

The 4th Infantry Division continued its attack to the east with the 8th CT on the left and the 22nd on the right. Both Combat Teams advanced rapidly. The 12th remained in reserve and was alerted for movement by motor to a forward assembly area in the vicinity of Hardheim early 1 April.

Casualties in March 1945:
Officers — Enlisted
KIA 9 — 174
MIA 0 — 8
SWA 3 — 69 (Seriously Wounded in Action)
LWA 29 — 480 (Lightly Wounded in Action)
Total 41 — 731
Prisoners: 3,540

Fit to Fight

To put things into perspective, following are the casualties for 4ID (approximate force of 16,000 troops) from June 6, 1944 to March 31, 1945:

Officers—Enlisted—Total
KIA 262—3,536—3,798
WIA (SWA/LWA): 19,140

With the war continuing, the 4ID suffered another 15 officers and 175 enlisted men killed in April 1945 and 667 were wounded, to bring the totals through April 30 to 3,988 killed and almost 20,000 wounded. These numbers do not include those who died or were injured from non-hostile causes. And there were still eight more days of the war in Europe after April 30, 1945.

Spotter plane

Artillery Forward Observers at work

APRIL 1945

4ID IN GERMANY

1 APRIL 1945—D+300: The Division Provost Marshal reported that he had located five Allied Prisoner of War enclosures in the Division Command Post area, a total of 384 prisoners of war. All the camps were reported short of rations, so arrangements were made to furnish the necessary food.

The disposition of the large number of American prisoners of war being released by our advancing troops presented a problem at this time. It was stated that those imprisoned more than sixty days would be evacuated through medical channels and those of less than sixty days through reinforcement channels.

An estimated battalion of antiaircraft artillery and small disorganized groups of enemy strongly defended Wurtzburg. Enemy resistance in the 4th Infantry Division sector was light and scattered.

The 4th Infantry Division continued the advance to the northeast in the direction of Wurzburg with the 8th and 22nd Infantry Regiments abreast and the 12th Infantry in division reserve. Increased resistance was encountered throughout the period and march units were harassed throughout the day and during the hours of darkness by enemy jet-propelled aircraft. The Division's objective was reached, and preparations made for support of the 12th Armored Division's attack on 2 April.

The 8th Infantry Regiment with the 29th Field Artillery Battalion; Company A, 70th Tank Battalion; Company A, 4th Engineer Combat Battalion; Company A, 4th Medical Battalion; and Company A, 99th Chemical Mortar Battalion attached, continued the advance at first light in the direction of Wurzburg following elements of the 12th Armored Division. A continuous shuttle movement was made throughout the day east through the 22nd Infantry Regiment's zone of action and then northeast toward the regimental objective immediately south of Wurzburg. By 1300, against increasing resistance of small arms, mortar fire, and direct fire from antiaircraft weapons, the leading elements of the combat team closed in the vicinity of the objective close behind the forward elements of the 12th Armored Division. Several attacks by jet-propelled enemy aircraft were made upon motor columns of the combat team throughout the day.

The 12th Infantry Regiment with the 42nd Field Artillery Battalion; Company B, 70th Tank Battalion; Company B, 4th Engineer Combat Battalion; Company B, 4th Medical Battalion; and Company B, 99th Chemical Mortar Battalion attached, remained in reserve. At 0655, the entire combat team began a shuttle movement forward and closed in an assembly area in the vicinity of Hardheim by 1930.

The 22nd Infantry Regiment with the 44th Field Artillery Battalion; Company C, 70th Tank Battalion; Company C, 4th Engineer Combat Battalion; Company C, 4th Medical Battalion; and Company C, 99th Chemical Mortar Battalion attached, advanced to the east beginning at 0600, then northeast toward the regimental objective in the vicinity of Grunsfeld. Small arms fire and a moderate amount of artillery fire was encountered in Heckfeld at 1020 but this did not deter the advance. By 1305 the advance units had reached Luada where a heavy amount of artillery was encountered. By the close of the period, the 2nd Battalion advanced as far as the village of Kurtzbronn where Company E took over 200 prisoners of war. In the interim, the 1st and 3rd Battalions continued on to the northeast, securing the regimental objective.

Upon verbal orders of the CG XXI Corps, two battalions of the 22nd Infantry were attached at 2250 to Combat Command R of the 12th Armored Division.

2 APRIL 1945—D+301: Elements of CT 8 encountered small arms resistance east of Neidinsfeld early in the period. At 1400, the 101st Cavalry met determined resistance consisting of bazooka, rocket, and mortar fire supported by direct fire from a tank or self-propelled gun in the vicinity of Osfeld. There was an increase in enemy air activity. An unknown number of enemy planes bombed at 0030 and between 1700 and 1745, twelve ME 109 and five FW 190 bombed and strafed the Division area. At least four enemy planes were destroyed by our antiaircraft artillery.

The 4th Infantry Division continued mopping up operations south of Wurtzburg with the 8th and 22nd Infantry. Over 1400 prisoners of war were captured. A bridgehead was affected across the Main river in the vicinity of Ochsenfurt by 2245.

CT 8 resumed operations at an early hour with the 2nd Battalion and one company of the 1st Battalion to clear scattered enemy resistance from Gullenberger Wald, a large wooded area southeast of Wuzburg. By mid-afternoon the 2nd Battalion had cleared enemy forces as far north as Hechberg. In the interim, the 1st Battalion advanced to the southeast and relieved elements of the 12th Armored Division in the vicinity of Oschenfurt. On fulfillment of the mission assigned to the 2nd Battalion, it returned to an assembly area in the vicinity of Rottenbauer closing prior to dark. Shortly after darkness fell, the 1st Battalion proceeded with operations to effect a river crossing in the vicinity of Oschenfurt and reported the mission accomplished by 2245.

CT 12 remained assembled in reserve in the vicinity of Hardheim.

The 1st and 2nd Battalions of the 22nd Infantry, attached to the 12th Armored Division, continued their attack in conjunction with operations of the 12th Armored Division and succeeded in clearing enemy forces from the high ground in the vicinity of Konigshofer with a large number of prisoners of war being captured. Dispositions of the remainder of CT 22 remained unchanged.

3 APRIL 1945—D+302: A general increase in enemy artillery and mortar fire with a predominance of 120 mm mortar, 75 mm, 88 mm, and 105 mm artillery was reported. Enemy units continued to show little organization and were comprised of numerous scattered remnants of minor detachments.

The 4th Infantry Division continued the attack against stiffening resistance on the right flank.

CT 8 moved the 2nd and 3rd Battalions to the south in the vicinity of the 1st Battalion's bridgehead. The 2nd Battalion effected a crossing at 1500 and the 3rd at 1730. The 1st Battalion became engaged in a small arms' fight in the wooded area east of Zeubelried. During mid-afternoon, a Bailey bridge was completed in the vicinity of Oschenfurt and CC R of the 12th Armored Division began crossing at 1600.

CT 12 initiated movement to a new assembly area in the vicinity of Gaubuttelbrunn.

The 1st and 2nd Battalions of the 22nd Infantry continued the attack and the 1st Battalion encountered determined resistance east of Konigshofen from enemy troops dressed in black uniforms. At 0900, the 1st and 2nd Battalions reverted to regimental control whereupon the 2nd Battalion was committed at 1115 to assist the 1st Battalion's attack in clearing the large, wooded area confronting them. Resistance continued heavy and progress was slow. At the close of the period, preparations were made to commit the 3rd Battalion.

4 APRIL 1945—D+303: A marked decrease in artillery and mortar fire was noted. The enemy remained defensive, holding several towns and strong points.

The 8th Infantry was subjected to a raid on the regimental command post area during the night of 3-4 April. The raiding force estimated at about 25 enemy soldiers armed with bazookas and incendiary grenades, succeeded in destroying approximately a dozen vehicles, killed one enlisted man, and caused a great deal of confusion within the CP. The 1st Battalion continued its attack to the northeast along the high ground overlooking the town of Erlach while operating in conjunction with Task Force Field of CC B 12th Armored Division. In the interim, the 2nd Battalion remained in position previously occupied, and the 3rd Battalion closed in the area previously held by the 1st Battalion.

CT 12 launched a coordinated attack with the 22nd Infantry Regiment at 1300. It encountered stiff enemy resistance from enemy entrenched in wooded areas.

Despite the stiff resistance encountered from SS troops that were well entrenched in high wooded areas, the 2nd Battalion of the 22nd Infantry was successful in occupying during the late afternoon, the town of Messelhasen.

From **Swede Henley's Diary—used with permission of his daughters:**

28-29 MARCH: CP in Lindenberg. Received orders to move across the Rhine on the 29th.

30 MARCH: Crossed Rhine River at 0530 on Pontoon Bridge at Worms—(what a relief to cross that bastard). Route—Worms, Burstaht, Lorsh, HeppenHeim, Laudenback. Set up CP in Landenback for 3 hours. Received orders to move to Michelback. Route—Hemsback, Weinheim, Morlenback, Weiher, Wald, Michelback. CP set up for night and was it a honey—electric lights, radio, and everything. Kraut fraulein look good but no fraternization. Received orders to move to Hebstahl by foot at motor beginning at 0800.

31 MARCH: Moved to Hebstahl. Closed at 1600 hours. CP in Beerhall and Inn. Route—Schonnaatenevag, Hedderback, Herschorn, Rothenberg, Beerfelden, Hebstahl. Received orders to move out at 0600 in morning for 50 mile attack. Company of tanks attached. Moving for speed and time now.

1 APRIL 1944: April Fool and Easter Sunday (Would like an egg for Easter)

Moved out on 50 mile march at 0615. Arrived at Lauda at 1400 and found bridge across Tauber river intact. Pushed on to Gerlachsheim and ran into hell. Captured or killed 350 Krauts. Pushed on to Grunsfeld and Krutzbrienn. Captured or killed 125 more Krauts.

2 APRIL: Attached with 1st Bn to 12 Arm. Div. to get thru passed Konigshofen. Opened road at 1900 but the sorry bastards used another road.

3 APRIL: Helped 1st Bn get unhitched from the Krauts. Fighting a bunch from NCO school and are they mean. They fight to the end.

4 APRIL: Attacked and took woods and Messelhausen after a helluva fight. Blue Bn helping 1st Bn.
- Found big television radio set—supposed to be largest in the world.

From **History of the 22nd Infantry Regiment in WWII** *by Chaplain Bill Boice:*

Upon termination of the period in which Combat Team 22 was an element of the Seventh U. S. Army reserve, and during which time the CT had again raised its combat efficiency by training, motor maintenance, and rehabilitation work, the unit was again committed to action against the Germans on the 30th of March 1945. The Twenty-Second Infantry Regiment, Fourth Infantry Division, was not to be an important element in the final thrust to defeat the Germans. After crossing the Rhine, the main objective was to attack to the Brenner Pass. It was established that the Germans were planning to stage a delaying action until their forces from northern Germany could form a defensive line in the Bavarian Alps in conjunction with the troops which they had fighting in the Po Valley and northern Italy.

The Brenner Pass was the only logical route through which the forces might again connect. This pass must be seized as rapidly as possible in an effort to prevent a uniting of forces and to isolate these enemy units in Italy from those in the Bavarian Alps and the rest of Germany. Though the regiment never actually reached the Brenner Pass, it did in approximately thirty-seven days disrupt enemy communications, transportation, supply and in turn force them into an utter state of confusion. The regiment in the month's drive attacked and drove the Germans back to the very edge of the Bavarian Alps in southern Germany. In order for this mission to be accomplished, objectives were sent down daily to the CT for its continuous drive to the southeast.

On the 30th of March, the regiment staged forward in rear of the 7th Army advance. Movement began by motor convoy about 0030 hours. The regiment was to move to an assembly area east of the Rhine. The route to be taken was via Neustadt, Baddurkheim, Heuchetheim, Worms, Heppenheim, Laudenbach. The column closed in shortly after dawn after travelling fifty miles, but immediately upon arrival all units were informed that the stop was to be brief, and a further move would be carried out that day.

Motorized patrols moved out at once and were followed by the main body. Because of poor roads and traffic congestion, the advance was slow, but forward elements pushed on with the mission of passing through the 12th Armored Division and securing the Army bridgehead thirty miles east of the Rhine. At dark, the Regiment secured for the night in the environs of Schonmattenwag, Hirschhorn, and Finkenbach.

The advance east was resumed early the morning of the 31st, with the mission of securing Eberbach. Preceded by strong motorized patrols, the attacking battalions easily reached these objectives with only slight resistance. This advance covered six miles. Elements of the 12th Armored Division and the 101st Cavalry Group, by their operations to the east, were greatly facilitating the advance of the Regiment.

The Combat Team mission on the 1st of April was to secure a crossing of the Tauber River, about 35 miles to the east, and secure an objective near Grunsfeld. The Regimental I & R Platoon reconnoitered routes for about twenty miles east and encountered units of the 12th Armored and returned. At 0600 hours, the Regiment, motorized only with organic transportation and several medium tanks, attacked east. The 2nd Battalion was completely motorized in order to affect a rapid advance. The unit pushed rapidly through Mudau, Buchen, Hettingen, Gerichstetten, Buch Ahorn, Heckfeld, and Lauda. The latter part of this move was made on foot against light resistance. Against increasing artillery and mortar opposition, the unit crossed the Tauber River during the early afternoon.

By late afternoon the 2nd Battalion had secured Grunsfeld and the high ground around the town.

In the meantime the 1st and 3rd Battalions had been shuttled forward, and both battalions attacked through the 2nd Battalion. The 1st Battalion pushed slightly more than 1,000 yards to the southeast of Grunsfeld and seized Krensheim.

The 3rd Battalion, moving through Lauda after dark, was struck by German fighter planes. Because the head of the column was not affected and the rear was, the column split in Lauda, and contact was lost. Capt. Reid, of Co. 'I', took command of the last section of the column and deployed the vehicles off the road to avoid strafing or bombing. In the eastern edge of Lauda was a railroad overpass, and men huddled silently beneath it as the German planes circled overhead looking for a target. In the distance, huge flames lit up the sky as the small town of Konigshofen burned. The planes could be heard firing their machine guns and blue streaks lined the sky as the incendiary bullets flashed forth in their mission of destruction. As always, some irresponsible GI lit a cigarette and the match flame flickered in the wind. Immediately shouts went forth, "Put out that damned cigarette. " It was too late; the planes thundered down, strafing the road, and lighting up the area with blue light.

After a short while, the rumbling motors were gone, and the column quickly moved down the road again. Each man knew the planes had only gone for a re-supply of ammunition and bombs, to return laden with their destructive missiles. Farther down the road, the column passed the area occupied by the 44th Field Artillery Battalion, and the planes were again heard. At once the 377th Antiaircraft Bn protecting the field artillery opened fire, and quick flashes of ack-ack burst in the sky. The column continued to move in spite of the aircraft, and several hours later arrived in the prearranged assembly area. During the day the Regiment had moved over fifty miles through very hilly terrain and over poor secondary roads.

In comparison to the previous encounters with the enemy forces, the past few weeks had been easy, casualties light, and the advance quick and continuous. This brought with it a new hope that Germany would soon collapse and the European War which had begun years before would finally cease.

There was ground yet to be gained, battles to be fought, and victories to be won. On the 2nd of April, the 1st and 2nd Battalion were attached to Combat Command 'R', of the 12th Armored Division. These two rifle battalions attacked to the south to clear the east bank of the Tauber River and help the armored command across the stream. Enemy artillery, rocket, and small arms fire was moderately heavy, but Marbach, Kutzbrunn, and Hofstetten were captured. Opposition to this attack to the south indicated a sizeable enemy force north of Bad Mergentheim and east of the Tauber River. CT 22, with only one rifle battalion remaining under its control, searched through, and mopped up its objective with motorized patrols.

Before noon the 3rd of April, the 1st and 2nd Battalions returned to the control of CT 22. The 3rd Battalion reverted to reserve and moved to an assembly area in Gerlachsheim. The day was utilized in position consolidation and the re-grouping of forces.

Well observed, heavy enemy rocket, mortar, and artillery fire on forward elements of the 1st and 2nd Battalions further indicated the general enemy defensive build-up south of the Combat Team.

Shortly after daylight, an enemy group of more than forty men slipped in between Companies 'B' and 'C', and a fight ensued. Three jeeps attempting to carry supplies to Co. 'B' were ambushed by these Germans and two men were killed, three wounded. Around 1430 hours, Co. 'F' with a detachment of tanks was sent down along the eastern edge of the woods to contact 'C' Company. Capt. Surratt, Battalion S3, was killed by a mortar shell just after he had succeeded in once again tying in the front lines of 'B' and 'C' Companies. Fighting was bitter, but within an hour, 'F' Company had managed to extricate Company 'C'.

An attack to the south on the following day was delayed pending the completion of plans and the issuance of orders. Shortly after noon, the 3rd Battalion attacked through the 1st Battalion across the Marbach-Hofstetten Road. Initially, progress was rapid, with only slight opposition, and Co. 'L' reached the edge of the woods about 1,100 yards northeast of Konigshofen, where it held, as Companies 'I' and 'K' pushed west to clear the wooded hill 300 yards right of Co. 'L'. Heavy small arms resistance was met on this hill, and the advance stopped. The command group from Co. 'M' and the 81mm mortar platoon moved into the town of Konigshofen and secured it for the night.

In talking to a couple of civilians living in the town, it was learned why the town had been burned. German SS Troops several days before had found civilians possessing the white flags of surrender, which they intended to display upon the arrival of the Yanks. The SS Troops immediately poured gasoline on the houses and set fire to them, telling the civilians that they would be shot if they ever attempted to surrender. Hundreds of people were homeless, and children gathered in the school building, crying that their homes and parents were gone. These were the houses seen burning from Lauda several nights before.

The 1st Battalion had, in the meantime, adjusted its positions to the rear of the 3rd Battalion, and the 2nd Battalion probed to the southeast in order to attain a position to the left rear, northwest, of the 1st Battalion. Before dark the 2nd Battalion had secured the town of Messelhausen.

From — War Stories: Volume II — Paris to VE Day...

Dominick Huster, Morris Plains, NJ
Co A, 1-22 Infantry Regiment
Hairy Escape

After crossing the Rhine, we were advancing on a small town by going through a large, open field when we came under fire from snipers in a small clump of trees in the middle of the field. We all hit the ground and started shooting in that direction. Suddenly, a rabbit jumped out and headed off to our right. Everyone in the company stopped shooting at the snipers and started shooting at the rabbit. I was a mortar gunner and fired my .45 caliber pistol — the barrel needed cleaning anyway. The rabbit escaped the hail of bullets unharmed. We took the town unopposed. Our marksmanship wasn't tested by the Germans.

Jim Roan, Fenton, MI
Company H, 12th Infantry Regiment
The Beginning of the End

As we went further into Germany, the destruction of cities was awful. We had to feel sorry for the civilians, especially the children. There was a lapse between the time that a city was taken and the time the army-trained civil administrators took over. The people needed food, shelter, and medical help. We always set up shop in the best structures available, and we had plenty of rations for our own needs and some left over. The roads were full of GI flatbed trucks crammed with what was left of the German army. Prisoners of war were crowded into these vehicles with little room to sit down. Some were wounded, and they spent a day or two traveling to their destinations. When they exited these vehicles, they had a hard time walking, and some died during transport.

We noted that there was always a crowd around. The civilians would cheer as they were transported by our troops. The U.S. Army did supply them with boxed rations, usually C or K rations, which we were being fed most of the time. We occasionally were treated with a hot meal when the kitchens caught up with us, and I can still picture the civilians patiently waiting in line with their buckets to dip into the slop that we dumped from our mess kits. We always took more food than we could consume just so they would have something to dip into.

5 APR 1945 TO 11 APR 1945 – D+304 TO D+310

5 APRIL 1945—D+304: At the close of the period, the enemy defended along a general line Theilheim—Wesytheim—Pepperndorf. Light resistance was met as elements of CT 8 entered Kitzingen. Our troops advanced to Eibelstadt and Lindelbach against scattered resistance. In CT 12 and 22 sectors, the enemy continued a stubborn defense consisting of small arms, automatic weapons, and bazooka fire. CT 22 advanced south on the high ground east of Konigshofen and met extremely stubborn resistance from an estimated 150 enemy well dug in on the reverse slope of the hill. Positions at this location were well camouflaged with natural material which blended well with the surrounding rocky terrain. Between 2150 and 2205 an unknown number of enemy planes dropped fragmentation and demolition bombs about 3,000 yards southwest of Ochsenfurt.

CT 8 continued the attack at 0800 in conjunction with Task Force Field of the 12th Armored Division with the 1st Battalion following closely behind advancing armored elements. The armored attack in the direction of Kitzengin progressed rapidly and by 0950 was closing on the outskirts of the city. The 1st Battalion moved into the town and two rifle companies mopped up within the city. The attack of the 3rd Battalion to the north progressed favorably and by the end of the period, all areas in the vicinity of Randersacker had been cleared of resistance. The 2nd Battalion remained in reserve in the vicinity of Ochsenfurt.

CT 12 continued the attack to the south and southwest at 0730 with the 2nd and 3rd Battalions abreast. The attack of the 3rd Battalion progressed favorably and an advance of three kilometers was made in the direction of Messelhausen. The attack of the 2nd Battalion met greater resistance and after heavy fighting throughout the period, the battalion succeeded in pushing through the woods, killing an estimated one hundred enemy. The 1st Battalion remained in regimental reserve in the vicinity of Euerhausen.

CT 22 continued the attack to the south with three battalions abreast. Progress in the entire regimental sector was negligible. The enemy employed 150 mm and 105 mm artillery, 120 mm and 80 mm mortars, small arms, and numerous automatic weapons. By the close of the period, the wooded areas to the south and north of Messelhausen had been cleared.

6 APRIL 1945—D+305: An enemy front line could not be clearly defined. CT 8 cleared the enemy from the area between Wurzburg, Kitzingen, and the Main river. CT 12 and 22 advanced to the south against small, scattered pockets of enemy resistance.

The 4th Infantry Division continued the attack, conducting mopping up operations in the left portion of the Division's zone of action, while attacking to the south with the 12th and 22nd Infantry Regiments abreast in the direction of Bad Mergentheim. Prior to the close of the period, the high ground overlooking the town had been secured by the 22nd Infantry Regiment.

The 8th Infantry continued mopping up operations within the zone of action north of Ochsenfurt.

The 12th Infantry continued the attack beginning at 0630 when the 2nd Battalion moved out, followed by the 3rd Battalion. Progress was continuous throughout the period against only scattered opposition. By nightfall the 2nd Battalion had advanced five kilometers and cleared Hassau. The 3rd Battalion reached Harthausen with elements reaching Helzbronn.

The 22nd Infantry continued the advance to the south. Prior to the close of the period, the leading elements of the 3rd Battalion had cleared the enemy from Edelfigen. The 2nd Battalion advanced against only light opposition and by 2300, two companies had secured the high ground overlooking the town of Bad Mergentheim from the north. The 1st Battalion mopped up the areas between the attacking battalions.

7 APRIL 1945—D+306: Enemy front lines remained fluid. The towns of Merkelsheim, Weikersheim, Rotteingen, and Bieberehren were believed to be enemy strong points. In CT 8's sector, the enemy remained entirely defensive. In CT 12's sector, the enemy was stubbornly defending the south flank of the Tauber river. In CT 22's sector the enemy was holding the hill southwest of Igersheim from well dug in positions. Between 2015 and 2100 seven JU 88 strafed the Division sector and three of them were shot down by our AA artillery.

The 8th Infantry continued mopping up operations.

The 12th Infantry initiated a coordinated attack at 0700 with the 1st and the 3rd Battalions abreast. Scattered enemy resistance was encountered throughout the day from a well-entrenched enemy employing small arms and mortar fire. At the close of the period, the two battalions were along the Tauber river. The small towns of Igersheim, Schaftersheim, Tauberrettersheim, and Rottingen were occupied while patrols reported the towns of Wierkersheim and Bieberehren to be strongly defended.

The 22nd Infantry attacked with its 2nd and 3rd Battalions. At an early hour, the 3rd Battalion occupied the town of Bad Mergentheim with only little resistance reported and during the afternoon continued its advance. The 1st Battalion remained in the vicinity of Gerlachsheim in division reserve.

8 APRIL 1945—D+307: The enemy was believed to have held a defensive line along the high ground south of the Tauber river. Early in the period, CT 22 routed the enemy from the castle at Burg Neuhaus. CT 12 met stubborn resistance in Rottingen and after a house-to-house fight, reported the town clear as of 1335. Fighting was still going on in Weikersheim at the close of the period. Several enemy planes strafed in the vicinity of Gerlachsheim at 2100.

The 8th Infantry in conjunction with the 12th Armored Division completed mopping up operations within their zone.

The 12th Infantry initiated strong patrols to the south along the Tauber river. The towns of Rottingen and Elpersheim were occupied during the day. The town of Weikersheim was strongly defended by a small but stubborn enemy force, but at the close of the day, Company K reported one-half of the town cleared.

The 22nd Infantry carried on extensive patrolling with Company F reaching as far south as the town of Apfelbach. The town of Igersheim was completely cleared during the afternoon.

9 APRIL 1945—D+308: Opposite CT 12, the enemy front lines extended along the high ground south of the Tauber river. In addition, the town of Bieberehren appeared to be defended by about 70 enemy. CT 12 cleared the towns of Elpersheim and Weikersheim. Considerable 75 mm or 88 mm fire from a self-propelled gun or tank fell in the area occupied by CT 12 during the period. Several towns along the front lines received intermittent fire.

10 APRIL 1945—D+309: No aggressive action from the enemy was reported. Laudenbach and Haagen were cleared late in the period. CT 22 advanced without contact until 1515 when an unknown number of enemy dug in positions were encountered. Artillery fire was light until near the end of the period. At 2230 enemy planes dropped flares on the high ground south of Elpersheim and later strafed and dropped two bombs in that vicinity.

The 4th Infantry Division attacked to the southeast with the 12th and 22nd Infantry Regiments abreast and secured the general line Bartenstein-Rottingen prior to the close of the period.

The 8th Infantry continued mopping up operations, apprehending small disorganized groups of the enemy.

The 12th Infantry assisted the 22nd Infantry by attacking at 1000 to seize Hill 401 and the town of Lauderbach. Enemy opposition was light and by 1900, the 3rd Battalion had secured the regimental objective.

The 22nd Infantry attacked at 0900 with the 2nd Battalion on the left and the 3rd on the right to seize the line Berkenstein-Niederstetten. By late afternoon, both battalions had established themselves upon the regimental objective.

The 324th Infantry Regiment with other elements was attached to the 4th Infantry Division at 1500.

11 APRIL 1945—D+310: In CT 22 and CT 324 sectors, strong points were at Wermisthausen, Queckbrown, Schrezberg, and Oberstetten. Troops of CT 12 while being relieved by CT 22 were pinned down by small arms, automatic weapons, and 20 mm antiaircraft artillery fire in the vicinity of Hill 401. Other elements of CT 12 received small arms and automatic weapons in the woods. At 1910, our troops in Laudenbach received small arms fire from enemy dug in southeast of the town. The advance of CT 22 was stubbornly resisted by enemy employing small arms, automatic, and direct fire weapons in dug in strong points. Two serious counterattacks were also repulsed, one of them in the vicinity of Malberbach. An unknown number of enemy planes dropped various demolition and antipersonnel bombs in the vicinity of Erlach and Marktbreit.

The 4th Infantry Division met stubborn resistance from artillery, small arms, and antiaircraft guns within the center zone of action from a determined enemy.

The 8th Infantry attacked at approximately 1000 with the 1st Battalion on the left and the 2nd Battalion on the right. The 1st Battalion moved to the towns of Willanzheim, Toefenstockheim, and Stadt Schwarzach. The 2nd Battalion was at the close of the period in the vicinity of Obernbreit. The 3rd Battalion was in division reserve in the vicinity of Ochsenfurt.

The 12th Infantry initiated an attack with the 1st Battalion at 0800 to clear the enemy from the woods and after hard fighting had cleared the enemy. The 2nd Battalion's main effort was initiated by Company E and at the close of the period, they were in the vicinity of Baldersheim. The 3rd Battalion in reserve closed in the town of Riedenheim.

The 22nd Infantry initiated an attack at approximately 0930 with the 3rd Battalion on the left and the 1st Battalion on the right. At the close of the period, the 3rd Battalion after a slow advance under heavy small arms fire, was holding the high ground. Throughout the day the 1st Battalion was under continuous artillery and some self-propelled fire from the vicinity of Hill 400. Not until during the late afternoon did the companies of the 1st Battalion reach the high ground after employing a combination of infantry and tanks.

From **Swede Henley's Diary — used with permission of his daughters:**

5 APRIL 1945: Ordered at 1430 to take Oberbalback. Jumped off and entered town at 1545. Ordered to go on for Loffelstelzen. Took objective at 1800. Send medic and patrol to Bad Mergentheim to see if town is clear and evacuate 4 Yanks in hospital. Found town clear.

6 APRIL 1945: Passed thru town to high ground to SE. CP in hotel at

Bad Mergentheim. What a place—second to none. Captured big radio station (propoganda).

7 APRIL 1945: CP in Bad Mergentheim—living like kings and enjoying life.
- Bad Mergentheim, Germany…a very pretty town—28 hospitals—the Krauts aren't hurting for anything. Hospital had cure for crud, but it did not work on Ruggles or Col. Lanham…too far gone.

8-9 APRIL 1945: Same

10 APRIL 1945: Ordered to attack to the southeast and clean out woods. Jumped off at 0900. Cleaned out Markelsheim, Elpersheim, Russelhaussen, Herrenzimmern, Adolzhausen, Bronn, Pfitzingen. SS Krauts burned town of Adolzhausen last night before they pulled out.

11 APRIL 1945: Held high ground. Ordered at 1750 to attack high ground on 1st Bn right flank. Moved CP to Pfitzingen.

From **History of the 22nd Infantry Regiment in WWII** *by Chaplain Bill Boice:*

The 3rd Battalion, which was meeting the stiffest resistance on the Konigshofen Ridge, was held to very small gains on the 4th and 5th of April. Heavy woods prevented the use of tanks in the attack, and intense, accurate small arms fire met every movement of the foot troops. As Capt. Reid later stated, "That was the doggonedest small arms fire 'Big Item Co.' will ever encounter." The ground on this ridge consisted of the heavy woods with rock piles parallel to the line of advance with holes cut in them for German automatic weapons. Almost every casualty suffered was by a direct hit in the head with one bullet. Lt. Neel, who led his machine gun platoon all the way from Northern France through Germany, was quite correct when he said, "In a battalion there are two machine gun platoons, one of which is always attached to each assault company, and there are always two assault companies, so while one rifle company is pulled into reserve to rest, the machine gun platoon is attached to the next assault company. In other words, a damn machine gunner never gets a rest."

The enemy were found to be paratroopers and as fanatical as any troop of German soldiers we had fought. They were young, from fifteen to nineteen, but they fought with a fanaticism of which we had read, but seldom had met. It was this group of men that against Co. 'C', had led one of the old-fashioned charges in which an officer stood up, and shouting and yelling, the men had charged forward, only to be cut down and hurled back by our machine guns, and finally by hand-to-hand bayonet fighting.

One of these young Hitler youth had a wound in his leg which prevented his crawling away, and he was sitting under a tree. In the clean-up of wounded after the attack had been repulsed, the battalion medics, as usual, were going from person to person, tagging them, administering first aid, evacuating litter cases, helping the wounded, and sending them to the safety of the rear areas where they could be treated by the surgeons. One of the medics started to approach the wounded German lad when the boy picked up a "potato masher", the common name for the German hand grenade, so called because it was shaped exactly like the old-fashioned wooden potato masher, with long wooden handle, for throwing. The medic stopped and pointed to the red cross arm band which he was wearing, then to his medical kit, then to the German. The German stared at him stonily, and as the medic again moved to approach him, he unscrewed the cap of his grenade and the medic hit the dirt, expecting the German to throw it. Instead, the lad held the grenade immediately under his chin until it went off, blowing his head completely and cleanly from his body. Such was the fanaticism of the Hitler youth.

Contact between our 2nd Battalion, still in Messelhausen, and CT 12 was established on the 6th of April, and, in agreement with plans, the 2nd Battalion reverted to regimental reserve at the time. As CT 12 pushed south, the 1st Battalion attacked and cleared the woods 1,000 yards north of Deubach and later advanced into the town itself.

The 3rd Battalion continued to meet heavy small arms resistance during the morning hours. About mid-day, the fire slackened, and a strong combat patrol was sent forward; this patrol returned with the information that the enemy was apparently withdrawing to previously prepared defenses around Bad Mergentheim. Patrols from the 1st Battalion had worked into the woods just south of Sailtheim and had heard voices and digging in various parts of the woods. Elements of the battalion were sent through the woods with tanks "firing like hell." 'C' Company attacked on a cross-country maneuver and captured Deubach while Co. 'B' advanced into the town shortly thereafter by coming down from the north.

The 2nd Battalion moved forward at approximately the same time as the 1st and seized Oberhalbach and Loffelstelzen.

The 3rd Battalion purposely delayed and then started cross country to Unterbalbach. As they left the Konigshofen Ridge, the German dead lay piled like cordwood over every conceivable defensive terrain feature. Some of the Germans had been dead for several days, and their skin was turning black, and the blood clotted clothing swarmed with flies. There was the foul stench of death in the atmosphere, while overhead a single bird chirped as if in mockery to the mortals below. Proceeding on across the open fields, the Battalion moved into Unterbalbach and Edelfingen. By night the CT was overlooking Bad Mergentheim from the north.

At once the 2nd Battalion sent a patrol into Bad Mergentheim to investigate and determine the enemy strength. Lt. Kornreich, of 'E' Company, led the patrol in about midnight. He was accompanied by Capt. Herrick, 2nd Bn. medical officer, who was to secure the release of three wounded American soldiers in the hospitals there. The patrol returned with the three wounded Americans and information that there was no organized resistance in Bad Mergentheim and that the vehicular bridge there still remained intact. With the information, the 2nd Battalion sent a larger patrol into Bad Mergentheim to penetrate through the town and reach the high ground to the south. This patrol returned with the information that the enemy was digging in south of Hill 307. Too, much to the surprise of the men in the patrol, the Burgomeister (town mayor) stated that the German civilians who lived in the town had, after a lengthy discussion, persuaded the German soldiers to surrender or to withdraw. The civilians were also responsible for keeping the bridge intact. These people realized that if the soldiers attempted to defend the town, American artillery, mortar, and tank fire would completely destroy both themselves and the town.

Lt. Col. "Lum" EDWARDS, Regimental S3, first received this information and immediately reported it to Lt. Col. JOHN F. RUGGLES, Combat Team Commander, who then ordered the Regiment to move into Bad Mergentheim and outpost the surrounding terrain. This action was initially carried out by the 3rd Battalion. Erroneously, a 3rd Battalion wire team jeep carrying Lt. Rose and his two forward linemen struck out down the main road into the town. They crossed the bridge and drove down across the railroad tracks into the center of town. Upon arrival at the town square, no GI's could be seen, and Lt. Rose turned to the driver and whispered, "My God, man, we're the only ones in town. Turn this jeep around and let's get the hell out of here; we might get killed." The wide-eyed occupants of the jeep quickly turned around and sped down the narrow streets. German civilians stared in amazement at the four passengers, not realizing their mistake. As the jeep left the edge of town, they met the lead scouts of one of the rifle companies moving toward the town. As the jeep drove by the advancing foot troops, the driver ironically leaned out of his jeep and said, "There's no one in there; we just cleaned out the town."

The 3rd Battalion moved on into the town, leaving 'I' Company to guard the hospitals, and the balance of the battalion moved on to Hill 374 southeast of the town. Bad Mergentheim was a hospital center and recuperation area for over a thousand Germans. Many homes had been converted into hospitals to care for the wounded.

The 2nd Battalion, following the 3rd Battalion, moved through the town to Hill 307, turned southeast, and moved to Hill 374 abreast and east of the 3rd Battalion.

The 1st Battalion had previously assembled in Oberbalbach and just before dark moved to Gerlachsheim as division reserve.

In conversations with the civilian populace of the town, it was not a rare occurrence to speak entirely in English. The German youth had been taught English in their schools as long as they could remember. Hitler had been preparing for this war and the defeat of the United States many years.

The town of Bad Mergentheim was a resort town somewhat similar to Hot Springs, Arkansas. It was situated along the Tauber River in between the surrounding hills. The streets within the town were narrow and the buildings and homes closely fitted. The buildings were not of large structure, usually only two floors with windows and large verandas opening into the streets. There were hotels, government buildings and hospitals throughout. In the edge of town and on the hillsides, large mansions could be seen, obviously owned by high government officials or business executives who came to Bad Mergentheim to relax and better their health. After the arrival of the Americans, life continued normally with only minor restrictions and curfews in effect. The German wounded remained within the hospitals, and German medical officers could be seen moving through the town on their routine check accompanied by a couple of our medics. In general, the people were very cooperative and quite thankful that their town had been spared the ravages of war.

From **War Stories Volume II: Paris to VE Day...**

Francis W. Glaze Jr., Clearwater, FL
HQ, 8th Infantry Regiment
One Scary Night

I believe it was in April 1945; the 8th Infantry Regiment was in reserve, and the Division was headed toward Munich, straddling the Autobahn. I had set up the Regimental HQ in the local bank—a sturdy two-story building in the middle of the village. The main street was typical German with two-story houses walling the street with an occasional alley or cross street. The houses had the typical large barn-type double doors fronting on the street. One of the large doors had a normal size "people" door for everyday use.

The I&R Platoon was responsible for security at one end of town, the communications platoon was responsible for the other end, and the security platoon was responsible for the immediate vicinity of Regimental HQ. I had been Duty Officer at HQ until relieved at 0200 hours. I had nothing much to report to my "relief," except some patrol action between us and the 2nd Battalion as well as a firefight in front of the 3rd Battalion. It was a relatively quiet night.

My Company CP was set up on the second floor of a private home down the street from and close by Regimental HQ. We had not made the German civilians evacuate although we did make them go to the cellars of the homes we had commandeered. I had gotten to my CP about 0215 hours and was taking off my shoes just prior to crawling into my sleeping bag. Just then I heard a Schmeiser machine pistol firing in the street up in the I&R area. I alerted my Company CP group, which consisted of the Company Executive Officer, the First Sergeant, two drivers, a radio operator, and my "dog-robber." We could hear firing, explosions, and all sorts of German noises in the street, so we headed down the stairs for the defense of the Regimental HQ.

I was leading, and when I got to the door we could hear hobnailed shoes marching by. It was pitch dark and as I opened the door, a German soldier just passing by stopped. He knew somebody was there but not who. He asked, "Sind sie ein Amerikaner?" I didn't want to say yes, or lie and say no, so I said nothing—just closed the door. I assume the German didn't want to go alone into the dark, so he kept on going. By now we had assumed that the 2nd and 3d Battalion's had been overrun, the Regimental HQ erased, and we were the sole survivors—so far. We went briefly into the inner court to find a route over the roofs and out of town to report the loss of the Regiment. Luckily, we couldn't get to the roof, so we very quietly went back upstairs to look out the windows at the street fighting.

We were no sooner there when there came a knocking at the front door accompanied by much shouting in German. It wasn't my house, so I felt it inappropriate to answer the door. Luckily the lady of the house and her grandfather came out of the cellar to open the door to greet the officer and his detail. He said one of his men had seen someone in the doorway—was it an American? She said that Americans had been there, but she had heard us come down and go out, so we were long gone. She was obviously on their side, so they continued on—mopping up stragglers.

They had no sooner left than the field phone rang—loud enough to awaken the dead or get us killed—whichever came first. I had to stop the ringing, but I was scared of who might be on the other end. I picked up the phone and said, "Hello." From the other end came, "Hello." (You can see our repartee was not up to par.) I responded, "Who's this?" The response was, "Who's this?"

I could see someone had to break the impasse, so I said, "Captain Glaze." The response was, "You don't sound like Captain Glaze."

It is alleged that my response was, "If you were as scared as I am you wouldn't sound like me either."

That must have been a clincher because then we got down to business.

The platoons were all on a party line, so they all started checking in. All the platoons were basically intact; fighting was going on in the street, but only the outposts seemed to be involved. They were evidently looking for a Regimental HQ, but they weren't strong enough to attempt a house-to-house search. It began to sound more like a raid than a general assault, so we decided that we should join the dance. In one minute, each point on the party line (there were about six) would send four to six grenades to the party, then cover the street while "me and mine" went out in the street, across and down an alley, to come in behind the Regimental HQ. Everything went as planned until we got to the end of the alley. Then I remembered that there was no recognition signal, and when we rounded the last building we would be in sight of our outpost behind the bank.

The real problem was that if the Germans had taken the HQ and held the outpost we would be shot; or if our people still held the outpost and we came running up, we would be shot. There was still some shooting going on in the street, but I couldn't see any action inside the bank, so I decided to earn my keep. I left my gun with the first sergeant and walked slowly forward with my arms in the air and softly saying, "Captain Glaze…Don't shoot," over and over, until I suddenly had a rifle muzzle in my gut.

It (the rifle muzzle) was then taken away with the comment, "It really is you, Captain. I'm damn glad to see you, Sir."

I went on by and through the back door of the bank to the stairs going up to the second floor. None of the staff was down at ground level; they were all on the second floor, twittering around, knotting sheets together, and close to panic.

As I went up the stairs I shouted, "What the Hell are you stupid sh--- doing? Get the Hell over to the street windows and shoot anything that moves until I tell you to stop!"

By then it was about all over but the shouting, and shortly we went about the business of counting the cost and paying the piper.

Harry Kuhn and two others were killed on our side versus four Germans; they took their wounded with them, and we had three wounded. We had over thirty jeeps, and the Germans had immobilized eighteen to twenty of them. By that time in the war, our mechanics were so experienced that fifteen jeeps were back in service by 1500 hours and the rest by 2400 hours. I always suspected that they stole or exchanged for two of the worst jeeps, but who was counting?

As I remember, the scariest moment of my life was crossing that street and then going up to the back of the Regimental HQ hoping that I wouldn't be shot by friendly fire. That's what happened, to the best of my memory. We didn't cover ourselves with glory, but most of us did survive.

Philip W. Tawes, Crisfield, MD
Company G, 2nd Battalion, 22nd Infantry Regiment
My German Prisoner

In the spring of 1945 we were chasing the German army. The 2nd Battalion, 22nd Infantry was ordered to secure a hill on the right flank of our army's route of advance. We carried out the assignment with problems.

Our platoons were digging foxholes in the event of a counter-attack. I was on my way to the Company CP and had to cross a wooded area.

I broke out of the heavy stuff into a man-made clearing. Sitting on the ground cross-legged was a German soldier, a pack and rifle beside him, a hunk of bread in one hand and a hunk of cheese in the other, and the friendliest grin on his face one could imagine. I took him prisoner and walked him to the next firebreak. Seeing movement at the bottom of the hill, I pointed him in that direction. I thought it was our CP, but he told me, "Nicht, nicht!" (No, no.)

I pointed on down the hill and then I got it when he said, "Comrades!"

I looked again, and there was a mess of German helmets. I hurried through the woods to the next firebreak. When I looked around, there was my prisoner, an even bigger smile on his face. I slung my rifle, shook his hand, and we walked down the hill side by side. We found the Company CP, and I remember how bad I felt turning him over to the prisoner guard detail. If I had his name and address, I would be sending him a "thank you" card every month.

Henry "Hank" Strecker (Deceased)
Company C, 1-12 Infantry
The war is coming to an end, and I get wounded...
Submitted by his daughter, Leslie Strecker Weisner

It was early April and the Germans were withdrawing from a little town. In the afternoon, the unit went on patrol in the woods across a river. After about an hour they met German rifle fire. The patrol, with Sgt. Joe Juarez in charge, had met the Germans head-on along a firebreak. The startled Germans yelled, "Kommen Sie hier." And Joe snapped back, "Du kommen Sie hier." Joe was fast on the trigger and shot two Germans. The others ran.

That night they spent in the houses of a small German town. Lil and Ellen, his sisters, had sent Hank a package of dry chicken noodle soup which he fixed on the stove. It tasted really good after a steady diet of rations. The next morning the men moved out at 10:00, crossing the river and getting into the corner of some woods where they could see the Germans on the ridge moving around among the bushes. An artillery officer came up and sent in some rounds before the men dug in for the night.

The next morning, the company attacked again, moving about one fourth of a mile. Support was called for and one or two light tanks came up and cleaned out the Germans. The tanks left and the infantrymen moved on. A wounded German was picked up as they headed along the woods and stopped at a clearing. Hank plopped down at the end of the column since everything had come to a stop for the moment. It was a beautiful spring day, bright and warm.

Someone was talking and moving in the woods behind him, and he looked out of curiosity to see who was coming. Five Germans were creeping through the forest. Hank grabbed his rifle and fired at the first, second, and third German, eight times before emptying it, as the Germans dashed off in all directions.

Henry noticed a coal shuttle helmet on the ground and what looked like a German coat lying in the ditch. Hank aimed and fired but was startled by the spray of a burp gun over his head. One of the Germans had sneaked back up on him. Hank ducked behind a tree and hurried to the front of the column to see what was holding them up. As he started back, he heard four or five shots and asked what had happened. The Germans had prowled back and were sniping—Germans ahead were holding things up, too.

It was April 12. They moved up and dug into a night defensive position. Hank heard an explosion in the rear and the TD's moved into their night lager. Only one TD lieutenant made it through and asked if a couple of squads of men could get the Germans out and clear a path for his TD. The patrol crept down to the edge of the woods and spotted two or three figures lying low, but they were afraid it might be their own men. A bullet snapped past Hank's helmet and he yelled, "Let 'em have it boys."

The GI's raced into the woods to get more cover. Hank emptied his BAR at them as the Germans behind the road bank jumped up and ran along the edge of the woods. He felt something hit his leg and thought that his trousers were torn by a branch as he ran in pursuit, but as he looked down it dawned on him. He must have been hit. He hobbled back and slumped into his hole until an aid man came and gave him a shot of morphine. He was thirsty and his squad buddies gave him some water, but water and morphine don't mix, and he got sick.

The squad was mostly replacements, younger than him and they were extremely upset that their experienced staff sergeant would have to leave them. They were saying things like, "How will we make it through without you?" and "Don't leave us." Mortars carrumped in on them. Hank felt terrible—his squad was upset and here he was in a front line hole—knowing he would be out of it after all the unbroken months of combat—if he could live to get out of it—by dusk.

They moved back to the firebreaks and were sitting in the woods. Hank was half asleep and frozen with fear when he saw what he thought was a German on the skyline above him. It was a GI. Jeeps came up, Hank climbed into one and they rolled back along the firebreak where the Germans still lurked, before getting into the town where the battalion aid station was located. An aide Lieutenant asked what the 12th Regiment boys were doing to the Krauts because the ones he was caring for were shot up so bad. The next day Hank was put in an ambulance and taken to an airfield. The GI's had to wait while some Germans were loaded in the first plane, ahead of the Americans. He had waited a long, long time to fulfill his childhood dream of an airplane ride and now, at last, he could hardly enjoy it.

They were flown to Rheims and processed by hospital train to Nancy. His bandage slipped and the wool blanket grated against his open wound along the way. It became infected and was drained with a tube and sewn up. Several days later the stitches were cut out—and the wound opened into a wide crescent scar above his knee. V-E Day dawned with Hank still in the hospital. To celebrate, the French set off dynamite behind the hospital. He was grateful but remembered, there was still the Pacific. While in the hospital, he was given the Purple Heart and one of the nurses gave him her Presidential Unit Citation pin, saying she wanted him to remember them when he wore it and tell people about the work the nurses had done.

Back in the States, his family (father, two sisters, and two younger brothers) were told by the neighbors that there was a telegram for them at the drugstore. No one wanted to retrieve the telegram, fearing the bad news that came in those days. Edward, who was just about to go into the Army—and to the Pacific, was persuaded to ride his bike and pick up the dreaded telegram. It is still in the family keepsakes and the terse form provided some measure of relief as it announced simply, "wounded in Germany." (The two other brothers, Edward and Alan also became sergeants during their Army service. At age eighty-four, Henry still wore his original wool uniform with insignia and medals to Veterans and Memorial Day services).

On recovery, Henry was sent to Worms and then back to the squad at Nuremberg and south to Zuggenheim on the way to Bamberg. Hank was happy to see his buddies again and catch up on the news. He had last seen them on the road to Crailsheim and Rothenburg. Fred Jackson told Hank about how he had captured two German soldiers and some civilians in the basement of a German house after a fight. The two Germans had come out of the basement with their hands up high and, as if to justify themselves, kept saying "Vee ver schleeeping..."

The guys gave Henry a wooden pipe, stamped with skull and crossbones, as a gift on his return. They had found it with boxes of others in a German military warehouse. Army detail began to creep in as combat became a memory. The Lieutenant wanted the sergeants to sew on their stripes and the men were scolded for wearing their wool knit caps or for not wearing the proper uniform.

It seemed odd, after only two showers and two hot meals, from Normandy to the end twelve months later...

In Henry's words... (these memories were preserved by his daughter)

Over the years, especially in November when the snow fell, I would remember Brownie Means, the man from Big Sky country, Montana and often wondered if he was ever able to ride horses again, which was mostly what he had talked about of home. It was sad, not knowing if he even lived through the war. In 1992, I attended my fiftieth Mt. Healthy High

School reunion. During the celebration dinner, different people stood up and told a little about themselves. There were only about 200 of us in the school and one woman got up and mentioned that she was originally from Broadus, Montana. I remembered by a strange coincidence, that was the place Brownie was from, and later asked her if she knew him or his family. She said she knew a Ward Means and the next time she was home in Broadus, she would try to give him my phone number and address.

A few months later she met Brownie, who she only knew as Ward, in the hardware store in Broadus. He had moved to Sheridan, Wyoming but was also paying a visit when they met. Ward called me and he and his wife drove all the way to Ohio to visit us. It was a very emotional meeting. Ward has a truly lovely wife and family, and his grandchildren are riding horses just like he did. The distance between our homes is far on a map but very close when measured by the heart.

On May 25, 1994, my wife Dee and I went to a mini-reunion of the Fourth Infantry Division at the Radisson Hotel in Columbus, Ohio. It was a four-day get together and there were several other conventions going on in the same hotel. On Friday evening, we were in the hospitality room on the second floor. Dee and I always like to welcome new members. I had just met a first-time fellow and while we were talking, a man with a gray beard and wearing a business suit walked in and then left. After I finished talking to the man I had just met, I asked the bartender if he knew the name of the man who just left. He said he thought it was Angle or something like that.

A light bulb lit up in my head as I said, "Was his first name Richard?" He said he didn't know. I ran straight down to the nearest elevator and down to the lobby. One of the men organizing the reunion was coming toward me and I asked him if he had seen a man with a beard. He said yes, he tried to get him to join the Fourth Infantry Division Association. I asked for his name, and he replied, Richard Engle. I was frantic. I thought after forty nine years of wondering if this man had lived, he got away from me.

I went to the girl at the desk and asked if she had a listing for Richard Engle. She said yes, but she could not give me his room number or phone number. I explained my situation and she said she would try to call his room.

After about an hour, I gave up. I figured he had gone somewhere, and I would try to reach him about nine the next morning. The next morning I called the operator, and she connected me to his room. I said, "Richard, you won't believe who this is." After I explained, he said he would come right down to our room. We had a wonderful conversation for about an hour.

They had sent him right back after he got hit in Normandy. The doctor told him that if he would have coughed on the way back from the front, he would have bled to death. Needless to say, we were two happy buddies. Richard had become a priest in 1956 and I had become a convert upon marrying my wife Dee in 1947. He was only at the Radisson that day to attend a Catholic convention and had seen the Fourth Infantry Division convention notice by coincidence. Father Engle had spent much of his life working with the VA. He is a close friend of our parish priest and visits whenever he is in town. He still has the bullet I handed him in 1944.

Editor's Note: *I was at this reunion, the fourth that I had attended, I now have 30 4ID Association reunions I have attended. I'm sure Hank Strecker and I spent time together at this one and others. While he served in WWII and I served in Vietnam, we both are part of the proud history of the 4th Infantry Division. My advice to veterans of all wars—join your division or regiment or whatever association that represents the unit you served with. You will renew old friendships, like Hank Strecker did, and make new friends that you served with but didn't know in person at that time. And Family members, encourage your veteran to attend, and go with him/her. You will hear and learn things you won't ever hear anywhere else.*

Henry Strecker earned the rank of Staff Sergeant. He received a Bronze Star for combat on the Siegfried Line, a Purple Heart and five battle stars along with the Combat Infantryman's Badge and Presidential Unit Citation. He thanks God every day for seeing him through the war and continued to correspond with Father Engle, Ward and Dora Means, and Herr Hubert Gees, who served opposite him in the Hurtgen Forest, until his death.

Another Editor's Note: *In 2024, probably within a month or two after this book you are reading is published, I will publish Henry Strecker's memoir, compiled by his daughter, Leslie Strecker Weisner. Title is* **Come Out Fighting** *— it is available on Amazon or on the bookstore at www.deedspublishing.com.*

We are getting close to the end of the war in Europe — less than a month to go.
12 APR 1945 TO 18 APR 1945 – D+311 TO D+317

12 APRIL 1945 — D+311: At the close of the period, CT 12 was clearing the town of Waldmannshofen. Bieberehren and Klingen were cleared during the period. CT 22's advance was stubbornly resisted by enemy in well prepared positions utilizing small arms, supported by artillery and direct fire weapons. At about 2205 the enemy counterattacked with an estimated rifle company in the vicinity of Blaufelden. It was considered possible that a reinforcement of enemy strength on the right flank was in progress. Artillery fire in CT 22's sector showed an increase during the period. During the hours of darkness, enemy planes bombed and strafed in the vicinity of Obernberit, Oschenfurt, and Willanzheim.

The 8th Infantry continued minor mopping up operations with the 1st and 2nd Battalions.

The 12th Infantry resumed the attack to the southeast at an early hour. The 1st Battalion cleared the woods and continued the advance across the Tauber river with supporting tanks.

The 22nd Infantry continued the attack at 0600 with the 1st and 3rd Battalions abreast. Throughout the period, progress of both battalions was held to a minimum by the enemy who employed small arms, antiaircraft, and self-propelled guns. The 1st Battalion occupied the town of Wermutshausen and the high ground to the northeast.

13 APRIL 1945—D+312: CT 22 reported stubborn resistance with good artillery support until approximately 2030. At 2045, elements of CT 12 forced the enemy to withdraw from Creglingen, but the enemy succeeded in destroying the bridge after this withdrawal. CT 324 advanced opposed only by harassing small arms and artillery fire, mines, and undefended road blocks. Enemy artillery fire showed a decrease during the period.

The 4th Infantry Division continued the attack and prior to the close of the period had secured the Division objective line extending from Freudenbach southwest to Flaufelden.

The 8th Infantry maintained positions in the vicinity of Markbreit.

The 12th Infantry resumed the attack at 0730. The 1st and 2nd Battalions continued their advance against light resistance and were successful in securing the regimental objective line in the vicinity of Freudenbach.

The 22nd Infantry resumed the attack at 0750 with three battalions abreast. Enemy opposition was negligible and by the close of the period, the regimental objective line in the vicinity of Lichtel had been secured and contact established with the 324th Infantry on the right.

14 APRIL 1945—D+313: Elements of CT 12 made contact with the enemy in the vicinity of Tauberscheckenbach and cleared the towns of Giekelhausen, Oberscheckenbach, Ohrenbach, and Gailshofen. CT 324 reported the enemy holding a line of strong points in the woods. The enemy resisted strenuously. The enemy employed small arms and automatic weapons fire supplemented with artillery support to delay the advance of CT 22. In approaching the wood line south and east of Ober Rimbach and east of Schmerbach, advance elements encountered stiffening resistance. At 1530 the enemy counterattacked with 175 men in the vicinity of Blaubach and was repulsed with heavy casualties. Approximately 120 rounds of artillery fell in CT 22's sector during the period.

The 4th Infantry Division resumed the attack and advanced approximately four to five kilometers in the direction of Rothenburg along the entire Division front.

The 8th Infantry began a shuttle movement at 1000 to the southeast within the new regimental zone of action following elements of the 12th Armored Division. All three battalions were shuttled forward during the day and by the end of the period had closed in the vicinity of Ergersheim. No enemy resistance was reported until 1845 when a small counterattack was reported in the vicinity of Illesheim.

The 12th Infantry initiated an attack to the southeast within the new regimental sector beginning at 0800 with the 1st and 2nd Battalions abreast. Progress was continuous throughout the day. The 2nd Battalion on the left advanced approximately eight kilometers when resistance increased on the left flank against Company G in the vicinity of Ohrenbach. The 1st Battalion pressed forward approximately five kilometers and secured the small communication center of Taubscheckenbach and the high ground to the northeast. The 3rd Battalion, in reserve, echeloned forward to the town of Gross Harbach.

The 22nd Infantry continued the attack with the 1st and 3rd Battalions at 0900, and initially had no contact with the enemy. Progress was continuous but slow, and enemy opposition increased in the wooded areas later in the day. By the close of the day, advances from two to three kilometers were made along the entire regimental front.

15 APRIL 1945—D+314: Opposite CT 8 and 12, the enemy defended on a line. Before CT 22, a clearly defined line did not exist, but the enemy was entrenched. In CT 324's sector, the enemy continued to defend a successive line of strong points. The enemy maintained a strong active defense, utilizing heavy small arms, automatic weapons, mortar, and artillery fires to delay our advance. During darkness, the enemy harassed CT 324 with light artillery, nebelwerfer, mortar, and small arms fire.

The 4th Infantry Division resumed the attack, advancing approximately two to five kilometers against stiffening resistance. It repulsed a counter attack late in the period in the vicinity of Weiler.

The 8th Infantry remained in assembly area to regroup and at 1645 jumped off with the 1st Battalion on the left and the 2nd Battalion on the right. Resistance increased as the combat team advanced, but by the close of the period, all elements were reported on their objective.

The 12th Infantry continued the attack at 0820 with the 2nd Battalion on the left and the 1st Battalion on the right and gained from two to four kilometers against moderate resistance. The 1st Battalion encountered many antipersonnel and antitank mines while the 2nd Battalion reported receiving small arms, artillery, and direct fire from the vicinity of Adelshofen. By the close of the period, this town had been cleared of the enemy.

The 22nd Infantry continued the attack at 0800. The 2nd Battalion's advance was slow but continuous with the battalion reporting gains of approximately two to three kilometers. The 3rd Battalion reported light to moderate resistance, advancing approximately three kilometers and clearing the towns of Wolfsbuch, Weiler, and Blumweiler.

16 APRIL 1945—D+315: The enemy continued its strong defense across the entire Division zone of action, withdrawing locally under the pressure of our attack. Our leading elements by-passed small groups of enemy. These pockets resumed the fight, and it was necessary that each one be attacked and eliminated separately. Stubborn resistance was encountered by CT 8 in the vicinity of Wildbad. CT 12 encountered considerable small arms and automatic weapons fire and one of its companies was pinned down for several hours on Hill 442. CT 22 and CT 324 encountered considerable rocket, artillery, mortar, direct fire, and small arms throughout the period.

The 4th Infantry Division resumed the attack early in the period, advancing against moderate to heavy resistance in the direction of Rothenburg. Many towns were cleared, and numerous prisoners of war were captured.

The 8th Infantry continued the attack at 0700 to destroy or capture all enemy forces in the woods. The 1st Battalion advanced from three to five kilometers against stubborn resistance of well concealed enemy in the woods. At the close of the period, Iber Dachstatten and the woods to the west had been cleared and the high ground east of Ermetzhoff occupied. The 2nd and 3rd Battalions cleared the woods against very stiff resistance.

The 12th Infantry jumped off at 0600 with the 1st and 2nd Battalions abreast, and during the day cleared Gattenhof, Hartershofen, Schweinsdorf, Bettwar, and Steinbach against light resistance which increased to stubborn resistance as they neared Rothenburg. At 1600 a patrol from the 1st Battalion rode into Rothenburg, flying a white flag, to ask the commander of the troops there to surrender the city. The German commander would not surrender the city, whereupon the attack was continued by both battalions.

The 22nd Infantry jumped off at 0700 with two battalions abreast with the mission of clearing the woods and assisting the 12th Infantry in the capture of Rothenburg. They advanced against stiff resistance from dug in enemy and strong points, receiving fire from direct fire weapons, small arms, and automatic weapons along their entire front. The following towns were cleared: Schwarzenbronn, Bohmweiler, Reuthasen, Leuzenbornn, Ober Eichroth, Funkstadt, and Leuzendorf. At the close of the period, they reported receiving direct fire from the woods west of Rothenburg and artillery and small arms fire from the vicinity of south and west of Rothenburg. The 1st Battalion remained in reserve in the vicinity of Speilbach.

17 APRIL 1945—D+316: The enemy continued its strong defense of towns and woods. In CT 8's sector, the enemy broke contact during the night and withdrew, leaving behind many stragglers who offered only slight resistance before surrendering. CT 12 encountered considerable fire but moved into Rothenberg, this town having rejected our surrender terms. Before CT 22, the enemy offered only disorganized and scattered resistance. In CT 324's sector, the enemy offered at the beginning only slight resistance but its defense of Brettheim was stubborn and tenacious.

The volume of artillery remained about the same as in the previous period. Mines and abatis were encountered in increasing numbers. The secondary roads vicinity of Ober Bachstetten were heavily mined. So it was for all entrances to towns. Mohenau and Colmberg were outstanding examples.

The 4th Infantry Division resumed the attack, secured the town of Rothenbrug together with numerous small villages. Gains of four to five kilometers were made along the entire right portion of the Division zone of action while, on the extreme left, leading elements of the 8th Infantry were reported to have advanced approximately fifteen kilometers and entered the city of Ansbach. The day's operations netted over 1,000 prisoners of war.

The 8th Infantry continued the attack at 0700 with elements of the 12th Armored Division operating within the left portion of the regimental zone of action. While the 1st Battalion advanced as a motorized task force, the 2nd and 3rd Battalions advanced against moderate resistance for ten kilometers as far as Ober Felden where positions were consolidated. In the interim, the 1st Battalion task force was successful in by-passing enemy road blocks and at the close of the period was reported in the outskirts of Ansbach, some eighteen kilometers from their line of departure.

The 12th Infantry continued the attack at first light. Beginning at 0630, the 1st Battalion assaulted Rothenburg, clearing the city by 1240. The 2nd Battalion advanced through the wooded area to the southeast in the direction of Gunsendorf which was cleared at 2115. The 3rd Battalion advanced against Heusitz and cleared it.

The 22nd Infantry continued the attack at 0730 with the 1st Battalion passing through the 3rd Battalion which in turn reverted to reserve. The 1st and 2nd Battalions attacked and advanced abreast. The towns of Buch, Lehrbach, and Herrewinden between three and four kilometers from the line of departure were secured.

18 APRIL 1945—D+317: The enemy continued to defend most of the towns by collecting and organizing some of the scattered remnants of its units in our sector. The enemy likewise managed to defend a hasty line south of Berbers Creek. Along the ridge of this vicinity considerable small arms, mortar, and antiaircraft artillery fire was directed against our leading elements. Encountering only light resistance, CT 12 cleared the towns of Heusitz and Bellerhausen. CT 22 reported only slight small arms resistance but considerable rocket and artillery fire during the hours of darkness. In CT 324's zone of advance, enemy contact did not become strong until late in the period at which time heavy resistance was encountered in attacking dug in positions.

The 4th Infantry Division resumed the attack within the new division zone of action and advanced from three to nine kilometers, clearing numerous towns and villages.

The 8th Infantry continued the attack with the 2nd and 3rd Battalions abreast. Resistance increased late in the period as fire was received from enemy positions extending from Leutershausen southwest to Schellingsfurst. At 1740 fighter bombers were employed to bomb and strafe Leutershausen and the 2nd Battalion was successful in advancing approximately six kilometers to the outskirts of Jochsberg while the 3rd Battalion advanced as far south as the wooded areas east and west of Buchwald. Patrols of the 101st Cavalry Squadron screened between advancing units. At the close of the period and under cover of darkness, the 3rd Battalion dispatched patrols into enemy's positions with a view of continuing the attack through the night. In the interim, the 1st Battalion remained in position in the southern outskirts of Ansbach awaiting relief by elements of the 12th Armored Division.

The 12th Infantry continued the attack at 0900 from positions held east of Rothenburg. Progress was continuous throughout the day against light resistance until late in the period when mortar and heavy caliber artillery fire increased considerably as leading units approached the ridge line extending from Frankenheim southwest to Pheuerbronn. Advances of approximately eight kilometers were made by the 2nd and 3rd Battalions before positions were consolidated. The 1st Battalion meanwhile closed within Gebsattel.

The 22nd Infantry continued the attack at approximately 0900 and advanced steadily south throughout the day against sporadic resistance to the vicinity of Renbach where the 1st Battalion consolidated its positions. At 1900 the 2nd and 3rd Battalions moved south and west to effect relief of the 1st and 2nd Battalions of the 324th Infantry. This relief was still in progress at the close of the period.

From Swede Henley's Diary—used with permission of his daughters...

12 APRIL 1945: Jumped off at 0730. F Co took high ground and then Wildentierback. E Co took Heinberg. G Co took Kruesfeld. Set up CP in castle at Niederstetten...prince and princess were there.

13 APRIL 1945: Held position.

14 APRIL 1945: Ordered to attack to SE and clear woods and take Leuzendorf. Cleared woods but didn't take Leuzendorf. CP in Unter Eichenroth.

15 APRIL 1945: Took Leuzendorf at 2030. Capturing a helluva lot of prisoners.

16-17-18 APRIL 1945: Jumped off—took Bossondorf—Resuch—Fernkstadt—Standorf—Gemmhagen -Metzholz—Bettenfeld—Buch—Lohrbach. Stopped by night awaiting a change in orders to attack to South.

17-18-19 APRIL 1945 (CONT'D): The Mayors acted all right—their towns were saved. (Remember Rossburg)

Chaplain Bill Boice and his driver/assistant Otto Oehring while visiting Otto's mother in Germany—see Love Thine Enemy story that follows

From Chaplain Bill Boice's **History of the 22nd Infantry Regiment in WWII:**

After enjoying a few days of luxury in Bad Mergentheim, the Combat Team forged ahead. The German armies were in such an utter state of confusion that they could only fight delaying actions, but every wood, hill, and town was a virtual strongpoint containing a small group of enemy who would fire enough to temporarily delay the unit.

Every day the huge silver army transport planes could be seen soaring overhead loaded with supplies for the armored columns spearheading the drive. It was an impossible task for the trucking and quartermaster companies to keep up with only bare necessities, because as long as the enemy was backing up, they knew the battles to be won were becoming fewer.

The landscape through Southern Germany was slow rolling hills spotted with small patches of woods and thousands of tiny villages. The towns were usually no more than a mile apart with roads connecting from all directions. The atmosphere sparkled with spring, and life returned to the trees. Overhead, birds could be seen and white billowy clouds lazily floated onward. Then suddenly the beautiful countryside would become a mass of bursting flame, black smoke, and shrieking metal; machine guns would drown out the sound of the birds; in the distance the deathly cough of mortars could be heard; and the powerful motors of the American tanks grumbled as they moved into firing positions. The enemy wanted to fight—so shall it be. In a few short hours the Combat Team moved on, leaving behind a hideous portrait of death and destruction.

(The following story is slightly out of sequence from Chaplain Boice's book, but it is close enough to this time period that I think it is a story each of you will enjoy).

LOVE THINE ENEMY – AN INTERLUDE

Otto Oehring was a quiet technician fifth grade who served as Chaplain's Assistant to Chaplain Boice. Oehring was considerably older than the average GI, distinctly German, and speaking English with a strong German accent. It was also easily apparent that he had succumbed to his ancestral tradition of baldheadedness.

Every attempt had been made to get Otto transferred to a station complement or a service command prior to leaving the States, but to no avail. The chaplain had learned that Mr. Steinway of New York, in one of his annual tours through Germany, had passed through the town of Heilbrounn, home of the Glass Piano Company, where he had picked Otto as a master piano craftsman, building of pianos, and had taken him to New York to help Steinway build their fine pianos.

And so Otto, two sisters, and a brother had left Germany and had settled in New York, becoming good and reasonably prosperous American citizens. The remainder of his family, we soon learned, consisted of an aged mother, a crippled sister, and three brothers, two of whom were officers in the German Army.

In the final campaign for Southern Germany, following the swift move across the Rhine River of the Division, the Regiment was ordered to seize the town of Bad Mergentheim. It was at this point we noticed Otto growing restive. This was so completely unlike him that we tried to fathom the reason, and soon discovered it was because we were a mere seventy kilometers from his home. He told us there had been no word from his mother, sisters, and brothers since the day Pearl Harbor was bombed.

Late one evening, the chaplain gave Otto instructions to get his work out of the way and to be ready to make a quick trip the following morning. The next morning, Mr. Mitchell, Army Red Cross Field Representative, the Chaplain, Otto, and Jonesy, the faithful driver, started toward the town of Heilbrounn, which we knew had been first bombed, then fiercely fought through, and finally "liberated" by American troops. The trip was uneventful but long, because all bridges had been knocked out and it was necessary to travel great distances in order to find fording places or bridges still intact.

In the middle of the afternoon, the party arrived on the outskirts of Heilbrounn. Otto tried to keep from showing his nervousness, his anticipation, and his fear without success. He knew as did we that Heilbrounn had been almost bombed out of existence by American heavy bombers on the 28th of December 1944.

We came into the city from the east, headed over the ridge down into the valley in which the city was located. We held our breath and then suddenly the shockingly appalling sight stunned us. Heilbrounn as a city had ceased to exist. Blackened, devastated piles of ruins stood before us. American bulldozers had pushed the debris from the streets, filled the shell craters, and what the bombers had not ruined, artillery completely finished. It was incredible that anything could have remained in the city during this period and lived.

We drove on down through town and there was not enough of the city left for Otto to get his bearings. We cruised around for some thirty minutes finally coming by chance close to the old section where the Glass Piano Factory had been, and then, we found his home. We stopped the jeep and went quietly behind Otto as he went past the little garden and the statue of Pan, piping by a little fish pond, to the door. The glass of the door was broken out, but in all of Heilbrounn, there were only two blocks of buildings left standing and this house was in the two blocks. There was a little metal sign on the door which said, "Mrs. E. Oehring", but the house seemed cold and was obviously lifeless.

The door was unlocked, and we went through. There was nothing there—no furniture, no living person, nothing, nor was there any trace of the family or where they could be found. Otto wanted to give up then, perhaps because he was afraid of the truth and what he was sure he must find. Having heard voices from one of the cellars next door, we persuaded him to talk to some of the civilians, and to ask them if they knew where his family had gone. The neighbor explained quickly that his aged mother and crippled sister had been in the basement of the house all through the bombing but that his brother had come back from Karlsruhe following the bombing and had taken the family to a little town called Kirchausen, which was only ten kilometers away.

We wasted no time in moving on west through the city under the ruined and twisted steel of the railroad overpass and west toward Kirchausen. It seemed strange to see this lovely German village completely untouched by war after the ruins of Heilbrounn. We inquired first at the drugstore, but the druggist was obviously too much upset at the sight of the hated American soldiers in his store to be of any practical assistance, so we went direct to the Burgomeister, who is always in touch with every event which affects the life of his village. The Burgomeister, not only aware of his own responsibility but of the power of the American Army, readily informed us that he knew where the family was living and so took us to the other side of the village to the family of Mrs. E. Lambert.

On the east edge of town close to the green gently sloping fields there was a small stucco bungalow with bright red shutters and hollyhocks growing in the yard. The first sight that greeted our eyes was a comely young German woman with darling blue-eyed twins in either arm. She stared at us for a moment with a highly frightened look on her face as we came through the gate and passed the hollyhocks toward the tree under which she was resting. Then she saw Otto—in American uniform, true, but still with a resemblance to the Oehrings that was unmistakable. She simply whispered softly, "It's Otto! I know it's Otto!"

Otto kissed her and hugged the twins of whom he had not even known. She guided him gently toward the door and we stood back, not wishing to intrude on this moment for these people whom a war could not separate. Inside the door the house was small but spotlessly clean and comfortably livable. We turned through the hall to the sitting room at the right and there, sitting quite alone, was one of the most distinguished-looking women we had ever seen. Her face was lined with wrinkles. Her eyes were China blue, and her head was crowned with luxurious waves of snow white hair. She wore a cheap black dress as if it were royal purple, and her hands were quietly folded as she sat and rocked and dreamed of a better day. And then she looked up.

Her quick eyes registered no surprise. She stood and held out her arms and cried, "Otto, Otto! Gott mitt uns! Mine Otto!" And then—we never quite knew how, for our eyes were dimmed with tears—Otto was in her arms, her boy again, not an American soldier in an enemy land, just her boy. It was a moment for them alone, and we went back out into the sunlight and stood by the hollyhocks, wondering at the sordidness of war and at the universality of love. Surely this was in the best tradition of Him who said, "Love thine enemy".

19 APR 1945 TO 25 APR 1945 – D+318 TO D+324

19 APRIL 1945—D+318: Before CT 8 the enemy withdrew during the night to positions south of Crailsheim—Ansbach—Railroad. No aggressive enemy action was reported by CT 12. High velocity direct fire was received however in the vicinity of Diebach. Following a rapid advance against only slight fire, a slight increase in harassing mortar and artillery fire was received by CT 22 toward the end of the period. Enemy artillery fire remained light, with concentrations falling mostly in the vicinity of towns.

The 8th Infantry continued the attack through the night. The 2nd and 3rd Battalions reported very light resistance initially but encountered numerous blown bridges and overpasses which slowed their advance. Resistance coming from the vicinity of Bindweiler and Rodenweiler increased later. The 1st Battalion, reinforced, motorized, initiated movement at 0630 and advanced against very light resistance consisting mainly of road blocks.

The 12th Infantry continued the attack at 0800 with the 2nd and 3rd Battalions and reported no active resistance until 0945. By 1400, Wattringen and Ober Ostheim were cleared against moderate resistance. The CT continued the advance, capturing Werbitz, Walkersdon, Gailrau, and cleared the woods to the south, capturing Erzberg, Bottenweiler, Wildenholz and Theuerbronn. The 1st Battalion remained in reserve in the vicinity of Gebsattel.

The 22nd Infantry consolidated positions in which they had relieved the 324th Infantry. During the period, the 2nd Battalion advanced approximately four kilometers, clearing Kauhnhard, Lunbach, Schainbach, Roosburg and Michelbach against determined resistance consisting of nebelwerfer, heavy mortar, artillery, and heavy small arms fire from the south. The 1st Battalion on the left flank advanced approximately three kilometers against stiff resistance, capturing Schonbronn and Gailroth. The 4th Reconnaissance Troop cleared Rotam See and maintained contact with the 63rd Infantry Division on the right.

20 APRIL 1945—D+319: Until late in the period, our advance encountered only light resistance.

The 8th Infantry continued the attack at 0700 advancing rapidly against very light resistance initially. As the attack progressed they met increasing enemy resistance in towns and along the edges of wooded areas with the enemy employing artillery, antitank, self-propelled 75 mm, and small arms fire. The CT continued to advance against light to moderate resistance, capturing many towns and villages, reporting advances of approximately 12 kilometers during the period.

The 12th Infantry continued the attack with the 2nd and 3rd Battalions and advanced rapidly, capturing many towns and villages with only sporadic resistance.

The 22nd Infantry continued the attack at 0635. The CT reported very slight resistance, making gains of from ten to twelve kilometers and capturing many towns. At 1945, the 1st Battalion reported leading elements in the outskirts of Crailsheim, where they received nebelwerfer, antitank, and some small arms fire.

21 APRIL 1945—D+320: Our leading elements advanced to the outskirts of Jagstzell.

Before CT 8 the enemy continued to withdraw, leaving small, isolated groups to cover the retreat of main bodies. CT 22 cleared the town of Crailsheim early in the period. After overcoming the resistance on the high ground southwest of Crailsheim, Task Force Rodwell proceeded hampered only by numerous road blocks, abatis, cratered roads, and blown bridges. Enemy artillery was light and scattered. One jet-propelled plane bombed and strafed the forward elements of CT 8 at 2335.

The 8th Infantry continued the attack to the south and protected the left flank of the division. Advances of up to fifteen kilometers were made. The 2nd Battalion had secured the village of Stocken while the 3rd Battalion closed within Riegersheun. The 1st Battalion remained in reserve in the vicinity of Riegelbach throughout the period.

Task Force " Rodwell " was constituted under the command of Brigadier General James S. Rodwell and consisted of the following units :

12th Infantry (motorized), 42nd FA Bn, 522nd FA Bn, 70th Tank Bn, 4th Reconnaissance Troop, and companies B of the 4th Medical Bn, 4th Engineer Combat Bn and 610th Tank Destroyer Bn. Beginning at 0800, this Task Force assembled in the vicinity of Schnelldorf and at 1030 leading elements began the advance to the south... By the close of the period, leading elements had reached the vicinity of Jagstell where large craters were encountered. Work continued throughout the night to make the road passable.

The 22nd Infantry continued the attack, beginning at first light with the 1st and 2nd Battalions assaulting the city of Crailsheim. By 1000, the town had been cleared with little or no opposition. During the remainder of the period, the 3rd Battalion continued its advance along the regimental left boundary for six kilometers and the 1st and 2nd Battalion echeloned forward, closing within the towns of Steinbach and Jagstheim.

22 APRIL 1945—D+321: Elements of CT 8 advanced with no real contact until they reached the edge of the woods north of Rindelbach and the outreaches of Ellwangen. At these two points the enemy began what was believed to be a last-ditch defense of the town of Ellwangen. Stubborn resistance consisting of all types of fire was continuous as soon as contact was made. Task Force Rodwell advanced steadily throughout the period, encountering the numerous terrain obstacles experienced in the previous period.

The first elements of the 4th Infantry Division moved at 0400 to secure the division objective in the vicinity of Aalen. By the close of the period, TF Rodwell had advanced twenty kilometers and was engaged with the enemy on the outskirts of the objective.

The 8th Infantry initiated movement beginning at 0400 when its 1st Battalion, motorized, began its advance. At 0700 the 2nd and 3rd Battalions continued the attack and advanced. Upon reaching the outskirts of Ellwangen, both battalions met determined resistance from a reported force of 600 enemy infantry SS troops defending the city. Repeated attempts to assault resulted in failure and a coordinated attack was planned on 23 April.

Forward elements of TF Rodwell continued on to the south at 0630. By 1230, at Leinan first, the Task Force was engaged in a short fire fight following which the enemy retreated towards Neuler on bicycles. In Neuler, leading elements met strong enemy resistance which resulted in some casualties and the loss of two tanks. By 1630 this resistance consisting of approximately 60 enemy, had been eliminated. The Task Force continued to move unopposed southeast out of Neuler and the enemy was again encountered in the vicinity of Aalen which was reported defended by 500 or 600 enemy armed with small arms and bazookas.

The 22nd Infantry continued the advance at 0700 with the 1st and 3rd Battalions abreast. They encountered no opposition and continued for approximately 14 kilometers to the vicinity of Adelmammsfeld.

23 APRIL 1945—D+322: The 12th Infantry Regiment reported the location of an Allied Prisoner of War camp containing approximately 350 prisoners.

The town of Ellwangen was completely and deliberately fortified. Extensive barbed wire obstacles were encountered along the edges of town. In rear of this line, there was a complete system of communications trenches. Roads leading to Ellwangen were mined and cratered with heavy road blocks at all defiles. In addition the surrounding area was well adapted to a strong defense because of the high hills around the town commanding the open fields beyond. The 5th SS Replacement Battalion continued the stubborn defense of Ellwangen until 2300 at which time a withdrawal to the south started.

The withdrawal continued during the early morning at which time some of the retreating elements were killed and captured in the vicinity of Westhausen where our troops were commanding the logical escape routes. Enemy rear guards in the town continued to engage our forces with small arms, automatic weapons, and panzerfaust until 1440.

Task Force Rodwell continued to advance through the town of Aalen against a strong delaying action by the enemy. At 1930, this resistance ceased and the enemy troops were observed fleeing into the woods. CT 22 continuing to advance on the right flank encountered mainly terrain obstacles such as road blocks, destroyed bridges, and craters.

The attack of the 8th Infantry continued with the 2nd and 3rd Battalions. The 1st Battalion cut the road in the vicinity of Schwabsberg and also the road running southeast out of Ellwangen, which put him in a position to inflict heavy casualties on the enemy. Ellwangen was reported cleared at 1440 after a strong rear guard action from the enemy. The 2nd Battalion continued to mop up small pockets of enemy while the two other battalions continued their advance. Approximately 15 square miles were cleared during the day, including the towns of Schwasberg, Dollsingen, Buch, and Westhausen.

Task Force Rodwell had coiled the complete column into Wasseralfingen north of Aalen during the night. The 1st and 3rd Battalions, reinforced by a company of tanks for each battalion, attacked the town of Aalen from the north. The advance was continued but slow during the entire morning. It was necessary to conduct a complete search of all buildings because by-passed enemy inflicted casualties on the following troops. The 2nd Battalion (motorized) used routes reconnoitered by the 4th Reconnaissance Troop west of Aalen and at 1400 launched an attack from this direction. This flanking movement broke the enemy resistance in Aalen and the three battalions quickly converged on each other.

The 22nd Infantry initiated movement at first light, the 1st Battalion in organic transportation, and the 3rd Battalion on foot, while the 2nd Battalion was shuttled forward. The 3rd Battalion advanced eleven kilometers without resistance.

24 APRIL 1945—D+323: The Division received a quota of 6 officers and 65 enlisted men to return to the United States as guards on Prison ships. Upon arrival in the United States, they were to have 45 day leaves and furloughs.

Early in the period, CT 8 reported the town of Ellwangen completely clear with remnants of the badly battered 5th SS Replacement and Training Battalion attempting to infiltrate south in an effort to escape. CT 22 experienced very little contact with the enemy during the daylight hours and overcame at 1630 the resistance in the town of Steinheim. Task Force Rodwell continued to advance rapidly south of Aalen.... As leading elements entered Hohenmemmingen, they received light small arms resistance and light artillery fire.

The 8th Infantry continued the attack at 0900. The 1st Battalion followed the TF Force while the 2nd Battalion advanced along the main highway from Aalen-Ober Kochen—Konigsbronn. The advance down this route was slowed considerably by mines, road blocks, and demolitions.

Task Force Rodwell continued the advance at 0800, moving along the route Ober Kochen—Ebnat—Gross Kochen—Oggenshausen—Giengen. Contact was established with the 3rd Infantry Division on the left flank at 1100 in the vicinity of Gross Kuchen. The advance of the TF was subjected to small arms fire, light artillery, and mortar fire. Road blocks, cratered roads, mines, and abatis continued to slow the advance. The TF closed into Giegen for the night.

The 22nd Infantry patrolled to Essingen where they engaged the enemy in a small arms fight. The CT resumed their advance at 0900 and encountered no active resistance until 1830.

25 APRIL 1945—D+324: As the period closed, leading elements of the 4th Infantry Division had advanced without contacting the enemy to just north or Landenburg, Waldkirch, and Weisingen. Reports were received of scattered small arms, presumably sniper fire, encountered by motorized elements of the 4th Infantry Division as they advanced through towns. Many prisoners of war, both in and out of uniform, were taken as mopping up activities in rear areas were carried out.

The 4th Infantry Division continued its advance and established contact with the 12th Armored Division in the vicinity of Gundel Fingen. At the close of the period, the bulk of the 8th and 12th Infantry Regiments were on the south side of the Danube river.

All three battalions of the 8th Infantry crossed the Danube river at Laningen and advanced to the southern edge of the bridgehead.

Task Force Rodwell was dissolved at 1600 and the 2nd and 3rd Battalions of the 12th Infantry crossed the Danube river in the rear of the 8th Infantry. The 1st Battalion at the close of the period was enroute by motor from Aalen.

The 22nd Infantry continued the advance to the southeast within its zone.

From Swede Henley's Diary—used with permission from his daughters…

19-20-21-22-23 APRIL: Took Lohrback, Schainback, Rossburg, Wallhausen, Groningen, Satteweiler, Satted and Auhop, Liefenback. 1st Bn took Crailsheim. 2nd Bn took airport to west—Alten-munster, Jagstheim, Honhardt, Rosenberg, Hohenberg, Adelmannsfelden, Pommertsweiler, Abtsgmund, Neuler, Dewangen.

23-30 APRIL: Rat race continued—gaining up to 20 miles a day.
• Traveled the autobahn—saw gobs of jet planes along road.

From Chaplain Bill Boice's History of the 22nd Infantry Regiment in WWII:

On April 20, the Combat Team, after a move of approximately 55 miles through the towns of Weikersheim, Ober Rimbach, Weiler, Rote See, and Beuerlbach, arrived upon the high ground overlooking Crailsheim from the north. Enroute numerous skirmishes were fought, but the advance was so rapid it would be repetitious to describe each encounter.

The First Battalion, under the command of Lt. Colonel George Goforth, led the advance on the 20th by moving into the northeast corner of Crailsheim. Here serious opposition was encountered from light artillery and sniper fire. One of the things which Americans will never forget was the order requiring every German house and building to fly a white flag or be destroyed. An advance patrol was usually sent into the town ahead of the combat troops and artillery, and the Burgomeister was informed that if the Germans defended the town or if American soldiers were harmed within its precincts, it would be burned to the ground.

If, on the other hand, the civilians did not interfere and forced the withdrawal of German troops to the other side of the town, it would be spared. In almost all cases, the Germans of Bavaria were anxious to have their homes spared, and the white flags went up at once. Usually a time limit of thirty minutes was set. It seemed strange, in the light of hysterical and arrogant speeches made by the Nazis through the years, to observe the servility of most of the civilians, although perhaps their reaction was only human.

It was now apparent that the once mighty German Army was disintegrating rapidly, and everyone, including the Germans themselves, realized they were completely defeated; still they fought on, a fact which we mightily resented, because it made every casualty we took and every casualty they sustained so completely useless. It increased our bitterness.

The First Battalion was ordered to take the town of Crailsheim, a city of perhaps some eight or ten thousand inhabitants. The Battalion drew up its ring of steel in preparation for the attack on the northern edge of the city and there stood fast. Lt. Colonel George Goforth, the Battalion Commander, ordered Lt. Jones, with two enlisted men, to approach the city officials and arrange for its surrender. This Lt. Jones immediately did. Upon approaching Crailsheim with an interpreter, he contacted the Burgomeister and gave to him the American terms for the surrender of the city.

The terms had apparently been received and accepted when, without warning, the three American soldiers were shot in the back and killed. When this information was given to Colonel Goforth, he issued orders with tenseness and a concealed fury which communicated itself to every man in the battalion. Instead of ordering that the city be attacked, he called for artillery fire, and he personally adjusted the mortars, ordering them to fire white phosphorous and to burn every building in the city. These orders were carried out, with Colonel Goforth observing. If occasionally the smoke and flames blew away and a building was revealed still standing, the Colonel adjusted the mortars and soon the building was in flames. The city of Crailsheim will long have cause to remember a Lieutenant named Jones and his funeral pyre. It was a cowardly and needless gesture on the part of the Germans; it was a furious and just retaliation from a combat battalion which had learned to hate the treachery of a defeated enemy. A city died, and remembered a Lieutenant named Jones.

As the city poured forth the black smoke of destruction, the First Battalion moved into the town. They now wanted to fight, to find the treacherous cowards who had only minutes before killed three men of the battalion. Company C with three tanks led the assault; Company B followed. This time there were no lead scouts, as each man wanted to be first. Street fighting had long ago become a perfected knack with these men. They quickly paired up and moved ahead, meticulously searching each possible hiding place for snipers. Darkness fell and the men, still boiling with anger, hunted the enemy by the light of the burning buildings. The night was overcast, and the white clouds reflected the firelight, illuminating the narrow streets. The population of the city knew that they had made a mistake and were paying for it.

While the fighting was going on in Crailsheim, the Second and Third Battalions moved up to secure the flanks and rear. The men of these battalions could clearly see the burning reflection and they, too, understood what had happened.

The Combat Team didn't remain long in Crailsheim; their job was ahead. Task Force "Rodwell," commanded by the assistant division commander, Brigadier General James S. Rodwell, passed through the CT the next day and temporarily led the advance.

This Task Force greatly facilitated in the further advance of the Combat Team for several days as it drove the Germans back or surrounded them, forcing a surrender.

Editor's Note from Bob...After I had become president of the 22nd Infantry Regiment Society in 1995, I was told this Crailsheim story by Dr. Boice and MG (Ret) John Ruggles, the Regimental commander at the time. Fifty years later, they both were still seething from the needless murder of LT Jones and two enlisted men by the SS troops at Crailsheim.

Fit to Fight

From **War Stories Volume II: Paris to VE Day**

Gordon Gullikson, Onalaska, WI
Company A, 1st Battalion, 22nd Infantry Regiment
No One Wants to Be the Last Man to Die

I don't think this qualifies as a war story, but it kind of showed me the attitude of our commanders, especially Lieutenant Colonel George Goforth. We were to attack this German-occupied town in the morning. We took off to find that German soldiers had left during the night and had the old men of the village cut down trees across the road as they left. (This was toward the end of the war.) Colonel Goforth had the same old men cut up the trees and haul them off the road so we could advance with our vehicles. If you ever heard swear words in German, this was classic—work all night to impede our progress and all day to help our progress.

We kept pushing the Germans in retreat and came to a small river. Goforth called Regiment and told them he would have to find a way to get across.

I said, "Colonel, there's a bridge about a half mile downstream."

He said, "Gordon, the war is about over. If we close on the Germans, they will have to stand and fight. We will just keep pushing them back as they retreat. No one wants to be the last man to die for his country."

That was a great lesson to me—I carried that over to Korea as a company commander—get as much support firepower from battalion and regiment to help you take your objective with the least number of casualties.

Fred Stromberg, Concord, CA
Company G, 2nd Battalion, 22nd Infantry Regiment
Hit With a Milk Bottle

Towards the last few months of the War, tanks rushed across Germany twenty to thirty miles per day, clustered with soldiers riding on top. We faced backwards with legs dangling over the end so a quick exit could be made if we encountered fire.

One such day, nearing dusk, we were traveling on a road through low hills when gunfire sprayed the tank. Bullets snapping just over my head caused me to jump off and roll to the side of the road for cover. My helmet fell off, and the tank behind ran over it.

Our CO came by in his jeep and pointed to a house some fifty yards or so away and told me to take the wounded over there and make it the CP for the night. I made my way over to the house. I opened a little white gate and then closed it behind me as I walked up a few steps to knock on the door. After I knocked hard, the door opened. A baby crying in the background made it hard for the well-dressed man to hear me. I shouted in the best German I knew, "Amerikaner Soldaten schlaffen hier." (American soldiers sleep here).

"Nein. Heraus mit Ihnen," (No. Go away,) he replied and slammed the door.

"Amerikaner Soldaten schlaffen hier."

"Nein. Heraus mit Ihnen."

Again, I pounded on the door. The door opened and before I could say a word, the man hit me on the head with a milk bottle. My basic training instructions of "always wear your helmet" came to mind.

I walked back to the tanks, told my story to the tank lieutenant, and asked him to bring his tank over to the door of the house. This he did as I stood on the steps and watched that giant tank crush the gate and stop at the steps. The huge monster swung its ugly cannon around and lowered it to a few inches above my head.

Once again I pounded on the door. It opened slowly. The Kraut peeked out and looked right down the muzzle of that cannon. "Gott im Himmel!" (God in heaven!)

We took over the upstairs for the CP. There was too much glass in my head from the broken milk bottle for the medics to remove, so I was driven to the battalion aid station. I was soon bandaged and sent back to the Company. No, I did not receive a Purple Heart for this, as the battalion did not prepare a casualty report. They felt the Army would not take it lightly for the cause of injury to read, "Hit on the head with a milk bottle."

Lewis Jacobson, Eagle River, WI
Company G, 2-22 Infantry
War can be hell

Near the end of WWII, we would commonly mount up on tanks and toward evening occupy homes overnight. On one occasion my squad rapidly dismounted, running up the walk to the house, looking for positions of comfort. As a result, the lady of the home fainted.

When I checked a bedroom, two of my men were on the bed. Across the room was a crib which I stretched out on, with my legs dangling over the side.

Shortly a toddler arrived, screaming because I was in his bed. The situation was so unbearable that I had to retreat to the kitchen. As a member of the 22nd Infantry, it marked the first time I had to retreat in the face of an unrelenting verbal onslaught by a two year old German toddler.

John C. Ausland (Deceased), La Crosse, WI
Headquarters Battery, 29th Field Artillery Battalion
Waiting Angrily for the War to End

This article, written by John Ausland, appeared in the
INTERNATIONAL HERALD TRIBUNE ON APRIL 11, 1994.

One reason people born after World War II find it difficult to understand why the final days of the war were so destructive is that they do not realize how angry we Allied soldiers had become — and to some extent still are.

Once our forces crossed the Rhine, it was clear that Germany was doomed. But Hitler, in his madness, vowed to fight on. German generals and admirals, whatever they thought, supported him. Their soldiers and sailors continued to fight in the misguided belief that they were defending their fatherland.

Anger became outrage and horror as our forces began to overrun concentration camps. As General Eisenhower emerged from one of them, he asked an American guard if he still had difficulty hating Germans.

Shortly before the 4th Infantry Division crossed the Rhine on March 29, at Worms, I went from artillery liaison officer with an infantry battalion to command of the 29th Field Artillery Battalion's fire direction center. I was in no mood to see any more of my friends in the infantry die. When our troops came under fire from a town, we would shell it heavily.

We were, as always, well aware that we could be causing civilian casualties. The fact that these would be the German enemy, and not French or Belgian friends, made our task easier. The glum faces we met, even in the towns we did not destroy, reminded us that we were not being welcomed as liberators.

With our forces sweeping eastward across Germany toward a Russian offensive even more ruthless than ours, the 4th Infantry Division advanced on a line of attack that took us west and south of Munich. Not far from Munich, the 8th Infantry Regiment ran into determined resistance in the town of Ellwangen.

Ellwangen was an SS military training center with a model defense. Its commander decided that his four hundred troops should defend it to the last man. When the commander of the 8th Infantry Regiment suggested by telephone that the German commander avoid a useless battle, he was rebuffed with an obscenity. With the 8th Infantry Regiment's staff planning an attack for the following morning, I suggested we try to force the town's surrender. On the night of April 22-23, the 4th Infantry Division and supporting corps artillery fired 1,500 shells into the town. We used delayed fuses so the shells would penetrate buildings before exploding, and we followed these with white phosphorus incendiary shells. Other shells scattered leaflets about how to surrender.

For many years I wondered what went on in Ellwangen that night. In 1992 the town archivist, Immo Eberl, sent me a lengthy account.

The military commander rejected the recommendation of the town's deputy mayor that he and his men leave the town. But after our bombardment began, the German commander had second thoughts. Changing into civilian clothes, he and his men quietly disappeared.

A tragic comedy then ensued as the civilian leaders tried to figure out how to communicate their wish to surrender. A proposal to send an emissary in an ambulance was abandoned when it was noted that a key bridge had been destroyed. A plan to raise a white flag on the church tower was delayed; no one could find the key to the church.

We ceased the bombardment early in the morning to see what the response was. An emissary soon appeared carrying a white flag, and our infantry took the town without an Allied casualty. The civilians had taken shelter in deep cellars. Fortunately, only a few were killed. Damage to buildings, however, was extensive.

A few days after Ellwangen, I visited a concentration camp that had just been taken near Landsberg. It is hard for me, even today, to describe what I saw there without crying. Hundreds of bodies, I wrote to my parents soon afterward, were laid out in neat, efficient rows. Some were burned. Some were shot. Some had been tortured and maimed. Others may have just died. All were unbelievably emaciated.

"This can never be explained or pardoned," I wrote, and "the leaders who caused, and the men who performed these crimes must die."

Shortly after that, we learned that Hitler was dead—a joyous moment—and the war in Europe finally ended. The rumors that Hitler would make a final stand in an Alpine retreat having proved wrong, we observed those beautiful snow-covered peaks in the distance and congratulated ourselves on not having to fight in them.

Our assumption that the war was over for us, however, proved wrong. Not long after VE Day, we learned that the 4th Infantry Division would be returning to the United States. There, after an intense training period, we were scheduled to go to the Pacific to participate in the conquest of Japan.

Having survived the fighting from Utah Beach to south of Munich, I could not help but wonder how long my luck would hold out. I am not inclined to question Harry Truman's decision to destroy Hiroshima and

Nagasaki. Had the fighting in the Pacific been prolonged with the death and destruction that would have ensued, it would have been even more difficult than it is proving now for Japanese and American veterans to escape their bitter memories and bury the past.

26 APR 1945 TO 2 MAY 1945 – D+325 TO D+331

26 APRIL 1945 — D+325: After the woods and the towns of Ellerbach and Dusmarshausen were cleared, our troops advanced rapidly without opposition.

The 8th Infantry with the 1st and 3rd Battalions advanced against light and scattered opposition for approximately ten kilometers, securing a line extending generally east from Dinkelscherben when positions were consolidated for the night.

The 12th Infantry attacked with its 2nd and 3rd Battalions. The 2nd Battalion met strong resistance consisting of heavy small arms and some mortar fire in the woods in the vicinity of Altenbaindt while the 3rd Battalion advanced behind elements of the 101st Cavalry Squadron. Company I mounted on supporting tanks closed in the vicinity of Horgau. The 1st Battalion in reserve closed in the vicinity of Ellerbach.

The 22nd Infantry began moving across the bridge on the Danube river and by dark the 2nd and 3rd Battalions had closed in an assembly area in the vicinity of Gundremmingen. The 1st Battalion remained at the bridge.

27 APRIL 1945 — D+326: A possible enemy front line existed along the east bank of the Lech river. Elsewhere our advance continued to the southeast against little or no enemy contact. CT 8 encountered small, scattered groups of stragglers who offered only token resistance. Upon approaching the river, heavy fire from small arms, automatic weapons, mortars, and artillery was received. CT 12 advanced making no contact until about 1600 when elements were fired on by small arms and automatic weapons from the vicinity of Bieburg. Early in the period, considerable artillery fire fell in CT 8's sector. At 2243, fire was received in the eastern edge of Zusmarshuasen from an estimated battalion of 150 mm guns. At 2300, a light barrage fell in Buch.

The 2nd Battalion of the 8th Infantry, after passing through elements of the 1st Battalion advanced with no resistance to the bridge site on the Lech river. They succeeded in crossing two companies, even though the enemy had blown the bridge. Strong resistance was encountered in the vicinity of the bridge site and heavy artillery and mortar fire was experienced along the east bank of the river. The 3rd Battalion operating in the left advanced against no resistance and was last reported in the vicinity of Aintingen.

The 12th Infantry continued the attack at 0610 with the 1st and 3rd Battalions and advanced with no resistance until they reached the vicinity of Biburg and Willishausen. At this point they received fire from an enemy strong point in the vicinity of Steppach. After reducing the strongpoint which contained several flak guns, they continued the advance to their objective.

The 22nd Infantry staged forward in assembly areas in order to control the main road to the west of the Division sector and to protect the autobahn in that vicinity.

28 April 1945 — D+327: A French Prisoner of War Enclosure with 60 French soldiers was reported by the 12th Infantry.

Generally around the bridgehead area, the enemy opposed our attempts to advance. CT 12 advanced to the southeast clearing enemy from its zone of action west of the Lech river. Resistance encountered consisted of considerable antiaircraft fire, some mortar fire, and small arms fire. In CT 8's sector, the enemy continued to harass our troops holding the bridgehead with small arms, mortar, and artillery fire.

The Division area was swept for by-passed pockets of enemy and a considerable number of prisoners were taken during this operation.

The 8th Infantry maintained their bridgehead across the Lech river and patrolled.

The 12th Infantry continued the advance at 0730 with the 1st and 3rd Battalions to the vicinity of the Lech river and consolidated positions for the crossing upon completion of the bridge.

The 22nd Infantry moved by shuttle to assembly areas in preparation for the crossing.

29 APRIL 1945—D+328: Throughout the day, our troops advanced rapidly to the southeast with little or no opposition. Groups of enemy surrendered readily without a fight after offering only token resistance. Two enemy planes were over the 4th Infantry Division sector at about 1730 and at least one was shot down by our antiaircraft artillery.

The 4th Infantry Division crossed the Lech river in force.

The 8th Infantry maintained the bridgehead. The 2nd Battalion after being passed through by the 12th and 22nd Infantry moved to Augsburg to relieve elements of the 3rd Infantry Division on security duty.

The 12th Infantry crossed the Lech river at 0800 and continued the advance for approximately 25 kilometers. The 1st and 2nd Battalions secured a general line along the western bank of the Amper river in the vicinity of Zankenhausen. The 3rd Battalion staged forward to Turkenfeld.

The 22nd Infantry crossed the Lech river at 0600, advancing to the northeast and then southeast. The CT advanced approximately 20 kilometers against very scattered resistance, securing a general line along the Amper river in the vicinity of Schongrising.

30 APRIL 1945—D+329: The rapid advance of our troops continued as only scattered small arms, road blocks, and demolished bridges were encountered. Enemy troops in increasing numbers surrendered readily without a fight. Over two thousand prisoners of war were taken during the period.

The 8th Infantry, less the 2nd Battalion sent to Augsburg, crossed the Lech river, and closed in assembly areas in the vicinity of Moorenweis-Galtendorf late in the period.

The 12th Infantry continued the advance to the southeast at 0600, crossing the Amper River in the vicinity of Wildenroth. Advancing against negligible resistance, the Combat Team secured bridges intact across the Loisach and Isar Rivers in the vicinity of Wolfratshausen after advancing approximately 25 kilometers.

The 22nd Infantry crossed the Amper River in the vicinity of Furstenfeldbruck at 0800 and continued the advance against passive resistance. The advance was halted late in the period along the Isar River line by blown bridges.

Notes about logistics:

The Division had covered a distance of approximately 250 miles during this period. This rapid advance created a serious transportation-supply problem. Vehicles were required to motorize elements of the Division and at the same time the lines of supply were lengthening, necessitating longer trips back to the supply dumps. A total of 113 trucks were used during the month of April for transportation other than normal supply.

CASUALTIES – APRIL 1945

Officers — Enlisted
KIA 15 — 175
MIA 0 — 16
SWA 5 — 68 (Seriously Wounded in Action)
LWA 23 — 571 (Lightly Wounded in Action)
Total 43 — 830
Prisoners: 26,091

Robert O. Babcock

Proof of the fact that you can get anything in Paris, this twin .50 caliber machine gun originally belonged to the Eighth Air Force—this gunner traded it for a field jacket.

MAY 1945

4ID IN GERMANY — VE DAY

1 MAY 1945 — D+330: No enemy front line existed, and no organized resistance was encountered, only scattered groups with small arms.

During the period of 30 April, the 4th Infantry Division with its attached units had secured positions along the Isar River and Isarwk Canal and captured intact the bridges across the river and the canal at Wolfratshausen. At 0800, the Division continued the attack with the 12th Infantry Regiment from the bridgehead secured across the Loisach River and the Isarwk Canal against a disorganized enemy. During the day, the Division advanced approximately ten kilometers and secured another bridgehead across the Isar River and Isarwk Canal.

The 8th Infantry shuttled forward with the 1st and 3rd Battalions while the 2nd Battalion remained in Augsburg to maintain order. The 1st Battalion closed in the vicinity of Starnberg early in the day while the 3rd Battalion closed in the vicinity of Gauting. Many enemy stragglers were captured as they attempted retreat from Munich to the southwest.

The 12th Infantry continued the attack at 0800 across the bridges seized intact over the Loisach River and the Isarwk Canal. Initially the regiment followed Combat Command R of the 12th Armored Division which had crossed over the 12th Infantry bridges and had passed through the regiment at 0730. The 1st and 3rd Battalions advanced approximately ten kilometers against scattered to heavy resistance, the 1st Battalion reaching Thankirchen, the 3rd Battalion reaching Hachenberg. Both battalions reported heavy resistance late in the day consisting of small arms, mortar, artillery, and antiaircraft gun fire. At 2030, the 2nd Battalion moved by motor to the vicinity of Aschelding.

The 22nd Infantry crossed the Isar River and Isarwk Canal with two companies of the 2nd Battalion starting at 0700. The 1st Battalion remained in the vicinity of Buchendorf as reserve. The 3rd Battalion maintained its positions in the vicinity of Baierbrun. The advance of the regiment was delayed throughout the day by blown bridges. Throughout the day, Corps Engineers worked feverishly to construct a bridge but due to the soft approaches to the bridge site and the swift current of the Isar River, the bridge was not completed at the close of the day. The bridges at Wolfratshausen were in constant use by CC R of the 12th Armored Division, the 101st Cavalry Squadron, and the 12th Infantry, making it impossible for the 22nd Infantry to cross.

2 MAY 1945—D+331: Enemy troops were encountered in large numbers but surrendered without offering resistance.

Prisoners of war for this period totaled over 5,000.

The 4th Infantry Division continued the attack with two regimental combat teams abreast. The fighting spirit of the enemy was broken. So many prisoners of war were taken that the progress of all units was slowed in endeavoring to handle them.

The 8th Infantry maintained peace and order in towns, cities, and on roads.

The 12th Infantry continued the advance to the southeast on the right of the Division. The CT advanced approximately 13 kilometers on the left and 6 kilometers on the right. Enemy resistance was scattered. The 2nd Battalion moved to an assembly area in the vicinity of Sachsenkam.

The 22nd Infantry began crossing the Isar River and Isarwk Canal over a treadway bridge at 1000. The progress was slow due to the soft, muddy approaches to the bridge site. No organized resistance was encountered by advancing troops until 1700 at which time the 4th Reconnaissance Troop was engaged by a group of dug-in enemy. The enemy was quickly overrun. At the end of the day, the 1st Battalion had advanced to the vicinity of Gusteig, the 3rd Battalion to the vicinity of Musbach and the 2nd Battalion to Holzkirchem.

From Swede Henley's Diary—used with permission of his daughters…

1 MAY 1945: Jumped off on another rat race and captured Gmund on lake at foothills of Alps. Captured 3000 prisoners.
- Want to go home—but not to C.B.I. (Editor note: China Burma India)

2-6 MAY: Relieved by 101st AB and moved to vicinity of Nurnberg. CP located at Roth. Passed thru Munich and you can mark that one off of the books.
- CP located in Baron's home. Guarding bridges and restoring law and order.
- Was the Baron mad when we ran him out of his house—the poor bastard.

From Chaplain Bill Boice's History of the 22nd Infantry Regiment in WWII…

The Combat Team, after leaving Crailsheim, continued to drive on to the southeast. Strong motorized combat patrols preceded the main body and located enemy pockets of resistance and reported that these could be destroyed.

All along the route of advance, German vehicles were found, some of which were still in good running condition. Capt. Crawford, of Antitank Company, and Lt. Milhous, from 'M' Company, located two German buses, and converted these into mobile kitchens. Actually, the mess sergeant and the company mechanics worked these two buses over and anchored the field ranges to the floor, after removing the seats. By so doing, these kitchens were able to prepare the meals while the motor column was moving. The mechanics continuously worked to repair the motors and keep them running.

Spare parts proved to be a problem, and the German vehicles apparently had no set standard of equipment or replacements. T/4 Don Wensink, of 'M' Co., who was by nature easy going and seldom infuriated, lost his temper more than once in trying to repair a German bus or truck. One cold morning after traveling some half-mile through snow knee-deep in order to locate a truck, Sgt. Wensink, in a tone of complete disgust, said, "These Krauts never made two pieces of equipment alike. If I ever see another German truck, I'm going to blow the damn thing to pieces before someone wants me to get it to run." In the last few weeks of the war, the entire CT was usually able to ride on some type of vehicle because there were so many captured vehicles available.

The advance crossed the Kocher River through Zang into Heidenheim. It was a beautiful city situated in the low, rolling hills of southern Germany. The 3rd Battalion was the first element of the Combat Team to move into the city. This they did the evening of April 24th, and by noon the next day the entire 4th Infantry Division had moved up into the city. The advance pushed on, and the CT crossed the Danube River near Lauingen on the 25th. The progress continued almost entirely uncontested until the Regiment reached the Lech River. Here the bridge was destroyed, and the Regiment assembled near Graben, awaiting completion of a bridge by the Engineers.

The only means which the enemy had to delay the advancing troops was the destruction of bridges which delayed the motorized columns. After crossing the Lech River, the CT proceeded to the Isar River and the bridge site just east of Unter-Schaftlarn. Here again the demolished bridges delayed the crossing. It was here that the Regiment captured a number of German women in the army uniform. When questioned by the IPW team, these women stated that they were typists and clerks for headquarters units. Enroute here, the Regiment had passed just south of

Munich, and the tall smoke stacks of the city's factories could be seen in the distance.

The 3rd and 45th Infantry Divisions were moving down the roads adjacent to the 22nd Regiment as they assaulted the city of Munchen. With the aid of field glasses, the white flags of truce could be seen hanging from the larger buildings. The 1st Battalion, which had the mission of blocking all roads from Munich into the Combat Team zone of action, secured important enemy installations, to include a supply dump of 10,000 liters of aviation gasoline and 100,000 liters of fuel oil.

The bridge across the Isar River was not completed until the 2nd of May. Shortly after it was completed, the 4th Reconnaissance Troop, with Co. 'K' mounted on their vehicles, led out in the renewed advance. The 2nd and 3rd Battalions followed up and rapidly swept through their zones of action, meeting only scattered token resistance. As before, the advance was further expedited by the use of captured enemy vehicles. With infantry mounted on vehicles of the 4th Reconnaissance Troop, tank destroyers of Company 'C', 610th Tank Destroyer (SP) Battalion, tanks of the 70th Tank Battalion, and by using organic and captured vehicles, the assault battalions were entirely motorized.

The resistance just north of Gmund was the heaviest reported and consisted of small arms, mortars, and artillery fire. By late afternoon, the Combat Team's advance to the southeast covered over twenty miles.

The Third Battalion, moving into Miesbach just before dark, met slight resistance. Captain Roche, Pfc. Kaiser, and his driver were well ahead of the advance when their jeep was fired upon by Germans on either side of the road. Panzerfausts, the German bazookas, hit around the jeep and Captain Roche told the driver to "get the hell out of there." Pfc. Kaiser had fallen from the jeep and was temporarily stunned. Captain Roche and the driver continued down the road and found a road block, forcing them to abandon the jeep.

Securing the machine gun, they returned through the woods to Miesbach and reported the incident to Major Kemp. Several days later, Kaiser returned to the Third Battalion and gave this account: When he noticed the jeep was gone and that he was alone, it was too late to escape. The

Germans had surrounded him and took his weapon. Kaiser, who had lived in Germany until 1938 before coming to the United States, spoke excellent German; however, he did not tell the enemy this; he told them that he had learned it in school. They took him to the next town to their command post where the commanding officer interviewed him and asked about the advance of the Americans. Several days later, Pfc. Kaiser returned to American lines and encountered elements of the 101st Airborne Division. He had persuaded some seventy-five Germans to accompany him and surrender.

The Combat Team, stopped for the night, deployed with the Third Battalion in Meisbach; the Second Battalion in Gusteig, Duenbach, Festenbach, and the First Battalion in Holzkirchen.

While the First Battalion was located temporarily in Holzkirchen, word came to the Battalion Commander, Lt. Colonel George Goforth, that a German woman in the town was asking the Americans to take over her supply of liquor. Her husband had been a liquor dealer and had samples of almost every kind of liquor stored in the basement of his house. Vermouth, gin, brandies of every sort, cognac, wine, and champagne were among the abundant samples that were stored.

Knowing that the Americans were on their way, the husband had rounded up the Russian slave laborers and had poured concrete into walls over the entire cache, sealing it completely and making it look as if it were a part of the cellar, in order to keep it from the Americans. Now, however, having been liberated, the Russians remembered the supply of liquor which they had worked so hard to preserve and now had but one purpose in mind, and that was to obtain it.

The woman had discovered that, armed with axes and sledge hammers, they were on their way to her home and, knowing the Russians and the German treatment of them, she had a pretty good idea that neither the liquor nor her home nor she herself would be spared, especially after the Russians had put some of the liquor inside. She was therefore asking the Americans to come at once and to take over the supply. Needless to say, she did not have to ask more than once, and the order went out for the S-4 to guard and, if need be, confiscate the liquor supply to prevent the Russians from taking it, since it was the obvious duty of the battalion to preserve order.

Since the battalion did not have enough men to waste to keep a constant guard on the cellar, it was decided that the most sensible thing to do was to liquidate the liquor. It was also felt that the most practical way to do this was to drink it. When the liquor was picked up, however, the German woman impudently asked the lieutenant in charge if the American government would pay her for it and presented a bill which represented the equivalent of about five thousand dollars.

The lieutenant, having been taught that a good soldier is never caught short, replied chivalrously and with no hesitation that he would be glad to sign such a receipt. He thereupon wrote out a complete and legitimate receipt and gave it into the hand of the woman, who was perfectly happy and satisfied. The receipt read: "This is to certify that the American Army has this day confiscated the liquor supply of this concern to the sum of five thousand dollars ($5,000), this sum to be deducted from the amount of money which the German Government owes the American Government from World War I."

As the personnel of the Combat Team dug in for the night of May 2-3, little did they realize that this day had been the last day of actual combat for them in the European Theater of Operations.

From **War Stories Volume II: Paris to VE Day**

William G. Cole, Tacoma, WA
Battery C, 29th Field Artillery Battalion
Memory Fragments from a Strange Two Days in Combat

Late in the war, perhaps in April of 1945, my forward observer party was with an infantry company of the 8th Infantry Regiment, and we were all involved in what seemed to me to be a bizarre series of combat events, which, for whatever reasons, I recall clearly and likely won't forget. Writing about them will help me clarify my memory and will be the first step in identifying the location. I have few clues to identify the time or place.

I recently told a friend that I had a dozen strange stories connected with the two or three days involved. He replied, "It was the Twilight Zone."

We were in the 7th Army in southern Germany. There was little resistance from the German forces. We moved very rapidly in the latter stages of the war in what was called a pursuit situation.

We entered a small German village early one day. It had been captured earlier that morning when an advance party, in a stealthy action, surprised the garrison and cleared the few buildings. Apparently, there was not time nor communication facilities for the Germans to inform their headquarters that the village had been occupied by us.

The village was in the valley of a small stream with rather steep hills on either side. It was on the side of the valley toward our rear areas and across the valley from our next objective. One narrow road along the valley passed through the village from our left to our right, crossing the stream as it entered and as it left the village.

The first action I remember was the sudden appearance of a German jeep type vehicle entering the village from the left. An outpost had tried to stop the vehicle, but the occupants tried to make a run for it. The vehicle had the top in place and side enclosures, which largely concealed the occupants. I was standing in the road at about the center of town as the vehicle approached. The people around me started firing at the jeep. I emptied the clip of my .45-caliber handgun but didn't hit anything. Someone hit the driver, who was dead when the vehicle left the road and stopped. The only passenger, a young officer, had bailed out as soon as the shooting started and was not injured. I may have fired my pistol at the enemy on other occasions, but I cannot specifically recall doing so.

Later, another small German vehicle approached, this time from the opposite direction. Our outpost was in a structure of some sort that I remember as a small farm building located at the sharp bend in the road as it turned to cross the bridge on its way into town. The vehicle was not moving fast as it passed our outpost. The infantrymen there fired a bazooka into the side of the vehicle. I don't think they gave the enemy any warning, but apparently they did not try to kill the occupants. The projectile hit the side of the vehicle just below the passenger-side front seat. It disabled the vehicle, burned a big hole in the seat of the passenger's uniform and burned his butt somewhat. He was lucky—he was able to walk.

He limped up the road ahead of his GI captors. I can still see it—a junior SS officer in a black uniform coming toward us, a very unimpressive little guy with the seat of his trousers burned out—a very satisfying sight to see. He spoke English, and later as he sat in the company command post, I asked him what he knew of the concentration camps. He professed total ignorance of such camps. I had nothing else to say to him. He didn't seem to be too unhappy. His war was likely over, and he had just survived in a close encounter with a bazooka shell.

The large, wooded hill to our front was our next objective. It must have been the first day that we arrived in that area at a position far up on the hill where the infantry, having encountered some opposition, was digging in. I don't remember going up the hill—I guess nothing much happened then. We were not with the lead elements of the company.

There appeared to be no great urgency to advance. The company commander was busy and didn't have time to tell me what he was being told. We were basically in a pursuit situation, the enemy in a rearguard delaying action. If we didn't clear the hill, their position would be outflanked soon. I was available and ready to get artillery fire if anyone wanted it. Artillery is not much help in such cases. You don't have a target other than a few enemy infantry close to you in the underbrush, and you don't dare adjust your artillery fire that close in. "Friendly" shells bursting in trees over one's infantry and oneself is to be avoided, if possible. Even if you can get the impacts a short distance ahead of you where they may be effective against the enemy (who may be a short distance behind his outposts), you are still shooting blind and still have the hazard of an occasional shell which falls short. (Every artillery shell that is fired, because of a number of variables, has a small probability of falling a significant distance too long or too short. Fire direction personnel have tables that have parameters by which the variation in range can be judged.)

An infantry NCO decided to fire mortars in the general direction of the enemy. I expressed my doubts to him. The first mortar rounds fell behind us. That was sufficient confirmation of my warnings, and no more mortar rounds were fired.

We spent one night on the hill and left it the following night. My memory retains the unusual events, and I'm not sure of the sequence. Our few skirmishes with the enemy probably took place on the second day. Panzerfaust projectiles were fired into our position. They are hand-held antitank rockets. They didn't do any damage, but they sure got our attention.

A German soldier, identified by his uniform as a paratrooper, got careless, I guess, and was taken prisoner. I was nearby when he was marched along ahead of his captor. A few yards from where I stood, the German saw a chance and ran for cover. The GI shouted at him before firing at him. By that time, the prisoner was moving fast in the underbrush and on his way to escape. I guess he preferred fighting to being a prisoner.

After dark on the second day, we came down the hill and back to the village. We moved along in single file, stopping often. At times, we heard German voices, but, presumably, neither side wanted a fight that night, and after minor exchanges of fire, we were disengaged.

The next day the outpost personnel in a small house about two hundred yards in front of the village found a large bomb in a crate, which the enemy had placed against the house, but abandoned when the outpost was alerted to their presence and drove them off.

I guess it was the infantry command who told me that an air strike—dive bomber—had been arranged against the village, which was about a mile down the valley to our left and partially visible to us. It may have been our fire direction center that let me know they were going to fire a red-smoke shell to mark the target for the P-47. I can never forget how badly I wanted to have the opportunity to adjust our gun on the target before it was marked with red smoke, but for whatever reason, I did not get the opportunity to do so. Where do you guess the red smoke shell landed? It fell in the valley, remote from any built-up area, but nearer to our village than to the target. The house containing our outpost was as close to the smoke as any other structure and the 500-pound bomb from the P-47 was placed somewhere in the vicinity of the smoke.

Later, I talked to an infantry officer who was at the outpost at the time. He was standing in the doorway of the building when the bomb exploded and was knocked across the room by the blast.

I don't remember the sequence—I just remember the explosion. Our guys fired mortars at a target in the vicinity of that same outpost and the mortar shells detonated some large amounts of explosive, perhaps bombs in crates.

An enemy tank appeared in a clearing well up on a hill, which was off to our right front, and began busting up our village. I was able to adjust artillery fire close to him, and undoubtedly we fired white phosphorous incendiary shells. We didn't get a direct hit, and he soon moved on to other things.

In the evening as I sat in the infantry command post in a village building, Captain Joe Gude, CO of Company C, 8th Infantry Regiment, came in and sat down. I had known him since early in the fighting and had been so impressed with him that I had mentioned him in letters I wrote during the war. Captain John Ausland, in his personal memoir of his experiences in our field artillery battalion, the 29th Field Artillery, had a lot of good things to say about Joe Gude.

Joe was prepared for the cold night. He had a bottle of Scotch inside the front of his field jacket. I asked him what he was doing there. He said he was taking his company up on the hill that night. He was cool and all business. Whether he started up the hill that night, I do not know.

I left the area that evening when I was relieved by Lieutenant George DeMeyers. I presume George was of Dutch ancestry, but it could have been Belgian. In either case, he had reason to hate the Germans. He never expressed himself to me on the subject, but he was very intense in his approach. I was told later that early the next morning the Germans mounted a counterattack across the open flood plain toward the village. DeMeyers was up to the challenge, as was the artillery he called upon.

As I remember the story, George's first transmission was, "Counterattack—request division artillery."

The artillery evidently was up and running because my memory of what I was told is that they adjusted their fire by battalion; that is, they fired all twelve guns of one battalion without delay on the location they had been given. This fire was sensed by the forward observer, which is a report of the location of the impact area in relation to the desired target. This is followed in turn by fire from twelve other guns of a second artillery battalion and then a third. This would make thirty-six 105mm howitzers pumping shells while, perhaps, the twelve 155mm howitzers of the division remained silent. Whatever the details were, the message I retain is that a massive amount of artillery fire was put on the target very quickly with much credit due the forward observer and the whole artillery command. The Germans got out of the area as best they could. One can thank God that he was not where the Germans were that morning.

I was always very glad that I had been relieved and didn't have to fire that mission and that George De Meyers did an apparently flawless job of it. If I had been associated with it, something would have gone wrong. I never fired such a mission and never saw one conducted in an emergency situation.

In thinking about it now, I wonder if such a large amount of artillery was justified. I don't really know all the facts, but if it accomplished the desired results, who am I to quibble?

It is very strange, considering the overall strategic situation, that the Germans would expose themselves to significant losses, which a counterattack across an open area would have produced. Maybe there was a local reason to buy a little time, or maybe some macho German paratroop officer had something to prove, as has been known to happen in our Army. At least the survivors can, fifty years later, swap stories.

3 MAY TO 8 MAY 1945 – D+332 TO D+337
VICTORY IN EUROPE DAY (VE DAY)

This is the week our 4ID Soldiers, and the whole world, have been looking for since September 1, 1939 when Germany invaded Poland, and personally since June 6, 1944 when the 4ID stormed the shores of Utah Beach on 6 June 1944.

Read on for the day that will be celebrated in Europe and the US next year on 8 May 2025—80 Years Ago. And stay with us as I summarize and wrap up before bringing this journey to an end.

3 MAY 1945—D+332: A quota of 4 officers and 30 enlisted men to return to the United States as guards on prisoner of war ships was received from the Seventh Army. Upon arrival in the US, the personnel were to be granted 45 days leaves or furloughs.

No contact was made with the enemy.

The 4th Infantry Division continued mopping up operations. Preparations were made to turn over the responsibility of the Division sector to the 101st Airborne Division. The 101st began movement into the 4th Infantry Division zone of action at 1000. Although no forward advances were made by any of the Division units during the day, many prisoners of war were taken. The enemy was surrendering in mass without a fight except in a few cases of small groups of fanatical SS troops.

The 8th Infantry continued to maintain peace and order in Division rear areas and to prevent looting. The 1st Battalion in Stamburg, the 2nd Battalion in Augsburg, and the 3rd Battalion in Gauting.

The 12th Infantry remained in the same areas as occupied during the previous day and continued mopping up operation throughout the day.

The 22nd Infantry continued mopping up operations until relieved by elements of the 101st Cavalry Reconnaissance Squadron at 1615. Upon being relieved, the entire regiment moved into an assembly area in the vicinity of Holzkirchen where preparations were made to move to new regimental areas in the vicinity of Nurnberg.

4 MAY 1945—D+333: The 4th Infantry Division was relieved from assignment to the Sixth Army Group, Seventh Army and XXI Corps and was assigned to the Third Army.

The 4th Infantry Division was relieved of responsibility by the 101st Airborne Division at 1200 and at 1000 had initiated the movement to its area of responsibility in the vicinity of Neumarkt which was in the Third Army zone.

The 8th Infantry continued its security mission and at 1200 was attached to the 101st Airborne Division.

The 12th Infantry was relieved by elements of the 101st Airborne Division by 1200 but remained in the area and made preparations for movement to new regimental areas in the vicinity of Sulzbach. An advance party initiated movement at 1300.

The 22nd Infantry began moving to the new assembly area in the vicinity of Schwabach at 1000 and closed therein at 2130.

5 MAY 1945—D+334: The 4th Infantry Division with the 70th Tank Battalion, 610th Tank Destroyer and the 377th AA Artillery continued movement into the new assigned division area: Hurnberg—Weisenburg—Ingalstadt—Regenburg—Sulzbach.

The 8th Infantry continued to maintain peace and order in the Gauting-Starnburg area. Preparations were made to receive relieving units of XXI Corps and to move in the vicinity of Burglingenfeld.

The 12th Infantry began movement from the area east of Bad Tolz to a new area in the vicinity of Sulzbach at 0850. It closed therein at 2130.

The 22nd Infantry initiated reconnaissance of the Nurnberg area and began relief of elements of the 16th Armored Division and other Third Army units guarding important installations in the Army railhead city of Nurnberg. The relieving of the different units was a slow undertaking due to the fact that reconnaissance parties had to find all the guarded installations before the relief could be accomplished.

6 MAY 1945—D+335: The Division command post opened at Amberg at 0700.

A teletype message signed by General Eisenhower was received during the day stating that the German military forces had signed the unconditional surrender to all Allied Forces, effective 090001 May 1945.

The 8th Infantry was relieved and all battalions assembled preparatory to moving to new assigned area. The 1st and 3rd Battalions continued to patrol the roads within the area.

The 12th Infantry initiated reconnaissance within the new area of occupation to contact other units guarding installations and patrolling the sector.

The 22nd Infantry continued to relieve all other units in the Nurnberg area and assume responsibility for the traffic control within the important Army supply center of Nurnberg.

The 4th Division Artillery with the 377 AA Bn, 610th Tank Destroyer Bn and 70th Tank Bn, initiated movement from Bad Tolz at an early hour to move to the new assigned area in the vicinity of Boilingries.

7 MAY 1945—D+336: The 8th Infantry remained under control of the 101st Airborne Division in assembly areas in the vicinity of Gauting in preparation to moving to new division area early 8 May.

The 12th Infantry took over the guarding and security of displaced person camps, captured enemy supply dumps, bridges, radio and telephone stations, and other installations within their sector in the vicinity of Sulzbach.

The 22nd Infantry continued to relieve other elements guarding enemy supply dumps and other installations in the vicinity of Nurnberg-Schwabach.

The 4th Division Artillery initiated the relief of other units in the vicinity of Boilingries. The 70th Tank Battalion and the 610th Tank Destroyer Battalion moved from assembly areas to the new Division area of occupation, closing therein at 1445.

8 MAY 1945—D+337 VE DAY (VICTORY IN EUROPE): The 4th Infantry Division continued to maintain law and order and to guard installations and also made preparation to assume responsibility for additional security missions.

The 8th Infantry moved to Burglengenfeld, closing therein at 1800. The regiment made plans for assuming responsibility for security of displaced persons' camps, captured enemy supply dumps, main supply route and bridges within their area early 09 May.

The 12th made plans for assuming responsibility for additional security missions in the vicinity of Neustadt and Eschenbach.

No change in the operations of the 22nd Infantry.

CASUALTIES – FROM 6 JUNE 1944 TO 9 MAY 1945

Officers — Enlisted — Total
KIA 263 — 3,595 — 3,858
Died of wounds 39 — 692 — 731
MIA 16 — 267 — 283
SWA 408 — 6,489 — 6,897 (Seriously Wounded in Action)
LWA 484 — 8,930 — 9,414 (Lightly Wounded in Action)
Captured 0 — 14 — 14
Total 1,210 — 19,987 — 21,197 Combat Casualties
Casualties equaled 149% of the authorized June 1944 strength of 14,253.
32% of the original June 1944 strength were killed in action or died of wounds.

From **Swede Henley's Diary — used with permission of his daughters ...**

7 MAY: Sitting on my can and the war has ended. V-E DAY MAY 7, 1945 AT ROTH, GERMANY 11 months 2 days of combat for the 22nd Inf.

8 MAY 1945: They announced it.

8-13 MAY: Still in Roth but planning on moving near Ausback soon.
• Ruggles got over the crud.

- Tommy Harrison stopped stuttering.
- Geo. Goforth lost all of his ailments & the doc said he was normal.
- Swede was laughing, as he was never hit—poor shots—the dirty bastards.

14 MAY: Moved to Dinkelsbuhl and set up CP in Golden Rose Hotel.

14-31 MAY: Dinkelsbuhl, Germany.

Cleaning up—guarding bridges. Received 918 prisoners of war. No. 1 camp located at Feuchtwangen.

No. 2 camp located at Ehringin (Herman Goering glider school)

This concludes Swede's diary—thanks a million to his daughters for letting us use it, and to Swede for being so faithful in writing it.

* * * * *

From Chaplain Bill Boice's **History of the 22nd Infantry Regiment in WWII**

At dawn the 3rd of May, the 2nd and 3rd Battalions swept through their respective zones with combat patrols but encountered no enemy. Division orders for the relief, movement, and assembly of the Regiment in the vicinity of Holzkirchen were received in the early afternoon. The Regiment was relieved shortly thereafter by elements of the 101st Airborne Division. The relief was complete by midnight. Totals compiled by the S2 Section showed that the Regiment had in the past two days processed 3,270 prisoners.

Orders came down during the night for a movement by the Combat Team to an area near Nurnberg, Germany. Immediately plans were drawn up, and at 0930 hours the 4th of May, leading units of the CT crossed the IP. The motorized column proceeded via the autobahn, superhighway of Germany, through Munich, Ingolstadt, to the assembly areas of Schwabach.

Upon arrival in the new area, planning was initiated, and preliminary orders were issued for the division of the area into separate battalion occupational sectors and for a thorough reconnaissance of the new area.

From 5-9 May, 1945, the 22nd Regiment was engaged in a non-tactical occupational and guarding mission in the Nurnberg and Ansbach area of Germany. The Regiment had no contact with the enemy from the 5th of May until 0001 hours the 9th, at which time the European War officially ended with the unconditional surrender of all German naval, land, and air forces.

On the 5th of May the Regiment divided its zone into four subordinate sectors of responsibility. Each of the three rifle battalions and the 4th Engineers, now attached to the 22nd, moved into and assumed control of one of these areas. The disposition of the units was as follows: Regimental Headquarters was in Schwabach, 1st Battalion Headquarters was in Nurnberg, 2nd Battalion Headquarters was in Roth, 3rd Battalion Headquarters was in Spalt, and the 4th Engineer Battalion was in Weidach. These positions were maintained until May 9th. A training schedule was set up, and the troops carried out all types of training. Motorized patrols daily swept through the Regimental zone of occupation.

Tom Reid, Marietta, GA
Cannon Company, 22nd Infantry Regiment and Company I, 3rd Battalion, 22nd Infantry Regiment
Last KIA in WWII, PFC Carl Baker

You can imagine my surprise upon reading the 22nd Infantry Regiment Society newsletter for September 1996, and learning that Private First Class Carl W. Baker of Item Company was the last official KIA in the 22nd Infantry in WWII on May 3, 1945—for I was the last Company Commander of Item Company in WWII.

Ever since the end of the War, I had always thought that the Regiment was in action on the following day, May 4, 1945. But with the passage of 51 years, I am willing to concede that my memory may not be as accurate in this respect as are the official records of the War Department.

Fit to Fight

No meaningful mention of Item Company, 22nd Infantry Regiment can be made without a reference to the contributions and outstanding leadership of two previous commanders of the company, Lieutenant General (Retired) Glenn Walker and Major Joe Samuels, who as a captain brought the company ashore in the first wave of D-Day, June 6, 1944 on Utah Beach, Normandy.

Joe Samuels commanded the company longer than any of the other Item Company commanders in combat. Glenn Walker commanded the company in its training days at Camp Gordon, Georgia, and then went on to successful command positions in the 22nd Infantry in WWII, fought in Korea, was commanding general of the 4th Infantry Division in Vietnam, and now resides in Mississippi. (Glen Walker died on May 3, 2002).

Their magnetic leadership left an indelible imprint on I Company. I was walking in their footsteps and trying to fill a large shoe size.

All through April 1945, we could see the end of the war in Europe coming. Our advances were swifter, more prisoners were being taken, and some days troops riding on tanks were making five to ten miles per day.

Everyone had talked about not wanting to be the last man killed in the war, but no one knew when that fateful day would arrive. On May 3, 1945, (May 4, by my recollection) Item Company was given the mission to seize the small village of Agatharied. We were now in southern Bavaria, about sixty miles south of Munich. Snow was still on the ground in the foothills of the Bavarian Alps.

Resistance was slight, the company had moved through the town, and I was ordered by the battalion commander to hold where I was. Suddenly a shot rang out and Private First Class Carl W. Baker, my company runner, fell. He was only a few feet away from me and was still alive. I took my radio and maps out of my jeep and told the driver to get him back to the aid station as fast as possible. He died on the way.

In a few minutes, I received an order to dig in where we were. The War was over, the Germans had surrendered, and PFC Carl W. Baker had become the last KIA in the 22nd Infantry Regiment.

Carl Baker was from Portland, Oregon, and wanted to be a forest ranger when the war was over. He was an outstanding soldier and could always be depended on to carry out any task he was given with dedication and dispatch. We often shared a cup of coffee or a K-ration. His death came hard to me.

Through the years since, I have often thought of Carl Baker, the gallant soldier of World War II who wanted to be a forest ranger and instead became the last KIA of the 22nd Infantry Regiment and 4th Infantry Division in WWII. He truly exemplified "Deeds not Words!"

From his book, *History of the 22nd Infantry Regiment in World War II.*

Bill Boice, Phoenix, AZ
Chaplain, 22nd Infantry Regiment
Letter Home as Hostilities End

When the announcement of cessation of hostilities was heard, Chaplain Boice sent down a letter to the men of the Regiment to be addressed to their families and mailed home. The letter read:

This evening Admiral Doenitz has announced to the German people the unconditional surrender of all German fighting forces. Had this surrender occurred the 1st of September on our wave of optimism when we hit the Siegfried Line, or immediately after the defeat of Von Rundstedt and the successful crossing of the Rhine, we would have been wild with joy. The news of Germany's surrender was received by all of us with a calmness very nearly approaching indifference about the feeling deep within our hearts.

There was no revelry last night, no drunkenness, no shouting, no flag waving, no horns blowing; there was a sober realization that it was all over, at least so far as Europe was concerned, and that we, by the strength of our arms and by our own courage, had, with the help of God, completely and finally defeated everything that the warped and twisted soul of a perverted nation could hurl at us.

We take no undue pride in what we have done, for we are sobered by the blood of our comrades, which cries up to us from every foot of ground from Normandy to Berlin and from Holland to Italy. We have done what we have had to do for you, as well as for our own peace of mind.

I am proud of my officers and fellow soldiers in the 22nd Infantry Regiment.

There is not one single fighting day of which we must be ashamed, or for which we must make excuses. No regiment in the ETO has more right to hold its head high and to march with shoulders back, colors streaming, than this one. Its record, its casualties, its achievements, and the respect it instilled, and the terror it struck in the heart of the German Army speak for themselves.

From his book, ***History of the 22nd Infantry Regiment in World War II***.

Bill Boice, Phoenix, AZ
Chaplain, 22nd Infantry Regiment
The Men Who Were Not There

And so, the war was over. It was a fact far too deep for us to grasp fully, and we realized somehow that we should be more grateful than we were, that probably we should do all of the little things which we were expected to do, like blowing horns and tooting whistles and perhaps getting drunk. But we didn't. We simply thought of the hundreds and hundreds of our friends who had given everything they had in order that we might see V-E Day. The men who were not there—the memory of them, the years we had trained with them, knowing their families, or perhaps the brief moments we had known some of them who came to us as replacements, the insight we had had into their very souls which can come only to a man who sees his soul laid bare and lives a thousand lives or dies a thousand deaths in a single day of combat.

Stretching back to the Turgen Sea to Bensheim and from Bensheim to Hamn, from Hamn to Henri Chappelle, and from Henri Chappelle to Marigny and from Marigny to St. Mére Eglise were rows of even white crosses dotted with occasional Stars of David, where school children on their way home left flowers on the graves. And always flying proudly, but somberly, were the Stars and Stripes, symbol of the devotion of the men who rest beneath.

The men were not there. Never completely gone from our minds were the little things we remembered—funny, crazy things they did, premonitions they had, ways they fought or talked, or maybe even things about them we hadn't liked; we supposed that we should feel our responsibility and we guessed, too, we were living on borrowed time, time loaned to us from these men who were not there. No more slopping through foxholes half-filled with water, clothes damp, and with such a constant hunger for something that we could never quite place or satisfy. No more of this. No more of it for them either. We had seen the gaping wounds that had sapped their lives.

We had seen the cemeteries; we knew how they were buried. We had seen these rows of lifeless objects, shattered mockeries of that which had been breathing, pulsating men, friends of ours, buried in the soil of France and Belgium and Luxembourg and Germany.

Strange that the soil of Germany was no different from the soil of France or America, nor were men any different. Men did what they had to do and hoped they could endure it. If they were lucky, they got back, or sometimes in the hellishness of combat they looked on the body of a soldier and said meaningfully, "Won't nothing bother him anymore."

There were some other men who were not there, men in hospitals in Michigan and Washington, Atlanta and Vancouver, men whose every footstep would bear testimony to war and everything it was and everything it did to men.

And so, the war was over. Perhaps we should have celebrated. Perhaps our celebration was the quiet realization that we were here, and they were not, for it was only by the grace of God, by hard fighting, and perhaps sometimes poor shooting that we had lived to see Victory in Europe.

Cal Grose (Deceased), Chapel Hill, NC
Medical Detachment, 3rd Battalion, 22nd Infantry Regiment
My Buddy

The war had ended and we were put up in a tent city around Nuremberg for a little R&R before going back to Paris to turn in our vehicles. The enlisted men had their section in tent city, and the officers had theirs. One day a captain came into my tent and ordered me to give up my cot. Being just a buck sergeant, I did so, but I did ask him why. He said they were looking for someone to be "Officer of the Day," and he wanted to hide so they could not choose him.

You notice I did not mention the officer's name, but I hope after this we will still be good buddies, because he is the brother I never had, and we have remained friends to this day—sorry, Sam Barrett (Regimental Dentist). (Editor's note from Bob—I met Cal Grose and Sam Barrett at the first 22nd Infantry Regiment Society reunion I hosted in 1996. They were still great friends then and remained that way until they both died a few years later. Always Steadfast and Loyal—Deeds not Words!)

Albert Schantz, Reading, PA
Company A, 1st Battalion, 22nd Infantry Regiment
Coming Home

We continued to force the Krauts back toward the east: First, to Rothenburg, then south and southeast through Crailsheim, Heidenheim, across the Danube River on April 25, 1945, then on to Wolfratshausen and Bad Tolz near the Bavarian Alps. We were six miles from the Austrian border when we received word that the Germans surrendered on May 8, 1945.

Morale increased when we learned about the surrender. There was a party mood, but we were glad the war was finished. We were looking forward to going home. Plus, there were no party "fixins" available anyway.

May 8, 1945, was declared "VE Day" (Victory in Europe Day). I remember that day very well. It snowed about eight inches, and we were occupying farmhouses. When we took over a house we forced the German occupants to sleep in the barn, and we slept in their beds. I slept in a bed with a straw mattress covered with a feather-filled quilt. The houses were attached to the barn so that the heat from the animals and the manure heated the house in winter.

A few days after VE Day, we boarded Army trucks and rode north through Munich, across the Danube River, to Amberg, then west to Ansbach, Germany, where we took control of a German fort. Here we processed German prisoners of war and discharged them so they could return to their homes. I was able to act as an interpreter for Germans who spoke no English, since I knew "Pennsylvania" German.

The worst war damage that I saw was in Munich, Germany. Munich must have been a beautiful city with statues in the middle of each intersection in the center of town. Many buildings and statues were bombed to rubble. It was sad... War is hell. There were very few people on the streets and sidewalks for a city of that size. One of my desires is to visit Munich now that it is rebuilt.

On June 23, 1945, we left Germany for Le Havre, France, in railroad boxcars. This mode of transportation was known as "40 and 8" in WWI. (Forty men or eight horses in a boxcar).

On our way west to Le Havre, our train stopped in a siding in a large railroad yard. I happened to look across several train tracks at another boxcar into a train that was also stopped. There in the open boxcar door was Bobby Walbert from Macungie, Pennsylvania. I knew Bobby from high school. I walked over to him, and we talked for a short time. He was in the 5th Infantry Division and was also headed for Le Havre, France.

Seeing someone familiar from back home was a happy occasion. It eased some of the homesickness.

We arrived in Le Havre on June 30, 1945, and boarded the General James Parker, a liberty ship, for our ride back to the good old USA. The entire 4th Infantry Division sailed on July 3, 1945. We experienced one rough day on the Atlantic Ocean. I didn't miss any meals, but I couldn't keep my breakfast down that rough morning. I wasn't alone at the rail. I was able to eat lunch and dinner without any problems. The ship was crowded, and many of us had to sleep on the open deck under blankets. The night air made us very wet, and we were glad it was summertime.

We arrived in New York Harbor on July 11, 1945. I can still see the Statue of Liberty as she came into view. How wonderful she looked. After we disembarked, the 4th Infantry Division was transported to Camp Kilmer, New Jersey, where a thick, delicious steak dinner awaited us. We were then fitted with new uniforms and attended lectures telling us what to expect back in the States.

The Army's plans were to retrain us and ship the 4th Infantry Division to the South Pacific to finish the war with Japan. Thanks to President Truman, who authorized dropping the Atomic Bombs on Japan, ending the War in the South Pacific on August 14, 1945 (VJ Day).

Clarence Brown, Buchanan, NY
4th Signal Company
Tent City

At the end of the war I was sent back to somewhere near Nuremberg where we had Italian prisoners digging up cable and German cable men repairing the cable that had been blown apart.

It was from there (with Selective Service points—married, a daughter, Bronze Star, etc.) that they told me that I was on my way home. They flew us from Nuremberg to Metz, France, to Tent City. (It wasn't really organized.) I then found out what they meant by "40 & 8." That was a freight car that would hold forty men or eight horses. We rode them for three days until we got to Le Havre…tent city again.

Then on a ship back to the States. Took four days. On board ship I was with a lot of American former POWs. The biggest thrill of my life came as we entered New York harbor. With the fireboat hoses spraying, tugboats blowing their whistles—we all shed a few tears of joy. We had made it back. It was then to Shanks, Dix, and deactivation. I was honorably discharged on my birthday (June 23, 1945) and went home to my wife and family in Buchanan, New York, where we still reside today.

Robert O. Babcock

SUMMARY OF 4ID'S FIGHT ACROSS EUROPE –

6 JUNE 1944 TO 8 MAY 1945: Let me give you a feeling for the killed and wounded statistics that we have covered over the past 11 months.

Every one of those 4ID Soldiers included in these statistics had parents, grandparents, and others at home praying for their safe return. Many did, too many did not. They did not die in vain, they died while stopping the evil that Adolph Hitler started in Europe on 1 September 1939.

These are not statistics, these are American Families, just like yours, who lost loved ones in WWII, and American Soldiers who wore the scars of wounds the rest of their lives.

Let us never forget—**FREEDOM IS NOT FREE**. It is paid for by patriotic Americans who love our country and the American way of life. They are always Steadfast and Loyal.

*****

To put things into perspective, following are the total casualties for the top six divisions who served in the European and Mediterranean theater of operations. You will note four of the top six served in North Africa, Sicily, and Italy before the D-Day invasion. Of those who served only in the European theater, the 4ID suffered the most casualties and ranked third among all divisions serving in the European and Mediterranean theaters. That is an indication of the amount of combat they were in.

CASUALTIES

The six divisions with the most battle casualties are presented below. Casualties are defined as killed in action, wounded in action, captured, and interned, and missing in action.

Casualties Division Theater
25,977 3rd Infantry Division Mediterranean & European

23,277 9th Infantry Division Mediterranean & European
22,660 4th Infantry Division European
20,993 45th Infantry Division Mediterranean & European
20,659 1st Infantry Division Mediterranean & European
20,620 29th Infantry Division European

Source: Army Battle Casualties and Nonbattle Deaths in World War II, Final Report, 1 December 1941 — 31 December 1946

REVIEW OF 4ID ACTIONS – D-DAY TO VE DAY

This is a high-level review of what the 4th Infantry Division accomplished between D-Day and V-E Day. My intent is to summarize what we have covered in this book. I have interspersed at the end of each major highlight, the casualty statistics for that time period of the war.

This will highlight the big picture fights that history remembers...

D-DAY, 6 JUNE 1944: 4ID, led by the 8th Infantry Regiment, was the first seaborne troops to land on the coast of Normandy, France at H-Hour, 0630 hours.

25 JUNE 1944: 4ID, along with 9ID, liberated the first port in France...Cherbourg.

Days and days of fighting through the hedgerows of Normandy took place before and after the liberation of Cherbourg.

- 4ID Battle Casualties — 6-30 June 1944 = 5,531 (our toughest casualty month of the war)

25 JULY 1944: 4ID, along with 2nd Armored Division, were the spearhead divisions in Operation Cobra, the St. Lo breakout where massive air bombardments stunned the Germans as our ground troops broke out of the hedgerows of Normandy and pursued the enemy toward Paris.

- 4ID Battle Casualties—July 1944 = 3,438 (our third toughest casualty month)

25 AUGUST 1944: The 12th Infantry Regiment of 4ID was the first Allied unit to enter Paris, followed close behind by the French 2nd Armored Division and the rest of the 4ID. After a day of celebration and clearing out pockets of German resistance, the 4ID continue their pursuit of the retreating Germans. Other units basked in the glory of a liberated Paris; the 4ID had a job to continue.
- 4ID Battle Casualties—August 1944 = 1,584 (our fifth toughest casualty month)

11 SEPTEMBER 1944: A patrol from the 22nd Infantry Regiment became the first Allied unit to breach the daunted Siegfried Line and move across into the German homeland. The next day, other 4ID units, along with MG Raymond Barton, became the first Allied unit on German soil.
- 4ID Battle Casualties—September 1944 = 1,267
- 4ID Battle Casualties—October 1944 = 350 (we were stopped, waiting for supplies to catch up)

NOVEMBER 1944: Starting in early November, the 12th Infantry Regiment of 4ID entered Germany's Hurtgen Forest, to help the 28th Infantry Division. At mid-month, the rest of the 4ID joined the fight which raged non-stop until early December. Virtually every 4ID Soldier, when asked what their toughest fight was, quickly said, "The Hurtgen Forest".
- 4ID Battle Casualties—November 1944 = 4,025 (our second toughest casualty month)

16 DECEMBER 1944: While resting and receiving replacements in Luxembourg for losses in the Hurtgen Forest (the average 4ID company had 150% casualties during the fight), the German counterattack that became known as The Battle of the Bulge, hit the weary and battered 4ID troops. Later, General George Patton wrote to the 4ID Commanding

General, ""Your fight in the Hürtgen Forest was an epic of stark infantry combat; but, in my opinion, your most recent fight—from the 16th to the 26th of December—when, with a depleted and tired division, you halted the left shoulder of the German thrust into the American lines and saved the City of Luxembourg and the tremendous supply establishments and road nets in that vicinity, is the most outstanding accomplishment of yourself and your division."

- 4ID Battle Casualties—December 1944 = 1,872 (our fourth toughest casualty month)
- 4ID Battle Casualties—January 1945 = 814

FEBRUARY 1945: Often occupying the same foxholes they dug in September, the 4ID once again penetrated the Siegfried Line and fought through Prum and other German strongholds as the Nazis resorted to defending their homeland against our relentless assault. This pursuit continued through March and April.

- 4ID Battle Casualties—February 1945 = 1,344
- 4ID Battle Casualties—March 1945 = 776
- 4ID Battle Casualties—April 1945 = 872

8 MAY 1945: After 336 days of combat, punctuated with only short rest periods, the 4ID was deep into Germany when Hitler committed suicide and the Germans surrendered unconditionally.

- 4ID Battle Casualties—May 1945 = 26

Total Battle Casualties: 21,879 (does not balance to above number which was adjusted after these numbers from 4ID Yearbook were printed)

Total Non-Battle Casualties: 12,430 (sickness, accidents, etc.)

Total Casualties: 34,309 (this includes some who were wounded multiple times)

Each and every one of these casualties had a Family worrying about him back at home and he carried the scars, if wounded, the rest of his life.

NEVER FORGET — FREEDOM IS NOT FREE

The above summary is the *Reader's Digest* version of the 4ID's fight across Europe in WWII. In this book, we have covered the day by day accounts. Hopefully it has been a journey that you learned from.

* * * * *

Now, stay with me and I'll wrap up the timeframe from May 1945 to March 1946 when the 4ID was temporarily deactivated at Camp Butner, NC before coming back in early 1947 for continuous active duty service ever since then. Today's (2024) 4ID is stationed at Fort Carson, CO.

Home from the Wars — men of the Division wave as the Hermitage, troop transport, pulls into New York Harbor on July 10, 1945.

4ID'S RETURN TO USA

CAMP BUTNER, NC, AND DEACTIVATION IN MARCH 1946

This wraps up the journey we've been taking to commemorate the 4th Infantry Division's preparation for and fight through WWII. This final chapter will cover what happened from VE Day through early March 1946 when the 4ID was deactivated at Camp Butner, NC.

Do not worry—that was a short-lived deactivation. We were back at work in 1947 and have been a key part of the US Army's force structure ever since then. Today, February 2024, 4ID Soldiers are on station at Fort Carson, CO, ready for any mission that comes their way.

* * * * *

Chaplain Bill Boice did a great job summarizing the wrap-up of WWII in his book, **History of the 22nd Infantry Regiment in WWII**. I think you can realistically say that all division units performed similar duties as what he describes for the 22nd Infantry Regiment…

AMERICA THE BEAUTIFUL

With the cessation of hostilities, the question most frequently heard was "when are we going home?" Rumors of long occupation duty, of immediate re-deployment to the Pacific theatre, and of certain shipment home were rampant.

On 12 May, orders for a shift of Zone came to the regiment, and a few days later, the shift was complete, but it was only a shift of position instead of the expected pre-return movement. Regimental headquarters moved into Heilbrounn and plunged into the mass of administrative details which had accumulated. The First Battalion, Canon Company, Anti-Tank Company, and Service Company were stationed in Ansbach, a comparatively undamaged German city of some fifty thousand people. The Hindenburg Barracks housed the troops adequately and under the rigorous cleaning details assumed the aspect of an American army camp.

The Second Battalion headquarters were in Dinkelsbuhl with the companies located nearby. The Third Battalion was at Neuen Dettelsau.

The Regiment remained in this position from the 15 May 1945 until 9 June 1945. The three battalions set up outposts in surrounding towns and daily motorized patrols scoured the area. Bridges and important installations were guarded. Personnel not engaged in guard duty were kept busy reconditioning equipment, resuming training schedules, and recovering physically from the drain of combat.

One of the greatest problems handled by the Regiment was that of Displaced Persons, mostly Russian, French, and Polish. These people had to be processed, housed, fed, and administrated in an orderly fashion. The largest DP Camp under the control of the regiment was located on a hill to the east, overlooking Ansbach.

German prisoners of war were processed and discharged, an enemy prison camp was maintained and carefully guarded, curfews were enforced, and careful liaison established with the Military Government in the execution of policies now established by them and carried out through the Combat Troops. This occupational zone for which the regiment was responsible included some 1300 square kilometers.

As could be expected, life was just beginning to assume comfortable routine when movement orders were received from Division headquarters. On 10 June 1945, the regiment moved by vehicle to an assembly area near the town of Schesslitz. All units in this new area pitched pup tents or pyramidal tents.

From the 11 June to 21 June 1945, the Regiment carried out its training schedule insofar as was practical. The war against the Japanese was still raging in the Pacific, and the probability was that the 22nd Regiment would be, in due time, redeployed to that zone of action. The training was carried on accordingly. Organized athletics, personal contests, field meets, and group games were included to build up the physical condition of the troops.

Supply, now a far greater problem than during combat, was under the control of Major James A. Burnside, Regimental S-4. Clothing and equipment were issued to the companies. Property inspections were made, and all equipment became accountable to company commanders and individuals. Un-serviceable or worn out equipment was turned in and replaced. Vehicles were overhauled to the fullest possible extent. Field pieces such as anti-tank guns and 105 cannons were cleaned, repaired, and turned into Division to be disposed of through channels. Officers from the Inspector General's Department periodically inspected company and battalion supply records.

In the headquarters of all companies and battalions, as well as Regiment, painstaking care was taken to bring all the administrative details up to date. Company officers, clerks, and 1st Sergeants worked meticulously day and night to straighten out long confused records. Sick books, duty rosters, and morning reports were brought up to date. Combat awards, long due men of the Regiment, were sent forward, and those awards previously approved were sent to the bearer. Administration had now become an important factor that was to be taken care of, as tedious as it often seemed. IG inspectors also checked these records and made corrections when and where they were necessary.

For the troops, Special Service Officers arranged long awaited recreation. Men were sent on passes to rest areas, USO shows were nearby, and movies were held nightly in open air theatres on hillsides or in barns.

Parades were organized, and Divisional and Regimental Reviews took place in the surrounding fields. Awards and promotions were presented to deserving men during these reviews. In the evening, Retreat was held, and orders for that evening and the following day were issued.

The Regiment in toto was striving to bring up to date a backlog of administrative work long encumbered by combat conditions and which must be made current in order to efficiently carry forward the competent record held by the Regiment.

On 22 June 1945, leading elements pulled out of the tent area and left by train in forty and eight box cars, forty men or eight horses as described by the French. Part of the Regiment was to move by vehicle, others by train. The vehicle convoy, made up of organic transportation, followed up a day later. The move was to be made from Bamberg, Germany, to Camp Old Gold in the vicinity of Le Havre, France. It was now apparent that the 22nd Infantry Regiment was to be redeployed to the United States through the French Port. The move, both by train and vehicle, even though it was to take four or five days, presented to all an opportunity to see the beautiful countryside without the conscious fear of sudden and complete destruction.

By the 27th of June 1945, the Regiment in its entirety had closed into Camp Old Gold. Processing began at once to prepare troops and equipment for the trans-Atlantic journey to the USA.

For almost a week, from 28 June until 2 July 1945, processing continued. Training periods became brief, and time was suitably used for cleaning, crating, and marking of clothes and equipment. The morale within the Regiment had risen to new heights. There were men and officers who had been overseas for more than three years; the Regiment had been overseas since January 1944. The unsurpassed combat efficiency of the units had temporarily shifted to garrison efficiency, and everybody did his utmost to prepare. Vehicles and several types of automatic weapons were turned in to Division for disposal through channels.

On July 2, 1945, the 3rd Battalion, less Company 'M', moved to the port of Le Havre and boarded the United States Army Transport 'James Parker'. The 3rd Battalion was to be the advance detail on board and pull the necessary details enroute. The following day, 3 July 1945, the remainder of the Regiment, less Company 'H' moved to the port and boarded the vessel. Companies 'H' and 'M' moved into the loading area and boarded the USAT 'Excelsior'.

At 1613 hours, the 'James Parker' was under way, bound for the States. During the voyage, all troops were allowed to spend their time eating, sleeping, lounging about on deck in the warm sunlight, or going to the movies. Card playing and reading seemed to be prevalent among the majority of the men. The second day out of Le Havre a slight storm was encountered, but other than this, the voyage was quite pleasant.

Shortly after dawn July 11, 1945, the eastern coast of the United States was sighted off the port side as the transport moved northward into the Hudson River and New York Harbor. At 1000 hours, the Statue of Liberty was passed, and welcoming ships encircled the 'James Parker'. At 1100 hours, the army transport docked at Pier 84, New York City, N. Y. By 1700 hours, the Regiment less Companies 'H' and 'M' had unloaded and moved either by bus or by train to Camp Kilmer, New Jersey.

Immediately upon arrival at Camp Kilmer, the processing, just prior to recuperation furloughs, began. Within twenty-four hours, the first contingent of men left Camp Kilmer by rail, bound for their nearest reception stations and their thirty day furlough.

Companies 'H' and 'M' embarked on the USAT 'Excelsior' on 3 July 1945 and shoved off about 1400 hours. After a pleasant voyage, the companies docked at Hampton Roads, Virginia, early in the afternoon of 12 July 1945. Within twenty-four hours, these men were also headed home for their long deserved thirty day recuperation furloughs.

At Camp Butner, the advance detail under command of Major Frederick T. Kent, Regimental S-2, arrived to make final arrangements pending the arrival of the main body. This detail, consisting of competent officers and enlisted men, had left Europe several days ahead of the regiment so that they could make the necessary preparations. When they arrived at the camp, they quickly established battalion and company areas, unpacked all TAT equipment, drew necessary supplies from Post Quartermaster, and made ready for the arrival of the Regiment.

By the 27 August 1945, the greater part of the Regiment was assembled at Camp Butner and an intensive training program got underway.

Even though hostilities had unofficially ceased in the Pacific and an inevitable armistice was close at hand, the training was to be carried on. The Regiment was scheduled to depart for the Pacific War Theatre in the early part of November 1945.

The 22nd Infantry Regiment, 4th Infantry Division, was now under the direction and control of the Second US Army. With the assembly of the Regiment, new problems presented themselves.

All enlisted men with eighty-five points or more were to be discharged as rapidly as possible. Officers possessing one hundred fifteen points, or more, were also eligible for discharge at this time if they desired. At once discharging began. Training was initiated with special emphasis placed on military courtesy, personal hygiene, athletics, and physical conditioning.

On 2 September 1945, word was received of the official surrender of all Japanese forces, land, sea, and air. This sudden cessation of hostilities would certainly cause wide changes in plans, but temporarily the action of the 22nd Infantry remained the same. Training was broadened to include weapons firing and qualification of all personnel in their individual arms and crew served weapons. About the middle of the month, orders were officially sent down that the Regiment would not go to the Pacific as previously planned but would stay in strategic reserve for a period of time then unknown.

The Army's Adjusted Service Rating, point score, dropped for both officers and enlisted men the 1st of October 1945. This placed virtually hundreds of men eligible for immediate release from the service. The change also meant that there was to be quite a turn-over of personnel within the Regiment. Shortly after 1 October 1945, a directive came down from Army Headquarters authorizing forty-five day furloughs for men not immediately due for discharge, provided that forty-five percent of TO strength remained for duty. With these two changes in effect, training became secondary, and administration became the top issue.

The remainder of October 1945 was spent in complying with the new discharge scores, the new furlough policy, and the indoctrination of new replacements being received almost daily. Parades and reviews were conducted throughout. Awards and decorations were made during such parades to the men who had been awarded them. Each of the nineteen companies organized information and education rooms for the use and benefit of all personnel.

With the coming of November, point scores for officers and enlisted men were again reduced, making another large number of men eligible for discharge. As before, administration took precedence over any other type of work, Company records were continuously being inspected, and new directives in regard to these records were being complied with. The 22nd Infantry was shifting from a Combat Team to a garrison Regiment.

During the month, the forty-five day furlough policy was stopped. The Regiment, still a part of the 4th Infantry Division, was shifted to the command of the First Army under the command of Lieutenant General Courtney H. Hodges. Again training schedules were formulated and carried out, to include all types of training and education. New weapons were introduced. Schools of various types were made available to both officers and enlisted men. Quotas were received and filled for these schools in an effort to bring the latest ideas within the Regiment.

BELGIUM FOURAGERE

V-J Day probably made the men of the Fourth Infantry Division as happy as any of the troops anywhere for the reason that it had been slated for an assault landing on the beaches of Japan, and toward this end, had been ordered to Camp Butner, North Carolina, immediately following a thirty day period of rest and recuperation.

It was a jubilant regiment that reassembled at Camp Butner; jubilant because the end of the War meant almost certainly they would not now go overseas.

It was amazing, this change of the fighting soldier to the garrison soldier. Within a matter of weeks, high point men began to be discharged. Soon some of the men who had contributed most to its success and ability were gone. Joe Samuels, George Goforth, Swede Henley, Hanshaw,

Sloninsky, Carol Kemp, Tom Harrison, Magruder, and hundreds of others soon took off their khakis and returned to as many walks of life.

These were lonely days, days in which comrades with whom we had lived and fought were separated from us. It was not an easy thing, this parting.

In the months which followed, the regiment changed personnel rapidly. Since our own men were being discharged, it was necessary to fill the complement with men from another source, although the Twenty-Second had many re-enlistments, chiefly because of the spirit of its officers and men. It received many fine officers and men from the 87th and 95th Divisions, which had been inactivated. Others came from the 76th, the 100th, and the 99th.

Throughout the winter months, routine training, orientation classes, and administration were carried on only with extreme difficulty due to the shortage of trained personnel.

On January 2, 1946, training was resumed following the Christmas Holidays. It was shortly thereafter that rumors reached the regiment that the Division might be inactivated. It seemed incredible to the men of the regiment, and no one believed that the War Department would seriously consider inactivating a Regular Army Division which was made up of three of the oldest Regiments in the Army. It soon became apparent that it was not rumor but fact, and the orders were received the first week of February with instructions that the inactivation would be completed by 1 March 1946. No reason was given.

In one terse order, the War Department had accomplished what an entire enemy army could not. The order, which was to inactivate the Fourth Infantry Division, Twenty-Second United States Infantry, had to be obeyed, and perhaps all this was a necessary and fitting rest for a gallant regiment which had turned its regimental motto, "Deeds Not Words, " into an accolade which few regiments could equal and none excel.

The days of February and March were unhappy, busy days in which the question of individual future came often to mind. Whether or not to stay in the Army, whether or not to accept a regular army commission, opportunities for advancement in return to civilian life, and separation from tried and true friends were uppermost in the minds of the regiment.

On the 20th of February 1946, Colonel John F. Ruggles, who had commanded from Sellerich, Germany, took a leave prior to his assignment to the Command and General Staff School at Fort Leavenworth, Kansas. This placed the Regiment in the hands of Lt. Colonel Arthur S. Teague. Great soldier, excellent tactician, leader of men, and loyal friend of both his officers and men, Art Teague was loved and respected by the Twenty-Second Infantry Regiment as were few men. He had served as an officer with the regiment almost five years. Thus, it was fitting that he should inactivate the regiment, and the men were glad that he was thus honored.

At the last formal review on the parade ground at Camp Butner, North Carolina, all sensed this was an historic occasion and certainly the last of its kind for the famous Fourth in World War II. General Courtney H. Hodges, Commanding General of the First Army, the Belgium Ambassador to the United States, a representative of the French Embassy, Major General Raymond O. Barton, Major General Harold W. Blakely, and Major General Melborn were guests of honor and present in the stands for the review. The Regiments formed and moved on to the parade ground, in order, the 22nd, the 12th and the 8th, followed by the Field Artillery, Engineers, and the special troop units. The day was gloomy and there was a slight drizzle as if Nature herself were weeping to watch such an organization die. There was grumbling in the ranks among the new men who had no loyalty to the Division, but there was a stillness that mirrored an ache in the hearts of the old Fourth Division men.

Colonel Ruggles, senior Regimental C. O. in the Division, was commander of troops.

Combat streamers were awarded to the Colors of the Regiment, and there was a thrill of pride within the heart of each man as the Regimental Colors dipped to receive the ribbons. And then the Belgium Ambassador was introduced. He was a tall, stately man who carried the dignity and the honor of brave Belgium upon his own shoulders. Scarcely had he started to speak when death-like stillness fell over the entire assembled Division,

It seemed as if each soldier sensed that there was something he wanted to hear.

The Ambassador spoke, "Belgium learned to love and honor the Fourth Infantry Division in the first World War when on the banks of the Marne the blood of your men mingled with the blood of our own, and the fierce Huns were stopped. Again in this war it was fitting that the Fourth Infantry Division should play so large a part in the liberation of Belgium, who had suffered so much at the hands of a cruel and ruthless enemy. We knew that you would come, and in that knowledge, liberty still lived within our hearts.

"Belgium salutes the brave men of the Fourth Infantry Division. She salutes Lt. Colonel Mabry, General Roosevelt, and Sgt. Joseph Garcia (our three Medal of Honor recipients as of that date). My country has conferred upon the men of this Division the highest honor it is in her power to bestow, and in honoring you, she honors herself. The red of the FOURAGERE is for the blood of your men shed for the liberty and for the freedom of Belgium. The green is for the constant memory of these men and what they did, and so the Fourth United States Infantry Division will always live in the heart of Belgium. Vive la America!"

No one stirred. Somehow it was fitting. Somehow it was appropriate that such an honor should come to the battle weary, exhausted, broken hearted, proud Division, and to her great fighting Regiments.

Then came the order, "Pass in review." The men marched stiffly and well, even in the mud and drizzle, and as the colors passed by, every person snapped to attention. As each one realized that this was the last time he would march as a member of the Double Deucers and of the famous Fourth Infantry Division, there was a stillness and heartache which can be occasioned only by the death of a well-beloved friend. "Eyes right." Heads snapped. The generals looked at the soldiers. The soldiers looked at the generals. Neither saw the other but rather the foxholes and hedgerows of Normandy, the crosses at St. Mere Eglise and Henri Chappelle, the match sticks and mud of Hurtgen. They saw marching in ranks, in file after file with perfect cadence and deathless spirit, all of the men who were not there. Not there? Certainly they were in the hearts and minds of those who remember, never to forget, in the love of those who would never cease missing them, in the freedom of every American.

And so the men marched off of the parade ground and into the cities and villages and farms, offices, or other Army posts. And with them went the Twenty-Second United States Infantry Regiment. A dead regiment? Certainly not. Not so long as a single man still lives and remembers. Sleeping, perhaps, but not dead. The Twenty-Second United States Infantry Regiment, the finest Regiment, the beloved Regiment, our Regiment, which gave life to the motto forever etched in our hearts…"Deeds Not Words."

* * * * *

I will stop here. The words of Chaplain Bill Boice can be transferred to those of every Soldier who served in any of the units of the 4th Infantry Division—**Steadfast and Loyal**, and of any unit or division that served so well in WWII or before or after. Those who served before these Soldiers in World War I, those of us who have served after them in the Cold War, Vietnam, War on Terror, and on active duty with 4ID today, have every bit as much pride in our division as you've read above.

I remain and will always be—Steadfast and Loyal…

Deeds not Words!

—Bob Babcock,
Past President, and Historian,
National 4ID Association

GRADUATION DAY — AND THIS WAS A TOUGH SCHOOL

ABOUT THE AUTHOR

Robert O. "Bob" Babcock was born and grew up in the small railroad town of Heavener in the mountains and forests of southeast Oklahoma. He received an ROTC commission from Pittsburg State University in 1965, trained with the 4th Infantry Division (4ID) at Fort Lewis, WA in 1965-1966, and served in Vietnam with B/1-22 Infantry, 4th Infantry Division as a rifle platoon leader and executive officer in 1966-1967. From 1968 to 2002, Bob was a Sales/Marketing Executive with IBM. Bob is a founding official partner of the Veterans History Project, part of the Library of Congress, preserving memories of America's veterans.

Bob completed his tenth year as president of the National 4th Infantry Division Association in 2023 and continues as their historian and liaison to the active duty 4th Infantry Division for over twenty-five years. He also served for ten years as president/founder of the current 22nd Infantry Regiment Society.

Bob is author of thirteen books, including seven that are 4ID focused, and is founder/CEO of Deeds Publishing LLC. Bob has published over 450 books for established and aspiring authors. He has five more 4ID related military history books on his list to write and publish over the next several years.

Bob is a member of multiple national and local veterans' organizations, including National 4th Infantry Division Association, 22nd Infantry Regiment Society, Atlanta Vietnam Veterans Business Association, and founded and leads the Veterans ministry at Mt. Bethel United Methodist Church. Bob and his wife, Jan, have four grown children and four grandchildren and live in Athens, GA.

4ID BIBLIOGRAPHY

Books About and Including 4th Infantry Division's Actions
    Originally published in: *"War Stories—Utah Beach to Pleiku"*
By Robert O. Babcock—2001
    Also check **www.deedspublishing.com** for updated 4ID history. As you become aware of other books to add to this list, please send the info to Bob Babcock at **bob@deedspublishing.com**
    Provided for your reference as you research the long and proud history of the 4ID—Current as of 1 April 2024

OVERALL HISTORY OF 4TH INFANTRY DIVISION – 1917 TO 2017

To War with the 4th: A Century of Frontline Combat with the U.S. 4th Infantry Division, from the Argonne to the Ardennes to Afghanistan by Martin King. Available on Amazon.com.

WORLD WAR I

The 4th Division in the World War by Christian A. Bach and Henry Noble

Hall. Issued by the Division, 1920. Out of Print. (Reprinted April 2017 by Deeds Publishing—www.deedspublishing.com).

About Face by Eleanor Elliott Brownell. World War I Press, Flint, MI, 2000. ISBN 0-9679784-0-8.

Soldiers Steadfast and Loyal by Michael Belis. Deeds Publishing. 2022. ISBN 978-1-950794-78-2. Available from www.deedspublishing.com and www.amazon.com. In depth details of one Medal of Honor and 185 Distinguished Service Cross 4th Division recipients in World War I.

WORLD WAR II

Hell in the Hürtgen: Ordeal and Triumph of an American Infantry Regiment by Dr. (retired CSM) Robert Rush. University Press of Kansas. ISBN 0-7006-1128-2.

History of the 22nd Infantry Regiment in World War II by Dr. (Chaplain) Bill Boice. Issued by the 22nd Infantry Regiment Society—World War II, 1956. (Reprinted January 2024 by www.deedspublishing.com)

History of the Twelfth Infantry Regiment in World War II by Colonel Gerden F. Johnson. Issued by the 4th Infantry Division Association, 1947. (Reprinted June 2017 and available at www.deedspublishing.com

If You Survive by George Wilson. Ivy Books Published by Ballantine Books, 1987. ISBN 0-8041-0003-9.

The Invasion Before Normandy—The Secret Battle of Slapton Sands by Edwin P. Hoyt. Robert Hale, London, 1985. ISBN 0-7090-3266-8.

June 6, 1944—The Voices of D-Day by Gerald Astor. St. Martin's Press, 1994. ISBN 0-312-11014-6.

The Last Offensive by Charles B. MacDonald. First Printed in 1973 by Center of Military History. Reprinted by BBD Special Editions, 1993. ISBN 0-7924-5858-3.

The Longest Day by Cornelius Ryan. Simon & Shuster Inc. April 1994 (Paperback version) ISBN 0671890913

Normandy 1944—A Young Rifleman's War by Dick Stodghill. Publish America, 2006. ISBN 1-4241-4913-4

Falling Out and Belonging: A Foot Soldier's Life by S. Joseph Krause. Author House 2006. ISBN 1-4259-2579-0

A Soldier's Journal: With the 22nd Infantry Regiment in World War II by David Rothbart. iBooks, 2003. ISBN 0-7434-5865-6.

A Soldier's Story by Omar N. Bradley. Henry Holt and Company, 1951.

Strike Swiftly! The 70th Tank Battalion from North Africa to Normandy to Germany by Marvin Jensen. Presidio Press, 1997. ISBN 0-89141-610-2.

Utah Beach to Cherbourg, 6-27 June 1944 by Center of Military History, 1948. CMH Pub 100-12. Available on the internet at www.army.mil/cmh-pg/books/wwii/wutah/utah.htm.

War Stories: Utah Beach to Pleiku by Robert O. Babcock. Deeds Publishing 2001, reprinted 2006. ISBN 0-9776018-1-1. Available at www.deedspublishing.com. (This book has been broken into three books, all available in e-book or autographed paperback at www.deedspublishing.com—new titles are:

War Stories Volume I: D-Day to Liberation of Paris—ISBN 978-1-941165-00-3;

War Stories Volume II: Paris to V-E Day—ISBN 978-1-941165-08-9;

War Stories Volume III: Vietnam 1966—1970—ISBN 978-1-944193-48-5. Also available on www.amazon.com.

World War II Order of Battle by Shelby L. Stanton. Gallahad Books, 1991. ISBN 0-88365-775-9.

Surviving the Odds—From D-Day to VE-Day with the 4th Division in Europe by Jack Capell. Regina Books, PO Box 280, Claremont, CA 91711. ISBN 978-1-930053-49-6.

A Chaplain's Duty by Rev. George W. Knapp and Gayle E. Knapp, Deeds Publishing, December 2010, ISBN 978-0-9826180-7-3.

A Soldier, My Dad by Neal Pizzano, Deeds Publishing, December 2011, ISBN 978-1-937565-12-1.

Reported Killed in Action by Lisa Beichl, Deeds Publishing, November 2015, ISBN 978-1-944193-04-1.

Finding my Father's Footsteps by Karen Marshall, Deeds Publishing, May 2024, ISBN 978-961505-19-3

Mr. 22nd Infantry – Lum Edwards by Michael Belis, Deeds Publishing, May 2024, ISBN 978-1-961505-21-6

12th Infantry Regiment RTO – Hurtgen to VE Day by R.J. Miles, Deeds Publishing, May 2024, ISBN 978-1-961505-18-6

Sainteny 1938 – 1963, From Shadow to Light by Jean-Paul Pitou, Deeds Publishing, May 2024, ISBN 978-1-961505-20-9

Fit to Fight

Come Out Fighting by Henry Strecker, Deeds Publishing, June 2024, ISBN 978-1-961505-22-3

Series of five yearbooks published in 1946 by the 4th Infantry Division (8th Infantry Regiment, 12th Infantry Regiment, 22nd Infantry Regiment, Division Artillery, Division HQ / Support Units). Reprinted in June 2017, available as PDF files at www.deedspublishing.com. Contact bob@deedspublishing.com for more details.

For information on self-published memoirs by 4th Infantry Division veterans, contact Bob Babcock at info@deedspublishing.com to get information on how to order the books, plus others as we become aware of them:

Deeds not Words: A Narrative of the 22nd Infantry in WWII by David Roderick

Kirtley's Chronicles by Dr. James Kirtley

Men of the Terrible Green Cross by Herb Fowle

Not a Hero, Just Lucky by Dib Taylor

Rifleman, Company G, 12th Infantry, WWII by Carlton H. Stauffer

Six Days in 1945 by Edwin D. Williams

Swede Henley's Diary by Swede Henley

And Then There Were None by Wes Trindal

World War II Army Journal by David Rothbart

From Dachau to D-Day by Werner Kleeman

Dear Dad by Kathy Williams (WWII story of Vietnam 4ID 2nd Brigade commander and Chief of Staff Jud Miller)

By-Line: Ernest Hemingway edited by William White. A Touchstone Book Published by Simon & Schuster, 1998. ISBN 0-684-83905-9.

Citizen Soldiers by Stephen E. Ambrose. A Touchstone Book Published by Simon & Schuster, 1998. ISBN 0-684-84801-5.

Cross Channel Attack by Gordon A. Harrison. First Printed in 1951 by Center of Military History. Reprinted by BBD Special Editions, 1993. ISBN 0-7924-5856-7.

Crusade in Europe by Dwight D. Eisenhower. Doubleday, 1948. ISBN 0-385-41619-9.

D-Day, June 6, 1944 by Stephen Ambrose. Simon & Shuster Inc. April 1995 (Paperback version) ISBN 068480137X

A Dark and Bloody Ground—The Hurtgen Forest and Roer River Dams 1944-1945 by Edward G. Miller. Texas A&M University Press, 1995. ISBN 0-89096-626-5.

Ernie's War, The Best of Ernie Pyle's World War II Dispatches by David Nichols. A Touchstone Book Published by Simon & Schuster, 1987. ISBN 0-671-64452-1.

The Forgotten Dead by Ken Small. Bloomsbury Publishing, Great Britain, 1999. ISBN 0-7475-4467-0.

The Good War, An Oral History of World War II by Studs Terkel. The New Press, 1984. ISBN 1-56584-343-6.

William C. Meadows. 2002. *The Comanche Code Talkers of World War II.*

Austin: University of Texas Press. ISBN 0-292-75274-1 paperback. 2nd paperback printing, 2003.

Unpacking Yesterday by Elizabeth Rieman. Deeds Publishing, 2020. ISBN 978-1-950794-22-5.

(If you know of other 4ID WWII books, please let me know at info@deedspublishing.com.)

VIETNAM

Return of the Warriors; subtitled *Vietnam War Veterans* Face *the Ghosts of Their Past on Their Personal Battlegrounds* by Bob Reilly. *Published in 2010 by Trafford Publishing.*

Absolution, Charlie Company, 3rd Battalion, 22nd Infantry by Charles J. Boyle, Sergeant Kirkland's Press, 1999 ISBN 1-887901-30-2.

The Army at War from the series, *The Vietnam Experience.* Boston Publishing Company, 1987. ISBN 0-939526-23-9.

The Battle for Chu Moor Mountain—April 1968 by Fred Childs, Deeds Publishing, 2014. ISBN 978-1-941165-43-0.

Five Years to DEROS by Harry Dilkes with Lewis A. Easterly. DPG Limited, 2000. (No ISBN) Library of Congress # 097-243959. (1-12 Infantry).

Flashback: A Journey in Time by John Michael Finn. 1st Books Library 2001. ISBN 0-75961-292-7.

Light Ruck, Vietnam 1969 by Tom Lacombe. Loft Press, 2002. ISBN 1-893846-56-3.

Nine Days in May by Warren Wilkins. University of Oklahoma Press, 2017. Available from www.amazon.com.

The Rise and Fall of an American Army, U.S. Ground Forces in Vietnam, 1965-1973 by Shelby L. Stanton. Presidio Press, 1985. ISBN 0-89141-576-9.

Summons of the Trumpet, U.S.- Vietnam in Perspective by Dave R. Palmer. Presidio Press, 1978. ISBN 0-89141-550-5.

Taking the Offensive — October 1966 to October 1967 by George L. MacGarrigle. Center of Military History, 1998. CMH Pub 91-4-1.

Time Heals No Wounds by Jack Leninger. Ivy Books Published by Ballantine 1993. ISBN 0-8041-0916-8.

Vietnam Combat Medic by Ron Donahey, Deeds Publishing 2018, ISBN 978-1-9473097-2-2.

Vietnam Order of Battle by Shelby Stanton. U.S. News Books, 1981. ISBN 0-89193-700-5.

War Stories: Utah Beach to Pleiku by Robert O. Babcock. Deeds Publishing, 2002. ISBN 0-9776018-1-1.

War Stories Volume III: Vietnam 1966-1970 by Robert O. Babcock. Deeds Publishing 2016. ISBN (subset of above book).

West to Cambodia by S.L.A. Marshall. Jove Books, 1968. ISBN 0-515-08890-0.

What Now, Lieutenant? by Robert O. Babcock. Deeds Publishing, 2007. ISBN 978-0-9776018-0-6. Available at www.deedspublishing.com or www.amazon.com.

Young Soldiers Amazing Warriors: Inside One of the Most Highly Decorated Battalions of Vietnam—December 20, 2013 by Robert H Sholly. Available at www.amazon.com.

Into the Storm by Donald Rawlinson. Deeds Publishing, 2019. ISBN 978-1-9473097-4-6. Available at www.deedspublishing.com or www.amazon.com.

I'm Ready to Talk by Robert O. Babcock, Deeds Publishing, 2019. ISBN 978-1-947309-98-2. Available at www.deedspublishing.com or www.amazon.com. (165 stories from 112 Vietnam vets from all branches of the service, units, and time periods from 1964 to 1975).

I'm Ready to Talk Two by Robert O. Babcock, Deeds Publishing, 2021. ISBN 978-1-950794-65-2. Available at www.deedspublishing.com or www.amazon.com. (More stories from Vietnam vets from all branches of the service, units, and time periods from 1964 to 1975).

It Don't Mean Nothin' by Eric Shelly, Deeds Publishing, 2022. ISBN 978-1-950794-83-6. Available at www.deedspublishing.com or www.amazon.com. Personal experiences of the author serving in Vietnam with Company A, 3rd Battalion, 12th Infantry Regiment of 4ID.

Duel with the Dragon at the Battle of Suoi Tre by Bill Comeau, Deeds Publishing, 2022. ISBN 978-1-950794-85-0. Available at www.deedspublishing.com or www.amazon.com. The story of Company A, 2nd Battalion, 12th Infantry Regiment of 4ID from training through their year fighting in Vietnam in 1966—1967.

Rucksack Grunt by Robert Kuhn. Self-Published—2021. Available in paperback and Kindle version on www.amazon.com. Covers Robert's service with 1-22 Infantry in Vietnam in 1971-1972 after 4ID had returned to the US but 1-22 remained in Vietnam.

Infantry Life in Vietnam's Central Highlands by Dennis Witt, Deeds Publishing, 2023. ISBN

OPERATION IRAQI FREEDOM

Ladies of the Ironhorse, The Voices of Those Who Wait at Home by Rhonda Eggleston. St. John's Press, 2005. ISBN 0-9710551-9-X.

Operation Iraqi Freedom I: A Year in the Sunni Triangle—The History of the 4th Infantry Division and Task Force Ironhorse in Iraq, April 2003 to April 2004 by Robert O. Babcock. St. John's Press, 2005. ISBN 0-9710551-8-1. Available at www.deedspublishing.com

My Son is Alive… by Roberta Quimby. Deeds Publishing, 2006. ISBN 978-0-9776018-4-4. Available at www.deedspublishing.com.

Wolfhound Reflections—A New Generation: Operation Iraqi Freedom 2007-2009 by JB Jaso III. Deeds Publishing, 2009. ISBN 978-0-9776018-8-2. Available at www.deedspublishing.com.

Operation Iraqi Freedom 07-09: Dispatches from Baghdad—The History of the 4th Infantry Division and Multi-National Division—Baghdad in Iraq by Robert O. Babcock (Details on availability can be gotten from Bob Babcock at www.deedspublishing.com).

Recon 701—the inner cordon unit during capture of Saddam Hussein by COL (Ret) Desmond V. Bailey with the troops of Golf Troop, 10th Cavalry, 4ID. Deeds Publishing 2022. ISBN 978-1-950794-84-3. Available at www.deedspublishing.com or www.amazon.com. Memories of the Soldiers in the unit working with Special Operations Forces in the hunt for and capture of Saddam Hussein.

We Got Him! By LTC (Ret) Steve Russell. First (limited) edition by Deeds

Publishing. 2011. ISBN 978-0-9834105-2-2. Available at www.deedspublishing.com. Simon & Schuster second edition available at www.amazon.com.

OPERATION ENDURING FREEDOM – AFGHANISTAN

Task Force Regulars, 1st Battalion, 22nd Infantry Regiment — Operation Enduring Freedom X-XI — July 2010 — July 2011, Kandahar Province, Afghanistan — yearbook, 2011. ISBN 978-1-937565-10-7. Available at www.deedspublishing.com.

Siren's Song: The Allure of War by Antonio Salinas. Deeds Publishing. February 2012. ISBN 978-1-937565-17-6. (2-12 Infantry, Afghanistan 2009)

Red Platoon: A True Story of American Valor by Clinton Romesha, Dutton, an Imprint of Random House, May 2016. ISBN 978-0-525-95505-4. Available at www.amazon.com. (MOH recipient)

8 Seconds of Courage: A Soldier's Story from Immigrant to the Medal of Honor by Flo Groberg, Simon & Schuster, November 2017. ISBN 978-1-5011-6588-1. Available at www.amazon.com.

WEB SITES OF INTEREST

The following web sites will be updated regularly with information about the 4th Infantry Division, how to become a member of the Association, these books, links to other web sites of interest, and other references as they become available:

National 4th Infantry Division Association: www.4thinfantry.org.

22nd Infantry Regiment Society: www.22ndinfantry.org.

1st Battalion, 22nd Infantry Regiment: www.1-22infantry.org.

If you are looking for other information on the history of the 4th Infantry Division, do not hesitate to contact our 4ID Association historian and past president (and author of this book) Bob Babcock at bob@deedspublishing.com. He will do his best to help in any way he can. Steadfast and Loyal.

Printed in the USA
CPSIA information can be obtained
at www.ICGtesting.com
LVHW051035220524
780544LV00002BA/3